Beginning C
From Novice to Professional, Fourth Edition

Ivor Horton

Apress®

ning C: From Novice to Professional, Fourth Edition

right © 2011 by Ivor Horton

978-1-4302-4362-5

978-1-4302-4363-2 (eBook)

emarked names, logos, and images may appear in this book. Rather than use a trademark symbol with
occurrence of a trademarked name, logo, or image we use the names, logos, and images only in an
rial fashion and to the benefit of the trademark owner, with no intention of infringement of the
mark.

se in this publication of trade names, trademarks, service marks, and similar terms, even if they are not
ified as such, is not to be taken as an expression of opinion as to whether or not they are subject to
rietary rights.

e the advice and information in this book are believed to be true and accurate at the date of publication,
er the authors nor the editors nor the publisher can accept any legal responsibility for any errors or
sions that may be made. The publisher makes no warranty, express or implied, with respect to the
rial contained herein.

resident and Publisher: Paul Manning
Lead Editor: Matthew Moodie
Technical Reviewer: Stan Lippman
Editorial Board: Steve Anglin, Mark Beckner, Ewan Buckingham, Gary Cornell, Morgan Ertel, Jonathan
   Gennick, Jonathan Hassell, Robert Hutchinson, Michelle Lowman, James Markham, Matthew
   Moodie, Jeff Olson, Jeffrey Pepper, Douglas Pundick, Ben Renow-Clarke, Dominic Shakeshaft,
   Gwenan Spearing, Matt Wade, Tom Welsh
Coordinating Editor: Tracy Brown Collins
Copy Editor: Jennifer Whipple
Compositor: Susan Glinert
ndexer: John Collin
Artist: Kinetic Publishing Services, LLC
Cover Designer: Anna Ishchenko

ibuted to the book trade worldwide by Springer Science+Business Media New York, 233 Spring Street,
Floor, New York, NY 10013. Phone 1-800-SPRINGER, fax (201) 348-4505, e-mail orders-ny@springer-
com, or visit www.springeronline.com.

nformation on translations, please e-mail rights@apress.com, or visit www.apress.com.

ss and friends of ED books may be purchased in bulk for academic, corporate, or promotional use.
ok versions and licenses are also available for most titles. For more information, reference our Special
Sales–eBook Licensing web page at www.apress.com/bulk-sales.

source code or other supplementary materials referenced by the author in this text is available to readers
ww.apress.com. For detailed information about how to locate your book's source code, go to
apress.com/source-code/.

This book is for the latest member of the family, Henry James Gilbey, who joined us on July 14, 2006. He hasn t shown much interest in programming so far, but he did smile when I asked him about it so I expect he will.

Contents at a Glance

Contents

About the Author

IVOR HORTON started out as a mathematician, but after graduating he was lured into messing around with computers by a well-known manufacturer. He has spent many happy years programming occasionally useful applications in a variety of languages as well as teaching scientists and engineers to do likewise. He has extensive experience in applying computers to problems in engineering design and manufacturing operations. He is the author of a number of tutorial books on programming in C, C++, and Java. When not writing programming books or providing advice to others, he leads a life of leisure.

Acknowledgments

I'd like to thank Gary Cornell for encouraging me to produce this new updated edition of *Beginning C: From Novice to Professional*. I'm particularly grateful to Stan Lippman for taking the time to cast his critical eye over the entire draft text; he did not pull any punches in his extensive review comments and the book is surely better as a result. My thanks to all the people at Apress, who have done their usual outstandingly professional job of converting my initial text with all its imperfections into this finished product. Any imperfections that remain are undoubtedly mine.

My sincere thanks to those readers of previous editions of this book who took the trouble to point out my mistakes and identify areas that could be better explained. I also greatly appreciate all those who wrote or e-mailed just to say how much they enjoyed the book or how it helped them get started in programming.

Last and certainly not least I'd like to thank my wife, Eve, who still provides limitless love, support, and encouragement for whatever I choose to do, and always understands when I can't quite make it to dinner on time.

Introduction

Welcome to *Beginning C: From Novice to Professional, Fourth Edition.* With this book you can become a competent C programmer. In many ways, C is an ideal language with which to learn programming. C is a very compact language, so there isn't a lot of syntax to learn before you can write real applications. In spite of its conciseness and ease, it's also an extremely powerful language that's still widely used by professionals. The power of C is such that it is used for programming at all levels, from device drivers and operating system components to large-scale applications. C compilers are available for virtually every kind of computer, so when you've learned C, you'll be equipped to program in just about any context. Finally, once you know C, you have an excellent base from which you can build an understanding of the object-oriented C++.

My objective in this book is to minimize what I think are the three main hurdles the aspiring programmer must face: coming to grips with the jargon that pervades every programming language, understanding how to *use* the language elements (as opposed to merely knowing what they are), and appreciating how the language is applied in a practical context.

Jargon is an invaluable and virtually indispensable means of communication for the expert professional as well as the competent amateur, so it can't be avoided. My approach is to ensure that you understand the jargon and get comfortable using it in context. In this way, you'll be able to more effectively use the documentation that comes along with most programming products, and also feel comfortable reading and learning from the literature that surrounds most programming languages.

Comprehending the syntax and effects of the language elements is obviously an essential part of learning a language, but appreciating *how* the language features work and *how* they are used is equally important. Rather than just using code fragments, I always provide you with practical working examples that show the relationship of each language feature to specific problems. These examples can then provide a basis for you to experiment and see the effects of changing the code in various ways.

Your understanding of programming in context needs to go beyond the mechanics of applying individual language elements. To help you gain this understanding, I conclude most chapters with a more complex program that applies what you've learned in the chapter. These programs will help you gain the competence and confidence to develop your own applications, and provide you with insight into how you can apply language elements in combination and on a larger scale. Most important, they'll give you an idea of what's involved in designing real programs and managing real code.

It's important to realize a few things that are true for learning any programming language. First, there *is* quite a lot to learn, but this means you'll gain a greater sense of satisfaction when you've mastered it. Second, it's great fun, so you really will enjoy it. Third, you can only learn programming by doing it, and this book helps you along the way. Finally, it's much easier than you think, so you positively *can* do it.

How to Use This Book

Because I believe in the hands-on approach, you'll write your first programs almost immediately. Every chapter has several programs that put a theory into practice, and these examples are key to the book. I advise you to type in and run all the examples that appear in the text because the very act of typing in programs is a tremendous aid to remembering the language elements. You should also attempt all the exercises that appear at the end of each chapter. When you get a program to work for the first time! particularly when you're trying to solve your own problems! you'll find that the great sense of accomplishment and progress make it all worthwhile.

We will start off at a gentle pace, but we'll gain momentum as we get further into the subject. Each chapter will cover quite a lot of ground, so take your time and make sure you understand everything before moving on. Experimenting with the code and trying out your own ideas is an important part of the learning process. Try modifying the programs and see what else you can make them do! that's when it gets really interesting. And don't be afraid to try things out! if you don't understand how something works, just type in a few variations and see what happens. A good approach is to read each chapter through, get an idea of its scope, and then go back and work through all the examples.

You might find some of the end-of-chapter programs quite difficult. Don't worry if it's not all completely clear on the first try. There are bound to be bits that you find difficult to understand at first, because they often apply what you've learned to rather complicated problems. And if you really get stuck, you can skip the end-of-chapter programs, move on to the next chapter, and come back to them later. You can even go through the entire book without worrying about them. The point of these programs is that they're a useful resource for you! even after you've finished the book.

Who This Book Is For

Beginning C: From Novice to Professional, Fourth Edition is designed to teach you how to write useful programs as quickly and easily as possible. This is the tutorial for you if

!   You're a newcomer to programming but you want to plunge straight into the C language and learn about programming and writing C programs right from the start.

!   You've done a little bit of programming before, so you understand the concepts behind it! maybe you've used BASIC or PASCAL. Now you're keen to learn C and develop your programming skills further.

This book doesn't assume any previous programming knowledge on your part, but it does move quickly from the basics to the real meat of the subject. By the end of *Beginning C*, you'll have a thorough grounding in programming the C language.

What You Need to Use This Book

To use this book, you'll need a computer with a C compiler and library installed so that you can execute the examples, and a program text editor for preparing your source code files. The compiler you use should provide good support for the International Standard for the C language, ISO/IEC 9899. You'll also need an editor for creating and modifying your code. You can use any plain text editor such as Notepad or vi to create your source program files. However, you'll get along better if your editor is designed for editing C code.

To get the most out of this book you need the willingness to learn, the desire to succeed, and the determination to continue when things are unclear and you can't see the way ahead. Almost everyone gets a little lost somewhere along the way when learning programming for the first time. When you find you are struggling to grasp some aspect of C, just keep at it! the fog will surely disperse and you'll wonder why you didn't understand the topic in the first place. You might believe that doing all this is going to be difficult, but I think you'll be surprised by how much you can achieve in a relatively short time. I'll help you to start experimenting on your own and become a successful programmer.

Conventions Used

I use a number of different styles of text and layout in the book to help differentiate between the different kinds of information. For the most part, their meanings will be obvious. Program code will appear like this:

```c
int main(void)
{
  printf("\nBeginning C");
  return 0;
}
```

When a code fragment is a modified version of a previous instance, I show the lines that have changed in bold type like this:

```c
int main(void)
{
  printf("\nBeginning C by Ivor Horton");
  return 0;
}
```

When code appears in the text, it has a different typestyle that looks like this: double.

I'll use different types of •brackets! in the program code. They aren't interchangeable, and their differences are very important. I'll refer to the symbols ( ) as **parentheses**, the symbols { } as **braces**, and the symbols [ ] as **square brackets**.

Important new words in the text are shown in **bold** type.

Code from the Book

All the code from the book and solutions to the exercises are available for download from the Apress web site at http://www.apress.com.

CHAPTER 1

■ ■ ■

Programming in C

C is a powerful and compact computer language that allows you to write programs that specify exactly what you want your computer to do. You're in charge: you create a program, which is just a set of instructions, and your computer will follow them.

Programming in C isn't difficult, as you're about to find out. I'm going to teach you all the fundamentals of C programming in an enjoyable and easy-to-understand way, and by the end of this chapter you'll have written your first few C programs. It's as easy as that!

In this chapter you'll learn the following:

! How to create C programs

! How C programs are organized

! How to write your own program to display text on the screen

Creating C Programs

There are four fundamental stages, or processes, in the creation of any C program:

! Editing

! Compiling

! Linking

! Executing

You'll soon know all these processes like the back of your hand (you'll be doing them so easily and so often), but first let's consider what each process is and how it contributes to the creation of a C program.

Editing

This is the process of creating and modifying C **source code**! the name given to the program instructions you write. Some C compilers come with a specific editor that can provide a lot of assistance in managing your programs. In fact, an editor often provides a complete environment for writing, managing, developing, and testing your programs. This is sometimes called an **integrated development environment**, or IDE.

You can also use other editors to create your source files, but they must store the code as plain text without any extra formatting data embedded in it. In general, if you have a compiler system with an editor included, it will provide a lot of features that make it easier to write and organize your source programs. There will usually be automatic facilities for laying out the program text appropriately, and color highlighting for important language elements, which not only makes your code more readable but also provides a clear indicator when you make errors when keying in such words.

If you're working in UNIX or Linux, the most common text editor is the vi editor. Alternately you might prefer to use the emacs editor.

On a PC you could use one of the many freeware and shareware programming editors. These will often provide a lot of help in ensuring your code is correct with syntax highlighting and autoindenting of your code. Don't use a word processor such as Microsoft Word, as these aren't suitable for producing program code because of the extra formatting information they store along with the text. Of course, you also have the option of purchasing one of the professionally created programming development environments that support C, such as those from Borland or Microsoft, in which case you will have very extensive editing capabilities. Before parting with your cash though, it's a good idea to check that the level of C that is supported is approximate to the current C standard. With some of the products out there that are primarily aimed at C++ developers, C has been left behind somewhat. A further possibility is to get the emacs editor for Windows. emacs is the editor of choice for some programming professionals.

Compiling

The compiler converts your source code into machine language and detects and reports errors in the compilation process. The input to this stage is the file you produce during your editing, which is usually referred to as a **source file**.

The compiler can detect a wide range of errors that are due to invalid or unrecognized program code, as well as structural errors where, for example, part of a program can never be executed. The output from the compiler is known as **object code** and is stored in files called **object files**, which usually have names with the extension .obj in the Microsoft Windows environment, or .o in the Linux/UNIX environment. The compiler can detect several different kinds of errors during the translation process, and most of these will prevent the object file from being created.

The result of a successful compilation is a file with the same name as that used for the source file, but with the .o or .obj extension.

If you're working in UNIX, at the command line, the standard command to compile your C programs will be cc (or the GNU's Not UNIX (GNU) compiler, which is gcc). You can use it like this:

```
cc -c myprog.c
```

where myprog.c is the program you want to compile. Note that if you omit the -c flag, your program will automatically be linked as well. The result of a successful compilation will be an object file.

Most C compilers will have a standard compile option, whether it's from the command line (such as cc myprog.c) or a menu option from within an IDE (where you'll find a Compile menu option).

Linking

The linker combines the various modules generated by the compiler from source code files, adds required code modules from program libraries supplied as part of C, and welds everything into an executable whole. The linker can also detect and report errors, for example, if part of your program is missing or a nonexistent library component is referenced.

In practice, if your program is of any significant size, it will consist of several separate source code files, which can then be linked. A large program may be difficult to write in one working session, and it may be impossible to work with as a single file. By breaking it up into a number of smaller source files that each provide a coherent part of what the whole program does, you can make the development of the program a whole lot easier. The source files can be compiled separately, which makes eliminating simple typographical errors a bit easier. Furthermore, the whole program can usually be developed incrementally. The set of source files that make up the program will usually be integrated under a **project name**, which is used to refer to the whole program.

Program libraries support and extend the C language by providing routines to carry out operations that aren't part of the language. For example, libraries contain routines that support operations such as performing input and output, calculating a square root, comparing two character strings, or obtaining date and time information.

A failure during the linking phase means that once again you have to go back and edit your source code. Success on the other hand will produce an executable file. In a Microsoft Windows environment, this executable file will have an .exe extension; in UNIX, there will be no such extension, but the file will be of an executable type.

Many IDEs also have a Build option, which will compile and link your program in one step. This option will usually be found, within an IDE, in the Compile menu; alternatively, it may have a menu of its own.

Executing

The execution stage is where you run your program, having completed all the previous processes successfully. Unfortunately, this stage can also generate a wide variety of error conditions that can include producing the wrong output or just sitting there and doing nothing, perhaps crashing your computer for good measure. In all cases, it's back to the editing process to check your source code.

Now for the good news: this is the stage where, at last, you get to see your computer doing exactly what you told it to do! In UNIX and Linux you can just enter the name of the file that has been compiled and linked to execute the program. In most IDEs, you'll find an appropriate menu command that allows you to run or execute your compiled program. This Run or Execute option may have a menu of its own, or you may find it under the Compile menu option. In Windows, you can run the .exe file for your program as you would any other executable.

The processes of editing, compiling, linking, and executing are essentially the same for developing programs in any environment and with any compiled language. Figure 1-1 summarizes how you would typically pass through processes as you create your own C programs.

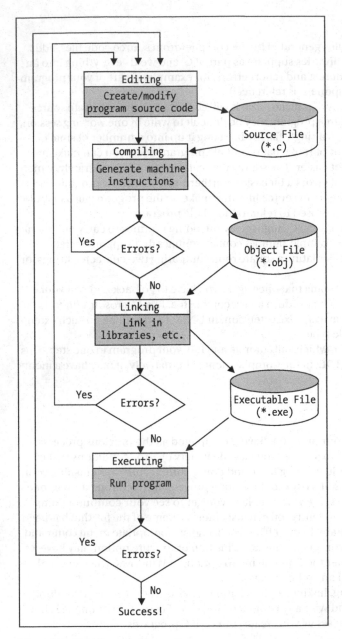

Figure 1-1. *Creating and executing a program*

Creating Your First Program

Let's step through the processes of creating a simple C program, from entering the program itself to executing it. Don't worry if what you type doesn't mean anything to you at this stage! I'll explain everything as we go along.

TRY IT OUT: AN EXAMPLE C PROGRAM

Run your editor, and type in the following program exactly as it's written. Be careful to use the punctuation exactly as you see here. The brackets used on the fourth and last lines are braces—the curly ones { }, not the square ones [ ] or the round ones ( )—it really does matter. Also, make sure you put the slashes the right way (/), as later you'll be using the backslash (\) as well. Don't forget the semicolon (;).

```
/* Program 1.1 Your Very First C Program - Displaying Hello World */
#include <stdio.h>

int main(void)
{
  printf("Hello world!");
  return 0;
}
```

When you've entered the preceding source code, save the program as hello.c. You can use whatever name you like instead of hello, but the extension must be .c. This extension is the common convention when you write C programs and identifies the contents of the file as C source code. Most compilers will expect the source file to have the extension .c, and if it doesn't, the compiler may refuse to process it.

Next you'll compile your program as described in the "Compiling" section previously in this chapter and link all the pieces necessary to create an executable program as discussed in the previous "Linking" section. This is typically carried out in a single operation, and once the source code has been compiled successfully, the linker will add code from the standard libraries that your program needs and create the single executable file for your program.

Finally, you can execute your program. Remember that you can do this in several ways. There is the usual method of double-clicking the .exe file from Windows Explorer if you're using Windows, but you will be better off opening a command-line window because the window showing the output will disappear when execution is complete. On all platforms, you can run your program from the command line. Just start a command-line session, change the current directory to the one that contains the executable file for your program, and then enter the program name to run it.

If everything worked without producing any error messages, you've done it! This is your first program, and you should see the following message on the screen:

```
Hello world!
```

Editing Your First Program

You could try altering the same program to display something else on the screen. For example, you might want to try editing the program to read like this:

```
/* Program 1.2 Your Second C Program */
#include<stdio.h>

int main(void)
{
  printf("If at first you don\'t succeed, try, try, try again!");
  return 0;
}
```

The \' sequence in the middle of the text to be displayed is called an **escape sequence**. Here it's a special way of including a single quote in the text because single quotes are usually used to indicate where a character constant begins and ends. You'll learn more about escape sequences in the •Control Characters! section later in this chapter. You can try recompiling the program, relinking it, and running it again once you've altered the source. With a following wind and a bit of luck you have now edited your first program. You've written a program using the editor, edited it, and compiled, linked, and executed it.

Dealing with Errors

To err is human, so there's no need to be embarrassed about making mistakes. Fortunately computers don't generally make mistakes themselves and they're actually very good at indicating where we've slipped up. Sooner or later your compiler is going to present you with a list (sometimes a list that's longer than you want) of the mistakes that are in your source code. You'll usually get an indication of the statements that are in error. When this happens, you must return to the editing stage, find out what's wrong with the incorrect code, and fix it.

Keep in mind that one error can result in error messages for subsequent statements that may actually be correct. This usually happens with statements that refer to something that is supposed to be defined by a statement containing an error. Of course, if a statement that defines something has an error, then what was supposed to be defined won't be.

Let's step through what happens when your source code is incorrect by creating an error in your program. Edit your second program example, removing the semicolon (;) at the end of the line with printf() in it, as shown here:

```
/* Program 1.2 Your Second C Program */
#include<stdio.h>

int main(void)
{
  printf("If at first you don\'t succeed, try, try, try again!")
  return 0;
}
```

If you now try to compile this program, you'll see an error message that will vary slightly depending on which compiler you're using. A typical error message is as follows:

```
Syntax error : missing ';' before '}'
HELLO.C - 1 error(s), 0 warning(s)
```

Here, the compiler is able to determine precisely what the error is, and where. There really should be a semicolon at the end of that printf() line. As you start writing your own programs, you'll probably get a lot of errors during compilation that are caused by simple punctuation mistakes. It's so easy to forget a comma or a bracket, or to just press the wrong key. Don't worry about this; a lot of experienced programmers make exactly the same mistakes! even after years of practice.

As I said earlier, just one mistake can sometimes result in a whole stream of abuse from your compiler, as it throws you a multitude of different things that it doesn't like. Don't get put off by the number of errors reported. After you consider the messages carefully, the basic approach is to go back and edit your source code to fix what you can, ignoring the errors that you can't understand. Then have another go at compiling the source file. With luck, you'll get fewer errors the next time around.

To correct your example program, just go back to your editor and reenter the semicolon. Recompile, check for any other errors, and your program is fit to be run again.

Dissecting a Simple Program

Now that you've written and compiled your first program, let's go through another that's very similar and see what the individual lines of code do. Have a look at this program:

```
/* Program 1.3 Another Simple C Program - Displaying a Quotation */
#include <stdio.h>

int main(void)
{
  printf("Beware the Ides of March!");
  return 0;
}
```

This is virtually identical to your first program. Even so, you could do with the practice, so use your editor to enter this example and see what happens when you compile and run it. If you type it in accurately, compile it, and run it, you should get the following output:

```
Beware the Ides of March!
```

Comments

Look at the first line of code in the preceding example:

```
/* Program 1.3 Another Simple C Program - Displaying a Quotation */
```

This isn't actually part of the program code, in that it isn't telling the computer to do anything. It's simply a **comment**, and it's there to remind you, or someone else reading your code, what the program does. Anything between /* and */ is treated as a comment. As soon as your compiler finds /* in your source file, it will simply ignore anything that follows (even if the text looks like program code) until it finds the matching */ that marks the end of the comment. This may be on the same line, or it can be several lines further on.

You should try to get into the habit of documenting your programs, using comments as you go along. Your programs will, of course, work without comments, but when you write longer programs you may not remember what they do or how they work. Put in enough comments to ensure that a month from now you (and any other programmer) can understand the aim of the program and how it works.

As I said, comments don't have to be in a line of their own. A comment is everything between /* and */, wherever /* and */ are in your code. Let's add some more comments to the program:

```
/* Program 1.3 Another Simple C Program - Displaying a Quotation */
#include <stdio.h>        /* This is a preprocessor directive    */

int main(void)            /* This identifies the function main() */
{                         /* This marks the beginning of main()  */
  printf("Beware the Ides of March!");  /* This line displays a quotation */
  return 0;               /* This returns control to the operating system */
}                         /* This marks the end of main()              */
```

You can see that using comments can be a very useful way of explaining what's going on in the program. You can place comments wherever you want in your program, and you can use them to explain the general objectives of the code as well as the specifics of how the code works. A single comment can spread over several lines; everything from the /* to the */ will be treated as a comment and ignored by the compiler. Here's how you could use a single comment to identify the author of the code and to assert your copyright:

```
/*
 * Written by Ivor Horton
 * Copyright 2006
 */
```

This is one comment spread over four lines. I have used asterisks to mark the beginning of each line of text here but they are not obligatory, just part of the comment as I wrote it. You can use anything you like to improve the readability of a comment, but don't forget that */ will be interpreted as the end of the comment.

Preprocessing Directives

Look at the following line of code:

```
#include <stdio.h>      /* This is a preprocessor directive    */
```

This is not strictly part of the executable program, but it is essential in this case! in fact, the program won't work without it. The symbol # indicates this is a **preprocessing directive**, which is an instruction to your compiler to do something before compiling the source code. The compiler handles these directives during an initial preprocessing phase before the compilation process starts. There are quite a few preprocessing directives, and they're usually placed at the beginning of the program source file.

In this case, the compiler is instructed to •include! in your program the contents of the file with the name stdio.h. This file is called a **header file**, because it's usually included at the head of a program. In this case the header file defines information about some of the functions that are provided by the standard C library but, in general, header files specify information that the compiler uses to integrate any predefined functions or other global objects with a program, so you'll be creating your own header files for use with your programs. In this case, because you're using the printf() function from the standard library, you have to include the stdio.h header file. This is because stdio.h contains the information that the compiler needs to understand what printf() means, as well as other functions that deal with input and output. As such, its name, stdio, is short for **standard input/output**. All header files in C have file names with the extension .h. You'll use other C header files later in the book.

■**Note** Although the header file names are not case sensitive, it's common practice to write them in #include directives in lowercase letters.

Every C compiler that conforms to the international standard (ISO/IEC 9899) for the language will have a set of standard header files supplied with it. These header files primarily contain declarations relating to standard library functions that are available with C. Although all C compilers that conform with the standard will support the same set of standard library functions and will have the same set of standard header files available, there may be extra library functions provided with a particular compiler that may not be available with other compilers, and these will typically provide functionality that is specific to the type of computer on which the compiler runs.

Defining the main() Function

The next five statements define the function main():

```
int main(void)          /* This identifies the function main() */
{                       /* This marks the beginning of main()  */
  printf("Beware the Ides of March!");  /* This line displays a quotation */
  return 0;             /* This returns control to the operating system */
}                       /* This marks the end of main()                 */
```

A **function** is just a named block of code between braces that carries out some specific set of operations. Every C program consists of one or more functions, and every C program must contain a function called main()! the reason being that a program will always start execution from the beginning of this function. So imagine that you've created, compiled, and linked a file called progname.exe. When you execute this program, the operating system calls the function main() for the program.

The first line of the definition for the function main() is as follows:

```
int main(void)          /* This identifies the function main() */
```

This defines the start of the function main(). Notice that there is *no* semicolon at the end of the line. The first line identifying this as the function main() has the word int at the beginning. What appears here defines the type of value to be returned by the function, and the word int signifies that the function main() returns an integer value. The integer value that is returned when the execution of main() ends represents a code that is returned to the operating system that indicates the program state. You end execution of the main() function and specify the value to be returned in the statement:

```
return 0;               /* This returns control to the operating system */
```

This is a **return** statement that ends execution of the main() function and returns that value 0 to the operating system. You return a zero value from main() to indicate that the program terminated normally; a nonzero value would indicate an abnormal return, which means, in other words, things were not as they should be when the program ended.

The parentheses that immediately follow the name of the function, main, enclose a definition of what information is to be transferred to main() when it starts executing. In this example, however, you can see that there's the word void between the parentheses, and this signifies that no data can be transferred to main(). Later, you'll see how data is transferred to main() and to other functions in a program.

The function main() can call other functions, which in turn may call further functions, and so on. For every function that's called, you have the opportunity to pass some information to it within the parentheses that follow its name. A function will stop execution when a return statement in the body of the function is reached, and control will then transfer to the calling function (or the operating system in the case of the function main()).

Keywords

In C, a **keyword** is a word with special significance, so you shouldn't use keywords for any other purposes in your program. For this reason, keywords are also referred to as **reserved words**. In the preceding example, int is a keyword and void and return are also keywords. C has several keywords, and you'll become familiar with more of them as you learn more of the language. You'll find a complete list of C keywords in Appendix C.

The Body of a Function

The general structure of the function `main()` is illustrated in Figure 1-2.

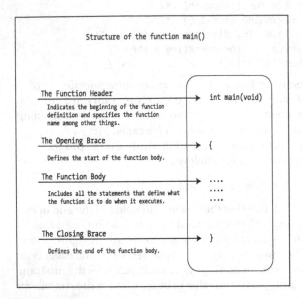

Structure of the function main()

The Function Header → `int main(void)`
Indicates the beginning of the function definition and specifies the function name among other things.

The Opening Brace → `{`
Defines the start of the function body.

The Function Body → `....` `....` `....`
Includes all the statements that define what the function is to do when it executes.

The Closing Brace → `}`
Defines the end of the function body.

Figure 1-2. *Structure of the function main()*

The **function body** is the bit between the opening and closing braces that follow the line where the function name appears. The function body contains all the statements that define what the function does. The example's `main()` function has a very simple function body consisting of just two statements:

```
{                       /* This marks the beginning of main()  */
  printf("Beware the Ides of March!");  /* This line displays a quotation */
  return 0;             /* This returns control to the operating system */
}                       /* This marks the end of main()            */
```

Every function must have a body, although the body can be empty and just consist of the opening and closing braces without any statements between them. In this case, the function will do nothing.

You may wonder where the use is for a function that does nothing. Actually, this can be very useful when you're developing a program that will have many functions. You can declare the set of (empty) functions that you think you'll need to write to solve the problem at hand, which should give you an idea of the programming that needs to be done, and then gradually create the program code for each function. This technique helps you to build your program in a logical and incremental manner.

■**Note** You can see that I've aligned the braces one below the other in Program 1.3. I've done this to make it clear where the block of statements that the braces enclose starts and finishes. Statements between braces are usually indented by a fixed amount—usually two or more spaces so that the braces stand out. This is good programming style, as the statements within a block can be readily identified.

Outputting Information

The body of the `main()` function in the example includes a statement that calls the `printf()` function:

```
printf("Beware the Ides of March!");  /* This line displays a quotation */
```

As I've said, `printf()` is a standard library function, and it outputs information to the display screen based on what appears between the parentheses that immediately follow the function name. In this case, the call to the function displays a simple piece of Shakespearean advice that appears between the double quotes; a string of characters between double quotes like this is called a **string literal**. Notice that this line *does* end with a semicolon.

Arguments

Items enclosed between the parentheses following a function name, as with the `printf()` function in the previous statement, are called **arguments**, which specify data that is to be passed to the function. When there is more than one argument to a function, they must be separated by commas.

In the previous example the argument to the function is the text string between double quotes. If you don't like the quotation that is specified here, you could display something else by simply including your own choice of words enclosed within double quotes inside the parentheses. For instance, you might prefer a line from *Macbeth*:

```
printf("Out, damned Spot! Out I say!");
```

Try using this in the example. When you've modified the source code, you need to compile and link the program again before executing it.

Note As with all executable statements in C (as opposed to defining or directive statements) the `printf()` line must have a semicolon at the end. As you've seen, a very common error, particularly when you first start programming in C, is to forget the semicolon.

Control Characters

You could alter the program to display two sentences on separate lines. Try typing in the following code:

```
/* Program 1.4 Another Simple C Program - Displaying a Quotation */
#include <stdio.h>

int main(void)
{
  printf("\nMy formula for success?\nRise early, work late, strike oil.");
  return 0;
}
```

The output from this program looks like this:

```
My formula for success?
Rise early, work late, strike oil.
```

Look at the `printf()` statement. At the beginning of the text and after the first sentence, you've inserted the characters \n. The combination \n actually represents one character: a newline character.

The backslash (\) is of special significance in a text string. As we saw before, it indicates the start of an **escape sequence**. Escape sequences are used to insert characters in a string that would otherwise be impossible to specify, such as tab and newline, or in some circumstances would confuse the compiler, such as placing a double quote, which you would normally use to delimit a string, within a string. The character following the backslash indicates what character the escape sequence represents. In this case, it's n for newline, but there are plenty of other possibilities. Obviously, if a backslash is of special significance, you need a way to specify a backslash in a text string. To do this, you simply use two backslashes: \\. Similarly, if you actually want to display a double quote character, you can use \".

Type in the following program:

```
/* Program 1.5 Another Simple C Program - Displaying Great Quotations */
#include <stdio.h>

int main(void)
{
  printf("\n\"It is a wise father that knows his own child.\" Shakespeare");
  return 0;
}
```

The output displays the following text:

```
"It is a wise father that knows his own child." Shakespeare
```

You can use the \a escape sequence in an output string to sound a beep to signal something interesting or important. Enter and run the following program:

```
/* Program 1.6 A Simple C Program – Important */
#include <stdio.h>

int main(void)
{
  printf("\nBe careful!!\a");
  return 0;
}
```

The output of this program is sound and vision. Listen closely and you should hear the beep through the speaker in your computer.

```
Be careful!!
```

The \a sequence represents the •bell! character. Table 1-1 shows a summary of the escape sequences that you can use.

Table 1-1. *Escape Sequences*

Escape Sequence	Description
\n	Represents a newline character
\r	Represents a carriage return
\b	Represents a backspace
\f	Represents a form-feed character
\t	Represents a horizontal tab

Table 1-1. *Escape Sequences*

Escape Sequence	Description
\v	Represents a vertical tab
\a	Inserts a bell (alert) character
\?	Inserts a question mark (?)
\"	Inserts a double quote (")
\'	Inserts a single quote (')
\\	Inserts a backslash (\)

Try displaying different lines of text on the screen and alter the spacing within that text. You can put words on different lines using \n, and you can use \t to space the text. You'll get a lot more practice with these as you progress through the book.

Developing Programs in C

The process of developing programs in C may not be evident if you've never written a program before. However, it's very similar to many other situations in life in which at the beginning it just isn't clear how you're going to achieve your objective. Normally you start with a rough idea of what you want to achieve, but you need to translate this into a more precise specification of what you want. Once you've reached this more precise specification, you can work out the series of steps that will lead to your final objective. So having an idea that you want to build a house just isn't enough. You need to know what kind of house you want, how large it's going to be, what kinds of materials you have to build it with, and where you want to build it. This kind of detailed planning is also necessary when you want to write a program.

Let's go through the basic steps that you need to follow when you're writing a program. The house analogy is a useful one, so we'll work with it for a while.

Understanding the Problem

The first step is to get a clear idea of what you want to do. It would be lunacy to start building your house before you had established what facilities it should provide: how many bedrooms, how many bathrooms, how big it's going to be, and so on. All these things affect the cost of the house in terms of materials and the work involved in building it. Generally it comes down to a compromise that best meets your needs within the constraints of the money, the workforce, and the time that's available for you to complete the project.

It's the same with developing a program of any size. Even for a relatively straightforward problem, you need to know what kind of input to expect, how the input is to be processed, and what kind of output is required!   and how it's going to look. The input could be entered with the keyboard, but it might also involve data from a disk file or information obtained over a telephone line or a network. The output could simply be displayed on the screen, or it could be printed; perhaps it might involve updating a data file on disk.

For more complex programs, you'll need to look at many more aspects of what the program is going to do. A clear definition of the problem that your program is going to solve is an absolutely essential part of understanding the resources and effort that are going to be needed for the creation of a finished product. Considering these details also forces you to establish whether the project is actually feasible.

Detailed Design

To get the house built, you'll need detailed plans. These plans enable the construction workers to do their job and the plans describe in detail how the house will go together! the dimensions, the materials to use, and so on. You'll also need a plan of what is to be done and when. For example, you'll want the foundation dug before the walls are built, so the plan must involve segmenting the work into manageable units to be performed in a logical sequence.

It's the same with a program. You'll need to specify what the program does by dividing it into a set of well-defined and manageable chunks that are reasonably self-contained. You'll also need to detail the way in which these chunks connect, as well as what information each chunk will need when it executes. This will enable you to develop the logic of each chunk relatively independently from the rest of the program. If you treat a large program as one huge process that you try to code as a single chunk, chances are that you'll never get it to work.

Implementation

Given the detailed design of a house, the work can start. Each group of construction workers will need to complete its part of the project at the right time. Each stage will need to be inspected to check that it's been done properly before the next stage begins. Omitting these checks could easily result in the whole house collapsing.

Of course, if a program is large, you'll write the source code one unit at a time. As one part is completed, you can write the code for the next. Each part will be based on the detailed design specifications, and you'll verify that each piece works, as much as you can, before proceeding. In this way, you'll gradually progress to a fully working program that does everything you originally intended.

Testing

The house is complete, but there are a lot of things that need to be tested: the drainage, the water and electricity supplies, the heating, and so on. Any one of these areas can have problems that the contractors need to go back and fix. This is sometimes an iterative process, in which problems with one aspect of the house can be the cause of things going wrong somewhere else.

The mechanism with a program is similar. Each of your program **modules**! the pieces that make up your program! will need to be tested individually. When they don't work properly, you need to debug them. **Debugging** is the process of finding and correcting errors in your program. This term is said to have originated in the days when finding the errors in a program involved tracing where the information went and how it was processed by using the circuit diagram for the computer. The story goes that it was discovered that a computer program error was caused by an insect shorting part of the circuit in the computer. The problem was caused by a bug. Subsequently, the term **bug** was used to refer to any error in a program.

With a simple program, you can often find an error simply by inspecting the code. In general, though, the process of debugging usually involves adding extra program code to produce output that will enable you to check what the sequence of events is and what intermediate values are produced in a program. With a large program, you'll also need to test the program modules in combination because, although the individual modules may work, there's no guarantee that they'll work together! The jargon for this phase of program development is **integration testing**.

Functions and Modular Programming

The word **function** has appeared a few times so far in this chapter with reference to main(), printf(), function body, and so on. Let's explore in a little more depth what functions are and why they're important.

Most programming languages, including C, provide a way of breaking up a program into segments, each of which can be written more or less independently of the others. In C these segments are called **functions**. The program code in the body of one function is insulated from that of other functions. A function will have a specific interface to the outside world in terms of how information is transferred to it and how results generated by the function are transmitted back from it. This interface is specified in the first line of the function, where the function name appears.

Figure 1-3 shows a simple example of a program to analyze baseball scores that is composed of four functions.

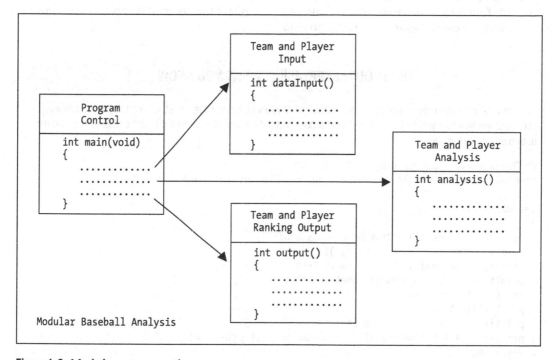

Figure 1-3. *Modular programming*

Each of the four functions does a specific, well-defined job. Overall control of the sequence of operations in the program is managed by one module, main(). There is a function to read and check the input data, and another function to do the analysis. Once the data has been read and analyzed, a fourth function has the task of outputting the team and player rankings.

Segmenting a program into manageable chunks is a very important aspect to programming, so let's go over the reasons for doing this:

! It allows each function to be written and tested separately. This greatly simplifies the process of getting the total program to work.

! Several separate functions are easier to handle and understand than one huge function.

! Libraries are just sets of functions that people tend to use all the time. Because they've been prewritten and pretested, you know they'll work, so you can use them without worrying about their code details. This will accelerate your program development by allowing you to concentrate on your own code, and it's a fundamental part of the philosophy of C. The richness of the libraries greatly amplifies the power of the language.

! You can accumulate your own libraries of functions that are applicable to the sort of programs that you're interested in. If you find yourself writing a particular function frequently, you can write a generalized version of it to suit your needs and build this into your own library. Then, whenever you need to use that particular function, you can simply use your library version.

! In the development of large programs, which can vary from a few thousand to millions of lines of code, development can be undertaken by teams of programmers, with each team working with a defined subgroup of the functions that make up the whole program.

You'll learn about C functions in greater detail in Chapter 8. Because the structure of a C program is inherently functional, you've already been introduced to one of the standard library functions in one of this chapter's earliest examples: the function printf().

TRY IT OUT: EXERCISING WHAT YOU KNOW

Let's now look at an example that puts into practice what you've learned so far. First, have a look at the following code and see whether you can understand what it does without running it. Then type it in and compile, link, and run it, and see what happens.

```c
/* Program 1.7 A longer program */
#include <stdio.h>     /* Include the header file for input and output */

int main(void)
{
  printf("Hi there!\n\n\nThis program is a bit");
  printf(" longer than the others.");
  printf("\nBut really it's only more text.\n\n\n\a\a");
  printf("Hey, wait a minute!! What was that???\n\n");
  printf("\t1.\tA bird?\n");
  printf("\t2.\tA plane?\n");
  printf("\t3.\tA control character?\n");
  printf("\n\t\t\b\bAnd how will this look when it prints out?\n\n");
  return 0;
}
```

The output will be as follows:

```
Hi there!


This program is a bit longer than the others.
But really it's only more text.


Hey, wait a minute!! What was that???

A bird?
A plane?
A control character?

        And how will this look when it prints out?
```

How It Works

The program looks a little bit complicated, but this is only because the text strings between parentheses include a lot of escape sequences. Each text string is bounded by a pair of double quotation marks. However, the program is just a succession of calls to the printf() function, and it demonstrates that output to the screen is controlled by what you pass to the printf() function. Let's look at this program in detail.

You include the stdio.h file from the standard library through the preprocessing directive:

```
#include <stdio.h>    /* Include the header file for input and output */
```

You can see that this is a preprocessing directive because it begins with #. The stdio.h file provides the definitions you need to be able to use the printf() function.

You then define the start of the function main() and specify that it returns an integer value with this line:

```
int main(void)
```

The opening brace on the next line indicates that the body of the function follows:

```
{
```

The next statement calls the standard library function printf() to output Hi there! to your display screen, followed by two blank lines and the phrase This program is a bit.

```
printf("Hi there!\n\n\nThis program is a bit");
```

The two blank lines are produced by the three \n escape sequences. Each of these starts a new line when the characters are written to the display. The first ends the line containing Hi there!, and the next two produce the two empty lines. The text This program is a bit appears on the fourth line of output. You can see that this one line of code produces a total of four lines of output on the screen.

The next line of output produced by the next printf() starts at the character position immediately following the last character in the previous output. The next statement outputs the text longer than the others with a space as the first character of the text:

```
printf(" longer than the others.");
```

This output will simply continue where the last line left off, following the t in bit. This means that you really do need the space at the beginning of the text, otherwise the computer will display This program is a bitlonger than the others, which isn't what you want.

The next statement starts its output on a new line immediately following the previous line, because of the \n at the beginning of the text string between double quotation marks:

```
printf("\nBut really it's only more text.\n\n\n\a\a");
```

It then displays the text and adds two empty lines (because of the three \n escape sequences) and beeps twice. The next output to the screen will start at the beginning of the line that follows the second empty line produced here.

The next output is produced by the following statement:

```
printf("Hey, wait a minute!! What was that???\n\n");
```

This outputs the text and then leaves one empty line. The next output will be on the line following the empty line.

Each of the next three statements inserts a tab, displays a number, inserts another tab followed by some text, and ends with a new line. This is useful for making your output easier to read.

```
printf("\t1.\tA bird?\n");
printf("\t2.\tA plane?\n");
printf("\t3.\tA control character?\n");
```

This produces three numbered lines of output.

The next statement initially outputs a new line character, so that there will be an empty line following the previous output. Two tabs are then sent to the display followed by two backspaces, which moves you back two spaces from the last tab position. Finally the text is displayed, and two newline characters are sent to the display.

```
printf("\n\t\t\b\bAnd how will this look when it prints out?\n\n");
```

The last statement in the body of the function is the following:

```
return 0;
```

This ends execution of main() and returns 0 to the operating system.

The closing brace marks the end of the function body:

```
}
```

Common Mistakes

Mistakes are a fact of life. When you write a computer program in C, the compiler must convert your source code to machine code, and so there must be some very strict rules governing how you use the language. Leave out a comma where one is expected, or add a semicolon where you shouldn't, and the compiler won't be able to translate your program into machine code.

You'll be surprised just how easy it is to introduce typographical errors into your program, even after years of practice. If you're lucky, these errors will be picked up when you compile or link your program. If you're really unlucky, they can result in your program apparently working fine but producing some intermittent erratic behavior. You can end up spending a lot of time tracking these errors down.

Of course, it's not only typographical errors that cause problems. You'll often find that your detailed implementation is just not right. Where you're dealing with complicated decisions in your program, it's easy to get the logic wrong. Your program may be quite accurate from a language point of view, and it may compile and run without a problem, but it won't produce the right answers. These kinds of errors can be the most difficult to find.

Points to Remember

It would be a good idea to review what you've gleaned from your first program. You can do this by looking at the overview of the important points in Figure 1-4.

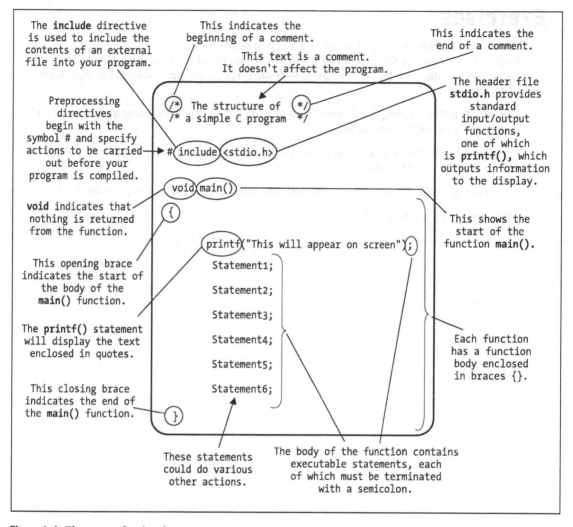

The **include** directive is used to include the contents of an external file into your program.

This indicates the beginning of a comment.

This text is a comment. It doesn't affect the program.

This indicates the end of a comment.

Preprocessing directives begin with the symbol # and specify actions to be carried out before your program is compiled.

The header file **stdio.h** provides standard input/output functions, one of which is **printf()**, which outputs information to the display.

void indicates that nothing is returned from the function.

This opening brace indicates the start of the body of the **main()** function.

This shows the start of the function **main()**.

The **printf()** statement will display the text enclosed in quotes.

Each function has a function body enclosed in braces {}.

This closing brace indicates the end of the **main()** function.

These statements could do various other actions.

The body of the function contains executable statements, each of which must be terminated with a semicolon.

```
/* The structure of */
/* a simple C program */
#include <stdio.h>
void main()
{
    printf("This will appear on screen");
    Statement1;
    Statement2;
    Statement3;
    Statement4;
    Statement5;
    Statement6;
}
```

Figure 1-4. *Elements of a simple program*

Summary

You've reached the end of the first chapter, and you've already written a few programs in C. You've covered quite a lot of ground, but at a fairly gentle pace. The aim of this chapter was to introduce a few basic ideas rather than teach you a lot about the C programming language. You should be confident about editing, compiling, and running your programs. You probably have only a vague idea about how to construct a C program at this point. It will become much clearer when you've learned a bit more about C and have written some programs with more meat to them.

In the next chapter you'll move on to more complicated things than just producing text output using the printf() function. You'll manipulate information and get some rather more interesting results. And by the way, the printf() function does a whole lot more than just display text strings! as you'll see soon.

Exercises

The following exercises enable you to try out what you've learned in this chapter. If you get stuck, look back over the chapter for help. If you're still stuck, you can download the solutions from the Source Code/Download section of the Apress web site (http://www.apress.com), but that really should be a last resort.

Exercise 1-1. Write a program that will output your name and address using a separate printf() statement for each line of output.

Exercise 1-2. Modify your solution for the previous exercise so that it produces all the output using only one printf() statement.

Exercise 1-3. Write a program to output the following text exactly as it appears here:

```
"It's freezing in here," he said coldly.
```

CHAPTER 2

■ ■ ■

First Steps in Programming

By now you're probably eager to create programs that allow your computer to really interact with the outside world. You don't just want programs that work as glorified typewriters, displaying fixed information that you included in the program code, and indeed there's a whole world of programming that goes beyond that.

Ideally, you want to be able to enter data from the keyboard and have the program squirrel it away somewhere. This would make the program much more versatile. Your program would be able to access and manipulate this data, and it would be able to work with different data values each time you execute it. This whole idea of entering different information each time you run a program is key to the whole enterprise of programming. A place to store an item of data that can vary in a program is not altogether surprisingly called a **variable**, and this is what this chapter covers.

This is quite a long chapter that covers a lot of ground. By the time you reach the end of it, you'll be able to write some really useful programs.

In this chapter you'll learn the following:

! How memory is used and what variables are

! How you can calculate in C

! What different types of variables there are and what you use them for

! What casting is and when you need to use it

! How to write a program that calculates the height of a tree!   any tree

Memory in Your Computer

First let's look at how the computer stores the data that's processed in your program. To understand this, you need to know a little bit about memory in your computer, so before you go into your first program, let's take a quick tour of your computer's memory.

The instructions that make up your program, and the data that it acts upon, have to be stored somewhere while your computer is executing that program. When your program is running, this storage place is the machine's memory. It's also referred to as **main memory**, or the **random access memory (RAM)** of the machine.

Your computer also contains another kind of memory called **read-only memory (ROM)**. As its name suggests, you can't change ROM: you can only read its contents or have your machine execute instructions contained within it. The information contained in ROM was put there when the machine was manufactured. This information is mainly programs that control the operation of the various devices attached to your computer, such as the display, the hard disk drive, the keyboard, and the floppy disk drive. On a PC, these programs are called the **basic input/output system (BIOS)** of your computer.

I don't need to refer to the BIOS in detail in this book. The interesting memory for your purposes is RAM; this is where your programs and data are stored when they execute. So let's learn a bit more about it.

You can think of your computer's RAM as an ordered sequence of boxes. Each of these boxes is in one of two states: either the box is full when it represents 1 or the box is empty when it represents 0. Therefore, each box represents one binary digit, either 0 or 1. The computer sometimes thinks of these in terms of **true** and **false**: 1 is true and 0 is false. Each of these boxes is called a **bit**, which is a contraction of *binary digit*.

■**Note** If you can't remember or have never learned about binary numbers, and you want to find out a little bit more, you'll find more detail in Appendix A. However, you needn't worry about these details if they don't appeal to you. The important point here is that the computer can only deal with 1s and 0s—it can't deal with decimal numbers directly. All the data that your program works with, including the program instructions themselves, will consist of binary numbers internally.

For convenience, the boxes or bits in your computer are grouped into sets of eight, and each set of eight bits is called a **byte**. To allow you to refer to the contents of a particular byte, each byte has been labeled with a number, starting from 0 for the first byte, 1 for the second byte, and going up to whatever number of bytes you have in your computer's memory. This label for a byte is called its **address**. Thus, each byte will have an address that's different from that of all the other bytes in memory. Just as a street address identifies a particular house, the address of a byte uniquely references that byte in your computer's memory.

To summarize, you have your memory building blocks (called bits) that are in groups of eight (called bytes). A bit can only be either 1 or 0. This is illustrated in Figure 2-1.

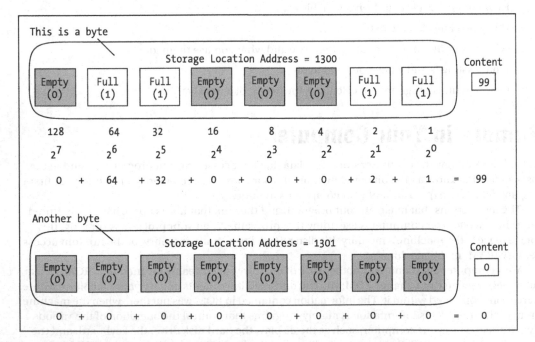

Figure 2-1. *Bytes in memory*

The amount of memory your computer has is expressed in terms of so many kilobytes, megabytes, or gigabytes. Here's what those words mean:

!   1 kilobyte (or 1KB) is 1,024 bytes.

!   1 megabyte (or 1MB) is 1,024 kilobytes, which is 1,048,576 bytes.

!   1 gigabyte (or 1GB) is 1,024 megabytes, which is 1,073,741,841 bytes.

You might be wondering why you don't work with simpler, more rounded numbers, such as a thousand, or a million, or a billion. The reason is this: there are 1,024 numbers from 0 to 1,023, and 1,023 happens to be 10 bits that are all 1 in binary: 11 1111 1111, which is a very convenient binary value. So while 1,000 is a very convenient decimal value, it's actually rather inconvenient in a binary machine!   it's 11 1110 1000, which is not exactly neat and tidy. The kilobyte (1,024 bytes) is therefore defined in a manner that's convenient for your computer, rather than for you. Similarly, for a megabyte, you need 20 bits, and for a gigabyte, you need 30 bits. One point of confusion can arise here, particularly with disk drive capacities. Disk drive manufacturers often refer to a disk as having a capacity of 537 megabytes or 18.3 gigabytes, when they really mean 537 million bytes and 18.3 billion bytes. Of course, 537 million bytes is only 512 megabytes and 18.3 billion bytes is only 17 gigabytes, so a manufacturer's specification of the capacity of a hard disk can be misleading.

Now that you know a bit about bytes, let's see how you can use this memory in your programs.

What Is a Variable?

A variable is a specific piece of memory in your computer that consists of one or more contiguous bytes. Every variable has a name, and you can use that name to refer to that place in memory to retrieve what it contains or store a new data value there.

Let's start with a program that displays your salary using the printf() function that you saw in Chapter 1. Assuming your salary is $10,000 per month, you can already write that program very easily:

```
/* Program 2.1 What is a Variable? */
#include <stdio.h>

int main(void)
{
  printf("My salary is $10000");
  return 0;
}
```

I'm sure you don't need any more explanation about how this works; it's almost identical to the programs you developed in Chapter 1. So how can you modify this program to allow you to customize the message depending on a value stored in memory? There are, as ever, several ways of doing this. What they all have in common, though, is that they use a variable.

In this case, you could allocate a piece of memory that you could call, say, salary, and store the value 10000 in it. When you want to display your salary, you could use the name you've given to the variable, which is salary, and the value that's stored in it (10000) would be displayed. Wherever you use a variable name in a program, the computer accesses the value that's stored there. You can access a variable however many times you need to in your program. And when your salary changes, you can simply change the value stored in the variable salary and the whole program will carry on working with the new value. Of course, all these values will be stored as binary numbers inside the computer.

You can have as many variables as you like in a program. The value that each variable contains, at any point during the execution of that program, is determined by the instructions contained in your program. The value of a variable isn't fixed, and it can change as many times as you need it to throughout a program.

Variables That Store Numbers

There are several different types of variables, and each type of variable is used for storing a particular kind of data. You'll start by looking at variables that you can use to store numbers. There are actually several different ways in which you can store numbers in your program, so let's start with the simplest.

Integer Variables

Let's look first at variables that store integers. An integer is any whole number without a decimal point. Examples of integers are as follows:

1

10,999,000,000

1

You will recognize these values as integers, but what I've written here isn't quite correct so far as your program is concerned. You can't include commas in an integer, so the second value would actually be written in a program as 10999000000.

Here are some examples of numbers that are *not* integers:

1.234

999.9

2.0

−0.0005

Normally, 2.0 would be described as an integer because it's a whole number, but as far as your computer is concerned it isn't because it contains a decimal point. For your program, you must write it as 2 with no decimal point. In a C program integers are always written without a decimal point; if there's a decimal point, it isn't recognized as an integer. Before I discuss variables in more detail (and believe me, there's a lot more detail!), let's look at a simple variable in action in a program, just so you can get a feel for how they're used.

TRY IT OUT: USING A VARIABLE

Let's go back to your salary. You can try writing the previous program using a variable:

```
/* Program 2.2 Using a variable  */
#include <stdio.h>

int main(void)
{
  int salary;            /* Declare a variable called salary        */
  salary = 10000;        /* A simple arithmetic assignment statement */
  printf("My salary is %d.", salary);
  return 0;
}
```

Type in this example and compile, link, and execute it. You'll get the following output:

```
My salary is 10000.
```

How It Works

The first three lines are exactly the same as in all the previous programs. Let's look at the new stuff.

The statement that identifies the memory that you're using to store your salary is the following:

```
int salary;          /* Declare a variable called salary        */
```

This statement is called a **variable declaration** because it declares the name of the variable. The name, in this program, is salary.

Caution Notice that the variable declaration ends with a semicolon. If you omit the semicolon, your program will generate an error when you compile it.

The variable declaration also specifies the type of data that the variable will store. You've used the keyword int to specify that the variable, salary, will be used to store an integer value. The keyword int precedes the name of the variable. As you'll see later, declarations for variables that store other kinds of data consist of another keyword specifying a data type followed by a variable name in a similar manner.

Note Remember, keywords are special C words that mean something specific to the compiler. You must not use them as variable names or your compiler will get confused.

The variable declaration is also a **definition** for the variable, salary, because it causes some storage to be allocated to store an integer value that can be referred to using the name salary. Of course, you have not specified what the value of salary should be yet, so at this point it will contain a junk value—whatever was left behind from when this bit of memory was used last.

The next statement is the following:

```
salary = 10000;
```

This is a simple **arithmetic assignment statement**. It takes the value to the right of the equal sign and stores it in the variable on the left of the equal sign. Here you're declaring that the variable salary will have the value 10000. You're storing the value on the right (10000) in the variable on the left (salary). The = symbol is called the **assignment operator** because it assigns the value on the right to the variable on the left.

You then have the familiar printf() statement, but it's a little different from how you've seen it in action before:

```
printf("My salary is %d.", salary);
```

There are now two **arguments** inside the parentheses, separated by a comma. An argument is a value that's passed to a function. In this program statement, the two arguments to the printf() function are as follows:

- Argument 1 is a **control string**, so called because it controls how the output specified by the following argument (or arguments) is to be presented. This is the character string between the double quotes. It is also referred to as a **format string** because it specifies the format of the data that is output.

- Argument 2 is the name of the variable salary. How the value of this variable will be displayed is determined by the first argument—the control string.

The control string is fairly similar to the previous example, in that it contains some text to be displayed. However, if you look carefully, you'll see %d embedded in it. This is called a **conversion specifier** for the variable.

Conversion specifiers determine how variables are displayed on the screen. In this case, you've used a d, which is a decimal specifier that applies to integer values (whole numbers). It just means that the second argument, salary, will be interpreted and output as a decimal (base 10) number.

■**Note** Conversion specifiers always start with a % character so that the printf( ) function can recognize them. Because a % in a control string always indicates the start of a conversion specifier, if you want to output a % character you must use the sequence %%.

TRY IT OUT: USING MORE VARIABLES

Let's try a slightly larger example:

```
/* Program 2.3 Using more variables */
#include <stdio.h>

int main(void)
{
  int brothers;            /* Declare a variable called brothers */
  int brides;              /* and a variable called brides       */

  brothers = 7;            /* Store 7 in the variable brothers   */
  brides = 7;              /* Store 7 in the variable brides      */

  /* Display some output */
  printf("%d brides for %d brothers", brides, brothers);
  return 0;
}
```

If you run this program you should get the following output:

```
7 brides for 7 brothers
```

How It Works

This program works in a very similar way to the previous example. You first declare two variables, brides and brothers, with the following statements:

```
  int brothers;            /* Declare a variable called brothers */
  int brides;              /* and a variable called brides       */
```

Both of these variables are declared as type int so they both store integer values. Notice that they've been declared in separate statements. Because they're both of the same type, you could have saved a line of code and declared them together like this:

```
int brothers, brides;
```

When you declare several variables in one statement, the variable names following the data type are separated by commas, and the whole line ends with a semicolon. This can be a convenient format, although there's a downside in that it isn't so obvious what each variable is for, because if they appear on a single line you can't add individual comments to describe each variable. However, you could write this single statement spread over two lines:

```
int brothers,        /* Declare a variable called brothers */
      brides;        /* and a variable called brides       */
```

By spreading the statement out over two lines, you're able to put the comments back in. The comments will be ignored by the compiler, so it's still the exact equivalent of the original statement without the comments. Of course, you might as well write it as two statements.

Note that the declarations appear at the beginning of the executable code for the function. You should put all the declarations for variables that you intend to use at the beginning.

The next two statements assign the same value, 7, to each of the variables:

```
brothers = 7;                /* Store 7 in the variable brothers  */
brides = 7;                  /* Store 7 in the variable brides    */
```

Note that the statements that declared these variables precede these statements. If one or other of the declarations were missing or appeared later in the code, the program wouldn't compile.

The next statement calls the printf() function with a control string as the first argument that will display a line of text. The %d conversion specifiers within this control string will be replaced by the values currently stored in the variables that appear as the second and third arguments to the printf() function call—in this case, brides and brothers:

```
printf("%d brides for %d brothers", brides, brothers);
```

The conversion specifiers are replaced in order by the values of the variables that appear as the second and subsequent arguments to the printf() function, so the value of brides corresponds to the first specifier, and the value of brothers corresponds to the second. This would be more obvious if you changed the statements that set the values of the variables as follows:

```
brothers = 8;                /* Store 8 in the variable brothers  */
brides = 4;                  /* Store 4 in the variable brides    */
```

In this somewhat dubious scenario, the printf() statement would show clearly which variable corresponds to which conversion specifier, because the output would be the following:

```
4 brides for 8 brothers
```

Naming Variables

The name that you give to a variable, conveniently referred to as a **variable name**, can be defined with some flexibility. A variable name is a sequence of one or more uppercase or lowercase letters, digits, and underscore characters (_) that begins with a letter (incidentally, the underscore character counts as a letter). Examples of legal variable names are as follows:

Radius

diameter

Auntie_May

Knotted_Wool

D678

Because a variable name can't begin with a digit, 8_Ball and 6_pack aren't legal names. A variable name can't include any other characters besides letters, underscores, and digits, so Hash! and Mary-Lou aren't allowed as names. This last example is a common mistake, but Mary_Lou would be quite acceptable. Because spaces aren't allowed in a name, Mary Lou would be interpreted as two variable names, Mary and Lou. Variables starting with one or two underscore characters are often used in the header files, so don't use the underscore as the first letter when naming your variables; otherwise, you run the risk of your name clashing with the name of a variable used in the standard library. For example, names such as _this and _that are best avoided.

Although you can call variables whatever you want within the preceding constraints, it's worth calling them something that gives you a clue to what they contain. Assigning the name x to a variable that stores a salary isn't very helpful. It would be far better to call it salary and leave no one in any doubt as to what it is.

■**Caution** The number of characters that you can have in a variable name will depend upon your compiler. A minimum of 31 characters must be supported by a compiler that conforms to the C language standard, so you can always use names up to this length without any problems. I suggest that you don't make your variable names longer than this anyway, as they become cumbersome and make the code harder to follow. Some compilers will truncate names that are too long.

Another very important point to remember when naming your variables is that variable names are case sensitive, which means that the names Democrat and democrat are distinct. You can demonstrate this by changing the printf() statement so that one of the variable names starts with a capital letter, as follows:

```
/* Program 2.3A Using more variables */
#include <stdio.h>

int main(void)
{
  int brothers;            /* Declare a variable called brothers */
  int brides;              /* and a variable called brides       */

  brothers = 7;            /* Store 7 in the variable brothers   */
  brides = 7;              /* Store 7 in the variable brides      */

  /* Display some output */
  printf("%d brides for %d brothers", Brides, brothers);
  return 0;
}
```

You'll get an error message when you try to compile this version of the program. The compiler interprets the two variable names brides and Brides as different, so it doesn't understand what Brides refers to. This is a common error. As I've said before, punctuation and spelling mistakes are one of the main causes of trivial errors.

You must also declare a variable before you use it, otherwise the compiler will not recognize it and will flag the statement as an error.

Using Variables

You now know how to name and declare your variables, but so far this hasn't been much more useful than anything you learned in Chapter 1. Let's try another program in which you'll use the values in the variables before you produce the output.

TRY IT OUT: DOING A SIMPLE CALCULATION

This program does a simple calculation using the values of the variables:

```
/* Program 2.4 Simple calculations */
#include <stdio.h>

int main(void)
{
  int Total_Pets;
  int Cats;
  int Dogs;
  int Ponies;
  int Others;

  /* Set the number of each kind of pet */
  Cats = 2;
  Dogs = 1;
  Ponies = 1;
  Others = 46;

  /* Calculate the total number of pets */
  Total_Pets = Cats + Dogs + Ponies + Others;

  printf("We have %d pets in total", Total_Pets);  /* Output the result */
  return 0;
}
```

This example produces this output:

```
We have 50 pets in total
```

How It Works

As in the previous examples, all the statements between the braces are indented by the same amount. This makes it clear that all these statements belong together. You should always organize your programs the way you see here: indent a group of statements that lie between an opening and closing brace by the same amount. It makes your programs much easier to read.

You first define five variables of type int:

```
int Total_Pets;
int Cats;
int Dogs;
int Ponies;
int Others;
```

Because each of these variables will be used to store a count of a number of animals, they are definitely going to be whole numbers. As you can see, they're all declared as type int.

Note that you could have declared all five variables in a single statement and include comments, as follows:

```
int Total_Pets,          /* The total number of pets      */
    Cats,                /* The number of cats as pets    */
    Dogs,                /* The number of dogs as pets    */
    Ponies,              /* The number of ponies as pets */
    Others;              /* The number of other pets      */
```

These are rather superfluous comments but they illustrate the point. The statement is spread over several lines so that you can add the comments in an orderly fashion. Notice that there are commas separating each of the variable names. Because the comments are ignored by the compiler, this is exactly the same as the following statement:

```
int Total_Pets, Cats, Dogs, Ponies, Others;
```

You can spread C statements over as many lines as you want. The semicolon determines the end of the statement, not the end of the line.

Now back to the program. The variables are given specific values in these four assignment statements:

```
Cats = 2;
Dogs = 1;
Ponies = 1;
Others = 46;
```

At this point the variable Total_Pets doesn't have an explicit value set. It will get its value as a result of the calculation using the other variables:

```
Total_Pets = Cats + Dogs + Ponies + Others;
```

In this arithmetic statement, you calculate the sum of all your pets on the right of the assignment operator by adding the values of each of the variables together. This total value is then stored in the variable Total_Pets that appears on the left of the assignment operator. The new value replaces any old value that was stored in the variable Total_Pets.

The printf() statement presents the result of the calculation by displaying the value of Total_Pets:

```
printf("We have %d pets in total", Total_Pets);
```

Try changing the numbers of some of the types of animals, or maybe add some more of your own. Remember to declare them, initialize their value, and include them in the Total_Pets statement.

Initializing Variables

In the previous example, you declared each variable with a statement such as this:

```
int Cats;                    /* The number of cats as pets    */
```

You set the value of the variable Cats using this statement:

```
Cats = 2;
```

This sets the value of the variable Cats to 2.

So what was the value before this statement was executed? Well, it could be anything. The first statement creates the variable called Cats, but its value will be whatever was left in memory from the last program that used this bit of memory. The assignment statement that appeared later set the value to 2, but it would be much better to initialize the variable when you declare it. You can do this with the following statement:

```
int Cats = 2;
```

This statement declares the variable Cats as type int *and* sets its initial value to 2.

Initializing variables as you declare them is a very good idea in general. It avoids any doubt about what the initial values are, and if the program doesn't work as it should, it can help you track down the errors. Avoiding leaving spurious values for variables when you create them also reduces the chances of your computer crashing when things do go wrong. Inadvertently working with junk values can cause all kinds of problems. From now on, you'll always initialize variables in the examples, even if it's just to 0.

Arithmetic Statements

The previous program is the first one that really did something. It is very simple! just adding a few numbers! but it is a significant step forward. It is an elementary example of using an arithmetic statement to perform a calculation. Now let's look at some more sophisticated calculations that you can do.

Basic Arithmetic Operations

In C, an arithmetic statement is of the following form:

```
Variable_Name = Arithmetic_Expression;
```

The arithmetic expression on the right of the = operator specifies a calculation using values stored in variables and/or explicit numbers that are combined using arithmetic operators such as addition (+), subtraction (–), multiplication (*), and division (/). There are also other operators you can use in an arithmetic expression, as you'll see.

In the previous example, the arithmetic statement was the following:

```
Total_Pets = Cats + Dogs + Ponies + Others;
```

The effect of this statement is to calculate the value of the arithmetic expression to the right of the = and store that value in the variable specified on the left.

In C, the = symbol defines an action. It doesn't specify that the two sides are equal, as it does in mathematics. It specifies that the value resulting from the expression on the right is to be stored in the variable on the left. This means that you could have the following:

```
Total_Pets = Total_Pets + 2;
```

This would be ridiculous as a mathematical equation, but in programming it's fine. Let's look at it in context. Imagine you'd rewritten the last part of the program to include the preceding statement. Here's a fragment of the program as it would appear with the statement added:

```
Total_Pets = Cats + Dogs + Ponies + Others;
Total_Pets = Total_Pets + 2;
printf("The total number of pets is: %d", Total_Pets);
```

After executing the first statement here, Total_Pets will contain the value 50. Then, in the second line, you extract the value of Total_Pets, add 2 to that value and store the result back in the variable Total_Pets. The final total that will be displayed is therefore 52.

■ Note In assignment operations, the expression on the right side of the = sign is evaluated first, and the result is then stored in the variable on the left. The new value replaces the value that was previously contained in the variable to the left of the assignment operator. The variable on the left of the assignment is called an lvalue, because it is a location that can store a value. The value that results from executing the expression on the right of the assignment is called an rvalue because it is simply a value that results from evaluating the expression.

Any expression that results in a numeric value is described as an **arithmetic expression**. The following are arithmetic expressions:

```
3
```

```
1 + 2
```

```
Total_Pets
```

```
Cats + Dogs - Ponies
```

Evaluating any of these expressions produces a single numeric value. Note that just a variable name is an expression that is evaluated to produce a value: the value that the variable contains. In a moment, you'll take a closer look at how an expression is made up, and you'll look into the rules governing its evaluation. First, though, you'll try some simple examples using the basic arithmetic operators that you have at your disposal. Table 2-1 shows these operators.

Table 2-1. *Basic Arithmetic Operators*

Operator	Action
+	Addition
-	Subtraction
*	Multiplication
/	Division
%	Modulus

You may not have come across the **modulus operator** before. It just calculates the remainder after dividing the value of the expression on the left of the operator by the value of the expression on the right. For this reason it's sometimes referred to as the **remainder operator**. The expression 12 % 5 would produce 2, because 12 divided by 5 leaves a remainder of 2. You'll look at this in more detail in the next section, •More on Division with Integers.! All these operators work as you'd expect, with the exception of division, which is slightly nonintuitive when applied to integers, as you'll see. Let's try some more arithmetic operations.

TRY IT OUT: SUBTRACTION AND MULTIPLICATION

Let's look at a food-based program that demonstrates subtraction and multiplication:

```
/* Program 2.5 Calculations with cookies */
#include <stdio.h>

int main(void)
{
  int cookies = 5;
  int cookie_calories = 125;    /* Calories per cookie */
  int total_eaten = 0;          /* Total cookies eaten */

  int eaten = 2;                /* Number to be eaten  */
  cookies = cookies - eaten;    /* Subtract number eaten from cookies */
  total_eaten = total_eaten + eaten;
  printf("\nI have eaten %d cookies.  There are %d cookies left",
                                                 eaten, cookies);

  eaten = 3;                    /* New value for cookies to be eaten  */
  cookies = cookies - eaten;    /* Subtract number eaten from cookies */
  total_eaten = total_eaten + eaten;
  printf("\nI have eaten %d more.  Now there are %d cookies left\n",
                                                 eaten, cookies);
  printf("\nTotal energy consumed is %d calories.\n",
                                    total_eaten*cookie_calories);
  return 0;
}
```

This program produces the following output:

```
I have eaten 2 cookies.  There are 3 cookies left
I have eaten three more.  Now there are 0 cookies left

Total energy consumed is 625 calories.
```

How It Works

You first declare and initialize three variables of type int:

```
  int cookies = 5;
  int cookie_calories = 125;    /* Calories per cookie */
  int total_eaten = 0;          /* Total cookies eaten */
```

You'll use the total_eaten variable to accumulate the total number of cookies eaten as execution of the program progresses, so you initialize it to 0.

The next variable that you declare and initialize holds the number of cookies to be eaten next:

```
  int eaten = 2;                     /* Number to be eaten */
```

You use the subtraction operator to subtract eaten from the value of cookies:

```
  cookies = cookies - eaten;         /* Subtract number eaten from cookies */
```

The result of the subtraction is stored back in the variable cookies, so the value of cookies will now be 3. Because you've eaten some cookies, you increment the count of the total that you've eaten by the value of eaten:

```
total_eaten = total_eaten + eaten;
```

You add the current value of eaten, which is 2, to the current value of total_eaten, which is 0. The result is stored back in the variable total_eaten.

The printf() statement displays the number of cookies that are left:

```
printf("\nI have eaten %d cookies.  There are %d cookies left",
                                                eaten, cookies);
```

I couldn't fit the statement in the space available, so after the comma following the first argument to printf(), I put the rest of the statement on a new line. You can spread statements out like this to make them easier to read or fit within a given width on the screen.

Note that you *cannot* split the string that is the first argument in this way. An explicit newline character isn't allowed in the middle of a string. When you need to split a string over two or more lines, each segment of the string on a line must have its own pair of double quotes delimiting it. For example, you could write the previous statement as follows:

```
printf("\nI have eaten %d cookies. "
                    " There are %d cookies left",
                                                eaten, cookies);
```

Where there are two or more strings immediately following one another like this, the compiler will join them together to form a single string.

You display the values stored in eaten and cookies using the conversion specifier, %d, for integer values. The value of eaten will replace the first %d in the output string, and the value of cookies will replace the second. The string will be displayed starting on a new line because of the \n at the beginning.

The next statement sets the variable eaten to a new value:

```
eaten = 3;                      /* New value for cookies to be eaten  */
```

The new value replaces the previous value stored in eaten, which was 2. You then go through the same sequence of operations as you did before:

```
cookies = cookies - eaten;      /* Subtract number eaten from cookies */
total_eaten = total_eaten + eaten;
printf("\nI have eaten %d more.  Now there are %d cookies left\n",
                                                eaten, cookies);
```

Finally, before executing the return statement that ends the program, you calculate and output the number of calories corresponding to the number of cookies eaten:

```
printf("\nTotal energy consumed is %d calories.\n",
                        total_eaten*cookie_calories);
```

Here the second argument to the printf() function is an arithmetic expression rather than just a variable. The compiler will arrange for the result of the expression total_eaten*cookie_calories to be stored in a temporary variable, and that value will be passed as the second argument to the printf() function. You can always use an expression for an argument to a function as long as it evaluates to a result of the required type.

Easy, isn't it? Let's take a look at division and the modulus operator.

TRY IT OUT: DIVISION AND THE MODULUS OPERATOR

Suppose you have a jar of 45 cookies and a group of seven children. You'll divide the cookies equally among the children and work out how many each child has. Then you'll work out how many cookies are left over.

```
/* Program 2.6 Cookies and kids */
#include <stdio.h>

int main(void)
{
  int cookies = 45;                    /* Number of cookies in the jar */
  int children = 7;                    /* Number of children           */
  int cookies_per_child = 0;           /* Number of cookies per child  */
  int cookies_left_over = 0;           /* Number of cookies left over  */

  /* Calculate how many cookies each child gets when they are divided up */
  cookies_per_child = cookies/children;  /* Number of cookies per child  */
  printf("You have %d children and %d cookies", children, cookies);
  printf("\nGive each child %d cookies.", cookies_per_child);

  /* Calculate how many cookies are left over */
  cookies_left_over = cookies%children;
  printf("\nThere are %d cookies left over.\n", cookies_left_over);
  return 0;
}
```

When you run this program you'll get this output:

```
You have 7 children and 45 cookies
Give each child 6 cookies.
There are 3 cookies left over.
```

How It Works

Let's go through this program step by step. Four integer variables, cookies, children, cookies_per_child, and cookies_left_over are declared and initialized with the following statements:

```
  int cookies = 45;                    /* Number of cookies in the jar */
  int children = 7;                    /* Number of children           */
  int cookies_per_child = 0;           /* Number of cookies per child  */
  int cookies_left_over = 0;           /* Number of cookies left over  */
```

The number of cookies is divided by the number of children by using the division operator / to produce the number of cookies given to each child:

```
  cookies_per_child = cookies/children;  /* Number of cookies per child */
```

The next two statements output what is happening, including the value stored in cookies_per_child:

```
  printf("You have %d children and %d cookies", children, cookies);
  printf("\nGive each child %d cookies.", cookies_per_child);
```

You can see from the output that `cookies_per_child` has the value 6. This is because the division operator always produces an integer result when the operands are integers. The result of dividing 45 by 7 is 6, with a remainder of 3. You calculate the remainder in the next statement by using the modulus operator:

```
cookies_left_over = cookies%children;
```

The expression to the right of the assignment operator calculates the remainder that results when the value of `cookies` is divided by the value of `children`.

Finally, you output the reminder in the last statement:

```
printf("\nThere are %d cookies left over.\n", cookies_left_over);
```

More on Division with Integers

Let's look at the result of using the division and modulus operators where one or other of the operands is negative. With division, if the operands have different signs, the result will be negative. Thus, the expression –45 / 7 produces the same result as the expression 45 / –7, which is –6. If the operands in a division are of the same sign, positive or negative, the result is positive. Thus, 45 / 7 produces the same result as –45 / –7, which is 6.

With the modulus operator, the sign of the result is always the same as the sign of the left operand. Thus, 45 % –7 results in the value 3, whereas –45 % 7 results in the value –3.

Unary Operators

The operators that you've dealt with so far have been **binary operators**. These operators are called binary operators because they operate on *two* data items. Incidentally, the items of data that an operator applies to are generally referred to as **operands**. For example, the multiplication is a binary operator because it has two operands and the effect is to multiply one operand value by the other. However, there are some operators that are unary, meaning that they only need one operand. You'll see more examples later, but for now you'll just take a look at the single most common unary operator.

The Unary Minus Operator

You'll find the unary operator very useful in more complicated programs. It makes whatever is positive negative, and vice versa. You might not immediately realize when you would use this, but think about keeping track of your bank account. Say you have $200 in the bank. You record what happens to this money in a book with two columns, one for money that you pay out and another for money that you receive. One column is your expenditure (negative) and the other is your revenue (positive).

You decide to buy a CD for $50 and a book for $25. If all goes well, when you compare the initial value in the bank and subtract the expenditure ($75), you should end up with what's left. Table 2-2 shows how these entries could typically be recorded.

Table 2-2. *Recording Revenues and Expenditures*

Entry	Revenue	Expenditure	Bank Balance
Check received	$200		$200
CD		$50	$150
Book		$25	$125
Closing balance	$200	$75	$125

If these numbers were stored in variables, you could enter both the revenue and expenditure as positive values and only make the number negative when you want to calculate how much is left. You could do this by simply placing a minus sign (–) in front of the variable name.

To output the amount you had spent as a negative value, you could write the following:

```
int expenditure = 75;
printf("Your balance has changed by %d.", -expenditure);
```

This would result in the following output:

```
Your balance has changed by -75.
```

The minus sign will remind you that you've spent this money rather than gained it. Note that the expression -expenditure doesn't change the value stored in expenditure! it's still 75. The value of the *expression* is –75.

The unary minus operator in the expression -expenditure specifies an action, the result of which is the value of expenditure with its sign inverted: negative becomes positive and positive becomes negative. Instructions must be executed in your program to evaluate this. This is subtly different from when you use the minus operator when you write a negative number such as –75 or –1.25. In this case, the minus doesn't result in an action and no instructions need to be executed when your program is running. It simply instructs the compiler to create the appropriate negative constant in your program.

Variables and Memory

So far you've only looked at integer variables without considering how much space they take up in memory. Each time you declare a variable, the computer allocates a space in memory big enough to store that particular type of variable. Every variable of a particular type will always occupy the same amount of memory! the same number of bytes! but different types of variables require different amounts of memory to be allocated.

Note The amount of memory occupied by variables of a given type will always be the same on a particular machine. However, in some instances a variable of a given type on one computer may occupy more memory than it does on another. This is because the C language specification leaves it up to the compiler writer to decide how much memory a variable of a particular type will occupy. This allows the compiler writer to choose the size of a variable to suit the hardware architecture of the computer.

You saw at the beginning of this chapter how your computer's memory is organized into bytes. Each variable will occupy some number of bytes in memory, so how many bytes are needed to store an integer? Well, 1 byte can store an integer value from 128 to +127. This would be enough for the integer values that you've seen so far, but what if you want to store a count of the average number of stitches in a pair of knee-length socks? One byte wouldn't be anywhere near enough. Consequently, not only do you have variables of different types in C that store different types of numbers, one of which happens to be integers, you also have several varieties of integer variables to provide for different ranges of integers to be stored.

As I describe each type of variable in the following sections, I include a table containing the range of values that can be stored and the memory the variable will occupy. I summarize all these in a complete table of all the variable types in the •Summary! section of this chapter.

Integer Variable Types

You have five basic flavors of variables that you can declare that can store signed integer values (I'll get to unsigned integer values in the next section). Each type is specified by a different keyword or combination of keywords, as shown in Table 2-3.

Table 2-3. *Type Names for Integer Variable Types*

Type Name	Number of Bytes	Range of Values
signed char	1	128 to +127
short int	2	32,768 to +32,767
int	4	2,147,438,648 to +2,147,438,647
long int	4	2,147,438,648 to +2,147,438,647
long long int	8	9,223,372,036,854,775,808 to +9,223,372,036,854,775,807

The type names short, long, and long long can be used as abbreviations for the type names short int, long int, and long long int, and these types are almost always written in their abbreviated forms. Table 2-3 reflects the typical size of each type of integer variable, although the amount of memory occupied by variables of these types depends on the particular compiler you're using.

■ **Note** The only specific requirement imposed by the international standard for C on the integer types is that each type in the table won't occupy less memory than the type that precedes it. Type unsigned char occupies the same memory as type char, which has sufficient memory to store any character in the execution set for the language implementation; this is typically 1 byte but could be more. Outside of these constraints, the compiler-writer has complete freedom to make the best use of the hardware arithmetic capabilities of the machine on which the compiler is executing.

Unsigned Integer Types

For each of the types that store signed integers, there is a corresponding type that stores unsigned integers that occupy the same amount of memory as the unsigned type. Each unsigned type name is essentially the signed type name prefixed with the keyword unsigned. Table 2-4 shows the unsigned integer types that you can use.

Table 2-4. *Type Names for Unsigned Integer Types*

Type Name	Number of Bytes	Range of Values
unsigned char	1	0 to 255
unsigned short int or unsigned short	2	0 to 65,535
unsigned int	4	0 to 4,294,967,295

Table 2-4. *Type Names for Unsigned Integer Types*

Type Name	Number of Bytes	Range of Values
`unsigned long int` or `unsigned long`	4	0 to 4,294,967,295
`unsigned long long int` or `unsigned long long`	8	0 to +18,446,744,073,709,551,615

You use unsigned integer types when you are dealing with values that cannot be negative! the number of players in a football team for example, or the number of pebbles on a beach. With a given number of bits, the number of different values that can be represented is fixed. A 32-bit variable can represent any of 4,294,967,296 different values. Thus, using an unsigned type doesn't provide more values than the corresponding signed type, but it does allow numbers to be represented that are twice as large.

Using Integer Types

Most of the time variables of type `int` or `long` should suffice for your needs, with occasional requirements for unsigned `int` or unsigned `long`. Here are some examples of declarations of these types:

```
unsigned int count = 10;
unsigned long inchesPerMile = 63360UL;
int balance = -500;
```

Notice the L at the end of the value for the variable of type `long`. This identifies the constant as type `long` rather than type `int`; constants of type `int` have no suffix. Similarly the constant of type unsigned `long` has UL appended to it to identify it as that type. I come back to suffixes in the section •Specifying Integer Constants! later in this chapter.

Variables of type `int` should have the size most suited to the computer on which the code is executing. For example, consider the following statement:

```
int cookies = 0;
```

This statement will typically declare a variable to store integers that will occupy 4 bytes, but it could be 2 bytes with another compiler. This variation may seem a little strange, but the `int` type is intended to correspond to the size of integer that the computer has been designed to deal with most efficiently, and this can vary not only between different types of machines, but also with the same machine architecture, as the chip technology evolves over time. Ultimately, it's the compiler that determines what you get. Although at one time many C compilers for the PC created `int` variables as 2 bytes, with more recent C compilers on a PC, variables of type `int` occupy 4 bytes. This is because all modern processors move data around at least 4 bytes at a time. If your compiler is of an older vintage, it may still use 2 bytes for type `int`, even though 4 bytes would now be better on the hardware you're using.

■**Note** The sizes of all these types are compiler-dependent. The international standard for the C language requires only that the size of `short` variables should be less than or equal to the size of type `int`, which in turn should be less than or equal to the size of type `long`.

If you use type `short`, you'll probably get 2-byte variables. The previous declaration could have been written as follows:

```
short cookies = 0;
```

Because the keyword short is actually an abbreviation for short int, you could write this as follows:

```
short int cookies = 0;
```

This is exactly the same as the previous statement. When you write just short in a variable declaration, the int is implied. Most people prefer to use this form! it's perfectly clear and it saves a bit of typing.

Note Even though type short and type int may occupy the same amount of memory on some machines, they're still different types.

If you need integers with a bigger range! to store the average number of hamburgers sold in one day, for instance! you can use the keyword long:

```
long Big_Number;
```

Type long defines an integer variable with a length of 4 bytes, which provides for a range of values from 2,147,438,648 to +2,147,438,647. As noted earlier, you can write long int if you wish instead of long, because it amounts to the same thing.

Specifying Integer Constants

Because you can have different kinds of integer variables, you might expect to have different kinds of integer constants, and you do. If you just write the integer value 100 for example, this will be of type int. If you want to make sure it is type long, you must append an uppercase or lowercase letter L to the numeric value. So the integer 100 as a long value is written as 100L. Although it's perfectly legal, a lowercase letter l is best avoided because it's easily confused with the digit 1.

To declare and initialize the variable Big_Number, you could write this:

```
long Big_Number = 1287600L;
```

An integer constant will also be type long by default if it's outside the range of type int. Thus, if your compiler implementation uses 2 bytes to store type int values, the values 1000000 and 33000 will be of type long by default, because they won't fit into 2 bytes.

You write negative integer constants with a minus sign, for example:

```
int decrease = -4;
long  below_sea_level = -100000L;
```

You specify integer constants to be of type long long by appending two Ls:

```
long long really_big_number = 123456789LL;
```

As you saw earlier, to specify a constant to be of an unsigned type you append a U, as in this example:

```
unsigned int count = 100U;
unsigned long value = 999999999UL;
```

You can also write integer values in hexadecimal form! that is, to base 16. The digits in a hexa-decimal number are the equivalent of decimal values 0 to 15, and they're represented by 0 through 9 and A though F (or a through f). Because there needs to be a way to distinguish between 99_{10} and 99_{16}, hexadecimal numbers are written with the prefix 0x or 0X. You would therefore write 99_{16} in your program as 0x99 or as 0X99.

Hexadecimal constants are most often used to specify bit patterns, because each hexadecimal digit corresponds to 4 binary bits. The bitwise operators that you'll see in Chapter 3 are usually used with hexadecimal constants that define masks. If you're unfamiliar with hexadecimal numbers, you can find a detailed discussion of them in Appendix A.

■**Note** An integer constant that starts with a zero, such as 014 for example, will be interpreted by your compiler as an octal number—a number to base 8. Thus 014 is the octal equivalent of the decimal value 12. If it is meant to be the decimal value 14 it will be wrong, so don't put a leading zero in your integers unless you really mean to specify an octal value.

Floating-Point Values

Floating-point variables are used to store floating-point numbers. Floating-point numbers hold values that are written with a decimal point, so you can represent fractional as well as integral values. The following are examples of floating-point values:

1.6   0.00008   7655.899

Because of the way floating-point numbers are represented, they hold only a fixed number of decimal digits; however, they can represent a very wide range of values!   much wider than integer types. Floating-point numbers are often expressed as a decimal value multiplied by some power of 10. For example, each of the previous examples of floating-point numbers could be expressed as shown in Table 2-5.

Table 2-5. *Expressing Floating-Point Numbers*

Value	With an Exponent	Can Also Be Written in C As
1.6	0.16×10^1	0.16E1
0.00008	0.8×10^{-4}	0.8E-4
7655.899	0.7655899×10^4	0.7655899E4

The center column shows how the numbers in the left column could be represented with an exponent. This isn't how you write them in C; it's just an alternative way of representing the same value designed to link to the right column. The right column shows how the representation in the center column would be expressed in C. The E in each of the numbers is for exponent, and you could equally well use a lowercase e. Of course, you can write each of these numbers in your program without an exponent, just as they appear in the left column, but for very large or very small numbers, the exponent form is very useful. I'm sure you would rather write 0.5E-15 than 0.0000000000000005, wouldn't you?

Floating-Point Variables

There are three different types of floating-point variables, as shown in Table 2-6.

Table 2-6. *Floating-Point Variable Types*

Keyword	Number of Bytes	Range of Values
float	4	±3.4E38 (6 decimal digits precision)
double	8	±1.7E308 (15 decimal digits precision)
long double	12	±1.19E4932 (18 decimal digits precision)

These are typical values for the number of bytes occupied and the ranges of values that are supported. Like the integer types, the memory occupied and the range of values are dependent on the machine and the compiler. The type long double is sometimes exactly the same as type double with some compilers. Note that the number of decimal digits of precision is only an approximation because floating-point values will be stored internally in binary form, and a decimal floating-point value does not always have an exact representation in binary.

A floating-point variable is declared in a similar way to an integer variable. You just use the keyword for the floating-point type that you want to use:

```
float Radius;
double Biggest;
```

If you need to store numbers with up to seven digits of accuracy (a range of 10_{-38} to 10_{+38}), you should use variables of type float. Values of type float are known as **single precision** floating-point numbers. This type will occupy 4 bytes in memory, as you can see from the table. Using variables of type double will allow you to store **double precision** floating-point values. Each variable of type double will occupy 8 bytes in memory and give you 15-digit precision with a range of 10_{-308} to 10_{+308}. Variables of type double suffice for the majority of requirements, but some specialized applications require even more accuracy and range. The long double type provides the exceptional range and precision shown in the table.

To write a constant of type float, you append an f to the number to distinguish it from type double. You could initialize the last two variables with these statements:

```
float Radius = 2.5f;
double Biggest = 123E30;
```

The variable Radius has the initial value 2.5, and the variable Biggest is initialized to the number that corresponds to 123 followed by 30 zeroes. Any number that you write containing a decimal point is of type double unless you append the F to make it type float. When you specify an exponent value with E or e, the constant need not contain a decimal point. For instance, 1E3f is of type float and 3E8 is of type double.

To specify a long double constant, you need to append an uppercase or lowercase letter L to the number as in the following example:

```
long double huge = 1234567.89123L;
```

Division Using Floating-Point Values

As you've seen, division operations with integer operands always produce an integer result. Unless the left operand of a division is an exact multiple of the right operand, the result will be inherently inaccurate. Of course, the way integer division works is an advantage if you're distributing cookies to children, but it isn't particularly useful when you want to cut a 10-foot plank into four equal pieces. This is a job for floating-point values.

Division operations with floating-point values will give you an exact result! at least, a result that is as exact as it can be with a fixed number of digits of precision. The next example illustrates how division operations work with variables of type float.

TRY IT OUT: DIVISION WITH VALUES OF TYPE FLOAT

Here's a simple example that just divides one floating-point value by another and displays the result:

```
/* Program 2.7 Division with float values */
#include <stdio.h>

int main(void)
{
  float plank_length = 10.0f;    /* In feet                  */
  float piece_count = 4.0f;      /* Number of equal pieces   */
  float piece_length = 0.0f;     /* Length of a piece in feet */

  piece_length = plank_length/piece_count;
  printf("A plank %f feet long can be cut into %f pieces %f feet long.",
                               plank_length, piece_count, piece_length);
  return 0;
}
```

This program should produce the following output:

```
A plank 10.000000 feet long can be cut into 4.000000 pieces 2.500000 feet long.
```

How It Works

You shouldn't have any trouble understanding how you chop the plank into equal pieces. Note that you've used a new format specifier for values of type float in the printf() statement:

```
printf("A plank %f feet long can be cut into %f pieces %f feet long.",
                               plank_length, piece_count, piece_length);
```

You use the format specifier %f to display floating-point values. In general, the format specifier that you use must correspond to the type of value that you're outputting. If you output a value of type float with the specifier %d that's intended for use with integer values, you'll get rubbish. This is because the float value will be interpreted as an integer, which it isn't. Similarly, if you use %f with a value of an integer type, you'll also get rubbish as output.

Controlling the Number of Decimal Places

In the last example, you got a lot of decimal places in the output that you really didn't need. You may be good with a rule and a saw, but you aren't going to be able to cut the plank with a length of 2.500000 feet rather than 2.500001 feet. You can specify the number of places that you want to see after the decimal point in the format specifier. To obtain the output to two decimal places, you would write the format specifier as %.2f. To get three decimal places, you would write %.3f.

You can change the printf() statement in the last example so that it will produce more suitable output:

```
printf("A plank %.2f feet long can be cut into %.0f pieces %.2f feet long.",
                              plank_length, piece_count, piece_length);
```

The first format specification corresponds to the plank_length variable and will produce output with two decimal places. The second specification will produce no decimal places! this makes sense here because the piece_count value is a whole number. The last specification is the same as the first. Thus, if you run the example with this version of the last statement, the output will be the following:

```
A plank 10.00 feet long can be cut into 4 pieces 2.50 feet long.
```

This is much more appropriate and looks a lot better.

Controlling the Output Field Width

The field width for the output, which is the total number of characters used for the value including spaces, has been determined by default. The printf() function works out how many character positions will be required for a value, given the number of decimal places you specify and uses that as the field width. However, you may want to decide the field width yourself. This will be the case if you want to output a column of values so they line up. If you let the printf() function work out the field width, you're likely to get a ragged column of output. A more general form of the format specifier for floating-point values can be written like this:

```
%[width][.precision][modifier]f
```

The square brackets here aren't part of the specification. They enclose bits of the specification that are optional, so you can omit the width or the .precision or the modifier or any combination of these. The width value is an integer specifying the total number of characters in the output: the field width. The precision value is an integer specifying the number of decimal places that are to appear after the decimal point. The modifier part is L when the value you are outputting is type long double, otherwise you omit it.

You could rewrite the printf() call in the last example to specify the field width as well as the number of digits you want after the decimal point, as in the following example:

```
printf("A %8.2f plank foot can be cut into %5.0f pieces %6.2f feet long.",
                              plank_length, piece_count, piece_length);
```

I changed the text a little to get it to fit across the page here. The first value now will have a field width of 8 and 2 decimal places after the decimal point. The second value, which is the count of the number of pieces, will have a field width of 5 characters and no decimal places. The third value will be presented in a field width of 6 with 2 decimal places.

When you specify the field width, the value will be right-aligned by default. If you want the value to be left-aligned in the field, just put a minus sign following the %. For instance, the specification %-10.4f will output a floating-point value left-aligned in a field width of 10 characters with 4 digits following the decimal point.

Note that you can specify a field width and the alignment in the field with a specification for outputting an integer value. For example, %-15d specifies an integer value will be presented left-aligned in a field width of 15 characters.

There's more to format specifiers than I've introduced here, and you'll learn more about them later. Try out some variations using the previous example. In particular, see what happens when the field width is too small for the value.

More Complicated Expressions

You know that arithmetic can get a lot more complicated than just dividing a couple of numbers. In fact, if that is all you are trying to do, you may as well use paper and pencil. Now that you have the tools of addition, subtraction, multiplication, and division at your disposal, you can start to do some really heavy calculations.

For these more complicated calculations, you'll need more control over the sequence of operations when an expression is evaluated. Parentheses provide you with this capability. They can also help to make expressions clearer when they're getting intricate.

You can use parentheses in arithmetic expressions, and they work much as you'd expect. Subexpressions contained within parentheses are evaluated in sequence from the innermost pair of parentheses to the outermost, with the normal rules that you're used to for operator precedence, where multiplication and division happen before addition or subtraction. Therefore, the expression 2 * (3 + 3 * (5 + 4)) evaluates to 60. You start with the expression 5 + 4, which produces 9. Then you multiply that by 3, which gives 27. Then you add 3 to that total (giving 30) and multiply the whole lot by 2.

You can insert spaces to separate operands from operators to make your arithmetic statements more readable, or you can leave them out when you need to make the code more compact. Either way, the compiler doesn't mind, as it will ignore the spaces. If you're not quite sure of how an expression will be evaluated according to the precedence rules, you can always put in some parentheses to make sure it produces the result you want.

TRY IT OUT: ARITHMETIC IN ACTION

This time you'll have a go at calculating the circumference and area of a circular table from an input value for its diameter radius. You may remember from elementary math the equations to calculate the area and circumference of a circle using π or pi (circumference = $2\pi r$ and area = πr^2, where r is the radius). If you don't, don't worry. This isn't a math book, so just look at how the program works.

```c
/* Program 2.8 calculations on a table */
#include <stdio.h>

int main(void)
{
  float radius = 0.0f;            /* The radius of the table        */
  float diameter = 0.0f;         /* The diameter of the table      */
  float circumference = 0.0f;    /* The circumference of the table */
  float area = 0.0f;             /* The area of a circle           */
  float Pi = 3.14159265f;
```

```
    printf("Input the diameter of the table:");
    scanf("%f", &diameter);          /* Read the diameter from the keyboard */
    radius = diameter/2.0f;          /* Calculate the radius                */
    circumference = 2.0f*Pi*radius;  /* Calculate the circumference         */
    area = Pi*radius*radius;         /* Calculate the area                  */
    printf("\nThe circumference is %.2f", circumference);
    printf("\nThe area is %.2f\n", area);
    return 0;
}
```

Here's some typical output from this example:

```
Input the diameter of the table: 6

The circumference is 18.85
The area is 28.27
```

How It Works

Up to the first printf(), the program looks much the same as those you've seen before:

```
    float radius = 0.0f;            /* The radius of the table        */
    float diameter = 0.0f;          /* The diameter of the table      */
    float circumference = 0.0f;     /* The circumference of the table */
    float area = 0.0f;              /* The area of a circle           */
    float Pi = 3.14159265f;
```

You declare and initialize five variables, where Pi has its usual value. Note how all the initial values have an f at the end because you're initializing values of type float. Without the f the values would be of type double. They would still work here, but you would be introducing some unnecessary conversion that the compiler would have to arrange, from type double to type float.

The next statement outputs a prompt for input from the keyboard:

```
    printf("Input the diameter of the table:");
```

The next statement deals with reading the value for the diameter of the table. You use a new standard library function, the scanf() function, to do this:

```
    scanf("%f", &diameter);          /* Read the diameter from the keyboard */
```

The scanf() function is another function that requires the <stdio.h> header file to be included. This function handles input from the keyboard. In effect it takes what you enter through the keyboard and interprets it as specified by the first argument, which is a control string between double quotes. In this case the control string is "%f" because you're reading a value of type float. It stores the result in the variable specified by the second argument, diameter in this instance. The first argument is a control string similar to what you've used with the printf() function, except that here it controls input rather than output. You'll learn more about the scanf() function in Chapter 10 and, for reference, Appendix D summarizes the control strings you can use with it.

You've undoubtedly noticed something new here: the & preceding the variable name diameter. This is called the address of operator, and it's needed to allow the scanf() function to store the value that is read in your variable, diameter. The reason for this is bound up with the way argument values are passed to a function. For the moment, I won't go into a more detailed explanation of this; you'll see more on this in Chapter 8. The only thing to remember is to use the address of operator (the & sign) before a variable when you're using the scanf() function, and not to use it when you use the printf() function.

Within the control string for the scanf() function, the % character identifies the start of a format specification for an item of data. The f that follows the % indicates that the input is a floating-point value. In general there can be several format specifications within the control string, in which case these determine the type of data for each of the subsequent arguments to the function in sequence. You'll see a lot more on how scanf() works later in the book, but for now the basic set of format specifiers you can use for reading data of various types are shown in the following table.

Format Specifiers for Reading Data

Action	Required Control String
To read a value of type short	%hd
To read a value of type int	%d
To read a value of type long	%ld
To read a value of type float	%f or %e
To read a value of type double	%lf or %le

In the %ld and %lf format specifiers, l is a lowercase letter L. Don't forget, you must *always* prefix the name of the variable that's receiving the input value with &. Also, if you use the wrong format specifier—if you read a value into a variable of type float with %d, for instance—the data value in your variable won't be correct, but you'll get no indication that a junk value has been stored.

Next, you have two statements that calculate the results you're interested in:

```
radius = diameter/2.0f;              /* Calculate the radius        */
circumference = 2.0f*Pi*radius;      /* Calculate the circumference */
area = Pi*radius*radius;             /* Calculate the area          */
```

The first statement calculates the radius as half of the value of the diameter that was entered. The second statement computes the circumference of the table, using the value that was calculated for the radius. The third statement calculates the area. Note that if you forget the f in 2.0f, you'll probably get a warning message from your compiler. This is because without the f, the constant is of type double, and you would be mixing different types in the same expression. You'll see more about this later.

The next two statements output the values you've calculated:

```
printf("\nThe circumference is %.2f", circumference);
printf("\nThe area is %.2f\n", area);
```

These two printf() statements output the values of the variables circumference and area using the format specifier %.2f. As you've already seen, in both statements the format control string contains text to be displayed, as well as a format specifier for the variable to be output. The format specification outputs the values with two decimal places after the point. The default field width will be sufficient in each case to accommodate the value that is to be displayed.

Of course, you can run this program and enter whatever values you want for the diameter. You could experiment with different forms of floating-point input here, and you could try entering something like 1E1f, for example.

Defining Constants

Although Pi is defined as a variable in the previous example, it's really a constant value that you don't want to change. The value of π is always a fixed number with an unlimited number of decimal digits. The only question is how many digits of precision you want to use in its specification. It would be nice to make sure its value stayed fixed in a program so it couldn't be changed by mistake.

There are a couple of ways in which you can approach this. The first is to define Pi as a symbol that's to be replaced in the program by its value during compilation. In this case, Pi isn't a variable at all, but more a sort of alias for the value it represents. Let's try that out.

TRY IT OUT: DEFINING A CONSTANT

Let's look at specifying PI as an alias for its value:

```
/* Program 2.9 More round tables */
#include <stdio.h>
#define PI    3.14159f           /* Definition of the symbol PI */

int main(void)
{
  float radius = 0.0f;
  float diameter = 0.0f;
  float circumference = 0.0f;
  float area = 0.0f;

  printf("Input the diameter of a table:");
  scanf("%f", &diameter);
  radius = diameter/2.0f;
  circumference = 2.0f*PI*radius;
  area = PI*radius*radius;
  printf("\nThe circumference is %.2f", circumference);
  printf("\nThe area is %.2f", area);
  return 0;
}
```

This produces exactly the same output as the previous example.

How It Works

After the comment and the #include directive for the header file, there is a preprocessing directive:

```
#definePI 3.14159f                     /* Definition of the symbol PI */
```

You've now defined PI as a symbol that is to be replaced in the code by 3.14159f. You've used PI rather than Pi, as it's a common convention in C to write identifiers that appear in a #define statement in capital letters. Wherever you reference PI within an expression in the program, the preprocessor will substitute the value you've specified for it in the #define directive. All the substitutions will be made before compiling the program. When the program is ready to be compiled, it will no longer contain references to PI, as all occurrences will have been replaced by the sequence of characters that you've specified in the #define directive. This all happens internally while your program is processed by the compiler. Your source program will not be changed; it will still contain the symbol PI.

The second possibility is to define Pi as a variable, but to tell the compiler that its value is fixed and must not be changed. You can fix the value of any variable by prefixing the type name with the keyword const when you declare the variable, for example:

```
const float Pi = 3.14159f;          /* Defines the value of Pi as fixed */
```

The advantage of defining Pi in this way is that you are now defining it as a constant numerical value. In the previous example PI was just a sequence of characters that replaced all occurrences of PI in your code.

Adding the keyword const in the declaration for Pi will cause the compiler to check that the code doesn't attempt to change its value. Any code that does so will be flagged as an error and the compilation will fail. Let's see a working example of this.

TRY IT OUT: DEFINING A VARIABLE WITH A FIXED VALUE

Try using a constant in a variation of the previous example but with the code shortened a little:

```
/* Program 2.10 Round tables again but shorter */
#include <stdio.h>

int main(void)
{
  float diameter = 0.0f;          /* The diameter of a table      */
  float radius = 0.0f;            /* The radius of a table        */
  const float Pi = 3.14159f;      /* Defines the value of Pi as fixed */

  printf("Input the diameter of the table:");
  scanf("%f", &diameter);
  radius = diameter/2.0f;
  printf("\nThe circumference is %.2f", 2.0f*Pi*radius);
  printf("\nThe area is %.2f", Pi*radius*radius);
  return 0;
}
```

How It Works

Following the declaration for the variable radius is this statement:

```
const float Pi = 3.14159f;          /* Defines the value of Pi as fixed */
```

This declares the variable Pi and defines a value for it; Pi is still a variable here, but the initial value you've given it can't be changed. The const modifier achieves this effect. It can be applied to any statement declaring a variable of any type to fix the value of that variable. Of course, the value must appear in the declaration in the same way as shown here: following an = sign after the variable name. The compiler will check your code for attempts to change variables that you've declared as const, and if it discovers that you've attempted to change a const variable it will complain. There are ways to trick the compiler to change const variables, but this defeats the whole point of using const in the first place.

The next two statements produce the output from the program:

```
printf("\nThe circumference is %.2f", 2.0f*Pi*radius);
printf("\nThe area is %.2f", Pi*radius*radius);
```

In this example, you've done away with the variables storing the circumference and area of the circle. The expressions for these now appear as arguments in the `printf()` statements where they're evaluated, and their values are passed directly to the function.

As you've seen before, the value that you pass to a function can be the result of evaluating an expression rather than the value of a particular variable. The compiler will create a temporary variable to hold the value and that will be passed to the function. The temporary variable is subsequently discarded. This is fine, as long as you don't want to use these values elsewhere.

Knowing Your Limitations

Of course, it may be important to be able to determine within a program exactly what the limits are on the values that can be stored by a given integer type. The header file `<limits.h>` defines symbols representing values for the limits for each type. Table 2-7 shows the symbols names corresponding to the limits for each signed type.

Table 2-7. *Symbols Representing Range Limits for Integer Types*

Type	Lower Limit	Upper Limit
char	CHAR_MIN	CHAR_MAX
short	SHRT_MIN	SHRT_MAX
int	INT_MIN	INT_MAX
long	LONG_MIN	LONG_MAX
long long	LLONG_MIN	LLONG_MAX

The lower limits for the unsigned integer types are all 0 so there are no symbols for these. The symbols corresponding to the upper limits for the unsigned integer types are UCHAR_MAX, USHRT_MAX, UINT_MAX, ULONG_MAX, and ULLONG_MAX.

To be able to use any of these symbols in a program you must have an #include directive for the `<limits.h>` header file in the source file:

```
#include <limits.h>
```

You could initialize a variable with the maximum possible value like this:

```
int number = INT_MAX;
```

This statement sets the value of number to be the maximum possible, whatever that may be for the compiler used to compile the code.

The `<float.h>` header file defines symbols that characterize floating-point values. Some of these are quite technical so I'll just mention those you are most likely to be interested in. The maximum and minimum positive values that can be represented by the three floating-point types are shown in Table 2-8.

You can also access the symbols FLT_DIG, DBL_DIG, and LDBL_DIG that indicate the number of decimal digits that can be represented by the binary mantissa of the corresponding types.

Let's explore in a working example how to access some of the symbols characterizing integers and floating-point values.

Table 2-8. *Symbols Representing Range Limits for Floating-Point Types*

Type	Lower Limit	Upper Limit
float	FLT_MIN	FLT_MAX
double	DBL_MIN	DBL_MAX
long double	LDBL_MIN	LDBL_MAX

TRY IT OUT: FINDING THE LIMITS

This program just outputs the values corresponding to the symbols defined in the header files:

```
/* Program 2.11 Finding the limits  */
#include <stdio.h>       /* For command line input and output  */
#include <limits.h>      /* For limits on integer types        */
#include <float.h>       /* For limits on floating-point types */

int main(void)
{
  printf("Variables of type char store values from %d to %d",
                                          CHAR_MIN, CHAR_MAX);
  printf("\nVariables of type unsigned char store values from 0 to %u",
                                          UCHAR_MAX);
  printf("\nVariables of type short store values from %d to %d",
                                          SHRT_MIN, SHRT_MAX);
  printf("\nVariables of type unsigned short store values from 0 to %u",
                                          USHRT_MAX);
  printf("\nVariables of type int store values from %d to %d", INT_MIN,
                                          INT_MAX);
  printf("\nVariables of type unsigned int store values from 0 to %u",
                                          UINT_MAX);
  printf("\nVariables of type long store values from %ld to %ld",
                                          LONG_MIN, LONG_MAX);
  printf("\nVariables of type unsigned long store values from 0 to %lu",
                                          ULONG_MAX);
  printf("\nVariables of type long long store values from %lld to %lld",
                                          LLONG_MIN, LLONG_MAX);
  printf("\nVariables of type unsigned long long store values from 0 to %llu",
                                          ULLONG_MAX);

  printf("\n\nThe size of the smallest non-zero value of type float is %.3e",
                                          FLT_MIN);
  printf("\nThe size of the largest value of type float is %.3e", FLT_MAX);
  printf("\nThe size of the smallest non-zero value of type double is %.3e",
                                          DBL_MIN);
  printf("\nThe size of the largest value of type double is %.3e", DBL_MAX);
  printf("\nThe size of the smallest non-zero value ~CCC
 of type long double is %.3Le", LDBL_MIN);
  printf("\nThe size of the largest value of type long double is %.3Le\n",
                                          LDBL_MAX);
```

```
    printf("\nVariables of type float provide %u decimal digits precision.",
                                                    FLT_DIG);
    printf("\nVariables of type double provide %u decimal digits precision.",
                                                    DBL_DIG);
    printf("\nVariables of type long double provide %u decimal digits precision.",
                                                    LDBL_DIG);

    return 0;
}
```

You'll get output somewhat similar to the following:

```
Variables of type char store values from -128 to 127
Variables of type unsigned char store values from 0 to 255
Variables of type short store values from -32768 to 32767
Variables of type unsigned short store values from 0 to 65535
Variables of type int store values from -2147483648 to 2147483647
Variables of type unsigned int store values from 0 to 4294967295
Variables of type long store values from -2147483648 to 2147483647
Variables of type unsigned long store values from 0 to 4294967295
Variables of type long long store values ~CCC
from -9223372036854775808 to 9223372036854775807
Variables of type unsigned long long store values from 0 to 18446744073709551615

The size of the smallest non-zero value of type float is 1.175e-038
The size of the largest value of type float is 3.403e+038
The size of the smallest non-zero value of type double is 2.225e-308
The size of the largest value of type double is 1.798e+308
The size of the smallest non-zero value of type long double is 3.362e-4932
The size of the largest value of type long double is 1.190e+4932

Variables of type float provide 6 decimal digits precision.
Variables of type double provide 15 decimal digits precision.
Variables of type long double provide 18 decimal digits precision.
```

How It Works

You output the values of symbols that are defined in the <limits.h> and <float.h> header files in a series of printf() function calls. Numbers in your computer are always limited in the range of values that can be stored, and the values of these symbols represent the boundaries for values of each numerical type. You have used the %u specifier to output the unsigned integer values. If you use %d for the maximum value of an unsigned type, values that have the leftmost bit (the sign bit for signed types) as 1 won't be interpreted correctly.

You use the %e specifier for the floating-point limits, which presents the values in exponential form. You also specify just three digits precision, as you don't need the full accuracy in the output. The L modifier is necessary when the value being displayed by the printf() function is type long double. Remember, this has to be a capital letter L; a small letter l won't do here. The %f specifier presents values without an exponent, so it's rather inconvenient for very large or very small values. If you try it in the example, you'll see what I mean.

Introducing the sizeof Operator

You can find out how many bytes are occupied by a given type by using the sizeof operator. Of course, sizeof is a keyword in C. The expression sizeof(int) will result in the number of bytes occupied by a variable of type int, and the value that results is an integer of type size_t. Type size_t is defined in the standard header file <stddef.h> (as well as possibly other header files such as <stdio.h>) and will correspond to one of the basic integer types. However, because the choice of type that corresponds to type `size_t` may differ between one C library and another, it's best to use variables of `size_t` to store the value produced by the `sizeof` operator, even when you know which basic type it corresponds to. Here's how you could store a value that results from applying the `sizeof` operator:

```
size_t size = sizeof(long long);
```

You can also apply the `sizeof` operator to an expression, in which case the result is the size of the value that results from evaluating the expression. In this context the expression would usually be just a variable of some kind.

The `sizeof` operator has uses other than just discovering the memory occupied by a value of a basic type, but for the moment let's just use it to find out how many bytes are occupied by each type.

TRY IT OUT: DISCOVERING THE NUMBER OF BYTES OCCUPIED BY A GIVEN TYPE

This program will output the number of bytes occupied by each numeric type:

```
/* Program 2.12 Finding the size of a type  */
#include <stdio.h>

int main(void)
{
  printf("\nVariables of type char occupy %d bytes", sizeof(char));
  printf("\nVariables of type short occupy %d bytes", sizeof(short));
  printf("\nVariables of type int occupy %d bytes", sizeof(int));
  printf("\nVariables of type long occupy %d bytes", sizeof(long));
  printf("\nVariables of type float occupy %d bytes", sizeof(float));
  printf("\nVariables of type double occupy %d bytes", sizeof(double));
  printf("\nVariables of type long double occupy %d bytes",
                                        sizeof(long double));
  return 0;
}
```

On my system I get the following output:

```
Variables of type char occupy 1 bytes
Variables of type short occupy 2 bytes
Variables of type int occupy 4 bytes
Variables of type long occupy 4 bytes
Variables of type float occupy 4 bytes
Variables of type double occupy 8 bytes
Variables of type long double occupy 12 bytes
```

How It Works

Because the `sizeof` operator results in an integer value, you can output it using the %d specifier. Note that you can also obtain the number of bytes occupied by a variable, `var_name`, with the expression `sizeof var_name`. Obviously, the space between the `sizeof` keyword and the variable name in the expression is essential.

Now you know the range limits and the number of bytes occupied by each numeric type with your compiler.

Choosing the Correct Type for the Job

You have to be careful to select the type of variable that you're using in your calculations so that it accommodates the range of values that you expect. If you use the wrong type, you may find that errors creep into your programs that can be hard to detect. This is best shown with an example.

TRY IT OUT: THE RIGHT TYPES OF VARIABLES

Here's an example of how things can go horribly wrong if you choose an unsuitable type for your variables:

```c
/* Program 2.13 Choosing the correct type for the job  1*/
#include <stdio.h>

int main(void)
{
  const float Revenue_Per_150 = 4.5f;
  short JanSold = 23500;                    /* Stock sold in January  */
  short FebSold = 19300;                    /* Stock sold in February */
  short MarSold = 21600;                    /* Stock sold in March    */
  float  RevQuarter = 0.0f;                 /* Sales for the quarter  */

  short QuarterSold = JanSold+FebSold+MarSold; /* Calculate quarterly total */

  /* Output monthly sales and total for the quarter */
  printf("\nStock sold in\n Jan: %d\n Feb: %d\n Mar: %d",
                                           JanSold,FebSold,MarSold);
  printf("\nTotal stock sold in first quarter: %d",QuarterSold);

  /* Calculate the total revenue for the quarter and output it */
  RevQuarter = QuarterSold/150*Revenue_Per_150;
  printf("\nSales revenue this quarter is:$%.2f\n",RevQuarter);
  return 0;
}
```

These are fairly simple calculations, and you can see that the total stock sold in the quarter should be 64400. This is just the sum of each of the monthly totals, but if you run the program, the output you get is this:

```
Stock sold in
 Jan: 23500
 Feb: 19300
 Mar: 21600
Total stock sold in first quarter: -1136
Sales revenue this quarter is:$-31.50
```

Obviously all is not right here. It doesn't take a genius or an accountant to tell you that adding three big, positive numbers together shouldn't give a negative result!

How It Works

First you define a constant that will be used in the calculation:

```c
const Revenue_Per_150 = 4.5f;
```

This defines the revenue obtained for every 150 items sold. There's nothing wrong with that.
Next, you declare four variables and assign initial values to them:

```
short JanSold = 23500;                    /* Stock sold in January  */
short FebSold = 19300;                    /* Stock sold in February */
short MarSold = 21600;                    /* Stock sold in March     */
float  RevQuarter = 0.0f;                 /* Sales for the quarter   */
```

The first three variables are of type short, which is quite adequate to store the initial value. The RevQuarter variable is of type float because you want two decimal places for the quarterly revenue.

The next statement declares the variable QuarterSold and stores the sum of the sales for each of the months:

```
short QuarterSold = JanSold+FebSold+MarSold; /* Calculate quarterly total */
```

Note that you're initializing this variable with the result of an expression. This is only possible because the values of these variables are known to the compiler, so this represents what is known as a **constant expression**. If any of the values in the expression were determined during execution of the program—from a calculation involving a value that was read in, for instance—this wouldn't compile. The compiler can only use initial values that are explicit or are produced by an expression that the compiler can evaluate.

In fact, the cause of the erroneous results is in the declaration of the QuarterSold variable. You've declared it to be of type short and given it the initial value of the sum of the three monthly figures. You know that their sum is 64400 and that the program outputs a negative number. The error must therefore be in this statement.

The problem arises because you've tried to store a number that's too large for type short. If you remember, the maximum value that a short variable can hold is 32,767. The computer can't interpret the value of QuarterSold correctly and happens to give a negative result. The solution to your problem is to use a variable of type long that will allow you to store much larger numbers.

Solving the Problem

Try changing the program and running it again. You need to change only two lines in the body of the function main(). The new and improved program is as follows:

```
/* Program 2.14 Choosing the correct type for the job  2 */
#include <stdio.h>

int main(void)
{
  const float Revenue_Per_150 = 4.5f;
  short JanSold =23500;                   /* Stock sold in January  */
  short FebSold =19300;                   /* Stock sold in February */
  short MarSold =21600;                   /* Stock sold in March     */
  float  RevQuarter = 0.0f;               /* Sales for the quarter */

  long QuarterSold = JanSold+FebSold+MarSold; /* Calculate quarterly total */

  /* Output monthly sales and total for the quarter */
  printf("Stock sold in\n Jan: %d\n Feb: %d\n Mar: %d\n",
                                       JanSold,FebSold,MarSold);
  printf("Total stock sold in first quarter: %ld\n",QuarterSold);

  /* Calculate the total revenue for the quarter and output it */
  RevQuarter = QuarterSold/150*Revenue_Per_150;
  printf("Sales revenue this quarter is:$%.2f\n",RevQuarter);
  return 0;
}
```

When you run this program, the output is more satisfactory:

```
Stock sold in
 Jan: 23500
 Feb: 19300
 Mar: 21600
Total stock sold in first quarter: 64400
Sales revenue this quarter is :$1930.50
```

The stock sold in the quarter is correct, and you have a reasonable result for revenue. Notice that you use %ld to output the total stock sold. This is to tell the compiler that it is to use a long conversion for the output of this value. Just to check the program, calculate the result of the revenue yourself with a calculator.

The result you should get is, in fact, $1,932. Somewhere you've lost a dollar and a half. Not such a great amount, but try saying that to an accountant. You need to find the lost $1.50. Consider what's happening when you calculate the value for revenue in the program.

```
RevQuarter = QuarterSold/150*Revenue_Per_150;
```

Here you're assigning a value to RevQuarter. The value is the result of the expression on the right of the = sign. The result of the expression will be calculated, step by step, according to the precedence rules you've already looked at in this chapter. Here you have quite a simple expression that's calculated from left to right, as division and multiplication have the same priority. Let's work through it:

- QuarterSold/150 is calculated as 64400 / 150, which should produce the result 429.333.

This is where your problem arises. QuarterSold is an integer and so the computer truncates the result of the division to an integer, ignoring the .333. This means that when the next part of the calculation is evaluated, the result will be slightly off.

- 429*Revenue_Per_150 is calculated as 429 * 4.5 which is 1930.50.

You now know where the error has occurred, but what can you do about it? You could change all of your variables to floating-point types, but that would defeat the purpose of using integers in the first place. The numbers entered really are integers, so you'd like to store them as such. Is there an easy solution to this? In this case there is. You can rewrite the statement as follows:

```
RevQuarter = Revenue_Per_150*QuarterSold/150;
```

Now the multiplication will occur first; and because of the way arithmetic with mixed operands works, the result will be of type float. The compiler will automatically arrange for the integer operand to be converted to floating-point. When you then divide by 150, that operation will execute with float values too, with 150 being converted to 150f. The net effect is that the result will now be correct.

However, there's more to it than that. Not only do you need to understand more about what happens with arithmetic between operands of different types, but also you need to understand how you can control conversions from one type to another. In C you have the ability to explicitly convert a value of one type to another type. This process is called **casting**.

Explicit Type Conversion

Let's look again at the original expression to calculate the quarterly revenue that you saw in Program 2.14 and see how you can control what goes on so that you end up with the correct result:

```
RevQuarter = QuarterSold/150*Revenue_Per_150;
```

You know that if the result is to be correct, this statement has to be amended so that the expression is calculated in floating-point form. If you can convert the value of QuarterSold to type float, the expression will be evaluated as floating-point and your problem will be solved. To convert the value of a variable to another type, place the type that you want to cast the value to in parentheses in front of the variable. Thus, the statement to calculate the result correctly will be the following:

```
RevQuarter = (float)QuarterSold/150.0f*Revenue_Per_150;
```

This is exactly what you require. You're using the right types of variables in the right places. You're also ensuring you don't use integer arithmetic when you want to keep the fractional part of the result of a division. An explicit conversion from one type to another is called a **cast**.

Automatic Conversion

Look at the output from the second version of the program again:

Sales revenue this quarter is :$1930.50

Even without the explicit cast in the expression, the result is in floating-point form, even though it is still wrong. This is because the compiler automatically converts one of the operands to be the same type as the other when it's dealing with an operation that involves values of different types

Binary arithmetic operations (add, subtract, multiply, divide, and remainder) can only be executed by your computer when both operands are of the same type. When you use operands in a binary operation that are of different types, the compiler arranges for the value that is of a type with a more limited range to be converted to the type of the other. This is referred to as an **implicit conversion**. So referring back to the expression to calculate revenue

```
QuarterSold / 150 * Revenue_Per_150
```

it evaluated as 64400 (int) / 150 (int), which equals 429 (int). Then 429 (int converted to float) is multiplied by 4.5 (float), giving 1930.5 (float).

An implicit conversion always applies when a binary operator involves operands of different types. With the first operation, the numbers are both of type int, so the result is of type int. With the second operation, the first value is type int and the second value is type float. Type int is more limited in its range than type float, so the value of type int is automatically cast to type float. Whenever there is a mixture of types in an arithmetic expression, your C compiler will use a set of specific rules to decide how the expression will be evaluated. Let's have a look at these rules now.

Rules for Implicit Conversions

The mechanism that determines which operand in a binary operation is to be changed to the type of the other is relatively simple. Broadly it works on the basis that the operand with the type that has the more restricted range of values will be converted to the type of the other operand, although in some instances both operands will be promoted.

To express accurately in words how this works is somewhat more complicated than the description in the previous paragraph, so you may want to ignore the fine detail that follows and maybe refer back to it if you need to. If you do want the full story, read on.

The compiler determines the implicit conversion to use by applying the following rules in sequence:

1. If one operand is of type `long double` the other operand will be converted to type `long double`.

2. Otherwise, if one operand is of type `double` the other operand will be converted to type `double`.

3. Otherwise, if one operand is of type `float` the other operand will be converted to type `float`.

4. Otherwise, if the operands are both of signed integer types, or both of unsigned integer types, the operand of the type of lower rank is converted to the type of the other operand.

   The unsigned integer types are ranked from low to high in the following sequence: `signed char`, `short`, `int`, `long`, `long long`.

   Each unsigned integer type has the same rank as the corresponding signed integer type, so type `unsigned int` has the same rank as type `int`, for example.

5. Otherwise, if the operand of the signed integer type has a rank that is less than or equal to the rank of the unsigned integer type, the signed integer operand is converted to the unsigned integer type.

6. Otherwise, if the range of values the signed integer type can represent includes the values that can be represented by the unsigned integer type, the unsigned operand is converted to the signed integer type.

7. Otherwise, both operands are converted to the unsigned integer type corresponding to the signed integer type.

Implicit Conversions in Assignment Statements

You can also cause an implicit conversion to be applied when the value of the expression on the right of the assignment operator is a different type to the variable on the left. In some circumstances this can cause values to be truncated so information is lost. For instance, if an assignment operation stores a value of type `float` or `double` to a variable of type `int` or `long`, the fractional part of the `float` or `double` will be lost, and just the integer part will be stored. The following code fragment illustrates this situation:

```
int number = 0;
float value = 2.5f;
number = value;
```

The value stored in `number` will be 2. Because you've assigned the value of decimal (2.5) to the variable, number, which is of type `int`, the fractional part, .5, will be lost and only the 2 will be stored. Notice how I've used a specifier f at the end of 2.5f.

An assignment statement that may lose information because an automatic conversion has to be applied will usually result in a warning from the compiler. However, the code will still compile, so there's a risk that your program may be doing things that will result in incorrect results. Generally, it's better to put explicit casts in your code wherever conversions that may result in information being lost are necessary.

Let's look at an example to see how the conversion rules in assignment operations work in practice. Look at the following code fragment:

```
double price = 10.0;          /* Product price per unit */
long count = 5L;              /* Number of items        */
float ship_cost = 2.5F;       /* Shipping cost per order */
int discount = 15;           /* Discount as percentage  */
long double total_cost = (count*price + ship_cost)*((100L - discount)/100.0F);
```

This declares the four variables that you see and computes the total cost of an order from the values set for these variables. I chose the types primarily to demonstrate implicit conversions, and these types would not represent a sensible choice in normal circumstances. Let's see what happens in the last statement to produce the value for total_cost:

1. count*price is evaluated first and count will be implicitly converted to type double to allow the multiplication to take place and the result will be of type double. This results from the second rule.

2. Next ship_cost is added to the result of the previous operation and, to make this possible, the value of ship_cost is converted to the value of the previous result, type double. This conversion also results from the second rule.

3. Next, the expression 100L - discount is evaluated, and to allow this to occur the value of discount will be converted to type long, the type of the other operand in the subtraction. This is a result of the fourth rule and the result will be type long.

4. Next, the result of the previous operation (of type long) is converted to type float to allow the division by 100.0F (of type float) to take place. This is the result of applying the third rule, and the result is of type float.

5. The result of step 2 is divided by the result of step 4, and to make this possible the float value from the previous operation is converted to type double. This is a consequence of applying the third rule, and the result is of type double.

6. Finally, the previous result is stored in the variable total_cost as a result of the assignment operation. An assignment operation always causes the type of the right operand to be converted to that of the left when the operand types are different, regardless of the types of the operands, so the result of the previous operation is converted to type long double. No compiler warning will occur because all values of type double can be represented as type long double.

More Numeric Data Types

To complete the set of numeric data types, I'll now cover those that I haven't yet discussed. The first is one that I mentioned previously: type char. A variable of type char can store the code for a single character. Because it stores a character code, which is an integer, it's considered to be an integer type. Because it's an integer type, you can treat the value stored just like any other integer so you can use it in arithmetic calculations.

The Character Type

Values of type char occupy the least amount of memory of all the data types. They typically require just 1 byte. The integer that's stored in a variable of type char can be interpreted as a signed or unsigned value, depending on your compiler. As an unsigned type, the value stored in a variable of type char can range from 0 to 255. As a signed type, a variable of type char can store values from –128 to +127. Of course, both ranges correspond to the same set of bit patterns: from 0000 0000 to 1111 1111. With unsigned values, all eight bits are data bits, so 0000 0000 corresponds to 0, and 1111 1111 corresponds to 255. With unsigned values, the leftmost bit is a sign bit, so –128 is the binary value 1000 0000, 0 is 0000 0000, and 127 is 0111 1111. The value 1111 1111 as a signed binary value is the decimal value –1.

Thus, from the point of view of representing character codes, which are bit patterns, it doesn't matter whether type char is regarded as signed or unsigned. Where it *does* matter is when you perform arithmetic operations on values of type char.

A char variable can hold any single character, so you can specify the initial value for a variable of type char by a character constant. A **character constant** is a character written between single quotes. Here are some examples:

```
char letter = 'A';
char digit = '9';
char exclamation = '!';
```

You can use escape sequences to specify character constants, too:

```
char newline = '\n';
char tab = '\t';
char single_quote = '\'';
```

Of course, in every case the variable will be set to the code for the character between single quotes. The actual code value will depend on your computer environment, but by far the most common is American Standard Code for Information Interchange (ASCII). You can find the ASCII character set in Appendix B.

You can also initialize a variable of type char with an integer value, as long as the value fits into the range for type char with your compiler, as in this example:

```
char character = 74;    /* ASCII code for the letter J */
```

A variable of type char has a sort of dual personality: you can interpret it as a character or as an integer. Here's an example of an arithmetic operation with a value of type char:

```
char letter = 'C';      /* letter contains the decimal code value 67 */
letter = letter + 3;    /* letter now contains 70, which is 'F'      */
```

Thus, you can perform arithmetic on a value of type char and still treat it as a character.

Character Input and Character Output

You can read a single character from the keyboard and store it in a variable of type char using the scanf() function with the format specifier %c, for example

```
char ch = 0;
scanf("%c", &ch);   /* Read one character */
```

As you saw earlier, you must add an #include directive for the <stdio.h> header file to any source file in which you use the scanf() function:

```
#include <stdio.h>
```

To write a single character to the command line with the printf() function, you use the same format specifier, %c:

```
printf("The character is %c", ch);
```

Of course, you can output the numeric value of a character, too:

```
printf("The character is %c and the code value is %d", ch, ch);
```

This statement will output the value in ch as a character and as a numeric value.

TRY IT OUT: CHARACTER BUILDING

If you're completely new to programming, you may be wondering how on earth the computer knows whether it's dealing with a character or an integer. The reality is that it doesn't. It's a bit like when Alice encounters Humpty Dumpty who says "When I use a word, it means just what I choose it to mean—neither more nor less." An item of data in memory can mean whatever you choose it to mean. A byte containing the value 70 is a perfectly good integer. It's equally correct to regard it as the code for the letter J.

Let's look at an example that should make it clear. Here, you'll use the conversion specifier %c, which indicates that you want to output a value of type char as a character rather than an integer.

```
/* Program 2.15 Characters and numbers */
#include <stdio.h>

int main(void)
{
  char first = 'T';
  char second = 20;

  printf("\nThe first example as a letter looks like this - %c", first);
  printf("\nThe first example as a number looks like this - %d", first);
  printf("\nThe second example as a letter looks like this - %c", second);
  printf("\nThe second example as a number looks like this - %d\n", second);
  return 0;
}
```

The output from this program is the following:

```
The first example as a letter looks like this - T
The first example as a number looks like this - 84
The second example as a letter looks like this - ¶
The second example as a number looks like this - 20
```

How It Works

The program starts off by declaring two variables of type char:

```
char first = 'T';
char second = 20;
```

You initialize the first variable with a character constant and the second variable with an integer.
The next four statements output the value of each variable in two ways:

```
printf("\nThe first example as a letter looks like this - %c", first_example);
printf("\nThe first example as a number looks like this - %d", first_example);
printf("\nThe second example as a letter looks like this - %c", second_example);
printf("\nThe second example as a number looks like this - %d\n", second_example);
```

The %c conversion specifier interprets the contents of the variable as a single character, and the %d specifier interprets it as an integer. The numeric values that are output are the codes for the corresponding characters. These are ASCII codes in this instance, and will be in most instances, so that's what you'll assume throughout this book.

As I've noted, not all computers use the ASCII character set, so you may get different values than those shown previously. As long as you use the notation character for a character constant, you'll get the character that you want regardless of the character coding in effect.

You could also output the integer values of the variables of type char as hexadecimal values by using the format specifier %x instead of %d. You might like to try that.

TRY IT OUT: ARITHMETIC WITH VALUES THAT ARE CHARACTERS

Let's look at another example in which you apply arithmetic operations to values of type char:

```
/* Program 2.16 Using type char  */
#include <stdio.h>

int main(void)
{
  char first = 'A';
  char second = 'B';
  char last = 'Z';

  char number = 40;

  char ex1 = first + 2;          /* Add 2 to 'A'        */
  char ex2 = second - 1;         /* Subtract 1 from 'B' */
  char ex3 = last + 2;           /* Add 2 to 'Z'        */

  printf("Character values      %-5c%-5c%-5c", ex1, ex2, ex3);
  printf("\nNumerical equivalents %-5d%-5d%-5d", ex1, ex2, ex3);
  printf("\nThe number %d is the code for the character %c\n", number, number);
  return 0;
}
```

When you run the program you should get the following output:

```
Character values      C    A    \
Numerical equivalents 67   65   92
The number 40 is the code for the character (
```

How It Works

This program demonstrates how you can happily perform arithmetic with char variables that you've initialized with characters. The first three statements in the body of main() are as follows:

```
  char first = 'A';
  char second = 'B';
  char last = 'Z';
```

These initialize the variables first, second, and last to the character values you see. The numerical value of these variables will be the ASCII codes for the respective characters. Because you can treat them as numeric values as well as characters, you can perform arithmetic operations with them.

The next statement initializes a variable of type char with an integer value:

```
char number = 40;
```

The initializing value must be within the range of values that a 1-byte variable can store; so with my compiler, where char is a signed type, it must be between 128 and 127. Of course, you can interpret the contents of the variable as a character. In this case, it will be the character that has the ASCII code value 40, which happens to be a left parenthesis.

The next three statements declare three more variables of type char:

```
char ex1 = first + 2;       /* Add 2 to 'A'      */
char ex2 = second - 1;      /* Subtract 1 from 'B' */
char ex3 = last + 2;        /* Add 2 to 'Z'      */
```

These statements create new values and therefore new characters from the values stored in the variables first, second, and last; the results of these expressions are stored in the variables ex1, ex2, and ex3.

The next two statements output the three variables ex1, ex2, and ex3 in two different ways:

```
printf("Character values     %-5c%-5c%-5c", ex1, ex2, ex3);
printf("\nNumerical equivalents %-5d%-5d%-5d", ex1, ex2, ex3);
```

The first statement interprets the values stored as characters by using the %-5c conversion specifier. This specifies that the value should be output as a character that is left-aligned in a field width of 5. The second statement outputs the same variables again, but this time interprets the values as integers by using the %-5d specifier. The alignment and the field width are the same but d specifies the output is an integer. You can see that the two lines of output show the three characters on the first line with their ASCII codes aligned on the line beneath.

The last line outputs the variable number as a character and as an integer:

```
printf("\nThe number %d is the code for the character %c\n", number, number);
```

To output the variable twice, you just write it twice—as the second and third arguments to the printf() function. It's output first as an integer value and then as a character.

This ability to perform arithmetic with characters can be very useful. For instance, to convert from uppercase to lowercase, you simply add the result of 'a'-'A' (which is 32 for ASCII) to the uppercase character. To achieve the reverse, just subtract 'a'-'A'. You can see how this works if you have a look at the decimal ASCII values for the alphabetic characters in Appendix B of this book. Of course, this operation depends on the character codes for a to z and A to Z being a contiguous sequence of integers. If this is not the case for the character coding used by your computer, this won't work. The EBCDIC code used on some IBM machines is an example of where you can't use this technique because there are discontinuities in the code values for letters.

The Wide Character Type

A variable of type wchar_t stores a multibyte character code and typically occupies 2 bytes. You would use type wchar_t when you are working with Unicode characters, for example. Type wchar_t is defined in the <stddef.h> standard header file, so you need to include this in source files that use this type. You can define a wide character constant by preceding what would otherwise be a character constant of type char with the modifier L. For example, here's how to declare a variable of type wchar_t and initialize it with the code for a capital A:

```
wchar_t w_ch = L'A';
```

Operations with type wchar_t work in much the same way as operations with type char. Since type wchar_t is an integer type, you can perform arithmetic operations with values of this type.

To read a character from the keyboard into a variable of type wchar_t, use the %lc format specification. Use the same format specifier to output a value of type wchar_t. Here's how you could read a character from the keyboard and then display it on the next line:

```
wchar_t wch = 0;
scanf("%lc", &wch);
printf("You entered %lc", wch);
```

Of course, you would need an #include directive for <stdio.h> for this fragment to compile correctly.

Enumerations

Situations arise quite frequently in programming when you want a variable that will store a value from a very limited set of possible values. One example is a variable that stores a value representing the current month in the year. You really would only want such a variable to be able to assume one of 12 possible values, corresponding to January through December. The enumeration in C is intended specifically for such purposes.

With an **enumeration** you can define a new integer type where variables of the type have a fixed range of possible values that you specify. Here's an example of a statement that defines a new type with the name Weekday:

```
enum Weekday {Monday, Tuesday, Wednesday, Thursday, Friday, Saturday, Sunday};
```

The name of the new type, Weekday in this instance, follows the enum keyword and this type name is referred to as the **tag** of the enumeration. Variables of type Weekday can have any of the values specified by the names that appear between the braces that follow the type name. These names are called **enumerators** or **enumeration constants** and there can be as many of these as you want. Each enumerator is identified by the unique name you assign, and the compiler will assign an integer value of type int to each name. An enumeration is an integer type because the enumerators that you specify will correspond to integer values that by default will start from zero with each successive enumerator having a value of one more than the previous enumerator. Thus, in this example, the values Monday through Sunday will map to values 0 through 6.

You could declare a new variable of type Weekday and initialize it like this:

```
enum Weekday today = Wednesday;
```

This declares a variable with the name today and it initializes it to the value Wednesday. Because the enumerators have default values, Wednesday will correspond to the value 2. The actual integer type that is used for a variable of an enumeration type is implementation-defined and the choice of type may depend on how many enumerators there are.

It is also possible to declare variables of the enumeration type when you define the type. Here's a statement that defines an enumeration type plus two variables:

```
enum Weekday {Monday, Tuesday, Wednesday, Thursday,
                    Friday, Saturday, Sunday} today, tomorrow;
```

This declares the enumeration type Weekday and two variables of that type, today and tomorrow. Naturally you could also initialize the variable in the same statement so you could write this:

```
enum Weekday {Monday, Tuesday, Wednesday, Thursday,
                    Friday, Saturday, Sunday} today = Monday, tomorrow = Tuesday;
```

This initializes today and tomorrow to Monday and Tuesday respectively.

Because variables of an enumeration type are of an integer type, they can be used in arithmetic expressions. You could write the previous statement like this:

```
enum Weekday {Monday, Tuesday, Wednesday, Thursday,
              Friday, Saturday, Sunday} today = Monday, tomorrow = today + 1;
```

Now the initial value for tomorrow is one more than that of today. However, when you do this kind of thing, it is up to you to ensure that the value that results from the arithmetic is a valid enumerator value.

■**Note** Although you specify a fixed set of possible values for an enumeration type, there is no checking mechanism to ensure that only these values are used in your program. It is up to you to make sure only valid enumeration values are used for a given enumeration type. One way to do this is to only assign values to variables of an enumeration type that are the enumeration constant names.

Choosing Enumerator Values

You can specify your own integer value for any or all of the enumerators explicitly. Although the names you use for enumerators must be unique, there is no requirement for the enumerator values themselves to be unique. Unless you have a specific reason for making some of the values the same, it is usually a good idea to ensure that they are unique. Here's how you could define the Weekday type so that the enumerator values start from 1:

```
enum Weekday {Monday=1, Tuesday, Wednesday, Thursday, Friday, Saturday, Sunday};
```

Now the enumerators Monday through Sunday will correspond to values 1 through 7. The enumerators that follow an enumerator with an explicit value will be assigned successive integer values. This can cause enumerators to have duplicate values, as in the following example:

```
enum Weekday {Monday=5, Tuesday=4, Wednesday,
              Thursday=10, Friday =3, Saturday, Sunday};
```

Monday, Tuesday, Thursday, and Friday have explicit values specified. Wednesday will be set to Tuesday+1 so it will be 5, the same as Monday. Similarly Saturday and Sunday will be set to 4 and 5 so they also have duplicate values. There's no reason why you can't do this, although unless you have a good reason for making some of the enumeration constants the same, it does tend to be confusing.

You can use an enumeration in any situation where you want a variable with a specific limited number of possible values. Here's another example of defining an enumeration:

```
enum Suit{clubs = 10, diamonds, hearts, spades);
enum Suit card_suit = diamonds;
```

The first statement defines the enumeration type Suit, so variables of this type can have one of the four values between the braces. The second statement defines a variable of type Suit and initializes it with the value diamonds, which will correspond to 11. You could also define an enumeration to identify card face values like this:

```
enum FaceValue { two=2, three, four, five, six, seven,
                 eight, nine, ten, jack, queen, king, ace};
```

In this enumeration the enumerators will have integer values that match the card value with ace as high.

When you output the value of a variable of an enumeration type, you'll just get the numeric value. If you want to output the enumerator name, you have to provide the program logic to do this. You'll be able to do this with what you learn in the next chapter.

Unnamed Enumeration Types

You can create variables of an enumeration type without specifying a tag, so there's no enumeration type name. For example

```
enum {red, orange, yellow, green, blue, indigo, violet} shirt_color;
```

There's no tag here so this statement defines an unnamed enumeration type with the possible enumerators from red to violet. The statement also declares one variable of the unnamed type with the name shirt_color.

You can assign a value to shirt_color in the normal way:

```
shirt_color = blue;
```

Obviously, the major limitation on unnamed enumeration types is that you must declare all the variables of the type in the statement that defines the type. Because you don't have a type name, there's no way to define additional variables of this type later in the code.

Variables to Store Boolean Values

The type _Bool stores Boolean values. A Boolean value typically arises from a comparison where the result may be true or false; you'll learn about comparisons and using the results to make decisions in your programs in Chapter 3. The value of a variable of type _Bool can be either 0 or 1, corresponding to the Boolean values false and true respectively, and because the values 0 and 1 are integers, type _Bool is regarded as an integer type. You declare a _Bool variable just like any other. For example

```
_Bool valid = 1;            /* Boolean variable initialized to true */
```

_Bool is not an ideal type name. The name bool would be less clumsy looking and more readable, but the Boolean type was introduced into the C language relatively recently so the type name was chosen to minimize the possibility of conflicts with existing code. If bool had been chosen as the type name, any program that used the name bool for some purpose most probably would not compile with a compiler that supported bool as a built-in type.

Having said that, you can use bool as the type name; you just need to add an #include directive for the standard header file <stdbool.h> to any source file that uses it. As well as defining bool to be the equivalent of _Bool, the <stdbool.h> header file also defines the symbols true and false to correspond to 1 and 0 respectively. Thus, if you include the header into your source file, you can rewrite the previous declaration as the following:

```
bool valid = true;         /* Boolean variable initialized to true */
```

This looks much clearer than the previous version so it's best to include the <stdbool.h> header unless you have a good reason not to.

You can cast between Boolean values and other numeric types. A nonzero numeric value will result in 1 (true) when cast to type _Bool, and 0 will cast to 0 (false). If you use a _Bool variable in an arithmetic expression, the compiler will insert an implicit conversion where necessary. Type _Bool has a rank lower than any of the other types, so in an operation involving type _Bool and a value of another type it is the _Bool value that will be converted to the other type.

I won't elaborate further on working with Boolean variables at this point. You'll learn more about using them in the next chapter.

The Complex Number Types

This section assumes you have learned about complex numbers at some point. If you have never heard of complex numbers, you can safely skip this section. In case you are a little rusty on complex numbers, I'll remind you of their basic characteristics.

A complex number is a number of the form a + bi (or a + bj if you are an electrical engineer) where i is the square root of minus one, and a and b are real numbers. a is the real part, and bi is the imaginary part of the complex number. A complex number can also be regarded as an ordered pair of real numbers (a, b).

Complex numbers can be represented in the complex plane, as illustrated in Figure 2-2.

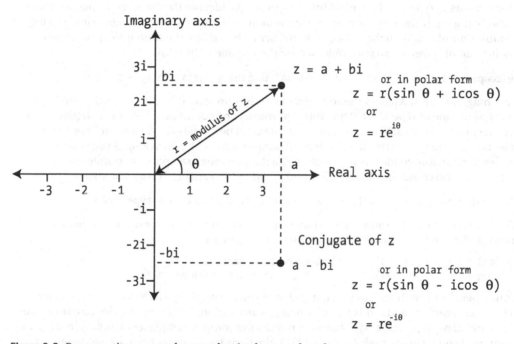

Figure 2-2. *Representing a complex number in the complex plane*

You can apply the following operations to complex numbers:

! *Modulus:* The modulus of a complex number a + bi is $\sqrt{(a^2 + b^2)}$.

! *Equality:* The complex numbers a + bi and c + di are equal if a equals c and b equals d.

! *Addition:* The sum of the complex numbers a + bi and c + di is (a + c) + (b + d)i.

! *Multiplication:* The product of the complex numbers a + bi and c + di is (ac - bd) + (ad + bc)i.

! *Division:* The result of dividing the complex number a + bi by c + di is (ac - bd) / (c2 + d2) + ((bc - ad)(c2 + d2))i.

! *Conjugate:* The conjugate of a complex number a + bi is a - bi. Note that the product of a complex number a + bi and its conjugate is a2 + b2.

Complex numbers also have a **polar representation**: a complex number can be written in polar form as r(sin θ+ icos θ) or as the ordered pair of real numbers (r,θ) where r and θ are as shown in Figure 2-2. From Euler's formula a complex number can also be represented as reiθ.

I'll just briefly introduce the idea of the types in the C language that store complex numbers because the applications for these are very specialized. You have three types that store complex numbers:

! `float _Complex` with real and imaginary parts of type `float`

! `double _Complex` with real and imaginary parts of type `double`

! `long double _Complex` with real and imaginary parts of type `long double`

You could declare a variable to store complex numbers like this:

```
double _Complex z1;              /* Real and imaginary parts are type double */
```

The somewhat cumbersome `_Complex` keyword was chosen for the complex number types for the same reasons as type `_Bool`: to avoid breaking existing code. But the `<complex.h>` header defines `complex` as being equivalent to `_Complex`, as well as many other functions and macros for working with complex numbers. With the `<complex.h>` header included into the source file, you can use `complex` instead of `_Complex`, so you could declare the variable `z1` like this:

```
double complex z1;               /* Real and imaginary parts are type double */
```

The imaginary unit, which is the square root of 1, is represented by the keyword `_Complex_I`, notionally as a value of type `float`. Thus you can write a complex number with the real part as 2.0 and the imaginary part as 3.0 as `2.0 + 3.0 * _Complex_I`. The `<complex.h>` header defines `I` to be the equivalent of `_Complex_I`, so you can use this much simpler representation as long as you have included the header in your source file. Thus you can write the previous example of a complex number as `2.0 + 3.0 * I`. You could therefore declare and initialize the variable `z1` with this statement:

```
double complex z1 = 2.0 + 3.0*I;   /* Real and imaginary parts are type double */
```

The `creal()` function returns the real part of a value of type `double complex` that is passed as the argument, and `cimag()` returns the imaginary part. For example

```
double real_part = creal(z1);    /* Get the real part of z1 */
double imag_part = cimag(z1);    /* Get the imaginary part of z1 */
```

You append an `f` to these function names when you are working with `float` complex values (`crealf()` and `cimagf()`) and a lowercase `L` when you are working with `long double` complex values (`creall()` and `cimagl()`). The `conj()` function returns the complex conjugate of its `double complex` argument, and you have the `conjf()` and `conjl()` functions for the other two complex types.

You use the `_Imaginary` keyword to define variables that store purely imaginary numbers; in other words there is no real component. There are three types for imaginary numbers, using the keywords `float`, `double`, and `long double`, analogous to the three complex types. The `<complex.h>` header defines `imaginary` as a more readable equivalent of `_Imaginary`, so you could declare a variable that stores imaginary numbers like this:

```
double imaginary ix = 2.4*I;
```

Casting an imaginary value to a complex type produces a complex number with a zero real part and a complex part the same as the imaginary number. Casting a value of an imaginary type to a real type other than `_Bool` results in 0. Casting a value of an imaginary type to type `_Bool` results in 0 for a zero imaginary value, and 1 otherwise.

You can write arithmetic expressions involving complex and imaginary values using the arithmetic operators +, , *, and /. Let's see them at work.

TRY IT OUT: WORKING WITH COMPLEX NUMBERS

Here's a simple example that creates a couple of complex variables and performs some simple arithmetic operations:

```
/* Program 2.17 Working with complex numbers
#include <complex.h>
#include <stdio.h>

int main(void)
{
  double complex cx = 1.0 + 3.0*I;
  double complex  cy = 1.0 - 4.0*I;
  printf("Working with complex numbers:");
  printf("\nStarting values: cx = %.2f%+.2fi  cy = %.2f%+.2fi",
                           creal(cx), cimag(cx), creal(cy), cimag(cy));

  double complex  sum = cx+cy;
  printf("\n\nThe sum cx + cy = %.2f%+.2fi",
                                   creal(sum),cimag(sum));

  double complex  difference = cx-cy;
  printf("\n\nThe difference cx - cy = %.2f%+.2fi",
                                   creal(difference),cimag(difference));

  double complex product = cx*cy;
  printf("\n\nThe product cx * cy = %.2f%+.2fi",
                                     creal(product),cimag(product));

  double complex quotient - cx/cy;
  printf("\n\nThe quotient cx / cy = %.2f%+.2fi",
                                      creal(quotient),cimag(quotient));

  double complex conjugate = conj(cx);
  printf("\n\nThe conjugate of cx =  %.2f%+.2fi",
                                   creal(conjugate) ,cimag(conjugate));

    return 0;
}
```

You should get the following output from this example:

```
Working with complex numbers:
Starting values: cx = 1.00+3.00i  cy = 1.00-4.00i

The sum cx + cy = 2.00-1.00i

The difference cx - cy = 0.00+7.00i

The product cx * cy = 13.00-1.00i

The quotient cx / cy = -0.65+0.41i

The conjugate of cx =  1.00-3.00i
```

How It Works

The code is fairly self-explanatory. After defining and initializing the variables cx and cy, you use the four arithmetic operators with these, and output the result in each case. You could equally well use the keyword _Complex instead of complex if you wish.

The output specification used for the imaginary part of each complex value is %+.2f. The + following the % specifies that the sign should always be output. If the + was omitted you would only get the sign in the output when the value is negative. The 2 following the decimal point specifies that two places after the decimal point are to be output.

If you explore the contents of the <complex.h> header that is supplied with your compiler you'll find it provides a wide range of other functions that operate on complex values.

The op= Form of Assignment

C is fundamentally a very concise language, so it provides you with abbreviated shortcuts for some operations. Consider the following line of code:

```
number = number + 10;
```

This sort of assignment, in which you're incrementing or decrementing a variable by some amount occurs very often so there's a shorthand version:

```
number += 10;
```

The += operator after the variable name is one example of a family of op= operators. This statement has exactly the same effect as the previous one and it saves a bit of typing. The op in op= can be any of the arithmetic operators:

```
+  -  *  /  %
```

If you suppose number has the value 10, you can write the following statements:

```
number *= 3;        /* number will be set to number*3 which is 30 */
number /= 3;        /* number will be set to number/3 which is 3  */
number %= 3;        /* number will be set to number%3 which is 1  */
```

The op in op= can also be a few other operators that you haven't encountered yet:

```
<<  >>  &  ^  |
```

I'll defer discussion of these to Chapter 3, however.

The op= set of operators always works in the same way. If you have a statement of the form

```
lhs op= rhs;
```

where rhs represents any expression on the right-hand side of the op= operator, then the effect is the same as a statement of the form

```
lhs = lhs op (rhs);
```

Note the parentheses around the rhs expression. This means that op applies to the value that results from evaluating the entire rhs expression, whatever it is. So just to reinforce your understanding of this, let's look at few more examples. The statement

```
variable *= 12;
```

is the same as

```
variable = variable * 12;
```

You now have two different ways of incrementing an integer variable by one. Both of the following statements increment count by 1:

```
count = count +1;
count += 1;
```

You'll learn about yet another way of doing this in the next chapter. This amazing level of choice tends to make it virtually impossible for indecisive individuals to write programs in C.

Because the op in op= applies to the result of evaluating the rhs expression, the statement

```
a /= b+1;
```

is the same as

```
a = a/(b+1);
```

Your computational facilities have been somewhat constrained so far. You've been able to use only a very basic set of arithmetic operators. You can get more power to your calculating elbow using standard library facilities, so before you come to the final example in this chapter, you'll take a look at some of the mathematical functions that the standard library offers.

Mathematical Functions

The math.h header file includes declarations for a wide range of mathematical functions. To give you a feel for what's available, you'll take a look at those that are used most frequently. All the functions return a value of type double.

You have the set of functions shown in Table 2-9 available for numerical calculations of various kinds. These all require arguments to be of type double.

Table 2-9. *Functions for Numerical Calculations*

Function	Operation
floor(x)	Returns the largest integer that isn't greater than x as type double
ceil(x)	Returns the smallest integer that isn't less than x as type double
fabs(x)	Returns the absolute value of x
log(x)	Returns the natural logarithm (base e) of x
log10(x)	Returns the logarithm to base 10 of x
exp(x)	Returns the value of e^x
sqrt(x)	Returns the square root of x
pow(x)	Returns the value x^y

Here are some examples of using these functions:

```
double x = 2.25;
double less = 0.0;
double more = 0.0;
double root = 0.0;
less = floor(x);    /* Result is 2.0 */
more = ceil(x);     /* Result is 3.0 */
root = sqrt(x);     /* Result is 1.5 */
```

You also have a range of trigonometric functions available, as shown in Table 2-10. Arguments and values returned are again of type double and angles are expressed in radians.

Table 2-10. *Functions for Trigonometry*

Function	Operation
sin(x)	Sine of x expressed in radians
cos(x)	Cosine of x
tan(x)	Tangent of x

If you're into trigonometry, the use of these functions will be fairly self-evident. Here are some examples:

```
double angle = 45.0;              /* Angle in degrees */
double pi = 3.14159265;
double sine = 0.0;
double cosine = 0.0;
sine = sin(pi*angle/180.0);       /*Angle converted to radians */
cosine = sin(pi*angle/180.0);     /*Angle converted to radians */
```

Because 180 degrees is the same angle as radians, dividing an angle measured in degrees by 180 and multiplying by the value of will produce the angle in radians, as required by these functions.

You also have the inverse trigonometric functions available: asin(), acos(), and atan(), as well as the hyperbolic functions sinh(), cosh(), and tanh(). Don't forget, you must include math.h into your program if you wish to use any of these functions. If this stuff is not your bag, you can safely ignore this section.

Designing a Program

Now it's time for the end-of-chapter real-life example. It would be a great idea to try out some of the numeric types in a new program. I'll take you through the basic elements of the process of writing a program from scratch. This involves receiving an initial specification of the problem, analyzing the problem, preparing a solution, writing the program, and, of course, running the program and testing it to make sure it works. Each step in the process can introduce problems, beyond just the theory.

The Problem

The height of a tree is of great interest to many people. For one thing, if a tree is being cut down, knowing its height tells you how far away *safe* is. This is very important to those with a nervous disposition. Your problem is to find out the height of a tree without using a very long ladder, which itself would introduce risk to life and limb. To find the height of a tree, you're allowed the help of a friend! preferably a short friend. You should assume that the tree you're measuring is taller than both you and your friend. Trees that are shorter than you present little risk, unless they're of the spiky kind.

The Analysis

Real-world problems are rarely expressed in terms that are directly suitable for programming. Before you consider writing a line of code, you need to be sure that you have a complete understanding of the problem and how it's going to be solved. Only then can you estimate how much time and effort will be involved in creating the solution.

The analysis phase involves gaining a full understanding of the problem and determining the logical process for solving it. Typically this requires a significant amount of work. It involves teasing out any detail in the specification of the problem that is vague or missing. Only when you fully understand the problem can you begin to express the solution in a form that's suitable for programming.

You're going to determine the height of a tree using some simple geometry and the heights of two people: you and one other. Let's start by naming the tall person (you) Lofty and the shorter person (your friend) Shorty. If you're vertically challenged, the roles can be reversed. For more accurate results, the tall person should be significantly taller than the short person. Otherwise the tall person could consider standing on a box. The diagram in Figure 2-3 will give you an idea of what you're trying to do in this program.

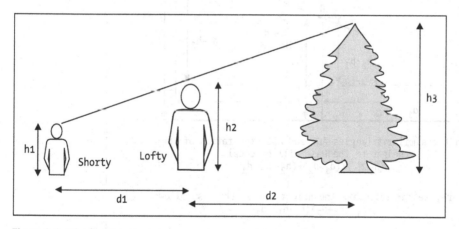

Figure 2-3. *The height of a tree*

Finding the height of the tree is actually quite simple. You can get the height of the tree, h_3, if you know the other dimensions shown in the illustration: h_1 and h_2, which are the heights of Shorty and Lofty, and d_1 and d_2, which are the distances between Shorty and Lofty and Lofty and the tree, respectively. You can use the technique of similar triangles to work out the height of the tree. You can see this in the simplified diagram in Figure 2-4.

Here, because the triangles are similar, height1 divided by distance1 is equal to height2 divided by distance2. Using this relationship, you can get the height of the tree from the height of Shorty and Lofty and the distances to the tree, as shown in Figure 2-5.

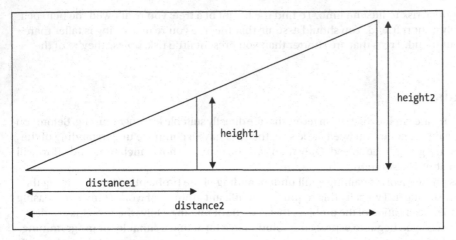

Figure 2-4. *Similar triangles*

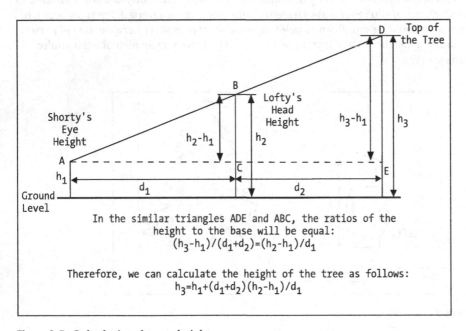

Figure 2-5. *Calculating the tree height*

The triangles ADE and ABC are the same as those shown in Figure 2-4. Using the fact that the triangles are similar, you can calculate the height of the tree as shown in the equation at the bottom of Figure 2-5.

This means that you can calculate the height of the tree in your program from four values:

! The distance between Shorty and Lofty, d_1 in the diagram. You'll use the variable shorty_to_lofty to store this value.

! The distance between Lofty and the tree, d_2 in the diagram. You'll use the variable lofty_to_tree to store this value.

! The height of Lofty to the top of his head, h_2 in the diagram. You'll use the variable lofty to store this value.

! The height of Shorty, but only up to the eyes, h_1 in the diagram. You'll use the variable shorty to store this value.

You can then plug these values into the equation for the height of the tree.

Your first task is to get these four values into the computer. You can then use your ratios to find out the height of the tree and finally output the answer. The steps are as follows:

1. Input the values you need.

2. Calculate the height of the tree using the equation in the diagram.

3. Display the answer.

The Solution

This section outlines the steps you'll take to solve the problem.

Step 1

Your first step is to get the values that you need to work out the height of the tree. This means that you have to include the stdio.h header file, because you need to use both printf() and scanf(). You then have to decide what variables you need to store these values in. After that, you can use printf() to prompt for the input and scanf() to read the values from the keyboard.

You'll provide for the heights of the participants to be entered in feet and inches for the convenience of the user. Inside the program, though, it will be easier to work with all heights and distances in the same units, so you'll convert all measurements to inches. You'll need two variables to store the heights of Shorty and Lofty in inches. You'll also need a variable to store the distance between Lofty and Shorty, and another to store the distance from Lofty to the tree! both distances in inches, of course.

In the input process, you'll first get Lofty's height as a number of whole feet and then as a number of inches, prompting for each value as you go along. You can use two more variables for this: one to store the feet value and the other to store the inches value. You'll then convert these into just inches and store the result in the variable you've reserved for Lofty's height. You'll do the same thing for Shorty's height (but only up to the height of his or her eyes) and finally the same for the distance between them. For the distance to the tree, you'll use only whole feet, because this will be accurate enough! and again you'll convert the distance to inches. You can reuse the same variables for each measurement in feet and inches that is entered. So here goes with the first part of the program:

```
/* Program 2.18  Calculating the height of a tree */
#include <stdio.h>

int main(void)
{
  long shorty = 0L;             /* Shorty's height in inches              */
  long lofty = 0L;              /* Lofty's height in inches               */
  long feet = 0L;
  long inches = 0L;
  long shorty_to_lofty = 0L; /* Distance from Shorty to Lofty in inches   */
  long lofty_to_tree = 0L;   /* Distance from Lofty to the tree in inches */
  const long inches_per_foot = 12L;
```

```
/* Get Lofty's height */
printf("Enter Lofty's height to the top of his/her head, in whole feet: ");
scanf("%ld", &feet);
printf("                ...and then inches: ");
scanf("%ld", &inches);
lofty = feet*inches_per_foot + inches;

/* Get Shorty's height up to his/her eyes */
printf("Enter Shorty's height up to his/her eyes, in whole feet: ");
scanf("%ld", &feet);
printf("                        ... and then inches: ");
scanf("%ld", &inches);
shorty = feet*inches_per_foot + inches;

/* Get the distance from Shorty to Lofty */
printf("Enter the distance between Shorty and Lofty, in whole feet: ");
scanf("%ld", &feet);
printf("                            ... and then inches: ");
scanf("%ld", &inches);
shorty_to_lofty = feet*inches_per_foot + inches;

/* Get the distance from Lofty to the tree */
printf("Finally enter the distance to the tree to the nearest foot: ");
  scanf("%ld", &feet);
lofty_to_tree = feet*inches_per_foot;

/* The code to calculate the height of the tree will go here */

/* The code to display the result will go here                */
  return 0;
}
```

Notice how the program code is spaced out to make it easier to read. You don't have to do it this way, but if you decide to change the program next year, it will make it much easier to see how the program works if it's well laid out. You should always add comments to your programs to help with this. It's particularly important to at least make clear what the variables are used for and to document the basic logic of the program.

You use a variable that you've declared as const to convert from feet to inches. The variable name, inches_per_foot, makes it reasonably obvious what's happening when it's used in the code. This is much better than using the •magic number! 12 explicitly. Here you're dealing with feet and inches, and most people will be aware that there are 12 inches in a foot. In other circumstances the significance of numeric constants may not be so obvious, though. If you're using the value 0.22 in a program calculating salaries, it's much less apparent what this might be; therefore, the calculation may seem rather obscure. If you create a const variable tax_rate that you've initialized to 0.22 and use that instead, then the mist clears.

Step 2

Now that you have all the data you need, you can calculate the height of the tree. All you need to do is implement the equation for the tree height in terms of your variables. You'll need to declare another variable to store the height of the tree.

You can now add the code that's shown here in bold type to do this:

```
/* Program 2.18  Calculating the height of a tree */
#include <stdio.h>

int main(void)
{
  long shorty = 0L;            /* Shorty's height in inches             */
  long lofty = 0L;             /* Lofty's height in inches              */
  long feet = 0L;              /* A whole number of feet                */
  long inches = 0L;
  long shorty_to_lofty = 0;    /* Distance from Shorty to Lofty in inches   */
  long lofty_to_tree = 0;      /* Distance from Lofty to the tree in inches */
  long tree_height = 0;        /* Height of the tree in inches              */
  const long inches_per_foot = 12L;

  /* Get Lofty's height */
  printf("Enter Lofty's height to the top of his/her head, in whole feet: ");
  scanf("%ld", &feet);
  printf("              ...and then inches: ");
  scanf("%ld", &inches);
  lofty = feet*inches_per_foot + inches;

  /* Get Shorty's height up to his/her eyes */
  printf("Enter Shorty's height up to his/her eyes, in whole feet: ");
  scanf("%ld", &feet);
   printf("                         ... and then inches: ");
  scanf("%ld", &inches);
  shorty = feet*inches_per_foot + inches;

  /* Get the distance from Shorty to Lofty */
  printf("Enter the distance between Shorty and Lofty, in whole feet: ");
  scanf("%ld", &feet);
  printf("                         ... and then inches: ");
  scanf("%ld", &inches);
  shorty_to_lofty = feet*inches_per_foot + inches;

  /* Get the distance from Lofty to the tree */
  printf("Finally enter the distance to the tree to the nearest foot: ");
  scanf("%ld", &feet);
  lofty_to_tree = feet*inches_per_foot;

  /* Calculate the height of the tree in inches */
  tree_height = shorty + (shorty_to_lofty + lofty_to_tree)*(lofty-shorty)/
                                                  shorty_to_lofty;

  /* The code to display the result will go here          */
  return 0;
}
```

The statement to calculate the height is essentially the same as the equation in the diagram. It's a bit messy, but it translates directly to the statement in the program to calculate the height.

Step 3

Finally, you need to output the answer. To present the result in the most easily understandable form, you'll convert the result that you've stored in tree_height! which is in inches! back into feet and inches:

```
/* Program 2.18 Calculating the height of a tree */
#include <stdio.h>

int main(void)
{
  long shorty = 0L;          /* Shorty's height in inches            */
  long lofty = 0L;           /* Lofty's height in inches             */
  long feet = 0L;
  long inches = 0L;
  long shorty_to_lofty = 0;  /* Distance from Shorty to Lofty in inches   */
  long lofty_to_tree = 0;    /* Distance from Lofty to the tree in inches */
  long tree_height = 0;      /* Height of the tree in inches             */
  const long inches_per_foot = 12L;

  /* Get Lofty's height */
  printf("Enter Lofty's height to the top of his/her head, in whole feet: ");
  scanf("%ld", &feet);
  printf("                                        ... and then inches: ");
  scanf("%ld", &inches);
  lofty = feet*inches_per_foot + inches;

  /* Get Shorty's height up to his/her eyes */
  printf("Enter Shorty's height up to his/her eyes, in whole feet: ");
  scanf("%ld", &feet);
  printf("                                  ... and then inches: ");
  scanf("%ld", &inches);
  shorty = feet*inches_per_foot + inches;

  /* Get the distance from Shorty to Lofty */
  printf("Enter the distance between Shorty and Lofty, in whole feet: ");
  scanf("%ld", &feet);
  printf("                                  ... and then inches: ");
  scanf("%ld", &inches);
  shorty_to_lofty = feet*inches_per_foot + inches;

  /* Get the distance from Lofty to the tree */
  printf("Finally enter the distance to the tree to the nearest foot: ");
  scanf("%ld", &feet);
  lofty_to_tree = feet*inches_per_foot;

  /* Calculate the height of the tree in inches */
  tree_height = shorty + (shorty_to_lofty + lofty_to_tree)*(lofty-shorty)/
                                                     shorty_to_lofty;

  /* Display the result in feet and inches            */
  printf("The height of the tree is %ld feet and %ld inches.\n",
                    tree_height/inches_per_foot, tree_height% inches_per_foot);
  return 0;
}
```

And there you have it. The output from the program looks something like this:

```
Enter Lofty's height to the top of his/her head, in whole feet first: 6
                              ... and then inches: 2
Enter Shorty's height up to his/her eyes, in whole feet: 4
                    ... and then inches: 6
Enter the distance between Shorty and Lofty, in whole feet : 5
                    ... and then inches: 0
Finally enter the distance to the tree to the nearest foot: 20
The height of the tree is 12 feet and 10 inches.
```

Summary

This chapter covered quite a lot of ground. By now, you know how a C program is structured, and you should be fairly comfortable with any kind of arithmetic calculation. You should also be able to choose variable types to suit the job at hand. Aside from arithmetic, you've added quite a bit of input and output capability to your knowledge. You should now feel at ease with inputting values into variables via scanf(). You can output text and the values of character and numeric variables to the screen. You won't remember it all the first time around, but you can always look back over this chapter if you need to. Not bad for the first two chapters, is it?

In the next chapter, you'll start looking at how you can control the program by making decisions depending on the values you enter. As you can probably imagine, this is key to creating interesting and professional programs.

Table 2-11 summarizes the real variable types you've used so far. You can look back at these when you need a reminder as you continue through the book.

Table 2-11. *Variable Types and Value Ranges*

Type	Number of Bytes	Range of Values
char	1	128 to +127 or 0 to +255
unsigned char	1	0 to +255
short	2	32,768 to +32,767
unsigned short	2	0 to +65,535
int	4	32,768 to +32,767 or 2,147,438,648 to +2,147,438,647
unsigned int	4	0 to +65,535 or 0 to +4,294,967,295
long	4	2,147,438,648 to +2,147,438,647
unsigned long	4	0 to +4,294,967,295
long long	8	9,223,372,036,854,775,808 to +9,223,372,036,854,775,807
unsigned long long	8	0 to +18,446,744,073,709,551,615
float	4	±3.4E38 (6 digits)
double	8	±1.7E308 (15 digits)
long double	12	±1.2E4932 (19 digits)

The types that store complex data are shown in Table 2-12.

Table 2-12. *Complex Types*

Type	Description
float _Complex	Stores a complex number with real and imaginary parts as type float
double _Complex	Stores a complex number with real and imaginary parts as type double
long double _Complex	Stores a complex number with real and imaginary parts as type long double
float _Imaginary	Stores an imaginary number as type float
double _Imaginary	Stores an imaginary number as type double
long double _Imaginary	Stores an imaginary number as type long double

The <complex.h> header file defines complex and imaginary as alternatives to the keywords _Complex and _Imaginary and it defines I to represent, i, the square root of 1.

You have seen and used some of the data output format specifications with the printf() function in this chapter and you'll find the complete set described in Appendix D. Appendix D also describes the input format specifiers that you use to control how data is interpreted when it's read from the keyboard by the scanf() function. Whenever you are unsure about how you deal with a particular kind of data for input or output, just look in Appendix D.

Exercises

The following exercises enable you to try out what you've learned in this chapter. If you get stuck, look back over the chapter for help. If you're still stuck, you can download the solutions from the Source Code/Download section of the Apress web site (http://www.apress.com), but that really should be a last resort.

Exercise 2-1. Write a program that prompts the user to enter a distance in inches and then outputs that distance in yards, feet, and inches.

Exercise 2-2. Write a program that prompts for input of the length and width of a room in feet and inches, and then calculates and outputs the floor area in square yards with two decimal places after the decimal point.

Exercise 2-3. You're selling a product that's available in two versions: type 1 is a standard version priced at $3.50, and type 2 is a deluxe version priced at $5.50. Write a program using only what you've learned up to now that prompts for the user to enter the product type and a quantity, and then calculates and outputs the price for the quantity entered.

Exercise 2-4. Write a program that prompts for the user's weekly pay in dollars and the hours worked to be entered through the keyboard as floating-point values. The program should then calculate and output the average pay per hour in the following form:

```
Your average hourly pay rate is 7 dollars and 54 cents.
```

CHAPTER 3

■ ■ ■

Making Decisions

In Chapter 2 you learned how to do calculations in your programs. In this chapter, you'll take great leaps forward in the range of programs you can write and the flexibility you can build into them. You'll add one of the most powerful programming tools to your inventory: the ability to compare the values of expressions and, based on the outcome, choose to execute one set of statements or another.

What this means is that you'll be able to control the sequence in which statements are executed in a program. Up until now, all the statements in your programs have been executed strictly in sequence. In this chapter you're going to change all that.

You are going to learn the following:

! How to make decisions based on arithmetic comparisons

! What logical operators are and how you can use them

! More about reading data from the keyboard

! How you can write a program that can be used as a calculator

The Decision-Making Process

You'll start with the essentials of in a program. Decision making in a program is concerned with choosing to execute one set of program statements rather than another. In everyday life you do this kind of thing all the time. Each time you wake up you have to decide whether it's a good idea to go to work. You may go through these questions:

Do I feel well?

If the answer is no, stay in bed. If the answer is yes, go to work.

You could rewrite this as follows:

If I feel well, I will go to work. Otherwise, I will stay in bed.

That was a straightforward decision. Later, as you're having breakfast, you notice it's raining, so you think:

If it is raining as hard as it did yesterday, I will take the bus. If it is raining harder than yesterday, I will drive to work. Otherwise, I will risk it and walk.

This is a more complex decision process. It's a decision based on several levels in the amount of rain falling, and it can have any of three different results.

As the day goes on, you're presented with more of these decisions. Without them you'd be stuck with only one course of action. Until now, in this book, you've had exactly the same problem with your programs. All the programs will run a straight course to a defined end, without making any decisions. This is a severe constraint on what your programs can do and one that you'll relieve now. First, you'll set up some basic building blocks of knowledge that will enable you to do this.

Arithmetic Comparisons

To make a decision, you need a mechanism for comparing things. This involves some new operators. Because you're dealing with numbers, comparing numerical values is basic to decision making. You have three fundamental **relational operators** that you use to compare values:

- ! < is less than
- ! == is equal to
- ! > is greater than

■ **Note** The equal to operator has *two* successive equal signs (==). You'll almost certainly use one equal sign on occasions by mistake. This will cause considerable confusion until you spot the problem. Look at the difference. If you type my_weight = your_weight, it's an assignment that puts the value from the variable your_weight into the variable my_weight. If you type the expression my_weight == your_weight, you're comparing the two values: you're asking whether they're exactly the same—you're not making them the same. If you use = where you intended to use == the compiler cannot determine that it is an error because either is usually valid.

Expressions Involving Relational Operators

Have a look at these examples:

```
5 < 4      1 == 2      5 > 4
```

These expressions are called **logical expressions** or **Boolean expressions** because each of them can result in just one of two values: either true or false. As you saw in the previous chapter, the value true is represented by 1; false is represented by 0. The first expression is false because 5 is patently not less than 4. The second expression is also false because 1 is not equal to 2. The third expression is true because 5 is greater than 4.

Because a relational operator produces a Boolean result, you can store the result in a variable of type _Bool. For example

```
_Bool result = 5 < 4;        /* result will be false */
```

If you #include the <stdbool.h> header file in the source file, you can use bool instead of the keyword _Bool, so you could write the statement like this:

```
bool result = 5 < 4;        /* result will be false */
```

Keep in mind that any nonzero numerical value will result in true when it is converted to type _Bool. This implies that you can assign the result of an arithmetic expression to a _Bool variable and store true if it is nonzero and false otherwise.

The Basic if Statement

Now that you have the relational operators for making comparisons, you need a statement allowing you to make a decision. The simplest is the if statement. If you want to compare your weight with that of someone else and print a different sentence depending on the result, you could write the body of a program as follows:

```
if(your_weight > my_weight)
  printf("You are heavier than me.\n");

if(your_weight < my_weight)
  printf("I am heavier than you.\n");

if(your_weight == my_weight)
  printf("We are exactly the same weight.\n");
```

Note how the statement following each if is indented. This is to show that it's dependent on the result of the if test. Let's go through this and see how it works. The first if tests whether the value in your_weight is greater than the value in my_weight. The expression for the comparison appears between the parentheses that immediately follow the keyword if. If the result of the comparison is true, the statement immediately after the if will be executed. This just outputs the following message:

```
You are heavier than me.
```

Execution will then continue with the next if.

What if the expression between the parentheses in the first if is false? In this case, the statement immediately following the if will be skipped, so the message won't be displayed. It will be displayed only if your_weight is greater than my_weight.

The second if works in essentially the same way. If the expression between parentheses after the keyword if is true, the following statement will be executed to output this message:

```
I am heavier than you.
```

This will be the case if your_weight is less than my_weight. If this isn't so, the statement will be skipped and the message won't be displayed. The third if is again the same. The effect of these statements is to print one message that will depend on whether your_weight is greater than, less than, or equal to my_weight. Only one message will be displayed because only one of these can be true.

The general form or syntax of the if statement is as follows:

```
if(expression)
  Statement1;

Next_statement;
```

Notice that the expression that forms the test (the if) is enclosed between parentheses and that there is no semicolon at the end of the first line. This is because both the line with the if keyword and the following line are tied together. The second line could be written directly following the first, like this:

```
if(expression) Statement1;
```

But for the sake of clarity, people usually put Statement1 on a new line.

The expression in parentheses can be any expression that results in a value of true or false. If the expression is true, Statement1 is executed, after which the program continues with Next_statement. If the expression is false, Statement1 is skipped and execution continues immediately with Next_statement. This is illustrated in Figure 3-1.

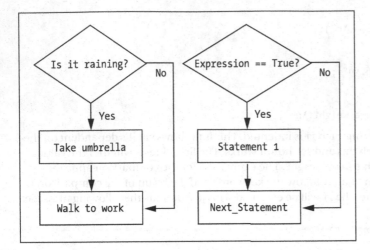

Figure 3-1. *The operation of the if statement*

You could have used the basic if statement to add some politically incorrect comments in the program that calculated the height of a tree at the end of the previous chapter. For example, you could have added the following code just after you'd calculated the height of the shortest person:

```
if(Shorty < 36)
  printf("\nMy, you really are on the short side, aren't you?");
```

Here, you have used the if statement to add a gratuitously offensive remark, should the individual be less than 36 inches tall.

Don't forget what I said earlier about what happens when a numerical value is converted to type _Bool. Because the control expression for an if statement is expected to produce a Boolean result, the compiler will arrange to convert the result of an if expression that produces a numerical result to type _Bool. You'll sometimes see this used in programs to test for a nonzero result of a calculation. Here's a statement that illustrates this:

```
if(count)
  printf("The value of count is not zero.");
```

This will only produce output if count is not 0, because a 0 value for count will mean the if expression is false.

TRY IT OUT: CHECKING CONDITIONS

Let's see the if statement in action. This program gets the user to enter a number between 1 and 10 and then tells the user how big that number is:

```
/* Program 3.1 A simple example of the if statement */
#include <stdio.h>

int main(void)
{
  int number = 0;
  printf("\nEnter an integer between 1 and 10: ");
  scanf("%d",&number);
```

```
  if(number > 5)
    printf("You entered %d which is greater than 5\n", number);

  if(number < 6)
    printf("You entered %d which is less than 6\n", number);
  return 0;
}
```

Sample output from this program is as follows:

```
Enter an integer between 1 and 10: 7
You entered 7 which is greater than 5
```

---

or

```
Enter an integer between 1 and 10: 3
You entered 3 which is less than 6
```

How It Works

As usual, you include a comment at the beginning as a reminder of what the program does. You include the stdio.h header file to allow you to use the printf() statement. You then have the beginning of the main() function of the program. This function doesn't return a value, as indicated by the keyword void:

```
/* Program 3.1 A simple example of the if statement*/
#include <stdio.h>

int main(void)
{
```

In the first three statements in the body of main(), you read an integer from the keyboard after prompting the user for the data:

```
  int number = 0;
  printf("\nEnter an integer between 1 and 10: \n");
  scanf("%d",&number);
```

You declare an integer variable called number that you initialize to 0, and then you prompt the user to enter a number between 1 and 10. This value is then read using the scanf() function and stored in the variable number.

The next statement is an if that tests the value that was entered:

```
  if(number > 5)
    printf("You entered %d which is greater than 5", number);
```

You compare the value in number with the value 5. If number is greater than 5, you execute the next statement, which displays a message, and you go to the next part of the program. If number isn't greater than 5, printf() is simply skipped. You've used the %d conversion specifier for integer values to output the number the user typed in.

You then have another if statement:

```
  if(number < 6)
    printf("You entered %d which is less than 6", number);
```

This compares the value entered with 6 and, if it's smaller, you execute the next statement to display a message. Otherwise, the printf() is skipped and the program ends. Only one of the two possible messages will be displayed because the number will always be less than 6 or greater than 5.

The if statement enables you to be selective about what input you accept and what you finally do with it. For instance, if you have a variable and you want to have its value specifically limited at some point, even though higher values may arise somehow in the program, you could write this:

```
if(x > 90)
  x = 90;
```

This would ensure that if anyone entered a value of x that was larger than 90, your program would automatically change it to 90. This would be invaluable if you had a program that could only specifically deal with values within a range. You could also check whether a value was lower than a given number and, if not, set it to that number. In this way, you could ensure that the value was within the given range.

Finally you have the return statement that ends the program and returns control to the operating system:

```
return 0;
```

Extending the if Statement: if-else

You can extend the if statement with a small addition that gives you a lot more flexibility. Imagine it rained a little yesterday. You could write the following:

If the rain today is worse than the rain yesterday,

I will take my umbrella.

Else

I will take my jacket.

Then I will go to work.

This is exactly the kind of decision-making the if-else statement provides. The syntax of the if-else statement is as follows:

```
if(expression)
  Statement1;
else
  Statement2;

Next_statement;
```

Here, you have an either-or situation. You'll always execute either Statement1 or Statement2 depending on whether expression results in the value true or false:

If expression evaluates to true, Statement1 is executed and the program continues with Next_statement.

If expression evaluates to false, Statement2 following the else keyword is executed, and the program continues with Next_statement.

The sequence of operations involved here is shown in Figure 3-2.

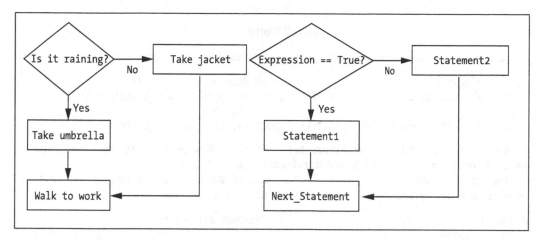

Figure 3-2. *The operation of the* if-else *statement*

TRY IT OUT: USING IF TO ANALYZE NUMBERS

Let's suppose that you're selling a product at a single-unit price of $3.50, and for order quantities greater than ten you offer a 5 percent discount. You can use the if-else statement to calculate and output the price for a given quantity.

```
/* Program 3.2 Using if statements to decide on a discount */
#include <stdio.h>

int main(void)
{
  const double unit_price = 3.50;          /* Unit price in dollars */
  int quantity = 0;
  printf("Enter the number that you want to buy:"); /* Prompt message */
  scanf(" %d", &quantity);                 /* Read the input        */

  /* Test for order quantity qualifying for a discount */
  if(quantity>10)                          /* 5% discount           */
    printf("The price for %d is $%.2f\n", quantity, quantity*unit_price*0.95);
  else                                     /* No discount           */
    printf("The price for %d is $%.2f\n", quantity, quantity*unit_price);
  return 0;
}
```

Typical output from this program is as follows:

```
Enter the number that you want to buy:20
The price for 20 is $66.50
```

How It Works

Once your program has read the order quantity, the if-else statement does all the work:

```
if(quantity>10)                              /* 5% discount        */
  printf("\nThe price for %d is $%.2f\n", quantity, quantity*unit_price*0.95);
else                                         /* No discount        */
  printf("\nThe price for %d is $%.2f\n", quantity, quantity*unit_price);
```

If quantity is greater than ten, the first printf() will be executed that applies a 5 percent discount. Otherwise, the second printf() will be executed that applies no discount to the price.

There are a few more things I could say on this topic, though. First of all, you can also solve the problem with a simple if statement by replacing the if-else statement with the following code:

```
double discount = 0.0;                       /* Discount allowed */
if(quantity>10)
    discount = 0.05;                         /* 5% discount      */
printf("\nThe price for %d is $%.2f\n", quantity,
                                quantity*unit_price*(1.0-discount));
```

This considerably simplifies the code. You now have a single printf() call that applies the discount that is set, either 0 or 5 percent. With a variable storing the discount value, it's also clearer what is happening in the code.

The second point worth making is that floating-point variables aren't ideal for calculations involving money because of the potential rounding that can occur. Providing that the amounts of money are not extremely large, one alternative is to use integer values and just store cents, for example

```
const long unit_price = 350L;                /* Unit price in cents */
int quantity = 0;
printf("Enter the number that you want to buy:");  /* Prompt message */
scanf(" %d", &quantity);                     /* Read the input     */

long discount = 0L;                          /* Discount allowed   */
if(quantity>10)
    discount = 5L;                           /* 5% discount        */
long total_price = quantity*unit_price*(100-discount)/100;
long dollars = total_price/100;
long cents = total_price%100;
printf("\nThe price for %d is $%ld.%ld\n", quantity, dollars,cents);
```

Of course, you also have the possibility of storing the dollars and cents for each monetary value in separate integer variables. It gets a little more complicated because you then have to keep track of when the cents value reaches or exceeds 100 during arithmetic operations.

Using Blocks of Code in if Statements

You can also replace either Statement1 or Statement2, or even both, by a block of statements enclosed between braces {}. This means that you can supply many instructions to the computer after testing the value of an expression using an if statement simply by placing these instructions together between braces. I can illustrate the mechanics of this by considering a real-life situation:

If the weather is sunny,

I will walk to the park, eat a picnic, and walk home.

Else

I will stay in, watch football, and drink beer.

The syntax for an if statement that involves statement blocks is as follows:

```
if(expression)
{
  StatementA1;
  StatementA2;
  ...
}
else
{
  StatementB1;
  StatementB2;
  ...
}

Next_statement;
```

All the statements that are in the block between the braces following the if condition will be executed if expression evaluates to true. If expression evaluates to false, all the statements between the braces following the else will be executed. In either case, execution continues with Next_statement. Have a look at the indentation. The braces aren't indented, but the statements between the braces are. This makes it clear that all the statements between an opening and a closing brace belong together.

■**Note** Although I've been talking about using a block of statements in place of a single statement in an if statement, this is just one example of a general rule. Wherever you can have a single statement, you can equally well have a block of statements between braces. This also means that you can nest one block of statements inside another.

Nested if Statements

It's also possible to have ifs within ifs. These are called **nested** ifs. For example

If the weather is good,

I will go out in the yard.

And if it's cool enough,

I will sit in the sun.

Else

I will sit in the shade.

Else

I will stay indoors.

I will then drink some lemonade.

In programming terms, this corresponds to the following:

```
if(expression1)              /* Weather is good?            */
{
  StatementA;                /* Yes - Go out in the yard    */
  if(expression2)            /* Cool enough?                */
    StatementB;              /* Yes - Sit in the sun        */
  else
    StatementC;              /* No - Sit in the shade       */
}
else
  StatementD;                /* Weather not good - stay in  */
Statement E;                 /* Drink lemonade in any event */
```

Here, the second if condition, expression2, is only checked if the first if condition, expression1, is true. The braces enclosing StatementA and the second if are necessary to make both of these statements a part of what is executed when expression1 is true. Note how the else is aligned with the if it belongs to. The logic of this is illustrated in Figure 3-3.

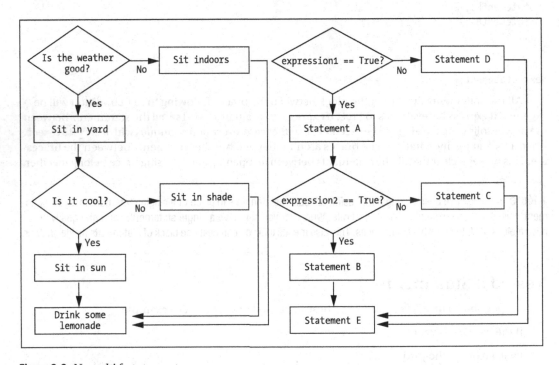

Figure 3-3. *Nested if statements*

TRY IT OUT: ANALYZING NUMBERS

You'll now exercise your if skills with a couple more examples. This program tests to see whether you enter an odd or an even number, and if the number is even, it then tests to see whether half that number is also even:

```
/* Program 3.3 Using nested ifs to analyze numbers */
#include <stdio.h>
#include <limits.h>                /* For LONG_MAX */
```

```
int main(void)
{
  long test = 0L;                  /* Stores the integer to be checked */

  printf("Enter an integer less than %ld:", LONG_MAX);
  scanf(" %ld", &test);

  /* Test for odd or even by checking the remainder after dividing by 2 */
  if(test % 2L == 0L)
  {
    printf("The number %ld is even", test);

    /* Now check whether half the number is also even */
    if((test/2L) % 2L == 0L)
    {
      printf("\nHalf of %ld is also even", test);
      printf("\nThat's interesting isn't it?\n");
    }
  }
  else
    printf("The number %ld is odd\n", test);
  return 0;
}
```

The output will look something like this:

```
Enter an integer less than 2147483647:20
The number 20 is even
Half of 20 is also even
That's interesting isn't it?
```

or this

```
Enter an integer less than 2147483647:999
The number 999 is odd
```

How It Works

The prompt for input makes use of the LONG_MAX symbol that's defined in the <limits.h> header file. This specifies the maximum value of type long. You can see from the output that on my system the upper limit for long values is 2147483647.

The first if condition tests for an even number:

```
if(test % 2L == 0L)
```

If you were to use 0 instead of 0L here, your compiler may insert code to convert 0, which is of type int, to a value of type long to allow the comparison for equality to be made. Using the constant 0L of type long avoids this unnecessary operation. For any even number, the remainder after dividing by 2 will be 0. If the expression is true, the block that follows will be executed:

```
{
  printf("The number %ld is even", test);

  /* Now check whether half the number is also even */
  if((test/2L) % 2L == OL)
  {
    printf("\nHalf of %ld is also even", test);
    printf("\nThat's interesting isn't it?\n");
  }
}
```

After outputting a message where the value is even, you have another if statement. This is called a nested if because it's inside the first if. The nested if condition divides the original value by 2 and tests whether the result is even, using the same mechanism as in the first if statement. There's an extra pair of parentheses in the nested if condition around the expression test/2L. These aren't strictly necessary, but they help to make what's going on clear. Making programs easier to follow is the essence of good programming style. If the result of the nested if condition is true, the two further printf() statements in the block following the nested if will be executed.

Try adding code to make the nested if an if-else that will output "Half of %ld is odd".

If the original input value isn't even, the statement following the else keyword will be executed:

```
else
  printf("The number %ld is odd\n", test);
```

■Note You can nest ifs anywhere inside another if, but I don't recommend this as a technique that you should use extensively. If you do, your program is likely to end up being very hard to follow and you are more likely to make mistakes.

To make the nested if statement output a message when the condition is false, you would need to insert the following after the closing brace:

```
else
  printf("\nHalf of %ld is odd", test);
```

More Relational Operators

You can now add a few more relational operators that you can use to compare expressions in if statements. These three additional operators make up the complete set:

! >= is greater than or equal to

! <= is less than or equal to

! != is not equal to

These are fairly self-explanatory, but let's consider some examples anyway, starting with a few arithmetic examples:

```
6 >= 5      5 <= 5      4 <= 5      4 != 5      10 != 10
```

These all result in the value true, except for the last one, which is false because 10 most definitely *is* equal to 10. These operators can be applied to values of type char and wchar_t as well as the other numerical types. If you remember, character types also have a numeric value associated with them. The ASCII table in Appendix B provides a full listing of all the standard ASCII characters and their numeric codes. Table 3-1 is an extract from Appendix B as a reminder for the next few examples.

Table 3-1. *Characters and ASCII Codes*

Character	ASCII Code (Decimal)
A	65
B	66
P	80
Q	81
Z	90
b	98

A char value may be expressed either as an integer or as a keyboard character between quotes, such as 'A'. Don't forget, numeric values stored as type char may be signed or unsigned, depending on how your compiler implements the type. When type char is unsigned, values can be from 128 to +127. When char is an unsigned type, values can be from 0 to 255. Here are a few examples of comparing values of type char:

```
'Z' >= 'A'        'Q' <= 'P'        'B' <= 'b'        'B' != 66
```

With the ASCII values of the characters in mind, the first expression is true, because 'Z', which has the code value 90, comes after 'A', which has the code value 65. The second is false, as 'Q' doesn't come before 'P'. The third is true. This is because in ASCII code lowercase letters are 32 higher than their uppercase equivalents. The last is false. The value 66 is indeed the decimal ASCII representation for the character 'B'.

TRY IT OUT: CONVERTING UPPERCASE TO LOWERCASE

Let's exercise the new logical operators in an example. Here you have a program that will convert any uppercase letter that is entered to a lowercase letter:

```
/* Program 3.4 Converting uppercase to lowercase */
#include <stdio.h>

int main(void)
{
  char letter = 0;                        /* Stores a character         */

  printf("Enter an uppercase letter:");   /* Prompt for input           */
  scanf("%c", &letter);                   /* Read a character           */
```

```
/* Check whether the input is uppercase */
  if(letter >= 'A')                        /* Is it A or greater?            */
    if(letter <= 'Z')                      /* and is it Z or lower?          */
    {                                      /* It is uppercase                */
      letter = letter - 'A'+ 'a';          /* Convert from upper- to lowercase */
      printf("You entered an uppercase %c\n", letter);
    }
    else                                   /* It is not an uppercase letter  */
      printf("Try using the shift key, Bud! I want a capital letter.\n");
  return 0;
}
```

Sample output from this program might be the following:

```
Enter an uppercase letter:G
You entered an uppercase g
```

---

or

```
Enter an uppercase letter:s
Try using the shift key, Bud! I want a capital letter.
```

How It Works

In the first three statements, you declare a variable of type char called letter, you prompt the user to input a capital letter, and you store the character entered in the variable letter:

```
char letter = 0;                          /* Stores a character            */

printf("Enter an uppercase letter:");     /* Prompt for input              */
scanf("%c", &letter);                     /* Read a character              */
```

If a capital letter is entered, the character in the letter variable must be between 'A' and 'Z', so the next if checks whether the character is greater than or equal to 'A':

```
if(letter >= 'A')                         /* Is it A or greater?           */
```

If the expression is true, you continue with the nested if that tests whether letter is less than or equal to 'Z':

```
if(letter <= 'Z')                         /* and is it Z or lower?         */
```

If this expression is true, you convert the character to lowercase and output a message by executing the block of statements following the if:

```
{                                         /* It is uppercase               */
  letter = letter - 'A'+ 'a';             /* Convert from upper- to lowercase */
  printf("You entered an uppercase %c\n", letter);
}
```

To convert to lowercase, you subtract the character code for 'A' from letter and add the character code for 'a'. If letter contained 'A', subtracting 'A' would produce 0, and adding 'a' would result in 'a'. If letter contained 'B', subtracting 'A' would produce 1, and adding 'a' would result in 'b'. You can see this conversion works for any uppercase letter. Note that although this works fine for ASCII, there are coding systems (such as EBCDIC) in which this won't work, because the letters don't have a contiguous sequence of codes. If you want to be sure that the conversion works for any code, you can use the standard library function tolower(). This converts the character passed as an argument to lowercase if it's an uppercase letter; otherwise, it returns the character code value unchanged. To use this function, you need to include the header file ctype.h in your program. This header file also declares the complementary function, toupper(), that will convert lowercase letters to uppercase.

If the expression letter <= 'Z' is false, you go straight to the statement following else and display a different message:

```
else                                 /* It is not an uppercase letter   */
   printf("Try using the shift key, Bud! I want a capital letter.\n");
```

There's something wrong, though. What if the character that was entered was less than 'A'? There's no else clause for the first if, so the program just ends without outputting anything. To deal with this, you must add another else clause at the end of the program. The complete nested if would then become the following:

```
if(letter >= 'A')                    /* Is it A or greater?           */
   if(letter <= 'Z')                 /* and is it Z or lower?         */
   {                                 /* It is uppercase               */
      letter = letter - 'A'+ 'a';    /* Convert from upper- to lowercase */
      printf("You entered an uppercase %c\n", letter);
   }
   else                              /* It is not an uppercase letter   */
      printf("Try using the shift key, Bud! I want a capital letter.\n");
else
   printf("You didn't enter an uppercase letter\n");
```

Now you always get a message. Note the indentation to show which else belongs to which if. The indentation doesn't determine what belongs to what. It just provides a visual cue. An else always belongs to the if that immediately precedes it that isn't already spoken for by another else.

So how would this look if you were working with wide characters? Not that different really:

```
/* Program 3.4A Converting uppercase to lowercase using wide characters */
#include <stdio.h>

int main(void)
{
  wchar_t letter = 0;                    /* Stores a character          */

  printf("Enter an uppercase letter:");  /* Prompt for input            */
  scanf("%lc", &letter);                 /* Read a character            */

  /* Check whether the input is uppercase */
  if(letter >= L'A')                     /* Is it A or greater?         */
    if(letter <= L'Z')                   /* and is it Z or lower?       */
    {                                    /* It is uppercase             */
      letter = letter - L'A'+ L'a';      /* Convert from upper- to lowercase */
      printf("You entered an uppercase %lc\n", letter);
    }
    else                                 /* It is not an uppercase letter   */
      printf("Try using the shift key, Bud! I want a capital letter.\n");
  return 0;
}
```

The type of the variable letter is now wchar_t and the character constants all have L in front to make them wide characters. The only other differences are the format specifications for input and output where you use %lc instead of %c.

Of course, you might want to be sure here that the conversion from uppercase to lowercase operation works regardless of the code values, but the tolower() and toupper() functions I mentioned earlier won't work with wide characters. However, the <wctype.h> header file defines the towlower() and towupper() functions that will. With the header file included you could write the statement that does the conversion as:

```
letter = towlower(letter); /* Convert from upper- to lowercase */
```

You used a nested if statement to check for two conditions in the example but, as you can imagine, this could get very confusing when you've got a lot of different criteria that you need to check for. The good news is that C allows you to use logical operators to simplify the situation.

Logical Operators

Sometimes it just isn't enough to perform a single test for a decision. You may want to combine two or more checks on values and, if they're all true, perform a certain action. Or you may want to perform a calculation if one or more of a set of conditions are true.

For example, you may only want to go to work if you're feeling well *and* it's a weekday. Just because you feel great doesn't mean you want to go in on a Saturday or a Sunday. Alternatively, you could say that you'll stay at home if you feel ill *or* if it's a weekend day. These are exactly the sorts of circumstances for which the logical operators are intended.

The AND Operator &&

You can look first at the logical AND operator, &&. This is another binary operator because it operates on two items of data. The && operator combines two logical expressions! that is, two expressions that have a value true or false. Consider this expression:

```
Test1 && Test2
```

This expression evaluates to true if both expressions Test1 and Test2 evaluate to true. If either or both of the operands for the && operator are false, the result of the operation is false.

The obvious place to use the && operator is in an if expression. Let's look at an example:

```
if(age > 12 && age < 20)
  printf("You are officially a teenager.");
```

The printf() statement will be executed only if age has a value between 13 and 19 inclusive.

Of course, the operands of the && operator can be _Bool variables. You could replace the previous statement with the following:

```
_Bool test1 = age > 12;
_Bool test2 = age < 20;
if(test1 && test2)
  printf("You are officially a teenager.");
```

The values of the two logical expressions checking the value of age are stored in the variables test1 and test2. The if expression is now much simpler using the _Bool variables as operands.

Naturally, you can use more than one of these logical operators in an expression:

```
if(age > 12 && age < 20 && savings > 5000)
  printf("You are a rich teenager.");
```

All three conditions must be true for the printf() to be executed. That is, the printf() will be executed only if the value of age is between 13 and 19 inclusive, and the value of savings is greater than 5000.

The OR Operator ||

The logical OR operator, ||, covers the situation in which you want to check for any of two or more conditions being true. If either or both operands of the || operator is true, the result is true. The result is false only when both operands are false. Here's an example of using this operator:

```
if(a < 10 || b > c || c > 50)
  printf("At least one of the conditions is true.");
```

The printf() will be executed only if *at least* one of the three conditions, a<10, b>c, or c<50, is true. When a, b, and c all have the value 9, for instance, this will be the case. Of course, the printf() will also be executed when two of the conditions are true, as well as all three.

You can use the && and || logical operators in combination, as in the following code fragment:

```
if((age > 12 && age < 20) || savings > 5000)
  printf ("Either you're a teenager, or you're rich, or possibly both.");
```

The printf() statement will be executed if the value of age is between 12 and 20 or the value of savings is greater than 5000, or both. As you can see, when you start to use more operators, things can get confusing. The parentheses around the expression that is the left operand of the || operator are not strictly necessary but I put them in to make the condition easier to understand. Making use of Boolean variables can help. You could replace the previous statement with the following:

```
bool age_test1 = age > 12;
bool age_test2 = age < 20;
bool age_check = test1 && test2;
bool savings_check = savings > 5000;
if((age_check || savings_check)
 printf ("Either you're a teenager, or you're rich, or possibly both.");
```

Now you have declared four Boolean variables using bool, which assumes the <stdbool.h> header has been included into the source file. You should be able to see that the if statement works with essentially the same test as before. Of course, you could define the value of age_check in a single step, like this:

```
bool age_check = age > 12 && age < 20;
bool savings_check = savings > 5000;
if((age_check || savings_check)
 printf ("Either you're a teenager, or you're rich, or possibly both.");
```

This reduces the number of variables you use and still leaves the code reasonably clear.

The NOT Operator !

Last but not least is the logical NOT operator, represented by !. The ! operator is a unary operator, because it applies to just one operand. The logical NOT operator reverses the value of a logical expression: true becomes false, and false becomes true. Suppose you have two variables, a and b, with the values 5 and 2 respectively; then the expression a>b is true. If you use the logical NOT operator, the expression !(a>b) is false. I recommend that you avoid using this operator as far as possible; it tends to result in code that becomes difficult to follow. As an illustration of how not to use NOT, you can rewrite the previous example as follows:

```
if((!(age >= 12) && !(age >= 20)) || !(savings <= 5000))
{
  printf("\nYou're either not a teenager and rich ");
  printf("or not rich and a teenager,\n");
  printf("or neither not a teenager nor not rich.");
}
```

As you can see, it becomes incredibly difficult to unravel the nots!

TRY IT OUT: A BETTER WAY TO CONVERT LETTERS

Earlier in this chapter you tried a program in which the user was prompted to enter an uppercase character. The program used a nested `if` to ensure that the input was of the correct type, and then wrote the small-letter equivalent or a remark indicating that the input was of the wrong type to the command line.

You can now see that all this was completely unnecessary, because you can achieve the same result like this:

```
/* Program 3.5   Testing letters the easy way */
#include <stdio.h>
int main(void)
{
  char letter =0;                         /* Stores an input character */

  printf("Enter an upper case letter:");  /* Prompt for input         */
  scanf(" %c", &letter);                  /* Read the input character  */

  if((letter >= 'A') && (letter <= 'Z'))  /* Verify uppercase letter  */
  {
    letter += 'a'-'A';                    /* Convert to lowercase      */
    printf("You entered an uppercase %c.\n", letter);
  }
  else
    printf("You did not enter an uppercase letter.\n");
  return 0;
}
```

The output will be similar to that from the earlier example.

How It Works

The output is similar but not exactly the same as the original program. In the corrected version of the program, you generated a different message when the input was less than 'A'. This version is rather better, though. Compare the mechanism to test the input in the two programs and you'll see how much neater the second solution is. This is the original version:

```
if(letter >= 'A')
  if(letter <= 'Z')
```

This is the new version:

```
if((letter >= 'A') && (letter <= 'Z'))   /* Verify uppercase letter  */
```

Rather than having confusing nested if statements, here you've checked that the character entered is greater than 'A' *and* less than 'Z' in one statement. Notice that you put extra parentheses around the two expressions to be checked. They aren't really needed in this case, but they don't hurt, and they leave you or any other programmer in no doubt as to the order of execution.

There's also a slightly simpler way of expressing the conversion to lowercase:

```
letter += 'a'-'A';                          /* Convert to lowercase     */
```

Now you use the += operator to add the difference between 'a' and 'A' to the character code value stored in letter.

If you add an #include directive for the <ctype.h> standard header file to the source, you could use the tolower() function to do the same thing:

```
letter = tolower(letter);
```

The lowercase letter that the tolower() function returns is stored back in the variable letter. The toupper() function that is also declared in <ctype.h> converts the argument to uppercase.

The Conditional Operator

There's another operator called the **conditional operator** that you can use to test data. It evaluates one of two expressions depending on whether a logical expression evaluates true or false.

Because three operands are involved! the logical expression plus two other expressions! this operator is also referred to as the **ternary operator**. The general representation of an expression using the conditional operator looks like this:

```
condition ? expression1 : expression2
```

Notice how the operator is arranged in relation to the operands. There is ? following the logical expression, condition, to separate it from the next operand, expression1. This is separated from the third operand, expression2, by a colon. The value that results from the operation will be produced by evaluating expression1 if condition evaluates to true, or by evaluating expression2 if condition evaluates to false. Note that only one of expression1 and expression2 will be evaluated. Normally this is of little significance, but sometimes this is important.

You can use the conditional operator in a statement such as this:

```
x = y > 7 ? 25 : 50;
```

Executing this statement will result in x being set to 25 if y is greater than 7, or to 50 otherwise. This is a nice shorthand way of producing the same effect as this:

```
if(y > 7)
  x = 25;
else
  x = 50;
```

The conditional operator enables you to express some things economically. An expression for the minimum of two variables can be written very simply using the conditional operator. For example, you could write an expression that compared two salaries and obtained the greater of the two, like this:

```
your_salary > my_salary ? your_salary : my_salary
```

Of course, you can use the conditional operator in a more complex expression. Earlier in Program 3.2 you calculated a quantity price for a product using an if-else statement. The price was

$3.50 per item with a discount of 5 percent for quantities over ten. You can do this sort of calculation in a single step with the conditional operator:

```
total_price = unit_price*quantity*(quantity>10 ? 1.0 : 0.95);
```

TRY IT OUT: USING THE CONDITIONAL OPERATOR

This discount business could translate into a short example. Suppose you have the unit price of the product still at $3.50, but you now offer three levels of discount: 15 percent for more than 50, 10 percent for more than 20, and the original 5 percent for more than 10. Here's how you can handle that:

```
/* Program 3.6 Multiple discount levels */
#include <stdio.h>

int main(void)
{
  const double unit_price = 3.50; /* Unit price in dollars    */
  const double discount1 = 0.05;   /* Discount for more than 10 */
  const double discount2 = 0.1;    /* Discount for more than 20 */
  const double discount3 = 0.15;   /* Discount for more than 50 */
  double total_price = 0.0;
  int quantity = 0;

  printf("Enter the number that you want to buy:");
  scanf(" %d", &quantity);

  total_price = quantity*unit_price*(1.0 -
                      (quantity>50 ? discount3 : (
                             quantity>20 ? discount2 : (
                                    quantity>10 ? discount1 : 0.0)))));

  printf("The price for %d is $%.2f\n", quantity, total_price);
  return 0;
}
```

Some typical output from the program is as follows:

```
Enter the number that you want to buy:60
The price for 60 is $178.50
```

How It Works

The interesting bit is the statement that calculates the total price for the quantity that's entered. The statement uses three conditional operators, so it takes a little unraveling:

```
total_price = quantity*unit_price*(1.0 -
                    (quantity>50 ? discount3 : (
                           quantity>20 ? discount2 : (
                                  quantity>10 ? discount1 : 0.0)))));
```

You can understand how this produces the correct result by breaking it into pieces. The basic price is produced by the expression quantity*unit_price, which simply multiplies the unit price by the quantity ordered. The result of this has to be multiplied by a factor that's determined by the quantity. If the quantity is over 50, the basic price must be multiplied by (1.0-discount3). This is determined by an expression like the following:

```
(1.0 - quantity > 50 ? discount3 : something_else)
```

If quantity is greater than 50 here, the expression will amount to (1.0-discount3), and the right side of the assignment is complete. Otherwise, it will be (1.0-something_else), where something_else is the result of another conditional operator.

Of course, if quantity isn't greater than 50, it may still be greater than 20, in which case you want something_else to be discount2. This is produced by the conditional operator that appears in the something_else position in the statement:

```
(quantity>20 ? discount2 : something_else_again)
```

This will result in something_else being discount2 if the value of quantity is over 20, which is precisely what you want, and something_else_again if it isn't. You want something_else_again to be discount1 if quantity is over 10, and 0 if it isn't. The last conditional operator that occupies the something_else_again position in the statement does this:

```
(quantity>10 ? discount1 : 0.0)
```

And that's it!

In spite of its odd appearance, you'll see the conditional operator crop up quite frequently in C programs. A very handy application of this operator that you'll see in examples in this book and elsewhere is to vary the contents of a message or prompt depending on the value of an expression. For example, if you want to display a message indicating the number of pets that a person has, and you want the message to change between singular and plural automatically, you could write this:

```
printf("You have %d pet%s.", pets, pets == 1 ? "" : "s" );
```

You use the %s specifier when you want to output a string. If pets is equal to 1, an empty string will be output in place of the %s; otherwise, "s" will be output. Thus, if pets has the value 1, the statement will output this message:

You have 1 pet.

However, if the variable pets is 5, you will get this output:

You have 5 pets.

You can use this mechanism to vary an output message depending on the value of an expression in many different ways: she instead of he, wrong instead of right, and so on.

Operator Precedence: Who Goes First?

With all the parentheses you've used in the examples in this chapter, now is a good time to come back to operator precedence. Operator precedence determines the sequence in which operators in an expression are executed. You have the logical operators &&, ==, !=, and ||, plus the comparison operators and the arithmetic operators. When you have more than one operator in an expression, how do you know which ones are used first? This order of precedence can affect the result of an expression substantially.

For example, suppose you are to process job applications and you want to only accept applicants who are 25 or older and have graduated from Harvard or Yale. Here's the age condition you can represent by this conditional expression:

```
Age >= 25
```

Suppose that you represent graduation by the variables Yale and Harvard, which may be true or false. Now you can write the condition as follows:

```
Age >= 25 && Harvard || Yale
```

Unfortunately, this will result in howls of protest because you'll now accept Yale graduates who are under 25. In fact, this statement will accept Yale graduates of any age. But if you're from Harvard, you must be 25 or over to be accepted. Because of operator precedence, this expression is effectively the following:

```
(Age >= 25 && Harvard) || Yale
```

So you take anybody at all from Yale. I'm sure those wearing a Y-front sweatshirt will claim that this is as it should be, but what you really meant was this:

```
Age >= 25 && (Harvard || Yale)
```

Because of operator precedence, you must put the parentheses in to force the order of operations to be what you want.

In general, the precedence of the operators in an expression determines whether it is necessary for you to put parentheses in to get the result you want, but if you are unsure of the precedence of the operators you are using, it does no harm to put the parentheses in. Table 3-2 shows the order of precedence for all the operators in C, from highest at the top to lowest at the bottom.

There are quite a few operators in the table that we haven't addressed yet. You'll see the operators ~, <<, >>, &, ^, and | later in this chapter in the •Bitwise Operators! section and you'll learn about the rest later in the book.

All the operators that appear in the same row in the table are of equal precedence. The sequence of execution for operators of equal precedence is determined by their associativity, which determines whether they're selected from left to right or from right to left. Naturally, parentheses around an expression come at the very top of the list of operators because they're used to override the natural priorities defined.

Table 3-2. *Operator Order of Precedence*

Operators	Description	Associativity
( )	Parenthesized expression	Left-to-right
[]	Array subscript	
.	Member selection by object	
->	Member selection by pointer	
+ -	Unary + and -	Right-to-left
++ --	Prefix increment and prefix decrement	
! ~	Logical NOT and bitwise complement	
*	Dereference	
&	Address-of	
sizeof	Size of expression or type	
(type)	Explicit cast to type such as (int) or (double)	
	Type casts such as (int) or (double)	
* / %	Multiplication and division and modulus (remainder)	Left-to-right
+ -	Addition and subtraction	Left-to-right
<< >>	Bitwise shift left and bitwise shift right	Left-to-right
< <=	Less than and less than or equal to	Left-to-right
> >=	Greater than and greater than or equal to	
== !=	Equal to and not equal to	Left-to-right
&	Bitwise AND	Left-to-right
^	Bitwise exclusive OR	Left-to-right
|	Bitwise OR	Left-to-right
&&	Logical AND	Left-to-right
||	Logical OR	Left-to-right
?:	Conditional operator	Right-to-left
=	Assignment	Right-to-left
+= -=	Addition assignment and subtraction assignment	
/= *=	Division assignment and multiplication assignment	
%=	Modulus assignment	
<<= >>=	Bitwise shift left assignment and bitwise shift right assignment	
&= |=	Bitwise AND assignment and bitwise OR assignment	
^=	Bitwise exclusive OR assignment	
,	Comma operator	Left-to-right

As you can see from Table 3-2, all the comparison operators are below the binary arithmetic operators in precedence, and the binary logical operators are below the comparison operators. As a result, arithmetic is done first, then comparisons, and then logical combinations. Assignments come last in this list, so they're only performed once everything else has been completed. The conditional operator squeezes in just above the assignment operators.

Note that the ! operator is highest within the set of logical operators. Consequently the parentheses around logical expressions are essential when you want to negate the value of a logical expression.

TRY IT OUT: USING LOGICAL OPERATORS WITHOUT CONFUSION

Suppose you want a program that will take applicant interviews for a large pharmaceutical corporation. The program should offer interviews to applicants who meet certain educational specifications. An applicant who meets any of the following criteria should be accepted for an interview:

1. Graduates over 25 who studied chemistry and who didn't graduate from Yale

2. Graduates from Yale who studied chemistry

3. Graduates from Harvard who studied economics and aren't older than 28

4. Graduates from Yale who are over 25 and who didn't study chemistry

One program to implement this policy is as follows:

```c
/* Program 3.7 Confused recruiting policy  */
#include <stdio.h>

int main(void)
{
  int age = 0;              /* Age of the applicant          */
  int college = 0;          /* Code for college attended     */
  int subject = 0;          /* Code for subject studied      */
  bool interview = false;   /* true for accept, false for reject */

  /* Get data on the applicant */
  printf("\nWhat college? 1 for Harvard, 2 for Yale, 3 for other: ");
  scanf("%d",&college);
  printf("\nWhat subject? 1 for Chemistry, 2 for economics, 3 for other: ");
  scanf("%d", &subject);
  printf("\nHow old is the applicant? ");
  scanf("%d",&age);

  /* Check out the applicant */
  if((age>25 && subject==1) && (college==3 || college==1))
    interview = true;
  if(college==2 &&subject ==1)
    interview = true;
  if(college==1 && subject==2 && !(age>28))
    interview = true;
  if(college==2 && (subject==2 || subject==3) && age>25)
    interview = true;

  /* Output decision for interview */
  if(interview)
    printf("\n\nGive 'em an interview");
  else
    printf("\n\nReject 'em");
  return 0;
}
```

The output from this program should be something like this:

```
What college? 1 for Harvard, 2 for Yale, 3 for other: 2
What subject? 1 for Chemistry, 2 for Economics, 3 for other: 1
How old is the applicant? 24

Give 'em an interview
```

How It Works

The program works in a fairly straightforward way. The only slight complication is with the number of operators and if statements needed to check a candidate out:

```
if((age>25 && subject==1) && (college==3 || college==1))
    interview =true;
if(college==2 &&subject ==1)
    interview = true;
if(college==1 && subject==2 && !(age>28))
    interview = true;
if(college==2 && (subject==2 || subject==3) && age>25)
    interview = true;
```

The final if statement tells you whether to invite the applicant for an interview or not; it uses the variable interview:

```
if(interview)
    printf("\n\nGive 'em an interview");
else
    printf("\n\nReject 'em");
```

The variable interview is initialized to false, but if any of the criteria is met, you assign the value true to it. The if expression is just the variable interview, so the expression is false when interview is 0 and true when interview has any nonzero value.

This could be a lot simpler, though. Let's look at the conditions that result in an interview. You can specify each criterion with an expression as shown in the following table:

Expressions for Selecting Candidates

Criterion	Expression
Graduates over 25 who studied chemistry and who didn't graduate from Yale	age>25 && college!=2
Graduates from Yale who studied chemistry	college==2 && subject==1
Graduates from Harvard who studied economics and aren't older than 28	college==1 && subject==2 && age<=28
Graduates from Yale who are over 25 and who didn't study chemistry	college==2 && age>25 && subject!=1

The variable interview should be set to true if any of these four conditions is true, so you can now combine them using the || operator to set the value of the variable interview:

```
interview = (age>25 && college!=2) || (college==2 && subject==1) ||
                        (college==1 && subject==2 && age<=28) ||
                            (college==2 && age>25 && subject!=1);
```

Now you don't need the `if` statements to check the conditions at all. You just store the logical value, `true` or `false`, which arises from combining these expressions. In fact, you could dispense with the variable `interview` altogether by just putting the combined expression for the checks into the last `if`:

```
if((age>25 && college!=2) || (college==2 && subject==1) ||
                    (college==1 && subject==2 && age<=28) ||
                        (college==2 && age>25 && subject!=1))
    printf("\n\nGive 'em an interview");
else
    printf("\n\nReject 'em");
```

So you end up with a much shorter, if somewhat less readable program.

Multiple-Choice Questions

Multiple-choice questions come up quite often in programming. One example is selecting a different course of action depending on whether a candidate is from one or other of six different universities. Another example is when you want to choose to execute a particular set of statements depending on which day of the week it is. You have two ways to handle multiple-choice situations in C. One is a form of the `if` statement described as the `else-if` that provides the most general way to deal with multiple choices. The other is the `switch` statement, which is restricted in the way a particular choice is selected; but where it does apply, it provides a very neat and easily understood solution. Let's look at the `else-if` statement first.

Using else-if Statements for Multiple Choices

The use of the `else-if` statement for selecting one of a set of choices looks like this:

```
if(choice1)
    /* Statement or block for choice 1 */
else if(choice2)
    /* Statement or block for choice 2 */
else if(choice3)
    /* Statement or block for choice 2 */

/* … and so on …    */
else
    /* Default statement or block  */
```

Each `if` expression can be anything as long as the result is `true` or `false`. If the first `if` expression, `choice1`, is false, the next `if` is executed. If `choice2` is false, the next `if` is executed. This continues until an expression is found to be true, in which case the statement or block of statements for that `if` is executed. This ends the sequence, and the statement following the sequence of `else-if` statements is executed next.

If all of the `if` conditions are `false`, the statement or block following the final `else` will be executed. You can omit this final `else`, in which case the sequence will do nothing if all the `if` conditions are false. Here's a simple illustration of this:

```
if(salary<5000)
  printf("Your pay is very poor.");     /* pay < 5000               */
else if(salary<15000)
  printf("Your pay is not good.");      /* 5000 <= pay < 15000    */
else if(salary<50000)
  printf("Your pay is not bad.");       /* 15000 <= pay < 50000   */
else if(salary<100000)
  printf("Your pay is very good.");     /* 50000 <= pay < 100000 */
else
  printf("Your pay is exceptional.");   /* pay > 100000              */
```

Note that you don't need to test for lower limits in the if conditions after the first. This is because if you reach a particular if, the previous test must have been false.

Because any logical expressions can be used as the if conditions, this statement is very flexible and allows you to express a selection from virtually any set of choices. The switch statement isn't as flexible, but it's simpler to use in many cases. Let's take a look at the switch statement.

The switch Statement

The switch statement enables you to choose one course of action from a set of possible actions, based on the result of an integer expression. Let's start with a simple illustration of how it works.

Imagine that you're running a raffle or a sweepstakes. Suppose ticket number 35 wins first prize, number 122 wins second prize, and number 78 wins third prize. You could use the switch statement to check for a winning ticket number as follows:

```
switch(ticket_number)
{
  case 35:
    printf("Congratulations! You win first prize!");
    break;
  case 122:
    printf("You are in luck - second prize.");
    break;
  case 78:
    printf("You are in luck - third prize.");
    break;
  default:
    printf("Too bad, you lose.");
}
```

The value of the expression in parentheses following the keyword switch, which is ticket_number in this case, determines which of the statements between the braces will be executed. If the value of ticket_number matches the value specified after one of the case keywords, the following statements will be executed. If ticket_number has the value 122, for example, this message will be displayed:

```
You are in luck - second prize.
```

The effect of the break statement following the printf() is to skip over the other statements within that block and continue with whatever statement follows the closing brace. If you were to omit the break statement for a particular case, when the statements for that case are executed, execution would continue with the statements for the next case. If ticket_number has a value that doesn't correspond to any of the case values, the statements that follow the default keyword are executed, so you simply get the default message. Both default and break are keywords in C.

The general way of describing the switch statement is as follows:

```
switch(integer_expression)
{
  case constant_expression_1:
    statements_1;
    break;
    ....
  case constant_expression_n:
    statements_n;
    break;
  default:
    statements;
}
```

The test is based on the value of integer_expression. If that value corresponds to one of the case values defined by the associated constant_expression_n values, the statements following that case value are executed. If the value of integer_expression differs from every one of the case values, the statements following default are executed. Because you can't reasonably expect to select more than one case, all the case values must be different. If they aren't, you'll get an error message when you try to compile the program. The case values must all be **constant expressions**, which are expressions that can be evaluated at compile time. This means that a case value can't be dependent on a value that's determined when your program executes. Of course, the test expression integer_expression can be anything at all, as long as it evaluates to an integer.

You can leave out the default keyword and its associated statements. If none of the case values match, then nothing happens. Notice, however, that all of the case values for the associated constant_expression must be different. The break statement jumps to the statement after the closing brace.

Notice the punctuation and formatting. There's no semicolon at the end of the first switch expression. The body of the statement is enclosed within braces. The constant_expression value for a case is followed by a colon, and each subsequent statement ends with a semicolon, as usual.

Because an enumeration type is an integer type, you can use a variable of an enumeration type to control a switch. Here's an example:

```
enum Weekday {Monday, Tuesday, Wednesday, Thursday, Friday, Saturday, Sunday};
enum Weekday today = Wednesday;
switch(today)
{
  case Sunday:
    printf("Today is Sunday.");
    break;
  case Monday:
    printf("Today is Monday.");
    break;
  case Tuesday:
    printf("Today is Tuesday.");
    break;
  case Wednesday:
    printf("Today is Wednesday.");
    break;
  case Thursday:
    printf("Today is Thursday.");
```

```
    break;
  case Friday:
    printf("Today is Friday.");
    break;
  case Saturday:
    printf("Today is Saturday.");
    break;
  }
```

This switch selects the case that corresponds to the value of the variable today, so in this case the message will be that today is Wednesday. There's no default case in the switch but you could put one in to guard against an invalid value for today.

You can associate several case values with one group of statements. You can also use an expression that results in a value of type char as the control expression for a switch. Suppose you read a character from the keyboard into a variable, ch, of type char. You can test this character in a switch like this:

```
switch(tolower(ch))
{
  case 'a': case 'e': case 'i': case 'o': case 'u':
    printf("The character is a vowel.");
    break;
  case 'b': case 'c': case 'd': case 'f': case 'g': case 'h': case 'j': case 'k':
  case 'l': case 'm': case 'n': case 'p': case 'q': case 'r': case 's': case 't':
  case 'v': case 'w': case 'x': case 'y': case 'z':
    printf("The character is a consonant.");
    break;
  default:
    printf("The character is not a letter.");
    break;
}
```

Because you use the function tolower() that is declared in the <ctype.h> header file to convert the value of ch to lowercase, you only need to test for lowercase letters. In the case in which ch contains the character code for a vowel, you output a message to that effect because for the five case values corresponding to vowels you execute the same printf() statement. Similarly, you output a suitable message when ch contains a consonant. If ch contains a code that's neither a consonant nor a vowel, the default case is executed.

Note the break statement after the default case. This isn't necessary, but it does have a purpose. By always putting a break statement at the end of the last case, you ensure that the switch still works correctly if you later add a new case at the end.

You could simplify the switch by making use of another function that's declared in the <ctype.h> header. The isalpha() function will return a nonzero integer (thus true) if the character that's passed as the argument is an alphabetic character, and it will return 0 (false) if the character isn't an alphabetic character. You could therefore produce the same result as the previous switch with the following code:

```
if(!isalpha(ch))
    printf("The character is not a letter.");
else
  switch(tolower(ch))
  {
    case 'a': case 'e': case 'i': case 'o': case 'u':
      printf("The character is a vowel.");
    break;
  default:
```

```
    printf("The character is a consonant.");
    break;
}
```

The if statement tests for ch not being a letter, and if this is so, it outputs a message. If ch is a letter, the switch statement will sort out whether it is a vowel or a consonant. The five vowel case values produce one output, and the default case produces the other. Because you know that ch contains a letter when the switch statement executes, if ch isn't a vowel, it must be a consonant.

As well as the tolower(), toupper(), and isalpha() functions that I've mentioned, the <ctype.h> header also declares several other useful functions for testing a character, as shown in Table 3-3.

Table 3-3. *Functions for Testing Characters*

Function	Tests For
islower()	Lowercase letter
isupper()	Uppercase letter
isalnum()	Uppercase or lowercase letter
iscntrl()	Control character
isprint()	Any printing character including space
isgraph()	Any printing character except space
isdigit()	Decimal digit ('0' to '9')
isxdigit()	Hexadecimal digit ('0' to '9', 'A' to 'F', 'a' to 'f')
isblank()	Standard blank characters (space, '\t')
isspace()	Whitespace character (space, '\n', '\t', '\v', '\r', '\f')
ispunct()	Printing character for which isspace() and isalnum() return false

In each case, the function returns a nonzero integer value (which is interpreted as true) if it finds what it's testing for and 0 (false) otherwise.

Let's look at the switch statement in action with an example.

TRY IT OUT: PICKING A LUCKY NUMBER

This example assumes that you're operating a lottery in which there are three winning numbers. Participants are required to guess a winning number, and the switch statement is designed to end the suspense and tell them about any valuable prizes they may have won:

```
/* Program 3.8 Lucky Lotteries    */
#include <stdio.h>

int main(void)
{
    int choice = 0;              /* The number chosen          */
```

```
/* Get the choice input */
printf("\nPick a number between 1 and 10 and you may win a prize! ");
scanf("%d",&choice);

/* Check for an invalid selection */
if((choice>10) || (choice <1))
    choice = 11;                        /* Selects invalid choice message */

switch(choice)
{
  case 7:
    printf("\nCongratulations!");
    printf("\nYou win the collected works of Amos Gruntfuttock.");
    break;                    /* Jumps to the end of the block   */

  case 2:
    printf("\nYou win the folding thermometer-pen-watch-umbrella.");
    break;                    /* Jumps to the end of the block   */

  case 8:
    printf("\nYou win the lifetime supply of aspirin tablets.");
    break;                    /* Jumps to the end of the block   */

  case 11:
    printf("\nTry between 1 and 10. You wasted your guess.");
                /* No break - so continue with the next statement */

  default:
    printf("\nSorry, you lose.\n");
    break;              /* Defensive break - in case of new cases */
  }
  return 0;
}
```

Typical output from this program will be the following:

```
Pick a number between 1 and 10 and you may win a prize! 3
Sorry, you lose.
```

or

```
Pick a number between 1 and 10 and you may win a prize! 7
Congratulations!
You win the collected works of Amos Gruntfuttock.
```

or, if you enter an invalid number

```
Pick a number between 1 and 10 and you may win a prize! 92
Try between 1 and 10. You wasted your guess.
Sorry, you lose.
```

How It Works

You do the usual sort of thing to start with. You declare an integer variable choice. Then you ask the user to enter a number between 1 and 10 and store the value the user types in choice:

```
int choice = 0;                    /* The number chosen           */
```

```
/* Get the choice input */
printf("\nPick a number between 1 and 10 and you may win a prize! ");
scanf("%d",&choice);
```

Before you do anything else, you check that the user has really entered a number between 1 and 10:

```
/* Check for an invalid selection */
if((choice>10) || (choice <1))
  choice = 11;                     /* Selects invalid choice message */
```

If the value is anything else, you automatically change it to 11. You don't have to do this, but to ensure the user is advised of his or her mistake, you set the variable choice to 11, which produces the error message generated by the printf() for that case value.

Next, you have the switch statement, which will select from the cases between the braces that follow depending on the value of choice:

```
switch(choice)
{
  ...
}
```

If choice has the value 7, the case corresponding to that value will be executed:

```
case 7:
  printf("\nCongratulations!");
  printf("\nYou win the collected works of Amos Gruntfuttock.");
  break;                          /* Jumps to the end of the block  */
```

The two printf() calls are executed, and the break will jump to the statement following the closing brace for the block (which ends the program, in this case, because there isn't one).

The same goes for the next two cases:

```
case 2:
  printf("\nYou win the folding thermometer-pen-watch-umbrella.");
  break;                          /* Jumps to the end of the block  */

case 8:
  printf("\nYou win the lifetime supply of aspirin tablets.");
  break;                          /* Jumps to the end of the block  */
```

These correspond to values for the variable choice of 2 or 8.

The next case is a little different:

```
case 11:
  printf("\nTry between 1 and 10, you wasted your guess.");
            /* No break - so continue with the next statement */
```

There's no break statement, so execution continues with the printf() for the default case after displaying the message. The upshot of this is that you get both lines of output if choice has been set to 11. This is entirely appropriate in this case, but usually you'll want to put a break statement at the end of each case. Remove the break statements from the program and try entering 7 to see why. You'll get all the output messages following any particular case.

The default case is as follows:

```
default:
    printf("\nSorry, you lose.\n");
    break;                  /* Defensive break - in case of new cases */
```

This will be selected if the value of choice doesn't correspond to any of the other case values. You also have a break statement here. Although it isn't strictly necessary, many programmers always put a break statement after the default case statements or whichever is the last case in the switch. This provides for the possibility of adding further case statements to the switch. If you were to forget the break after the default case in such circumstances the switch won't do what you want. The case statements can be in any order in a switch, and default doesn't have to be the last.

TRY IT OUT: YES OR NO

Let's see the switch statement in action controlled by a variable of type char where the value is entered by the user. You'll prompt the user to enter the value 'y' or 'Y' for one action and 'n' or 'N' for another. On its own, this program may be fairly useless, but you've probably encountered many situations in which a program has asked just this question and then performed some action as a result (saving a file, for example):

```
/* Program 3.9 Testing cases */
#include <stdio.h>

int main(void)
{
  char answer = 0;               /* Stores an input character */

  printf("Enter Y or N: ");
  scanf(" %c", &answer);

  switch(answer)
  {
    case 'y': case 'Y':
      printf("\nYou responded in the affirmative.");
      break;

    case 'n': case 'N':
      printf("\nYou responded in the negative.");
      break;

    default:
      printf("\nYou did not respond correctly...");
      break;
  }
  return 0;
}
```

Typical output from this would be the following:

```
Enter Y or N: y
You responded in the affirmative.
```

How It Works

When you declare the variable answer as type char, you also take the opportunity to initialize it to 0. You then ask the user to type something in and store that value as usual:

```
char answer = 0;                    /* Stores an input character */

printf("Enter Y or N: ");
scanf(" %c", &answer);
```

The switch statement uses the character stored in letter to select a case:

```
switch(answer)
{
  ...
}
```

The first case in the switch provides for the possibility of the user entering an uppercase or a lowercase letter Y:

```
case 'y': case 'Y':
  printf("\nYou responded in the affirmative.");
  break;
```

Both values 'y' and 'Y' will result in the same printf() being executed. In general, you can put as many cases together like this as you want. Notice the punctuation for this. The two cases just follow one another and each has a terminating colon after the case value.

The negative input is handled in a similar way:

```
case 'n': case 'N':
  printf("\nYou responded in the negative.");
  break;
```

If the character entered doesn't correspond with any of the case values, the default case is selected:

```
default:
  printf("\nYou did not respond correctly...");
  break;
```

Note the break statement after the printf() statements for the default case, as well as the legal case values. As before, this causes execution to break off at that point and continue after the end of the switch statement. Again, without it you'd get the statements for succeeding cases executed and, unless there's a break statement preceding the valid cases, you'd get the following statement (or statements), including the default statement, executed as well.

Of course, you could also use the toupper() or tolower() function to simplify the cases in the switch. By using one or the other you can nearly halve the number of cases:

```
switch(toupper(answer))
{
  case 'Y':
    printf("\nYou responded in the affirmative.");
    break;
  case 'N':
    printf("\nYou responded in the negative.");
    break;
  default:
    printf("\nYou did not respond correctly...");
    break;
}
```

Remember, you need an #include directive for <ctype.h> if you want to use the toupper() function.

The goto Statement

The if statement provides you with the ability to choose one or the other of two blocks of statements, depending on a test. This is a powerful tool that enables you to alter the naturally sequential nature of a program. You no longer have to go from A to B to C to D. You can go to A and then decide whether to skip B and C and go straight to D.

The goto statement, on the other hand, is a blunt instrument. It directs the flow of statements to change *unconditionally!* do not pass Go, do not collect $200, go directly to jail. When your program hits a goto, it does just that. It goes to the place you send it, without checking any values or asking the user whether it is really what he or she wants.

I'm only going to mention the goto statement very briefly, because it isn't as great as it might at first seem. The problem with goto statements is that they seem too easy. This might sound perverse, but the important word is *seems*. It feels so simple that you can be tempted into using it all over the place, where it would be better to use a different statement. This can result in heavily tangled code.

When you use the goto statement, the position in the code to be moved to is defined by a statement label at that point. A statement label is defined in exactly the same way as a variable name, which is a sequence of letters and digits, the first of which must be a letter. The statement label is followed by a colon (:) to separate it from the statement it labels. If you think this sounds like a case label in a switch, you would be right. Case labels are statement labels.

Like other statements, the goto statement ends with a semicolon:

```
goto there;
```

The destination statement must have the same label as appears in the goto statement, which is there in this case. As I said, the label is written preceding the statement it applies to, with a colon separating the label from the rest of the statement, as in this example:

```
there: x=10;                   /* A labeled statement */
```

The goto statement can be used in conjunction with an if statement, as in the following example:

```
...
if(dice == 6)
  goto Waldorf;
else
  goto Jail;                       /* Go to the statement labeled Jail */

Waldorf:
  comfort = high;
  ...
  /* Code to prevent falling through to Jail */

Jail:                    /* The label itself. Program control is sent here */
  comfort = low;
  ...
```

You roll the dice. If you get 6, you go to the Waldorf; otherwise, you go to Jail. This might seem perfectly fine but, at the very least, it's confusing. To understand the sequence of execution, you need to hunt for the destination labels. Imagine your code was littered with gotos. It would be very difficult to follow and perhaps even more difficult to fix when things go wrong. So it's best to avoid the goto statement as far as possible. In theory it's always possible to avoid using the goto statement, but there are one or two instances in which it's a useful option. You'll look into loops in Chapter 4, but for now, know that exiting from the innermost loop of a deeply nested set of loops can be much simpler with a goto statement than with other mechanisms.

Bitwise Operators

Before you come to the big example for the chapter, you'll examine a group of operators that look something like the logical operators you saw earlier but in fact are quite different. These are called the **bitwise operators**, because they operate on the bits in integer values. There are six bitwise operators, as shown in Table 3-4.

Table 3-4. *Bitwise Operators*

Operator	Description
&	Bitwise AND operator
|	Bitwise OR operator
^	Bitwise Exclusive OR (EOR) operator
~	Bitwise NOT operator, also called the 1's complement operator
>>	Bitwise shift right operator
<<	Bitwise shift left operator

All of these only operate on integer types. The ~ operator is a unary operator！ it applies to one operand！ and the others are binary operators.

The bitwise AND operator, &, combines the corresponding bits of its operands in such a way that if both bits are 1, the resulting bit is 1; otherwise, the resulting bit is 0. Suppose you declare the following variables:

```
int x = 13;
int y = 6;
int z = x&y;                    /* AND the bits of x and y */
```

After the third statement, z will have the value 4 (binary 100). This is because the corresponding bits in x and y are combined as follows:

x	0	0	0	0	1	1	0	1
y	0	0	0	0	0	1	1	0
x&y	0	0	0	0	0	1	0	0

Obviously the variables would have more bits than I have shown here, but the additional bits would all be 0. There is only one instance where corresponding bits in the variables x and y are both 1 and that is the third bit from the right; this is the only case where the result of ANDing the bits is 1.

Caution It's important not to get the bitwise operators and the logical operators muddled. The expression x & y will produce quite different results from x && y in general. Try it out and see.

The bitwise OR operator, |, results in 1 if either or both of the corresponding bits are 1; otherwise, the result is 0. Let's look at a specific example. If you combine the same values using the | operator in a statement such as this

```
int z = x|y;                    /* OR the bits of x and y */
```

the result would be as follows:

x	0	0	0	0	1	1	0	1
y	0	0	0	0	0	1	1	0
x|y	0	0	0	0	1	1	1	1

The value stored in z would therefore be 15 (binary 1111).

The bitwise EOR operator, ^, produces a 1 if both bits are different, and 0 if they're the same. Again, using the same initial values, the statement

```
int z = x^y;                    /*Exclusive OR the bits of x and y */
```

would result in z containing the value 11 (binary 1011), because the bits combine as follows:

x	0	0	0	0	1	1	0	1
y	0	0	0	0	0	1	1	0
x^y	0	0	0	0	1	0	1	1

The unary operator, ~, flips the bits of its operand, so 1 becomes 0, and 0 becomes 1. If you apply this operator to x with the value 13 as before, and you write

```
int z = ~x;                     /* Store 1's complement of x */
```

then z will have the value 14. The bits are set as follows:

x	0	0	0	0	1	1	0	1
~x	1	1	1	1	0	0	1	0

The value 11110010 is 14 in 2's complement representation of negative integers. If you're not familiar with the 2's complement form, and you want to find out about it, it is described in Appendix A.

The shift operators shift the bits in the left operand by the number of positions specified by the right operand. You could specify a shift-left operation with the following statements:

```
int value = 12;
int shiftcount = 3;                 /* Number of positions to be shifted */
int result = value << shiftcount;   /* Shift left shiftcount positions   */
```

The variable result will contain the value 96. The binary number in value is 00001100. The bits are shifted to the left three positions, and 0s are introduced on the right, so the value of value << shiftcount, as a binary number, will be 01100000.

The right shift operator moves the bits to the right, but it's a little more complicated than left shift. For unsigned values, the bits that are introduced on the left (in the vacated positions as the bits are shifted right) are filled with zeros. Let's see how this works in practice. Suppose you declare a variable:

```
unsigned int value = 65372U;
```

As a binary value in a 2-byte variable, this is:
Suppose you now execute the following statement:

    1111 1111 0101 1100

```
unsigned int result = value >> 2;    /* Shift right two bits */
```

The bits in value will be shifted two places to the right, introducing zeros at the left end, and the resultant value will be stored in result. In binary this will be 0, which is the decimal value 16343.

0011 1111 1101 0111

For signed values that are negative, where the leftmost bit will be 1, the result depends on your system. In most cases, the sign bit is propagated, so the bits introduced on the right are 1 bits, but on some systems zeros are introduced in this case too. Let's see how this affects the result.

Suppose you define a variable with this statement:

```
int new_value = -164;
```

This happens to be the same bit pattern as the unsigned value that you used earlier; remember that this is the 2's complement representation of the value:

1111 1111 0101 1100

Suppose you now execute this statement:

```
int new_result = new_value >> 2;      /* Shift right two bits */
```

This will shift the value in new_value two bit positions to the right and the result will be stored in new_result. If, as is usually the case, the sign bit is propagated, 1s will be inserted on the left as the bits are shifted to the right, so new_result will end up as

1111 1111 1101 0111

This is the decimal value –41, which is what you might expect because it amounts to –164/4. If the sign bit isn't propagated, however, as can occur on some computers, the value in new_result will be

0011 1111 1101 0111

So shifting right two bits in this case has changed the value –164 to +16343! perhaps a rather unexpected result.

The op= Use of Bitwise Operators

You can use all of the binary bitwise operators in the op= form of assignment. The exception is the operator ~, which is a unary operator. As you saw in Chapter 2, a statement of the form

```
lhs op= rhs;
```

is equivalent to the statement

```
lhs = lhs op (rhs);
```

This means that if you write

```
value <<= 4;
```

the effect is to shift the contents of the integer variable, value, left four bit positions. It's exactly the same as the following:

```
value = value << 4;
```

You can do the same kind of thing with the other binary operators. For example, you could write the following statement:

```
value &= 0xFF;
```

where value is an integer variable. This is equivalent to the following:

```
value = value & 0xFF;
```

The effect of this is to keep the rightmost eight bits unchanged and to set all the others to zero.

Using Bitwise Operators

The bitwise operators look interesting in an academic kind of way, but what use are they? They don't come up in everyday programs, but in some areas they become very useful. One major use of the bitwise AND, &, and the bitwise OR, |, is in operations to test and set individual bits in an integer variable. With this capability you can use individual bits to store data that involves one of two choices. For example, you could use a single integer variable to store several characteristics of a person. You could store whether the person is male or female with one bit, and you could use three other bits to specify whether the person can speak French, German, or Italian. You might use another bit to record whether the person's salary is $50,000 or more. So in just four bits you have a substantial set of data recorded. Let's see how this would work out.

The fact that you only get a 1 bit when both of the bits being combined are 1 means that you can use the & operator to select a part of an integer variable or even just a single bit. You first define a value, usually called a **mask**, that you use to select the bit or bits that you want. It will contain a bit value of 1 for the bit positions you want to keep and a bit value of 0 for the bit positions you want to discard. You can then AND this mask with the value that you want to select from. Let's look at an example. You can define masks with the following statements:

```
unsigned int male      = 0x1;   /* Mask selecting first (rightmost) bit */
unsigned int french    = 0x2;   /* Mask selecting second bit            */
unsigned int german    = 0x4;   /* Mask selecting third bit             */
unsigned int italian   = 0x8;   /* Mask selecting fourth bit            */
unsigned int payBracket = 0x10;  /* Mask selecting fifth bit             */
```

In each case, a 1 bit will indicate that the particular condition is true. These masks in binary each pick out an individual bit, so you could have an unsigned int variable, personal_data, which would store five items of information about a person. If the first bit is 1, the person is male, and if the first bit is 0, the person is female. If the second bit is 1, the person speaks French, and if it is 0, the person doesn't speak French, and so on for all five bits at the right end of the data value.

You could therefore test the variable, personal_data, for a German speaker with the following statement:

```
if(personal_data & german)
  /* Do something because they speak German */
```

The expression personalData & german will be nonzero! that is, true! if the bit corresponding to the mask, german, is 1; otherwise, it will be 0.

Of course, there's nothing to prevent you from combining several expressions involving using masks to select individual bits with the logical operators. You could test whether someone is a female who speaks French or Italian with the following statement:

```
if(!(personal_data & male) && ((personal_data & french) ||
                                (personal_data & italian)))
  /* We have a French or Italian speaking female */
```

As you can see, it's easy enough to test individual bits or combinations of bits. The only other thing you need to understand is how to set individual bits. The OR operator swings into action here.

You can use the OR operator to set individual bits in a variable using the same mask as you use to test the bits. If you want to set the variable personal_data to record a person as speaking French, you can do it with this statement:

```
personal_data |= french;            /* Set second bit to 1 */
```

Just to remind you, the preceding statement is exactly the same as the following statement:

```
personal_data = personal_data|french;  /* Set second bit to 1 */
```

The second bit from the right in personal_data will be set to 1, and all the other bits will remain as they were. Because of the way the | operator works, you can set multiple bits in a single statement:

```
personal_data |= french|german|male;
```

This sets the bits to record a French- and German-speaking male. If the variable personalData previously recorded that the person spoke Italian, that bit would still be set, so the OR operator is additive. If a bit is already set, it will stay set.

What about resetting a bit? Suppose you want to change the male bit to female. This amounts to resetting a 1 bit to 0, and it requires the use of the ! operator with the bitwise AND:

```
personal_data &= !male;             /* Reset male to female */
```

This works because !male will have a 0 bit set for the bit that indicates male and all the other bits as 1. Thus, the bit corresponding to male will be set to 0: 0 ANDed with anything is 0, and all the other bits will be as they were. If another bit is 1, then 1&1 will still be 1. If another bit is 0, then 0&1 will still be 0.

I've used the example of using bits to record specific items of personal data. If you want to program a PC using the Windows application programming interface (API), you'll often use individual bits to record the status of various window parameters, so the bitwise operators can be very useful in this context.

TRY IT OUT: USING BITWISE OPERATORS

Let's exercise some of the bitwise operators in a slightly different example, but using the same principles discussed previously. This example illustrates how you can use a mask to select multiple bits from a variable. You'll write a program that sets a value in a variable and then uses the bitwise operators to reverse the sequence of hexadecimal digits. Here's the code:

```
/* Program 3.10 Exercising bitwise operators */
#include <stdio.h>

int main(void)
{
  unsigned int original = 0xABC;
  unsigned int result = 0;
  unsigned int mask = 0xF;       /* Rightmost four bits                   */

  printf("\n original = %X", original);

  /* Insert first digit in result */
  result |= original&mask;       /* Put right 4 bits from original in result */

  /* Get second digit */
  original >>= 4;                /* Shift original right four positions   */
  result <<= 4;                  /* Make room for next digit              */
  result |= original&mask;       /* Put right 4 bits from original in result */

  /* Get third digit */
  original >>= 4;                /* Shift original right four positions   */
  result <<= 4;                  /* Make room for next digit              */
  result |= original&mask;       /* Put right 4 bits from original in result */
  printf("\t result = %X\n", result);
  return 0;
}
```

This will produce the following output:

```
original = ABC  result = CBA
```

How It Works

This program uses the idea of masking, previously discussed. The rightmost hexadecimal digit in `original` is obtained by ANDing the value with `mask` in the expression `original&mask`. This sets all the other hexadecimal digits to 0. Because the value of `mask` as a binary number is

```
0000  0000  0000  1111
```

you can see that only the first four bits on the right are kept. Any of these four bits that is 1 in `original` will stay as 1 in the result, and any that are 0 will stay as 0. All the other bits will be 0 because 0 ANDed with anything is 0.

Once you've selected the rightmost four bits, you then store the result with the following statement:

```
result |= original&mask;       /* Put right 4 bits from original in result */
```

The content of `result` is ORed with the hexadecimal digit that's produced by the expression on the right side.

To get at the second digit in `original`, you need to move it to where the first digit was. You do this by shifting `original` right by four bit positions:

```
original >>= 4;                /* Shift original right four positions      */
```

The first digit is shifted out and is lost.

To make room for the next digit from `original`, you shift the contents of `result` left by four bit positions with this statement:

```
result <<= 4;                  /* Make room for next digit                 */
```

Now you want to insert the second digit from `original`, which is now in the first digit position, into `result`. You do this with the following statement:

```
result |= original&mask;       /* Put right 4 bits from original in result */
```

To get the third digit you just repeat the process. Clearly, you could repeat this for as many digits as you want.

Designing a Program

You've reached the end of Chapter 3 successfully, and now you'll apply what you've learned so far to build a useful program.

The Problem

The problem is to write a simple calculator that can add, subtract, multiply, divide, and find the remainder when one number is divided by another. The program must allow the calculation that is to be performed to be keyed in a natural way, such as 5.6 * 27 or 3 + 6.

The Analysis

All the math involved is simple, but the processing of the input adds a little complexity. You need to make checks on the input to make sure that the user hasn't asked the computer to do something impossible. You must allow the user to input a calculation in one go, for example

```
34.87 + 5
```

or

```
9 * 6.5
```

The steps involved in writing this program are as follows:

1. Get the user's input for the calculation that the user wants the computer to perform.
2. Check that input to make sure that it's understandable.
3. Perform the calculation.
4. Display the result.

The Solution

This section outlines the steps you'll take to solve the problem.

Step 1

Getting the user input is quite easy. You'll be using `printf()` and `scanf()`, so you need the `<stdio.h>` header file. The only new thing I'll introduce is in the way in which you'll get the input. As I said earlier, rather than asking the user for each number individually and then asking for the operation to be performed, you'll get the user to type it in more naturally. You can do this because of the way `scanf()` works, but I'll discuss the details of that after you've seen the first part of the program. Let's kick off the program with the code to read the input:

```
/*Program 3.11 A calculator*/
#include <stdio.h>

int main(void)
{
  double number1 = 0.0;        /* First operand value a decimal number  */
  double number2 = 0.0;        /* Second operand value a decimal number */
  char operation = 0;          /* Operation - must be +, -, *, /, or %  */

  printf("\nEnter the calculation\n");
  scanf("%lf %c %lf", &number1, &operation, &number2);

  /* Plus the rest of the code for the program */
  return 0;
}
```

The `scanf()` function is fairly clever when it comes to reading data. You don't actually need to enter each input data item on a separate line. All that's required is one or more whitespace characters between each item of input. (You create a whitespace character by pressing the spacebar, the Tab key, or the Enter key.)

Step 2

Next, you must check to make sure that the input is correct. The most obvious check to perform is that the operation to be performed is valid. You've already decided that the valid operations are +, -, /, *, and %, so you need to check that the operation is one of these.

You also need to check the second number to see if it's 0 if the operation is either / or %. If the right operand is 0, these operations are invalid. You could do all these checks using `if` statements, but a `switch` statement provides a far better way of doing this because it is easier to understand than a sequence of `if` statements:

```
/*Program 3.11 A calculator*/
#include <stdio.h>

int main(void)
{
  double number1 = 0.0;        /* First operand value a decimal number  */
  double number2 = 0.0;        /* Second operand value a decimal number */
  char operation = 0;          /* Operation - must be +, -, *, /, or %  */
```

```
  printf("\nEnter the calculation\n");
  scanf("%lf %c %lf", &number1, &operation, &number2);

  /* Code to check the input goes here */
  switch(operation)
  {
    case '+':                       /* No checks necessary for add       */
      break;

    case '-':                       /* No checks necessary for subtract */
      break;

    case '*':                       /* No checks necessary for multiply */
      break;

    case '/':
      if(number2 == 0)              /* Check second operand for zero     */
        printf("\n\n\aDivision by zero error!\n");
      break;

    case '%':                       /* Check second operand for zero     */
      if((long)number2 == 0)
        printf("\n\n\aDivision by zero error!\n");
      break;

    default:                        /* Operation is invalid if we get to here */
      printf("\n\n\aIllegal operation!\n");
      break;
  }
  /* Plus the rest of the code for the program */
  return 0;
}
```

Because you're casting the second operand to an integer when the operator is %, it isn't sufficient to just check the second operand against 0! you must check that number2 doesn't have a value that will result in 0 when it's cast to type long.

Steps 3 and 4

So now that you've checked the input, you can calculate the result. You have a choice here. You could calculate each result in the switch and store it to be output after the switch, or you could simply output the result for each case. Let's go for the latter approach. The code you need to add is as follows:

```
/*Program 3.11 A calculator*/
#include <stdio.h>

int main(void)
{
  double number1 = 0.0;          /* First operand value a decimal number  */
  double number2 = 0.0;          /* Second operand value a decimal number */
  char operation = 0;            /* Operation - must be +, -, *, /, or % */
```

```
    printf("\nEnter the calculation\n");
    scanf("%lf %c %lf", &number1, &operation, &number2);

    /* Code to check the input goes here */
    switch(operation)
    {
      case '+':                        /* No checks necessary for add       */
        printf("= %lf\n", number1 + number2);
        break;

      case '-':                        /* No checks necessary for subtract */
        printf("= %lf\n", number1 - number2);
        break;

      case '*':                        /* No checks necessary for multiply */
        printf("= %lf\n", number1 * number2);
        break;

      case '/':
        if(number2 == 0)               /* Check second operand for zero     */
          printf("\n\n\aDivision by zero error!\n");
        else
          printf("= %lf\n", number1 / number2);
        break;

      case '%':                        /* Check second operand for zero     */
        if((long)number2 == 0)
          printf("\n\n\aDivision by zero error!\n");
        else
          printf("= %ld\n", (long)number1 % (long)number2);
        break;

      default:                         /* Operation is invalid if we get to here */
        printf("\n\n\aIllegal operation!\n");
        break;
    }
    return 0;
}
```

Notice how you cast the two numbers from double to long when you calculate the modulus. This is because the % operator only works with integers in C.

All that's left is to try it out! Here's some typical output:

```
Enter the calculation
25*13
= 325.000000
```

Here's another example:

```
Enter the calculation
999/3.3
= 302.727273
```

And just one more

```
Enter the calculation
7%0
```

```
Division by zero error!
```

Summary

This chapter ends with quite a complicated example. In the first two chapters you really just looked at the groundwork for C programs. You could do some reasonably useful things, but you couldn't control the sequence of operations in the program once it had started. In this chapter you've started to feel the power of the language and how you can use data entered by the user or results calculated during execution to determine what happens next.

You've learned how to compare variables and then use if, if-else, else-if, and switch statements to affect the outcome. You also know how to use logical operators to combine comparisons between your variables. You should now understand a lot more about making decisions and taking different paths through your program code.

In the next chapter, you'll learn how to write even more powerful programs: programs that can repeat a set of statements until some condition is met. By the end of Chapter 4, you'll think your calculator is small-fry.

Exercises

The following exercises enable you to try out what you've learned in this chapter. If you get stuck, look back over the chapter for help. If you're still stuck, you can download the solutions from the Source Code/Download area of the Apress web site (http://www.apress.com), but that really should be a last resort.

Exercise 3-1. Write a program that will first allow a user to choose one of two options:

1. Convert a temperature from degrees Celsius to degrees Fahrenheit.

2. Convert a temperature from degrees Fahrenheit to degrees Celsius.

The program should then prompt for the temperature value to be entered and output the new value that results from the conversion. To convert from Celsius to Fahrenheit you can multiply the value by 1.8 and then add 32. To convert from Fahrenheit to Celsius, you can subtract 32 from the value, then multiply by 5, and divide the result by 9.

Exercise 3-2. Write a program that prompts the user to enter the date as three integer values for the month, the day in the month, and the year. The program should then output the date in the form 31st December 2003 when the user enters 12 31 2003, for example.

You will need to work out when *th*, *nd*, *st*, and *rd* need to be appended to the day value. Don't forget 1st, 2nd, 3rd, 4th; but 11th, 12th, 13th, 14th; and 21st, 22nd, 23rd, and 24th.

Exercise 3-3. Write a program that will calculate the price for a quantity entered from the keyboard, given that the unit price is $5 and there is a discount of 10 percent for quantities over 30 and a 15 percent discount for quantities over 50.

Exercise 3-4. Modify the last example in the chapter that implemented a calculator so that the user is given the option to enter y or Y to carry out another calculation, and n or N to end the program. (Note: You'll have to use a goto statement for this at this time, but you'll learn a better way of doing this in the next chapter).

CHAPTER 4

■ ■ ■

Loops

In the last chapter you learned how to compare items and base your decisions on the result. You were able to choose how the computer reacted based on the input to a program. In this chapter, you'll learn how you can repeat a block of statements until some condition is met. This is called a **loop**.

The number of times that a loop is repeated can be controlled simply by a count! repeating the statement block a given number of times! or it can be more complex! repeating a block until some condition is met, such as the user entering **quit**, for instance. The latter would enable you to program the calculator example in the previous chapter to repeat as many times as required without having to use a goto statement.

In this chapter, you'll learn the following:

- ! How you can repeat a statement, or a block of statements, as many times as you want

- ! How you can repeat a statement or a block of statements until a particular condition is fulfilled

- ! How you use the for, while, and do-while loops

- ! What the increment and decrement operators do, and how you can use them

- ! How you can write a program that plays a Simple Simon game

How Loops Work

As I said, the programming mechanism that executes a series of statements repeatedly a given number of times, or until a particular condition is fulfilled, is called a **loop**. The loop is a fundamental programming tool, along with the ability to compare items. Once you can compare data values and repeat a block of statements, you can combine these capabilities to control how many times the block of statements is executed. For example, you can keep performing a particular action until two items that you are comparing are the same. Once they *are* the same, you can go on to perform a different action.

In the lottery example in Chapter 3 in Program 3.8, you could give the user exactly three guesses! in other words, you could let him continue to guess until a variable called number_of_guesses, for instance, equals 3. This would involve a loop to repeat the code that reads a guess from the keyboard and checks the accuracy of the value entered. Figure 4-1 illustrates the way a typical loop would work in this case.

More often than not, you'll find that you want to apply the same calculation to different sets of data values. Without loops, you would need to write out the instructions to be performed as many times as there were sets of data values to be processed, which would not be very satisfactory. A loop allows you to use the same program code for any number of sets of data to be entered.

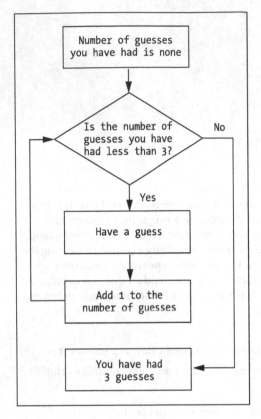

Figure 4-1. *Logic of a typical loop*

Before I discuss the various types of loops that you have available in C, I'll first introduce two new arithmetic operators that you'll encounter frequently in C programs: the **increment operator** and the **decrement operator**. These operators are often used with loops, which is why I'll discuss them here. I'll start with the briefest of introductions to the increment and decrement operators and then go straight into an example of how you can use them in the context of a loop. Once you're comfortable with how loops work, you'll return to the increment and decrement operators to investigate some of their idiosyncrasies.

Introducing the Increment and Decrement Operators

The increment operator (++) and the decrement operator (--) will increment or decrement the value stored in the integer variable that they apply to by 1. Suppose you have defined an integer variable, number, that currently has the value 6. You can increment it by 1 with the following statement:

```
++number;                          /* Increase the value by 1 */
```

After executing this statement, number will contain the value 7. Similarly, you could decrease the value of number by one with the following statement:

```
--number;                                  /* Decrease the value by 1 */
```

These operators are different from the other arithmetic operators you have encountered. When you use any of the other arithmetic operators, you create an expression that will result in a value, which may be stored in a variable or used as part of a more complex expression. They do not directly modify the value stored in a variable. When you write the expression –number, for instance, the result of evaluating this expression is 6 if number has the value +6, but the value stored in number is unchanged. On the other hand, the expression --number *does* modify the value in number. This expression will decrement the value in number by 1, so number will end up as 5 if it was originally 6.

There's much more you'll need to know about the increment and decrement operators, but I'll defer that until later. Right now, let's get back to the main discussion and take a look at the simplest form of loop, the for loop. There are other types of loops as you'll see later, but I'll give the for loop a larger slice of time because once you understand it the others will be easy.

The for Loop

You can use the for loop in its basic form to execute a block of statements a given number of times. Let's suppose you want to display the numbers from 1 to 10. Instead of writing ten printf() statements, you could write this:

```
int count;
for(count = 1 ; count <= 10 ; ++count)
  printf("\n%d", count);
```

The for loop operation is controlled by the contents of the parentheses that follow the keyword for. This is illustrated in Figure 4-2. The action that you want to repeat each time the loop repeats is the statement immediately following the first line that contains the keyword for. Although you have just a single statement here, this could equally well be a block of statements between braces.

Figure 4-2 shows the three **control expressions** that are separated by semicolons and that control the operation of the loop.

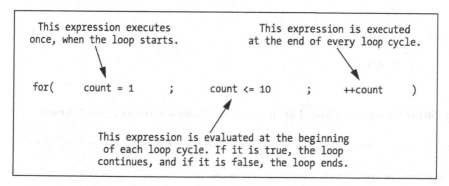

Figure 4-2. *Control expressions in a for loop*

The effect of each control expression is shown in Figure 4-2, but let's take a much closer look at exactly what's going on.

! The first control expression is executed only once, when the loop starts. In the example, the first expression sets a variable, count, to 1. This is the expression count = 1.

! The second control expression must be a logical expression that produces a result of true or false; in this case, it's the expression count <= 10. The second expression is evaluated before each loop iteration starts. If the expression evaluates to true, the loop continues, and if it's false, the loop ends and execution of the program continues with the first statement following the loop block or loop statement. Remember that false is a zero value, and any nonzero value is true. Thus, the example loop will execute the printf() statement as long as count is less than or equal to 10. The loop will end when count reaches 11.

! The third control expression, ++count in this case, is executed at the end of each iteration. Here you use the increment operator to add 1 to the value of count. On the first iteration, count will be 1, so the printf() will output 1. On the second iteration, count will have been incremented to 2, so the printf() will output the value 2. This will continue until the value 10 has been displayed. At the start of the next iteration, count will be incremented to 11, and because the second control expression will then be false, the loop will end.

Notice the punctuation. The for loop control expressions are contained within parentheses, and each expression is separated from the next by a semicolon. You can omit any of the control expressions, but if you do you must still include the semicolon. For example, you could declare and initialize the variable count to 1 outside the loop:

```
int count = 1;
```

Now you don't need to specify the first control expression at all, and the for loop could look like this:

```
for( ; count <= 10 ; ++count)
  printf("\n%d", count);
```

As a trivial example, you could make this into a real program simply by adding a few lines of code:

```
/* Program 4.1 List ten integers */
#include <stdio.h>

int main(void)
{
  int count = 1;
  for( ; count <= 10 ; ++count)
    printf("\n%d", count);
  printf("\nWe have finished.\n");
  return 0;
}
```

This program will list the numbers from 1 to 10 on separate lines and then output this message:

```
We have finished.
```

The flow chart in Figure 4-3 illustrates the logic of this program.

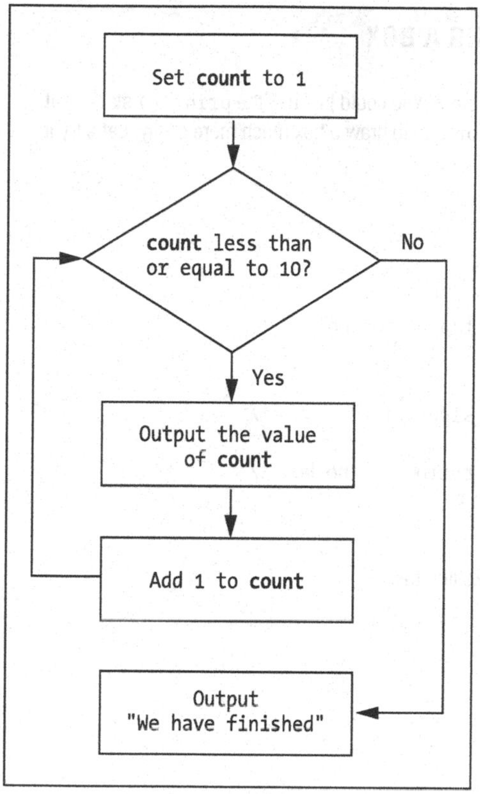

Figure 4-3. *The logic of Program 4.1*

In this example, it's easy to see what the variable count starts out as, so this code is quite OK. In general, though, unless the variable controlling the loop is initialized very close to the loop statement itself, it's better to initialize it in the first control expression. That way, there's less potential for error.

You can also declare the loop variable within the first loop control expression, in which case the variable is local to the loop and does not exist once the loop has finished. You could write the main() function like this:

```
int main(void)
{
  for(int count = 1 ; count <= 10 ; ++count)
    printf("\n%d", count);
  printf("\nWe have finished.\n");
  return 0;
}
```

Now count is declared within the first for loop expression. This means that count does not exist once the loop ends, so you could not output its value after the loop. When you really do need access to the loop control variable outside the loop, you just declare it in a separate statement preceding the loop, as in Program 4.1.

Let's try a slightly different example.

TRY IT OUT: DRAWING A BOX

Suppose that you want to draw a box on the screen using * characters. You could just use the printf() statement a lot of times, but the typing would be exhausting. You can use a for loop to draw a box much more easily. Let's try it:

```
/* Program 4.2 Drawing a box */
#include <stdio.h>

int main(void)
{
  printf("\n**************");           /* Draw the top of the box    */

  for(int count = 1 ; count <= 8 ; ++count)
    printf("\n*            *");         /* Draw the sides of the box  */

  printf("\n**************\n");         /* Draw the bottom of the box */
  return 0;
}
```

No prizes for guessing, but the output for this program looks like this:

```
**************
*            *
*            *
*            *
*            *
*            *
*            *
*            *
*            *
**************
```

How It Works

The program itself is really very simple. The first printf() statement outputs the top of the box to the screen:

```
  printf("\n**************");           /* Draw the top of the box    */
```

The next statement is the for loop:

```
  for(int count = 1 ; count <= 8 ; ++count)
    printf("\n*            *");   /* Draw the sides of the box  */
```

This repeats the printf() statement eight times to output the sides of the box. You probably understand this, but let's look again at how it works and pick up a bit more jargon. The loop control is the following:

```
for(int count = 1 ; count <= 8 ; ++count)
```

The operation of the loop is controlled by the three expressions that appear between the parentheses following the keyword for. The first expression is the following:

```
int count = 1
```

This creates and initializes the **loop control variable**, or **loop counter**, which in this case is an integer variable, count. You could have used other types of variables for this, but integers are convenient for the job. The next loop control expression is the following:

```
count <= 8
```

This is the **continuation condition** for the loop. This is checked *before* each loop iteration to see whether the loop should continue. If the expression is true, the loop continues. If it's false, the loop ends and execution continues with the statement following the loop. In this example, the loop continues as long as the variable count is less than or equal to 8. The last expression is the following:

```
++count
```

This statement increments the loop counter at the end of each loop iteration. The loop statement that outputs the sides of the box will therefore be executed eight times. After the eighth iteration, count will be incremented to 9 and the continuation condition will be false, so the loop will end.

Program execution will then continue by executing the statement that follows the loop:

```
printf("\n*************\n");    /* Draw the bottom of the box */
```

This outputs the bottom of the box on the screen.

■**Tip** Whenever you find yourself repeating something more than a couple of times, it's worth considering a loop. They'll usually save you time and memory.

General Syntax of the for Loop

The general pattern of the for loop is as follows:

```
for(starting_condition; continuation_condition ; action_per_iteration)
  Statement;

Next_statement;
```

The statement to be repeated is represented by Statement. In general, this could equally well be a block of statements (a group of statements) enclosed between a pair of braces.

The starting_condition usually (but not always) sets an initial value to a loop control variable. The loop control variable is typically, but not necessarily, a counter of some kind that tracks how often the loop has been repeated. You can also declare and initialize several variables of the same type here with the declarations separated by commas; in this case all the variables will be local to the loop and will not exist once the loop ends.

The continuation_condition is a logical expression evaluating to true or false. This determines whether the loop should continue to be executed. As long as this condition has the value true, the loop continues. It typically checks the value of the loop control variable, but any logical expression can be placed here, as long as you know what you're doing.

As you've already seen, the continuation_condition is tested at the beginning of the loop rather than at the end. This obviously makes it possible to have a for loop whose statements aren't executed at all if the continuation_condition starts out as false.

The action_per_iteration is executed at the end of each loop iteration and is usually (but again not necessarily) an increment or decrement of one or more loop control variables. Where several variables are modified, you separate the expression by commas. At each iteration of the loop, the statement or block of statements immediately following the for statement is executed. The loop is terminated, and execution continues with Next_statement as soon as the continuation_condition is false.

Here's an example of a loop with two variables declared in the first loop control condition:

```
for(int i = 1, j = 2 ; i<=5 ; i++, j = j+2)
  printf("\n %5d", i*j);
```

The output produced by this fragment will be the values 2, 8, 18, 32, and 50 on separate lines.

More on the Increment and Decrement Operators

Now that you've seen an increment operator in action, let's delve a little deeper and find out what else these increment and decrement operators can do. They're both **unary operators**, which means that they're used with only one operand. You know they're used to increment (increase) or decrement (decrease) a value stored in a variable of one of the integer types by 1.

The Increment Operator

Let's start with the increment operator. It takes the form ++ and adds 1 to the variable it acts on. For example, assuming your variables are of type int, the following three statements all have exactly the same effect:

```
count = count + 1;
count += 1;
++count;
```

Each of these statement increments the variable count by 1. The last form is clearly the most concise.

Thus, if you declare a variable count and initialize it to 1

```
int count = 1;
```

and then you repeat the following statement six times in a loop

```
++count;
```

by the end of the loop, count will have a value of 7.

You can also use the increment operator in an expression. The action of this operator in an expression is to increment the value of the variable and then use the incremented value in the expression. For example, suppose count has the value 5 and you execute the statement

```
total = ++count + 6;
```

The variable count will be incremented to 6 and the variable total will be assigned the value 12, so the one statement modifies two variables. The variable count, with the value 5, has 1 added to it, making it 6, and then 6 is added to this value to produce 12 for the expression on the right side of the assignment operator. This value is stored in total.

CHAPTER 4 ■ LOOPS

The Prefix and Postfix Forms of the Increment Operator

Up to now you've written the operator ++ in front of the variable to which it applies. This is called the **prefix form**. The operator can also be written *after* the variable to which it applies, and this is referred to as the **postfix form**. In this case, the effect is significantly different from the prefix form when it's used in an expression. If you write count++ in an expression, the incrementing of the variable count occurs *after* its value has been used. This sounds more complicated than it is.

Let's look at a variation on the earlier example:

```
total = 6 + count++;
```

With the same initial value of 5 for count, total is assigned the value 11. This is because the initial value of count is used to evaluate the expression on the right of the assignment (6 + 5). The variable count is incremented by 1 after its value has been used in the expression. The preceding statement is therefore equivalent to these two statements:

```
total = 6 + count;
++count;
```

Note, however, that when you use the increment operator in a statement by itself (as in the preceding second statement, which increments count), it doesn't matter whether you write the prefix or the postfix version of the operator. They both have the same effect.

Where you have an expression such as a++ + b! or worse, a+++b! it's less than obvious what is meant to happen or what the compiler will achieve. The expressions are actually the same, but in the second case you might really have meant a + ++b, which is different because it evaluates to one more than the other two expressions.

For example, if a = 10 and b = 5, then in the statement

```
x = a++ + b;
```

x will have the value 15 (from 10 + 5) because a is incremented after the expression is evaluated. The next time you use the variable a, however, it will have the value 11.

On the other hand, if you execute the following statement, with the same initial values for a and b

```
y = a + (++b);
```

y will have the value 16 (from 10 + 6) because b is incremented before the statement is evaluated.

It's a good idea to use parentheses in all these cases to make sure there's no confusion. So you should write these statements as follows:

```
x = (a++) + b;
y = a + (++b);
```

The Decrement Operator

The decrement operator works in much the same way as the increment operator. It takes the form -- and subtracts 1 from the variable it acts on. It's used in exactly the same way as ++. For example, assuming the variables are of type int, the following three statements all have exactly the same effect:

```
count = count - 1;
count -= 1;
--count;
```

They each decrement the variable count by 1. For example, if count has the value 10, then the statement

```
total = --count + 6;
```

results in the variable total being assigned the value 15 (from 9 + 6). The variable count, with the initial value of 10, has 1 subtracted from it so that its value is 9. Then 6 is added to the new value, making the value of the expression on the right of the assignment operator 15.

Exactly the same rules that I discussed in relation to the prefix and postfix forms of the increment operator apply to the decrement operator. For example, if count has the initial value 5, then the statement

```
total = --count + 6;
```

results in total having the value 10 (from 4 + 6) assigned, whereas

```
total = 6 + count-- ;
```

sets the value of total to 11 (from 6 + 5). Both operators are usually applied to integers, but you'll also see, in later chapters, how they can be applied to certain other data types in C.

The for Loop Revisited

Now that you understand a bit more about ++ and --, let's move on with another example that uses a loop.

TRY IT OUT: SUMMING NUMBERS

This is a more useful and interesting program than drawing a box with asterisks (unless what you really need is a box drawn with asterisks). Have you ever wanted to know what all the house numbers on your street totaled? Here you're going to read in an integer value and then use a for loop to sum all the integers from 1 to the value that was entered:

```
/* Program 4.3   Sum the integers from 1 to a user-specified number */
#include <stdio.h>

int main(void)
{
  long sum = 0L;                    /* Stores the sum of the integers       */
  int count = 0;                    /* The number of integers to be summed */

  /* Read the number of integers to be summed */
  printf("\nEnter the number of integers you want to sum: ");
  scanf(" %d", &count);

  /* Sum integers from 1 to count */
  for(int i = 1 ; i <= count ; i++)
    sum += i;

  printf("\nTotal of the first %d numbers is %ld\n", count, sum);
  return 0;
}
```

The typical output you should get from this program is the following:

```
Enter the number of integers you want to sum: 10

Total of the first 10 integers is 55
```

How It Works

You start by declaring and initializing two variables that you'll need during the calculation:

```
long sum = OL;              /* Stores the sum of the integers    */
int count = 0;              /* The number of integers to be summed */
```

You use sum to hold the final value of your calculations. You declare it as type long to allow the maximum total you can deal with to be as large an integer as possible. The variable count will store the integer that's entered as the number of integers to be summed, and you'll use this value to control the number of iterations in the for loop.

You deal with the input by means of the following statements:

```
printf("\nEnter the number of integers you want to sum: ");
scanf(" %d", &count);
```

After the prompt, you read in the integer that will define the sum required. If the user enters **4**, for instance, the program will compute the sum of 1, 2, 3, and 4.

The sum is calculated in the following loop:

```
for(int i = 1 ; i <= count ; i++)
  sum += i;
```

The loop variable i is declared and initialized to 1 by the starting condition in the for loop. On each iteration the value of i is added to sum, and then i is incremented so the values 1, 2, 3, and so on, up to the value stored in count, will be added to sum. The loop ends when the value of i exceeds the value of count.

As I've hinted by saying •not necessarily! in my descriptions of how the for loop is controlled, there is a lot of flexibility about what you can use as control expressions. The next program demonstrates how this flexibility might be applied to shortening the previous example slightly.

TRY IT OUT: THE FLEXIBLE FOR LOOP

This example demonstrates how you can carry out a calculation within the third control expression in a for loop.

```
/* Program 4.4 Summing integers - compact version */
#include <stdio.h>

int main(void)
{
  long sum = OL;              /* Stores the sum of the integers    */
  int count = 0;             /* The number of integers to be summed */
```

```
/* Read the number of integers to be summed */
printf("\nEnter the number of integers you want to sum: ");
scanf(" %d", &count);

/* Sum integers from 1 to count */
for(int i = 1 ; i<= count ; sum += i++ );

printf("\nTotal of the first %d numbers is %ld\n", count, sum);
return 0;
}
```

Typical output would be the following:

```
Enter the number of integers you want to sum: 6

Total of the first 6 numbers is 21
```

How It Works

This program will execute exactly the same as the previous program. The only difference is that you've placed the operation that accumulates the sum in the third control expression for the loop:

```
for(int i = 1 ; i<= count ; sum += i++ );
```

The loop statement is empty: it's just the semicolon after the closing parenthesis. This expression adds the value of i to sum and then increments i ready for the next iteration. It works this way because you've used the postfix form of the increment operator. If you use the prefix form here, you'll get the wrong answer, because the total in sum will include the number count+1 from the first iteration of the loop, instead of just count.

Modifying the for Loop Variable

Of course, you aren't limited to incrementing the loop control variable by 1. You can change it by any value, positive or negative. You could sum the first n integers backward if you wish, as in the following example:

```
/* Program 4.5 Summing integers backward */
#include <stdio.h>
int main(void)
{
  long sum = 0L;                    /* Stores the sum of the integers    */
  int count = 0;                    /* The number of integers to be summed */

  /* Read the number of integers to be summed */
  printf("\nEnter the number of integers you want to sum: ");
  scanf(" %d", &count);

  /* Sum integers from count to 1 */
  for(int i = count ; i >= 1 ; sum += i--);

  printf("\nTotal of the first %d numbers is %ld\n", count, sum);
  return 0;
}
```

This produces the same output as the previous example. The only change is in the loop control expressions. The loop counter is initialized to count, rather than to 1, and it's *decremented* on each iteration. The effect is to add the values count, count-1, count-2, and so on, down to 1. Again, if you used the prefix form, the answer would be wrong, because you would start with adding count-1 instead of just count.

Just to keep any mathematically inclined readers happy, I should mention that it's quite unnecessary to use a loop to sum the first *n* integers. The following tidy little formula for the sum of the integers from 1 to *n* will do the trick much more efficiently:

```
n*(n+1)/2
```

However, it wouldn't teach you much about loops, would it?

A for Loop with No Parameters

As I've already mentioned, you have no obligation to put any parameters in the for loop statement at all. The minimal for loop looks like this:

```
for( ;; )
  statement;
```

Here, as previously, statement could also be a block of statements enclosed between braces, and in this case it usually will be. Because the condition for continuing the loop is absent, as is the initial condition and the loop increment, the loop will continue indefinitely. As a result, unless you want your computer to be indefinitely doing nothing, statement must contain the means of exiting from the loop. To stop repeating the loop, the loop body must contain two things: a test of some kind to determine whether the condition for ending the loop has been reached, and a statement that will end the current loop iteration and continue execution with the statement following the loop.

The break Statement in a Loop

You encountered the break statement in the context of the switch statement in Chapter 3. Its effect was to stop executing the code within the switch block and continue with the first statement following the switch. The break statement works in essentially the same way within the body of a loop! any kind of loop. For instance

```
char answer = 0;
for( ;; )
{
  /* Code to read and process some data */
  printf("Do you want  to enter some more(y/n): ");
  scanf("%c", &answer);
  if(tolower(answer) == 'n')
    break;                            /* Go to statement after the loop */
}
/* Statement after the loop */
```

Here you have a loop that will execute indefinitely. The scanf() statement reads a character into answer, and if the character entered is **n** or **N**, the break statement will be executed. The effect is to stop executing the loop and to continue with the first statement following the loop. Let's see this in action in another example.

TRY IT OUT: A MINIMAL FOR LOOP

This example computes the average of an arbitrary number of values:

```c
/* Program 4.6 The almost indefinite loop - computing an average */
#include <stdio.h>
#include <ctype.h>              /* For tolower() function */

int main(void)
{
  char answer = 'N';          /* Records yes or no to continue the loop */
  double total = 0.0;         /* Total of values entered              */
  double value = 0.0;         /* Value entered                        */
  int count = 0;              /* Number of values entered             */

  printf("\nThis program calculates the average of"
                              " any number of values.");

  for( ;; )                   /* Indefinite loop */
  {
    printf("\nEnter a value: ");   /* Prompt for the next value */
    scanf(" %lf", &value);         /* Read the next value       */
    total += value;                /* Add value to total        */
    ++count;                       /* Increment count of values */

    /* check for more input */
    printf("Do you want to enter another value? (Y or N): ");
    scanf(" %c", &answer);         /* Read response Y or N    */

    if(tolower(answer) == 'n')     /* look for any sign of no */
      break;                       /* Exit from the loop      */
  }
  /* output the average to 2 decimal places */
  printf("\nThe average is %.2lf\n", total/count );
  return 0;
}
```

Typical output from this program is the following:

```
This program calculates the average of any number of values.
Enter a value: 2.5
Do you want to enter another value? (Y or N): y

Enter a value: 3.5
Do you want to enter another value? (Y or N): y

Enter a value: 6
Do you want to enter another value? (Y or N): n

The average is 4.00
```

How It Works

The general logic of the program is illustrated in Figure 4-4.

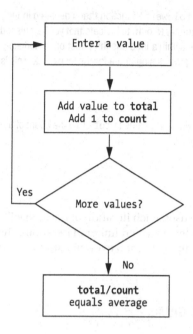

Figure 4-4. *Basic logic of the program*

You've set up the loop to continue indefinitely because the for loop has no end condition specified—or indeed any loop control expressions:

```
for( ;; )                          /* Indefinite loop */
```

Therefore, so far as the loop control is concerned, the block of statements enclosed between the braces will be repeated indefinitely.

You display a prompt and read an input value in the loop with these statements:

```
printf("\nEnter a value: ");       /* Prompt for the next value */
scanf(" %lf", &value);             /* Read the next value       */
```

Next, you add the value entered to your variable total:

```
total += value;                    /* Add value to total        */
```

You then increment the count of the number of values:

```
++count;                           /* Increment count of values */
```

Having read a value and added it to the total, you check with the user to see if more input is to be entered:

```
/* check for more input */
printf("Do you want to enter another value? (Y or N): ");
scanf(" %c", &answer);             /* Read response Y or N      */
```

This prompts for either **Y** or **N** to be entered. The character entered is checked in the if statement:

```
if(tolower(answer) == 'n')        /* look for any sign of no */
   break;                         /* Exit from the loop      */
```

The character stored in answer is converted to lowercase by the `tolower()` function that's declared in the `<ctype.h>` header file, so you only need to test for n. If you enter a character **N**, or **n**, to indicate that you've finished entering data, the break statement will be executed. Executing break within a loop has the effect of immediately ending the loop so that execution continues with the statement following the closing brace for the loop block. This is the statement:

```
printf("\nThe average is %.2lf\n", total/count);
```

This statement calculates the average of the values entered by dividing the value in total by the count of the number of values. The result is then displayed.

Limiting Input Using a for Loop

You can use a for loop to limit the amount of input from the user. Each iteration of the loop will permit some input to be entered. When the loop has completed a given number of iterations, the loop ends so no more data can be entered. You can write a simple program to demonstrate how this can work. The program will implement a guessing game.

TRY IT OUT: A GUESSING GAME

This program is going to get the user to guess the number that the program has picked as the lucky number. It uses one for loop and plenty of if statements. I've also thrown in a conditional operator, just to make sure you haven't forgotten how to use it!

```
/* Program 4.7  A Guessing Game */
#include <stdio.h>

int main(void)
{
  int chosen = 15;                  /* The lucky number           */
  int guess = 0;                    /* Stores a guess             */
  int count = 3;                    /* The maximum number of tries */

  printf("\nThis is a guessing game.");
  printf("\nI have chosen a number between 1 and 20"
                          " which you must guess.\n");

  for( ; count>0 ; --count)
  {
    printf("\nYou have %d tr%s left.", count, count == 1 ? "y" : "ies");
    printf("\nEnter a guess: ");    /* Prompt for a guess  */
    scanf("%d", &guess);            /* Read in a guess     */

    /* Check for a correct guess */
    if(guess == chosen)
    {
```

```
    printf("\nYou guessed it!\n");
        return 0;                          /* End the program    */
    }

    /* Check for an invalid guess */
    if(guess<1 || guess > 20)
        printf("I said between 1 and 20.\n ");
    else
        printf("Sorry. %d is wrong.\n", guess);
    }
    printf("\nYou have had three tries and failed. The number was %d\n",
                                                          chosen);

    return 0;
}
```

Some sample output would be the following:

```
This is a guessing game.
I have chosen a number between 1 and 20 which you must guess.

You have 3 tries left.
Enter a guess: 5
Sorry. 5 is wrong.

You have 2 tries left.
Enter a guess: 18
Sorry. 18 is wrong.

You have 1 try left.
Enter a guess: 7
Sorry. 7 is wrong.

You have had three tries and failed. The number was 15
```

How It Works

You first declare and initialize three variables of type int, chosen, guess, and count:

```
int chosen = 15;              /* The lucky number          */
int guess = 0;                /* Stores a guess            */
int count = 3;                /* The maximum number of tries */
```

These are to store, respectively, the number that's to be guessed, the number that's the user's guess, and the number of guesses the user is permitted. Notice that you've created a variable to store the chosen number. You could just have used the number 15 in the program, but doing it this way makes it much easier to alter the value of the number that the user must guess. It also makes it obvious what is happening in the code when you use the variable chosen.

You provide the user with an initial explanation of the program:

```
printf("\nThis is a guessing game.");
printf("\nI have chosen a number between 1 and 20"
                         " which you must guess.\n");
```

The number of guesses that can be entered is controlled by this loop:

```
for( ; count>0 ; --count)
  {
    ...
  }
```

All the operational details of the game are within this loop, which will continue as long as `count` is positive, so the loop will repeat `count` times.

There's a prompt for a guess to be entered, and the guess itself is read by these statements:

```
printf("\nYou have %d tr%s left.", count, count == 1 ? "y" : "ies");
printf("\nEnter a guess: ");       /* Prompt for a guess  */
scanf("%d", &guess);               /* Read in a guess     */
```

The first `printf()` looks a little complicated, but all it does is insert "y" after "tr" in the output when `count` is 1, and "ies" after "tr" in the output in all other cases. You must, after all, get your plurals right.

After reading a `guess` value using `scanf()`, you check whether it's correct with these statements:

```
/* Check for a correct guess */
if(guess == chosen)
{
  printf("\nYou guessed it!");
  return 0;                        /* End the program     */
}
```

If the guess is correct, you display a suitable message and execute the `return` statement. The `return` statement ends the function `main()`, and so the program ends. You'll learn more about the `return` statement when I discuss functions in greater detail in Chapter 8.

The program will reach the last check in the loop only if the guess is incorrect:

```
/* Check for an invalid guess */
if(guess<1 || guess > 20)
  printf("I said between 1 and 20.\n ");
else
  printf("Sorry. %d is wrong.\n", guess);
```

This group of statements tests whether the value entered is within the prescribed limits. If it isn't, a message is displayed reiterating the limits. If it's a valid guess, a message is displayed to the effect that it's incorrect.

The loop ends after three iterations and thus three guesses. The statement after the loop is the following:

```
printf("\nYou have had three tries and failed. The number was %d\n",
                                                       chosen);
```

This will be executed only if all three guesses were wrong. It displays an appropriate message, revealing the number to be guessed, and then the program ends.

This program is designed so that you can easily change the value of the variable `chosen` and have endless fun. Well, endless fun for a short while, anyway.

Generating Pseudo-Random Integers

The previous example would have been much more entertaining if the number to be guessed could have been generated within the program so that it was different each time the program executed. Well, you can do that using the `rand()` function that's declared in the `<stdlib.h>` header file:

```
int chosen = 0;
chosen = rand();   /* Set to a random integer */
```

Each time you call the rand() function, it will return a random integer. The value will be from 0 to a maximum of RAND_MAX, the value of which is defined in <stdlib.h>. The integers generated by the rand() function are described as **pseudo-random** numbers because truly random numbers can arise only in natural processes and can't be generated algorithmically.

The sequence of numbers that's generated by the rand() function uses a starting seed number, and for a given seed the sequence will always be the same. If you use the function with the default seed value, as in the previous snippet, you'll always get exactly the same sequence, which won't make the game very challenging but is useful when you are testing a program. However, C provides another standard function, srand(), which you can call to initialize the sequence with a particular seed that you pass as an argument to the function. This function is also declared in the <stdlib.h> header.

At first sight, this doesn't seem to get you much further with the guessing game, as you now need to generate a different seed each time the program executes. Yet another library function can help with this: the time() function that's declared in the <time.h> header file. The time() function returns the number of seconds that have elapsed since January 1, 1970, as an integer, and because time always marches on, you can get a different value returned by the time() function each time the program executes. The time() function requires an argument to be specified that you'll specify as NULL. NULL is a symbol that's defined in <stdlib.h>, but I'll defer further discussion of it until Chapter 7.

Thus to get a different sequence of pseudo-random numbers each time a program is run, you can use the following statements:

```
srand(time(NULL));              /* Use clock value as starting seed */
int chosen = 0;
chosen = rand();                /* Set to a random integer 0 to RAND_MAX */
```

The value of the upper limit, RAND_MAX, is likely to be quite large! often the maximum value that can be stored as type int. When you need a more limited range of values, you can scale the value returned by rand() to provide values within the range that you want. Suppose you want to obtain values in a range from 0 up to, but not including, limit. The simplest approach to obtaining values in this range is like this:

```
srand(time(NULL));              /* Use clock value as starting seed   */
int limit = 20.0;               /* Upper limit for pseudo-random values */
int chosen = 0;
chosen = rand()%limit;          /* 0 to limit-1 inclusive             */
```

Of course, if you want numbers from 1 to limit, you can write this:

```
chosen = 1+rand()%limit;        /* 1 to limit   inclusive             */
```

This works reasonably well with the implementation of rand() in my compiler and library. However, this isn't a good way in general of limiting the range of numbers produced by a pseudo-random number generator. This is because you're essentially chopping off the high-order bits in the value that's returned and implicitly assuming that the bits that are left will also represent random values. This isn't necessarily the case.

You could try using rand() in a variation of the previous example:

```
/*  Program 4.7A  A More Interesting Guessing Game */
#include <stdio.h>
#include <stdlib.h>              /* For rand() and srand() */
#include <time.h>                /* For time() function    */
```

```
int main(void)
{
  int chosen = 0;              /* The lucky number                 */
  int guess = 0;               /* Stores a guess                   */
  int count = 3;               /* The maximum number of tries      */
  int limit = 20;              /* Upper limit for pseudo-random values */


  srand(time(NULL));           /* Use clock value as starting seed */
  chosen = 1 + rand()%limit;   /* Random int 1 to limit            */

  printf("\nThis is a guessing game.");
  printf("\nI have chosen a number between 1 and 20"
                          " which you must guess.\n");


  for( ; count>0 ; --count)
  {
    printf("\nYou have %d tr%s left.", count, count == 1 ? "y" : "ies");
    printf("\nEnter a guess: ");       /* Prompt for a guess */
    scanf("%d", &guess);               /* Read in a guess    */

    /* Check for a correct guess */
    if(guess == chosen)
    {
      printf("\nYou guessed it!\n");
      return 0;                        /* End the program */
    }

    /* Check for an invalid guess */
    if(guess<1 || guess > 20)
      printf("I said between 1 and 20.\n ");
    else
      printf("Sorry. %d is wrong.\n", guess);
  }
  printf("\nYou have had three tries and failed. The number was %ld\n",
                                                    chosen);
  return 0;
}
```

This program should give you a different number to guess most of the time.

More for Loop Control Options

You've seen how you can increment or decrement the loop counter by 1 using the ++ and -- operators. You can increment or decrement the loop counter by any amount that you wish. Here's an example of how you can do this:

```
long sum = 0L;
for(int n = 1 ; n<20 ; n += 2)
  sum += n;
printf("Sum is %ld", sum);
```

The loop in the preceding code fragment sums all the odd integers from 1 to 20. The third control expression increments the loop variable n by 2 on each iteration. You can write any expression here, including any assignment. For instance, to sum every seventh integer from 1 to 1000, you could write the following loop:

```
for(int n = 1 ; n<1000 ; n = n+7)
  sum += n;
```

Now the third loop control expression increments n by 7 at the end of each iteration, so you'll get the sum 1 + 8 + 15 + 22 + and so on up to 1000.

You aren't limited to a single loop control expression. You could rewrite the loop in the first code fragment, summing the odd numbers from 1 to 20, like this:

```
for(int n = 1 ; n<20 ; sum += n, n += 2)
  ;
```

Now the third control expression consists of two expressions separated by a comma. These will execute in sequence at the end of each loop iteration. So first the expression

```
sum +=n
```

will add the current value of n to sum. Next, the second expression

```
n += 2
```

will increment n by 2. Because these expressions execute in sequence from left to right, you must write them in the sequence shown. If you reverse the sequence, the result will be incorrect.

You aren't limited to just two expressions either. You can have as many expressions here as you like, as long as they're separated by commas. Of course, you should make use of this only when there is a distinct advantage in doing so. Too much of this can make your code hard to understand.

The first and second control expressions can also consist of several expressions separated by commas, but the need for this is quite rare.

Floating-Point Loop Control Variables

The loop control variable can also be a floating-point variable. Here's a loop to sum the fractions from 1/1 to 1/10:

```
double sum = 0.0;
for(double x = 1.0 ; x<11 ; x += 1.0)
  sum += 1.0/x;
```

You'll find this sort of thing isn't required very often. It's important to remember that fractional values often don't have an exact representation in floating-point form, so it's unwise to rely on equality as the condition for ending a loop, for example

```
for(double x = 0.0 ; x != 2.0 ; x+= 0.2)      /* Indefinite loop!!! */
  printf("\nx = %.2lf",x);
```

This loop is supposed to output the values of x from 0.0 to 2.0 in steps of 0.2, so there should be 11 lines of output. Because 0.2 doesn't have an exact representation as a binary floating-point value, x never has the value 2.0, so this loop will take over your computer and run indefinitely (until you stop it; use Ctrl+C under Microsoft Windows).

The while Loop

That's enough of the for loop. Now that you've seen several examples of for loops, let's look at a different kind of loop: the while loop. With a while loop, the mechanism for repeating a set of statements allows execution to continue for as long as a specified logical expression evaluates to true. In English, I could represent this as follows:

```
While this condition is true
   Keep on doing this
```

Alternatively, here's a particular example:

```
While you are hungry
   Eat sandwiches
```

This means that you ask yourself •Am I hungry?! before eating the next sandwich. If the answer is yes, then you eat a sandwich and then ask yourself •Am I still hungry?! You keep eating sandwiches until the answer is no, at which point you go on to do something else! drink some coffee, maybe. One word of caution: enacting a loop in this way yourself is probably best done in private.

The general syntax for the while loop is as follows:

```
while( expression )
   Statement1;

Statement2;
```

As always, Statement1 could be a block of statements.
The logic of the while loop is shown in Figure 4-5.

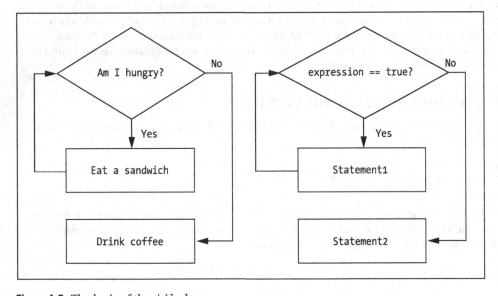

Figure 4-5. *The logic of the while loop*

Just like the for loop, the condition for continuation of the while loop is tested at the start, so if expression starts out false, none of the loop statements will be executed. If you answer the first question ••No, I'm not hungry,! then you don't get to eat any sandwiches at all, and you move straight on to the coffee.

TRY IT OUT: USING THE WHILE LOOP

The while loop looks fairly straightforward, so let's go right into applying it in that old favorite, humming and summing house numbers:

```
/* Program 4.8 While programming and summing integers */
#include <stdio.h>

int main(void)
{
  long sum = 0L;                /* The sum of the integers          */
  int i = 1;                    /* Indexes through the integers     */
  int count = 0;                /* The count of integers to be summed */

  /* Get the count of the number of integers to sum */
  printf("\nEnter the number of integers you want to sum: ");
  scanf(" %d", &count);

  /* Sum the integers from 1 to count */
  while(i <= count)
    sum += i++;

  printf("Total of the first %d numbers is %ld\n", count, sum);
  return 0;
}
```

Typical output from this program is the following:

```
Enter the number of integers you want to sum: 7
Total of the first 7 numbers is 28
```

How It Works

Well, really this works pretty much the same as when you used the for loop. The only aspect of this example worth discussing is the while loop:

```
while(i <= count)
  sum += i++;
```

The loop contains a single statement action that accumulates the total in sum. This continues to be executed with i values up to and including the value stored in count. Because you have the postfix increment operator here (the ++ comes after the variable), i is incremented *after* its value is used to compute sum on each iteration. What the statement really means is this:

```
sum += i;
i++;
```

So the value of sum isn't affected by the increment of i until the next loop iteration.

I'll try to explain this in relatively plain English, so that you understand what's really happening.

- *Entering the* while *loop*: When you enter the while loop, i is 1 and count has the value corresponding to whatever you've typed in (let's say **3**). When the loop starts, you first check whether i <= count is true. In this case, it amounts to 1<=3, which is true, so you execute the loop statement:

```
sum += i++;
```

- *First time through the* while *loop:* First, the value of i (which is 1) is added to the variable sum. The variable sum was equal to 0, so it's now equal to 1. Because you've used the postfix increment operator, the variable i is incremented after the value to be stored in sum has been calculated. So i is now 2, and you return to the beginning of the loop. You check the while expression and see whether the value in i is still less than or equal to count. Because i is now 2, which is indeed less than 3, you execute the loop statement again.

- *Second time* through *the* while *loop*: In the second loop iteration, you add the new value of i (which is now 2) to the old value of sum (which is 1) and store the result in sum. The variable sum now equals 3. You add 1 to i so i now has the value 3, and you go back to the beginning of the loop to check whether the control expression is still true.

- *Third time through the* while *loop*: At this point i is equal to count, so you can still continue the loop. You add the new value of i (which is 3) to the old value of sum (which is also 3) and store the result in sum, which now has the value 6. You add 1 to i, so i now has the value 4, and you go back to check the loop expression once more.

- *Last time through the* while *loop*: Now i, which has the value 4, is greater than count, which has the value 3, so the expression i <= count is false, and you leave the loop.

This example used the increment operator as postfix. How could you change the preceding program to use the prefix form of the ++ operator? Have a try and see whether you can work it out. The answer is given in the next section.

Using ++ As a Prefix Operator

The obvious bit of code that will change will be the while loop:

```
sum += ++i;
```

Try just changing this statement in Program 4.8. If you run the program now you get the wrong answer:

```
Enter the number of integers you want to sum: 3
Total of the first 3 numbers is 9
```

This is because the ++ operator is adding 1 to the value of i before it stores the value in sum. The variable i starts at 1 and is increased to 2 on the first iteration, whereupon that value is added to sum.

To make the first loop iteration work correctly, you need to start i off as 0. This means that the first increment would set the value of i to 1, which is what you want. So you must change the declaration of i to the following:

```
int i = 0;
```

However, the program still doesn't work properly, because it continues doing the calculation until the value in i is greater than count, so you get one more iteration than you need. The alteration you need to fix this is to change the control expression so that the loop continues while i is less than but not equal to count:

```
while(i < count)
```

Now the program will produce the correct answer. This example should help you really understand postfixing and prefixing these operators.

Nested Loops

Sometimes you may want to place one loop inside another. You might want to count the number of occupants in each house on a street. You step from house to house, and for each house you count the number of occupants. Going through all the houses could be an outer loop, and for each iteration of the outer loop you would have an inner loop that counts the occupants.

The simplest way to understand how a nested loop works is to look at a simple example.

TRY IT OUT: USING NESTED LOOPS

To demonstrate a nested loop, you'll use a simple example based on the summing integers program. Originally, you produced the sums of all the integers from 1 up to the value entered. Now for every house, you'll produce the sum of all the numbers from the first house, 1, up to the current house. If you look at the program output, it will become clearer.

```c
/* Program 4.9 Sums of integers step-by-step */
#include <stdio.h>

int main(void)
{
  long sum = 0L;                    /* Stores the sum of integers     */
  int count = 0;                    /* Number of sums to be calculated */

  /* Prompt for, and read the input count */
  printf("\nEnter the number of integers you want to sum: ");
  scanf(" %d", &count);

  for(int i = 1 ; i <= count ; i++)
  {
    sum = 0L;                       /* Initialize sum for the inner loop */

    /* Calculate sum of integers from 1 to i */
    for(int j = 1 ; j <= i ; j++)
      sum += j;

    printf("\n%d\t%ld", i, sum);    /* Output sum of 1 to i */
  }
  return 0;
}
```

You should see some output like this:

```
Enter the number of integers you want to sum: 5

1               1
2               3
3               6
4               10
5               15
```

As you can see, if you enter **5**, the program calculates the sums of the integers from 1 to 1, from 1 to 2, from 1 to 3, from 1 to 4, and from 1 to 5.

How It Works

The program calculates the sum from 1 to each integer value, for all values from 1 up to the value of count that you enter. The important thing to grasp about this nested loop is that the inner loop completes all its iterations *for each iteration* of the outer loop. Thus, the outer loop sets up the value of i that determines how many times the inner loop will repeat:

```
for(int i = 1 ; i <= count ; i++)
{
  sum = OL;                              /* Initialize sum for the inner loop */

  /* Calculate sum of integers from 1 to i */
  for(int j = 1 ; j <= i ; j++)
    sum += j;

  printf("\n%d\t%ld", i, sum);          /* Output sum of 1 to i */
}
```

The outer loop starts off by initializing i to 1, and the loop is repeated for successive values of i up to count. For each iteration of the outer loop, and therefore for each value of i, sum is initialized to 0, the inner loop is executed, and the result displayed by the printf() statement. The inner loop accumulates the sum of all the integers from 1 to the current value of i:

```
/* Calculate sum of integers from 1 to i */
for(int j = 1 ; j <= i ; j++)
  sum += j;
```

Each time the inner loop finishes, the printf() to output the value of sum is executed. Control then goes back to the beginning of the outer loop for the next iteration.

Look at the output again to see the action of the nested loop. The first loop simply sets the variable sum to 0 each time around, and the inner loop adds up all the numbers from 1 to the current value of i. You could modify the nested loop to use a while loop for the inner loop and to produce output that would show what the program is doing a little more explicitly.

TRY IT OUT: NESTING A WHILE LOOP WITHIN A FOR LOOP

In the previous example you nested a for loop inside a for loop. In this example you'll nest a while loop inside a for loop.

```
/* Program 4.10 Sums of integers with a while loop nested in a for loop */
#include <stdio.h>

int main(void)
{
  long sum = 1L;                 /* Stores the sum of integers      */
  int j = 1;                     /* Inner loop control variable     */
  int count = 0;                 /* Number of sums to be calculated */
```

```
  /* Prompt for, and read the input count */
  printf("\nEnter the number of integers you want to sum: ");
  scanf(" %d", &count);

  for(int i = 1 ; i <= count ; i++)
  {
    sum = 1L;                       /* Initialize sum for the inner loop */
    j=1;                            /* Initialize integer to be added    */
    printf("\n1");

    /* Calculate sum of integers from 1 to i */
    while(j < i)
    {
      sum += ++j;
      printf("+%d", j);            /* Output +j - on the same line */
    }
    printf(" = %ld\n", sum);        /* Output  = sum  */
  }
  return 0;
}
```

This program produces the following output:

```
Enter the number of integers you want to sum: 5

1 = 1

1+2 = 3

1+2+3 = 6

1+2+3+4 = 10

1+2+3+4+5 = 15
```

How It Works

The differences are inside the outer loop:

```
  for(int i = 1 ; i <= count ; i++)
  {
    sum = 1L;                       /* Initialize sum for the inner loop */
    j=1;                            /* Initialize integer to be added    */
    printf("\n1");

    /* Calculate sum of integers from 1 to i */
    while(j < i)
    {
      sum += ++j;
      printf("+%d", j);            /* Output +j - on the same line */
    }
    printf(" = %ld\n", sum);        /* Output  = sum  */
  }
```

The outer loop control is exactly the same as before. The difference is what occurs during each iteration. The variable sum is initialized to 1 within the outer loop, because the while loop will add values to sum starting with 2. The integer to be added is stored in j, which is also initialized to 1. The first printf() in the outer loop just outputs a newline character followed by 1, the first integer in the set to be summed. The inner loop adds the integers from 2 up to the value of i. For each integer value in j that's added to sum, the printf() in the inner loop outputs +j on the same line as the 1 that was output first. Thus the inner loop will output +2, then +3, and so on for as long as j is less than i. Of course, for the first iteration of the outer loop, i is 1, so the inner loop will not execute at all, because j<i (1 < 1) is false from the beginning.

When the inner loop ends, the last printf() statement is executed. This outputs an equal sign followed by the value of sum. Control then returns to the beginning of the outer loop for the next iteration.

Nested Loops and the goto Statement

You've learned how you can nest one loop inside another, but it doesn't end there. You can nest as many loops one inside another as you want, for instance

```
for(int i = 0 ; i<10 ; ++i)
  for(int j = 0 ; j<20 ; ++k)      /* Loop executed 10 times          */
    for(int k = 0 ; k<30 ; ++k)    /* Loop executed 10x20 times       */
    {                              /* Loop body executed 10x20x30 times */
      /* Do something useful */
    }
```

The inner loop controlled by j will execute once for each iteration of the outer loop that is controlled by i. The innermost loop controlled by k will execute once for each iteration of the loop controlled by j. Thus the body of the innermost loop will be executed 6,000 times.

Occasionally with deeply nested loops like this you'll want to break out of all the nested loops from the innermost loop and then continue with the statement following the outermost loop. A break statement in the innermost loop will only break out of that loop, and execution will continue with the loop controlled by j. To escape the nested loops completely using break statements therefore requires quite complicated logic to break out of each level until you escape the outermost loop. This is one situation in which the goto can be very useful because it provides a way to avoid all the complicated logic. For example

```
for(int i = 0 ; i<10 ; ++i)
  for(int j = 0 ; j<20 ; ++k)      /* Loop executed 10 times          */
    for(int k = 0 ; k<30 ; ++k)    /* Loop executed 10x20 times       */
    {                              /* Loop body executed 10x20x30 times */
      /* Do something useful */
      if(must_escape)
        goto out;
    }
out: /*Statement following the nested loops */
```

This fragment presumes that must_escape can be altered within the innermost loop to signal that the whole nested loop should end. If the variable must_escape is true, you execute the goto statement to branch directly to the statement with the label out. So you have a direct exit from the complete nest of loops without any complicated decision-making in the outer loop levels.

The do-while Loop

The third type of loop is the do-while loop. Now you may be asking why you need this when you already have the for loop and the while loop. Well, there's actually a very subtle difference between the do-while loop and the other two. The test for whether the loop should continue is at the *end* of the loop so the loop statement or statement block always executes at least once.

The while loop tests at the beginning of the loop. So before any action takes place, you check the expression. Look at this fragment of code:

```
int number = 4;

while(number < 4)
{
  printf("\nNumber = %d", number);
  number++;
}
```

Here, you would never output anything. The control expression number < 4 is false from the start, so the loop block is never executed.

The do-while loop, however, works differently. You can see this if you replace the preceding while loop with a do-while loop and leave the rest of the statements the same:

```
int number = 4;

do
{
  printf("\nNumber = %d", number);
  number++;
}
while(number < 4);
```

Now when you execute this loop, you get number = 4 displayed. This is because the expression number < 4 is only checked at the end of the first iteration of the loop.

The general representation of the do-while loop is as follows:

```
do
  Statement;
while(expression);
```

Notice the semicolon after the while statement in a do-while loop. There isn't one in the while loop. As always, a block of statements between braces can be in place of Statement. In a do-while loop, if the value of expression is true (nonzero), the loop continues. The loop will exit only when the value of expression becomes false (zero). You can see how this works more clearly in Figure 4-6.

Here, you can see that you eat a sandwich *before* you check whether you're hungry. You'll always eat at least one sandwich so this loop is not to be used as part of a calorie-controlled diet.

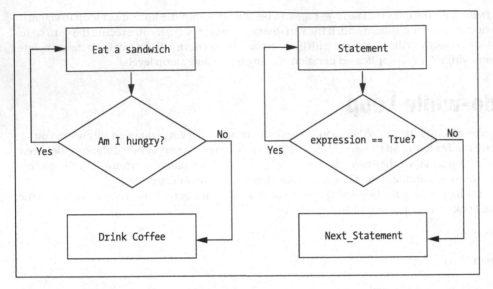

Figure 4-6. *Operation of the do-while loop*

TRY IT OUT: USING A DO-WHILE LOOP

You can try out the do-while loop with a little program that reverses the digits of a positive number:

```
/* Program 4.11 Reversing the digits */
#include <stdio.h>
int main(void)
{
  int number = 0;                    /* The number to be reversed */
  int rebmun = 0;                    /* The reversed number       */
  int temp = 0;                      /* Working storage           */

  /* Get the value to be reversed */
  printf("\nEnter a positive integer: ");
  scanf(" %d", &number);

  temp = number;                     /* Copy to working storage   */

  /* Reverse the number stored in temp */
  do
  {
    rebmun = 10*rebmun + temp % 10;  /* Add the rightmost digit      */
    temp = temp/10;                  /* Remove the rightmost digit */
  } while(temp);                     /* Continue while temp>0       */

  printf("\nThe number %d reversed is  %d rebmun ehT\n",
                                     number, rebmun );

  return 0;
}
```

The following is a sample of output from this program:

```
Enter a positive integer: 43

The number 43 reversed is 34 rebmun ehT
```

How It Works

The best way to explain what's going on here is to take you through a small example. Assume that the number 43 is entered by the user.

After reading the input integer and storing it in the variable number, the program copies the value in number to the variable temp:

```
temp = number;                          /* Copy to working storage  */
```

This is necessary, because the process of reversing the digits destroys the original value, and you want to output the original integer along with the reversed version.

The reversal of the digits is done in the do-while loop:

```
do
{
  rebmun = 10*rebmun + temp % 10;   /* Add the rightmost digit    */
  temp = temp/10;                   /* Remove the rightmost digit */
} while(temp);                      /* Continue while temp>0      */
```

The do-while loop is most appropriate here because any number will have at least one digit. You get the rightmost digit from the value stored in temp by using the modulus operator, %, to get the remainder after dividing by 10. Because temp originally contains 43, temp%10 will be 3. You assign the value of 10*rebmun + temp%10 to rebmun. Initially, the value of the variable rebmun is 0, so on the first iteration 3 is stored in rebmun.

You've now stored the rightmost digit of your input in rebmun, and so you now remove it from temp by dividing temp by 10. Because temp contains 43, temp/10 will be rounded down to 4.

At the end of the loop the while(temp) condition is checked, and because temp contains the value 4, it is true. Therefore, you go back to the top of the loop to begin another iteration.

■**Note** Remember, any nonzero integer will convert to true. The Boolean value false corresponds to zero.

This time, the value stored in rebmun will be 10 times rebmun, which is 30, plus the remainder when temp is divided by 10, which is 4, so the result is that rebmun becomes 34. You again divide temp by 10, so it will contain 0. Now when you arrive at the end of the loop iteration, temp is 0, which is false, so the loop finishes and you've reversed the number. You can see how this would work with numbers with more digits. An example of the output from the program running with a longer number entered is as follows:

```
Enter a positive integer: 1234

The number 1234 reversed is 4321 rebmun ehT
```

This form of loop is used relatively rarely, compared with the other two forms. Keep it in the back of your mind, though; when you need a loop that always executes at least once, the do-while loop delivers the goods.

The continue Statement

Sometimes a situation will arise in which you don't want to end a loop, but you want to skip the current iteration and continue with the next. The continue statement in the body of a loop does this and is written simply as follows:

```
continue;
```

Of course, continue is a keyword, so you must not use it for other purposes. Here's an example of how the continue statement works:

```
for(int day = 1; day<=7 ; ++day)
{
  if(day == 3)
    continue;
  /* Do something useful with day */
}
```

This loop will execute with values of day from 1 to 7. When day has the value 3, however, the continue statement will execute, and the rest of the current iteration is skipped and the loop continues with the next iteration when day will be 4.

You'll see more examples of using continue later in the book.

Designing a Program

It's time to try your skills on a bigger programming problem and to apply some of what you've learned in this chapter and the previous chapters. You'll also see a few new standard library functions that you're sure to find useful.

The Problem

The problem that you're going to solve is to write a game of Simple Simon. Simple Simon is a memory-test game. The computer displays a sequence of digits on the screen for a short period of time. You then have to memorize them, and when the digits disappear from the screen, you must enter exactly the same sequence of digits. Each time you succeed, you can repeat the process to get a longer list of digits for you to try. The objective is to continue the process for as long as possible.

The Analysis

The program must generate a sequence of integers between 0 and 9 and display the sequence on the screen for one second before erasing it. The player then has to try to enter the identical sequence of digits. The sequences gradually get longer until the player gets a sequence wrong. A score is then calculated based on the number of successful tries and the time taken, and the player is asked if he would like to play again.

The logic of the program is quite straightforward. You could express it in general terms in the flow chart shown in Figure 4-7.

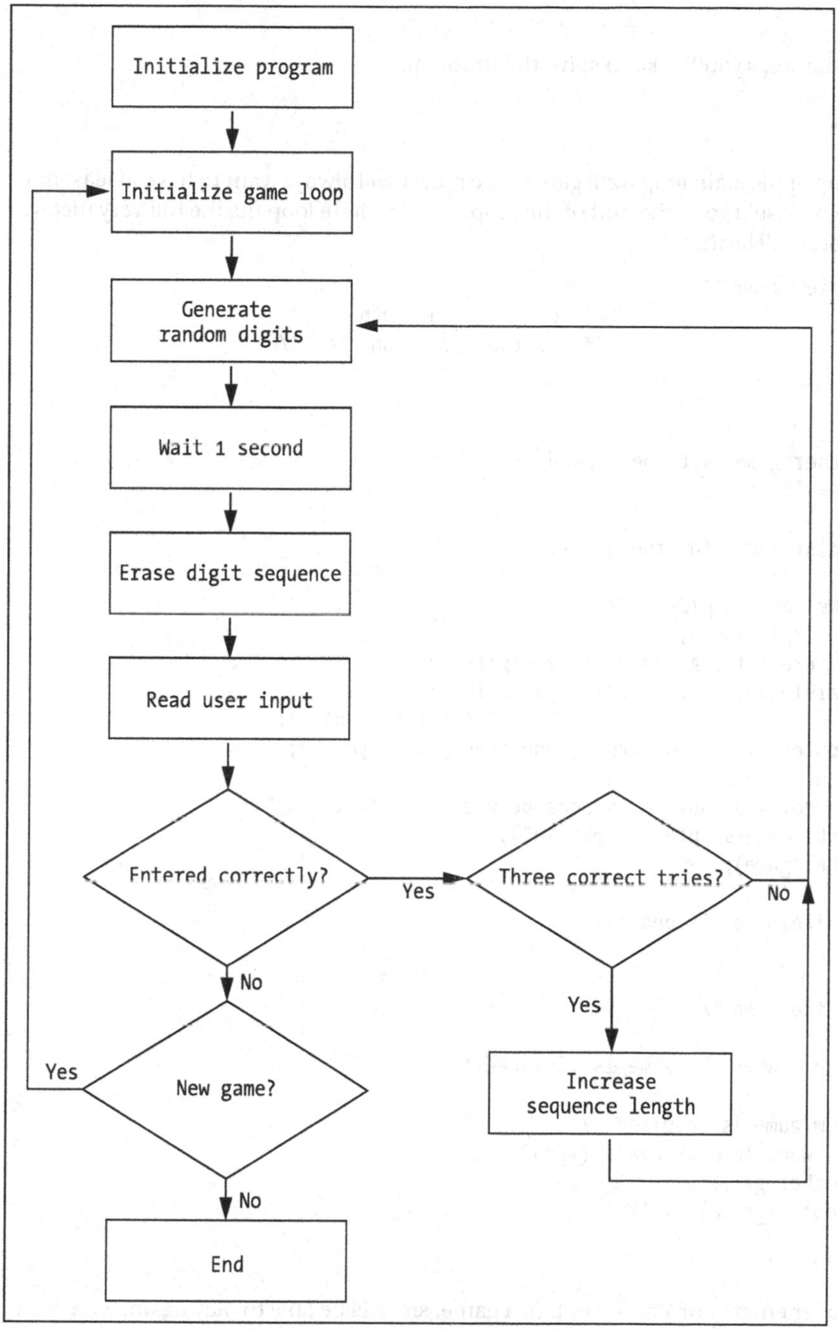

Figure 4-7. *The basic logic of the Simple Simon program*

Each box describes an action in the program, and the diamond shapes represent decisions. Let's use the flow chart as the basis for coding the program.

The Solution

This section outlines the steps you'll take to solve the problem.

Step 1

You can start by putting in the main loop for a game. The player will always want to have at least one game, so the loop check should go at the end of the loop. The do-while loop fits the bill very nicely. The initial program code will be this:

```
/* Program 4.12 Simple Simon */
#include <stdio.h>                    /* For input and output   */
#include <ctype.h>                    /* For toupper() function */

int main(void)
{
  /* Records if another game is to be played */
  char another_game = 'Y';

  /* Rest of the declarations for the program */

  /* Describe how the game is played */
  printf("\nTo play Simple Simon, ");
  printf("watch the screen for a sequence of digits.");
  printf("\nWatch carefully, as the digits are only displayed"
                                          " for a second! ");
  printf("\nThe computer will remove them, and then prompt you ");
  printf("to enter the same sequence.");
  printf("\nWhen you do, you must put spaces between the digits. \n");
  printf("\nGood Luck!\nPress Enter to play\n");
  scanf("%c", &another_game);

  /* One outer loop iteration is one game */
  do
  {
    /* Code to play the game */

    /* Output the score when the game is finished */

    /* Check if a new game is required */
    printf("\nDo you want to play again (y/n)? ");
    scanf("%c", &another_game);
  } while(toupper(another_game) == 'Y');
  return 0;
}
```

As long as the player enters y or Y at the end of a game, she will be able to play again. Note how you can automatically concatenate two strings in the printf() statement:

```
  printf("\nWatch carefully, as the digits are only displayed"
                                          " for a second! ");
```

This is a convenient way of splitting a long string over two or more lines. You just put each piece of the string between its own pair of double-quote characters, and the compiler will take care of assembling them into a single string.

Step 2

Next, you can add a declaration for another variable, called `correct`, that you'll need in the program to record whether the entry from the player is correct or not. You'll use this variable to control the loop that plays a single game:

```c
/* Program 4.12 Simple Simon */
#include <stdio.h>                    /* For input and output   */
#include <ctype.h>                    /* For toupper() function */
#include <stdbool.h>                  /* For bool, true, false */

int main(void)
{
  /* Records if another game is to be played */
  char another_game = 'Y';

  /* true if correct sequence entered, false otherwise */
  bool correct = true;

  /* Rest of the declarations for the program */

  /* Describe how the game is played */
  printf("\nTo play Simple Simon, ");
  printf("watch the screen for a sequence of digits.");
  printf("\nWatch carefully, as the digits are only displayed"
                                          " for a second! ");
  printf("\nThe computer will remove them, and then prompt you ");
  printf("to enter the same sequence.");
  printf("\nWhen you do, you must put spaces between the digits. \n");
  printf("\nGood Luck!\nPress Enter to play\n");
  scanf("%c", &another_game);

  /* One outer loop iteration is one game */
  do
  {
    correct = true;            /* By default indicates correct sequence entered */

    /* Other code to initialize the game */

    /* Inner loop continues as long as sequences are entered correctly */
    while(correct)
    {
      /* Play the game */
    }

    /* Output the score when the game is finished */

    /* Check if new game required*/
    printf("\nDo you want to play again (y/n)? ");
    scanf("%c", &another_game);
  } while(toupper(another_game) == 'Y');
  return 0;
}
```

You are using the _Bool variable, correct, here, but because you have added an #include directive for the <stdbool.h> header, you can use bool as the type name. The <stdbool.h> header also defines the symbols true and false to correspond to 1 and 0 respectively.

Caution The code will compile as it is, and you should compile it to check it out, but you should not run it yet. As you develop your own programs, you'll want to make sure that the code will at least compile along each step of the way. If you wrote all the program code in one attempt, you could end up with hundreds of errors to correct, and as you correct one problem, more may appear. This can be very frustrating. By checking out the program incrementally, you can minimize this issue, and the problems will be easier to manage. This brings us back to our current program. If you run this, your computer will be completely taken over by the program, because it contains an infinite loop. The reason for this is the inner while loop. The condition for this loop is always true because the loop doesn't do anything to change the value of correct. However, you'll be adding that bit of the program shortly.

Step 3

Now you have a slightly more difficult task to do: generating the sequence of random digits. There are two problems to be tackled here. The first is to generate the sequence of random digits. The second is to check the player's input against the computer-generated sequence.

The main difficulty with generating the sequence of digits is that the numbers have to be random. You've already seen that you have a standard function, rand(), available that returns a random integer each time you call it. You can get a random digit by just getting the remainder after dividing by 10, by using the % operator.

To ensure that you get a different sequence each time the program is executed, you'll also need to call srand() to initialize the sequence with the value returned by the time() function in the way you've already seen. Both the rand() and srand() functions require that you include the <tdlib.h> header file into the program, and the time() function requires an #include directive for <time.h>.

Now let's think about this a bit more. You'll need the sequence of random digits twice: once to display it initially before you erase it, and the second time to check against the player's input. You could consider saving the sequence of digits as an integer value of type unsigned long long. The problem with this is that the sequence could get very long if the player is good, and it could exceed the upper limit for integer values of type unsigned long long. There is another possible approach. The rand() function can produce the same sequence of numbers twice. All you need to do is to start the sequence each time with the same seed by calling srand(). This means that you won't need to store the sequence of numbers. You can just generate the same sequence twice.

Now let's add some more code to the program, which will generate the sequence of random digits and check them against what the player enters:

```
/* Program 4.12 Simple Simon */
#include <stdio.h>             /* For input and output    */
#include <ctype.h>            /* For toupper() function  */
#include <stdbool.h>         /* For bool, true, false   */
#include <stdlib.h>          /* For rand() and srand()  */
#include <time.h>            /* For time() function     */

int main(void)
{
    /* Records if another game is to be played */
    char another_game = 'Y';
```

```
/* true if correct sequence entered, false otherwise */
bool correct = true;

/* Number of sequences entered successfully */
int counter = 0;

int sequence_length = 0;       /* Number of digits in a sequence        */
time_t seed = 0;               /* Seed value for random number sequence */
int number = 0;                /* Stores an input digit                 */

/* Rest of the declarations for the program */

/* Describe how the game is played */
printf("\nTo play Simple Simon, ");
printf("watch the screen for a sequence of digits.");
printf("\nWatch carefully, as the digits are only displayed"
                                            " for a second! ");
printf("\nThe computer will remove them, and then prompt you ");
printf("to enter the same sequence.");
printf("\nWhen you do, you must put spaces between the digits. \n");
printf("\nGood Luck!\nPress Enter to play\n");
scanf("%c", &another_game);

/* One outer loop iteration is one game */
do
{
  correct = true;          /* By default indicates correct sequence entered  */
  counter = 0;             /* Initialize count of number of successful tries */
  sequence_length = 2;     /* Initial length of a digit sequence             */

  /* Other code to initialize the game */

  /* Inner loop continues as long as sequences are entered correctly */
  while(correct)
  {
    /* On every third successful try, increase the sequence length  */
    sequence_length += counter++%3 == 0;

    /* Set seed to be the number of seconds since Jan 1,1970        */
    seed = time(NULL);

    /* Generate a sequence of numbers and display the number        */
    srand((unsigned int)seed);     /* Initialize the random sequence */
    for(int i = 1; i <= sequence_length; i++)
      printf("%d ", rand() % 10); /* Output a random digit */

    /* Wait one second */

    /* Now overwrite the digit sequence */

    /* Prompt for the input sequence */
```

```
      /* Check the input sequence of digits against the original  */
      srand((unsigned int)seed);        /* Restart the random sequence  */
      for(int i = 1; i <= sequence_length; i++)
      {
        scanf("%d", &number);           /* Read an input number          */
        if(number != rand() % 10)       /* Compare against random digit */
        {
          correct = false;              /* Incorrect entry               */
          break;                        /* No need to check further...   */
        }
      }
      printf("%s\n", correct ? "Correct!" : "Wrong!");
    }

    /* Output the score when the game is finished */

    /* Check if new game required*/
    printf("\nDo you want to play again (y/n)? ");
    scanf("%c", &another_game);
  } while(toupper(another_game) == 'Y');
  return 0;
}
```

You've declared five new variables that you need to implement the while loop that will continue to execute as long as the player is successful. Each iteration of this loop displays a sequence that the player must repeat. The counter variable records the number of times that the player is successful, and sequence_length records the current length of a sequence of digits. Although you initialize these variables when you declare them, you must also initialize their values in the do-while loop to ensure that the initial conditions are set for every game. You declare a variable, seed, of type long, that you'll pass as an argument to srand() to initialize the random number sequence returned by the function rand(). The value for seed is obtained in the while loop by calling the standard library function time().

At the beginning of the while loop, you can see that you increase the value stored in sequence_length by adding the value of the expression counter++%3 == 0 to it. This expression will be 1 when the value of counter is a multiple of 3, and 0 otherwise. This will increment the sequence length by 1 after every third successful try. The expression also increments the value in counter by 1 after the expression has been evaluated.

There are some other things to notice about the code. The first is the conversion of seed from type time_t to type unsigned int when you pass it to the srand() function. This is because srand() requires that you use type unsigned int, but the time() function returns a value of type time_t. Because the number of seconds since January 1, 1970, is in excess of 800,000,000, you need a 4-byte variable to store it. Second, you obtain a digit between 0 and 9 by taking the remainder when you divide the random integer returned by rand() by 10. This isn't the best way of obtaining random digits in the range 0 to 9, but it's a very easy way and is adequate for our purposes. Although numbers generated by srand() are randomly distributed, the low order decimal digit for the numbers in the sequence are not necessarily random. To get random digits we should be dividing the whole range of values produced by srand() into ten segments and associating one of the digits 0 to 9 with each segment. The digit corresponding to a given pseudo-random number can then be selected based on the segment in which the number lies.

The sequence of digits is displayed by the for loop. The loop just outputs the low-order decimal digit of the value returned by rand(). You then have some comments indicating the other code that you still have to add that will delay the program for one second and then erase the sequence from the screen. This is followed by the code to check the sequence that was entered by the player. This reinitializes the random number–generating process by calling srand() with the same seed value that was used at the outset. Each digit entered is compared with the low-order digit of the value returned by the function rand(). If there's a discrepancy, correct is set to false so the while loop will end.

Of course, if you try to run this code as it is, the sequence won't be erased, so it isn't usable yet. The next step is to add the code to complete the while loop.

Step 4

You must now erase the sequence, after a delay of one second. How can you get the program to wait? One way is to use another standard library function. The library function clock() returns the time since the program started, in units of clock ticks. The <time.h> header file defines a symbol CLOCKS_PER_SEC that's the number of clock ticks in one second. All you have to do is wait until the value returned by the function clock() has increased by CLOCKS_PER_SEC, whereupon one second will have passed. You can do this by storing the value returned by the function clock() and then checking, in a loop, when the value returned by clock() is CLOCKS_PER_SEC more than the value that you saved. With a variable now to store the current time, the code for the loop would be as follows:

```
for( ;clock() - now < CLOCKS_PER_SEC; );          /* Wait one second */
```

You also need to decide how you can erase the sequence of computer-generated digits. This is actually quite easy. You can move to the beginning of the line by outputting the escape character '\r', which is a carriage return. All you then need to do is output a sufficient number of spaces to overwrite the sequence of digits. Let's fill out the code you need in the while loop:

```
/* Program 4.12 Simple Simon */
#include <stdio.h>                    /* For input and output   */
#include <ctype.h>                    /* For toupper() function */
#include <stdbool.h>                  /* For bool, true, false  */
#include <stdlib.h>                   /* For rand() and srand() */
#include <time.h>                     /* For time() and clock() */

int main(void)
{
  /* Records if another game is to be played */
  char another_game = 'Y';

  /* true if correct sequence entered, false otherwise */
  int correct = true;

  /* Number of sequences entered successfully      */
  int counter = 0;

  int sequence_length = 0;     /* Number of digits in a sequence        */
  time_t seed = 0;             /* Seed value for random number sequence */
  int number = 0;              /* Stores an input digit                 */
```

```c
/* Stores current time - seed for random values */
time_t now = 0;
/* Rest of the declarations for the program */

/* Describe how the game is played */
printf("\nTo play Simple Simon, ");
printf("watch the screen for a sequence of digits.");
printf("\nWatch carefully, as the digits are only displayed"
                                        " for a second! ");
printf("\nThe computer will remove them, and then prompt you ");
printf("to enter the same sequence.");
printf("\nWhen you do, you must put spaces between the digits. \n");
printf("\nGood Luck!\nPress Enter to play\n");
scanf("%c", &another_game);

/* One outer loop iteration is one game */
do
{
  correct = true;          /* By default indicates correct sequence entered */
  counter = 0;             /* Initialize count of number of successful tries */
  sequence_length = 2;     /* Initial length of a digit sequence            */

  /* Other code to initialize the game */

  /* Inner loop continues as long as sequences are entered correctly */
  while(correct)
  {
    /* On every third successful try, increase the sequence length */
    sequence_length += counter++%3 == 0;

    /* Set seed to be the number of seconds since Jan 1,1970     */
    seed = time(NULL);

    now = clock();          /* record start time for sequence */

    /* Generate a sequence of numbers and display the number */
    srand((unsigned int)seed);      /* Initialize the random sequence */
    for(int i = 1; i <= sequence_length; i++)
      printf("%d ", rand() % 10);   /* Output a random digit            */

    /* Wait one second */
    for( ;clock() - now < CLOCKS_PER_SEC; );

    /* Now overwrite the digit sequence */
    printf("\r");           /* go to beginning of the line */
    for(int i = 1; i <= sequence_length; i++)
      printf("  ");          /* Output two spaces            */

    if(counter == 1)        /* Only output message for the first try */
      printf("\nNow you enter the sequence  - don't forget"
                                        " the spaces\n");
    else
      printf("\r");          /* Back to the beginning of the line     */
```

```
    /* Check the input sequence of digits against the original  */
    srand((unsigned int)seed);          /* Restart the random sequence  */
    for(int i = 1; i <= sequence_length; i++)
    {
      scanf("%d", &number);              /* Read an input number        */
      if(number != rand() % 10)          /* Compare against random digit */
      {
        correct = false;                 /* Incorrect entry             */
        break;                           /* No need to check further... */
      }
    }
    printf("%s\n", correct ? "Correct!" : "Wrong!");
  }

  /* Output the score when the game is finished */

  /* Check if new game required*/
  printf("\nDo you want to play again (y/n)? ");
  scanf("%c", &another_game);
} while(toupper(another_game) == 'Y');
return 0;
}
```

You record the time returned by clock() before you output the sequence. The for loop that's executed when the sequence has been displayed continues until the value returned by clock() exceeds the time recorded in now by CLOCKS_PER_SEC, which of course will be one second.

Because you haven't written a newline character to the screen at any point when you displayed the sequence, you're still on the same line when you complete the output of the sequence. You can move the cursor back to the start of the line by executing a carriage return without a linefeed, and outputting "\r" does just that. You then output two spaces for each digit that was displayed, thus overwriting each of them with blanks. Immediately following that, you have a prompt for the player to enter the sequence that was displayed. You output this message only the first time around; otherwise it gets rather tedious. On the second and subsequent tries, you just back up to the beginning of the now blank line, ready for the user's input.

Step 5

All that remains is to generate a score to display, once the player has gotten a sequence wrong. You'll use the number of sequences completed and the number of seconds it took to complete them to calculate this score. You can arbitrarily assign 100 points to each digit correctly entered and divide this by the number of seconds the game took. This means the faster the player is, the higher the score, and the more sequences the player enters correctly, the higher the score.

Actually, there's also one more problem with this program that you need to address. If one of the numbers typed by the player is wrong, the loop exits and the player is asked if he wants to play again. However, if the digit in error isn't the last digit, you could end up with the next digit entered as the answer to the question •Do you want to play again (y/n)?! because these digits will still be in the keyboard buffer. What you need to do is remove any information that's still in the keyboard buffer. So there are two problems: first, how to address the keyboard buffer, and second, how to clean out the buffer.

■**Note** The **keyboard buffer** is memory that's used to store input from the keyboard. The scanf() function looks in the keyboard buffer for input rather than getting it directly from the keyboard itself.

With standard input and output! that is, from the keyboard and to the screen! there are actually two buffers: one for input and one for output. The standard input and output streams are called stdin and stdout respectively. So to identify the input buffer for the keyboard you just use the name stdin. Now that you know how to identify the buffer, how do you remove the information in it? Well, there's a standard library function, fflush(), for clearing out buffers. Although this function tends to be used for files, which I'll cover later in the book, it will actually work for any buffer at all. You simply tell the function which stream buffer you want cleared out by passing the name of the stream as the argument. So to clean out the contents of the input buffer, you simply use this statement:

```
fflush(stdin);                        /* Flush the stdin buffer */
```

Here's the complete program, which includes calculating the scores and flushing the input buffer:

```
/* Program 4.12 Simple Simon */
#include <stdio.h>              /* For input and output    */
#include <ctype.h>             /* For toupper() function */
#include <stdbool.h>           /* For bool, true, false   */
#include <stdlib.h>            /* For rand() and srand() */
#include <time.h>              /* For time() and clock() */

int main(void)
{
  /* Records if another game is to be played */
  char another_game = 'Y';

  /* true if correct sequence entered, false otherwise */
  int correct = false;

  /* Number of sequences entered successfully        */
  int counter = 0;

  int sequence_length = 0;    /* Number of digits in a sequence       */
  time_t seed = 0;            /* Seed value for random number sequence */
  int number = 0;             /* Stores an input digit                */

  time_t now = 0;             /* Stores current time - seed for random values */
  int time_taken = 0;         /* Time taken for game in seconds            */

  /* Describe how the game is played */
  printf("\nTo play Simple Simon, ");
  printf("watch the screen for a sequence of digits.");
  printf("\nWatch carefully, as the digits are only displayed"
                                        " for a second! ");
  printf("\nThe computer will remove them, and then prompt you ");
  printf("to enter the same sequence.");
  printf("\nWhen you do, you must put spaces between the digits. \n");
  printf("\nGood Luck!\nPress Enter to play\n");
  scanf("%c", &another_game);
```

```
/* One outer loop iteration is one game */
do
{
  correct = true;          /* By default indicates correct sequence entered */
  counter = 0;             /* Initialize count of number of successful tries*/
  sequence_length = 2;     /* Initial length of a digit sequence           */
  time_taken = clock();  /* Record current time at start of game         */

  /* Inner loop continues as long as sequences are entered correctly */
  while(correct)
  {
    /* On every third successful try, increase the sequence length */
    sequence_length += counter++%3 == 0;

    /* Set seed to be the number of seconds since Jan 1,1970  */
    seed = time(NULL);

    now = clock();                   /* record start time for sequence  */

    /* Generate a sequence of numbers and display the number */
    srand((unsigned int)seed);        /* Initialize the random sequence */
    for(int i = 1; i <= sequence_length; i++)
      printf("%d ", rand() % 10);     /* Output a random digit          */

    /* Wait one second */
    for( ;clock() - now < CLOCKS_PER_SEC; );

    /* Now overwrite the digit sequence */
    printf("\r");                    /* go to beginning of the line */
    for(int i = 1; i <= sequence_length; i++)
      printf("  ");                  /* Output two spaces */

    if(counter == 1)          /* Only output message for the first try */
      printf("\nNow you enter the sequence  - don't forget"
                                      " the spaces\n");
    else
      printf("\r");                  /* Back to the beginning of the line */

    /* Check the input sequence of digits against the original */
    srand((unsigned int)seed);       /* Restart the random sequence    */
    for(int i = 1; i <= sequence_length; i++)
    {
      scanf("%d", &number);          /* Read an input number          */
      if(number != rand() % 10)      /* Compare against random digit */
      {
        correct = false;             /* Incorrect entry          */
        break;                       /* No need to check further... */
      }
    }
  }
  printf("%s\n", correct? "Correct!" : "Wrong!");
}
```

```
/* Calculate total time to play the game in seconds)*/
time_taken = (clock() - time_taken) / CLOCKS_PER_SEC;

/* Output the game score */
printf("\n\n Your score is %d", --counter * 100 / time_taken);

fflush(stdin);

/* Check if new game required*/
printf("\nDo you want to play again (y/n)? ");
scanf("%c", &another_game);

} while(toupper(another_game) == 'Y');
return 0;
}
```

The declaration required for the function fflush() is in the <stdio.h> header file for which you already have an #include directive. Now you just need to see what happens when you actually play:

```
To play Simple Simon, watch the screen for a sequence of digits.
Watch carefully, as the digits are only displayed for a second!
The computer will remove them, and then prompt you to enter the same sequence.
When you do, you must put spaces between the digits.

Good Luck!
Press Enter to play


Now you enter the sequence  - don't forget the spaces
2 1 4
Correct!
8 7 1
Correct!
4 1 6
Correct!
7 9 6 6
Correct!
7 5 4 6
Wrong!


 Your score is 16
Do you want to play again (y/n)? n
```

Summary

In this chapter, I covered all you need to know about repeating actions using loops. With the powerful set of programming tools you've learned up to now, you should be able to create quite complex programs of your own. You have three different loops you can use to repeatedly execute a block of statements:

! The for loop, which you typically use for counting loops where the value of a control variable is incremented or decremented by a given amount on each iteration until some final value is reached.

! The while loop, which you use when the loop continues as long as a given condition is true. If the loop condition is false at the outset, the loop block will not be executed at all.

! The do-while loop, which works like the while loop except that the loop condition is checked at the end of the loop block. Consequently the loop block is always executed at least once.

In keeping with this chapter topic, I'll now reiterate some of the rules and recommendations I've presented in the book so far:

! Before you start programming, work out the logic of the process and computations you want to perform, and write it down! preferably in the form of a flow chart. Try to think of lateral approaches to a problem; there may be a better way than the obvious approach.

! Understand operator precedence in order to get complex expressions right. Whenever you are not sure about operator precedence, use parentheses to ensure expressions do what you want. Use parentheses to make complex expressions more readily understood.

! Comment your programs to explain all aspects of their operation and use. Assume the comments are for the benefit of someone else reading your program with a view to extend or modify it. Explain the purpose of each variable as you declare it.

! Program with readability foremost in your mind.

! In complicated logical expressions, avoid using the operator ! as much as you can.

! Use indentation to visually indicate the structure of your program.

Prepared with this advice, you can now move on to the next chapter! after you've completed all the exercises, of course!

Exercises

The following exercises enable you to try out what you've learned in this chapter. If you get stuck, look back over the chapter for help. If you're still stuck, you can download the solutions from the Source Code/Downloads section of the Apress web site (http://www.apress.com), but that really should be a last resort.

Exercise 4-1. Write a program that will generate a multiplication table of a size entered by the user. A table of size 4, for instance, would have four rows and four columns. The rows and columns would be labeled from 1 to 4. Each cell in the table will contain the product of the corresponding row and column numbers, so the value in the position corresponding to the third row and the fourth column would contain 12.

Exercise 4-2. Write a program that will output the printable characters for character code values from 0 to 127. Output each character code along with its symbol with two characters to a line. Make sure the columns are aligned. (Hint: You can use the isgraph() function that's declared in ctype.h to determine when a character is printable.)

Exercise 4-3. Extend the previous program to output the appropriate name, such as •newline,! •space,! •tab,! and so on, for each whitespace character.

Exercise 4-4. Use nested loops to output a box bounded by asterisks as in Program 4.2, but with a width and height that's entered by the user. For example, a box ten characters wide and seven characters high would display as follows:

```
**********
*        *
*        *
*        *
*        *
*        *
**********
```

Exercise 4-5. Modify the guessing game implemented in Program 4.7 so that the program will continue with an option to play another game when the player fails to guess the number correctly and will allow as many games as the player requires.

CHAPTER 5

■ ■ ■

Arrays

You'll often need to store many data values of a particular kind in your programs. For example, if you were writing a program to track the performance of a basketball team, then you might want to store the scores for a season of games and the scores for individual players. You could then output the scores for a particular player over the season or work out an ongoing average as the season progresses. Armed with what you've learned so far, you could write a program that does this using a different variable for each score. However, if there are a lot of games in the season, this will be rather tedious because you'll need as many variables for each player as there are games. All your basketball scores are really the same kind of thing. The values are different, but they're all basketball scores. Ideally, you would want to group these values together under a single name! perhaps the name of the player! so that you wouldn't have to define separate variables for each item of data.

In this chapter, I'll show you how to do just that using arrays in C. I'll then show you how powerful referencing a set of values through a single name can be when you write programs that process arrays.

In this chapter you'll learn the following:

! What arrays are

! How to use arrays in your programs

! How memory is used by an array

! What a multidimensional array is

! How to write a program to work out your hat size

! How to write a game of tic-tac-toe

An Introduction to Arrays

The best way to show you what an array is and how powerful it can be is to go through an example in which you can see how much easier a program becomes when you use an array. For this example, you'll look at ways in which you can find the average score of the students in a class.

Programming Without Arrays

To find the average score of a class of students, assume that there are only ten students in the class (mainly to avoid having to type in a lot of numbers). To work out the average of a set of numbers, you add them all together and then divide by how many you have (in this case, by 10):

```
/* Program 5.1 Averaging ten numbers without storing the numbers */
#include <stdio.h>

int main(void)
{
  int number = 0;                  /* Stores a number              */
  int count = 10;                  /* Number of values to be read */
  long sum = 0L;                   /* Sum of the numbers           */
  float average = 0.0f;            /* Average of the numbers       */

  /* Read the ten numbers to be averaged */
  for(int i = 0; i < count; i ++)
  {
    printf("Enter grade: ");
    scanf("%d", &number);          /* Read a number */
    sum += number;                 /* Add it to sum */
  }

  average = (float)sum/count;      /* Calculate the average */

  printf("\nAverage of the ten numbers entered is: %f\n", average);
  return 0;
}
```

If you're interested only in the average, then you don't have to remember what the previous grades were. All you're interested in is the sum of them all, which you then divide by count, which has the value 10. This simple program uses a single variable, number, to store each grade as it is entered within the loop. The loop repeats for values of i of 1, 2, 3, and so on, up to 9, so there are ten iterations. You've done this sort of thing before, so the program should be clear.

But let's assume that you want to develop this into a more sophisticated program in which you'll need the values you enter later. Perhaps you might want to print out each person's grade, with the average grade next to it. In the previous program, you had only one variable. Each time you add a grade, the old value is overwritten, and you can't get it back.

So how do you store the results? You could do this is by declaring ten integers to store the grades in, but then you can't use a for loop to enter the values. Instead, you have to include code that will read the values individually. This would work, but it's quite tiresome:

```
/* Program 5.2 Averaging ten numbers - storing the numbers the hard way */
#include <stdio.h>

int main(void)
{
  int number0 = 0, number1 = 0, number2 = 0, number3 = 0, number4 = 0;
  int number5 = 0, number6 = 0, number7 = 0, number8 = 0, number9 = 0;

  long sum = 0L;            /* Sum of the numbers      */
  float average = 0.0f;     /* Average of the numbers */

  /* Read the ten numbers to be averaged */
  printf("Enter the first five numbers,\n");
  printf("use a space or press Enter between each number.\n");
  scanf("%d%d%d%d%d", &number0, &number1, &number2, &number3, &number4);
  printf("Enter the last five numbers,\n");
  printf("use a space or press Enter between each number.\n");
  scanf("%d%d%d%d%d", &number5, &number6, &number7, &number8, &number9);
```

```
/* Now we have the ten numbers, we can calculate the average */
sum = number0 + number1+ number2 + number3 + number4+
        number5 + number6 + number7 + number8 + number9;
average = (float)sum/10.0f;

printf("\nAverage of the ten numbers entered is: %f\n", average);
return 0;
}
```

This is more or less OK for ten students, but what if your class has 30 students, or 100, or 1,000? How can you do it then? Well, this is where this approach would become wholly impractical and arrays become essential.

What Is an Array?

An **array** is a fixed number of data items that are all of the same type. The data items in an array are referred to as **elements**. These are the most important feature of an array!   there is a fixed number of elements and the elements of each array are all of type int, or of type long, or all of type whatever. So you can have arrays of elements of type int, arrays of elements of type float, arrays of elements of type long, and so on.

The following array declaration is very similar to how you would declare a normal variable that contains a single value, except that you've placed a number between square brackets [ ] following the name:

```
long numbers[10];
```

The number between square brackets defines how many elements you want to store in your array and is called the array **dimension**. The important feature here is that each of the data items stored in the array is accessed by the same name; in this case, numbers.

If you have only one variable name but are storing ten values, how do you differentiate between them? Each individual value in the array is identified by what is called an **index value**. An index value is an integer that's written after the array name between square brackets [ ]. Each element in an array has a different **index value**, which are sequential integers starting from 0. The index values for the elements in the preceding numbers array would run from 0 to 9. The index value 0 refers to the first element and the index value 9 refers to the last element. To access a particular element, just write the appropriate index value between square brackets immediately following the array name. Therefore, the array elements would be referred to as numbers[0], numbers[1], numbers[2], and so on, up to numbers[9]. You can see this in Figure 5-1.

Don't forget, index values start from 0, not 1. It's a common mistake to assume that they start from 1 when you're working with arrays for the first time, and this is sometimes referred to as *the off-by-one error*. In a ten-element array, the index value for the last element is 9. To access the fourth value in your array, you use the expression numbers[3]. You can think of the index value for an array element as the offset from the first element. The first element is the first element, so it has an offset of 0. The second element has an offset of 1 from the first element, the third element has an offset of 2 from the first element, and so on.

To access the value of an element in the numbers array, you could also place an expression in the square brackets following the array name. The expression would have to result in an integer value that corresponds to one of the possible index values. For example, you could write numbers[i-2]. If i had the value 3, this would access numbers[1], the second element in the array. Thus there are two ways to specify an index to access a particular element of an array. You can use a simple integer to explicitly reference the element that you want to access. Alternatively, you can use an integer expression that's evaluated during the execution of the program. When you use an expression the only constraints are that it must produce an integer result and the result must be a legal index value for the array.

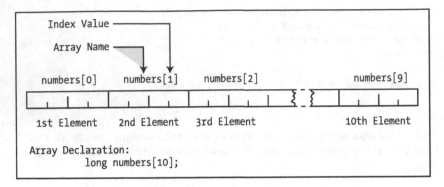

Figure 5-1. *Accessing the elements of an array*

Note that if you use an index value in your program that's outside the legal range for an array, the program won't work properly. The compiler can't check for this, so your program will still compile, but execution is likely to be less than satisfactory. At best you'll just pick up a junk value from somewhere so that the results are incorrect and may vary from one run to the next. At worst the program may overwrite something important and lock up your computer so a reboot becomes necessary. It is also possible that the effect will be much more subtle with the program sometimes working and sometimes not, or the program may appear to work but the results are wrong but not obviously so. It is therefore most important to check carefully that your array indexes are within bounds.

Using Arrays

That's a lot of theory, but you still need to solve your average score problem. Let's put what you've just learned about arrays into practice in that context.

TRY IT OUT: AVERAGES WITH ARRAYS

Now that you understand arrays, you can use an array to store all the scores you want to average. This means that all the values will be saved, and you'll be able to reuse them. You can now rewrite the program to average ten scores:

```
/* Program 5.3 Averaging ten numbers - storing the numbers the easy way */
#include <stdio.h>

int main(void)
{
  int numbers[10];                    /* Array storing 10 values     */
  int count = 10;                     /* Number of values to be read */
  long sum = 0L;                      /* Sum of the numbers          */
  float average = 0.0f;               /* Average of the numbers      */

  printf("\nEnter the 10 numbers:\n");          /* Prompt for the input */

  /* Read the ten numbers to be averaged */
  for(int i = 0; i < count; i ++)
  {
    printf("%2d> ",i+1);
    scanf("%d", &numbers[i]);         /* Read a number */
```

```
  sum += numbers[i];                    /* Add it to sum */
  }

  average = (float)sum/count;           /* Calculate the average */

  printf("\nAverage of the ten numbers entered is: %f\n", average);
  return 0;
}
```

The output from the program looks something like this:

```
Enter the ten numbers:
 1> 450
 2> 765
 3> 562
 4> 700
 5> 598
 6> 635
 7> 501
 8> 720
 9> 689
10> 527

Average of the ten numbers entered is: 614.700000
```

How It Works

You start off the program with the ubiquitous #include directive for <stdio.h> because you want to use printf() and scanf(). At the beginning of main(), you declare an array of ten integers and then the other variables that you'll need for calculation:

```
int numbers[10];              /* Array storing 10 values     */
int count = 10;               /* Number of values to be read */
long sum = 0L;                /* Sum of the numbers          */
float average = 0.0f;         /* Average of the numbers      */
```

You then prompt for the input to be entered with this statement:

```
printf("\nEnter the 10 numbers:\n");   /* Prompt for the input */
```

Next, you have a loop to read the values and accumulate the sum:

```
for(int i = 0; i < count; i++)
{
  printf("%2d> ",i+1);
  scanf("%d", &numbers[i]);           /* Read a number */
  sum += numbers[i];                  /* Add it to sum */
}
```

The for loop is in the preferred form with the loop continuing as long as i is not equal to the limit, count. In general you should write your for loops like this if you can. Because the loop counts from 0 to 9, rather than from 1 to 10, you can use the loop variable i directly to reference each of the members of the array. The printf() call outputs the current value of i+1 followed by >, so it has the effect you see in the output. By using %2d as the format specifier, you ensure that each value is output in a two-character field, so the numbers are aligned. If you had used %d instead, the output for the tenth value would have been out of alignment.

You read each value entered into element i of the array using the scanf() function; the first value will be stored in number[0], the second number entered will be stored in number[1], and so on up to the tenth value entered, which will be stored in number[9]. For each iteration of the loop, the value that was read is added to sum.

When the loop ends, you calculate the average and display it with these statements:

```
average = (float)sum/count;           /* Calculate the average */

printf("\nAverage of the ten numbers entered is: %f\n", average);
```

You've calculated the average by dividing the sum by count, which has the value 10. Notice how, in the call to printf(), you've told the compiler to convert sum (which is declared as type long) into type float. This is to ensure that the division is done using floating-point values, so you don't discard any fractional part of the result.

TRY IT OUT: RETRIEVING THE NUMBERS STORED

You can expand it a little to demonstrate one of the advantages. I've made only a minor change to the original program (highlighted in the following code in **bold**), but now the program displays all the values that were typed in. Having the values stored in an array means that you can access those values whenever you want and process them in many different ways.

```
/* Program 5.4 Reusing the numbers stored */
#include <stdio.h>

int main(void)
{
  int numbers[10];                /* Array storing 10 values    */
  int count = 10;                 /* Number of values to be read */
  long sum = 0L;                  /* Sum of the numbers         */
  float average = 0.0f;           /* Average of the numbers     */

  printf("\nEnter the 10 numbers:\n");      /* Prompt for the input */

  /* Read the ten numbers to be averaged */
  for(int i = 0; i < count; i++)
  {
    printf("%2d> ",i+1);
    scanf("%d", &numbers[i]);      /* Read a number */
    sum += numbers[i];             /* Add it to sum */
  }

  average = (float)sum/count;      /* Calculate the average */

  for(int i = 0; i < count; i++)
    printf("\nGrade Number %d was %d", i+1, numbers[i]);

  printf("\nAverage of the ten numbers entered is: %f\n", average);
  return 0;
}
```

Typical output from this program would be as follows:

```
Enter the ten numbers:
 1> 56
 2> 64
 3> 34
 4> 51
 5> 52
 6> 78
 7> 62
 8> 51
 9> 47
10> 32

Grade No 1 was 56
Grade No 2 was 64
Grade No 3 was 34
Grade No 4 was 51
Grade No 5 was 52
Grade No 6 was 78
Grade No 7 was 62
Grade No 8 was 51
Grade No 9 was 47
Grade No 10 was 32
Average of the ten numbers entered is: 52.700001
```

How It Works

I'll just explain the new bit where you reuse the elements of the array in a loop:

```
for(int i = 0; i < count; i++)
    printf("\nGrade Number %d was %d", i+1, number[i]);
```

You simply add another for loop to step through the elements in the array and output each value. You use the loop control variable to produce the sequence number for the value of the number of the element and to access the corresponding array element. These values obviously correspond to the numbers you typed in. To get the grade numbers starting from 1, you use the expression i+1 in the output statement so you get grade numbers from 1 to 10 as i runs from 0 to 9.

Before you go any further with arrays, you need to look into how your variables are stored in the computer's memory. You also need to understand how an array is different from the variables you've seen up to now.

A Reminder About Memory

Let's quickly recap what you learned about memory in Chapter 2. You can think of the memory of your computer as an ordered line of elements. Each element is in one of two states: either the element is on (let's call this state 1) or the element is off (this is state 0). Each element holds one binary digit and is referred to as a **bit**. Figure 5-2 shows a sequence of bytes in memory.

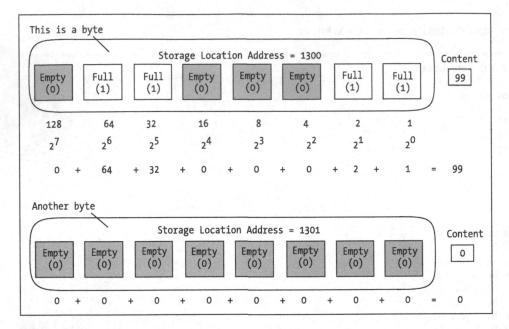

Figure 5-2. *Bytes in memory*

For convenience, the bits in Figure 5-2 are grouped into sets of eight, and a group of eight bits is called a **byte**. To identify each byte so that its contents may be accessed, the byte is labeled with a number starting from 0 for the first byte in memory and going up to whatever number of bytes there are in memory. This label for a byte is called its address.

You've already been using the address of operator, &, extensively with the scanf() function. You've been using this as a prefix to the variable name, because the function needs to store data that is entered from the keyboard into the variable. Just using the variable name by itself as an argument to a function makes the value stored in the variable available to the function. Prefixing the variable name with the address of operator and using that as the argument to the function makes the address of the variable available to the function. This enables the function to store information at this address and thus modify the value that's stored in the variable. The best way to get a feel for the address of operator is to use it a bit more, so let's do that.

TRY IT OUT: USING THE ADDRESS OF OPERATOR

Each variable that you use in a program takes up a certain amount of memory, measured in bytes, and the exact amount of memory is dependent on the type of the variable. Let's try finding the address of some variables of different types with the following program:

```
/* Program 5.5 Using the & operator */
#include<stdio.h>

int main(void)
{
  /* declare some integer variables */
  long a = 1L;
  long b = 2L;
  long c = 3L;
```

```
/* declare some floating-point variables */
double d = 4.0;
double e = 5.0;
double f = 6.0;

printf("A variable of type long occupies %d bytes.", sizeof(long));
printf("\nHere are the addresses of some variables of type long:");
printf("\nThe address of a is: %p  The address of b is: %p", &a, &b);
printf("\nThe address of c is: %p", &c);
printf("\n\nA variable of type double occupies %d bytes.", sizeof(double));
printf("\nHere are the addresses of some variables of type double:");
printf("\nThe address of d is: %p  The address of e is: %p", &d, &e);
printf("\nThe address of f is: %p\n", &f);
return 0;
}
```

Output from this program will be something like this:

```
A variable of type long occupies 4 bytes.
Here are the addresses of some variables of type long:
The address of a is: 0064FDF4  The address of b is: 0064FDF0
The address of c is: 0064FDEC

A variable of type double occupies 8 bytes.
Here are the addresses of some variables of type double:
The address of d is: 0064FDE4  The address of e is: 0064FDDC
The address of f is: 0064FDD4
```

The addresses that you get will almost certainly be different from these. What you get will depend on what operating system you're using and what other programs are running at the time. The actual address values are determined by where your program is loaded in memory, and this can differ from one execution to the next.

How It Works

You declare three variables of type long and three of type double:

```
/* declare some integer variables */
long a = 1L;
long b = 2L;
long c = 3L;

/* declare some floating-point variables */
double d = 4.0;
double e = 5.0;
double f = 6.0;
```

Next, you output the size of variables of type long, followed by the addresses of the three variables of that type that you created:

```
printf("A variable of type long occupies %d bytes.", sizeof(long));
printf("\nHere are the addresses of some variables of type long:");
printf("\nThe address of a is: %p  The Address of b is: %p", &a, &b);
printf("\nThe address of c is: %p", &c);
```

The address of operator is the & that precedes the name of each variable. You also used a new format specifier, %p, to output the address of the variables. This format specifier is for outputting a memory address, and the value is presented in hexadecimal format. A memory address is typically 16, 32, or 64 bits, and the size of the address will determine the maximum amount of memory that can be referenced. A memory address on my computer is 32 bits and is presented as eight hexadecimal digits; on your machine it may be different.

You then output the size of variables of type double, followed by the addresses of the three variables of that type that you also created:

```
printf("\n\nA variable of type double occupies %d bytes.", sizeof(double));
printf("\nHere are the addresses of some variables of type double:");
printf("\nThe address of d is: %p  The address of e is: %p", &d, &e);
printf("\nThe address of f is: %p\n", &f);
```

In fact, the interesting part isn't the program itself so much as the output. Look at the addresses that are displayed. You can see that the value of the address gets steadily lower in a regular pattern, as shown in Figure 5-3. On my computer, the address of b is 4 lower than that of a, and c is also lower than b by 4. This is because each variable of type long occupies 4 bytes. There's a similar situation with the variables d, e, and f, except that the difference is 8. This is because 8 bytes are used to store a value of type double.

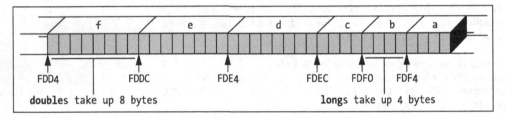

Figure 5-3. *Addresses of variables in memory*

■**Caution** If the addresses for the variables are separated by greater amounts than the size value, it is most likely because you compiled the program as a **debug** version. In debug mode your compiler may allocate extra space to store additional information about the variable that will be used when you're executing the program in debug mode.

Arrays and Addresses

In the following array, the name number identifies the address of the area of memory where your data is stored, and the specific location of each element is found by combining this with the index value, because the index value represents an offset of a number of elements from the beginning of the array.

```
long number[4];
```

When you declare an array, you give the compiler all the information it needs to allocate the memory for the array. You tell it the type of value, which will determine the number of bytes that each element will require, and how many elements there will be. The array name identifies where in memory the array begins. An index value specifies how many elements from the beginning you have to go to address the element you want. The address of an array element is going to be the address where the array starts, plus the index value for the element multiplied by the number of bytes required to store each element of the type stored in the array. Figure 5-4 represents the way that array variables are held in memory.

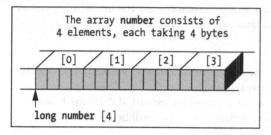

Figure 5-4. *The organization of an array in memory*

You can obtain the address of an array element in a fashion similar to ordinary variables. For an integer variable called value, you would use the following statement to print its address:

```
printf("\n%p", &value);
```

To output the address of the third element of an array called number, you could write the following:

```
printf("\n%p", &number[2]);
```

Remember that you use the value 2 that appears within the square brackets to reach the third element. Here, you've obtained the address of the element with the address of operator. If you used the same statement without the &, you would display the actual value stored in the third element of the array, not its address.

I can show this using some working code. The following fragment sets the value of the elements in an array and outputs the address and contents of each element:

```
int data[5];
for(int i = 0 ; i<5 ; i++)
{
  data[i] = 12*(i+1);
  printf("\ndata[%d] Address: %p  Contents: %d", i, &data[i], data[i]);
}
```

The for loop variable i iterates over all the legal index values for the data array. Within the loop, the value of the element at index position i is set to 12*(i+1). The output statement displays the current element with its index value, the address of the current array element determined by the current value of i, and the value stored within the element. If you make this fragment into a program, the output will be the following:

```
data[0] Address: 0x0012ff58  Contents: 12
data[1] Address: 0x0012ff5c  Contents: 24
data[2] Address: 0x0012ff60  Contents: 36
data[3] Address: 0x0012ff64  Contents: 48
data[4] Address: 0x0012ff68  Contents: 60
```

The value of i is displayed between the square brackets following the array name. You can see that the address of each element is 4 greater than the previous element so each element occupies 4 bytes.

Initializing an Array

Of course, you may want to assign initial values for the elements of your array, even if it's only for safety's sake. Predetermining initial values in the elements of your array can make it easier to detect when things go wrong. To initialize the elements of an array, you just specify the list of initial values between braces and separated by commas in the declaration. For example

```
double values[5] = { 1.5, 2.5, 3.5, 4.5, 5.5 };
```

declares the array values with five elements. The elements are initialized with values[0] having the value 1.5, value[1] having the initial value 2.5, and so on.

To initialize the whole array, there should be one value for each element. If there are fewer initializing values than elements, the elements without initializing values will be set to 0. Thus, if you write

```
double values[5] = { 1.5, 2.5, 3.5 };
```

the first three elements will be initialized with the values between braces, and the last two elements will be initialized with 0.

If you put more initializing values than there are array elements, you'll get an error message from the compiler. However, you are not obliged to supply the size of the array when you specify a list of initial values. The compiler can deduce the number of elements from the list of values:

```
int primes[] = { 2, 3, 5, 7, 11, 13, 17, 19, 23, 29};
```

Here the size of the array is determined by the number of initial values in the list so the primes array will have ten elements.

Finding the Size of an Array

You've already seen that the sizeof operator computes the number of bytes that a variable of a given type occupies. You can apply the sizeof operator to a type name like this:

```
printf("\nThe size of a variable of type long is %d bytes.", sizeof(long));
```

The parentheses around the type name following the sizeof operator are required. If you leave them out, the code won't compile.

You can also apply the sizeof operator to a variable and it will compute the number of bytes occupied by that variable. For example, suppose you declare the variable value with the following statement:

```
double value = 1.0;
```

You can now output the number of bytes occupied by value with this statement:

```
printf("\nThe size of value is %d bytes.", sizeof value);
```

Note that no parentheses around the operand for sizeof are necessary in this case, but you can include them if you wish. This statement will output the following line:

```
The size of value is 8 bytes.
```

This is because a variable of type double occupies 8 bytes in memory. Of course, you can store the size value you get from applying the sizeof operator:

```
int value_size = sizeof value;
```

The sizeof operator works with arrays too. You can declare an array with the following statement:

```
double values[5] = { 1.5, 2.5, 3.5, 4.5, 5.5 };
```

Now you can output the number of bytes that the array occupies with the following statement:

```
printf("\nThe size of the array, values, is %d bytes.", sizeof values);
```

This will produce the following output:

```
The size of the array, values, is 40 bytes.
```

You can also obtain the number of bytes occupied by a single element of the array with the expression sizeof values[0]. This expression will have the value 8. Of course, any legal index value for an element could be used to produce the same result. You can therefore use the sizeof operator to calculate the number of elements in an array:

```
int element_count = sizeof values/sizeof values[0];
```

After executing this statement, the variable element_count will contain the number of elements in the array values.

Because you can apply the sizeof operator to a data type, you could have written the previous statement to calculate the number of array elements as follows:

```
int element_count = sizeof values/sizeof(double);
```

This would produce the same result as before because the array is of type double and sizeof(double) would have produced the number of bytes occupied by a double value. Because there is the risk that you might accidentally use the wrong type, it's probably better to use the former statement in practice.

Although the sizeof operator doesn't require the use of parentheses when applied to a variable, it's common practice to use them anyway, so the earlier example could be written as follows:

```
int ElementCount = sizeof(values)/sizeof(values[0]);
printf("The size of the array is %d elements ", sizeof(values));
printf("and there are %d elements of %d bytes each",
                           ElementCount, sizeof(values[0]));
```

The output from these statements will be the following:

```
The size of the array is 40 bytes and there are 5 elements of 8 bytes each
```

Multidimensional Arrays

Let's stick to two dimensions for the moment and work our way up. A two-dimensional array can be declared as follows:

```
float carrots[25][50];
```

This declares an array, carrots, containing 25 rows of 50 floating-point elements. Similarly, you can declare another two-dimensional array of floating-point numbers with this statement:

```
float numbers[3][5];
```

Like the vegetables in the field, you tend to visualize these arrays as rectangular arrangements because it's convenient to do so. You can visualize this array as having three rows and five columns. They're actually stored in memory sequentially by row, as shown in Figure 5-5.

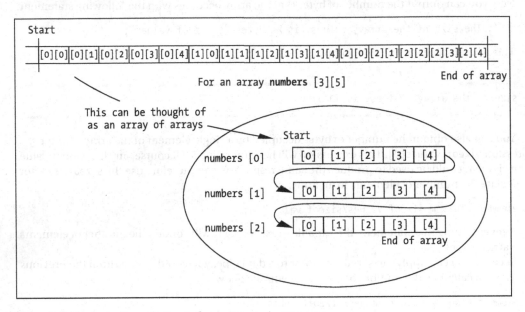

Figure 5-5. *Organization of a 3 × 5 element array in memory*

It's easy to see that the rightmost index varies most rapidly. Figure 5-5 also illustrates how you can envisage a two-dimensional array as a one-dimensional array of elements, in which each element is itself a one-dimensional array. You can view the numbers array as a one-dimensional array of three elements, where each element in an array contains five elements of type float. The first row of five elements of type float is located in memory at an address labeled numbers[0], the next row at numbers[1], and the last row of five elements at numbers[2].

The amount of memory allocated to each element is, of course, dependent on the type of variables that the array contains. An array of type double will need more memory to store each element than an array of type float or type int. Figure 5-6 illustrates how the array numbers[4][10] with four rows of ten elements of type float is stored.

Because the array elements are of type float, which on my machine occupy 4 bytes, the total memory occupied by this array on my computer will be 4 × 10 × 4 bytes, which amounts to a total of 160 bytes.

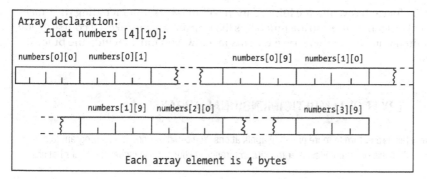

Figure 5-6. *Memory occupied by a 4 × 10 array*

Initializing Multidimensional Arrays

Let's first consider how you initialize a two-dimensional array. The basic structure of the declaration, with initialization, is the same as you've seen before, except that you can optionally put all the initial values for each row between braces {}:

```
int numbers[3][4] = {
                    { 10, 20, 30, 40 },        /* Values for first row  */
                    { 15, 25, 35, 45 },        /* Values for second row */
                    { 47, 48, 49, 50 }         /* Values for third row  */
                };
```

Each set of values that initializes the elements in a row is between braces, and the whole lot goes between another pair of braces. The values for a row are separated by commas, and each set of values for a row is separated from the next set by a comma.

If you specify fewer initializing values than there are elements in a row, the values will be assigned to elements in sequence, starting with the first in the row. The remaining elements in a row that are left when the initial values have all been assigned will be initialized to 0.

For arrays of three or more dimensions, the process is extended. A three-dimensional array, for example, will have three levels of nested braces, with the inner level containing sets of initializing values for a row:

```
int numbers[2][3][4] = {
                    {                                   /* First block of 3 rows  */
                        { 10, 20, 30, 40 },
                        { 15, 25, 35, 45 },
                        { 47, 48, 49, 50 }
                    },
                    {                                   /* Second block of 3 rows */
                        { 10, 20, 30, 40 },
                        { 15, 25, 35, 45 },
                        { 47, 48, 49, 50 }
                    }
                };
```

As you can see, the initializing values are between an outer pair of braces that enclose two blocks of three rows, each between braces. Each row is also between braces, so you have three levels of nested braces for a three-dimensional array. This is true generally; for instance, a six-dimensional array will have six levels of nested braces enclosing the initial values for the elements. You can omit the braces around the list for each row and the initialization will still work; but including the braces for the row values is much safer because you are much less likely to make a mistake. Of course, if you want to supply fewer initial values than there are elements in a row, you must include the braces around the row values.

TRY IT OUT: MULTIDIMENSIONAL ARRAYS

Let's move away from vegetables and turn to more practical applications. You could use arrays in a program to help you work out your hat size. With this program, just enter the circumference of your head in inches, and your hat size will be displayed:

```c
/* Program 5.6 Know your hat size - if you dare... */
#include <stdio.h>
#include <stdbool.h>

int main(void)

{
   /* The size array stores hat sizes from 6 1/2 to 7 7/8 */
   /* Each row defines one character of a size value so   */
   /* a size is selected by using the same index for each */
   /* the three rows. e.g. Index 2 selects 6 3/4.         */
   char size[3][12] = {                    /* Hat sizes as characters */
      {'6', '6', '6', '6', '7', '7', '7', '7', '7', '7', '7', '7'},
      {'1', '5', '3', '7', ' ', '1', '1', '3', '1', '5', '3', '7'},
      {'2', '8', '4', '8', ' ', '8', '4', '8', '2', '8', '4', '8'}
                      };

   int headsize[12] =                   /* Values in 1/8 inches    */
      {164,166,169,172,175,178,181,184,188,191,194,197};

   float cranium = 0.0;        /* Head circumference in decimal inches */
   int your_head = 0;          /* Headsize in whole eighths            */
   int i = 0;                  /* Loop counter                         */
   bool hat_found = false;     /* Indicates when a hat is found to fit */

   /* Get the circumference of the head */
   printf("\nEnter the circumference of your head above your eyebrows "
       "in inches as a decimal value: ");
   scanf(" %f", &cranium);

   /* Convert to whole eighths of an inch */
   your_head = (int)(8.0*cranium);

   /* Search for a hat size */
   /* A fit is when your_head is greater that one headsize element */
   /* and less than or equal to the next. The size the the second  */
   /* headsize value.                                              */
   for (i = 1 ; i < 12 ; i++)

      /* Find head size in the headsize array */
      if(your_head > headsize[i-1] && your_head <= headsize[i])
```

```
      {
        hat_found = true;
          break;
      }

    if(your_head == headsize[0])   /* Check for min size fit    */
    {
      i = 0;
      hat_found = true;
    }
    if(hat_found)
      printf("\nYour hat size is %c %c%c%c\n",
              size[0][i], size[1][i], (size[1][i]==' ') ? ' ' : '/', size[2][i]);
    /* If no hat was found, the head is too small, or too large    */
    else
    {
      if(your_head < headsize[0])          /* check for too small    */
        printf("\nYou are the proverbial pinhead. No hat for"
                                          " you I'm afraid.\n");
      else                                /* It must be too large  */
        printf("\nYou, in technical parlance, are a fathead."
                                " No hat for you, I'm afraid.\n");
    }
    return 0;
}
```

Typical output from this program would be this

```
Enter the circumference of your head above your eyebrows in inches as a decimal
 value: 22.5
Your hat size is 7 1/4
```

---

or possibly this

```
Enter the circumference of your head above your eyebrows in inches as a decimal
 value: 29
You, in technical parlance, are a fathead. No hat for you I'm afraid.
```

How It Works

Before I start discussing this example, I should give you a word of caution. Don't use it to assist large football players to determine their hat size unless they're known for their sense of humor.

The example looks a bit complicated because of the nature of the problem, but it does illustrate using arrays. Let's go through what's happening.

The first declaration in the body of main() is as follows:

```
char size[3][12] = {                   /* Hat sizes as characters */
    {'6', '6', '6', '6', '7', '7', '7', '7', '7', '7', '7', '7'},
    {'1', '5', '3', '7', ' ', '1', '1', '3', '1', '5', '3', '7'},
    {'2', '8', '4', '8', ' ', '8', '4', '8', '2', '8', '4', '8'}
                      };
```

Apart from hats that are designated as "one size fits all" or as small, medium, and large, hats are typically available in sizes from 6 1/2 to 7 7/8 in increments of 1/8. The size array shows one way in which you could store such sizes in the program. This array corresponds to 12 possible hat sizes, each of which is made up of three values. For each hat size you store three characters, making it more convenient to output the fractional sizes. The smallest hat size is 6 1/2, so the first three characters corresponding to the first size are in size[0][0], size[1][0], and size[2][0]. They contain the characters '6', '1', and '2', representing the size 6 1/2. The biggest hat size is 7 7/8, and it's stored in size[0][11], size[1][11], size[2][11].

You then declare the array headsize, which provides the reference head dimensions in this declaration:

```
int headsize[12] =        /* Values in 1/8 inches    */
                 {164,166,169,172,175,178,181,184,188,191,194,197};
```

The values in the array are all whole eighths of an inch. They correspond to the values in the size array containing the hat sizes. This means that a head size of 164 eighths of an inch (about 20.5 inches) will give a hat size of 6 1/2, and at the other end of the scale, 197 eighths corresponds to a hat size of 7 7/8.

Notice that the head sizes don't run consecutively. You could get a head size of 171, for example, which doesn't fall into a definite hat size. You need to be aware of this later in the program so that you can decide which is the closest hat size for the head size.

After declaring your arrays, you then declare all the variables you're going to need:

```
float cranium = 0.0;        /* Head circumference in decimal inches */
int your_head = 0;          /* Headsize in whole eighths            */
int i = 0;                  /* Loop counter                         */
bool hat_found = false;     /* Indicates when a hat is found to fit */
```

Notice that cranium is declared as type float, but the rest are all type int. This becomes important later. You declare the variable hat_found as type bool so you use the symbol false to initialize this. The hat_found variable will record when you have found a size that fits.

Next, you prompt for your head size to be entered in inches, and the value is stored in the variable cranium (remember it's type float, so you can store values that aren't whole numbers):

```
printf("\nEnter the circumference of your head above your eyebrows "
    "in inches as a decimal value: ");
scanf(" %f", &cranium);
```

The value stored in cranium is then converted into eighths of an inch with this statement:

```
your_head = (int)(8.0*cranium);
```

Because cranium contains the circumference of a head in inches, multiplying by 8.0 results in the number of eighths of an inch that that represents. Thus the value stored in your_head will then be in the same units as the values stored in the array headsize. Note that you need the cast to type int here to avoid a warning message from the compiler. The code will still work if you omit the cast, but the compiler must then insert the cast to type int. Because this cast potentially loses information, the compiler will issue a warning. The parentheses around the expression (8.0*cranium) are also necessary; without them, you would only cast the value 8.0 to type int, not the whole expression.

You use the value stored in your_head to find the closest value in the array headsize that isn't less than that value:

```
for (i = 1 ; i < 12 ; i++)
    /* Find head size in the headsize array */
    if(your_head > headsize[i-1] && your_head <= headsize[i])
    {
```

```
        hat_found = true;
        break;
    }
```

The process is a simple one and is carried out in this for loop. The loop index i runs from the second element in the array to the last element. This is because you use i-1 to index the array in the if expression. On each loop iteration, you compare your head size with a pair of successive values stored in the headsize array to find the element value that is greater than or equal to your input size with the preceding value less than your input size. The index found will correspond to the hat size that fits.

If your input size corresponds exactly to the size corresponding to the first element in the array, this size will fit but will not be discovered within the loop. You therefore check for this situation with the if statement:

```
if(your_head == headsize[0])  /* Check for min size fit    */
{
  i = 0;
  hat_found = true;
}
```

If the size in your_head matches that in the first element of the headsize array then you have a hat that fits, so you set i to 0 and hat_found to true.

Next you output the hat size if the value of hat_found is true:

```
if(hat_found)
  printf("\nYour hat size is %c %c%c%c\n",
        size[0][i], size[1][i], (size[1][i]==' ') ? ' ' : '/', size[2][i]);
```

As I said, the hat sizes are stored in the array size as characters to simplify the outputting of fractions. The printf() here uses the conditional operator to decide when to print a blank and when to print a slash (/) for the fractional output value. The fifth element of the headsize array corresponds to a hat size of exactly 7. You don't want it to print 7 /; you just want 7. Therefore, you customize the printf() depending on whether the element size[1][i] contains ' '. In this way, you omit the slash for any size where the numerator of the fractional part is a space, so this will still work even if you add new sizes to the array.

Of course, it may be that no hat was found because either the head is too small or too large for the hat sizes available, so the else clause for the if statement deals with that situation, because the else executes if hat_found is false:

```
/* If no hat was found, the head is too small, or too large    */
else
{
  if(your_head < headsize[0])          /* check for too small   */
    printf("\nYou are the proverbial pinhead. No hat for"
                          " you I'm afraid.\n");
  else                                 /* It must be too large  */
    printf("\nYou, in technical parlance, are a fathead."
                          " No hat for you, I'm afraid.\n");
}
```

If the value in your_head is less than the first headsize element, the head is too small for the available hats; otherwise it must be too large.

Remember, when you use this program, if you lie about the size of your head, your hat won't fit. The more mathematically astute, and any hatters reading this book, will appreciate that the hat size is simply the diameter of a notionally circular head. Therefore, if you have the circumference of your head in inches, you can produce your hat size by dividing this value by π.

Designing a Program

Now that you've learned about arrays, let's see how you can apply them in a bigger problem. Let's try writing another game.

The Problem

The problem you're set is to write a program that allows two people to play tic-tac-toe (also known as noughts and crosses) on the computer.

The Analysis

Tic-tac-toe is played on a 3 × 3 grid of squares. Two players take turns entering either an **X** or an **O** in the grid. The player that first manages to get three of his or her symbols in a line horizontally, vertically, or diagonally is the winner. You know how the game works, but how does that translate into designing your program? You'll need the following:

! *A 3 × 3 grid in which to store the turns of the two players*: That's easy. You can just use a two-dimensional array with three rows of three elements.

! *A way for a square to be selected when a player takes his or her turn*: You can label the nine squares with digits from 1 to 9. A player will just need to enter the number of the square to select it.

! *A way to get the two players to take alternate turns*: You can identify the two players as 1 and 2, with player 1 going first. You can then determine the player number by the number of the turn. On odd-numbered turns it's player 1. On even-numbered turns it's player 2.

! *Some way of specifying where to place the player symbol on the grid and checking to see if it s a valid selection*: A valid selection is a digit from 1 to 9. If you label the first row of squares with 1, 2, and 3, the second row with 4, 5, and 6, and the third row with 7, 8, and 9, you can calculate a row index and a column index from the square number. If you subtract 1 from the player's choice of square number, the square numbers are effectively 0 through 8, as shown in the following image:

Original

1	2	3
4	5	6
7	8	9

Subtract 1

0	1	2
3	4	5
6	7	8

Then the expression choice/3 gives the row number, as you can see here:

Original less 1

0	1	2
3	4	5
6	7	8

Divide by 3

0	0	0
1	1	1
2	2	2

The expression choice%3 will give the column number:

Original less 1

0	1	2
3	4	5
6	7	8

Remainder after divide by 3

0	1	2
0	1	2
0	1	2

! *A method of finding out if one of the players has won*: After each turn, you'll need to check to see if any row, column, or diagonal in the board grid contains identical symbols. If it does, the last player has won.

! *A way to detect the end of the game*: Because the board has nine squares, a game consists of up to nine turns. The game ends when a winner is discovered, or after nine turns.

The Solution

This section outlines the steps you'll take to solve the problem.

Step 1

You can first add the code for the main game loop and the code to display the board:

```
/* Program 5.7 Tic-Tac-Toe */
#include <stdio.h>

int main(void)
{
  int player = 0;                    /* Player number - 1 or 2 */
  int winner = 0;                    /* The winning player      */

  char board[3][3] = {               /* The board */
              {'1','2','3'},         /* Initial values are reference numbers */
              {'4','5','6'},         /* used to select a vacant square for   */
              {'7','8','9'}          /* a turn.                              */
                     };
```

```
/* The main game loop. The game continues for up to 9 turns */
/* As long as there is no winner                            */
for(int i = 0; i<9 && winner==0; i++)
{
  /* Display the board */
  printf("\n\n");
  printf(" %c | %c | %c\n", board[0][0], board[0][1], board[0][2]);
  printf("---+---+---\n");
  printf(" %c | %c | %c\n", board[1][0], board[1][1], board[1][2]);
  printf("---+---+---\n");
  printf(" %c | %c | %c\n", board[2][0], board[2][1], board[2][2]);

  player = i%2 + 1; /* Select player */

  /* Code to play the game */
}
/* Code to output the result */
return 0;
}
```

Here, you've declared the following variables: i, for the loop variable; player, which stores the identifier for the current player, 1 or 2; winner, which contains the identifier for the winning player; and the array board, which is of type char. The array is of type char because you want to place the symbols 'X' or 'O' in the squares. The array is initialized with the characters for the digits that identify the squares. The main game loop continues for as long as the loop condition is true. It will be false if winner contains a value other than 0 (which indicates that a winner has been found) or the loop counter is equal to or greater than 9 (which will be the case when all nine squares on the board have been filled).

When you display the grid in the loop, you use vertical bars and underline characters to delineate the squares. When a player selects a square, the symbol for that player will replace the digit character.

Step 2

Next, you can implement the code for the player to select a square and to ensure that the square is valid:

```
/* Program 5.7 Tic-Tac-Toe */
#include <stdio.h>

int main(void)
{
  int player = 0;          /* Player number - 1 or 2          */
  int winner = 0;          /* The winning player              */
  int choice = 0;          /* Square selection number for turn */
  int row = 0;             /* Row index for a square          */
  int column = 0;          /* Column index for a square       */

  char board[3][3] = {     /* The board */
            {'1','2','3'},  /* Initial values are reference numbers */
            {'4','5','6'},  /* used to select a vacant square for   */
            {'7','8','9'}   /* a turn.                              */
                  };
```

```
/* The main game loop. The game continues for up to 9 turns */
/* As long as there is no winner                            */
for(int i = 0; i<9 && winner==0; i++)
{
  /* Display the board */
  printf("\n\n");
  printf(" %c | %c | %c\n", board[0][0], board[0][1], board[0][2]);
  printf("---+---+---\n");
  printf(" %c | %c | %c\n", board[1][0], board[1][1], board[1][2]);
  printf("---+---+---\n");
  printf(" %c | %c | %c\n", board[2][0], board[2][1], board[2][2]);

  player = i%2 + 1; /* Select player   */

  /* Get valid player square selection */
  do
  {
    printf("\nPlayer %d, please enter the number of the square "
           "where you want to place your %c: ",
            player,(player==1)?'X':'O');
    scanf("%d", &choice);

    row = --choice/3;                 /* Get row index of square    */
    column = choice%3;                /* Get column index of square */
  }while(choice<0 || choice>9 || board[row][column]>'9');

  /* Insert player symbol */
  board[row][column] = (player == 1) ? 'X' : 'O';

  /* Code to check for a winner */
}
/* Code to output the result */
return 0;
}
```

You prompt the current player for input in the do-while loop and read the square number into the variable choice that you declared as type int. You'll use this value to compute the row and column index values in the array. The row and column index values are stored in the integer variables row and column, and you compute these values using the expressions you saw earlier. The do-while loop condition verifies that the square selected is valid. There are three possible ways that an invalid choice could be made: the integer entered for the square number could be less than the minimum, 1, or greater than the maximum, 9, or it could select a square that already contains 'X' or 'O'. In the latter case, the contents of the square will have a value greater than the character '9', because the character codes for 'X' and 'O' are greater than the character code for '9'. If the choice that is entered fails on any of these conditions, you just repeat the request to select a square.

Step 3

You can add the code to check for a winning line next. This needs to be executed after every turn:

```c
/* Program 5.7 Tic-Tac-Toe */
#include <stdio.h>

int main(void)
{
  int player = 0;              /* Player number - 1 or 2               */
  int winner = 0;              /* The winning player                   */
  int choice = 0;              /* Square selection number for turn     */
  int row = 0;                 /* Row index for a square               */
  int column = 0;              /* Column index for a square            */
  int line=0;                  /* Row or column index in checking loop */

  char board[3][3] = {         /* The board */
              {'1','2','3'},    /* Initial values are reference numbers */
              {'4','5','6'},    /* used to select a vacant square for   */
              {'7','8','9'}     /* a turn.                              */
                     };

  /* The main game loop. The game continues for up to 9 turns */
  /* As long as there is no winner                            */
  for(int i = 0; i<9 && winner==0; i++)
  {
    /* Display the board */
    printf("\n\n");
    printf(" %c | %c | %c\n", board[0][0], board[0][1], board[0][2]);
    printf("---+---+---\n");
    printf(" %c | %c | %c\n", board[1][0], board[1][1], board[1][2]);
    printf("---+---+---\n");
    printf(" %c | %c | %c\n", board[2][0], board[2][1], board[2][2]);

    player = i%2 + 1;                   /* Select player    */

    /* Get valid player square selection          */
    do
    {
      printf("\nPlayer %d, please enter the number of the square "
             "where you want to place your %c: ",
                 player,(player==1)?'X':'O');
      scanf("%d", &choice);

      row = --choice/3;                 /* Get row index of square    */
      column = choice%3;                /* Get column index of square */
    }while(choice<0 || choice>9 || board[row][column]>'9');

    /* Insert player symbol */
    board[row][column] = (player == 1) ? 'X' : 'O';

    /* Check for a winning line - diagonals first */
    if((board[0][0]==board[1][1] && board[0][0]==board[2][2]) ||
       (board[0][2]==board[1][1] && board[0][2]==board[2][0]))
      winner = player;
```

```
      else
        /* Check rows and columns for a winning line */
        for(line = 0; line <= 2; line ++)
          if((board[line][0]==board[line][1] && board[line][0]==board[line][2])||
             (board[0][line]==board[1][line] && board[0][line]==board[2][line]))
            winner = player;
  }
  /* Code to output the result */
  return 0;
}
```

To check for a winning line, you can compare one element in the line with the other two to test for equality. If all three are identical, then you have a winning line. You check both diagonals in the board array with the if expression, and if either diagonal has identical symbols in all three elements, you set winner to the current player. The current player, identified in player, must be the winner because he or she was the last to place a symbol on a square. If neither diagonal has identical symbols, you check the rows and the columns in the else clause, using a for loop. The for loop contains one statement, an if statement that checks both a row and a column for identical elements. If either is found, winner is set to the current player. Each value of the loop variable line is used to index a row and a column. Thus the for loop will check the row and column corresponding to index value 0, which is the first row and column, then the second row and column, and finally the third row and column corresponding to line having the value 2. Of course, if winner is set to a value here, the main loop condition will be false, so the loop will end and you'll continue with the code following the main loop.

Step 4

The final task is to display the grid with the final position and to display a message for the result. If winner is 0, the game is a draw; otherwise, winner contains the player number of the winner:

```
/* Program 5.7 Tic-Tac-Toe */
#include <stdio.h>

int main(void)
{
  int player = 0;              /* Player number - 1 or 2               */
  int winner = 0;              /* The winning player                   */
  int choice = 0;              /* Square selection number for turn     */
  int row = 0;                 /* Row index for a square               */
  int column = 0;              /* Column index for a square            */
  int line=0;                  /* Row or column index in checking loop */

  char board[3][3] = {         /* The board */
              {'1','2','3'},    /* Initial values are reference numbers */
              {'4','5','6'},    /* used to select a vacant square for   */
              {'7','8','9'}     /* a turn.                              */
                    };

  /* The main game loop. The game continues for up to 9 turns */
  /* As long as there is no winner                            */
  for(int i = 0; i<9 && winner==0; i++)
  {
```

```c
/* Display the board */
printf("\n\n");
printf(" %c | %c | %c\n", board[0][0], board[0][1], board[0][2]);
printf("---+---+---\n");
printf(" %c | %c | %c\n", board[1][0], board[1][1], board[1][2]);
 printf("---+---+---\n");
printf(" %c | %c | %c\n", board[2][0], board[2][1], board[2][2]);

player = i%2 + 1;                      /* Select player */

/* Get valid player square selection */
do
{
  printf("\nPlayer %d, please enter the number of the square "
         "where you want to place your %c: ",
             player,(player==1)?'X':'O');
  scanf("%d", &choice);

  row = --choice/3;                  /* Get row index of square    */
  column = choice%3;                 /* Get column index of square */
}while(choice<0 || choice>9 || board[row][column]>'9');

/* Insert player symbol */
board[row][column] = (player == 1) ? 'X' : 'O';

/* Check for a winning line - diagonals first */
if((board[0][0]==board[1][1] && board[0][0]==board[2][2]) ||
   (board[0][2]==board[1][1] && board[0][2]==board[2][0]))
  winner = player;
else
  /* Check rows and columns for a winning line */
  for(line = 0; line <= 2; line ++)
    if((board[line][0]==board[line][1] &&
        board[line][0]==board[line][2])||
       (board[0][line]==board[1][line] &&
        board[0][line]==board[2][line]))
      winner = player;
}
/* Game is over so display the final board */
printf("\n\n");
printf(" %c | %c | %c\n", board[0][0], board[0][1], board[0][2]);
printf("---+---+---\n");
printf(" %c | %c | %c\n", board[1][0], board[1][1], board[1][2]);
printf("---+---+---\n");
printf(" %c | %c | %c\n", board[2][0], board[2][1], board[2][2]);

/* Display result message */
if(winner == 0)
  printf("\nHow boring, it is a draw\n");
else
  printf("\nCongratulations, player %d, YOU ARE THE WINNER!\n",
                                               winner);

return 0;
}
```

Typical output from this program and a very bad player No. 2 would be as follows:

```
 1 | 2 | 3
---+---+---
 4 | 5 | 6
---+---+---
 7 | 8 | 9

Player 1, please enter your go: 1

 X | 2 | 3
---+---+---
 4 | 5 | 6
---+---+---
 7 | 8 | 9

Player 2, please enter your go: 2

 X | 0 | 3
---+---+---
 4 | 5 | 6
---+---+---
 7 | 8 | 9

Player 1, please enter your go: 5

 X | 0 | 3
---+---+---
 4 | X | 6
---+---+---
 7 | 8 | 9

Player 2, please enter your go: 3

 X | 0 | 0
---+---+---
 4 | X | 6
---+---+---
 7 | 8 | 9

Player 1, please enter your go: 9

 X | 0 | 0
---+---+---
 4 | X | 6
---+---+---
 7 | 8 | X

Congratulations, player 1, YOU ARE THE WINNER!
```

Summary

This chapter explored the ideas behind arrays. An array is a fixed number of elements of the same type and you access any element within the array using the array name and one or more index values. Index values for an array are integer values starting from 0, and there is one index for each array dimension.

Combining arrays with loops provides a very powerful programming capability. Using an array, you can process a large number of data values of the same type within a loop, so the amount of program code you need for the operation is essentially the same, regardless of how many data values there are. You have also seen how you can organize your data using multidimensional arrays. You can structure an array such that each array dimension selects a set of elements with a particular characteristic, such as the data pertaining to a particular time or location. By applying nested loops to multidimensional arrays, you can process all the array elements with a very small amount of code.

Up until now, you've mainly concentrated on processing numbers. The examples haven't really dealt with text to any great extent. You're going to change that in the next chapter, where you're going to write programs that can process and analyze strings of characters.

Exercises

The following exercises enable you to try out what you've learned in this chapter. If you get stuck, look back over the chapter for help. If you're still stuck, you can download the solutions from the Source Code/Downloads area of the Apress web site (http://www.apress.com), but that really should be a last resort.

Exercise 5-1. Write a program that will read five values of type double from the keyboard and store them in an array. Calculate the reciprocal of each value (the reciprocal of a value x is 1.0/x) and store it in a separate array. Output the values of the reciprocals, and calculate and output the sum of the reciprocals.

Exercise 5-2. Define an array, data, with 100 elements of type double. Write a loop that will store the following sequence of values in corresponding elements of the array:

1/(2*3*4) 1/(4*5*6) 1/(6*7*8) … up to 1/(200*201*202)

Write another loop that will calculate the following:

data[0]-data[1]+data[2]-data[3]+… -data[99]

Multiply the result of this by 4.0, add 3.0, and output the final result. Do you recognize the value that you get?

Exercise 5-3. Write a program that will read five values from the keyboard and store them in an array of type float with the name amounts. Create two arrays of five elements of type long with the names dollars and cents. Store the whole number part of each value in the amounts array in the corresponding element of dollars and the fractional part of the amount as a two-digit integer in cents (e.g., 2.75 in amounts[1] would result in 2 being stored in dollars[1] and 75 being stored in cents[1]). Output the values from the two arrays of type long as monetary amounts (e.g., $2.75).

Exercise 5-4. Define a two-dimensional array, data[12][5], of type double. Initialize the elements in the first column with values from 2.0 to 3.0 inclusive in steps of 0.1. If the first element in a row has the value x, populate the remaining elements in each row with the values $1/x$, x^2, x^3, and x^4. Output the values in the array with each row on a separate line and with a heading for each column.

CHAPTER 6

■ ■ ■

Applications with Strings and Text

In the last chapter you were introduced to arrays and you saw how using arrays of numerical values could make many programming tasks much easier. In this chapter you'll extend your knowledge of arrays by exploring how you can use arrays of characters. You'll frequently have a need to work with a text string as a single entity. As you'll see, C doesn't provide you with a string data type as some other languages do. Instead, C uses an array of elements of type char to store a string.

In this chapter I'll show you how you can create and work with variables that store strings, and how the standard library functions can greatly simplify the processing of strings.

You'll learn the following:

! How you can create string variables

! How to join two or more strings together to form a single string

! How you compare strings

! How to use arrays of strings

! How you work with wide character strings

! What library functions are available to handle strings and how you can apply them

! How to write a simple password-protection program

What Is a String?

You've already seen examples of string constants! quite frequently in fact. A **string constant** is a sequence of characters or symbols between a pair of double-quote characters. Anything between a pair of double quotes is interpreted by the compiler as a string, including any special characters and embedded spaces. Every time you've displayed a message using printf(), you've defined the message as a string constant. Examples of strings used in this way appear in the following statements:

```
printf("This is a string.");
printf("This is on\ntwo lines!");
printf("For \" you write \\\".");
```

These three example strings are shown in Figure 6-1. The decimal value of the character codes that will be stored in memory are shown below the characters.

"This is a string."

T	h	i	s		i	s		a		s	t	r	i	n	g	.	\0
84	104	105	115	32	105	115	32	97	32	115	116	114	105	110	103	46	00

"This is on\ntwo lines!"

T	h	i	s		i	s		o	n	\n	t	w	o		l	i	n	e	s	!	\0
84	104	105	115	32	105	115	32	111	110	115	116	119	111	32	108	105	110	101	115	33	00

"For \" you write \\\"."

F	o	r		"		y	o	u		w	r	i	t	e		\	"	.	\0
70	111	114	32	34	32	121	111	117	32	119	114	105	116	101	32	92	34	46	00

Figure 6-1. *Examples of strings in memory*

The first string is a straightforward sequence of letters followed by a period. The printf() function will output this string as the following:

This is a string.

The second string has a newline character, \n, embedded in it so the string will be displayed over two lines:

This is on
two lines!

The third string may seem a little confusing but the output from printf() should make is clearer:

For " you write \".

You must write a double quote within a string as the escape sequence \" because the compiler will interpret an explicit " as the end of the string. You must also use the escape sequence \\ when you want to include a backslash in a string because a backslash in a string always signals to the compiler the start of an escape sequence.

As Figure 6-1 shows, a special character with the code value 0 is added to the end of each string to mark where it ends. This character is known as the **null character** (not to be confused with NULL, which you'll see later), and you write it as \0.

Note Because a string in C is always terminated by a \0 character, the length of a string is always one greater than the number of characters in the string.

There's nothing to prevent you from adding a \0 character to the end of a string yourself, but if you do, you'll simply end up with two of them. You can see how the null character \0 works with a simple example. Have a look at the following program:

```
/* Program 6.1 Displaying a string */
#include <stdio.h>

int main(void)
{
  printf("The character \0 is used to terminate a string.");
  return 0;
}
```

If you compile and run this program, you'll get this output:

```
The character
```

It's probably not quite what you expected: only the first part of the string has been displayed. The output ends after the first two words because the printf() function stops outputting the string when it reaches the first null character, \0. Even though there's another \0 at the end of string, it will never be reached. The first \0 that's found always marks the end of the string.

String- and Text-Handling Methods

Unlike some other programming languages, C has no specific provision within its syntax for variables that store strings, and because there are no string variables, C has no special operators for processing strings. This is not a problem, though, because you're quite well-equipped to handle strings with the tools you have at your disposal already.

As I said at the beginning of this chapter, you use an array of type char to hold strings. This is the simplest form of string variable. You could declare a char array variable as follows:

```
char saying[20];
```

The variable saying that you've declared in this statement can accommodate a string that has up to 19 characters, because you must allow one element for the termination character. Of course, you can also use this array to store 20 characters that aren't a string.

Caution Remember that you must always declare the dimension of an array that you intend to use to store a string as at least one greater than the number of characters that you want to allow the string to have because the compiler will automatically add \0 to the end of a string constant.

You could also initialize the preceding string variable in the following declaration:

```
char saying[] = "This is a string.";
```

Here you haven't explicitly defined the array dimension. The compiler will assign a value to the dimension sufficient to hold the initializing string constant. In this case it will be 18, which corresponds to 17 elements for the characters in the string, plus an extra one for the terminating \0. You could, of course, have put a value for the dimension yourself, but if you leave it for the compiler to do, you can be sure it will be correct.

You could also initialize just part of an array of elements of type char with a string, for example:

```
char str[40] = "To be";
```

Here, the compiler will initialize the first five elements from str[0] to str[4] with the characters of the specified string in sequence, and str[5] will contain the null value '\0'. Of course, space is allocated for all 40 elements of the array, and they're all available to use in any way you want.

Initializing a char array and declaring it as constant is a good way of handling standard messages:

```
const char message[] = "The end of the world is nigh";
```

Because you've declared message as const, it's protected from being modified explicitly within the program. Any attempt to do so will result in an error message from the compiler. This technique for defining standard messages is particularly useful if they're used in various places within a program. It prevents accidental modification of such constants in other parts of your program. Of course, if you do need to be able to change the message, then you shouldn't specify the array as const.

When you want to refer to the string stored in an array, you just use the array name by itself. For instance, if you want to output the string stored in message using the printf() function, you could write this:

```
printf("\nThe message is: %s", message);
```

The %s specification is for outputting a null-terminating string. At the position where the %s appears in the first argument, the printf() function will output successive characters from the message array until it finds the '\0' character. Of course, an array with elements of type char behaves in exactly the same way as an array of elements of any other type, so you use it in exactly the same way. Only the special string handling functions are sensitive to the '\0' character, so outside of that there really is nothing special about an array that holds a string.

The main disadvantage of using char arrays to hold a variety of different strings is the potentially wasted memory. Because arrays are, by definition, of a fixed length, you have to declare each array that you intend to use to store strings with its dimension set to accommodate the maximum string length you're likely to want to process. In most circumstances, your typical string length will be somewhat less than the maximum, so you end up wasting memory. Because you normally use your arrays here to store strings of different lengths, getting the length of a string is important, especially if you want to add to it. Let's look at how you do this using an example.

TRY IT OUT: FINDING OUT THE LENGTH OF A STRING

In this example, you're going to initialize two strings and then find out how many characters there are in each, excluding the null character:

```
/* Program 6.2 Lengths of strings  */
#include <stdio.h>
int main(void)
{
  char str1[] = "To be or not to be";
  char str2[] = ",that is the question";
  int count = 0;                  /* Stores the string length              */
  while (str1[count] != '\0')     /* Increment count till we reach the string */
    count++;                      /*  terminating character.               */
  printf("\nThe length of the string \"%s\" is %d characters.", str1, count);
```

```
    count = 0;                         /* Reset to zero for next string      */
    while (str2[count] != '\0')        /* Count characters in second string  */
      count++;
    printf("\nThe length of the string \"%s\" is %d characters.\n", str2, count);
    return 0;
}
```

The output you will get from this program is the following:

```
The length of the string "To be or not to be" is 18 characters.
The length of the string ",that is the question" is 21 characters.
```

How It Works

First you have the inevitable declarations for the variables that you'll be using:

```
char str1[] = "To be or not to be";
char str2[] = ",that is the question";
int count = 0;                         /* Stores the string length           */
```

You declare two arrays of type char that are each initialized with a string. The compiler will set the size of each array to accommodate the string including its terminating null. You also declare and initialize a counter, count, to use in the loops in the program. Of course, you could have omitted the dimension for each array and left the compiler to figure out what is required, as you saw earlier.

Next, you have a while loop that determines the length of the first string:

```
while (str1[count] != '\0')     /* Increment count till we reach the string */
  count++;                       /*   terminating character.                 */
```

Using a loop in the way you do here is very common in programming with strings. To find the length, you simply keep incrementing a counter in the while loop as long as you haven't reached the end of string character. You can see how the condition for the continuation of the loop is whether the terminating '\0' has been reached. At the end of the loop, the variable count will contain the number of characters in the string, excluding the terminating null.

I have shown the while loop comparing the value of the str1[count] element with '\0' so the mechanism for finding the end of the string is clear to you. However, this loop would typically be written like this:

```
while(str1[count])
  count++;
```

The ASCII code value for the '\0' character is zero which corresponds to the Boolean value false. All other ASCII code values are nonzero and therefore correspond to the Boolean value true. Thus the loop will continue as long as str1[count] is not '\0', which is precisely what you want.

Now that you've determined the length, you display the string with the following statement:

```
printf("\nThe length of the string \"%s\" is %d characters.", str1, count);
```

This also displays the count of the number of characters that the string contains, excluding the terminating null. Notice that you use the new format specifier, %s that we saw earlier. This outputs characters from the string until it reaches the terminating null. If there was no terminating character, it would continue to output characters until it found one somewhere in memory. In some cases, that can mean *a lot* of output. You also use the escape character, \", to include a double quote in the string. If you don't precede the double-quote character with the backslash, the compiler will think it marked the end of the string that is the first argument to the printf() function, and the statement will cause an error message to be produced.

You find the length of the second string and display the result in exactly the same way as the first string.

Operations with Strings

The code in the previous example is designed to show you the mechanism for finding the length of a string, but you never have to write such code in practice. As you'll see very soon, the strlen() function in the standard library will determine the length of a null-terminated string for you. So now that you know how to find the lengths of strings, how can you manipulate them?

Unfortunately you can't use the assignment operator to copy a string in the way you do with int or double variables. To achieve the equivalent of an arithmetic assignment with strings, one string has to be copied element by element to the other. In fact, performing any operation on string variables is very different from the arithmetic operations with numeric variables you've seen so far. Let's look at some common operations that you might want to perform with strings and how you would achieve them.

Appending a String

Joining one string to the end of another is a common requirement. For instance, you might want to assemble a single message from two or more strings. You might define the error messages in a program as a few basic text strings to which you append one of a variety of strings to make the message specific to a particular error. Let's see how this works in the context of an example.

TRY IT OUT: JOINING STRINGS

You could rework the last example to append the second string to the first:

```
/* Program 6.3 Joining strings */
#include <stdio.h>

int main(void)
{
  char str1[40] = "To be or not to be";
  char str2[] = ",that is the question";
  int count1 = 0;                    /* Length of str1 */
  int count2 = 0;                    /* Length of str2 */

  /* find the length of the first string */
  while (str1[count1]        )   /* Increment count till we reach the string */
    count1++;                      /* terminating character.                  */

  /* Find the length of the second string */
  while (str2[count2])             /* Count characters in second string */
    count2++;

  /* Check that we have enough space for both strings  */
  if(sizeof str1 < count1 + count2 + 1)
    printf("\nYou can't put a quart into a pint pot.");
  else
  { /* Copy 2nd string to end of the first  */
    count2 = 0;                     /* Reset index for str2 to 0   */
    while(str2[count2])            /* Copy up to null from str2   */
      str1[count1++] = str2[count2++];
```

```
    str1[count1] = '\0';      /* Make sure we add terminator  */
    printf("\n%s\n", str1 );  /* Output combined string       */
  }
  return 0;
}
```

The output from this program will be the following:

```
To be or not to be, that is the question
```

How It Works

This program first finds the lengths of the two strings. It then checks that str1 has enough elements to hold both strings plus the terminating null character:

```
if(sizeof str1 < count1 + count2 + 1)
  printf("\nYou can't put a quart into a pint pot.");
```

Notice how you use the sizeof operator to get the total number of bytes in the array by just using the array name as an argument. The value that results from the expression sizeof str1 is the number of characters that the array will hold, because each character occupies 1 byte.

If you discover that the array is too small to hold the contents of both strings, then you display a message. The program will then end as you fall through the closing brace in main(). It's essential that you do not try to place more characters in the array than it can hold, as this will overwrite some memory that may contain important data. This is likely to crash your program. You should never append characters to a string without first checking that there is sufficient space in the array to accommodate them.

You reach the else block only if you're sure that both strings will fit in the first array. Here, you reset the variable count2 to 0 and copy the second string to the first array with the following statements:

```
  else
  {  /* Copy 2nd string to end of the first  */
    count2 = 0;                  /* Reset index for str2 to 0  */
    while(str2[count2])          /* Copy up to null from str2  */
      str1[count1++] = str2[count2++];

    str1[count1] = '\0';         /* Make sure we add terminator */
    printf("\n%s\n", str1 );     /* Output combined string       */
  }
```

The variable count1 starts from the value that was left by the loop that determined the length of the first string, str1. This is why you use two separate variables to count the number of characters in each of the two strings. Because the array is indexed from 0, the value that's stored in count1 will point to the element containing '\0' at the end of the first string. So when you use count1 to index the array str1, you know that you're starting at the end of the message proper and that you'll overwrite the null character with the first character of the second string.

You then copy characters from str2 to str1 until you find the '\0' in str2. You still have to add a terminating '\0' to str1 because it isn't copied from str2. The end result of the operation is that you've added the contents of str2 to the end of str1, overwriting the terminating null character for str1 and adding a terminating null to the end of the combined string.

You could replace the three lines of code that did the copying with a more concise alternative:

```
while ((str1[count1++] = str2[count2++]));
```

This would replace the loop you have in the program as well as the statement to put a '\0' at the end of str1. This statement would copy the '\0' from str2 to str1, because the copying occurs in the loop continuation condition. Let's consider what happens at each stage.

1. Assign the value of str2[count2] to str1[count1]. An assignment expression has a value that is the value that was stored in the left operand of the assignment operator. In this case it is the character that was copied into str1[count1].

2. Increment each of the counters by 1, using the postfix form of the ++ operator.

3. Check whether the value of the assignment expression—which will be the last character stored in str1—is true or false. The loop ends after the '\0' has been copied to str1, which will result in the value of the assignment being false.

Arrays of Strings

It may have occurred to you by now that you could use a two-dimensional array of elements of type char to store strings, where each row is used to hold a separate string. In this way you could arrange to store a whole bunch of strings and refer to any of them through a single variable name, as in this example:

```
char sayings[3][32] = {
                  "Manners maketh man.",
                  "Many hands make light work.",
                  "Too many cooks spoil the broth."
              };
```

This creates an array of three rows of 32 characters. The strings between the braces will be assigned in sequence to the three rows of the array, sayings[0], sayings[1], and sayings[2]. Note that you don't need braces around each string. The compiler can deduce that each string is intended to initialize one row of the array. The last dimension is specified to be 32, which is just sufficient to accommodate the longest string, including its terminating \0 character. The first dimension specifies the number of strings.

When you're referring to an element of the array! sayings[i][j], for instance! the first index, i, identifies a row in the array, and the second index, j, identifies a character within a row. When you want to refer to a complete row containing one of the strings, you just use a single index value between square brackets. For instance, sayings[1] refers to the second string in the array, "Many hands make light work.".

Although you must specify the last dimension in an array of strings, you can leave it to the compiler to figure out how many strings there are:

```
char sayings[][32] = {
                      "Manners maketh man.",
                      "Many hands make light work.",
                      "Too many cooks spoil the broth."
                  };
```

I've omitted the value for the size of the first dimension in the array here so the compiler will deduce this from the initializers between braces. Because you have three initializing strings, the compiler will make the first array dimension 3. Of course, you must still make sure that the last dimension is large enough to accommodate the longest string, including its terminating null character.

You could output the three sayings with the following code:

```
for(int i = 0 ; i<3 ; i++)
```

```
printf("\n%s", sayings[i]);
```

You reference a row of the array using a single index in the expression sayings[i]. This effectively accesses the one-dimensional array that is at index position i in the sayings array.

You could change the last example to use a two-dimensional array.

TRY IT OUT: ARRAYS OF STRINGS

Let's change the previous example so that it stores the two initial strings in a single array and incorporate the more concise coding for finding string lengths and copying strings:

```
/* Program 6.4 Arrays of strings */
#include <stdio.h>

int main(void)
{
  char str[][40] = {
                    "To be or not to be"  ,
                    ", that is the question"
                   };
  int count[] = {0, 0};                 /* Lengths of strings */

  /* find the lengths of the strings */
  for(int i = 0 ; i<2 ; i++)
    while (str[i][count[i]])
      count[i]++;

  /* Check that we have enough space for both strings  */
  if(sizeof str[0] < count[0] + count[1] + 1)
    printf("\nYou can't put a quart into a pint pot.");
  else
  {  /* Copy 2nd string to first */
    count[1] = 0;
    while((str[0][count[0]++] = str[1][count[1]++]));

    printf("\n%s\n", str[0]);    /* Output combined string */
  }
  return 0;
}
```

Typical output from this program is the following:

```
To be or not to be, that is the question
```

How It Works

You declare a single two-dimensional char array instead of the two one-dimensional arrays you had before:

```
char str[][40] = {
                  "To be or not to be",
                  ",that is the question"
                 };
```

The first initializing string is stored with the first index value as 0, and the second initializing string is stored with the first index value as 1. Of course, you could add as many initializing strings as you want between the braces, and the compiler would adjust the first array dimension to accommodate them.

The string lengths are now stored as elements in the count array. With count as an array we are able to find the lengths of both strings in the same loop:

```
for(int i = 0 ; i<2 ; i++)
  while (str[i][count[i]])
    count[i]++;
```

The outer for loop iterates of the two strings and the inner while loop iterates over the characters in the current string selected by i. This approach obviously applies to any number of strings in the str array; naturally the number of elements in the count array must be the same as the number of strings. A disadvantage of this approach is that if your strings are significantly less than 40 characters long, you waste quite a bit of memory in the array. In the next chapter you'll learn how you can avoid this and store each string in the most efficient manner.

String Library Functions

Now that you've struggled through the previous examples, laboriously copying strings from one variable to another, it's time to reveal that there's a standard library for string functions that can take care of all these little chores. Still, at least you know what's going on when you use the library functions.

The string functions are declared in the <string.h> header file, so you'll need to put

```
#include <string.h>
```

at the beginning of your program if you want to use them. The library actually contains quite a lot of functions, and your compiler may provide an even more extensive range of string library capabilities than is required by the C standard. I'll discuss just a few of the essential functions to demonstrate the basic idea and leave you to explore the rest on your own.

Copying Strings Using a Library Function

First, let's return to the process of copying the string stored in one array to another, which is the string equivalent of an assignment operation. The while loop mechanism you carefully created to do this must still be fresh in your mind. Well, you can do the same thing with this statement:

```
strcpy(string1, string2);
```

The arguments to the strcpy() function are char array names. What the function actually does is copy the string specified by the second argument to the string specified by the first argument, so in the preceding example string2 will be copied to string1, replacing what was previously stored in string1. The copy operation will include the terminating '\0'. It's your responsibility to ensure that the array string1 has sufficient space to accommodate string2. The function strcpy() has no way of checking the sizes of the arrays, so if it goes wrong it's all your fault. Obviously, the sizeof operator is important because you'll most likely check that everything is as it should be:

```
if(sizeof(string2) <= sizeof (string1))
  strcpy(string1, string2);
```

You execute the strcpy() operation only if the length of the string2 array is less than or equal to the length of the string1 array.

You have another function available, strncpy(), that will copy the first n characters of one string to another. The first argument is the destination string, the second argument is the source string, and the third argument is an integer of type size_t that specifies the number of characters to be copied. Here's an example of how this works:

```
char destination[] = "This string will be replaced";
char source[] = "This string will be copied in part";
size_t n = 26;                   /* Number of characters to be copied */
strncpy(destination, source, n);
```

After executing these statements, destination will contain the string "This string will be copied", because that corresponds to the first 26 characters from source. A '\0' character will be appended after the last character copied. If source has fewer than 26 characters, the function will add '\0' characters to make up the count to 26.

Note that when the length of the source string is greater than the number of characters to be copied, no additional '\0' character is added to the destination string by the strncpy() function. This means that the destination string may not have a termination null character in such cases, which can cause major problems with further operations with the destination string.

Determining String Length Using a Library Function

To find out the length of a string you have the function strlen(), which returns the length of a string as an integer of type size_t. To find the length of a string in Program 6.3 you wrote this:

```
while (str2[count2])
  count2++;
```

Instead of this rigmarole, you could simply write this:

```
count2 = strlen(str2);
```

Now the counting and searching that's necessary to find the end of the string is performed by the function, so you no longer have to worry about it. Note that it returns the length of the string *excluding* the '\0', which is generally the most convenient result. It also returns the value as size_t which corresponds to an unsigned integer type, so you may want to declare the variable to hold the result as size_t as well. If you don't, you may get warning messages from your compiler.

Just to remind you, type size_t is a type that is defined in the standard library header file <stddef.h>. This is also the type returned by the operator sizeof. The type size_t will be defined to be one of the unsigned integer types you have seen, typically unsigned int. The reason for implementing things this way is code portability. The type returned by sizeof and the strlen() function, among others, can vary from one C implementation to another. It's up to the compiler writer to decide what it should be. Defining the type to be size_t and defining size_t in a header file enables you to accommodate such implementation dependencies in your code very easily. As long as you define count2 in the preceding example as type size_t, you have code that will work in every standard C implementation, even though the definition of size_t may vary from one implementation to another.

So for the most portable code, you should write the following:

```
size_t count2 = 0;
count2 = strlen(str2);
```

As long as you have #include directives for <string.h> and <stddef.h>, this code will compile with the ISO/IEC standard C compiler.

Joining Strings Using a Library Function

In Program 6.3, you copied the second string onto the end of the first using the following rather complicated looking code:

```
count2 = 0;
while(str2[count2])
  str1[count1++] = str2[count2++];
str1[count1] = '\0';
```

Well, the string library gives a slight simplification here, too. You could use a function that joins one string to the end of another. You could achieve the same result as the preceding fragment with the following exceedingly simple statement:

```
strcat(str1, str2);              /* Copy str2 to the end of str1 */
```

This function copies str2 to the end of str1. The strcat() function is so called because it performs string catenation; in other words it joins one string onto the end of another. As well as appending str2 to str1, the strcat() function also returns str1.

If you only want to append part of the source string to the destination string, you can use the strncat() function. This requires a third argument of type size_t that indicates the number of characters to be copied, for instance

```
strncat(str1, str2, 5);    /* Copy 1st 5 characters of str2 to the end of str1 */
```

As with all the operations that involve copying one string to another, it's up to you to ensure that the destination array is sufficiently large to accommodate what's being copied to it. This function and others will happily overwrite whatever lies beyond the end of your destination array if you get it wrong.

All these string functions return the destination string. This allows you to use the value returned in another string operation, for example

```
size_t length = 0;
length = strlen(strncat(str1, str2, 5));
```

Here the strncat() function copies five characters from str2 to the end of str1. The function returns the array str1, so this is passed as an argument to the strlen() function. This will then return the length of the new version of str1 with the five characters from str2 appended.

TRY IT OUT: USING THE STRING LIBRARY

You now have enough tools to do a good job of rewriting Program 6.3:

```
/* Program 6.5 Joining strings - revitalized */
#include <stdio.h>
#include <string.h>
#define STR_LENGTH 40

int main(void)
{
  char str1[STR_LENGTH] = "To be or not to be";
  char str2[STR_LENGTH] = ",that is the question";

  if(STR_LENGTH > strlen(str1) + strlen(str2)) /* Enough space ?          */
    printf("\n%s\n", strcat(str1, str2));   /* yes, so display joined string */
```

```
    else
       printf("\nYou can't put a quart into a pint pot.");
    return 0;
}
```

This program will produce exactly the same output as before.

How It Works

Well, what a difference a library makes. It actually makes the problem trivial, doesn't it? You've defined a symbol for the size of the arrays using a #define directive. If you want to change the array sizes in the program later, you can just modify the definition for STR_LENGTH. You simply check that you have enough space in your array by means of the if statement:

```
if(STR_LENGTH > strlen(str1) + strlen(str2)) /* Enough space ?              */
   printf("\n%s\n", strcat(str1, str2));    /* yes, so display joined string  */
else
   printf("\nYou can't put a quart into a pint pot.");
```

If you do have enough space, you join the strings using the strcat() function within the argument to the printf(). Because the strcat() function returns str1, the printf() displays the result of joining the strings. If str1 is too short, you just display a message. Note that the comparison uses the > operator—this is because the array length must be at least one greater than the sum of the two string lengths to allow for the terminating '\0' character.

Comparing Strings

The string library also provides functions for comparing strings and deciding whether one string is greater than or less than another. It may sound a bit odd applying such terms as •greater than! and •less than! to strings, but the result is produced quite simply. Successive corresponding characters of the two strings are compared based on the numerical value of their character codes. This mechanism is illustrated graphically in Figure 6-2, in which the character codes are shown as hexadecimal values.

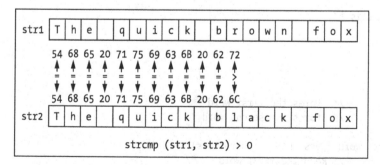

Figure 6-2. *Comparing two strings*

If two strings are identical, then of course they're equal. The first pair of corresponding characters that are different in two strings determines whether the first string is less than or greater than the second. So, for example, if the character code for the character in the first string is less than the character code for the character in the second string, the first string is less than the second. This mechanism for comparison generally corresponds to what you expect when you're arranging strings in alphabetical order.

The function strcmp(str1, str2) compares two strings. It returns a value of type int that is less than, equal to, or greater than 0, corresponding to whether str1 is less than, equal to, or greater than str2. You can express the comparison illustrated in Figure 6-2 in the following code fragment:

```
char str1[] = "The quick brown fox";
char str2[] = "The quick black fox";
if(strcmp(str1, str2) < 0)
  printf("str1 is less than str2");
```

The printf() statement will execute only if the strcmp() function returns a negative integer. This will be when the strcmp() function finds a pair of corresponding characters in the two strings that do not match and the character code in str1 is less than the character code in str2.

The strncmp() function compares up to n characters of the two strings. The first two arguments are the same as for the strcmp() function and the number of characters to be compared is specified by a third argument that's an integer of type size_t. This function would be useful if you were processing strings with a prefix of ten characters, say, that represented a part number or a sequence number. You could use the strncmp() function to compare just the first ten characters of two strings to determine which should come first:

```
if(strncmp(str1, str2, 10) <= 0)
  printf("\n%s\n%s", str1, str2);
else
  printf("\n%s\n%s", str2, str1);
```

These statements output strings str1 and str2 arranged in ascending sequence according to the first ten characters in the strings.

Let's try comparing strings in a working example.

TRY IT OUT: COMPARING STRINGS

You can demonstrate the use of comparing strings in an example that compares just two words that you enter from the keyboard:

```
/* Program 6.6 Comparing strings */
#include <stdio.h>
#include <string.h>

int main(void)
{
  char word1[20];                /* Stores the first word  */
  char word2[20];                /* Stores the second word */

  printf("\nType in the first word (less than 20 characters):\n1: ");
  scanf("%19s", word1);          /* Read the first word    */
  printf("Type in the second word (less than 20 characters):\n 2: ");
  scanf("%19s", word2);          /* Read the second word   */

  /* Compare the two words */
  if(strcmp(word1,word2) == 0)
    printf("You have entered identical words");
```

```
      else
         printf("%s precedes %s",
                           (strcmp(word1, word2) < 0) ? word1 : word2,
                           (strcmp(word1, word2) < 0) ? word2 : word1);
      return 0;
   }
```

The program will read in two words and then tell you which word comes before the other alphabetically. The output looks something like this:

```
Type in the first word (less than 20 characters):
 1: apple
Type in the second word (less than 20 characters):
 2: banana
apple precedes banana
```

How It Works

You start the program with the `#include` directives for the header files for the standard input and output library, and the string handling library:

```
#include <stdio.h>
#include <string.h>
```

In the body of `main()`, you first declare two character arrays to store the words that you'll read in from the keyboard:

```
char word1[20];              /* Stores the first word  */
char word2[20];              /* Stores the second word */
```

You set the size of the arrays to 20. This should be enough for an example, but there's a risk that this may not be sufficient. As with the `strcpy()` function, It's *your* responsibility to allocate enough space for what the user may key in. The function `scanf()` will limit the number of characters read if you specify a width with the format specification. While this ensures the array limit will not be exceeded, any characters in excess of the width you specify will be left in the input stream and will be read by the next input operation for the stream.

The next task is to get two words from the user; so after a prompt you use `scanf()` twice to read a couple of words from the keyboard:

```
printf("\nType in the first word (less than 20 characters):\n 1: ");
scanf("%19s", word1);                /* Read the first word    */
printf("Type in the second word (less than 20 characters):\n 2: ");
scanf("%19s", word2);                /* Read the second word   */
```

The width specification of 19 characters ensures that the array size of 20 elements will not be exceeded. Notice how in this example you haven't used an & operator before the variables in the arguments to the `scanf()` function. This is because the name of an array by itself is an address. It corresponds to the address of the first element in the array. You could write this explicitly using the & operator like this:

```
scanf("%s", &word1[0]);
```

Therefore, `&word1[0]` is equal to `word1`! I'll go into more detail on this in the next chapter.

Finally, you use the `strcmp()` function to compare the two words that were entered:

```
if(strcmp(word1,word2) == 0)
   printf("You have entered identical words");
```

```
else
  printf("%s precedes %s",
                  (strcmp(word1, word2) < 0) ? word1 : word2,
                  (strcmp(word1, word2) < 0) ? word2 : word1);
```

If the value returned by the strcmp() function is 0, the two strings are equal and you display a message to this effect. If not, you print out a message specifying which word precedes the other. You do this using the conditional operator to specify which word you want to print first and which you want to print second.

Searching a String

The <string.h> header file declares several string-searching functions, but before I get into these, we'll take a peek at the subject of the next chapter, namely pointers. You'll need an appreciation of the basics of this in order to understand how to use the string-searching functions.

The Idea of a Pointer

As you'll learn in detail in the next chapter, C provides a remarkably useful type of variable called a **pointer**. A pointer is a variable that contains an address! that is, it contains a reference to another location in memory that can contain a value. You already used an address when you used the function scanf(). A pointer with the name pNumber is defined by the second of the following two statements:

```
int Number = 25;
int *pNumber = &Number;
```

Figure 6-3 illustrates what happens when these two statements are executed.

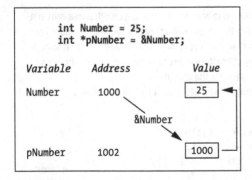

Figure 6-3. *An example of a pointer*

You declare a variable, Number, with the value 25, and a pointer, pNumber, which contains the address of Number. You can now use the variable pNumber in the expression *pNumber to obtain the value contained in Number. The * is the dereference operator and its effect is to access the data stored at the address specified by a pointer.

The main reason for introducing this idea here is that the functions I'll discuss in the following sections return pointers, so you could be a bit confused by them if there was no explanation here at all. If you end up confused anyway, don't worry! all will be illuminated in the next chapter.

Searching a String for a Character

The strchr() function searches a given string for a specified character. The first argument to the function is the string to be searched (which will be the address of a char array), and the second argument is the character that you're looking for. The function will search the string starting at the beginning and return a pointer to the first position in the string where the character is found. This is the address of this position in memory and is of type char* described as •pointer to char.! So to store the value that's returned you must create a variable that can store an address of a character. If the character isn't found, the function will return a special value NULL, which is the equivalent of 0 for a pointer and represents a pointer that doesn't point to anything.

You can use the strchr() function like this:

```
char str[] = "The quick brown fox";  /* The string to be searched        */
char c = 'q';                          /* The character we are looking for */
char *pGot_char = NULL;                /* Pointer initialized to zero      */
pGot_char = strchr(str, c);            /* Stores address where c is found  */
```

You define the character that you're looking for by the variable c of type char. Because the strchr() function expects the second argument to be of type int, the compiler will convert the value of c to this type before passing it to the function.

You could just as well define c as type int like this:

```
int c = 'q';   /* Initialize with character code for q */
```

Functions are often implemented so that a character is passed as an argument of type int because it's simpler to work with type int than type char.

Figure 6-4 illustrates the result of this search using the strchr() function.

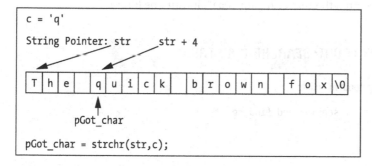

Figure 6-4. *Searching for a character*

The address of the first character in the string is given by the array name str. Because 'q' appears as the fifth character in the string, its address will be str + 4, an offset of 4 bytes from the first character. Thus, the variable pGot_char will contain the address str + 4.

Using the variable name pGot_char in an expression will access the address. If you want to access the character that's stored at that address too, then you must dereference the pointer. To do this, you precede the pointer variable name with the dereference operator *, for example:

```
printf("Character found was %c.", *pGot_char);
```

I'll go into more detail on using the dereferencing operator further in the next chapter.

Of course, in general it's always possible that the character you're searching for might not be found in the string, so you should take care that you don't attempt to dereference a NULL pointer.

If you do try to dereference a NULL pointer, your program will crash. This is very easy to avoid with an if statement, like this:

```
if(pGot_char != NULL)
  printf("Character found was %c.", *pGot_char);
```

Now you only execute the printf() statement when the variable pGot_char isn't NULL.

The strrchr() function is very similar in operation to the strchr() function, except that it searches for the character starting from the end of the string. Thus, it will return the address of the *last* occurrence of the character in the string, or NULL if the character isn't found.

Searching a String for a Substring

The strstr() function is probably the most useful of all the searching functions declared in string.h. It searches one string for the first occurrence of a substring and returns a pointer to the position in the first string where the substring is found. If it doesn't find a match, it returns NULL. So if the value returned here isn't NULL, you can be sure that the searching function that you're using has found an occurrence of what it was searching for. The first argument to the function is the string that is to be searched, and the second argument is the substring you're looking for.

Here is an example of how you might use the strstr() function:

```
char text[] = "Every dog has his day";
char word[] = "dog";
char *pFound = NULL;
pFound = strstr(text, word);
```

This searches text for the first occurrence of the string stored in word. Because the string "dog" appears starting at the seventh character in text, pFound will be set to the address text + 6. The search is case sensitive, so if you search the text string for "Dog", it won't be found.

TRY IT OUT: SEARCHING A STRING

Here's some of what I've been talking about in action:

```
/* Program 6.7 A demonstration of seeking and finding  */
#include <stdio.h>
#include <string.h>
int main(void)
{
  char str1[] = "This string contains the holy grail.";
  char str2[] = "the holy grail";
  char str3[] = "the holy grill";

  /* Search str1 for the occurrence of str2 */
  if(strstr(str1, str2) == NULL)
    printf("\n\"%s\" was not found.", str2);
  else
    printf("\n\"%s\" was found in \"%s\"",str2, str1);

  /* Search str1 for the occurrence of str3 */
  if(strstr(str1, str3) == NULL)
    printf("\n\"%s\" was not found.", str3);
```

```
  else
    printf("\nWe shouldn't get to here!");
  return 0;
}
```

This program produces the following output:

```
"the holy grail" was found in "This string contains the holy grail."
"the holy grill" was not found.
```

How It Works

Note the #include directive for <string.h>. This is necessary when you want to use any of the string processing functions.

You have three strings defined: str1, str2, and str3:

```
char str1[] = "This string contains the holy grail.";
char str2[] = "the holy grail";
char str3[] = "the holy grill";
```

In the first if statement, you use the library function strstr() to search for the occurrence of the second string in the first string:

```
if(strstr(str1, str2) == NULL)
  printf("\n\"%s\" was not found.", str2);
else
  printf("\n\"%s\" was found in \"%s\"",str2, str1);
```

You display a message corresponding to the result by testing the returned value of strstr() against NULL. If the value returned is equal to NULL, this indicates the second string wasn't found in the first, so a message is displayed to that effect. If the second string *is* found, the else is executed. In this case, a message is displayed indicating that the string was found.

You then repeat the process in the second if statement and check for the occurrence of the third string in the first:

```
if(strstr(str1, str3) == NULL)
  printf("\n\"%s\" was not found.", str3);
else
  printf("\nWe shouldn't get to here!");
```

If you get output from the first or the last printf() in the program, something is seriously wrong.

Analyzing and Transforming Strings

If you need to examine the internal contents of a string, you can use the set of standard library functions that are declared the <ctype.h> header file that I introduced in Chapter 3. These provide you with a very flexible range of analytical functions that enable you to test what kind of character you have. They also have the advantage that they're independent of the character code on the computer you're using. Just to remind you, Table 6-1 shows the functions that will test for various categories of characters.

Table 6-1. *Character Classification Functions*

Function	Tests For
islower()	Lowercase letter
isupper()	Uppercase letter
isalpha()	Uppercase or lowercase letter
isalnum()	Uppercase or lowercase letter or a digit
iscntrl()	Control character
isprint()	Any printing character including space
isgraph()	Any printing character except space
isdigit()	Decimal digit ('0' to '9')
isxdigit()	Hexadecimal digit ('0' to '9', 'A' to 'F', 'a' to 'f')
isblank()	Standard blank characters (space, '\t')
isspace()	Whitespace character (space, '\n', '\t', '\v', '\r', '\f')
ispunct()	Printing character for which isspace() and isalnum() return false

The argument to a function is the character to be tested. All these functions return a nonzero value of type int if the character is within the set that's being tested for; otherwise, they return 0. Of course, these return values convert to true and false respectively so you can use them as Boolean values. Let's see how you can use these functions for testing the characters in a string.

TRY IT OUT: USING THE CHARACTER CLASSIFICATION FUNCTIONS

The following example determines how many digits and letters there are in a string that's entered from the keyboard:

```
/* Program 6.8 Testing characters in a string */
#include <stdio.h>
#include <ctype.h>

int main(void)
{
  char buffer[80];              /* Input buffer             */
  int i = 0;                    /* Buffer index             */
  int num_letters = 0;          /* Number of letters in input */
  int num_digits = 0;           /* Number of digits in input  */

  printf("\nEnter an interesting string of less than 80 characters:\n");
  gets(buffer);                 /* Read a string into buffer  */

  while(buffer[i] != '\0')
  {
    if(isalpha(buffer[i]))
      num_letters++;            /* Increment letter count     */
```

```
    if(isdigit(buffer[i++]))
      num_digits++;                     /* Increment digit count      */
  }
  printf("\nYour string contained %d letters and %d digits.\n",
                                    num_letters, num_digits);
  return 0;
}
```

The following is typical output from this program:

```
Enter an interesting string of less than 80 characters:
I was born on the 3rd of October 1895

Your string contained 24 letters and 5 digits.
```

How It Works

This example is quite straightforward. You read the string into the array, buffer, with the following statement:

```
gets(buffer);
```

The string that you enter is read into the array buffer using a new standard library function, gets(). So far, you've used only scanf() to accept input from the keyboard, but it's not very useful for reading strings because it interprets a space as the end of an input value. The gets() function has the advantage that it will read all the characters entered from the keyboard, including blanks, up to when you press the Enter key. This is then stored as a string into the area specified by its argument, which in this case is the buffer array. A '\0' will be appended to the string automatically.

As with any input or output operation, things can go wrong. If an error of some kind prevents the gets() function from reading the input successfully, it will return NULL (normally, it returns the address passed as the argument—buffer, in this case). You could therefore check that the read operation was successful using the following code fragment:

```
if(gets(buffer) == NULL)
{
  printf("Error reading input.");
  return 1;                          /* End the program */
}
```

This will output a message and end the program if the read operation fails for any reason. Errors on keyboard input are relatively rare, so you won't include this testing when you're reading from the keyboard in your examples; but if you are reading from a file, verifying that the read was successful is essential.

A disadvantage of the gets() function is that it will read a string of any length and attempt to store it in buffer. There is no check that buffer has sufficient space to store the string so there's another opportunity to crash the program. To avoid this you could use the fgets() function, which allows you to specify the maximum length of the input string. This is a function that is used for any kind of input stream, as opposed to gets() which only reads from the standard input stream stdin; so you also have to specify a third argument to fgets() indicating the stream that is to be read. Here's how you could use fgets() to read a string from the keyboard:

```
if(fgets(buffer, sizeof(buffer), stdin) == NULL)
{
  printf("Error reading input.");
  return 1;                          /* End the program */
}
```

The fgets() function reads a maximum of one less than the number of characters specified by the second argument. It then appends a \0 character to the end of the string in memory, so the second argument in this case is sizeof(buffer). Note that there is another important difference between fgets() and gets(). For both functions, reading a newline character ends the input process, but fgets() stores a '\n' character when a newline is entered, whereas gets() does not. This means that if you are reading strings from the keyboard, strings read by fgets() will be one character longer than strings read by gets(). It also means that just pressing the Enter key as the input will result in an empty string "\0" with gets(), but will result in the string "\n\0" with fgets(). You'll use fgets() in the next example in this chapter, Program 6.9, where you have to take account of the newline character that is stored as part of the string. You'll also see more about the fgets() function in Chapter 12.

The statements that analyze the string are as follows:

```
while(buffer[i] != '\0')
{
  if(isalpha(buffer[i]))
    num_letters++;              /* Increment letter count   */
  if(isdigit(Buffer[i++]))
    num_digits++;               /* Increment digit count    */
}
```

The input string is tested character by character in the while loop. Checks are made for alphabetic characters and digits in the two if statements. When either is found, the appropriate counter is incremented. Note that you increment the index to the buffer array in the second if. Remember, because you're using the postfix form of the increment operator, the check is made using the current value of i, and then i is incremented.

You could implement this without using if statements:

```
while(buffer[i] != '\0')
{
  num_letters += isalpha(buffer[i]) != 0;
  num_digits += isdigit(buffer[i++]) != 0;
}
```

The test functions return a nonzero value (not necessarily 1, though) if the argument belongs to the group of characters being tested for. The value of the logical expressions to the right of the assignment operators will be true if the character does belong to the category you're testing for; otherwise, it will be false.

The way you've coded the example isn't a particularly efficient way of doing things, because you test for a digit even if you've already discovered the current character is alphabetic. You could try to improve on this if the TV is really bad one night.

Converting Characters

You've already seen that the standard library also includes two conversion functions that you get access to through <ctype.h>. The toupper() function converts from lowercase to uppercase, and the tolower() function does the reverse. Both functions return either the converted character or the same character for characters that are already in the correct case. You can therefore convert a string to uppercase using this statement:

```
for(int i = 0 ; (buffer[i] = toupper(buffer[i])) != '\0' ; i++);
```

This loop will convert the entire string to uppercase by stepping through the string one character at a time, converting lowercase to uppercase and leaving uppercase characters unchanged. The loop stops when it reaches the string termination character '\0'. This sort of pattern in which everything is done inside the loop control expressions is quite common in C.

Let's try a working example that applies these functions to a string.

TRY IT OUT: CONVERTING CHARACTERS

You can use the function `toupper()` in combination with the `strstr()` function to find out whether one string occurs in another, ignoring case. Look at the following example:

```c
/* Program 6.9 Finding occurrences of one string in another  */
#include <stdio.h>
#include <string.h>
#include <ctype.h>

int main(void)
{
  char text[100];              /* Input buffer for string to be searched */
  char substring[40];          /* Input buffer for string sought         */

  printf("\nEnter the string to be searched (less than 100 characters):\n");
  fgets(text, sizeof(text), stdin);

  printf("\nEnter the string sought (less than 40 characters):\n");
  fgets(substring, sizeof(substring), stdin);

  /* overwrite the newline character in each string */
  text[strlen(text)-1] = '\0';
  substring[strlen(substring)-1] = '\0';

  printf("\nFirst string entered:\n%s\n", text);
  printf("\nSecond string entered:\n%s\n", substring);

  /* Convert both strings to uppercase. */
  for(int i = 0 ; (text[i] = toupper(text[i])) ; i++);
  for(int i = 0 ; (substring[i] = toupper(substring[i])) ; i++);

    printf("\nThe second string %s found in the first.",
           ((strstr(text, substring) == NULL) ? "was not" : "was"));
  return 0;
}
```

Typical operation of this example will produce the following:

```
Enter the string to be searched(less than 100 characters):
Cry havoc, and let slip the dogs of war.

Enter the string sought (less than 40 characters ):
The Dogs of War

First string entered:
Cry havoc, and let slip the dogs of war

Second string entered:
The Dogs of War

The second string was found in the first.
```

How It Works

This program has three distinct phases: getting the input strings, converting both strings to uppercase, and searching the first string for an occurrence of the second.

First of all, you use printf() to prompt the user for the input, and you use the fgets() function introduced in the discussion of the previous example to read the input into text and substring:

```
printf("\nEnter the string to be searched(less than 100 characters):\n");
fgets(text. sizeof(text), stdin);
printf("\nEnter the string sought (less than 40 characters ):\n");
gets(substring, sizeof(substring), stdin);
```

You use the fgets() function here because it will read in any string from the keyboard, including spaces, the input being terminated when the Enter key is pressed. The input process will only allow 99 characters to be entered for the first string, text, and 39 characters for the second string, substring. If more characters are entered they will be ignored so the operation of the program is safe.

You'll recall that fgets() stores the newline character that ends the input process. This doesn't matter particularly for the first string but it matters a lot for the second string you are searching for. For example, if the string you want to find is "dogs", the fgets() function will actually store "dogs\n", which is not the same at all. You therefore remove the newline from each string by overwriting it with a '\0' character:

```
text[strlen(text)-1] = '\0';
substring[strlen(substring)-1] = '\0';
```

The newline character is the next to last character in each string and the index for this position is the string length less 1.

Of course, if you exceed the limits for input, the strings will be truncated and the results are unlikely to be correct. This will be evident from the listing of the two strings that is produced by the following:

```
printf("\nFirst string entered:\n%s\n", text);
printf("\nSecond string entered:\n%s\n", substring);
```

The conversion of both strings to uppercase is accomplished using the following statements:

```
for(int i = 0 ; (text[i] = toupper(text[i])) ; i++);
for(int i = 0 ; (substring[i] = toupper(substring[i])) ; i++);
```

You use for loops to do the conversion and the work is done entirely within the control expressions for the loops. The first for loop initializes i to 0, and then converts the ith character of text to uppercase in the loop condition and stores that result back in the same position in text. The loop continues as long as the character code stored in text[i] in the second loop control expression is nonzero, which will be for any character except NULL. The index i is incremented in the third loop control expression. This ensures that there's no confusion as to when the incrementing of i takes place. The second loop works in exactly the same way to convert substring to uppercase.

With both strings in uppercase, you can test for the occurrence of substring in text, regardless of the case of the original strings. The test is done inside the output statement that reports the result:

```
printf("\nThe second string %s found in the first.",
            ((strstr(text, substring) == NULL) ? "was not" : "was"));
```

The conditional operator chooses either "was not" or "was" to be part of the output string, depending on whether the strstr() function returns NULL. You saw earlier that the strstr() function returns NULL when the string specified by the second argument isn't found in the first. Otherwise, it returns the address where the string was found.

Converting Strings to Numerical Values

The <stdlib.h> header file declares functions that you can use to convert a string to a numerical value. Each of the functions in Table 6-2 requires an argument that's a pointer to a string or an array of type char that contains a string that's a representation of a numerical value.

Table 6-2. *Functions That Convert Strings to Numerical Values*

Function	Returns
atof()	A value of type double that is produced from the string argument
atoi()	A value of type int that is produced from the string argument
atol()	A value of type long that is produced from the string argument
atoll()	A value of type long long that is produced from the string argument

These functions are very easy to use, for example

```
char value_str[] = "98.4";
double value = 0;
value = atof(value_str);          /* Convert string to floating-point */
```

The value_str array contains a string representation of a value of type double. You pass the array name as the argument to the atof() function to convert it to type double. You use the other three functions in a similar way.

These functions are particularly useful when you need to read numerical input in the format of a string. This can happen when the sequence of the data input is uncertain, so you need to analyze the string in order to determine what it contains. Once you've figured out what kind of numerical value the string represents, you can use the appropriate library function to convert it.

Working with Wide Character Strings

Working with wide character strings is just as easy as working with the strings you have been using up to now. You store a wide character string in an array of elements of type wchar_t and a wide character string constant just needs the L modifier in front of it. Thus you can declare and initialize a wide character string like this:

```
wchar_t proverb[] = L"A nod is as good as a wink to a blind horse.";
```

As you saw back in Chapter 2, a wchar_t character occupies 2 bytes. The proverb string contains 44 characters plus the terminating null, so the string will occupy 90 bytes.

If you wanted to write the proverb string to the screen using printf() you must use the %S format specifier rather than %s that you use for ASCII string. If you use %s, the printf() function will assume the string consists of single-byte characters so the output will not be correct. Thus the following statement will output the wide character string correctly:

```
printf("The proverb is:\n%S", proverb);
```

Operations on Wide Character Strings

The <wchar.h> header file declares a range of functions for operating on wide character strings that parallel the functions you have been working with that apply to ordinary strings. Table 6-3 shows the functions declared in <wchar.h> that are the wide character equivalents to the string functions I have already discussed in this chapter.

Table 6-3. *Functions That Operate on Wide Character Strings*

Function	Description
wcslen(const wchar_t* ws)	Returns a value of type size_t that is the length of the wide character string ws that you pass as the argument. The length excludes the termination L'\0' character.
wcscpy(wchar_t* destination, const wchar_t source)	Copies the wide character string source to the wide character string destination. The function returns source.
wcsncpy(wchar_t* destination, const wchar_t source, size_t n)	Copies n characters from the wide character string source to the wide character string destination. If source contains less than n characters, destination is padded with L'\0' characters. The function returns source.
wcscat(whar_t* ws1, whar_t* ws2)	Appends a copy of ws2 to ws1. The first character of ws2 overwrites the terminating null at the end of ws1. The function returns ws1.
wcsncmp(const wchar_t* ws1, const wchar_t* ws2)	Compares the wide character string pointed to by ws1 with the wide character string pointed to by ws2 and returns a value of type int that is less than, equal to, or greater than 0 if the string ws1 is less than, equal to, or greater than the string ws2.
wcscmp(const wchar_t* ws1, const wchar_t* ws2, size_t n)	Compares up to n characters from the wide character string pointed to by ws1 with the wide character string pointed to by ws2. The function returns a value of type int that is less than, equal to, or greater than 0 if the string of up to n characters from ws1 is less than, equal to, or greater than the string of up to n characters from ws2.
wcschr(const wchar_t* ws, wchar_t wc)	Returns a pointer to the first occurrence of the wide character, wc, in the wide character string pointed to by ws. If wc is not found in ws, the NULL pointer value is returned.
wcsstr(const wchar_t* ws1, const wchar_t* ws2)	Returns a pointer to the first occurrence of the wide character string ws2 in the wide character string ws1. If ws2 is not found in ws1, the NULL pointer value is returned.

As you see from the descriptions, all these functions work in essentially the same way as the string functions you have already seen. Where the const keyword appears in the specification of the type of argument you can supply to a function, it implies that the argument will not be modified by the function. This forces the compiler to check that the function does not attempt to change such arguments. You'll see more on this in Chapter 7 when you explore how you create your own functions in more detail.

The <wchar.h> header also declares the fgetws() function that reads a wide character string from a stream such as stdin, which by default corresponds to the keyboard. You must supply three arguments to the fgetws() function, just like the fgets() function you use for reading for single-byte strings:

! The first argument is a pointer to an array of wchar_t elements that is to store the string.

! The second argument is a value n of type size_t that is the maximum number of characters that can be stored in the array.

! The third argument is the stream from which the data is to be read, which will be stdin when you are reading a string from the keyboard.

The function reads up to n-1 characters from the stream and stores them in the array with an L'\0' appended. Reading a newline in less than n-1 characters from the stream signals the end of input. The function returns a pointer to the array containing the string.

Testing and Converting Wide Characters

The <wchar.h> header also declares functions to test for specific subsets of wide characters, analogous to the functions you have seen for characters of type char. These are shown in Table 6.4.

Table 6-4. *Wide Character Classification Functions*

Function	Tests For
iswlower()	Lowercase letter
iswupper()	Uppercase letter
iswalnum()	Uppercase or lowercase letter
iswcntrl()	Control character
iswprint()	Any printing character including space
iswgraph()	Any printing character except space
iswdigit()	Decimal digit (L'0' to L'9')
iswxdigit()	Hexadecimal digit (L'0' to L'9', L'A' to L'F', L'a' to L'f')
iswblank()	Standard blank characters (space, L'\t')
iswspace()	Whitespace character (space, L'\n', L'\t', L'\v', L'\r', L'\f')
iswpunct()	Printing character for which iswspace() and iswalnum() return false

You also have the case-conversion functions, towlower() and towupper(), that return the lowercase or uppercase equivalent of the wchar_t argument.

You can see some of the wide character functions in action with a wide character version of Program 6.9.

TRY IT OUT: CONVERTING WIDE CHARACTERS

This example uses the wide character equivalents of `fgets()`, `toupper()`, and `wcsstr()`. The code that has changed from Program 6.9 is shown in bold type.

```c
/* Program 6.9A Finding occurrences of one wide character string in another   */
#include <stdio.h>
#include <wchar.h>

int main(void)
{
  wchar_t text[100];            /* Input buffer for string to be searched */
  wchar_t substring[40];        /* Input buffer for string sought          */

  printf("\nEnter the string to be searched(less than 100 characters):\n");
  fgetws(text, 100, stdin);
  printf("\nEnter the string sought (less than 40 characters ):\n");
  fgetws(substring, 40, stdin);

  /* overwrite the newline character in each string */
  text[wcslen(text)-1] = L'\0';
  substring[wcslen(substring)-1] = L'\0';

  printf("\nFirst string entered:\n%S\n", text);
  printf("\nSecond string entered:\n%S\n", substring);

  /* Convert both strings to uppercase. */
  for(int i = 0 ; (text[i] = towupper(text[i])) ; i++);
  for(int i = 0 ; (substring[i] = towupper(substring[i])) ; i++);

    printf("\nThe second string %s found in the first.",
            ((wcsstr(text, substring) == NULL) ? "was not" : "was"));
  return 0;
}
```

The output will be the same as for the previous example.

How It Works

This works in the same way as the previous example except that it stores the input as wide character strings and makes use of wide character functions. The example is so similar there is not much to say about it. Of course, the arrays now have elements of type `wchar_t` and the names of the functions are slightly different. Reading from the keyboard into the wide character arrays is accomplished by the `fgetws()` function where you supply the limit on the number of characters that can be stored and the name of the stream as the second and third arguments. We replace the newline character in each string with the wide character version of the null terminator, `L'\0'`. Prefixing a character literal with L makes it a literal of type `wchar_t`. Of course, the statements that output the strings use %S because we are outputting wide character strings.

Designing a Program

You've almost come to the end of this chapter. All that remains is to go through a larger example to use some of what you've learned so far.

The Problem

You are going to develop a program that will read a paragraph of text of an arbitrary length that is entered from the keyboard, and determine the frequency of which each word in the text occurs, ignoring case. The paragraph length won't be completely arbitrary, as you'll have to specify some limit for the array size within the program, but you can make the array that holds the text as large as you want.

The Analysis

To read the paragraph from the keyboard, you need to be able to read input lines of arbitrary length and assemble them into a single string that will ultimately contain the entire paragraph. You don't want lines truncated either, so fgets() looks like a good candidate for the input operation. If you define a symbol at the beginning of the code that specifies the array size to store the paragraph, you will be able to change the capacity of the program by changing the definition of the symbol.

The text will contain punctuation, so you will have to deal with that somehow if you are to be able to separate one word from another. It would be easy to extract the words from the text if each word is separated from the next by one or more spaces. You can arrange for this by replacing all characters that are not characters that appear in a word with spaces. You'll remove all the punctuation and any other odd characters that are lying around in the text. We don't need to retain the original text, but if you did you could just make a copy before eliminating the punctuation.

Separating out the words will be simple. All you need to do is extract each successive sequence of characters that are not spaces as a word. You can store the words in another array. Since you want to count word occurrences, ignoring case, you can store each word as lowercase. As you find a new word, you'll have to compare it with all the existing words you have found to see if it occurs previously. You'll only store it in the array if it is not already there. To record the number of occurrences of each word, you'll need another array to store the word counts. This array will need to accommodate as many counts as the number of words you have provided for in the program.

The Solution

This section outlines the steps you'll take to solve the problem. The program boils down to a simple sequence of steps that are more or less independent of one another. At the moment, the approach to implementing the program will be constrained by what you have learned up to now, and by the time you get to Chapter 9 you'll be able to implement this much more efficiently.

Step 1

The first step is to read the paragraph from the keyboard. As this is an arbitrary number of input lines it will be necessary to involve an indefinite loop. Let's first define the variables that we'll be using to code up the input mechanism:

```
/* Program 6.10 Analyzing text */
#include <stdio.h>
#include <string.h>

#define TEXTLEN   10000     /* Maximum length of text        */
#define BUFFERSIZE 100       /* Input buffer size             */

int main(void)
{
  char text[TEXTLEN+1];
  char buffer[BUFFERSIZE];
  char endstr[] = "*\n";              /* Signals end of input        */

  printf("Enter text on an arbitrary number of lines.");
  printf("\nEnter a line containing just an asterisk to end input:\n\n");

  /* Read an arbitrary number of lines of text */
  while(true)
  {
    /* A string containing an asterisk followed by newline */
    /* signals end of input                         */
    if(!strcmp(fgets(buffer, BUFFERSIZE, stdin), endstr))
      break;

    /* Check if we have space for latest input */
    if(strlen(text)+strlen(buffer)+1 > TEXTLEN)
      {
        printf("Maximum capacity for text exceeded. Terminating program.");
        return 1;
      }
    strcat(text, buffer);
  }

  /* Plus the rest of the program code ... */

  return 0;
}
```

You can compile and run this code as it stands if you like. The symbols TEXTLEN and BUFFERSIZE specify the capacity of the text array and the buffer array respectively. The text array will store the entire paragraph, and the buffer array stores a line of input. We need some way for the user to tell the program when he is finished entering text. As the initial prompt for input indicates, entering a single asterisk on a line will do this. The single asterisk input will be read by the fgets() function as the string "*\n" because the function stores newline characters that arise when the Enter key is pressed. The endstr array stores the string that marks the end of the input so you can compare each input line with this array.

The entire input process takes place within the indefinite while loop that follows the prompt for input. A line of input is read in the if statement:

```
if(!strcmp(fgets(buffer, BUFFERSIZE, stdin), endstr))
  break;
```

The fgets() function reads a maximum of BUFFERSIZE-1 characters from stdin. If the user enters a line longer than this, it won't really matter. The characters that are in excess of BUFFERSIZE-1 will be left in the input stream and will be read on the next loop iteration. You can check that this works by setting BUFFERSIZE at 10, say, and entering lines longer than ten characters.

Because the fgets() function returns a pointer to the string that you pass as the first argument, you can use fgets() as the argument to the strcmp() function to compare the string that was read with endstr. Thus, the if statement not only reads a line of input, it also checks whether the end of the input has been signaled by the user.

Before you append the new line of input to what's already stored in text, you check that there is still sufficient free space in text to accommodate the additional line. To append the new line, just use the strcat() library function to concatenate the string stored in buffer with the existing string in text.

Here's an example of output that results from executing this input operation:

```
Enter text on an arbitrary number of lines.
Enter a line containing just an asterisk to end input:

Mary had a little lamb,
Its feet were black as soot,
And into Mary's bread and jam,
His sooty foot he put.
  *
```

Step 2

Now that you have read all the input text, you can replace the punctuation and any newline characters recorded by the fgets() function by spaces. The following code goes immediately before the return statement at the end of the previous version of main():

```
/* Replace everything except alpha and single quote characters by spaces */
for(int i = 0 ; i < strlen(text) ; i++)
{
  if(text[i] == quote || isalnum(text[i]))
    continue;
  text[i] = space;
}
```

The loop iterates over the characters in the string stored in the text array. We are assuming that words can only contain letters, digits, and single-quote characters, so anything that is not in this set is replaced by a space character. The isalnum() that returns true for a character that is a letter or a digit is declared in the <ctype.h> header file so you must add an #include statement for this to the program. You also need to add declarations for the variables quote and space, following the declaration for endstr:

```
const char space = ' ';
const char quote = '\'';
```

You could, of course, use character literals directly in the code, but defining variables like this helps to make the code a little more readable.

Step 3

The next step is to extract the words from the text array and store them in another array. You can first add a couple more definitions for symbols that relate to the array you will use to store the words. These go immediately after the definition for BUFFERSIZE:

```
#define MAXWORDS   500      /* Maximum number of different words */
#define WORDLEN    15       /* Maximum word length              */
```

You can now add the declarations for the additional arrays and working storage that you'll need for extracting the words from the text, and you can put these after the existing declarations at the beginning of main():

```
char words[MAXWORDS][WORDLEN+1];
int nword[MAXWORDS];            /* Number of word occurrences */
char word[WORDLEN+1];           /* Stores a single word       */
int wordlen = 0;                /* Length of a word           */
int wordcount = 0;              /* Number of words stored      */
```

The words array stores up to MAXWORDS word strings of length WORDLEN, excluding the terminating null. The nword array hold counts of the number of occurrences of the corresponding words in the words array. Each time you find a new word, you'll store it in the next available position in the words array and set the element in the nword array that is at the same index position to 1. When you find a word that you have found and stored previously in words, you just need to increment the corresponding element in the nword array.

You'll extract words from the text array in another indefinite while loop because you don't know in advance how many words there are. There is quite a lot of code in this loop so we'll put it together incrementally. Here's the initial loop contents:

```
/* Find unique words and store in words array */
int index = 0;
while(true)
{
  /* Ignore any leading spaces before a word */
  while(text[index] == space)
    ++index;

  /* If we are at the end of text, we are done */
  if(text[index] == '\0')
    break;

  /* Extract a word */
  wordlen = 0;            /* Reset word length */
  while(text[index] == quote || isalpha(text[index]))
  {
    /* Check if word is too long */
    if(wordlen == WORDLEN)
    {
      printf("Maximum word length exceeded. Terminating program.");
      return 1;
    }
    word[wordlen++] = tolower(text[index++]);  /* Copy as lowercase    */
  }
  word[wordlen] = '\0';                        /* Add string terminator */
}
```

This code follows the existing code in main(), immediately before the return statement at the end.

The index variable records the current character position in the text array. The first operation within the outer loop is to move past any spaces that are there so that index refers to the first character of a word. You do this in the inner while loop that just increments index as long as the current character is a space.

It's possible that the end of the string in text has been reached, so you check for this next. If the current character at position index is '\0', you exit the loop because all words must have been extracted.

Extracting a word just involves copying any character that is alphanumeric or a single quote. The first character that is not one of these marks the end of a word. You copy the characters that make up the word into the word array in another while loop, after converting each character to lowercase using the tolower() function from the standard library. Before storing a character in word, you check that the size of the array will not be exceeded. After the copying process, you just have to append a terminating null to the characters in the word array.

The next operation to be carried out in the loop is to see whether the word you have just extracted already exists in the words array. The following code does this and goes immediately before the closing brace for the while loop in the previous code fragment:

```
/* Check for word already stored */
bool isnew = true;
for(int i = 0 ; i< wordcount ; i++)
  if(strcmp(word, words[i]) == 0)
  {
    ++nword[i];
    isnew = false;
    break;
  }
```

The isnew variable records whether the word is present and is first initialized to indicate that the latest word you have extracted is indeed a new word. Within the for loop you compare word with successive strings in the words array using the strcmp() library function that compares two strings. The function returns 0 if the strings are identical; as soon as this occurs you set isnew to false, increment the corresponding element in the nword array, and exit the for loop.

The last operation within the indefinite loop that extracts words from text is to store the latest word in the words array, but only if it is new, of course. The following code does this:

```
if(isnew)
{
  /* Check if we have space for another word */
  if(wordcount >= MAXWORDS)
  {
    printf("\n Maximum word count exceeded. Terminating program.");
    return 1;
  }

  strcpy(words[wordcount], word);    /* Store the new word  */
  nword[wordcount++] = 1;            /* Set its count to 1  */
}
```

This code also goes after the previous code fragment, but before the closing brace in the indefinite while loop. If the isnew indicator is true, you have a new word to store, but first you verify that there is still space in the words array. The strcpy() function copies the string in word to the element of the words array selected by wordcount. You then set the value of the corresponding element of the nword array that holds the count of the number of times a word has been found in the text.

Step 4

The last code fragment that you need will output the words and their frequencies of occurrence. Following is a complete listing of the program with the additional code from steps 3 and 4 highlighted in bold font:

```
/* Program 6.10 Analyzing text */
#include <stdio.h>
#include <stdbool.h>
#include <string.h>
#include <ctype.h>

#define TEXTLEN    10000    /* Maximum length of text            */
#define BUFFERSIZE 100      /* Input buffer size                 */
#define MAXWORDS   500      /* Maximum number of different words */
#define WORDLEN    15       /* Maximum word length               */

int main(void)
{
  char text[TEXTLEN+1];
  char buffer[BUFFERSIZE];
  char endstr[] = "*\n";             /* Signals end of input      */

  const char space = ' ';
  const char quote = '\'';

  char words[MAXWORDS][WORDLEN+1];
  int nword[MAXWORDS];               /* Number of word occurrences */
  char word[WORDLEN+1];              /* Stores a single word       */
  int wordlen = 0;                   /* Length of a word           */
  int wordcount = 0;                 /* Number of words stored     */

  printf("Enter text on an arbitrary number of lines.");
  printf("\nEnter a line containing just an asterisk to end input:\n\n");

  /* Read an arbitrary number of lines of text */
  while(true)
  {
    /* A string containing an asterisk followed by newline */
    /* signals end of input                                */
    if(!strcmp(fgets(buffer, BUFFERSIZE, stdin), endstr))
      break;

    /* Check if we have space for latest input */
    if(strlen(text)+strlen(buffer)+1 > TEXTLEN)
      {
        printf("Maximum capacity for text exceeded. Terminating program.");
        return 1;
      }
    strcat(text, buffer);
  }

  /* Replace everything except alpha and single quote characters by spaces */
  for(int i = 0 ; i < strlen(text) ; i++)
  {
    if(text[i] == quote || isalnum(text[i]))
      continue;
    text[i] = space;
  }
```

```
/* Find unique words and store in words array */
int index = 0;
while(true)
{
  /* Ignore any leading spaces before a word */
  while(text[index] == space)
    ++index;

  /* If we are at the end of text, we are done */
  if(text[index] == '\0')
    break;

  /* Extract a word */
  wordlen = 0;            /* Reset word length */
  while(text[index] == quote || isalpha(text[index]))
  {
    /* Check if word is too long */
    if(wordlen == WORDLEN)
    {
      printf("Maximum word length exceeded. Terminating program.");
      return 1;
    }
    word[wordlen++] = tolower(text[index++]);  /* Copy as lowercase      */
  }
  word[wordlen] = '\0';                        /* Add string terminator */

  /* Check for word already stored */
  bool isnew = true;
  for(int i = 0 ; i< wordcount ; i++)
    if(strcmp(word, words[i]) == 0)
    {
      ++nword[i];
      isnew = false;
      break;
    }

  if(isnew)
  {
    /* Check if we have space for another word */
    if(wordcount >= MAXWORDS)
    {
      printf("\n Maximum word count exceeded. Terminating program.");
      return 1;
    }

    strcpy(words[wordcount], word);   /* Store the new word   */
    nword[wordcount++] = 1;           /* Set its count to 1  */
  }
}
```

```
/* Output the words and frequencies */
for(int i = 0 ; i<wordcount ; i++)
{
  if( !(i%3) )                         /* Three words to a line */
    printf("\n");
  printf("  %-15s%5d", words[i], nword[i]);
}

return 0;
}
```

The seven lines highlighted in bold output the words and corresponding frequencies. This is very easily done in a for loop that iterates over the number of words. The loop code arranges for three words plus frequencies to be output per line by writing a newline character to stdout if the current value of i is a multiple of 3. The expression i%3 will be zero when i is a multiple of 3, and this value maps to the bool value false, so the expression !(i%3) will be true.

The program ends up as a main() function of more than 100 statements. When you learn the complete C language you would organize this program very differently with the code segmented into several much shorter functions. By Chapter 9 you'll be in a position to do this, and I would encourage you to revisit this example when you reach the end of Chapter 9. Here's a sample of output from the complete program:

```
Enter text on an arbitrary number of lines.
Enter a line containing just an asterisk to end input:

When I makes tea I makes tea, as old mother Grogan said.
And when I makes water I makes water.
Begob, ma'am, says Mrs Cahill, God send you don't make them in the same pot.
*
```

when	2	i	4	makes	4
tea	2	as	1	old	1
mother	1	grogan	1	said	1
and	1	water	2	begob	1
ma'am	1	says	1	mrs	1
cahill	1	god	1	send	1
you	1	don't	1	make	1
them	1	in	1	the	1
same	1	pot	1		

Summary

In this chapter, you applied the techniques you acquired in earlier chapters to the general problem of dealing with character strings. Strings present a different, and perhaps more difficult, problem than numeric data types.

Most of the chapter dealt with handling strings using arrays, but I also mentioned pointers. These will provide you with even more flexibility in dealing with strings, and many other things besides, as you'll discover as soon as you move on to the next chapter.

Exercises

The following exercises enable you to try out what you've learned in this chapter. If you get stuck, look back over the chapter for help. If you're still stuck, you can download the solutions from the Source Code/Downloads section of the Apress web site (http://www.apress.com), but that really should be a last resort.

Exercise 6-1. Write a program that will prompt for and read a positive integer less than 1000 from the keyboard, and then create and output a string that is the value of the integer in words. For example, if 941 is entered, the program will create the string "Nine hundred and forty one".

Exercise 6-2. Write a program that will allow a list of words to be entered separated by commas, and then extract the words and output them one to a line, removing any leading or trailing spaces. For example, if the input is

```
John  ,  Jack ,   Jill
```

then the output will be

```
John
Jack
Jill
```

Exercise 6-3. Write a program that will output a randomly chosen thought for the day from a set of at least five thoughts of your own choosing.

Exercise 6-4. A **palindrome** is a phrase that reads the same backward as forward, ignoring whitespace and punctuation. For example, •Madam, I'm Adam! and •Are we not drawn onward, we few? Drawn onward to new era?! are palindromes. Write a program that will determine whether a string entered from the keyboard is a palindrome.

CHAPTER 7

■■■

Pointers

You had a glimpse of pointers in the last chapter and just a small hint at what you can use them for. Here, you'll delve a lot deeper into the subject of pointers and see what else you can do with them.

I'll cover a lot of new concepts here, so you may need to repeat some things a few times. This is a long chapter, so spend some time on it and experiment with the examples. Remember that the basic ideas are very simple, but you can apply them to solving complicated problems. By the end of this chapter, you'll be equipped with an essential element for effective C programming.

In this chapter you'll learn the following:

! What a pointer is and how it's used

! What the relationship between pointers and arrays is

! How to use pointers with strings

! How you can declare and use arrays of pointers

! How to write an improved calculator program

A First Look at Pointers

You have now come to one of the most extraordinarily powerful tools in the C language. It's also potentially the most confusing, so it's important you get the ideas straight in your mind at the outset and maintain a clear idea of what's happening as you dig deeper.

Back in Chapters 2 and 5 I discussed memory. I talked about how your computer allocates an area of memory when you declare a variable. You refer to this area in memory using the variable name in your program, but once your program is compiled and running, your computer references it by the address of the memory location. This is the number that the computer uses to refer to the •box! in which the value of the variable is stored.

Look at the following statement:

```
int number = 5;
```

Here an area of memory is allocated to store an integer, and you can access it using the name number. The value 5 is stored in this area. The computer references the area using an address. The specific address where this data will be stored depends on your computer and what operating system and compiler you're using. Even though the variable name is fixed in the source program, the address is likely to be different on different systems.

Variables that can store addresses are called **pointers**, and the address that's stored in a pointer is usually that of another variable, as illustrated in Figure 7-1. You have a pointer P that contains the address of another variable, called number, which is an integer variable containing the value 5. The address that's stored in P is the address of the first byte of number.

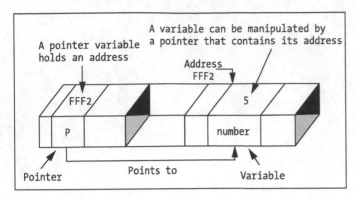

Figure 7-1. *How a pointer works*

The first thing to appreciate is that it's not enough to know that a particular variable, such as P, is a pointer. You, and more importantly, the compiler, must know the *type* of data stored in the variable to which it points. Without this information it's virtually impossible to know how to handle the contents of the memory to which it points. A pointer to a value of type char is pointing to a value occupying 1 byte, whereas a pointer to a value of type long is usually pointing to the first byte of a value occupying 4 bytes. This means that every pointer will be associated with a specific variable type, and it can be used only to point to variables of that type. So pointers of type •pointer to int! can point only to variables of type int, pointers of type •pointer to float! can point only to variables of type float, and so on. In general a pointer of a given type is written type * for any given type name type.

The type name void means absence of any type, so a pointer of type void * can contain the address of a data item of any type. Type void * is often used as an argument type or return value type with functions that deal with data in a type-independent way. Any kind of pointer can be passed around as a value of type void * and then cast to the appropriate type when you come to use it. The address of a variable of type int can be stored in a pointer variable of type void * for example. When you want to access the integer value at the address stored in the void * pointer, you must first cast the pointer to type int *. You'll meet the malloc() library function later in this chapter that returns a pointer of type void *.

Declaring Pointers

You can declare a pointer to a variable of type int with the following statement:

```
int *pointer;
```

The type of the variable with the name pointer is int *. It can store the address of any variable of type int. This statement just creates the pointer but doesn't initialize it. Uninitialized pointers are particularly hazardous, so you should always initialize a pointer when you declare it. You can initialize pointer so that it doesn't point to anything by rewriting the declaration like this:

```
int *pointer = NULL;
```

NULL is a constant that's defined in the standard library and is the equivalent of zero for a pointer. NULL is a value that's guaranteed not to point to any location in memory. This means that it implicitly prevents the accidental overwriting of memory by using a pointer that doesn't point to anything specific. NULL is defined in the header files <stddef.h>, <stdlib.h>, <stdio.h>, <string.h>, <time.h>, <wchar.h>, and <locale.h>, and you must have at least one of these headers included in your source file for NULL to be recognized by the compiler.

If you want to initialize your variable pointer with the address of a variable that you've already declared, you use the address of operator &:

```
int number = 10;
int *pointer = &number;
```

Now the initial value of pointer is the address of the variable number. Note that the declaration of number must precede the declaration of the pointer. If this isn't the case, your code won't compile. The compiler needs to have already allocated space and thus an address for number to use it to initialize the pointer variable.

There's nothing special about the declaration of a pointer. You can declare regular variables and pointers in the same statement, for example

```
double value, *pVal, fnum;
```

This statement declares two double precision floating-point variables, value and fnum, and a variable, pVal of type •pointer to double.! With this statement it is obvious that only the second variable, pVal, is a pointer, but consider this statement:

```
int *p, q;
```

This declares a pointer, p, and a variable, q, that is of type int. It is a common mistake to think that both p and q are pointers.

Accessing a Value Through a Pointer

You use the **indirection operator**, *, to access the value of the variable pointed to by a pointer. This operator is also referred to as the **dereference operator** because you use it to •dereference! a pointer. Suppose you declare the following variables:

```
int number = 15;
int *pointer = &number;
int result = 0;
```

The pointer variable contains the address of the variable number, so you can use this in an expression to calculate a new value for total, like this:

```
result = *pointer + 5;
```

The expression *pointer will evaluate to the value stored at the address contained in the pointer. This is the value stored in number, 15, so result will be set to 15 + 5, which is 20.

So much for the theory. Let's look at a small program that will highlight some of the characteristics of this special kind of variable.

TRY IT OUT: DECLARING POINTERS

In this example, you're simply going to declare a variable and a pointer. You'll then see how you can output their addresses and the values they contain.

```
/* Program 7.1 A simple program using pointers */
#include <stdio.h>

int main(void)
{
  int number = 0;                 /* A variable of type int initialized to 0 */
  int *pointer = NULL;            /* A pointer that can point to type int     */

  number = 10;
  printf("\nnumber's address: %p", &number);         /* Output the address */
  printf("\nnumber's value: %d\n\n", number);        /* Output the value   */

  pointer = &number;              /* Store the address of number in pointer   */

  printf("pointer's address: %p", &pointer);          /* Output the address */
  printf("\npointer's size: %d bytes", sizeof(pointer)); /* Output the size    */
  printf("\npointer's value: %p", pointer);  /* Output the value (an address) */
  printf("\nvalue pointed to: %d\n", *pointer);        /* Value at the address */
  return 0;
}
```

The output from the program will look something like the following. Remember, the actual address is likely to be different on your machine:

```
number's address: 0012FEE4
number's value: 10

pointer's address: 0012FEE0
pointer's size: 4 bytes
pointer's value: 0012FEE4
value pointed to: 10
```

How It Works

You first declare a variable of type int and a pointer:

```
  int number = 0;                 /* A variable of type int initialized to 0 */
  int *pointer = NULL;            /* A pointer that can point to type int     */
```

The pointer called pointer is of type "pointer to int." Pointers need to be declared just like any other variable. To declare the pointer called pointer, you put an asterisk (*) in front of the variable name in the declaration. The asterisk defines pointer as a pointer, and the type, int, fixes it as a pointer to integer variables. The initial value, NULL, is the equivalent of 0 for a pointer—it doesn't point to anything.

After the declarations, you store the value 10 in the variable called number and then output its address and its value with these statements:

```
number = 10;
printf("\nnumber's address: %p", &number);        /* Output the address */
printf("\nnumber's value: %d\n\n", number);        /* Output the value    */
```

To output the address of the variable called number, you use the output format specifier %p. This outputs the value as a memory address in hexadecimal form.

The next statement obtains the address of the variable number and stores that address in pointer, using the address of operator &:

```
pointer = &number;                 /* Store the address of number in pointer   */
```

Remember, the only kind of value that you should store in pointer is an address.

Next, you have four printf() statements that output, respectively, the address of pointer (which is the first byte of the memory location that pointer occupies), the number of bytes that the pointer occupies, the value stored in pointer (which is the address of number), and the value stored at the address that pointer contains (which is the value stored in number).

Just to make sure you're clear about this, let's go through these line by line. The first output statement is as follows:

```
printf("pointer's address: %p", &pointer);
```

Here, you output the address of pointer. Remember, a pointer itself has an address, just like any other variable. You use %p as the conversion specifier to display an address, and you use the & (address of) operator to reference the address that the pointer variable occupies.

Next you output the size of pointer:

```
printf("\npointer's size: %d bytes", sizeof(pointer)); /* Output the size    */
```

You can use the sizeof operator to obtain the number of bytes a pointer occupies, just like any other variable, and the output on my machine shows that a pointer occupies 4 bytes, so a memory address on my machine is 32 bits.

The next statement outputs the value stored in pointer:

```
printf("\npointer's value: %p", pointer);
```

The value stored in pointer is the address of number. Because this is an address, you use %p to display it and you use the variable name, pointer, to access the address value.

The last output statement is as follows:

```
printf("\nvalue pointed to: %d", *pointer);
```

Here, you use the pointer to access the value stored in number. The effect of the * operator is to access the data contained in the address stored at pointer. You use %d because you know it's an integer value. The variable pointer stores the address of number, so you can use that address to access the value stored in number. As I said, the * operator is called the **indirection operator**, or sometimes the **dereferencing operator**.

While we've noted that the addresses shown will be different on different computers, they'll often be different at different times on the same computer. The latter is due to the fact that your program won't always be loaded at the same place in memory. The addresses of number and pointer are where in the computer the variables are stored. Their values are what is actually stored at those addresses. For the variable called number, it's an actual integer value (10), but for the variable called pointer, it's the address of number. Using *pointer actually gives you access to the value of number. You're accessing the value of the variable, number, indirectly.

You'll certainly have noticed that your indirection operator, *, is also the symbol for multiplication. Fortunately, there's no risk of confusion for the compiler. Depending on where the asterisk appears, the compiler will understand whether it should interpret it as an indirection operator or as a multiplication sign.

Figure 7-2 illustrates using a pointer.

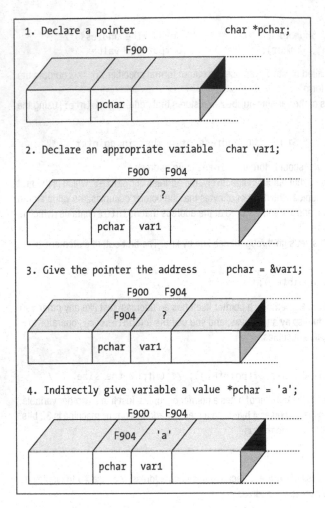

1. Declare a pointer   char *pchar;

2. Declare an appropriate variable   char var1;

3. Give the pointer the address   pchar = &var1;

4. Indirectly give variable a value *pchar = 'a';

Figure 7-2. *Using a pointer*

Using Pointers

Because you can access the contents of number through the pointer pointer, you can use a dereferenced pointer in arithmetic statements. For example

```
*pointer += 25;
```

This statement increments the value of whatever variable pointer currently addresses by 25. The * indicates you're accessing the contents of whatever the variable called pointer is pointing to. In this case, it's the contents of the variable called number.

The variable pointer can store the address of any variable of type int. This means you can change the variable that pointer points to by a statement such as this:

```
pointer = &another_number;
```

If you repeat the same statement that you used previously:

```
*pointer += 25;
```

the statement will operate with the new variable, another_number. This means that a pointer can contain the address of any variable of the same type, so you can use one pointer variable to change the values of many other variables, as long as they're of the same type as the pointer.

TRY IT OUT: USING POINTERS

Let's exercise this newfound facility in an example. You'll use pointers to increase values stored in some other variables.

```
/* Program 7.2  What's the pointer */
#include <stdio.h>

int main(void)
{
  long num1 = 0L;
  long num2 = 0L;
  long *pnum = NULL;

  pnum = &num1;                          /* Get address of num1         */
  *pnum = 2;                             /* Set num1 to 2               */
  ++num2;                                /* Increment num2              */
  num2 += *pnum;                         /* Add num1 to num2            */

  pnum = &num2;                          /* Get address of num2         */
  ++*pnum;                               /* Increment num2 indirectly */

  printf("\nnum1 = %ld  num2 = %ld  *pnum = %ld  *pnum + num2 = %ld\n",
                            num1, num2, *pnum, *pnum + num2);
  return 0;
}
```

When you run this program, you should get the following output:

```
num1 = 2  num2 = 4  *pnum = 4  *pnum + num2 = 8
```

How It Works

The comments should make the program easy to follow up to the printf(). First, in the body of main(), you have these declarations:

```
  long num1 = 0;
  long num2 = 0;
  long *pnum = NULL;
```

This ensures that you set out with initial values for the two variables, num1 and num2, at 0. The third statement above declares an integer pointer, pnum, which is initialized with NULL.

■Caution You should always initialize your pointers when you declare them. Using a pointer that isn't initialized to store an item of data is dangerous. Who knows what you might overwrite when you use the pointer to store a value?

The next statement is an assignment:

```
pnum = &num1;                                    /* Get address of num1      */
```

The pointer pnum is set to point to num1 here, because you take the address of num1 using the & operator. The next two statements are the following:

```
*pnum = 2;                                       /* Set num1 to 2            */
++num2;                                          /* Increment num2           */
```

The first statement exploits your newfound power of the pointer, and you set the value of num1 to 2 indirectly by dereferencing pnum. Then the variable num2 gets incremented by 1 in the normal way, using the increment operator.

The statement is the following:

```
num2 += *pnum;                                   /* Add num1 to num2         */
```

This adds the contents of the variable pointed to by pnum, to num2. Because pnum still points to num1, num2 is being increased by the value of num1.

The next two statements are the following:

```
pnum = &num2;                                    /* Get address of num2      */
++*pnum;                                          /* Increment num2 indirectly */
```

First, the pointer is reassigned to point to num2. The variable num2 is then incremented indirectly through the pointer. You can see that the expression ++*pnum increments the value pointed to by pnum without any problem However, if you want to use the postfix form, you have to write (*pnum)++. The parentheses are essential—assuming that you want to increment the value rather than the address. If you omit them, the increment would apply to the address contained in pnum. This is because the operators ++ and unary * (and unary &, for that matter) share the same precedence level and are evaluated right to left. The compiler would apply the ++ to pnum first, incrementing the address, and only then dereference it to get the value. This is a common source of error when incrementing values through pointers, so it's probably a good idea to use parentheses in any event.

Finally, before the return statement that ends the program, you have the following printf() statement:

```
printf("\nnum1 = %ld  num2 = %ld  *pnum = %ld  *pnum + num2 = %ld",
                        num1, num2, *pnum, *pnum + num2);
```

This displays the values of num1, num2, num2 incremented by 1 through pnum and, lastly, num2 in the guise of pnum, with the value of num2 added.

Pointers can be confusing when you encounter them for the first time. It's the multiple levels of meaning that are the source of the confusion. You can work with addresses or values, pointers or variables, and sometimes it's hard to work out what exactly is going on. The best thing to do is to keep writing short programs that use the things I've described: getting values using pointers, changing values, printing addresses, and so on. This is the only way to really get confident about using pointers.

I've mentioned the importance of operator precedence again in this discussion. Don't forget that Table 3-2 in Chapter 3 shows the precedence of all the operators in C, so you can always refer back to it when you are uncertain about the precedence of an operator.

Let's look at an example that will show how pointers work with input from the keyboard.

TRY IT OUT: USING A POINTER WITH SCANF()

Until now, when you've used `scanf()` to input values, you've used the & operator to obtain the address to be transferred to the function. When you have a pointer that already contains an address, you simply need to use the pointer name as a parameter. You can see this in the following example:

```
/* Program 7.3  Pointer argument to scanf */
#include <stdio.h>

int main(void)
{
  int value = 0;
  int *pvalue = NULL;

  pvalue = &value;                    /* Set pointer to refer to value  */

  printf ("Input an integer: ");
  scanf(" %d", pvalue);               /* Read into value via the pointer */

  printf("\nYou entered %d\n", value);       /* Output the value entered */
  return 0;
}
```

This program will just echo what you enter. How unimaginative can you get? Typical output could be something like this:

```
Input an integer: 10
You entered 10
```

How It Works

Everything should be pretty clear up to the `scanf()` statement:

```
scanf(" %d", pvalue);
```

You normally store the value entered by the user at the address of the variable. In this case, you could have used &value. But here, the pointer pvalue is used to hand over the address of value to scanf(). You already stored the address of value in pvalue with this assignment:

```
pvalue = &value;                      /* Set pointer to refer to value  */
```

pvalue and &value are the same, so you can use either.
You then just display value:

```
printf("\nYou entered %d", value);
```

Although this is a rather pointless example, it isn't pointerless, as it illustrates how pointers and variables can work together.

Testing for a NULL Pointer

The pointer declaration in the last example is the following:

```
int *pvalue = NULL;
```

Here, you initialize pvalue with the value NULL. As I said previously, NULL is a special constant in C, and it's the pointer equivalent to 0 with ordinary numbers. The definition of NULL is contained in <stdio.h> as well as a number of other header files, so if you use it, you must ensure that you include one of these header files.

When you assign 0 to a pointer, it's the equivalent of setting it to NULL, so you could write the following:

```
int *pvalue = 0;
```

Because NULL is the equivalent of zero, if you want to test whether the pointer pvalue is NULL, you can write this:

```
if(!pvalue)
{
  ...
}
```

When pvalue is NULL, !pvalue will be true, so the block of statement will be executed only if pvalue is NULL. Alternatively you can write the test as follows:

```
if(pvalue == NULL)
{
  ...
}
```

Pointers to Constants

You can use the const keyword when you declare a pointer to indicate that the value pointed to must not be changed. Here's an example of a declaration of a const pointer:

```
long value = 9999L;
const long *pvalue = &value;      /* Defines a pointer to a constant */
```

Because you have declared the value pointed to by pvalue to be const, the compiler will check for any statements that attempt to modify the value pointed to by pvalue and flag such statements as an error. For example, the following statement will now result in an error message from the compiler:

```
*pvalue = 8888L;                  /* Error - attempt to change const location */
```

You have only asserted that what pvalue points to must not be changed. You are quite free to do what you want with value:

```
value = 7777L;
```

The value pointed to has changed but you did not use the pointer to make the change. Of course, the pointer itself is not constant, so you can still change what it points to:

```
long number = 8888L;
pvalue = &number;                 /* OK - changing the address in pvalue      */
```

This will change the address stored in pvalue to point to number. You still cannot use the pointer to change the value that is stored though. You can change the address stored in the pointer as much as you like but using the pointer to change the value pointed to is not allowed.

Constant Pointers

Of course, you might also want to ensure that the address stored in a pointer cannot be changed. You can arrange for this to be the case by using the const keyword slightly differently in the declaration of the pointer. Here's how you could ensure that a pointer always points to the same thing:

```
int count = 43;
int *const pcount = &count;            /* Defines a constant */
```

The second statement declares and initializes pnumber and indicates that the address stored must not be changed. The compiler will therefore check that you do not inadvertently attempt to change what the pointer points to elsewhere in your code, so the following statements will result in an error message when you compile:

```
int item = 34;
pcount = &item;                    /* Error - attempt to change a constant pointer */
```

You can still change the value that pcount points to using pcount though:

```
*pcount = 345;                     /* OK - changes the value of count */
```

This references the value stored in count through the pointer and changes its value to 345. You could also use count directly to change the value.

You can create a constant pointer that points to a value that is also constant:

```
int item = 25;
const int *const pitem = &item;
```

pitem is a constant pointer to a constant so everything is fixed. You cannot change the address stored in pitem and you cannot use pitem to modify what it points to.

Naming Pointers

You've already started to write some quite large programs. As you can imagine, when your programs get even bigger, it's going to get even harder to remember which variables are normal variables and which are pointers. Therefore, it's quite a good idea to use names beginning with p for use as pointer names. If you follow this method religiously, you stand a reasonable chance of knowing which variables are pointers.

Arrays and Pointers

You'll need a clear head for this bit. Let's recap for a moment and recall what an array is and what a pointer is:

An **array** is a collection of objects of the same type that you can refer to using a single name. For example, an array called scores[50] could contain all your basketball scores for a 50-game season. You use a different index value to refer to each element in the array. scores[0] is your first score and scores[49] is your last. If you had ten games each month, you could use a multi-dimensional array, scores[12][10]. If you start play in January, the third game in June would be referenced by scores[5][2].

A **pointer** is a variable that has as its value the address of another variable or constant of a given type. You can use a pointer to access different variables at different times, as long as they're all of the same type.

These seem quite different, and indeed they are, but arrays and pointers are really very closely related and they can sometimes be used interchangeably. Let's consider strings. A string is just an array of elements of type char. If you want to input a single character with scanf(), you could use this:

```
char single;
scanf("%c", &single);
```

Here you need the address of operator for scanf() to work because scanf() needs the address of the location where the input data is to be stored.

However, if you're reading in a string, you can write this:

```
char multiple[10];
scanf("%s", multiple);
```

Here you don't use the & operator. You're using the array name just like a pointer. If you use the array name in this way without an index value, it refers to the address of the first element in the array.

Always keep in mind, though, that arrays are *not* pointers, and there's an important difference between them. You can change the address contained in a pointer, but you can't change the address referenced by an array name.

Let's go through several examples to see how arrays and pointers work together. The following examples all link together as a progression. With practical examples of how arrays and pointers can work together, you should find it fairly easy to get a grasp of the main ideas behind pointers and their relationship to arrays.

TRY IT OUT: ARRAYS AND POINTERS

Just to further illustrate that an array name by itself refers to an address, try running the following program:

```
/* Program 7.4  Arrays and pointers - A simple program*/
#include <stdio.h>

int main(void)
{
  char multiple[] = "My string";

  char *p = &multiple[0];
  printf("\nThe address of the first array element  : %p", p);

  p = multiple;
  printf("\nThe address obtained from the array name: %p\n", p);
  return 0;
}
```

On my computer, the output is as follows:

```
The address of the first array element  : 0x0013ff62
The address obtained from the array name: 0x0013ff62
```

How It Works

You can conclude from the output of this program that the expression &multiple[0] produces the same value as the expression multiple. This is what you might expect because multiple evaluates to the address of the first byte of the array, and &multiple[0] evaluates to the first byte of the first element of the array, and it would be surprising if these were not the same. So let's take this a bit further. If p is set to multiple, which has the same value as &multiple[0], what does p + 1 equal? Let's try the following example.

TRY IT OUT: ARRAYS AND POINTERS TAKEN FURTHER

This program demonstrates the effect of adding an integer value to a pointer.

```
/* Program 7.5 Arrays and pointers taken further */
#include <stdio.h>

int main(void)
{
  char multiple[] = "a string";
  char *p = multiple;

  for(int i = 0 ; i<strlen(multiple) ; i++)
    printf("\nmultiple[%d] = %c  *(p+%d) = %c  &multiple[%d] = %p  p+%d = %p",
                    i, multiple[i], i, *(p+i), i, &multiple[i], i, p+i);
  return 0;
}
```

The output is the following:

```
multiple[0] = a  *(p+0) = a  &multiple[0] = 0x0013ff63  p+0 = 0x0013ff63
multiple[1] =    *(p+1) =    &multiple[1] = 0x0013ff64  p+1 = 0x0013ff64
multiple[2] = s  *(p+2) = s  &multiple[2] = 0x0013ff65  p+2 = 0x0013ff65
multiple[3] = t  *(p+3) = t  &multiple[3] = 0x0013ff66  p+3 = 0x0013ff66
multiple[4] = r  *(p+4) = r  &multiple[4] = 0x0013ff67  p+4 = 0x0013ff67
multiple[5] = i  *(p+5) = i  &multiple[5] = 0x0013ff68  p+5 = 0x0013ff68
multiple[6] = n  *(p+6) = n  &multiple[6] = 0x0013ff69  p+6 = 0x0013ff69
multiple[7] = g  *(p+7) = g  &multiple[7] = 0x0013ff6a  p+7 = 0x0013ff6a
```

How It Works

Look at the list of addresses to the right in the output. Because p is set to the address of multiple, p + n is essentially the same as multiple + n, so you can see that multiple[n] is the same as *(multiple + n). The addresses differ by 1, which is what you would expect for an array of elements that each occupy one byte. You can see from the two columns of output to the left that *(p + n), which is dereferencing the address that you get by adding an integer n to the address in p, evaluates to the same thing as multiple[n].

TRY IT OUT: DIFFERENT TYPES OF ARRAYS

That's interesting, but you already knew that the computer could add numbers together without much problem. So let's change to a different type of array and see what happens:

```
/* Program 7.6 Different types of arrays */
#include <stdio.h>

int main(void)
{
  long multiple[] = {15L, 25L, 35L, 45L};
  long * p = multiple;

  for(int i = 0 ; i<sizeof(multiple)/sizeof(multiple[0]) ; i++)
    printf("\naddress p+%d (&multiple[%d]): %d   *(p+%d) value: %d",
                      i,           i,   p+i,     i,     *(p+i));
  printf("\n    Type long occupies: %d bytes\n", sizeof(long));
  return 0;
}
```

If you compile and run this program, you get an entirely different result:

```
address p+0 (&multiple[0]): 1310552   *(p+0) value: 15
address p+1 (&multiple[1]): 1310556   *(p+1) value: 25
address p+2 (&multiple[2]): 1310560   *(p+2) value: 35
address p+3 (&multiple[3]): 1310564   *(p+3) value: 45
    Type long occupies: 4 bytes
```

How It Works

I have spaced out the second and subsequent arguments to the printf() function so you can more easily see the correspondence between format specifiers and the arguments. This time the pointer, p, is set to the address that results from multiple, where multiple is an array of elements of type long. The pointer will initially contain the address of the first byte in the array, which is also the first byte of the element multiple[0]. This time the addresses are displayed using the %d specifier so they will be decimal values. This will make is easier to see the difference between successive addresses.

Look at the output. With this example, p is 1310552 and p+1 is equal to 1310556. You can see that 1310556 is 4 greater than 1310552 although you only added 1. This isn't a mistake. The compiler realizes that when you add 1 to an address value, what you actually want to do is access the next variable of that type. This is why, when you declare a pointer, you have to specify the *type* of variable that's to be pointed to. Remember that char data is stored in 1 byte and that variables declared as long typically occupy 4 bytes. As you can see, on my computer variables declared as long are 4 bytes. Incrementing a pointer to type long by 1 on my computer increments the address by 4, because a value of type long occupies 4 bytes. On a computer that stores type long in 8 bytes, incrementing a pointer to long by 1 will increase the address value by 8.

Note that you could use the array name directly in this example. You could write the for loop as

```
for(int i = 0 ; i<sizeof(multiple)/sizeof(multiple[0]) ; i++)
  printf(
    "\naddress multiple+%d (&multiple[%d]): %d   *(multiple+%d) value: %d",
                  i,            i,  multiple+i,       i, *(multiple+i));
```

This works because the expressions multiple and multiple+i both evaluate to an address. We output the values of these addresses and output the value at these addresses by using the * operator. The arithmetic with addresses works the same here as it did with the pointer p. Incrementing multiple by 1 results in the address of the next element in the array, which is 4 bytes further along in memory. However, don't be misled; an array name is just a fixed address and is not a pointer.

Multidimensional Arrays

So far, you've looked at one-dimensional arrays; but is it the same story with arrays that have two or more dimensions? Well, to some extent it is. However, the differences between pointers and array names start to become more apparent. Let's consider the array that you used for the tic-tac-toe program at the end of Chapter 5. You declared the array as follows:

```
char board[3][3] = {
                      {'1','2','3'},
                      {'4','5','6'},
                      {'7','8','9'}
                    };
```

You'll use this array for the examples in this section, to explore multidimensional arrays in relation to pointers.

TRY IT OUT: USING TWO-DIMENSIONAL ARRAYS

You'll look first at some of the addresses related to your array, board, with this example:

```
/* Program 7.7 Two-Dimensional arrays and pointers */
#include <stdio.h>

int main(void)
{
  char board[3][3] = {
                        {'1','2','3'},
                        {'4','5','6'},
                        {'7','8','9'}
                      };

  printf("address of board       : %p\n", board);
  printf("address of board[0][0] : %p\n", &board[0][0]);
  printf("but what is in board[0] : %p\n", board[0]);
  return 0;
}
```

The output might come as a bit of a surprise to you:

```
address of board       : 0x0013ff67
address of board[0][0] : 0x0013ff67
but what is in board[0] : 0x0013ff67
```

How It Works

As you can see, all three output values are the same, so what can you deduce from this? The answer is quite simple. When you declare a one-dimensional array, placing [n1] after the array name tells the compiler that it's an array with n1 elements. When you declare a two-dimensional array by placing [n2] for the second dimension after the [n1] for the first dimension, the compiler creates an array of size n1, in which each element is an array of size n2.

As you learned in Chapter 5, when you declare a two-dimensional array, you're creating an array of subarrays. So when you access this two-dimensional array using the array name with a single index value, board[0] for example, you're actually referencing the address of one of the subarrays. Using the two-dimensional array name by itself references the address of the beginning of the whole array of subarrays, which is also the address of the beginning of the first subarray.

To summarize

```
board
board[0]
&board[0][0]
```

all have the same value, but they aren't the same thing.

This also means that the expression board[1] results in the same address as the expression board[1][0]. This should be reasonably easy to understand because the latter expression is the first element of the second subarray, board[1].

The problems start when you use pointer notation to get to the values within the array. You still have to use the indirection operator, but you must be careful. If you change the preceding example to display the value of the first element, you'll see why:

```c
/* Program 7.7 A Two-Dimensional arrays */
#include <stdio.h>

int main(void)
{
  char board[3][3] = {
                        {'1','2','3'},
                        {'4','5','6'},
                        {'7','8','9'}
                     };

  printf("value of board[0][0] : %c\n", board[0][0]);
  printf("value of *board[0]    : %c\n", *board[0]);
  printf("value of **board      : %c\n", **board);
  return 0;
}
```

The output from this program is as follows:

```
value of board[0][0] : 1
value of *board[0]    : 1
value of **board      : 1
```

As you can see, if you use board as a means of obtaining the value of the first element, you need to use two indirection operators to get it: **board. You were able to use just one * in the previous program because you were dealing with a one-dimensional array. If you used only the one *, you would get the address of the first element of the array of arrays, which is the address referenced by board[0].

The relationship between the multidimensional array and its subarrays is shown in Figure 7-3.

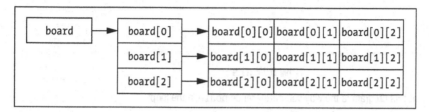

Figure 7-3. *Referencing an array, its subarrays, and its elements*

As Figure 7-3 shows, board refers to the address of the first element in the array of subarrays, and board[0], board[1], and board[2] refer to the addresses of the first element in the corresponding subarrays. Using two index values accesses the value stored in an element of the array. So, with this clearer picture of what's going on in your multidimensional array, let's see how you can use board to get to all the values in that array. You'll do this in the next example.

TRY IT OUT: GETTING ALL THE VALUES IN A TWO-DIMENSIONAL ARRAY

This example takes the previous example a bit further using a for loop:

```
/* Program 7.8  Getting the values in a two-dimensional array */
#include <stdio.h>

int main(void)
{
  char board[3][3] = {
                       {'1','2','3'},
                       {'4','5','6'},
                       {'7','8','9'}
                      };

  /* List all elements of the array */
  for(int i = 0; i < 9; i++)
    printf(" board: %c\n", *(*board + i));
  return 0;
}
```

The output from the program is as follows:

```
board: 1
board: 2
board: 3
board: 4
board: 5
board: 6
board: 7
board: 8
board: 9
```

How It Works

The thing to notice about this program is the way you dereference board in the loop:

```
printf(" board: %c\n", *(*board + i));
```

As you can see, you use the expression *(*board + i) to get the value of an array element. The expression between the parentheses, *board + i, produces the address of the element in the array that is at offset i. Dereferencing this results in the value at this address. It's important that the brackets are included. Leaving them out would give you the value pointed to by board (i.e., the value stored in the location referenced by the address stored in board) with the value of i added to this value. So if i had the value 2, you would simply output the value of the first element of the array plus 2. What you actually want to do, and what your expression does, is to add the value of i to the *address* contained in board, and then dereference this new address to obtain a value.

To make this clearer, let's see what happens if you omit the parentheses in the example. Try changing the initial values for the array so that the characters go from '9' to '1'. If you leave out the brackets in the expression in the printf() call, so that it reads like this

```
printf(" board: %c\n", **board + i);
```

you should get output that looks something like this:

```
board: 9
board: :
board: ;
board: <
board: =
board: >
board: ?
board: @
board: A
```

This output results because you're adding the value of i to the contents of the first element of the array, board. The characters you get come from the ASCII table, starting at '9' and continuing to 'A'.

Also, if you us the expression **(board + i), this too will give erroneous results. In this case, **(board + 0) points to board[0][0], whereas **(board + 1) points to board[1][0], and **(board + 2) points to board[2][0]. If you use higher increments, you access memory locations outside the array, because there isn't a fourth element in the array of arrays.

Multidimensional Arrays and Pointers

So now that you've used the array name using pointer notation for referencing a two-dimensional array, let's use a variable that you've declared as a pointer. As I've already stated, this is where there's a significant difference. If you declare a pointer and assign the address of the array to it, then you can use that pointer to access the members of the array.

TRY IT OUT: MULTIDIMENSIONAL ARRAYS AND POINTERS

You can see this in action here:

```
/* Program 7.9  Multidimensional arrays and pointers*/
#include <stdio.h>

int main(void)
{
  char board[3][3] = {
                       {'1','2','3'},
                       {'4','5','6'},
                       {'7','8','9'}
                      };

  char *pboard = *board;              /* A pointer to char */

  for(int i = 0; i < 9; i++)
    printf(" board: %c\n", *(pboard + i));
  return 0;
}
```

Here, you get the same output as before:

```
board: 1
board: 2
board: 3
board: 4
board: 5
board: 6
board: 7
board: 8
board: 9
```

How It Works

Here, you initialize pboard with the address of the first element of the array, and then you just use normal pointer arithmetic to move through the array:

```
  char *pboard = *board;              /* A pointer to char */

  for(int i = 0; i < 9; i++)
    printf(" board: %c\n", *(pboard + i));
```

Note how you dereference board to obtain the address you want (with *board), because board, by itself, is the address of the array board[0], not the address of an element. You could have initialized pboard by using the following:

```
char *pboard = &board[0][0];
```

This amounts to the same thing. You might think you could initialize pboard using this statement:

```
pboard = board;                    /* Wrong level of indirection! */
```

This is wrong. You should at least get a compiler warning if you do this. Strictly speaking, this isn't legal, because pboard and board have different levels of **indirection**. That's a great jargon phrase that just means that pboard refers to an address that contains a value of type char, whereas board refers to an address *that refers to an address* containing a value of type char. There's an extra level with board compared to pboard. Consequently, pboard needs one * to get to the value and board needs two. Some compilers will allow you to get away with this and just give you a warning about what you've done. However, it is an error, so you shouldn't do it!

Accessing Array Elements

Now you know that, for a two-dimensional array, you have several ways of accessing the elements in that array. Table 7-1 lists these ways of accessing your board array. The left column contains row index values to the board array, and the top row contains column index values. The entry in the table corresponding to a given row index and column index shows the various possible expressions for referring to that element.

Table 7-1. *Pointer Expressions for Accessing Array Elements*

board	0	1	2
0	board[0][0] *board[0] **board	board[0][1] *(board[0]+1) *(*board+1)	board[0][2] *(board[0]+2) *(*board+2)
1	board[1][0] *(board[0]+3) *board[1] *(*board+3)	board[1][1] *(board[0]+4) *(board[1]+1) *(*board+4)	board[1][2] *(board[0]+5) *(board[1]+2) *(*board+5)
2	board[2][0] *(board[0]+6) *(board[1]+3) *board[2] *(*board+6)	board[2][1] *(board[0]+7) *(board[1]+4) *(board[2]+1) *(*board+7)	board[2][2] *(board[0]+8) *(board[1]+5) *(board[2]+2) *(*board+8)

Let's see how you can apply what you've learned so far about pointers in a program that you previously wrote without using pointers. Then you'll be able to see how the pointer-based implementation differs. You'll recall that in Chapter 5 you wrote an example that worked out your hat size. Let's see how you could have done things a little differently.

Here's a rewrite of the hat sizes example using pointer notation:

```
/* Program 7.10  Understand pointers to your hat size - if you dare */
#include <stdio.h>
#include <stdbool.h>

int main(void)
{
  char size[3][12] = {                 /* Hat sizes as characters */
       {'6', '6', '6', '6', '7', '7', '7', '7', '7', '7', '7', '7'},
       {'1', '5', '3', '7', ' ', '1', '1', '3', '1', '5', '3', '7'},
       {'2', '8', '4', '8', ' ', '8', '4', '8', '2', '8', '4', '8'}
                      };

    int headsize[12] =                   /* Values in 1/8 inches    */
       {164,166,169,172,175,178,181,184,188,191,194,197};

    char *psize = *size;
    int *pheadsize = headsize;

    float cranium = 0.0;              /* Head circumference in decimal inches */
    int your_head = 0;               /* Headsize in whole eighths        */
    bool hat_found = false;          /* Indicates when a hat is found to fit */
    bool too_small = false;          /* Indicates headsize is too small     */

    /* Get the circumference of the head */
    printf("\nEnter the circumference of your head above your eyebrows"
                                    " in inches as a decimal value: ");
    scanf(" %f", &cranium);
    /* Convert to whole eighths of an inch */
    your_head = (int)(8.0*cranium);
    /* Search for a hat size */
    for(int i = 0 ; i < 12 ; i++)
    {
      /* Find head size in the headsize array */
      if(your_head > *(pheadsize+i))
        continue;

      /* If it is the first element and the head size is  */
      /* more than 1/8 smaller then the head is too small */
      /*  for a hat                                       */
      if((i == 0) && (your_head < (*pheadsize)-1))
      {
        printf("\nYou are the proverbial pinhead. No hat for"
                                        "you I'm afraid.\n");
        too_small = true;
        break;                        /* Exit the loop */
      }

      /* If head size is more than 1/8 smaller than the current */
      /* element in headsize array, take the next element down  */
```

```
        /* as the head size                                  */
    if( your_head < *(pheadsize+i)-1)
       i--;

    printf("\nYour hat size is %c %c%c%c\n",
                        *(psize + i),         /* First row of size  */
                        *(psize + 1*12 + i),  /* Second row of size */
                        (i==4) ?' ' : '/',
                        *(psize+2*12+i));     /* Third row of size  */
    hat_found=true;
    break;
  }
  if(!hat_found && !too_small)
     printf("\nYou, in technical parlance, are a fathead."
                                " No hat for you, I'm afraid.\n");

  return 0;
}
```

The output from this program is the same as in Chapter 5, so I won't repeat it. It's the code that's of interest, so let's look at the new elements in this program.

How It Works

This program works in essentially the same way as the example from Chapter 5. The differences arise because the implementation is now in terms of the pointers pheadsize and psize that contain the addresses of the start of the headsize and size arrays respectively. The value in your_head is compared with the values in the array in the following statement:

```
    if(your_head > *(pheadsize+i))
       continue;
```

The expression on the right side of the comparison, *(pheadsize+i), is equivalent to headsize[i] in array notation. The bit between the parentheses adds i to the address of the beginning of the array. Remember that adding an integer i to an address will add i times the length of each element. Therefore, the subexpression between parentheses produces the address of the element corresponding to the index value i. The dereference operator * then obtains the contents of this element for the comparison operation with the value in the variable your_head.

If you examine the printf() in the middle, you'll see the effect of two array dimensions on the pointer expression that access an element in a particular row:

```
    printf("\nYour hat size is %c %c%c%c\n",
                        *(psize + i),         /* First row of size  */
                        *(psize + 1*12 + i),  /* Second row of size */
                        (i==4) ?' ' : '/',
                        *(psize+2*12+i));     /* Third row of size  */
```

The first expression is *(psize + i) that accesses the ith element in the first row of size so this is equivalent to size[0][i]. The second expression is *(psize + 1*12 + i) that accesses the ith element in the second row of size so it is equivalent to size[1][i]. I have written the expression to show that the address of the start of the second row is obtained by adding the row size to psize. You then add i to that to get the element within the second row. To get the element in the third row of the size array you use the expression *(psize + 2*12 + i), which is equivalent to size[2][i].

Using Memory As You Go

Pointers are an extremely flexible and powerful tool for programming over a wide range of applications. The majority of programs in C use pointers to some extent. C also has a further facility that enhances the power of pointers and provides a strong incentive to use them in your code; it permits memory to be allocated dynamically when your program executes. Allocating memory dynamically is possible only because you have pointers available.

Think back to the program in Chapter 5 that calculated the average scores for a group of students. At the moment, it works for only ten students. Suppose you want to write the program so that it works for any number of students without knowing the number of students in the class in advance, and so it doesn't use any more memory than necessary for the number of student scores specified. **Dynamic memory allocation** allows you to do just that. You can create arrays at runtime that are large enough to hold the precise amount of data that you require for the task.

When you explicitly allocate memory at runtime in a program, space is reserved for you in a memory area called the **heap**. There's another memory area called the **stack** in which space to store function arguments and local variables in a function is allocated. When the execution of a function is finished, the space allocated to store arguments and local variables is freed. The memory in the heap is controlled by you. As you'll see in this chapter, when you allocate memory on the heap, it is up to you to keep track of when the memory you have allocated is no longer required and free the space you have allocated to allow it to be reused.

Dynamic Memory Allocation: The malloc() Function

The simplest standard library function that allocates memory at runtime is called `malloc()`. You need to include the `<stdlib.h>` header file in your program when you use this function. When you use the `malloc()` function, you specify the number of bytes of memory that you want allocated as the argument. The function returns the address of the first byte of memory allocated in response to your request. Because you get an address returned, a pointer is a useful place to put it.

A typical example of dynamic memory allocation might be this:

```
int *pNumber = (int *)malloc(100);
```

Here, you've requested 100 bytes of memory and assigned the address of this memory block to pNumber. As long as you haven't modified it, any time that you use the variable pNumber, it will point to the first int location at the beginning of the 100 bytes that were allocated. This whole block can hold 25 int values on my computer, where they require 4 bytes each.

Notice the cast, (int *), that you use to convert the address returned by the function to the type •pointer to int.! You've done this because malloc() is a general-purpose function that's used to allocate memory for any type of data. The function has no knowledge of what you want to use the memory for, so it actually returns a pointer of type •pointer to void,! which, as I indicated earlier, is written as void *. Pointers of type void * can point to any kind of data. However, you can't dereference a pointer of type •pointer to void! because what it points to is unspecified. Many compilers will arrange for the address returned by malloc() to be automatically cast to the appropriate type, but it doesn't hurt to be specific.

You could request any number of bytes, subject only to the amount of free memory on the computer and the limit on malloc() imposed by a particular implementation. If the memory that you request can't be allocated for any reason, malloc() returns a pointer with the value NULL. Remember that this is the equivalent of 0 for pointers. It's always a good idea to check any dynamic memory request immediately using an if statement to make sure the memory is actually there before you try to use it. As with money, attempting to use memory you don't have is generally catastrophic. For that reason, writing

```
if(pNumber == NULL)
{
   /*Code to deal with no memory allocated */
}
```

with a suitable action if the pointer is NULL is a good idea. For example, you could at least display a message "Not enough memory" and terminate the program. This would be much better than allowing the program to continue, and crashing when it uses a NULL address to store something. In some instances, though, you may be able to free up a bit of memory that you've been using elsewhere, which might give you enough memory to continue.

Using the sizeof Operator in Memory Allocation

The previous example is all very well, but you don't usually deal in bytes; you deal in data of type int, type double, and so on. It would be very useful to allocate memory for 75 items of type int, for example. You can do this with the following statement:

```
pNumber = (int *) malloc(75*sizeof(int));
```

As you've seen already, sizeof is an operator that returns an unsigned integer of type size_t that's the count of the number of bytes required to store its argument. It will accept a type keyword such as int or float as an argument between parentheses, in which case the value it returns will be the number of bytes required to store an item of that type. It will also accept a variable or array name as an argument. With an array name as an argument, it returns the number of bytes required to store the whole array. In the preceding example, you asked for enough memory to store 75 data items of type int. Using sizeof in this way means that you automatically accommodate the potential variability of the space required for a value of type int between one C implementation and another.

TRY IT OUT: DYNAMIC MEMORY ALLOCATION

You can put the concept of dynamic memory allocation into practice by using pointers to help calculate prime numbers. In case you've forgotten, a prime number is an integer that's exactly divisible only by 1 or by the number itself.

The process for finding a prime is quite simple. First, you know by inspection that 2, 3, and 5 are the first three prime numbers, because they aren't divisible by any lower number other than 1. Because all the other prime numbers must be odd (otherwise they would be divisible by 2), you can work out the next number to check by starting at the last prime you have and adding 2. When you've checked out that number, you add another 2 to get the next to be checked, and so on.

To check whether a number is actually prime rather than just odd, you could divide by all the odd numbers less than the number that you're checking, but you don't need to do as much work as that. If a number is *not* prime, it must be divisible by one of the primes lower than the number you're checking. Because you'll obtain the primes in sequence, it will be sufficient to check a candidate by testing whether any of the primes that you've already found is an exact divisor.

You'll implement this program using pointers and dynamic memory allocation:

```
/* Program 7.11  A dynamic prime example          */
#include <stdio.h>
#include <stdlib.h>
#include <stdbool.h>

int main(void)
{
   unsigned long *primes = NULL;      /* Pointer to primes storage area  */
   unsigned long trial = 0;           /* Integer to be tested            */
```

```
  bool found = false;              /* Indicates when we find a prime   */
  size_t total = 0;                /* Number of primes required        */
  size_t count = 0;                /* Number of primes found           */

  printf("How many primes would you like - you'll get at least 4?  ");
  scanf("%u", &total);             /* Total is how many we need to find */
  total = total<4U ? 4U:total;     /* Make sure it is at least 4        */

  /* Allocate sufficient memory to store the number of primes required */
  primes = (unsigned long *)malloc(total*sizeof(unsigned long));
  if(primes == NULL)
  {
    printf("\nNot enough memory. Hasta la Vista, baby.\n");
    return 1;
  }

  /* We know the first three primes    */
  /* so let's give the program a start. */
  *primes = 2UL;                   /* First prime                      */
  *(primes+1) = 3UL;               /* Second prime                     */
  *(primes+2) = 5UL;               /* Third prime                      */
  count = 3U;                      /* Number of primes stored          */
  trial = 5U;                      /* Set to the last prime we have    */

  /* Find all the primes required */
  while(count<total)
  {
    trial += 2UL;                  /* Next value for checking          */

    /* Try dividing by each of the primes we have       */
    /* If any divide exactly - the number is not prime  */
    for(size_t i = 0 ; i < count ; i++)
      if(!(found = (trial % *(primes+i))))
        break;                     /* Exit if no remainder             */

    if(found)                      /* we got one - if found is true */
      *(primes+count++) = trial;   /* Store it and increment count  */
  }

  /* Display primes 5-up */
  for(size_t i = 0 ; i < total ; i ++)
  {
    if(!(i%5U))
      printf("\n");                /* Newline after every 5            */
    printf ("%12lu", *(primes+i));
  }
  printf("\n");                    /* Newline for any stragglers    */
  return 0;
}
```

The output from the program looks something like this:

How many primes would you like - you'll get at least 4? 25

2	3	5	7	11
13	17	19	23	29
31	37	41	43	47
53	59	61	67	71
73	79	83	89	97

How It Works

With this example, you can enter the number of prime numbers you want the program to generate. The pointer variable `primes` refers to a memory area that will be used to store the prime numbers as they're calculated. However, no memory is defined initially in the program. The space is allocated after you've entered the number of primes that you want:

```
printf("How many primes would you like - you'll get at least 4?  ");
scanf("%u", &total);            /* Total is how many we need to find */
total = total<4U ? 4U:total;    /* Make sure it is at least 4        */
```

After the prompt, the number that you enter is stored in `total`. The next statement then ensures that `total` is at least 4. This is because you'll define and store the three primes that you know (2, 3, and 5) by default.

You then use the value in `total` to allocate the appropriate amount of memory to store the primes:

```
primes = (unsigned long *)malloc(total*sizeof(unsigned long));
if (primes == NULL)
{
  printf("\nNot enough memory. Hasta la Vista, baby.\n");
  return 0;
}
```

Primes grow in size faster than the count so you store them as type `unsigned long` although if you want to maximize the range you can deal with you could use `unsigned long long`. Because you're going to store each prime as type `long`, the number of bytes you require is `total*sizeof(unsigned long)`. If the `malloc()` function returns NULL, no memory was allocated, so you display a message and end the program.

The maximum number of primes that you can specify depends on two things: the memory available on your computer, and the amount of memory that your compiler's implementation of `malloc()` can allocate at one time. The former is probably the major constraint. The argument to `malloc()` is of type `size_t` so the integer type that corresponds to `size_t` will limit the number of bytes you can specify. If `size_t` corresponds to a 4-byte unsigned integer, you will be able to allocate up to 4,294,967,295 bytes at one time.

Once you have the memory allocated for the primes, you define the first three primes and store them in the first three positions in the memory area pointed to by `primes`:

```
*primes = 2UL;              /* First prime             */
*(primes+1) =3UL;           /* Second prime            */
*(primes+2) = 5UL;          /* Third prime             */
```

As you can see, referencing successive memory locations is simple. Because `primes` is of type "pointer to `unsigned long`," `primes+1` refers to the address of the second location—the address being `primes` plus the number of bytes required to store one data item of type `unsigned long`. To store each value, you use the indirection operator; otherwise, you would be modifying the address itself.

Now that you have three primes, you set the variable count to 3 and initialize the variable trial with the last prime you stored:

```
count = 3U;                    /* Number of primes stored   */
trial = 5UL;                   /* Set to the last prime we have */
```

The value in trial will be incremented by 2 to get the next value to be tested when you start searching for the next prime.

All the primes are found in the while loop:

```
while(count<total)
{
  ...
}
```

The variable count is incremented within the loop as each prime is found, and when it reaches the value total, the loop ends.

Within the while loop, you first increase the value in trial by 2UL, and then you test whether the value is prime:

```
trial += 2UL;                  /* Next value for checking   */

/* Try dividing by each of the primes we have      */
/* If any divide exactly - the number is not prime  */
for(size_t i = 0 ; i < count ; i++)
  if(!(found = (trial % *(primes+i))))
    break;                     /* Exit if no remainder      */
```

The for loop does the testing. Within this loop the remainder after dividing trial by each of the primes that you have so far is stored in found. If the division is exact, the remainder will be 0, and therefore found will be set to false. If you find any remainder is 0, this means that the value in trial isn't a prime and you can continue with the next candidate.

The value of an assignment expression is the value that's stored in the variable on the left of the assignment operator. Thus, the value of the expression (found = (trial % *(primes+i))) will be the value that's stored in found as a result of this. This will be false for an exact division, so the expression !(found = (trial % *(primes+i))) will be true in this case, and the break statement will be executed. Therefore, the for loop will end if any previously stored prime divides into trial with no remainder.

If none of the primes divides into trial exactly, the for loop will end when all the primes have been tried, and found will contain the result of converting the last remainder value, which will be some positive integer, to type bool. If trial had a factor, the loop will have ended via the break statement and found will contain false. Therefore, you can use the value stored in found at the completion of the for loop to determine whether you've found a new prime:

```
if(found)                      /* we got one - if found is true */
  *(primes+count++) = trial;   /* Store it and increment count  */
```

If found is true, you store the value of trial in the next available slot in the memory area. The address of the next available slot is primes+count. Remember that the first slot is primes, so when you have count number of primes, the last prime occupies the location primes+count-1. The statement storing the new prime also increments the value of count after the new prime has been stored.

The while loop just repeats the process until you have all the primes requested. You then output the primes five on a line:

```
for(size_t i = 0 ; i < total ; i ++)
{
  if(!(i%5U))
     printf("\n");                        /* Newline after every 5       */
  printf ("%12lu", *(primes+i));
}
printf("\n");                             /* Newline for any stragglers   */
```

The for loop will output total number of primes. The printf() that displays each prime value just appends the output to the current line, but the if statement outputs a newline character after every fifth iteration, so there will be five primes displayed on each line. Because the number of primes may not be an exact multiple of five, you output a newline after the loop ends to ensure that there's always at least one newline character at the end of the output.

Memory Allocation with the calloc() Function

The calloc() function that is declared in the <stdlib.h> header offers a couple of advantages over the malloc() function. First, it allocates memory as an array of elements of a given size, and second, it initializes the memory that is allocated so that all bits are zero. The calloc() function requires you to supply two argument values, the number of elements in the array, and the size of the array element, both arguments being of type size_t. The function still doesn't know the type of the elements in the array so the address of the area that is allocated is returned as type void *.

Here's how you could use calloc() to allocate memory for an array of 75 elements of type int:

```
int *pNumber = (int *) calloc(75, sizeof(int));
```

The return value will be NULL if it was not possible to allocate the memory requested, so you should still check for this. This is very similar to using malloc() but the big plus is that you know the memory area will be initialized to zero.

To make Program 7.11 use calloc() instead of malloc() to allocate the memory required, you only need to change one statement, shown in bold. The rest of the code is identical:

```
/* Allocate sufficient memory to store the number of primes required */
primes = (unsigned long *)calloc(total, sizeof(unsigned long));
if (primes == NULL)
{
   printf("\nNot enough memory. Hasta la Vista, baby.\n");
   return 1;
}
```

Releasing Dynamically Allocated Memory

When you allocate memory dynamically, you should always release the memory when it is no longer required. Memory that you allocate on the heap will be automatically released when your program ends, but it is better to explicitly release the memory when you are done with it, even if it's just before you exit from the program. In more complicated situations, you can easily have a **memory leak**. A memory leak occurs when you allocate some memory dynamically and you do not retain the reference to it, so you are unable to release the memory. This often occurs within a loop, and because you do not release the memory when it is no longer required, your program consumes more and more of the available memory and eventually may occupy it all.

Of course, to free memory that you have allocated using malloc() or calloc(), you must still be able to use the address that references the block of memory that the function returned. To release the memory for a block of dynamically allocated memory whose address you have stored in the pointer pNumber, you just write the statement:

```
free(pNumber);
```

The free() function has a formal parameter of type void *, and because any pointer type can be automatically converted to this type, you can pass a pointer of any type as the argument to the function. As long as pNumber contains the address that was returned by malloc() or calloc() when the memory was allocated, the entire block of memory that was allocated will be freed for further use.

If you pass a null pointer to the free() function the function does nothing. You should avoid attempting to free the same memory area twice, as the behavior of the free() function is undefined in this instance and therefore unpredictable. You are most at risk of trying to free the same memory twice when you have more than one pointer variable that references the memory you have allocated, so take particular care when you are doing this.

Let's modify the previous example so that it uses calloc() and frees the memory at the end of the program.

TRY IT OUT: FREEING DYNAMICALLY ALLOCATED MEMORY

You'll implement this program using pointers and dynamic memory allocation:

```c
/* Program 7.11A  Allocating and freeing memory             */
#include <stdio.h>
#include <stdlib.h>
#include <stdbool.h>

int main(void)
{
    unsigned long *primes - NULL;      /* Pointer to primes storage area  */
    unsigned long trial = 0;           /* Integer to be tested            */

    bool found = false;                /* Indicates when we find a prime  */
    size_t total = 0;                  /* Number of primes required       */
    size_t count = 0;                  /* Number of primes found          */

    printf("How many primes would you like - you'll get at least 4? ");
    scanf("%u", &total);               /* Total is how many we need to find */
    total = total<4U ? 4U:total;       /* Make sure it is at least 4       */

    /* Allocate sufficient memory to store the number of primes required */
    primes = (unsigned long *)calloc(total, sizeof(unsigned long));
    if (primes == NULL)
    {
        printf("\nNot enough memory. Hasta la Vista, baby.\n");
        return 1;
    }

    /* Code to determine the primes as before...*/
```

```
/* Display primes 5-up */
for(int i = 0 ; i < total ; i ++)
{
  if(!(i%5U))
    printf("\n");                          /* Newline after every 5      */
  printf ("%12lu", *(primes+i));
}
printf("\n");                              /* Newline for any stragglers */

free(primes);                              /* Release the memory         */
return 0;
}
```

The output from the program will be the same as the previous version, given the same input. Only the two lines in bold font are different from the previous version. The program now allocates memory using `calloc()` with the first argument as the size of type `long`, and the second argument as `total`, which the number of primes required. Immediately before the `return` statement that ends the program, you free the memory that you allocated previously by calling the `free()` function with `primes` as the argument.

Reallocating Memory

The `realloc()` function enables you to reuse memory that you previously allocated using `malloc()` or `calloc()` (or `realloc()`). The `realloc()` function expects two argument values to be supplied: a pointer containing an address that was previously returned by a call to `malloc()`, `calloc()` or `realloc()`, and the size in bytes of the new memory that you want allocated.

The `realloc()` function releases the previously allocated memory referenced by the pointer that you supply as the first argument, then reallocates the same memory area to fulfill the new requirement specified by the second argument. Obviously the value of the second argument should not exceed the number of bytes that was previously allocated. If it is, you will only get a memory area allocated that is equal to the size of the previous memory area.

Here's a code fragment illustrating how you might use the `realloc()` function:

```
long *pData = NULL;                     /* Stores the data                */
size_t count = 0;                       /* Number of data items           */
size_t oldCount = 0;                    /* previous count value           */
while(true)
{
  oldCount = count;                     /* Save previous count value      */
  printf("How many values would you like?  ");
  scanf("%u", &count);                  /* Total is how many we need to find */

  if(count == 0)                        /* If none required, we are done  */
  {
    if(!pData)                          /* If memory is allocated         */
      free(pData);                      /* release it                     */
    break;                              /* Exit the loop                  */
  }

  /* Allocate sufficient memory to store count values */
  if((pData && (count <= oldCount)      /* If there's big enough old memory... */
    pData = (long *)realloc(pData, sizeof(long)*count); /* reallocate it.  */
```

```
  else
  {                                      /* There wasn't enough old memory    */
    if(pData)                            /* If there's old memory...          */
      free(pData);                       /* release it.                       */

    /* Allocate a new block of memory */
    pData = (long *)calloc(count, sizeof(long));
  }
  if (pData == NULL)                     /* If no memory was allocated...      */
  {
    printf("\nNot enough memory.\n");
    return 1;                            /* abandon ship!                      */
  }
  /* Read and process the data and output the result... */
}
```

This should be easy to follow from the comments. The loop reads an arbitrary number of items of data, the number being supplied by the user. Space is allocated dynamically by reusing the previously allocated block if it exists and if it is large enough to accommodate the new requirement. If the old block is not there, or is not big enough, the code allocates a new block using `calloc()`.

As you see from the code fragment, there's quite a lot of work involved in reallocating memory because you typically need to be sure that an existing block is large enough for the new requirement. Most of the time in such situations it will be best to just free the old memory block explicitly and allocate a completely new block.

Here are some basic guidelines for working with memory that you allocate dynamically:

! Avoid allocating lots of small amounts of memory. Allocating memory on the heap carries some overhead with it, so allocating many small blocks of memory will carry much more overhead than allocating fewer larger blocks.

! Only hang on to the memory as long as you need it. As soon as you are finished with a block of memory on the heap, release the memory.

! Always ensure that you provide for releasing memory that you have allocated. Decide where in you code you will release the memory when you write the code that allocates it.

! Make sure you do not inadvertently overwrite the address of memory you have allocated on the heap before you have released it; otherwise your program will have a memory leak. You need to be especially careful when allocating memory within a loop.

Handling Strings Using Pointers

You've used array variables of type char to store strings up to now, but you can also use a variable of type •pointer to char! to reference a string. This approach will give you quite a lot of flexibility in handling strings, as you'll see. You can declare a variable of type •pointer to char! with a statement such as this:

```
char *pString = NULL;
```

At this point, it's worth noting yet again that a pointer is just a variable that can store the address of another memory location. So far, you've created a pointer but not a place to store a string. To store a string, you need to allocate some memory. You can declare a block of memory that you intend to use to store string data and then use pointers to keep track of where in this block you've stored the strings.

String Input with More Control

It's often desirable to read text with more control than you get with the scanf() function. The getchar() function that's declared in <stdio.h> provides a much more primitive operation in that it reads only a single character at a time, but it does enable you to control when you stop reading characters. This way, you can be sure that you don't exceed the memory you have allocated to store the input.

The getchar() function reads a single character from the keyboard and returns it as type int. You can read a string terminated by '\n' into an array, buffer, like this:

```
char buffer[100];                       /* String input buffer */
char *pbuffer = buffer;                 /* Pointer to buffer    */
while((*pbuffer++ = getchar()) != '\n');

*pbuffer = '\0';                        /* Add null terminator */
```

All the input is done in the while loop condition. The getchar() function reads a character and stores it in the current address in pbuffer. The address in pbuffer is then incremented to point to the next character. The value of the assignment expression, ((*pbuffer++ = getchar()), is the value that was stored in the operation. As long as the character that was stored isn't '\n', the loop will continue. After the loop ends, the '\0' character is added in the next available position. Note that this retains the '\n' character as part of the string. If you don't want to do this, you can adjust the address where you store the '\0' to overwrite the '\n'.

This doesn't prevent the possibility of exceeding the 100 bytes available in the array, so you can use this safely only when you're sure that the array is large enough. However, you could rewrite the loop to check for this:

```
size_t index = 0;
for(; index<sizeof(buffer) ; i++)
  if((*(pbuffer+index) = getchar()) == '\n')
  {
    *(pbuffer + index++) = '\0';
    break;
  }
if( (index ==sizeof(buffer) &&( (*(pbuffer+index-1) != '\0) )
    {
      printf("\nYou ran out of space in the buffer.");
      return 1;
    }
```

The index variable indicates the next available element in the buffer array. The read operations now take place in a for loop that terminates, either when the end of the buffer array is reached, or when a '\n' character is read and stored. The '\n' character is replaced by '\0' within the loop. Note that index is incremented after '\0' is stored. This ensures that index still reflects the next available position in buffer, although of course, if you fill the buffer, this will be beyond the last element in the array.

When the loop ends, you have to determine why; it could be because you finished reading the string, but it also could be because you ran out of space in buffer. When you run out of space, index will be equal to the number of elements in buffer and the last element in buffer will not be a terminating null. Therefore the left operand of the && operation in the if expression will be true if you have filled buffer, and the right operand will be true if the last element in buffer is not a terminating null. It is possible that you read a string that exactly fits, in which case the last element will be a terminating null, in which case the if expression will be false, which is the way it should be.

Using Arrays of Pointers

Of course, when you are dealing with several strings, you can use an array of pointers to store references to the strings on the heap. Suppose that you wanted to read three strings from the keyboard and store them in the buffer array. You could create an array of pointers to store the locations of the three strings:

```
char *pS[3] = { NULL };
```

This declares an array, pS, of three pointers. You learned in Chapter 5 that if you supply fewer initial values than elements in an array initializer list, the remaining elements will be initialized with 0. Thus just putting a list with one value, NULL, will initialize all the elements of an array of pointers of any size to NULL.

Let's see how this works in an example.

TRY IT OUT: ARRAYS OF POINTERS

The following example is a rewrite of the previous program, and it demonstrates how you could use an array of pointers to achieve the same result:

```c
/* Program 7.12 Arrays of Pointers to Strings */
#include <stdio.h>
const size_t BUFFER_LEN = 512;              /* Size of input buffer    */

int main(void)
{
  char buffer[BUFFER_LEN];                  /* Store for strings       */
  char *pS[3] = { NULL };                   /* Array of string pointers */
  char *pbuffer = buffer;                   /* Pointer to buffer       */
  size_t index = 0;                         /* Available buffer position*/

  printf("\nEnter 3 messages that total less than %u characters.",
                                            BUFFER_LEN-2);

  /* Read the strings from the keyboard */
  for(int i=0 ; i<3 ; i++)
  {
    printf("\nEnter %s message\n", i>0? "another" : "a" );
    pS[i] = &buffer[index];                 /* Save start of string        */

    /* Read up to the end of buffer if necessary */
    for( ; index<BUFFER_LEN ; index++)        /* If you read \n ... */
      if((*(pbuffer+index) = getchar()) == '\n')
        {
          *(pbuffer+index++) = '\0';          /* ...substitute \0   */
          break;
        }
```

```
    /* Check for buffer capacity exceeded */
    if((index == BUFFER_LEN) && ((*(pbuffer+index-1) != '\0') || (i<2)))
    {
      printf("\nYou ran out of space in the buffer.");
      return 1;
    }
  }

  printf("\nThe strings you entered are:\n\n");
  for(int i = 0 ; i<3 ; i++)
    printf("%s\n", pS[i]);

  printf("The buffer has %d characters unused.\n",
                    BUFFER_LEN-index);
  return 0;
}
```

Here's some sample output from this program:

```
Enter a message
Hello World!

Enter another message
Today is a great day for learning about pointers.

Enter another message
That's all.

The strings you entered are:
Hello World!
Today is a great day for learning about pointers.
That's all.
The buffer has 437 characters unused.
```

How It Works

The first thing of note in this example is that you use the variable BUFFER_LEN defined at global scope as the dimension for the array buffer:

```
const size_t BUFFER_LEN = 512;                /* Size of input buffer    */
```

The variable must be defined as const to allow you to use it as an array dimension; array dimensions can only be specified by constant expressions.

The declarations at the beginning of main() are as follows:

```
  char buffer[BUFFER_LEN];           /* Store for strings         */
  char *pS[3] = { NULL };            /* Array of string pointers  */
  char *pbuffer = buffer;            /* Pointer to buffer         */
  size_t index = 0;                  /* Available buffer position */
```

buffer is an array of BUFFER_LEN elements of type char that will hold all the input strings. pS is an array of three pointers that will store the addresses of the strings in buffer. pbuffer is a pointer that is initialized with the address of the first byte in buffer. You'll use pbuffer to move through the buffer array as you fill it with input characters. The index variable records the position of the currently unused element in buffer.

The first for loop reads in three strings. The first statement in the loop is this:

```
printf("\nEnter %s message\n", i>0? "another" : "a" );
```

Here, you use a snappy way to alter the prompt in the printf() after the first iteration of the for loop, using your old friend the conditional operator. This outputs "a" on the first iteration, and "another" on all subsequent iterations.

The next statement saves the address currently stored in pbuffer:

```
pS[i] = pbuffer;                              /* Save start of  string    */
```

This assignment statement is storing the address stored in the pointer pbuffer in an element of the pS pointer array.

The statements for reading the string and appending the string terminator are the following:

```
for( ; index<BUFFER_LEN ; index++)
  if((*(pbuffer+index) - getchar()) == '\n')      /* If you read \n ... */
    {
      *(pbuffer+index++) = '\0';                    /* ...substitute \0   */
      break;
    }
```

This is the for loop you saw in the previous section that will read up to the end of buffer if necessary. If a '\n' is read, it is replaced by '\0' and the loop ends. After the loop you check for buffer being full without reaching the end of the string:

```
if((index == BUFFER_LEN) && ((*(pbuffer+index-1) != '\0') || (i<2)))
  {
    printf("\nYou ran out of space in the buffer.");
    return 1;
  }
```

This is the code you saw explained in the previous section.

By reading the strings using getchar() you have a great deal of control over the input process. This approach isn't limited to just reading strings; you can use it for any input where you want to deal with it character by character. You could choose to remove spaces from the input or look for special characters such as commas that you might use to separate one input value from the next.

```
printf("\nThe strings you entered are:\n\n");
for(int i = 0 ; i<3 ; i++)
  printf("%s\n", pS[i]);
```

In the loop, you output the strings that each of the elements in the pS point to.

If you were to develop this example just a little further, you would be able to allow input of any number of messages, limited only by the number of string pointers provided for in the array.

In the last printf(), you output the number of characters left in the string:

```
printf("The buffer has %d characters unused.\n",
                 BUFFER_LEN-index);
```

Subtracting index from the number of elements in the buffer array gives the number of elements unused.

At the outset, you initialize your pointers to NULL. You can also initialize a pointer with the address of a constant string:

```
char *pString = "To be or not to be";
```

This statement allocates sufficient memory for the string, places the constant string in the memory allocated and, after allocating space for it, sets the value of the pointer pS as the address of the first byte of the string. The problem with this is that there is nothing to prevent you from modifying the string with a statement such as the following:

```
*(pString+3) = 'm';
```

The const keyword doesn't help in this case. If you declare pString as const, it's the pointer that is constant, not what it points to.

TRY IT OUT: GENERALIZING STRING INPUT

Let's try rewriting the example to generalize string input. You can extend the program to read an arbitrary number of strings up to a given limit and ensure that you don't read strings that are longer than you've provided for. Here's the program:

```
/* Program 7.13 Generalizing string input */
#include <stdio.h>
#include <stdlib.h>
#include <string.h>

const size_t BUFFER_LEN = 128;          /* Length of input buffer   */
const size_t NUM_P = 100;               /* maximum number of strings */

int main(void)
{
  char buffer[BUFFER_LEN];              /* Input buffer             */
  char *pS[NUM_P] = { NULL };           /* Array of string pointers */
  char *pbuffer = buffer;               /* Pointer to buffer        */
  int i = 0;                            /* Loop counter             */

  printf("\nYou can enter up to %u messages each up to %u characters.",
                                      NUM_P, BUFFER_LEN-1);

  for(i = 0 ; i<NUM_P ; i++)
  {
    pbuffer = buffer ; /* Set pointer to beginning of buffer */
    printf("\nEnter %s message, or press Enter to end\n",
                                            i>0? "another" : "a");

    /* Read a string of up to BUFFER_LEN characters */
    while((pbuffer - buffer < BUFFER_LEN-1) &&
          ((*pbuffer++ = getchar()) != '\n'));

    /* check for empty line indicating end of input */
    if((pbuffer - buffer) < 2)
      break;
```

```
    /* Check for string too long */
    if((pbuffer - buffer) == BUFFER_LEN && *(pbuffer-1)!= '\n')
    {
      printf("String too long - maximum %d characters allowed.",
                                              BUFFER_LEN);
      i--;
      continue;
    }
    *(pbuffer - 1) = '\0';                    /* Add terminator            */

    pS[i] = (char*)malloc(pbuffer-buffer);  /* Get memory for string     */
    if(pS[i] == NULL)                       /* Check we actually got some...*/
    {
      printf("\nOut of memory - ending program.");
      return 1;                             /* ...Exit if we didn't      */
    }

    /* Copy string from buffer to new memory */
    strcpy(pS[i], buffer);
  }

  /* Output all the strings */
  printf("\nIn reverse order, the strings you entered are:\n");
  while(--i >= 0)
  {
    printf("\n%s", pS[i] );              /* Display strings last to first  */
    free(pS[i]);                         /* Release the memory we got      */
    pS[i] = NULL;                        /* Set pointer back to NULL for safety*/
  }
  return 0;
}
```

The output is very similar to the previous two examples:

```
Enter a message, or press Enter to end
Hello

Enter another message, or press Enter to end
World!

Enter another message, or press Enter to end

In reverse order, the strings you entered are:
World!
Hello
```

How It Works

This has expanded a little bit, but there are quite a few extras compared to the original version. You now handle as many strings as you want, up to the number that you provide pointers for, in the array pS. The dimension of this array is defined at the beginning, to make it easy to change:

```
const size_t NUM_P = 100;                 /* maximum number of strings */
```

If you want to alter the maximum number of strings that the program will handle, you just need to change the value set for this variable.

At the beginning of `main()`, you have the declarations for the variables you need:

```
char buffer[BUFFER_LEN];              /* Input buffer            */
char *pS[NUM_P] = { NULL };           /* Array of string pointers */
char *pbuffer = buffer;               /* Pointer to buffer       */
int i = 0;                            /* Loop counter            */
```

The `buffer` array is now just an input buffer that will contain each string as you read it. Therefore, the `#define` directive for `BUFFER_LEN` now defines the maximum length of string you can accept. You then have the declaration for your pointer array of length `NUM_P`, and your pointer, `pbuffer`, for working within `buffer`. Finally, you have a couple of loop control variables.

Next you display a message explaining what the input constraints are:

```
printf("\nYou can enter up to %u messages each up to %u characters.",
                                         NUM_P, BUFFER_LEN-1);
```

The maximum input message length allows for the terminating null to be appended.

The first `for` loop reads the strings and stores them. The loop control is as follows:

```
for(i = 0 ; i<NUM_P ; i++)
```

This ensures that you can input only as many strings as there are pointers that you've declared. Once you've entered the maximum number of strings, the loop ends and you fall through to the output section of the program.

Within the loop, a string is entered using a similar mechanism with `getchar()` to those that you've seen before but with an additional condition:

```
/* Read a string of up to BUFFER_LEN characters */
while((pbuffer - buffer < BUFFER_LEN-1) &&
        ((*pbuffer++ = getchar()) != '\n'));
```

The whole process takes place in the condition for the continuation of the `while` loop. A character obtained by `getchar()` is stored at the address pointed to by `pbuffer`, which starts out as the address of `buffer`. The `pbuffer` pointer is then incremented to point to the next available space, and the character that was stored as a result of the assignment is compared with `'\n'`. If it's `'\n'`, the loop terminates. The loop will also end if the expression `pbuffer-buffer < BUFFER_LEN-1` is false. This will occur if the next character to be stored will occupy the last position in the `buffer` array.

The input process is followed by the check in the following statement:

```
if((pbuffer - buffer) < 2)
  break;
```

This detects an empty line because if you just press the Enter key only one character will be entered: the `'\n'`. In this case, the `break` statement immediately exits the `for` loop and begins the output process.

The next `if` statement checks whether you attempted to enter a string longer than the capacity of `buffer`:

```
if((pbuffer - buffer) == BUFFER_LEN && *(pbuffer-1)!= '\n')
{
  printf("String too long - maximum %d characters allowed.",
                                         BUFFER_LEN);

  i--;
  continue;
}
```

Because you end the while loop when the last position in the buffer array has been used, if you attempt to enter more characters than the capacity of buffer, the expression pbuffer-buffer will be equal to BUFFER_LEN. Of course, this will also be the case if you enter a string that fits exactly, so you must also check the last character in buffer to see if it's '\n'. If it isn't, you tried to enter too many characters, so you decrement the loop counter after displaying a message and go to the next iteration.

The next statement is the following:

```
*(pbuffer - 1) = '\0';                    /* Add terminator          */
```

This places the '\0' in the position occupied by the '\n' character, because pbuffer was left pointing to the first free element in the array buffer.

Once a string has been entered, you use the malloc() function to request sufficient memory to hold the string exactly:

```
pS[i] = (char*)malloc(pbuffer-buffer);  /* Get memory for string    */
if (pS[i] == NULL)                      /* Check we actually got some */
{
  printf("\nOut of memory - ending program.");
  return 0;                             /* ...Exit if we didn't      */
}
```

The number of bytes required is the difference between the address currently pointed to by pbuffer, which is the first vacant element in buffer, and the address of the first element of buffer. The pointer returned from malloc() is stored in the current element of the pS array, after casting it to type char. If you get a NULL pointer back from malloc(), you display a message and end the program.

You copy the string from the buffer to the new memory you obtained using the following statement:

```
strcpy(pS[i], buffer);
```

This uses the library function, strcpy(), to copy the contents of buffer to the memory pointed to by pS[i]. Take care not to confuse the arguments when using the strcpy() function; the second argument is the source and the first argument is the destination for the copy operation. Getting them mixed up is usually disastrous, because copying continues until a '\0' is found.

Once you exit the loop, either because you entered an empty string or because you used all the pointers in the array pS, you generate the output:

```
printf("\nIn reverse order, the strings you entered are:\n");
while(--i >= 0)
{
  printf("\n%s", pS[i] );                /* Display strings last to first */
  free(pS[i]);                           /* Release the memory we got    */
  pS[i] = NULL;                          /* Set pointer back to NULL for safety */
}
```

The index i will have a value one greater than the number of strings entered. So after the first loop condition check, you can use it to index the last string. The loop continues counting down from this value and the last iteration will be with i at 0, which will index the first string.

You could use the expression *(pS + i) instead of pS[i], but using array notation is much clearer.

You use the function, free(), after the last printf(). This function is complementary to malloc(), and it releases memory previously allocated by malloc(). It only requires the pointer to the memory allocated as an argument. Although memory will be freed at the end of the program automatically, it's good practice to free memory as soon as you no longer need it. Of course, once you have freed memory in this way, you can't use it, so it's a good idea to set the pointer to NULL immediately, as was done here.

Caution Errors with pointers can produce catastrophic results. If an uninitialized pointer is used to store a value before it has been assigned an address value, the address used will be whatever happens to be stored in the pointer location. This could overwrite virtually anywhere in memory.

TRY IT OUT: SORTING STRINGS USING POINTERS

Using the functions declared in the string.h header file, you can demonstrate the effectiveness of using pointers through an example showing a simple method of sorting:

```
/* Program 7.14 Sorting strings */
#include <stdio.h>
#include <stdlib.h>
#include <stdbool.h>
#include <string.h>
#define BUFFER_LEN 100              /* Length of input buffer         */
#define NUM_P 100                   /* maximum number of strings      */

int main(void)
{
  char buffer[BUFFER_LEN];          /* space to store an input string */
  char *pS[NUM_P] = { NULL };       /* Array of string pointers       */
  char *pTemp = NULL;               /* Temporary pointer              */
  int i = 0;                        /* Loop counter                   */
  bool sorted = false;              /* Indicated when strings are sorted */
  int last_string = 0;              /* Index of last string entered   */

  printf("\nEnter successive lines, pressing Enter at the"
              " end of each line.\nJust press Enter to end.\n\n");
  while((*fgets(buffer, BUFFER_LEN, stdin) != '\n') && (i < NUM_P))
  {
    pS[i] = (char*)malloc(strlen(buffer) + 1);
    if(pS[i]==NULL)                 /* Check for no memory allocated  */
    {
      printf(" Memory allocation failed. Program terminated.\n");
      return 1;
    }
    strcpy(pS[i++], buffer);
  }
  last_string = i;                  /* Save last string index         */
```

```
/* Sort the strings in ascending order */
while(!sorted)
{
  sorted = true;
  for(i = 0 ; i<last_string-1 ; i++)
    if(strcmp(pS[i], pS[i + 1]) > 0)
      {
        sorted = false;           /* We were out of order     */
        pTemp= pS[i];             /* Swap pointers pS[i]      */
        pS[i] = pS[i + 1];        /*        and               */
        pS[i + 1]  = pTemp;       /*      pS[i + 1]            */
      }
}

/* Displayed the sorted strings */
printf("\nYour input sorted in order is:\n\n");
for(i = 0 ; i<last_string ; i++)
{
  printf("%s\n", pS[i] );
  free( pS[i] );
  pS[i] = NULL;
}
  return 0;
}
```

Assuming you enter the same input data, the output from this program is as follows:

```
Enter successive lines, pressing Enter at the end of each line.
Just press Enter to end.

Many a mickle makes a muckle.
A fool and your money are soon partners.
Every dog has his day.
Do unto others before they do it to you.
A nod is as good as a wink to a blind horse.


Your input sorted in order is:

A fool and your money are soon partners.
A nod is as good as a wink to a blind horse.
Do unto others before they do it to you.
Every dog has his day.
Many a mickle makes a muckle.
```

How It Works

This example will really sort the wheat from the chaff. You use the input function fgets(), which reads a complete string up to the point you press Enter and then adds '\0' to the end. Using fgets() rather than the gets() function ensures that the capacity of buffer will not be exceeded. The first argument is a pointer to the memory area where you want the string to be stored, the second is the maximum number of character that can be stored, and the third argument is the stream to be read, the standard input stream in this case. Its return value is either the address where the input string is stored—buffer, in this case—or NULL if an error occurs. Don't forget, fgets() differs from gets() in that it stores the newline character that terminates the input before appending the string terminator '\0' whereas fgets() does not.

The overall operation of this program is quite simple, and it involves three distinct activities:

- Read in all the input strings.

- Sort the input strings in order.

- Display the input strings in alphabetical order.

After the initial prompt lines are displayed, the input process is handled by these statements:

```
while((*fgets(buffer, BUFFER_LEN, stdin) != '\n') && (i < NUM_P))
{
  pS[i] = (char*)malloc(strlen(buffer) + 1);
  if(pS[i]==NULL)                       /* Check for no memory allocated     */
  {
    printf(" Memory allocation failed. Program terminated.\n");
    return 1;
  }
  strcpy(pS[i++], buffer);
}
```

The input process continues until an empty line is entered or until you run out of space in the pointer array. Each line is read into buffer using the fgets() function. This is inside the while loop condition, which allows the loop to continue for as long as fgets() doesn't read a string containing just '\n' and the total number of lines entered doesn't exceed the pointer array dimension. The string just containing '\n' will be a result of you pressing Enter without entering any text. You use the * to get at the contents of the pointer address returned by fgets(). This is the same as dereferencing buffer, of course.

As soon as you collect each input line in buffer, you allocate the correct amount of memory to accommodate the line by using the malloc() function. You get the count of the number of bytes that you need by using the strlen() function and adding 1 for the '\0' at the end. After verifying that you did get the memory allocated, you copy the string from buffer to the new memory using the library function strcpy().

You then save the index for the last string:

```
 last_string = i;                       /* Save last string index            */
```

This is because you're going to reuse the loop counter i, and you need to keep track of how many strings you have.

Once you have all your strings safely stowed away, you sort them using the simplest, and probably the most inefficient, sort going—but it's easy to follow. This takes place within these statements:

```
while(!sorted)
{
  sorted = true;
  for(i = 0 ; i < last_string - 1 ; i++)
    if(strcmp(pS[i], pS[i + 1]) > 0)
    {
      sorted = false;              /* We were out of order          */
      pTemp= pS[i];                /* Swap pointers pS[i]           */
      pS[i] = pS[i + 1];           /*        and                    */
      pS[i + 1]  = pTemp;          /*        pS[i + 1]              */
    }
}
```

The sort takes place inside the `while` loop that continues as long as `sorted` is false. The sort proceeds by comparing successive pairs of strings using the `strcmp()` function inside the `for` loop. If the first string is greater than the second string, you swap pointer values. Using pointers, as you have here, is a very economical way of changing the order. The strings themselves remain undisturbed exactly where they were in memory. It's just the sequence of their addresses that changes in the pointer array, pS. This mechanism is illustrated in Figure 7-4. The time needed to swap pointers is a fraction of that required to move all the strings around.

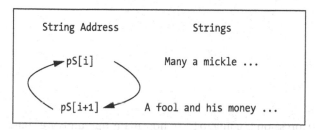

Figure 7-4. *Sorting using pointers*

The swapping continues through all the string pointers. If you have to interchange any strings as you pass through them, you set `sorted` to `false` to repeat the whole thing. If you repeat the whole thing without interchanging any, then they're in order and you've finished the sort. You track the status of this with the `bool` variable `sorted`. This is set to `true` at the beginning of each cycle, but if any interchange occurs, it gets set back to `false`. If you exit a cycle with `sorted` still `true`, it means that no interchanges occurred, so everything must be in order; therefore, you exit from the `while` loop.

The reason this sort is none too good is that each pass through all the items only moves a value by one position in the list. In the worst case, when you have the first entry in the last position, the number of times you have to repeat the process is one less than the number of entries in the list. This inefficient but nevertheless famous method of sorting is known as a **bubble sort**.

Handling strings and other kinds of data using pointers in this way is an extremely powerful mechanism in C. You can throw the basic data (the strings, in this case) into a bucket of memory in any old order, and then you can process them in any sequence you like without moving the data at all. You just change the pointers. You could use ideas from this example as a base for programs for sorting any text. You had better find a better sort of sort, though.

Designing a Program

Congratulations! You made it through a really tough part of the C language, and now I can show you an application using some of what you've learned. I'll follow the usual process, taking you through the analysis and design, and writing the code step by step. Let's look at the final program for this chapter.

The Problem

The problem you'll address is to rewrite the calculator program that you wrote in Chapter 3 with some new features, but this time using pointers. The main improvements are as follows:

! Allow the use of signed decimal numbers, including a decimal point with an optional leading sign, - or +, as well as signed integers.

! Permit expressions to combine multiple operations such as 2.5 + 3.7 - 6/6.

! Add the ^ operator, which will be raised to a power, so 2 ^ 3 will produce 8.

! Allow a line to operate on the previous result. If the previous result is 2.5, then writing =*2 + 7 will produce the result 12. Any input line that starts with an assignment operator will automatically assume the left operand is the previous result.

You're also going to cheat a little by not taking into consideration the precedence of the operators. You'll simply evaluate the expression that's entered from left to right, applying each operator to the previous result and the right operand. This means that the expression

```
1 + 2*3 - 4*-5
```

will be evaluated as

```
((1 + 2)*3 - 4)*(-5)
```

The Analysis

You don't know in advance how long an expression is going to be or how many operands are going to be involved. You'll get a complete string from the user and then analyze this to see what the numbers and operators are. You'll evaluate each intermediate result as soon as you have an operator with a left and a right operand.

The steps are as follows:

1. Read an input string entered by the user and exit if it is quit.
2. Check for an = operator, and if there is one skip looking for the first operand.
3. Search for an operator followed by an operand, executing each operator in turn until the end of the input string.
4. Display the result and go back to step 1.

The Solution

This section outlines the steps you'll take to solve the problem.

Step 1

As you saw earlier in this chapter, the scanf() function doesn't allow you to read a complete string that contains spaces, as it stops at the first whitespace character. You'll therefore read the input expression using the gets() function that's declared in the <stdio.h> library header file. This will read an entire line of input, including spaces. You can actually combine the input and the overall program loop together as follows:

```
/* Program 7.15 An improved calculator */
#include <stdio.h>                        /* Standard input/output  */
#include <string.h>                       /* For string functions   */
#define BUFFER_LEN 256                     /* Length of input buffer */

int main(void)
{
  char input[BUFFER_LEN];                  /* Input expression       */
```

```
    while(strcmp(fgets(input, BUFFER_LEN, stdin), "quit\n") != 0)
    {
        /* Code to implement the calculator */
    }
    return 0;
}
```

You can do this because the function strcmp() expects to receive an argument that's a pointer to a string, and the function fgets() actually returns a pointer to the string that the user has typed in! &input[0] in this case. The strcmp() function will compare the string that's entered with "quit\n" and will return 0 if they're equal. This will end the loop.

You set the input string to a length of 256. This should be enough because most computers keyboard buffers are 255 characters. (This refers to the maximum number of characters that you can type in before having to press Enter.)

Once you have your string, you could start analyzing it right away, but it would be better if you removed any spaces from the string. Because the input string is well-defined, you don't need spaces to separate the operator from the operands. Let's add code inside the while loop to remove any spaces:

```
/* Program 7.15 An improved calculator */
#include <stdio.h>                              /* Standard input/output  */
#include <string.h>                             /* For string functions   */
#define BUFFER_LEN 256                          /* Length of input buffer */

int main(void)
{
    char input[BUFFER_LEN];                     /* Input expression       */
    unsigned int index = 0; /* Index of the current character in input    */
    unsigned int to = 0;    /* To index for copying input to itself       */
    size_t input_length = 0;     /* Length of the string in input         */
    while(strcmp(fgets(input, BUFFER_LEN, stdin), "quit\n") != 0)
    {
        input_length = strlen(input);      /* Get the input string length */
        input[--input_length] = '\0';      /* Remove newline at the end   */

        /* Remove all spaces from the input by copy the string to itself */
        /* including the string terminating character                 */
        for(to = 0, index = 0 ; index<=input_length ; index++)
        if(*(input+index) != ' ')                /* If it is not a space   */
            *(input+to++) = *(input+index);      /* Copy the character     */

        input_length = strlen(input);       /* Get the new string length   */
        index = 0;                          /* Start at the first character */

        /* Code to implement the calculator */
    }
    return 0;
}
```

You've added declarations for the additional variables that you'll need. The variable input_length has been declared as type size_t to be compatible with the type returned by the strlen() function. This avoids possible warning messages from the compiler.

The fgets() function stores a newline character when you press the Enter to end entry of as line. You don't want the code that analyzes the string to be looking at the newline character, so you overwrite it with '\0'. The index expression for the input array decrements the length value returned by the strlen() and uses the result to reference the element containing newline.

You remove spaces by copying the string stored in input to itself. You need to keep track of two indexes in the copy loop: one for the position in input where the next nonspace character is to be copied to, and one for the position of the next character to be copied. In the loop you don't copy spaces; you just increment index to move to the next character. The to index gets incremented only when a character is copied. After the loop is entered, you store the new string length in input_length and reset index to reference to the first character in input.

You could equally well write the loop here using array notation:

```
for(to = 0, index = 0 ; index<=input_length ; index++)
   if(input[index] != ' ')                    /* If it is not a space */
      input[to++] = input[index];             /* Copy the character   */
```

For my taste, the code is clearer using array notation, but you'll continue using pointer notation as you need the practice.

Step 2

The input expression has two possible forms. It can start with an assignment operator, indicating that the last result is to be taken as the left operand, or it can start with a number with or without a sign. You can differentiate these two situations by looking for the '=' character first. If you find one, the left operand is the previous result.

The code you need to add next in the while loop will look for an '=', and if it doesn't find one it will look for a substring that is numeric that will be the left operand:

```
/* Program 7.15 An improved calculator */
#include <stdio.h>                 /* Standard input/output               */
#include <string.h>                /* For string functions                */
#include <ctype.h>                 /* For classifying characters          */
#include <stdlib.h>                /* For converting strings to numeric values */
#define BUFFER_LEN 256             /* Length of input buffer              */

int main(void)
{
  char input[BUFFER_LEN];                  /* Input expression            */
  char number_string[30];        /* Stores a number string from input        */
  unsigned int index = 0;        /* Index of the current character in input  */
  unsigned int to = 0;           /* To index for copying input to itself     */
  size_t input_length = 0;       /* Length of the string in input            */
  unsigned int number_length = 0;   /* Length of the string in number_string */
  double result = 0.0;              /* The result of an operation            */

  while(strcmp(fgets(input, BUFFER_LEN, stdin), "quit\n") != 0)
  {
    input_length = strlen(input);          /* Get the input string length */
    input[--input_length] = '\0';          /* Remove newline at the end   */

    /* Remove all spaces from the input by copying the string to itself */
    /* including the string terminating character                       */
    for(to = 0, index = 0 ; index<=input_length ; index++)
      if(*(input+index) != ' ')                 /* If it is not a space   */
        *(input+to++) = *(input+index);         /* Copy the character     */
```

```
   input_length = strlen(input);              /* Get the new string length   */
   index = 0;                                 /* Start at the first character */

   if(input[index]== '=')                     /* Is there =?                 */
     index++;                                  /* Yes so skip over it         */
   else
   {                                          /* No - look for the left operand */
     /* Look for a number that is the left operand for */
     /* the first operator                             */

     /* Check for sign and copy it */
     number_length = 0;                            /* Initialize length       */
     if(input[index]=='+' || input[index]=='-')    /* Is it + or -?           */
       *(number_string+number_length++) = *(input+index++); /* Yes so copy it */

     /* Copy all following digits */
     for( ; isdigit(*(input+index)) ; index++)          /* Is it a digit? */
       *(number_string+number_length++) = *(input+index);  /* Yes - Copy it  */

     /* copy any fractional part */
     if(*(input+index)=='.')                            /* Is it decimal point? */
     { /* Yes so copy the decimal point and the following digits */
       *(number_string+number_length++) = *(input+index++);   /* Copy point */

       for( ; isdigit(*(input+index)) ; index++)        /* For each digit */
           *(number_string+number_length++) = *(input+index);    /* copy it */
     }
     *(number_string+number_length) = '\0';       /* Append string terminator */

     /* If we have a left operand, the length of number_string */
     /* will be > 0. In this case convert to a double so we    */
     /* can use it in the calculation                          */
     if(number_length>0)
       result = atof(number_string);            /* Store first number as result */
   }

   /* Code to analyze the operator and right operand */
   /* and produce the result                         */
 }
 return 0;
}
```

You include the <ctype.h> header for the character analysis functions and the <stdlib.h> header because you use the function atof(), which converts a string passed as an argument to a floating-point value. You've added quite a chunk of code here, but it consists of a number of straightforward steps.

The if statement checks for '=' as the first character in the input:

```
if(input[index]== '=')                     /* Is there =?                 */
  index++;                                  /* Yes so skip over it         */
```

If you find one, you increment index to skip over it and go straight to looking for the operand. If '=' isn't found, you execute the else, which looks for a numeric left operand.

You copy all the characters that make up the number to the array number_string. The number may start with a unary sign, '-' or '+', so you first check for that in the else block. If you find it, then you copy it to number_string with the following statement:

```
if(input[index]=='+' || input[index]=='-')              /* Is it + or -? */
    *(number_string+number_length++) = *(input+index++); /* Yes so copy it */
```

If a sign isn't found, then index value, recording the current character to be analyzed in input, will be left exactly where it is. If a sign is found, it will be copied to number_string and the value of index will be incremented to point to the next character.

One or more digits should be next, so you have a for loop that copies however many digits there are to number_string:

```
for( ; isdigit(*(input+index)) ; index++)              /* Is it a digit? */
    *(number_string+number_length++) = *(input+index);  /* Yes - Copy it  */
```

This will copy all the digits of an integer and increment the value of index accordingly. Of course, if there are no digits, the value of index will be unchanged.

The number might not be an integer. In this case, there must be a decimal point next, which may be followed by more digits. The if statement checks for the decimal point. If there is one, then the decimal point and any following digits will also be copied:

```
if(*(input+index)=='.')                                /* Is it decimal point? */
{ /* Yes so copy the decimal point and the following digits */
    *(number_string+number_length++) = *(input+index++);    /* Copy point */

    for( ; isdigit(*(input+index)) ; index++)          /* For each digit */
        *(number_string+number_length++) = *(input+index);  /* copy it */
}
```

You must have finished copying the string for the first operand now, so you append a string-terminating character to number_string.

```
*(number_string+number_length) = '\0';        /* Append string terminator */
```

While there may not be a value found, if you've copied a string representing a number to number_string, the value of number_length must be positive because there has to be at least one digit. Therefore, you use the value of number_length as an indicator that you have a number:

```
if(number_length>0)
    result = atof(number_string);             /* Store first number as result */
```

The string is converted to a floating-point value of type double by the atof() function. Note that you store the value of the string in result. You'll use the same variable later to store the result of an operation. This will ensure that result always contains the result of an operation, including that produced at the end of an entire string. If you haven't stored a value here, because there is no left operand, result will already contain the value from the previous input string.

Step 3

At this point, what follows in the input string is very well-defined. It must be an operator followed by a number. The operator will have the number that you found previously as its left operand, or the previous result. This •op-number! combination may also be followed by another, so you have a possible succession of op-number combinations through to the end of the string. You can deal with this in a loop that will look for these combinations:

```
/* Program 7.15 An improved calculator */
#include <stdio.h>              /* Standard input/output                */
#include <string.h>             /* For string functions                 */
#include <ctype.h>              /* For classifying characters           */
#include <stdlib.h>             /* For converting strings to numeric values */
#define BUFFER_LEN 256          /* Length of input buffer               */

int main(void)
{
  char input[BUFFER_LEN];              /* Input expression               */
  char number_string[30];              /* Stores a number string from input */
  char op = 0;                         /* Stores an operator             */

  unsigned int index = 0;       /* Index of the current character in input  */
  unsigned int to = 0;          /* To index for copying input to itself     */
  size_t input_length = 0;      /* Length of the string in input            */
  unsigned int number_length = 0;   /* Length of the string in number_string */
  double result = 0.0;          /* The result of an operation               */
  double number = 0.0;          /* Stores the value of number_string        */

  while(strcmp(fgets(input, BUFFER_LEN, stdin), "quit\n") != 0)
  {
    input_length = strlen(input);            /* Get the input string length */
    input[--input_length] = '\0';            /* Remove newline at the end   */

    /* Remove all spaces from the input by copying the string to itself */
    /* including the string terminating character                       */
    /* Code to remove spaces as before...                               */

    /* Code to check for '=' and analyze & store the left operand as before.. */

    /* Now look for 'op number' combinations */
    for(;index < input_length;)
    {
      op = *(input+index++);                        /* Get the operator */
      /* Copy the next operand and store it in number */
      number_length = 0;                    /* Initialize the length  */

      /* Check for sign and copy it */
      if(input[index]=='+' || input[index]=='-')         /* Is it + or -? */
      *(number_string+number_length++) = *(input+index++); /* Yes - copy it. */

      /* Copy all following digits */
      for( ; isdigit(*(input+index)) ; index++)         /* For each digit */
       *(number_string+number_length++) = *(input+index);   /* copy it.       */

      /* copy any fractional part */
      if(*(input+index)=='.')                     /* Is it a decimal point? */
      { /* Copy the  decimal point and the following digits */
        *(number_string+number_length++) = *(input+index++);   /* Copy point */
        for( ; isdigit(*(input+index)) ; index++)            /* For each digit */
         *(number_string+number_length++) = *(input+index);   /* copy it.   */
      }
```

```
      *(number_string+number_length) = '\0';              /* terminate string */

      /* Convert to a double so we can use it in the calculation */
      number = atof(number_string);
    }
  /* code to produce result */
  }
  return 0;
}
```

In the interest of not repeating the same code ad nauseam, there are some comments indicating where the previous bits of code that you added are located in the program. I'll list the complete source code with the next addition to the program.

The for loop continues until you reach the end of the input string, which will be when you have incremented index to be equal to input_length. On each iteration of the loop, you store the operator in the variable op of type char:

```
      op = *(input+index++);                              /* Get the operator */
```

With the operator out of the way, you then extract the characters that form the next number. This will be the right operand for the operator. You haven't verified that the operator is valid here, so the code won't spot an invalid operator at this point.

The extraction of the string for the number that's the right operand is exactly the same as that for the left operand. The same code is repeated. This time, though, the double value for the operand is stored in number:

```
  number = atof(number_string);
```

You now have the left operand stored in result, the operator stored in op, and the right operand stored in number. Consequently, you're now prepared to execute an operation of the form

```
 result=(result op number)
```

When you've added the code for this, the program will be complete.

Step 4

You can use a switch statement to select the operation to be carried out based on the operand. This is essentially the same code that you used in the previous calculator. You'll also display the output and add a prompt at the beginning of the program on how the calculator is used. Here's the complete code for the program, with the last code you're adding in bold:

```
/* Program 7.15 An improved calculator */
#include <stdio.h>             /* Standard input/output                */
#include <string.h>            /* For string functions                 */
#include <ctype.h>             /* For classifying characters           */
#include <stdlib.h>            /* For converting strings to numeric values */
#include <math.h>              /* For power() function                 */
#define BUFFER_LEN 256         /* Length of input buffer               */

int main(void)
{
  char input[BUFFER_LEN];      /* Input expression                     */
  char number_string[30];      /* Stores a number string from input    */
  char op = 0;                 /* Stores an operator                   */
```

```
unsigned int index = 0;          /* Index of the current character in input  */
unsigned int to = 0;             /* To index for copying input to itself     */
size_t input_length = 0;         /* Length of the string in input            */
unsigned int number_length = 0;  /* Length of the string in number_string    */
double result = 0.0;             /* The result of an operation               */
double number = 0.0;             /* Stores the value of number_string        */

printf("\nTo use this calculator, enter any expression with"
                                  " or without spaces");
printf("\nAn expression may include the operators:");
printf("\n          +, -, *, /, %%, or ^(raise to a power).");
printf("\nUse = at the beginning of a line to operate on ");
printf("\nthe result of the previous calculation.");
printf("\nUse quit by itself to stop the calculator.\n\n");

/* The main calculator loop */
while(strcmp(fgets(input, BUFFER_LEN, stdin), "quit\n") != 0)
{
  input_length = strlen(input);          /* Get the input string length */
  input[--input_length] = '\0';          /* Remove newline at the end   */

  /* Remove all spaces from the input by copying the string to itself */
  /* including the string terminating character                       */
  for(to = 0, index = 0 ; index<=input_length ; index++)
  if(*(input+index) != ' ')                    /* If it is not a space */
    *(input+to++) = *(input+index);            /* Copy the character   */

  input_length = strlen(input);              /* Get the new string length */
  index = 0;                                 /* Start at the first character */

  if(input[index]== '=')                     /* Is there =?               */
    index++;                                 /* Yes so skip over it       */
  else
  {                                          /* No - look for the left operand */
    /* Look for a number that is the left operand for the 1st operator */

    /* Check for sign and copy it */
    number_length = 0;                            /* Initialize length    */
    if(input[index]=='+' || input[index]=='-')            /* Is it + or -? */
      *(number_string+number_length++) = *(input+index++); /* Yes so copy it */

    /* Copy all following digits */
    for( ; isdigit(*(input+index)) ; index++)          /* Is it a digit? */
      *(number_string+number_length++) = *(input+index);   /* Yes - Copy it  */

    /* copy any fractional part */
    if(*(input+index)=='.')                         /* Is it decimal point? */
    { /* Yes so copy the decimal point and the following digits */
      *(number_string+number_length++) = *(input+index++);    /* Copy point */

      for( ; isdigit(*(input+index)) ; index++)          /* For each digit */
        *(number_string+number_length++) = *(input+index);  /* copy it      */
    }
```

```
  *(number_string+number_length) = '\0';        /* Append string terminator */

  /* If we have a left operand, the length of number_string */
  /* will be > 0. In this case convert to a double so we    */
  /* can use it in the calculation                          */
  if(number_length>0)
    result = atof(number_string);          /* Store first number as result */
}

/* Now look for 'op number' combinations */
for(;index < input_length;)
{
  op = *(input+index++);                               /* Get the operator */
  /* Copy the next operand and store it in number */
  number_length = 0;                           /* Initialize the length   */

  /* Check for sign and copy it */
  if(input[index]=='+' || input[index]=='-')            /* Is it + or -?  */
  *(number_string+number_length++) = *(input+index++); /* Yes - copy it. */

  /* Copy all following digits */
  for( ; isdigit(*(input+index)) ; index++)            /* For each digit */
    *(number_string+number_length++) = *(input+index); /* copy it.       */

  /* copy any fractional part */
  if(*(input+index)=='.')                         /* Is it a decimal point? */
  { /* Copy the  decimal point and the following digits */
    /* Copy point       */
    *(number_string+number_length++) = *(input+index++);
    for( ; isdigit(*(input+index)) ; index++)          /* For each digit */
      *(number_string+number_length++) = *(input+index); /* copy it.     */
  }
  *(number_string+number_length) = '\0';                 /* terminate string */

  /* Convert to a double so we can use it in the calculation */
  number = atof(number_string);

  /* Execute operation, as 'result op= number' */
  switch(op)
  {
    case '+':                                         /* Addition       */
      result += number;
      break;
    case '-':                                         /* Subtraction    */
      result -= number;
      break;
    case '*':                                         /* Multiplication */
      result *= number;
      break;
    case '/':                                         /* Division       */
      /* Check second operand for zero */
      if(number == 0)
        printf("\n\n\aDivision by zero error!\n");
```

```
        else
          result /= number;
        break;
      case '%':                          /* Modulus operator - remainder  */
        /* Check second operand for zero */
        if((long)number == 0)
          printf("\n\n\aDivision by zero error!\n");
        else
          result = (double)((long)result % (long)number);
        break;
      case '^':                          /* Raise to a power          */
        result = pow(result, number);
        break;
      default:                           /* Invalid operation or bad input */
        printf("\n\n\aIllegal operation!\n");
        break;
    }
  }
  printf("= %f\n", result);                      /* Output the result */
  }
  return 0;
}
```

The switch statement is essentially the same as in the previous calculator program, but with some extra cases. Because you use the power function pow() to calculate resultnumber, you have to add an #include directive for the header file math.h.

Typical output from the calculator program is as follows:

```
To use this calculator, enter any expression with or without spaces
An expression may include the operators:
            +, -, *, /, %, or ^(raise to a power).
Use = at the beginning of a line to operate on
the result of the previous calculation.
Use quit by itself to stop the calculator.

2.5+3.3/2
= 2.900000
= *3
= 8.700000
= ^4
= 5728.976100
1.3+2.4-3.5+-7.8
= -7.600000
=*-2
= 15.200000
= *-2
= -30.400000
= +2
= -28.400000
quit
```

And there you have it!

Summary

This chapter covered a lot of ground. You explored pointers in detail. You should now understand the relationship between pointers and arrays (both one-dimensional and multidimensional arrays) and have a good grasp of their uses. I introduced the malloc(), calloc(), and realloc() functions for dynamically allocating memory, which provides the potential for your programs to use just enough memory for the data being processed in each run. You also saw the complementary function free() that you use to release memory previously allocated by malloc(), calloc(), or realloc(). You should have a clear idea of how you can use pointers with strings and how you can use arrays of pointers.

The topics I've discussed in this chapter are fundamental to a lot of what follows in the rest of the book, and of course to writing C programs effectively, so you should make sure that you're quite comfortable with the material in this chapter before moving on to the next chapter. The next chapter is all about structuring your programs.

Exercises

The following exercises enable you to try out what you've learned in this chapter. If you get stuck, look back over the chapter for help. If you're still stuck, you can download the solutions from the Source Code area of the Apress web site (http://www.apress.com), but that really should be a last resort.

Exercise 7-1. Write a program to calculate the average for an arbitrary number of floating-point values that are entered from the keyboard. Store all values in memory that's allocated dynamically before calculating and displaying the average. The user shouldn't be required to specify in advance how many values there will be.

Exercise 7-2. Write a program that will read an arbitrary number of proverbs from the keyboard and store them in memory that's allocated at runtime. The program should then output the proverbs ordered by their length, starting with the shortest and ending with the longest.

Exercise 7-3. Write a program that will read a string from the keyboard and display it after removing all spaces and punctuation characters. All operations should use pointers.

Exercise 7-4. Write a program that will read a series of temperature recordings as floating-point values for an arbitrary number of days, in which six recordings are made per day. The temperature readings should be stored in an array that's allocated dynamically and that's the correct dimensions for the number of temperature values that are entered. Calculate the average temperature per day, and then output the recordings for each day together, with the average on a single line with one decimal place after the point.

CHAPTER 8

■ ■ ■

Structuring Your Programs

I mentioned in Chapter 1 that breaking up a program into reasonably self-contained units is basic to the development of any program of a practical nature. When confronted with a big task, the most sensible thing to do is break it up into manageable chunks. You can then deal with each small chunk fairly easily and be reasonably sure that you've done it properly. If you design the chunks of code carefully, you may be able to reuse some of them in other programs.

One of the key ideas in the C language is that every program should be segmented into functions that are relatively short. Even with the examples you've seen so far that were written as a single function, `main()`, other functions are also involved because you've still used a variety of standard library functions for input and output, for mathematical operations, and for handling strings.

In this chapter, you'll look at how you can make your programs more effective and easier to develop by introducing more functions of your own.

In this chapter you'll learn:

! How data is passed to a function

! How to return results from your functions

! How to define your own functions

! The advantages of pointers as arguments to functions

Program Structure

As I said right at the outset, a C program consists of one or more functions, the most important of which is the function `main()` where execution starts. When you use library functions such as `printf()` or `scanf()`, you see how one function is able to call up another function in order to carry out some particular task and then continue execution back in the calling function when the task is complete. Except for side effects on data stored at global scope, each function in a program is a self-contained unit that carries out a particular operation. When a function is called, the code within the body of that function is executed, and when the function has finished executing, control returns to the point at which that function was called. This is illustrated in Figure 8-1, where you can see an idealized representation of a C program structured as five functions. It doesn't show any details of the statements involved! just the sequence of execution.

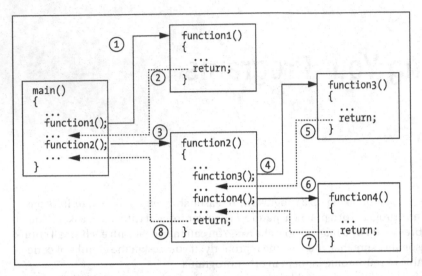

Figure 8-1. *Execution of a program made up of several functions*

The program steps through the statements in sequence in the normal way until it comes across a call to a particular function. At that point, execution moves to the start of that function! that is, the first statement in the body of the function. Execution of the program continues through the function statements until it hits a `return` statement or reaches the closing brace marking the end of the function body. This signals that execution should go back to the point immediately after where the function was originally called.

The set of functions that make up a program link together through the function calls and their `return` statements to perform the various tasks necessary for the program to achieve its purpose. Figure 8-1 shows each function in the program executed just once. In practice, each function can be executed many times and can be called from several points within a program. You've already seen this in the examples that called the `printf()` and `scanf()` functions several times.

Before you look in more detail at how to define your own functions, I need to explain a particular aspect of the way variables behave that I've glossed over so far.

Variable Scope and Lifetime

In all the examples up to now, you've declared the variables for the program at the beginning of the block that defines the body of the function `main()`. But you can actually define variables at the beginning of *any* block. Does this make a difference? •It most certainly does, Stanley,! as Ollie would have said. Variables exist only within the block in which they're defined. They're created when they are declared, and they cease to exist at the next closing brace.

This is also true of variables that you declare within blocks that are inside other blocks. The variables declared at the beginning of an outer block also exist in the inner block. These variables are freely accessible, as long as there are no other variables with the same name in the inner block, as you'll see.

Variables that are created when they're declared and destroyed at the end of a block are called **automatic variables**, because they're automatically created and destroyed. The extent within the program code where a given variable is visible and can be referenced is called the variable's **scope**. When you use a variable within its scope, everything is OK. But if you try to reference a variable outside its scope, you'll get an error message when you compile the program because the variable doesn't exist outside of its scope. The general idea is illustrated in the following code fragment:

```
{
  int a = 0;                                          /* Create a       */
  /* Reference to a is OK here      */
  /* Reference to b is an error here */
  {
    int b = 10;                                       /* Create b       */
    /* Reference to a and b is OK here */
  }                                                   /* b dies here    */
  /* Reference to b is an error here */
  /* Reference to a is OK here       */
}                                                     /* a dies here    */
```

All the variables that are declared within a block die and no longer exist after the closing brace of the block. The variable a is visible within both the inner and outer blocks because it's declared in the outer block. The variable b is visible only within the inner block because it's declared within that block.

While your program is executing, a variable is created and memory is allocated for it. At some point, which for automatic variables is the end of the block in which the variable is declared, the memory that the variable occupies is returned back to the system. Of course, while functions called within the block are executing, the variable continues to exist; it is only destroyed when execution reaches the end of the block in which it was created. The time period during which a variable is in existence is referred to as the **lifetime** of the variable.

Let's explore the implications of a variable's scope through an example.

TRY IT OUT: UNDERSTANDING SCOPE

Let's take a simple example that involves a nested block that happens to be the body of a loop:

```
/* Program 8.1 A microscopic program about scope */
#include <stdio.h>
int main(void)
{
  int count1 = 1;                              /* Declared in outer block */

  do
  {
    int count2 = 0;                            /* Declared in inner block */
    ++count2;
    printf("\ncount1 = %d     count2 = %d", count1,count2);
  } while( ++count1 <= 8 );

  /* count2 no longer exists */

  printf("\ncount1 = %d\n", count1);
  return 0;
}
```

You will get the following output from this program:

```
count1 = 1    count2 = 1
count1 = 2    count2 = 1
count1 = 3    count2 = 1
count1 = 4    count2 = 1
count1 = 5    count2 = 1
count1 = 6    count2 = 1
count1 = 7    count2 = 1
count1 = 8    count2 = 1
count1 = 9
```

How It Works

The block that encloses the body of main() contains an inner block that is the do-while loop. You declare and define count2 inside the loop block:

```
  do
  {
    int count2 = 0; /* Declared in inner block */
    ++count2;
    printf("\ncount1 = %d      count2 = %d", count1,count2);
  } while( ++count1 <= 8 );
```

As a result, the value of count2 is never more than 1. During each iteration of the loop, the variable count2 is created, initialized, incremented, and destroyed. It only exists from the statement that declares it down to the closing brace for the loop. The variable count1, on the other hand, exists at the main() block level. It continues to exist while it is incremented, so the last printf() produces the value 9.

Try modifying the program to make the last printf() output the value of count2. It won't compile. You'll get an error because, at the point where the last printf() is, count2 no longer exists. From this you may guess, correctly, that failing to initialize automatic variables before you use them can cause untold chaos, because the memory that they occupy may be reallocated to something else at the end of their existence. As a consequence, next time around, your uninitialized variables may contain anything but what you expect.

TRY IT OUT: MORE ABOUT SCOPE

Let's try a slight modification of the last example:

```
/* Program 8.2 More scope in this one */
#include <stdio.h>
int main(void)
{
  int count = 0;                              /* Declared in outer block */
  do
  {
    int count = 0;                /* This is another variable called count */
    ++count;                      /* this applies to inner count         */
    printf("\ncount = %d ", count);
  }
  while( ++count <= 8 );                       /* This works with outer count */
```

```
/* Inner count is dead, this is outer */
printf("\ncount = %d\n", count);
return 0;
}
```

Now you've used the same variable name, count, at the main() block level and in the loop block. Observe what happens when you compile and run this:

```
count = 1
count = 1
count = 1
count = 1
count = 1
count = 1
count = 1
count = 1
count = 9
```

How It Works

The output is boring, but interesting at the same time. You actually have two variables called count, but inside the loop block the local variable will "hide" the version of count that exists at the main() block level. The compiler will assume that when you use the name count, you mean the one that was declared in the current block. Inside the while loop, only the local version of count can be reached, so that is the variable being incremented. The printf() inside the loop block displays the local count value, which is always 1, for the reasons given previously. As soon as you exit from the loop, the outer count variable becomes visible, and the last printf() displays its exit value from the loop as 9.

Clearly, the variable that is controlling the loop is the one declared at the beginning of main(). This little example demonstrates why it isn't a good idea to use the same variable name for two different variables in a function, even though it's legal. At best, it's most confusing. At worst, you'll be thinking "that's another fine mess I've gotten myself into."

Variable Scope and Functions

The last point to note, before I get into the detail of creating functions, is that the body of every function is a block (which may contain other blocks, of course). As a result, the automatic variables that you declare within a function are local to the function and don't exist elsewhere. Therefore, the variables declared within one function are quite independent of those declared in another function or in a nested block. There's nothing to prevent you from using the same name for variables in different functions; they will remain quite separate.

This becomes more significant when you're dealing with large programs in which the problem of ensuring unique variables can become a little inconvenient. It's still a good idea to avoid any unnecessary or misleading overlapping of variable names in your various functions and, of course, you should try to use names that are meaningful to make your programs easy to follow. You'll see more about this as you explore functions in C more deeply.

Functions

You've already used built-in functions such as printf() or strcpy() quite extensively in your programs. You've seen how these built-in functions are executed when you reference them by name and how you are able to transfer information to a function by means of arguments between parentheses following the function name. With the printf() function, for instance, the first argument is usually a string literal, and the succeeding arguments (of which there may be none) are a series of variables or expressions whose values are to be displayed.

You've also seen how you can receive information back from a function in two ways. The first way is through one of the function arguments in parentheses. You provide an address of a variable through an argument to a function, and the function places a value in that variable. When you use scanf() to read data from the keyboard, for instance, the input is stored in an address that you supply as an argument. The second way is that you can receive information back from a function as a **return value**. With the strlen() function, for instance, the length of the string that you supply as the argument appears in the program code in the position where the function call is made. Thus, if str is the string "example", in the expression 2*strlen(str), the value 7, which the function returns, replaces the function call in the expression. The expression will therefore amount to 2*7. Where a function returns a value of a given type, the function call can appear as part of any expression where a variable of the same type could be used.

Of necessity you've written the function main() in all your programs, so you already have the basic knowledge of how a function is constructed. So let's look at what makes up a function in more detail.

Defining a Function

When you create a function, you need to specify the **function header** as the first line of the function definition, followed by the executable code for the function enclosed between braces. The block of code between braces following the function header is called the **function body**.

! The function header defines the name of the function, the function parameters (in other words, what types of values are passed to the function when it's called), and the type for the value that the function returns.

! The function body determines what calculations the function performs on the values that are passed to it.

The general form of a function is essentially the same as you've been using for main(), and it looks like this:

```
Return_type  Function_name( Parameters - separated by commas )
{
    Statements;
}
```

The statements in the function body can be absent, but the braces must be present. If there are no statements in the body of a function, the return type must be void, and the function will have no effect. You'll recall that I said that the type void means •absence of any type,! so here it means that the function doesn't return a value. A function that does not return a value must also have the return type specified as void. Conversely, for a function that does not have a void return type, every return statement in the function body must return a value of the specified return type.

Although it may not be immediately apparent, presenting a function with a content-free body is often useful during the testing phase of a complicated program. This allows you to run the program with only selected functions actually doing something; you can then add the function bodies, step by step, until the whole thing works.

The parameters between parentheses are placeholders for the argument values that you must specify when you call a function. The term **parameter** refers to a placeholder in the function definition that specifies the type of value that should be passed to the function when it is called. A parameter consists of the type followed by the parameter name that is used within the body of the function to refer to that value when the function executes. The term **argument** refers to the value that you supply corresponding to a parameter when you call a function. I'll explain parameters in more detail in the •Function Parameters! section later in this chapter.

■**Note** The statements in the body of a function can also contain nested blocks of statements. But you can't define a function inside the body of another function.

The general form for calling a function is the following expression:

```
Function_name(List of Arguments - separated by commas)
```

You simply use the function's name followed by a list of arguments separated by commas in parentheses, just as you've been doing with functions such as printf() and scanf(). A function call can appear as a statement on a line by itself, like this:

```
printf("A fool and your money are soon partners,");
```

A function that's called like this can be a function that returns a value. In this case the value that's returned is simply discarded. A function that has been defined with a return type of void can *only* be called like this.

A function that returns a value can, and usually does, participate in an expression. For example

```
result = 2.0*sqrt(2.0);
```

Here, the value that's returned by the sqrt() function (declared in the <math.h> header file) is multiplied by 2.0 and the result is stored in the variable result. Obviously, because a function with a void return type doesn't return anything, it can't possibly be part of an expression.

Naming a Function

The name of a function can be any legal name in C that isn't a reserved word (such as int, double, sizeof, and so on) and isn't the same as the name of another function in your program. You should take care not to use the same names as any of the standard library functions because this would prevent you from using the library function of the same name, and it would also be very confusing.

One way of differentiating your function names from those in the standard library is to start them with a capital letter, although some programmers find this rather restricting. A legal name has the same form as that of a variable: a sequence of letters and digits, the first of which must be a letter. As with variable names, the underline character counts as a letter. Other than that, the name of a function can be anything you like, but ideally the name that you choose should give some clue as to what the function does. Examples of valid function names that you might create are as follows:

```
cube_root    FindLast    Explosion    Back2Front
```

You'll often want to define function names (and variable names, too) that consist of more than one word. There are two common approaches you can adopt that happen to be illustrated in the first two examples:

! Separate each of the words in a function name with an underline character.

! Capitalize the first letter of each word.

Both approaches work well. Which one you choose is up to you, but it's a good idea to pick an approach and stick to it. You can, of course, use one approach for functions and the other for variables. Within this book, both approaches have been sprinkled around to give you a feel for how they look. By the time you reach the end of the book, you'll probably have formed your own opinion as to which approach is best.

Function Parameters

Function parameters are defined within the function header and are placeholders for the arguments that need to be specified when the function is called. The parameters for a function are a list of parameter names and their types, and successive parameters are separated by commas. The entire list of parameters is enclosed between the parentheses that follow the function name.

Parameters provide the means by which you pass information *from* the calling function *into* the function that is called. These parameter names are local to the function, and the values that are assigned to them when the function is called are referred to as arguments. The computation in the body of the function is then written using these parameter names, which will have the values of the arguments when the function executes. Of course, a function may also have locally defined automatic variables declared within the body of the function. Finally, when the computation has finished, the function will exit and return an appropriate value back to the original calling statement.

Some examples of typical function headers are shown in Table 8-1.

Table 8-1. *Examples of Function Headers*

Function Header	Description
`bool SendMessage(char *text)`	This function has one parameter, text, which is of type •pointer to char,! and it returns a value of type bool.
`void PrintData(int count, double *data)`	This function has two parameters, one of type int and the other of type •pointer to double.! The function does not return a value.
`char message GetMessage(void)`	This function has no parameters and returns a pointer of type char.

You call a function by using the function name followed by the arguments to the function between parentheses. When you actually call the function by referencing it in some part of your program, the arguments that you specify in the call will replace the parameters in the function. As a result, when the function executes, the computation will proceed using the values that you supplied as arguments. The arguments that you specify when you call a function need to agree in type, number, and sequence with the parameters that are specified in the function header. The relationship and information passing between the calling and called function is illustrated in Figure 8-2.

If the type of an argument to a function does not match the type of the corresponding parameter, the compiler will insert a conversion of the argument value to the parameter type where this is possible. This may result in truncation of the argument value, when you pass a value of type double for a parameter of type int, for example, so this is a dangerous practice. If the compiler cannot convert an argument to the required type, you will get an error message.

If there are no parameters to a function, you can specify the parameter list as void, as you have been doing in the case of the main() function.

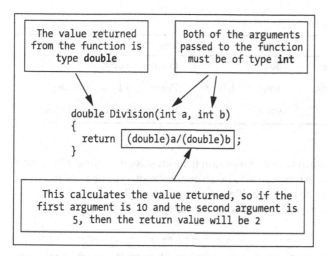

Figure 8-2. *Passing arguments to a function*

Specifying the Return Value Type

Let's take another look at the general form of a function:

```
Return_type  Function_name(List of Parameters - separated by commas)
{
    Statements;
}
```

The Return_type specifies the type of the value returned by the function. If the function is used in an expression or as the right side of an assignment statement, the return value supplied by the function will effectively be substituted for the function in its position. The type of value to be returned by a function can be specified as any of the legal types in C, including pointers. The type can also be specified as void, meaning that no value is returned. As noted earlier, a function with a void return type can't be used in an expression or anywhere in an assignment statement.

The return type can also be type void *, which is a •pointer to void.! The value returned in this case is an address value but with no specified type. This type is used when you want the flexibility to be able to return a pointer that may be used for a variety of purposes, as in the case of the malloc() function for allocating memory. The most common return types are shown in Table 8-2.

Table 8-2. *Common Return Types*

Type	Meaning	Type	Meaning
int	Integer, 2 or 4 bytes	int *	Pointer to int
short	Integer, 2 bytes	short *	Pointer to short
long	Integer, 4 bytes	long *	Pointer to long
long long	Integer, 8 bytes	long long *	Pointer to long
char	Character, 1 byte	char *	Pointer to char
float	Floating-point, 4 bytes	float *	Pointer to float

Table 8-2. *Common Return Types (Continued)*

Type	Meaning	Type	Meaning
double	Floating-point, 8 bytes	double *	Pointer to double
long double	Floating-point, 12 bytes	long double *	Pointer to long double
void	No value	void *	Pointer to undefined type

Of course, you can also specify the return type to a function to be an unsigned integer type, or a pointer to an unsigned integer type. A return type can also be an enumeration type or a pointer to an enumeration type. If a function has its return type specified as other than void, it must return a value. This is achieved by executing a return statement to return the value.

■**Note** In Chapter 11 you will be introduced to objects called structs that provide a way to work with aggregates of several data items as a single unit. A function can have parameters that are structs to pointers to a struct type and can also return a struct or a pointer to a struct.

The return Statement

The return statement provides the means of exiting from a function and resuming execution of the calling function at the point from which the call occurred. In its simplest form, the return statement is just this:

```
return;
```

In this form, the return statement is being used in a function where the return type has been declared as void. It doesn't return any value. However, the more general form of the return statement is this:

```
return expression;
```

This form of return statement must be used when the return value type for the function has been declared as some type other than void. The value that's returned to the calling program is the value that results when expression is evaluated.

■**Caution** You'll get an error message if you compile a program that contains a function defined with a void return type that tries to return a value. You'll get an error message from the compiler if you use a bare return in a function where the return type was specified to be other than void.

The return expression can be any expression, but it should result in a value that's the same type as that declared for the return value in the function header. If it isn't of the same type, the compiler will insert a conversion from the type of the return expression to the one required where this is possible. The compiler will produce an error message if the conversion isn't possible.

There can be more than one return statement in a function, but each return statement must supply a value that is convertible to the type specified in the function header for the return value.

■**Note** The calling function doesn't have to recognize or process the value returned from a called function. It's up to you how you use any values returned from function calls.

TRY IT OUT: USING FUNCTIONS

It's always easier to understand new concepts with an example, so let's start with a trivial illustration of a program that consists of two functions. You'll write a function that will compute the average of two floating-point variables, and you'll call that function from main(). This is more to illustrate the mechanism of writing and calling functions than to present a good example of their practical use.

```c
/* Program 8.3 Average of two float values */
#include <stdio.h>

/* Definition of the function to calculate an average */
float average(float x, float y)
{
   return (x + y)/2.0f;
}

/* main program - execution always starts here */
int main(void)
{
  float value1 = 0.0F;
  float value2 = 0.0F;
  float value3 = 0.0F;

  printf("Enter two floating-point values separated by blanks: ");
  scanf("%f %f", &value1, &value2);
  value3 = average(value1, value2);
  printf("\nThe average is: %f\n",  value3);
  return 0;
}
```

Typical output of this program would be the folllowing:

```
Enter two floating-point values separated by blanks: 2.34 4.567

The average is: 3.453500
```

How It Works

Let's go through this example step by step. Figure 8-3 describes the order of execution in the example.

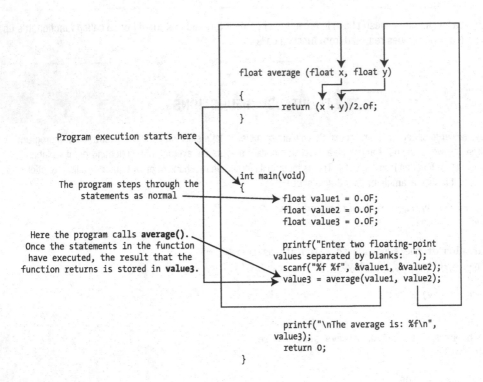

Figure 8-3. *Order of execution*

As you already know, execution begins at the first executable statement of the function main(). The first statement in the body of main() is the following:

```
printf("Enter two floating-point values separated by blanks: ");
```

There's nothing new here—you simply make a call to the function printf() with one argument, which happens to be a string. The actual value transferred to printf() will be a pointer containing the address of the beginning of the string that you've specified as the argument. The printf() function will then display the string that you've supplied as that argument.

The next statement is also a familiar one:

```
scanf("%f %f",&value1, &value2);
```

This calls the input function scanf(). There are three arguments: a string, which is therefore effectively a pointer, as in the previous statement; the address of the first variable, which again is effectively a pointer; and the address of the second variable—again, effectively a pointer. As I've discussed, scanf() must have the addresses for those last two arguments to allow the input data to be stored in them. You'll see why a little later in this chapter.

Once you've read in the two values, the assignment statement is executed:

```
value3 = average(value1, value2);
```

This calls the average() function, which expects two values of type float as arguments, and you've correctly supplied value1 and value2, which are both of type float.

The first executable statement that actually does something is this:

```
printf("Enter two floating-point values separated by blanks: ");
```

There's nothing new here—you simply make a call to the function printf() with one argument, which happens to be a string. The actual value transferred to printf() will be a pointer containing the address of the beginning of the string that you've specified as the argument. The printf() function will then display the string that you've supplied as that argument.

The next statement is also a familiar one:

```
scanf("%f %f",&value1, &value2);
```

This calls the input function scanf(). There are three arguments: a string, which is therefore effectively a pointer, as in the previous statement; the address of the first variable, which again is effectively a pointer; and the address of the second variable—again, effectively a pointer. As I've discussed, scanf() must have the addresses for those last two arguments to allow the input data to be stored in them. You'll see why a little later in this chapter.

Once you've read in the two values, the assignment statement is executed:

```
value3 = average(value1, value2);
```

This calls the average() function, which expects two values of type float as arguments, and you've correctly supplied value1 and value2, which are both of type float. These two values are accessed as x and y in the body of average() when it executes. The result that is returned by the function is then stored in value3. The last printf() call then outputs the value of value3.

The Pass-By-Value Mechanism

There's a very important point to be made in Program 8.3, which is illustrated in Figure 8-4.

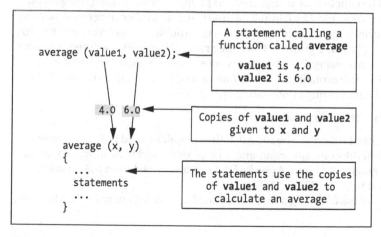

Figure 8-4. *Passing arguments to a function*

The important point is this: *copies* of the values of value1 and value2 are transferred to the function as arguments, *not the variables themselves*. This means that the function can't change the values stored in value1 or value2. For instance, if you input the values 4.0 and 6.0 for the two variables, the compiler will create separate copies of these two values on the stack, and the average() function will have access to these copies when it's called. This mechanism is how all argument values are passed to functions in C, and it's termed the **pass-by-value mechanism**.

The only way that a called function can change a variable belonging to the calling function is by receiving an argument value that's the address of the variable. When you pass an address as an argument to a function, it's still only a copy of the address that's actually passed to the function, not the original. However, the copy is still the address of the original variable. I'll come back to this point later in the chapter in the section •Pointers As Arguments and Return Values.!

The average() function is executed with the values from value1 and value2 substituted for the parameter names in the function, which are x and y, respectively. The function is defined by the following statements:

```
float average(float x, float y)
{
  return (x + y)/2.0f;
}
```

The function body has only one statement, which is the return statement. But this return statement does all the work you need. It contains an expression for the value to be returned that works out the average of x and y. This value then appears in place of the function in the assignment statement back in main(). So, in effect, a function that returns a value acts like a variable of the same type as the return value.

Note that without the f on the constant 2.0, this number would be of type double and the whole expression would be evaluated as type double. Because the compiler would then arrange to cast this to type float for the return value, you would get a warning message during compilation because data could be lost when the value is converted from type double to type float before it is returned.

Instead of assigning the result of the function to value3, you could have written the last printf() statement as follows:

```
printf("\nThe average is: %f", average(value1, value2));
```

Here the function average() would receive copies of the values of the arguments. The return value from the function would be supplied as an argument to printf() directly, even though you haven't explicitly created a place to store it. The compiler would take care of allocating some memory to store the value returned from average(). It would also take the trouble to make a copy of this to hand over to the function printf() as an argument. Once the printf() had been executed, however, you would have had no means of accessing the value that was returned from the function average().

Another possible option is to use explicit values in a function call. What happens then? Let's stretch the printf() statement out of context now and rewrite it like this:

```
printf("\nThe average is: %f", average(4.0, 6.0));
```

In this case if the literal 4.0 and 6.0 don't already exist, the compiler would typically create a memory location to store each of the constant arguments to average(), and then supply copies of those values to the function!   exactly as before. A copy of the result returned from the function average() would then be passed to printf().

Figure 8-5 illustrates the process of calling a function named useful() from main() and getting a value returned.

```
      void main()
      {
        ...
  ┌───► x = useful (y, z);
  │       ...
  │     }
  │     long useful ( int a, int b )
  │     {
  │       long c; /* A local variable we are using to hold a result */
  │       ...           /* In here would be useful statements */
  └────── return c:
      }
```

Figure 8-5. *Argument passing and the return value*

The arrows in the figure show how the values correspond between main() and useful(). Notice that the value returned from useful() is finally stored in the variable x in main(). The value that's returned from useful() is stored in the variable c that is local to the useful() function. This variable ceases to exist when execution of the useful() function ends, but the returned value is still safe because a copy of the value is returned, not the original value stored in c. Thus, returning a value from a function works in the same way as passing an argument value.

Function Declarations

In a variation of Program 8.3, you could define the function main() first and then the function average():

```
#include <stdio.h>

int main(void)
{
  /* Code in main() ... */
}

float average(float x, float y)
{
  return (x + y)/2.0;
}
```

As it stands this won't compile. When the compiler comes across the call to the average() function, it will have no idea what to do with it, because at that point the average() function has not been defined. For this to compile you must add something before the definition of main() that tells the compiler about the average() function.

A **function declaration** is a statement that defines the essential characteristics of a function. It defines its name, its return value type, and the type of each of its parameters. You can actually write it exactly the same as the function header and just add a semicolon at the end if you want. A function declaration is also called a **function prototype**, because it provides all the external specifications for the function. A function prototype enables the compiler to generate the appropriate instructions at each point where you use the function and to check that you use it correctly in each case. When you include a header file in a program, the header file adds the function prototypes for library functions to the program. For example, the header file <stdio.h> contains function prototypes for printf() and scanf(), among others.

To get the variation of Program 8.3 to compile, you just need to add the function prototype for average() before the definition of main():

```
#include <stdio.h>
float average(float, float);                    /* Function prototype */

int main(void)
{
  /* Code in main() ... */
}

float average(float x, float y)
{
  return (x + y)/2.0;
}
```

Now the compiler can compile the call to average() in main() because it knows all its characteristics, its name, its parameter types, and its return type. Technically, you could put the declaration for the function average() within the body of main(), prior to the function call, but this is never done. Function prototypes generally appear at the beginning of a source file prior to the definitions of any of the functions. The function prototypes are then external to all of the functions in the source file, and their scopes extend to the end of the source file, thereby allowing any of the functions in the file to call any function regardless of where you've placed the definitions of the functions.

It's good practice to always include declarations for all of the functions in a program source file, regardless of where they're called. This approach will help your programs to be more consistent in design, and it will prevent any errors occurring if, at any stage, you choose to call a function from another part of your program. Of course, you never need a function prototype for main() because this function is only called by the host environment when execution of a program starts.

Pointers As Arguments and Return Values

You've already seen how it's possible to pass a pointer as an argument to a function. More than that, you've seen that this is essential if a function is to modify the value of a variable that's defined in the calling function. In fact, this is the only way it can be done. So let's explore how all this works out in practice with another example.

TRY IT OUT: FUNCTIONS USING ORDINARY VARIABLES

Let's first take an elementary example of a function that doesn't use a pointer argument. Here, you're going to try to change the contents of a variable by passing it as an argument to a function, changing it, and then returning it. You'll output its value both within the function and back in main() to see what the effect is.

```
/* Program 8.4 The change that doesn't */
#include <stdio.h>

int change(int number);                 /* Function prototype         */

int main(void)
{
  int number = 10;                      /* Starting Value             */
  int result = 0;                       /* Place to put the returned value */
```

```
  result = change(number);
  printf("\nIn main, result = %d\tnumber = %d", result, number);
  return 0;
}

/* Definition of the function change() */
int change(int number)
{
  number = 2 * number;
  printf("\nIn function change, number = %d\n", number);
  return number;
}
```

The output from this program is the following:

```
In function change, number = 20
In main, result = 20     number = 10
```

How It Works

This example demonstrates that you can't change the world without pointers. You can only change the values locally within the function.

The first thing of note in this example is that you put the prototype for the function change() outside of main() along with the #include directive:

```
#include <stdio.h>

int change(int number);                    /* Function prototype              */
```

This makes the function declaration *global*, and if you had other functions in the example they would all be able to use this function.

In main() you set up an integer variable, number, with an initial value of 10. You also have a second variable, result, which you use to store the value that you get back from the function change():

```
  int number = 10;                  /* Starting Value              */
  int result = 0;                   /* Place to put the returned value */
```

You then call the function change() and pass the value of the variable number to it:

```
  result = change(number);
```

The function change() is defined as follows:

```
int change(int number)
{
  number = 2 * number;
  printf("\nIn function change, number = %d", number);
  return number;
}
```

Within the body of the function change(), the first statement doubles the value stored in the argument that has been passed to it from main(). You even use the same variable name in the function that you used in main() to reinforce the idea that you want to change the original value. The function change() displays the new value of number before it returns it to main() by means of the return statement.

In `main()` you also display what you got back from `change()` and the value of number.

```
printf("\nIn main, result = %d\tnumber = %d", result, number);
```

Look at the output, though. It demonstrates how vain and pathetic the attempt to change a variable value by passing it to a function has been. Clearly, the variable number in `change()` has the value 20 on return from the function. It's displayed both in the function and as a returned value in `main()`. In spite of our transparent subterfuge of giving them the same name, the variables with the name number in `main()` and `change()` are evidently quite separate, so modifying one has no effect on the other.

TRY IT OUT: USING POINTERS IN FUNCTIONS

Let's now modify the last example to use pointers, and with a following wind, you should succeed in modifying the value of a variable in `main()`.

```
/* Program 8.5 The change that does    */
#include <stdio.h>

int change(int *pnumber);                /* Function prototype              */

int main(void)
{
  int number = 10;                 /* Starting Value                */
  int *pnumber = &number;          /* Pointer to starting value     */
  int result = 0;                  /* Place to put the returned value */

  result = change(pnumber);
  printf("\nIn main, result = %d\tnumber = %d", result, number);
  return 0;
}

/* Definition of the function change() */
int change(int *pnumber)
{
  *pnumber *= 2;
  printf("\nIn function change, *pnumber = %d\n", *pnumber );
  return *pnumber;
}
```

The output from this program looks like this:

```
In function change, *pnumber = 20
In main, result = 20    number = 20
```

How It Works

There are relatively few changes to the last example. You define a pointer in main() with the name pnumber that is initialized to the address of the variable number, which holds the starting value:

```
int *pnumber = &number;            /* Pointer to starting value    */
```

The prototype of the function change() has been modified to take account of the parameter being a pointer:

```
int change(int *pnumber);              /* Function prototype         */
```

The definition of the function change() has also been modified to use a pointer:

```
int change(int *pnumber)
{
  *pnumber *= 2;
  printf("\nIn function change, *pnumber = %d", *pnumber );
  return *pnumber;
}
```

This pointer, pnumber, has the same name as the pointer in main(), although this is of no consequence to the way the program works. You could call it anything you like, as long as it's a pointer of the correct type, because the name is local to this function.

Within the function change(), the arithmetic statement has been changed to this:

```
*pnumber *= 2;
```

Using the *= operator isn't strictly necessary, but it makes it a lot less confusing, provided you can remember what *= does at this point. It's exactly the same as this:

```
*pnumber - 2*(*pnumber);
```

The output now demonstrates that the pointer mechanism is working correctly and that the function change() is indeed modifying the value of number in main(). Of course, when you submit a pointer as an argument, it's still passed by value. Therefore, the compiler doesn't pass the original pointer; it makes a copy of the address stored in the pointer variable to hand over to the function. Because the copy will be the same address as the original, it still refers to the variable number, so everything works OK.

If you're unconvinced of this, you can demonstrate it for yourself quite easily by adding a statement to the function change() that modifies the pointer pnumber. You could set it to NULL, for instance. You can then check in main() that pnumber still points to number. Of course, you'll have to alter the return statement in change() to get the correct result.

const Parameters

You can qualify a function parameter using the const keyword, which indicates that the function will treat the argument that is passed for this parameter as a constant. Because arguments are passed by value, this is only useful when the parameter is a pointer. Typically you apply the const keyword to a parameter that is a pointer to specify that a function will not change the value pointed to. In other words, the code in the body of the function will not modify the value pointed to by the pointer argument. Here's an example of a function with a const parameter:

```
bool SendMessage(const char* pmessage)
{
  /* Code to send the message */
  return true;
}
```

The compiler will verify that the code in the body of the function does not use the pmessage pointer to modify the message text. You could specify the pointer itself as const too, but this makes little sense because the address is passed by value so you cannot change the original pointer in the calling function.

Specifying a pointer parameter as const has another useful purpose. Because the const modifier implies that the function will not change the data that is pointed to, the compiler knows that an argument that is a pointer to constant data should be safe. On the other hand, if you do not use the const modifier with the parameter, so far as the compiler is concerned, the function may modify the data pointed to by the argument. A good C compiler will at least give you a warning message when you pass a pointer to constant data as the argument for a parameter that you did not declare as const.

■**Tip** If your function does not modify the data pointed to by a pointer parameter, declare the function parameter as const. That way the compiler will verify that your function indeed does not change the data. It will also allow a pointer to a constant to be passed to the function without issuing a warning or an error message.

To specify the address that a pointer contains as const, you place the const keyword after the * in the pointer type specification. Here is a code fragment containing a couple of examples of pointer declaration that will illustrate the difference between a pointer to a constant and a constant pointer:

```
int value1 = 99;
int value2 = 88;

const int pvalue = &value1;       /* pointer to constant */
int const cpvalue = &value1;      /* Constant pointer    */

pvalue = &value2;                 /* OK: pointer is not constant   */
*pvalue = 77;                     /* Illegal: data is constant */

cpvalue = &value2;                /* Illegal: pointer is constant   */
*cpvalue = 77;                     /* OK: data is not constant */
```

If you wanted the parameter to the SendMessage() function to be a constant pointer, you would code it as:

```
bool SendMessage(char *const pmessage)
{
  /* Code to send the message    */
  /* Can change the message here */
  return true;
}
```

Now the function body can change the message but not the address in pmessage. As I said, pmessage will contain a copy of the address so you might as well declare the parameter with using const in this case.

TRY IT OUT: PASSING DATA USING POINTERS

You can exercise this method of passing data to a function using pointers in a slightly more practical way, with a revised version of the function for sorting strings from Chapter 7. You can see the complete code for the program here, and then I'll discuss it in detail. The source code defines three functions in addition to main():

```c
/* Program 8.6 The functional approach to string sorting*/
#include <stdio.h>
#include <stdlib.h>
#include <stdbool.h>
#include <string.h>

bool str_in(char **);                    /* Function prototype for str_in    */
void str_sort(const char *[], int);      /* Function prototype for str_sort  */
void swap( void **p1,  void **p2);       /* Swap two pointers                */
void str_out(char *[], int);             /* Function prototype for str_out   */

const size_t BUFFER_LEN =  256;
const size_t NUM_P = 50;

/* Function main - execution starts here */
int main(void)
{
  char *pS[NUM_P];                /* Array of string pointers     */
  int count = 0;                  /* Number of strings read       */

  printf("\nEnter successive lines, pressing Enter at the end of"
                      " each line.\nJust press Enter to end.\n");

  for(count = 0; count < NUM_P ; count++)   /* Max of NUM_P strings    */
    if(!str_in(&pS[count]))                  /* Read a string           */
      break;                                 /* Stop input on 0 return  */

  str_sort( pS, count);             /* Sort strings     */
  str_out( pS, count);              /* Output strings   */
  return 0;
}

/*****************************************************
*      String input routine                         *
*  Argument is a pointer to a pointer to a constant  *
*  string which is const char**                      *
*  Returns false for empty string and returns true   *
*  otherwise. If no memory is obtained or if there   *
*  is an error reading from the keyboard, the program *
*  is terminated by calling exit().                  *
*****************************************************/
bool str_in(char **pString)
{
  char buffer[BUFFER_LEN];                /* Space to store input string  */
```

```
  if(gets(buffer) == NULL )              /* NULL returned from gets()?   */
  {
    printf("\nError reading string.\n");
    exit(1);                             /* Error on input so exit       */
  }

  if(buffer[0] == '\0')                  /* Empty string read?           */
    return false;

  *pString = (char*)malloc(strlen(buffer) + 1);

  if(*pString == NULL)                   /* Check memory allocation      */
  {
    printf("\nOut of memory.");
    exit(1);                             /* No memory allocated so exit  */
  }

  strcpy(*pString, buffer);              /* Copy string read to argument */
  return true;
}

/**************************************************
 *        String sort routine                     *
 * First argument is array of pointers to constant *
 * strings which is of type const char*[].         *
 * Second argument is the number of elements in the *
 * pointer array - i.e. the number of strings      *
 **************************************************/
void str_sort(const char *p[], int n)
{
  char *pTemp = NULL;                    /* Temporary pointer            */
  bool sorted = false;                   /* Strings sorted indicator     */
  while(!sorted)                         /* Loop until there are no swaps */
  {
    sorted = true;                       /* Initialize to indicate no swaps */
    for(int i = 0 ; i<n-1 ; i++ )
      if(strcmp(p[i], p[i + 1]) > 0)
      {
        sorted = false;                  /* indicate we are out of order */
        swap(&p[i], &p[i+1]);            /* Swap the pointers            */
      }
  }
}

/****************************************
 *        Swap two pointers             *
 * The arguments are type pointer to void* *
 * so pointers can be any type*.         *
 ****************************************/
```

```
void swap( void **p1,  void **p2)
{
  void *pt = *p1;
  *p1 = *p2;
  *p2 = pt;
}

/***************************************************
 *        String output routine                    *
 * First argument is an array of pointers to strings *
 * which is the same as char**                      *
 * The second argument is a count of the number of  *
 * pointers in the array i.e. the number of strings *
 ***************************************************/
void str_out(char *p[] , int n)
{
  printf("\nYour input sorted in order is:\n\n");
  for(int i = 0 ; i<n ; i++)
  {
    printf("%s\n", p[i]);          /* Display a string        */
    free(p[i]);                    /* Free memory for the string */
    p[i] = NULL;
  }
  return;
}
```

Typical output from this program would be the following:

```
Enter successive lines, pressing Enter at the end of each line.
Just press Enter to end.
Mike
Adam
Mary
Steve


Your input sorted in order is:

Adam
Mary
Mike
Steve
```

How It Works

This example works in a similar way to the sorting example in Chapter 7. It looks like a lot of code, but I've added quite a few comment lines in fancy boxes that occupy space. This is good practice for longer programs that use several functions, so that you can be sure you know what each function does.

The whole set of statements for all the functions makes up your source file. At the beginning of the program source file, before you define main(), you have your #include statements for the libraries that you're using and your function prototypes. Each of these is effective from the point of their occurrence to the end of your file, because they're defined outside of all of the functions. They are therefore effective in all of your functions.

The program consists of four functions in addition to the function main(). The prototypes of the functions defined are as follows:

```
bool str_in(const char **);          /* Function prototype for str_in    */
void str_sort(const char *[], int);  /* Function prototype for str_sort  */
void swap( void **p1,  void **p2);   /* Swap two pointers                */
void str_out(char *[], int);         /* Function prototype for str_out   */
```

The first parameter for the str_sort() function has been specified as const, so the compiler will verify that the function body does not attempt to change the values pointed to. Of course, the parameter in the function definition must also be specified as const, otherwise the code won't compile. You can see that the parameter names aren't specified here. You aren't obliged to put the parameter names in a function prototype, but it's usually better if you do. I omitted them in this example to demonstrate that you can leave them out but I recommend that you include them in your programs. You can also use different parameter names in the function prototype from those in the function definition.

■**Tip** It can be useful to use longer, more explanatory names in the prototype and shorter names in the function definition to keep the code more concise.

The prototypes in this example declare a function str_in() to read in all the strings, a function str_sort() to sort the strings, and a function str_out() to output the sorted strings in their new sequence. The swap() function, which I'll come to in a moment, will swap the addresses stored in two pointers. Each function prototype declares the types of the parameters and the return value type for that function.

The first declaration is for str_in(), and it declares the parameter as type char **, which is a "pointer to a pointer to a char." Sound complicated? Well, if you take a closer look at exactly what's going on here, you'll understand how simple this really is.

In main(), the argument to this function is &pS[i]. This is the address of pS[i]—in other words, a pointer to pS[i]. And what is pS[i]? It's a pointer to char. Put these together and you have the type as declared: char**, which is a "pointer to a pointer to char." You have to declare it this way because you want to modify the contents of an element in the pS array from within the function str_in. This is the only way that the str_in() function can get access to the pS array. If you use only one * in the parameter type definition and just use pS[i] as the argument, the function receives whatever is contained in pS[i], which isn't what you want at all. This mechanism is illustrated in Figure 8-6.

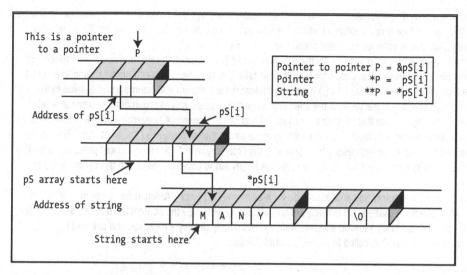

Figure 8-6. *Determining the pointer type*

Of course, type const char** is the same as type const char*[ ], which is an array of elements of type const char*. You could use either type specification here.

You can now take a look at the internal working of the function.

The str_in() Function

First, note the detailed comment at the beginning. This is a good way of starting out a function and highlighting its basic purpose. The function definition is as follows:

```c
bool str_in(char **pString)
{
  char buffer[BUFFER_LEN];            /* Space to store input string  */

  if(gets(buffer) == NULL)            /* NULL returned from gets()?   */
  {
    printf("\nError reading string.\n");
    return false;                     /* Read error                   */
  }

  if(buffer[0] == '\0')               /* Empty string read?           */
    return false;

  *pString = (char*)malloc(strlen(buffer) + 1);

  if(*pString == NULL)                /* Check memory allocation      */
  {
    printf("\nOut of memory.");
    exit(1);                          /* No memory allocated so exit  */
  }

  strcpy(*pString, buffer);           /* Copy string read to argument */
  return true;
}
```

When the function str_in() is called from main(), the address of pS[i] is passed as the argument. This is the address of the current free array element in which the address of the next string that's entered should be stored. Within the function, this is referred to as the parameter pString.

The input string is stored in buffer by the function gets(). This function returns NULL if an error occurs while reading the input, so you first check for that. If input fails, you terminate the program by calling to exit(), which is declared in stdlib.h. The exit() function terminates the program and returns a status value to the oper-ating system that depends on the value of the integer argument you pass. A zero argument will result in a value passed to the operating system that indicates a successful end to the program. A nonzero value will indicate that the program failed in some way. You check the first character in the string obtained by gets() against '\0'. The function replaces the newline character that results from pressing the Enter key with '\0'; so if you just press the Enter key, the first character of the string will be '\0'. If you get an empty string entered, you return the value false to main().

Once you've read a string, you allocate space for it using the malloc() function and store its address in *pString. After checking that you did actually get some memory, you copy the contents of buffer to the memory that was allocated. If malloc() fails to allocate memory, you simply display a message and call exit().

The function str_in() is called in main() within this loop:

```
for(count = 0; count < NUM_P ; count++)      /* Max of NUM_P strings    */
  if(!str_in(&pS[count]))                    /* Read a string           */
    break;                                   /* Stop input on 0 return  */
```

Because all the work is done in the str_in() function, all that's necessary here is to continue the loop until you get false returned from the function, which will cause the break to be executed, or until you fill up the pointer array pS, which is indicated by count reaching the value NUM_P, thus ending the loop. The loop also counts how many strings are entered in count.

Having safely stored all the strings, main() then calls the function str_sort() to sort the strings with this statement:

```
str_sort( pS, count );                              /* Sort strings            */
```

The first argument is the array name, pS, so the address of the first location of the array is transferred to the function. The second argument is the count of the number of strings so the function will know how many there are to be sorted. Let's now look at how the str_sort() function works.

The str_sort() Function

The function str_sort() is defined by these statements:

```
void str_sort(const char *p[], int n)
{
  char *pTemp = NULL;                 /* Temporary pointer                */
  bool sorted = false;                /* Strings sorted indicator         */
  while(!sorted)                      /* Loop until there are no swaps    */
  {
    sorted = true;                    /* Initialize to indicate no swaps */
    for(int i = 0 ; i < n-1 ; i++ )
      if(strcmp(p[i], p[i + 1] ) > 0)
      {
        sorted = false;               /* indicate we are out of order     */
        swap(&p[i], &p[i+1]);         /* Swap the pointers                */
      }
  }
}
```

Within the function, the parameter variable p has been defined as an array of pointers. This will be replaced, when the function is called, by the address for pS that's transferred as an argument. You haven't specified the dimension for p. This isn't necessary because the array is one dimensional. The address is passed to the function as the first argument, and the second argument defines the number of elements that you want to process. If the array had two or more dimensions, you would have to specify all dimensions except the first. This would be necessary to enable the compiler to know the shape of the array. The first parameter is const because the function does not change the strings, it simply rearranges their addresses.

You declare the second parameter, n, in the function str_sort() as type int, and this will have the value of the argument count when the function is called. You declare a variable named sorted that will have the value true or false to indicate whether or not the strings have been sorted. Remember that all the variables declared within the function body are local to that function.

The strings are sorted in the for loop using the swap() function that interchanges the addresses in two pointers. You can see how the sorting process works in Figure 8-7. Notice that only the pointers are altered. In this illustration, I used the input data you saw previously, and this input happens to be completely sorted in one pass. However, if you try this process on paper with a more disordered sequence of the same input strings, you'll see that more than one pass is often required to reach the correct sequence.

Note that there is no return statement in the definition of the str_sort() function. Coming to the end of the function body during execution is equivalent of executing a return statement without a return expression.

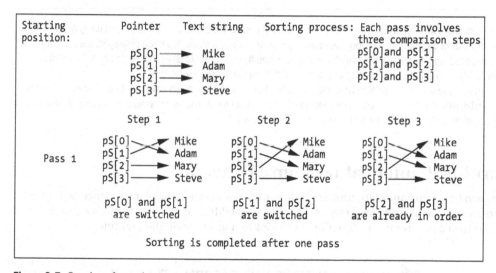

Figure 8-7. *Sorting the strings*

The swap() Function

The swap() function called by sort() is a short utility function that swaps two pointers:

```
void swap( void **p1, void **p2)
{
  void *pt = *p1;
  *p1 = *p2;
  *p2 = pt;
}
```

As you know, pointers are passed by value, just like any other type of argument so to be able to change a pointer, you must pass a pointer to a pointer as the function argument. The parameters here are of type void**, which is "pointer to void*". Any pointer of the form type* will convert to type void* so this function can swap two pointers of any given type. The swapping process is simple. The address stored at the location specified by p1 is stored in pt. The address stored in p2 is transferred to p1. Finally p2 is set to the original address from p1, now in pt.

The str_out() Function

The last function called by main() is str_out(), which displays the sorted strings:

```
void str_out(char *p[] , int n)
{
  printf("\nYour input sorted in order is:\n\n");
  for(int i = 0 ; i<n ; i++)
  {
    printf("%s\n", p[i]);          /* Display a string          */
    free(p[i]);                    /* Free memory for the string */
    p[i] = NULL;
  }
  return;
}
```

In this function, the parameter n receives the value of count and the strings are displayed using n as the count for the number of strings. The for loop outputs all the strings. Once a string has been displayed, the memory is no longer required, so you release the memory that it occupied by calling the library function free(). You also set the pointer to NULL to avoid any possibility of referring to that memory again by mistake.

You've used a return statement at the end of the function, but you could have left it out. Because the return type is void, reaching the end of the block enclosing the body of the function is the equivalent of return. (Remember, though, that this isn't the case for functions that return a value.)

Returning Pointer Values from a Function

You've seen how you can return numeric values from a function. You've just learned how to use pointers as arguments and how to store a pointer at an address that's passed as an argument. You can also return a pointer from a function. Let's look first at a very simple example.

TRY IT OUT: RETURNING VALUES FROM A FUNCTION

You'll use increasing your salary as the basis for the example, as it's such a popular topic.

```
/* Program 8.7 A function to increase your salary */
#include <stdio.h>

long *IncomePlus(long* pPay);          /* Prototype for increase function */

int main(void)
{
  long your_pay = 30000L;               /* Starting salary           */
  long *pold_pay = &your_pay;           /* Pointer to pay value       */
  long *pnew_pay = NULL;                /* Pointer to hold return value */
```

```
    pnew_pay = IncomePlus( pold_pay );
    printf("\nOld pay = $%ld", *pold_pay);
    printf("   New pay = $%ld\n", *pnew_pay);
    return 0;
}


/* Definition of function to increment pay */
long *IncomePlus(long *pPay)
{
    *pPay += 10000L;                    /* Increment the value for pay   */
    return pPay;                        /* Return the address            */
}
```

When you run the program, you'll get this output:

```
Old pay = $40000    New pay = $40000
```

How It Works

In main(), you set up an initial value in the variable your_pay and define two pointers for use with the function IncomePlus(), which is going to increase your_pay. One pointer is initialized with the address of your_pay, and the other is initialized to NULL because it's going to receive the address returned by the function IncomePlus().

Look at the output. It looks like a satisfactory result, except that there's something not quite right. If you overlook what you started with ($30,000), it looks as though you didn't get any increase at all. Because the function IncomePlus() modifies the value of your_pay through the pointer pold_pay, the original value has been changed. Clearly, both pointers, pold_pay and pnew_pay, refer to the same location: your_pay. This is a result of the statement in the function IncomePlus():

```
return pPay;
```

This returns the pointer value that the function received when it was called. This is the address contained in pold_pay. The result is that you inadvertently increase the original amount that you were paid—such is the power of pointers.

TRY IT OUT: USING LOCAL STORAGE

Let's look at what happens if you use local storage in the function IncomePlus() to hold the value that is returned. After a small modification, the example becomes this:

```
/* Program 8.8 A function to increase your salary that doesn't   */
#include <stdio.h>

long *IncomePlus(long* pPay);            /* Prototype for increase function */

int main(void)
{
    /* Code as before...              */
    return 0;
}
```

```
/* Definition of function to increment pay */
long *IncomePlus(long *pPay)
{
  long pay = 0;                 /* Local variable for the result */

  pay = *pPay + 10000;          /* Increment the value for pay   */
  return &pay;                  /* Return the address            */
}
```

How It Works

You will probably get a warning message when you compile this example. When I run this I now get the following result (it's likely to be different on your machine and you may even get the correct result):

```
Old pay = $30000   New pay = $27467656
```

Numbers like $27,467,656 with the word "pay" in the same sentence tend to be a bit startling. You would probably hesitate before complaining about this kind of error. As I said, you may get different results on your computer, possibly the correct result this time. You should get a warning from your compiler with this version of the program. With my compiler, I get the message "Suspicious pointer conversion". This is because I'm returning the address of the variable pay, which goes out of scope on exiting the function IncomePlus(). This is the cause of the remarkable value for the new value of pay—it's junk, just a spurious value left around by something. This is an easy mistake to make, but it can be a hard one to find if the compiler doesn't warn you about the problem.

Try combining the two printf() statements in main() into one:

```
printf("\nOld pay = $%ld   New pay = $%ld\n", *pold_pay, *pnew_pay);
```

On my computer it now produces the following output:

```
Old pay = $30000   New pay = $40000
```

This actually looks right, in spite of the fact that you know there's a serious error in the program. In this case, although the variable pay is out of scope and therefore no longer exists, the memory it occupied hasn't been reused yet. In the example, evidently something uses the memory previously used by the variable pay and produces the enormous output value. Here's an absolutely 100 percent cast-iron rule for avoiding this kind of problem.

■**Cast-Iron Rule** Never return the address of a local variable in a function.

So how should you implement the IncomePlus() function? Well, the first implementation is fine if you recognize that it does modify the value at the address that is passed to it. If you don't want this to happen, you could just return the new value for the pay rather than a pointer. The calling program would then need to store the value that's returned, not an address.

If you want the new pay value to be stored in another location, the IncomePlus() function could conceivably allocate space for it using malloc() and then return the address of this memory. However, you should be cautious about doing this because responsibility for freeing the memory would then be left to the calling function. It would be better to pass two arguments to the function, one being the address of the initial pay and the other being the address of the location in which the new pay is to be stored. That way, the calling function has control of the memory.

Separating the allocation of memory at runtime from the freeing of the memory is sometimes a recipe for something called a **memory leak**. This arises when a function that allocates memory dynamically but doesn't release it gets called repeatedly in a loop. This results in more and more of the available memory being occupied, until in some instances there is none left so the program crashes. As far as possible, you should make the function that allocates memory responsible for releasing it. When this is not possible, put in place the code to release the memory when you code the dynamic memory allocation.

You can look at a more practical application of returning pointers by modifying Program 8.6. You could write the routine str_in() in this example as follows:

```
char *str_in(void)
{
  char buffer[BUFFER_LEN];           /* Space to store input string */
  char *pString = NULL;              /* Pointer to string           */

  if(gets(buffer) == NULL)           /* NULL returned from gets()?  */
  {
    printf("\nError reading string.\n");
    exit(1);                         /* Error on input so exit      */
  }

  if(buffer[0] == '\0')              /* Empty string read?          */
    return NULL;

  pString = (char*)malloc(strlen(buffer) + 1);

  if(pString == NULL)                /* Check memory allocation     */
  {
    printf("\nOut of memory.");
    exit(1);                         /* No memory allocated so exit */
  }
  return strcpy(pString, buffer);    /* Return pString              */
}
```

Of course, you would also have to modify the function prototype to this:

```
char *str_in(void);
```

Now there are no parameters because you've declared the parameter list as void, and the return value is now a pointer to a character string rather than an integer.

You would also need to modify the for loop in main(), which invokes the function to

```
for(count=0; count < NUM_P ; count++)        /* Max of NUM_P strings       */
  if((pS[count] = str_in())== NULL)          /* Stop input on NULL return */
    break;
```

You now compare the pointer returned from str_in() and stored in pS[count] with NULL, as this will indicate that an empty string was entered or that a string was not read because of a read error. The example would still work exactly as before, but the internal mechanism for input would be a little different. Now the function returns the address of the allocated memory block into which the string has been copied. You might imagine that you could use the address of `buffer` instead, but remember that `buffer` is local to the function, so it goes out of scope on return from the function. You could try it if you like to see what happens.

Choosing one version of the function `str_in()` or the other is, to some extent, a matter of taste, but on balance this latter version is probably better because it uses a simpler definition of the parameter, which makes it easier to understand. Note, however, that it does allocate memory that has to be released somewhere else in the program. When you need to do this it's best to code the function that will release the memory in tandem with coding the function that allocates it. That way, there's less risk of a memory leak.

Incrementing Pointers in a Function

When you use an array name as an argument to a function, a *copy* of the address of the beginning of the array is transferred to the function. As a result, you have the possibility of treating the value received as a pointer in the fullest sense, incrementing or decrementing the address as you wish. For example, you could rewrite the `str_out()` function in Program 8.6 as follows:

```
void str_out(char *p[] , int n)
{
  printf("\nYour input sorted in order is:\n\n");
  for(int i = 0 ; i<n ; i++)
  {
    printf("%s\n", *p);          /* Display a string            */
    free(*p);                    /* Free memory for the string */
    *p++ = NULL;
  }
  return;
}
```

You replace array notation with pointer notation in the `printf()` and `free()` function calls. You wouldn't be able to do this with an array declared within the function body, but because you have a copy of the original array address, it's possible here. You can treat the parameter just like a regular pointer. Because the address you have at this point is a copy of the original in `main()`, this doesn't interfere with the original array address `pS` in any way.

There's little to choose between this version of the function and the original. The former version, using array notation, is probably just a little easier to follow. However, operations expressed in pointer notation often execute faster than array notation.

Summary

You're not done with functions yet, so I'll postpone diving into another chunky example until the end of the next chapter, which covers further aspects of using functions. So let's pause for a moment and summarize the key points that you need to keep in mind when creating and using functions:

! C programs consist of one or more functions, one of which is called `main()`. The function `main()` is where execution always starts, and it's called by the operating system through a user command.

! A function is a self-contained named block of code in a program. The name of a function is in the same form as identifiers, which is a unique sequence of letters and digits, the first of which must be a letter (an underline counts as a letter).

! A function definition consists of a header and a body. The header defines the name of the function, the type of the value returned from the function, and the types and names of all the parameters to the function. The body contains the executable statements for the function, which define what the function actually does.

! All the variables that are declared in a function are local to that function.

! A function prototype is a declaration statement terminated by a semicolon that defines the name, the return type, and the parameter types for a function. A function prototype is required to provide information about a function to the compiler when the definition of a function doesn't precede its use in executable code.

! Before you use a function in your source file, you'd either define the function or declare the function with a function prototype.

! Specifying a pointer parameter as const indicates to the compiler that the function does not modify the data pointed to by the function.

! Arguments to a function should be of a type that's compatible with the corresponding parameters specified in its header. If you pass a value of type double to a function that expects an integer argument, the value will be truncated, removing the fractional part.

! A function that returns a value can be used in an expression just as if it were a value of the same type as the return value.

! *Copies* of the argument values are transferred to a function, not the original values in the calling function. This is referred to as the **pass-by-value mechanism** for transferring data to a function.

! If you want a function to modify a variable that's declared in its calling function, the address of the variable needs to be transferred as an argument.

That covers the essentials of creating your own functions. In the next chapter, you'll add a few more techniques for using functions. You'll also work through a more substantial example of applying functions in a practical context.

Exercises

The following exercises enable you to try out what you've learned in this chapter. If you get stuck, look back over the chapter for help. If you're still stuck, you can download the solutions from the Source Code area of the Apress web site (http://www.apress.com), but that really should be a last resort.

Exercise 8-1. Define a function that will calculate the average of an arbitrary number of floating-point values that are passed to the function in an array. Demonstrate the operation of this function by implementing a program that will accept an arbitrary number of values entered from the keyboard, and output the average.

Exercise 8-2. Define a function that will return a string representation of an integer that is passed as the argument. For example, if the argument is 25, the function will return "25". If the argument is –98, the function will return "-98". Demonstrate the operation of your function with a suitable version of main().

Exercise 8-3. Extend the function that you defined for the previous example to accept an additional argument that specifies the field width for the result, and return the string representation of the value right-justified within the field. For example, if the value to be converted is –98 and the field width argument is 5, the string that is returned should be " -98". Demonstrate the operation of this function with a suitable version of main().

Exercise 8-4. Define a function that will return the number of words in a string that is passed as an argument. (Words are separated by spaces or punctuation characters. Assume the string doesn't contain embedded single or double quotes! that is, no words such as •isn't.!) Define a second function that will segment a string that's passed as the first argument to the function into words, and return the words stored in the array that's passed as the second argument. Define a third function that will return the number of letters in a string that's passed as the argument. Use these functions to implement a program that will read a string containing text from the keyboard and then output all the words from the text ordered from the shortest to the longest.

CHAPTER 9

■ ■ ■

More on Functions

Now that you've completed Chapter 8, you have a good grounding in the essentials of creating and using functions. In this chapter you'll build on that foundation by exploring how functions can be used and manipulated; in particular, you'll investigate how you can access a function through a pointer. You'll also be working with some more flexible methods of communicating between functions.

In this chapter you'll learn the following:

! What pointers to functions are and how you use them

! How to use static variables in functions

! How to share variables between functions

! How functions can call themselves without resulting in an indefinite loop

! How to write an Othello-type game (also known as Reversi)

Pointers to Functions

Up to now, you've considered pointers as an exceptionally useful device for manipulating data and variables that contain data. It's a bit like handling things with a pair of tongs. You can manipulate a whole range of hot items with just one pair of tongs. However, you can also use pointers to handle *functions* at a distance. Because a function has an address in memory where it starts execution (i.e., its starting address), the basic information to be stored in a pointer to a function is going to be that address.

If you think about it, though, this isn't going to be enough. If a function is going to be called through a pointer, information also has to be available about the number and type of the arguments to be supplied, and the type of return value to be expected. The compiler can't deduce these just from the address of the function. This means that declaring a pointer to a function is going to be a little more complicated than declaring a pointer to a data type. Just as a pointer holds an address and must also define a type, a function pointer holds an address and must also define a prototype.

Declaring a Pointer to a Function

The declaration for a pointer to a function looks a little strange and can be confusing, so let's start with a simple example:

```
int (*pfunction) (int);
```

This declares a pointer to a function. It doesn't point to anything! yet; this statement just defines the pointer variable. The name of the pointer is pfunction, and it's intended to point to functions that have one parameter of type int and that return a value of type int to the calling program. Furthermore, you can *only* use this particular pointer to point to functions with these characteristics. If you want a pointer to functions that accept a float argument and return float values, you need to declare another pointer with the required characteristics. The components of the declaration are illustrated in Figure 9-1.

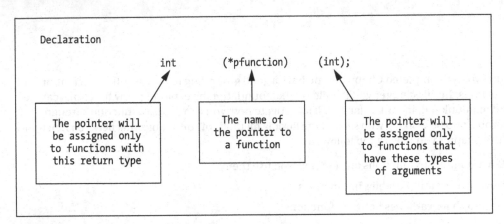

Figure 9-1. *Declaring a pointer to a function*

There are a lot of parentheses in a •pointer to function! declaration. In this example, the *pfunction part of the declaration must be between parentheses.

■Note If you omit the parentheses, you'll have a declaration for a function called pfunction() that returns a value that's a pointer to int, which isn't what you want.

With •pointer to function! declarations, you must always put the * plus the pointer name between parentheses. The second pair of parentheses just encloses the parameter list in the same way as it does with a standard function declaration.

Because a pointer to a function can point only to functions with a given return type and a given number of parameters of given types, the variation in what it can point to is just the function name.

Calling a Function Through a Function Pointer

Suppose that you define a function that has the following prototype:

```
int sum(int a, int b);                    /* Calculates a+b */
```

This function has two parameters of type int and returns a value of type int so you could store its address in a function pointer that you declare like this:

```
int (*pfun)(int, int) = sum;
```

This declares a function pointer with the name pfun that will store addresses of functions with two parameters of type int and a return value of type int. The statement also initializes pfun with the address of the function sum(). To supply an initial value you just use the name of a function that has the required prototype.

You can now call sum() through the function pointer like this:

```
int result = pfun(45, 55);
```

This statement calls the sum() function through the pfun pointer with argument values of 45 and 55. You use the value returned by sum() as the initial value for the variable result so result will be 100. Note that you just use the function pointer name just like a function name to call the function that it points to; no dereference operator is required.

Suppose you define another function that has the following prototype:

```
int product(int a, int b);          /* Calculates a*b */
```

You can store the address of product() in pfun with the following statement:

```
pfun = product;
```

With pfun containing the address of product(), you can call product through the pointer

```
result = pfun(5, 12);
```

After executing this statement, result will contain the value 60.

Let's try a simple example and see how it works.

TRY IT OUT: USING POINTERS TO FUNCTIONS

In this example, you'll define three functions that have the same parameter and return types and use a pointer to a function to call each of them in turn.

```
/* Program 9.1 Pointing to functions */
#include <stdio.h>

/* Function prototypes */
int sum(int, int);
int product(int, int);
int difference(int, int);

int main(void)
{
  int a = 10;                       /* Initial value for a            */
  int b = 5;                        /* Initial value for b            */
  int result = 0;                   /* Storage for results            */
  int (*pfun)(int, int);            /* Function pointer declaration    */

  pfun = sum;                       /* Points to function sum()       */
  result = pfun(a, b);              /* Call sum() through pointer      */
  printf("\npfun = sum          result = %d", result);

  pfun = product;                   /* Points to function product()   */
  result = pfun(a, b);              /* Call product() through pointer  */
  printf("\npfun = product      result = %d", result);
```

```
  pfun = difference;                    /* Points to function difference()   */
  result = pfun(a, b);                  /* Call difference() through pointer */
  printf("\npfun = difference     result = %d\n", result);
  return 0;
}

int sum(int x, int y)
{
  return x + y;
}

int product(int x, int y)
{
  return x * y;
}

int difference(int x, int y)
{
  return x - y;
}
```

The output from this program looks like this:

```
pfun = sum          result = 15
pfun = product      result = 50
pfun = difference   result = 5
```

How It Works

You declare and define three different functions to return the sum, the product, and the difference between two integer arguments. Within main( ), you declare a pointer to a function with this statement:

```
  int (*pfun)(int, int);                /* Function pointer declaration       */
```

This pointer can be assigned to point to any function that accepts two int arguments and also returns a value of type int. Notice the way you assign a value to the pointer:

```
  pfun = sum;                           /* Points to function sum()           */
```

You just use a regular assignment statement that has the name of the function, completely unadorned, on the right side! You don't need to put in the parameter list or anything. If you did, it would be wrong, because it would then be a function call, not an address, and the compiler would complain. A function is very much like an array in its usage here. If you want the address of an array, you just use the name by itself, and if you want the address of a function you also use the name by itself.

In main( ), you assign the address of each function, in turn, to the function pointer pfun. You then call each function using the pointer pfun and display the result. You can see how to call a function using the pointer in this statement:

```
  result = pfun(a, b);                  /* Call sum() through pointer         */
```

You just use the name of the pointer as though it were a function name, followed by the argument list between parentheses. Here, you're using the "pointer to function" variable name as though it were the original function name, so the argument list must correspond with the parameters in the function header for the function you're calling. This is illustrated in Figure 9-2.

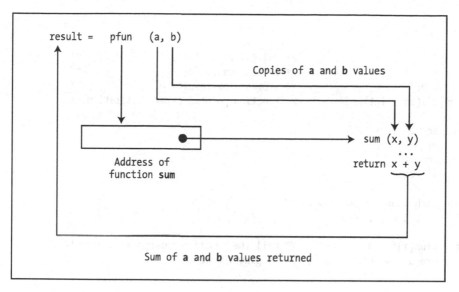

Figure 9-2. *Calling a function through a pointer*

Arrays of Pointers to Functions

Of course, a function pointer is a variable like any other. You can therefore create an array of pointers to functions.

To declare an array of function pointers, you just put the array dimension after the function pointer array name, for instance

```
int (*pfunctions[10]) (int);
```

This declares an array, pfunctions, with ten elements. Each element in this array can store the address of a function with a return type of int and two parameters of type int. Let's see how this would work in practice.

TRY IT OUT: ARRAYS OF POINTERS TO FUNCTIONS

You can demonstrate how you can use an array of pointers to functions with a variation on the last example:

```
/* Program 9.2 Arrays of Pointers to functions    */
#include <stdio.h>

/* Function prototypes    */
int sum(int, int);
int product(int, int);
int difference(int, int);
```

```
int main(void)
{
  int a = 10;                          /* Initial value for a                     */
  int b = 5;                           /* Initial value for b                     */
  int result = 0;                      /* Storage for results                     */
  int (*pfun[3])(int, int);            /* Function pointer array declaration */

  /* Initialize pointers */
  pfun[0] = sum;
  pfun[1] = product;
  pfun[2] = difference;

  /* Execute each function pointed to */
  for(int i = 0 ; i < 3 ; i++)
  {
    result = pfun[i](a, b);            /* Call the function through a pointer */
    printf("\nresult = %d", result);   /* Display the result                     */
  }

  /* Call all three functions through pointers in an expression */
  result = pfun[1](pfun[0](a, b), pfun[2](a, b));
  printf("\n\nThe product of the sum and the difference = %d\n",
                                               result);

  return 0;
}

/* Definitions of sum(), product() and difference() as before... */
```

The output from this program is as follows:

```
result = 15
result = 50
result = 5

The product of the sum and the difference = 75
```

How It Works

The major difference between this and the last example is the pointer array, which you declare as follows:

```
  int (*pfun[3])(int, int);            /* Function pointer array declaration */
```

This is similar to the previous declaration for a single pointer variable, but with the addition of the array dimension in square brackets following the pointer name. If you want a two-dimensional array, two sets of square brackets would have to appear here, just like declarations for ordinary array types. You still enclose the parameter list between parentheses, as you did in the declaration of a single pointer. Again, in parallel with what happens for ordinary arrays, all the elements of the array of "pointers to functions" are of the same type and will accept only the argument list specified. So, in this example, they can all only point to functions that take two arguments of type int and return an int value.

When you want to assign a value to a pointer within the array, you write it in the same way as an element of any other array:

```
pfun[0] = sum;
```

Apart from the function name on the right of the equal sign, this could be a normal data array. It's used in exactly the same way. You could have chosen to initialize all the elements of the array of pointers within the declaration itself:

```
int (*pfun[3])(int, int) = { sum, product, difference };
```

This would have initialized all three elements and would have eliminated the need for the assignment statements that perform the initialization. In fact, you could have left out the array dimension, too, and gotten it by default:

```
int (*pfun[])(int, int) = { sum, product, difference };
```

The number of initializing values between the braces would determine the number of elements in the array. Thus an initialization list for an array of function pointers works in exactly the same way as an initialization list for any other type of array.

When it comes to calling a function that an array element points to, you write it as follows:

```
result = pfun[i](a, b);   /* Call the function through a pointer */
```

This, again, is much like the previous example, with just the addition of the index value in square brackets that follow the pointer name. You index this array with the loop variable i as you've done many times before with ordinary data arrays.

Look at the output. The first three lines are generated in the for loop, where the functions sum(), product(), and difference() are each called in turn through the corresponding element of the pointer array. The last line of output is produced using the value result from the following statement:

```
result = pfun[1](pfun[0](a, b), pfun[2](a, b));
```

This statement shows that you can incorporate function calls through pointers into expressions, in the same way that you might use a normal function call. Here, you call two of the functions through pointers, and their results are used as arguments to a third function that's called through a pointer. Because the elements of the array correspond to the functions sum(), product(), and difference() in sequence, this statement is equivalent to the following:

```
result = product(sum(a, b), difference(a, b));
```

The sequence of events in this statement is as follows:

1. Execute sum(a, b) and difference(a, b) and save the return values.

2. Execute the function product() with the returned values from step 1 as arguments, and save the value returned.

3. Store the value obtained from step 2 in the variable result.

Pointers to Functions As Arguments

You can also pass a pointer to a function as an argument. This allows a different function to be called, depending on which function is addressed by the pointer that's passed as the argument.

TRY IT OUT: POINTERS TO FUNCTIONS AS ARGUMENTS

You could produce a variant of the last example that will pass a pointer to a function as an argument to a function.

```c
/* Program 9.3 Passing a Pointer to a function    */
#include <stdio.h>

/* Function prototypes */
int sum(int,int);
int product(int,int);
int difference(int,int);
int any_function(int(*pfun)(int, int), int x, int y);

int main(void)
{
  int a = 10;                      /* Initial value for a */
  int b = 5;                       /* Initial value for b */
  int result = 0;                  /* Storage for results */
  int (*pf)(int, int) = sum;       /* Pointer to function */

  /* Passing a pointer to a function */
  result = any_function(pf, a, b);

  printf("\nresult = %d", result );

  /* Passing the address of a function      */
  result = any_function(product,a, b);

  printf("\nresult = %d", result );

  printf("\nresult = %d\n", any_function(difference, a, b));
  return 0;
}

/* Definition of a function to call a function */
int any_function(int(*pfun)(int, int), int x, int y)
{
  return pfun(x, y);
}

/* Definition of the function sum          */
int sum(int x, int y)
{
  return x + y;
}

/* Definition of the function product      */
int product(int x, int y)
{
  return x * y;
}
```

```
/* Definition of the function difference */
int difference(int x, int y)
{
  return x - y;
}
```

The output looks like this:

```
result = 15
result = 50
result = 5
```

How It Works

The function that will accept a "pointer to a function" as an argument is any_function(). The prototype for this function is the following:

```
int any_function(int(*pfun)(int, int), int x, int y);
```

The function named any_function() has three parameters. The first parameter type is a pointer to a function that accepts two integer arguments and returns an integer. The last two parameters are integers that will be used in the call of the function specified by the first parameter. The function any_function() itself returns an integer value that will be the value obtained by calling the function indicated by the first argument.

Within the definition of any_function(), the function specified by the pointer argument is called in the return statement:

```
int any_function(int(*pfun)(int, int), int x, int y)
{
  return pfun(x, y);
}
```

The name of the pointer pfun is used, followed by the other two parameters as arguments to the function to be called. The value of pfun and the values of the other two parameters x and y all originate in main().

Notice how you initialize the function pointer pf that you declared in main():

```
int (*pf)(int, int) = sum;    /* Pointer to function */
```

You place the name of the function sum() as the initializer after the equal sign. As you saw earlier, you can initialize function pointers to the addresses of specific functions just by putting the function name as an initializing value.

The first call to any_function() involves passing the value of the pointer pf and the values of the variables a and b to any_function():

```
result = any_function(pf, a, b);
```

The pointer is used as an argument in the usual way, and the value returned by any_function() is stored in the variable result. Because of the initial value of pf, the function sum() will be called in any_function(), so the returned value will be the sum of the values of a and b.

The next call to any_function() is in this statement:

```
result = any_function(product,a, b);
```

Here, you explicitly enter the name of a function, `product`, as the first argument, so within `any_function()` the function `product` will be called with the values of a and b as arguments. In this case, you're effectively persuading the compiler to create an internal pointer to the function `product` and passing it to `any_function()`.

The final call of `any_function()` takes place in the argument to the `printf()` function call:

```
printf("\nresult = %d\n", any_function(difference, a, b));
```

In this case, you're also explicitly specifying the name of a function, `difference`, as an argument to `any_function()`. The compiler knows from the prototype of `any_function()` that the first argument should be a pointer to a function. Because you specify the function name, `difference`, explicitly as an argument, the compiler will generate a pointer to this function for you and pass that pointer to `any_function()`. Lastly, the value returned by `any_function()` is passed as an argument to the function `printf()`. When all this unwinds, you eventually get the difference between the values of a and b displayed.

Take care not to confuse the idea of passing an address of a function as an argument to a function, such as in this expression,

```
any_function(product, a, b)
```

with the idea of passing a value that is returned from a function, as in this statement,

```
printf("\n%d", product(a, b));
```

In the former case, you're passing the address of the function `product()` as an argument, and if and when it gets called depends on what goes on inside the body of the function `any_function()`. In the latter case, however, you're calling the function `product()` before you call `printf()` and passing the result obtained as an argument to `printf()`.

Variables in Functions

Structuring a program into functions not only simplifies the process of developing the program, but also extends the power of the language to solve problems. Carefully designed functions can often be reused making the development of new applications faster and easier. The standard library illustrates the power of reusable functions. The power of the language is further enhanced by the properties of variables within a function and some extra capabilities that C provides in declaring variables. Let's take a look at some of these now.

Static Variables: Keeping Track Within a Function

So far, all the variables you've used have gone out of scope at the end of the block in which they were defined, and their memory on the stack then becomes free for use by another function. These are called **automatic variables** because they're automatically created at the point where they're declared, and they're automatically destroyed when program execution leaves the block in which they were declared. This is a very efficient process because the memory containing data in a function is only retained for as long as you're executing statements within the function in which the variable is declared.

However, there are some circumstances in which you might want to retain information from one function call to the next within a program. You may wish to maintain a count of something within a function, such as the number of times the function has been called or the number of lines of output that have been written. With just automatic variables you have no way of doing this.

However, C does provide you with a way to do this with **static variables**. You could declare a static variable count, for example, with this declaration:

```
static int count = 0;
```

The word static in this statement is a keyword in C. The variable declared in this statement differs from an automatic variable in two ways. First of all, despite the fact that it may be defined within the scope of a function, this static variable doesn't get destroyed when execution leaves the function. Second, whereas an automatic variable is initialized each time its scope is entered, the initialization of a variable declared as static occurs only once, right at the beginning of the program. Although a static variable is visible only within the function that contains its declaration, it is essentially a global variable and therefore treated in the same way.

■**Note** You can make any type of variable within a function a static variable.

TRY IT OUT: USING STATIC VARIABLES

You can see static variables in action in the following very simple example:

```c
/* Program 9.4 Static versus automatic variables */
#include <stdio.h>

/* Function prototypes */
void test1(void);
void test2(void);

int main(void)
{
  for(int i = 0; i < 5; i++ )
  {
    test1();
    test2();
  }
  return 0;
}

/* Function test1 with an automatic variable */
void test1(void)
{
  int count = 0;
  printf("\ntest1   count = %d ", ++count );
}

/* Function test2 with a static variable */
void test2(void)
{
  static int count = 0;
  printf("\ntest2   count = %d ", ++count );
}
```

This produces the following output:

```
test1    count = 1
test2    count = 1
test1    count = 1
test2    count = 2
test1    count = 1
test2    count = 3
test1    count = 1
test2    count = 4
test1    count = 1
test2    count = 5
```

How It Works

As you can see, the two variables called count are quite separate. The changes in the values of each show clearly that they're independent of one another. The static variable count is declared in the function test2():

```
static int count = 0;
```

Although you specify an initial value, here the variable would have been initialized to 0 anyway because you declared it as static.

■**Note** All static variables are initialized to 0 unless you initialize them with some other value.

The static variable count is used to count the number of times the function is called. This is initialized when program execution starts, and its current value when the function is exited is maintained. It isn't reinitialized on subsequent calls to the function. Because the variable has been declared as static, the compiler arranges things so that the variable will be initialized only once. Because initialization occurs before program startup, you can always be sure a static variable has been initialized when you use it.

The automatic variable count in the function test1() is declared as follows:

```
int count = 0;
```

Because this is an automatic variable, it isn't initialized by default, and if you don't specify an initial value, it will contain a junk value. This variable gets reinitialized to 0 at each entry to the function, and it's discarded on exit from test1(); therefore, it never reaches a value higher than 1.

Although a static variable will persist for as long as the program is running, it will be visible only within the scope in which it is declared, and it can't be referenced outside of that original scope.

Sharing Variables Between Functions

You also have a way of sharing variables between all your functions. In the same way that you can declare constants at the beginning of a program file, so that they're outside the scope of the functions that make up the program, you can also declare variables like this. These are called **global variables** because they're accessible anywhere. Global variables are declared in the normal way; it's the position of the declaration that's significant and determines whether they're global.

TRY IT OUT: USING GLOBAL VARIABLES

By way of a demonstration, you can modify the previous example to share the count variable between the functions as follows:

```
/* Program 9.5 Global variables */
#include <stdio.h>

int count = 0;                          /* Declare a global variable   */

/* Function prototypes */
void test1(void);
void test2(void);

int main(void)
{
  int count = 0;                        /* This hides the global count */

  for( ; count < 5; count++)
  {
    test1();
    test2();
  }
  return 0;
}

/* Function test1 using the global variable   */
void test1(void)
{
  printf("\ntest1   count = %d ", ++count);
}

/* Function test2 using a static variable */
void test2(void)
{
  static int count;               /* This hides the global count */
  printf("\ntest2   count = %d ", ++count);
}
```

The output will be this:

```
test1   count = 1
test2   count = 1
test1   count = 2
test2   count = 2
test1   count = 3
test2   count = 3
test1   count = 4
test2   count = 4
test1   count = 5
test2   count = 5
```

How It Works

In this example you have three separate variables called count. The first of these is the global variable count that's declared at the beginning of the file:

```
#include <stdio.h>

int count = 0;
```

This isn't a static variable (although you could make it static if you wanted to), but because it is global it will be initialized by default to 0 if you don't initialize it. It's potentially accessible in any function from the point where it's declared to the end of the file, so it's accessible in any of the functions here.

The second variable is an automatic variable count that's declared in main():

```
int count = 0;                          /* This hides the global count */
```

Because it has the same name as the global variable, the global variable count can't be accessed from main(). Any use of the name count in main() will refer to the variable declared within the body of main(). The local variable count *hides* the global variable.

The third variable is a static variable count that's declared in the function test2():

```
static int count;                       /* This hides the global count */
```

Because this is a static variable, it will be initialized to 0 by default. This variable also hides the global variable of the same name, so only the static variable count is accessible in test2().

The function test1() works using the global count. The functions main() and test2() use their local versions of count, because the local declaration hides the global variable of the same name.

Clearly, the count variable in main() is incremented from 0 to 4, because you have five calls to each of the functions test1() and test2(). This has to be different from the count variables in either of the called functions; otherwise, they couldn't have the values 1 to 5 that are displayed in the output.

You can further demonstrate that this is indeed the case by simply removing the declaration for count in test2() as a static variable. You'll then have made test1() and test2() share the global count, and the values displayed will run from 1 to 10. If you then put a declaration back in test2() for count as an initialized automatic variable with the statement

```
int count = 0;
```

the output from test1() will run from 1 to 5, and the output from test2() will remain at 1, because the variable is now automatic and will be reinitialized on each entry to the function.

Global variables can replace the need for function arguments and return values. They look very tempting as the complete alternative to automatic variables. However, you should use global variables sparingly. They can be a major asset in simplifying and shortening some programs, but using them excessively will make your programs prone to errors. It's very easy to modify a global variable and forget what consequences it might have throughout your program. The bigger the program, the more difficult it becomes to avoid erroneous references to global variables. The use of local variables provides very effective insulation for each function against the possibility of interference from the activities of other functions. You could try removing the local variable count from main() in Program 9.5 to see the effect of such an oversight on the output.

■**Caution** As a rule, it's unwise to use the same names in C for local and global variables. There's no particular advantage to be gained, other than to demonstrate the effect, as I've done in the example.

Functions That Call Themselves: Recursion

It's possible for a function to call itself. This is termed **recursion**. You're unlikely to come across a need for recursion very often, so I won't dwell on it, but it can be a very effective technique in some contexts, providing considerable simplification of the code needed to solve particular problems. There are a few bad jokes based on the notion of recursion, but we won't dwell on those either.

Obviously, when a function calls itself there's the immediate problem of how the process stops. Here's a trivial example of a function that obviously results in an indefinite loop:

```
void Looper(void)
{
  printf("\nLooper function called.");
  Looper();                              /* Recursive call to Looper() */
}
```

Calling this function would result in an indefinite number of lines of output because after executing the printf() call, the function calls itself. There is no mechanism in the code that will stop the process.

This is similar to the problem you have with an indefinite loop, and the answer is similar too: a function that calls itself must also contain the means of stopping the process. Let's see how it works in practice.

TRY IT OUT: RECURSION

The primary uses of recursion tend to arise in complicated problems, so it's hard to come up with original but simple examples to show how it works. Therefore, I'll follow the crowd and use the standard illustration: the calculation of the **factorial** of an integer. A factorial of any integer is the product of all the integers from 1 up to the integer itself. So here you go:

```
/* Program 9.6 Calculating factorials using recursion */
#include <stdio.h>

unsigned long factorial(unsigned long);

int main(void)
{
  unsigned long number = 0L;
  printf("\nEnter an integer value: ");
  scanf(" %lu", &number);
  printf("\nThe factorial of %lu is %lu\n", number, factorial(number));
  return 0;
}

/* Our recursive factorial function */
unsigned long factorial(unsigned long n)
{
  if(n < 2L)
    return n;

  return n*factorial(n - 1);
}
```

Typical output from the program looks like this:

```
Enter an integer value: 4

The factorial of 4 is 24
```

How It Works

This is very simple once you get your mind around what's happening. Let's go through a concrete example of how it works. Assume you enter the value 4. Figure 9-3 shows the sequence of events.

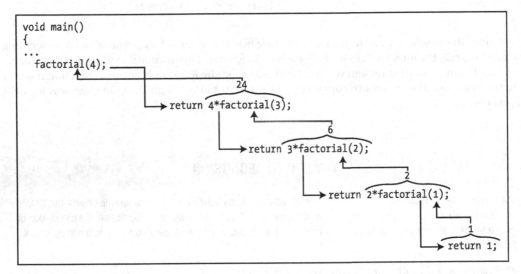

Figure 9-3. *Recursive function calls*

Within the statement

```
printf("\nThe factorial of %lu is %lu", number, factorial(number));
```

the function `factorial()` gets called from `main()` with `number` having the value 4 as the argument.

Within the `factorial()` function itself, because the argument is greater than 1, the statement executed is

```
return n*factorial(n - 1L);
```

This is the second `return` statement in the function, and it calls `factorial()` again with the argument value 3 from within the arithmetic expression. This expression can't be evaluated, and the `return` can't be completed until the value is returned from this call to the function `factorial()` with the argument 3.

This continues, as shown in Figure 9-3, until the argument in the last call of the `factorial()` function is 1. In this case, the first `return` statement

```
return n;
```

is executed and the value 1 is returned to the previous call point. This call point is, in fact, inside the second `return` in the `factorial()` function, which can now calculate `2 * 1` and return to the previous call.

In this way, the whole process unwinds, ending up with the value required being returned to main() where it's displayed. So for any given number n, you'll have n calls to the function factorial(). For each call, a copy of the argument is created, and the location to be returned to is stored. This can get expensive as far as memory is concerned if there are many levels of recursion. A loop to do the same thing would be cheaper and faster. If you do need or want to use recursion, the most important thing to remember is that there has to be a way to end the process. In other words, there must be a mechanism for *not* repeating the recursive call. In this example the check for whether the argument is 1 provides the way for the sequence of recursive calls of the factorial() function to end.

Note that factorial values grow very quickly. With quite modest input values, you'll exceed the capacity of an unsigned long integer and start getting the wrong results.

Functions with a Variable Number of Arguments

It can't have escaped your notice that some functions in the standard libraries accept a variable number of arguments. The functions printf() and scanf() are obvious examples. You may come up with a need to do this yourself from time to time, so the standard library <stdarg.h> provides you with routines to write some of your own.

The immediately obvious problem with writing a function with a variable number of parameters is how to specify its prototype. Suppose you're going to produce a function to calculate the average of two or more values of type double. Clearly, calculating the average of fewer than two values wouldn't make much sense. The prototype would be written as follows:

```
double average(double v1, double v2, ...);
```

The **ellipsis** (that's the fancy name for the three periods after the second parameter type) indicates that a variable number of arguments may follow the first two fixed arguments. You must have at least one fixed argument. The remaining specifications are as you would usually find with a function prototype. The first two arguments are of type double, and the function returns a double result.

The second problem with variable argument lists that hits you between the eyes next is how you reference the arguments when writing the function. Because you don't know how many there are, you can't possibly give them names. The only conceivable way to do this is indirectly, through pointers. The <stdarg.h> library header provides you with routines that are usually implemented as macros to help with this, but they look and operate like functions, so I'll discuss them as though they were. You need to use three of these when implementing your own function with a variable number of arguments. They are called va_start(), va_arg(), and va_end(). The first of these has the following form:

```
void va_start(va_list parg, last_fixed_arg);
```

The name, va_start, is obtained from **variable argument start**. This function accepts two arguments: a pointer parg of type va_list, and the name of the last fixed parameter that you specified for the function you're writing. The va_list type is a type that is also defined in <stdarg.h> and is designed to store information required by the routines provided that support variable argument lists.

So using the function average() as an illustration, you can start to write the function as follows:

```
double average(double v1, double v2,...)
{
  va_list parg;                 /* Pointer for variable argument list */
  /* More code to go here... */
  va_start( parg, v2);
  /* More code to go her. . . */
}
```

You first declare the variable parg of type va_list. You then call va_start() with this as the first argument and specify the last fixed parameter v2 as the second argument. The effect of the call to va_start() is to set the variable parg to point to the first variable argument that is passed to the function when it is called. You still don't know what type of value this represents, and the standard library is no further help in this context. You must determine the type of each variable argument, either implicitly! all variable arguments assumed to be of a given type, for instance! or by deducing the type of each argument from information contained within one of the fixed arguments.

The average() function deals with arguments of type double, so the type isn't a problem. You now need to know how to access the value of each of the variable arguments, so let's see how this is done by completing the function average():

```
/* Function to calculate the average of a variable number of arguments */
double average( double v1, double v2,...)
{
  va_list parg;              /* Pointer for variable argument list */
  double sum = v1+v2;        /* Accumulate sum of the arguments    */
  double value = 0;          /* Argument value                     */
  int count = 2;             /* Count of number of arguments       */

  va_start(parg,v2);         /* Initialize argument pointer        */
  while((value = va_arg(parg, double)) != 0.0)
  {
    sum += value;
    count++;
  }
  va_end(parg);              /* End variable argument process      */
  return sum/count;
}
```

You can work your way through this step by step. After declaring parg, you declare the variable sum as double and as being initialized with the sum of the first two fixed arguments, v1 and v2. You'll accumulate the sum of all the argument values in sum. The next variable, value, declared as double will be used to store the values of the variable arguments as you obtain them one by one. You then declare a counter, count, for the total number of arguments and initialize this with the value 2 because you know you have at least that many values from the fixed arguments. After you call va_start() to initialize parg, most of the action takes place within the while loop. Look at the loop condition:

```
while((value = va_arg(parg, double)) != 0.0)
```

The loop condition calls another function from stdarg.h, va_arg(). The first argument to va_arg() is the variable parg you initialized through the call to va_start(). The second argument is a specification of the type of the argument you expect to find. The function va_arg() returns the value of the current argument specified by parg, and this is stored in value. It also updates the pointer parg to point to the next argument in the list, based on the type you specified in the call. It's essential to have some means of determining the types of the variable arguments. If you don't specify the correct type, you won't be able to obtain the next argument correctly. In this case, the function is written assuming the arguments are all double. Another assumption you're making is that all the arguments will be nonzero except for the last. This is reflected in the condition for continuing the loop, being that value isn't equal to 0. Within the loop you have familiar statements for accumulating the sum in sum and for incrementing count.

When an argument value obtained is 0, the loop ends and you execute the statement

```
va_end(parg);                      /* End variable argument process       */
```

The call to va_end() is essential to tidy up loose ends left by the process. It resets the parg point to NULL. If you omit this call, your program may not work properly. Once the tidying up is complete, you can return the required result with the statement

```
return sum/count;
```

TRY IT OUT: USING VARIABLE ARGUMENT LISTS

After you've written the function average(), it would be a good idea to exercise it in a little program to make sure it works:

```
/* Program 9.7 Calculating an average using variable argument lists */
#include <stdio.h>
#include <stdarg.h>

double average(double v1 , double v2,...);          /* Function prototype */

int main(void)
{
  double Val1 = 10.5, Val2 = 2.5;
  int num1 = 6, num2 = 5;
  long num3 = 12, num4 = 20;

  printf("\n Average = %lf", average(Val1, 3.5, Val2, 4.5, 0.0));
  printf("\n Average = %lf", average(1.0, 2.0, 0.0));
  printf("\n Average = %lf\n", average( (double)num2, Val2,(double)num1,
                                 (double)num4,(double)num3, 0.0));
  return 0;
}

/* Function to calculate the average of a variable number of arguments */
double average( double v1, double v2,...)
{
  va_list parg;               /* Pointer for variable argument list */
  double sum = v1+v2;         /* Accumulate sum of the arguments    */
  double value = 0;           /* Argument value                     */
  int count = 2;              /* Count of number of arguments       */

  va_start(parg,v2);          /* Initialize argument pointer        */

  while((value = va_arg(parg, double)) != 0.0)
  {
    sum += value;
    count++;
  }
  va_end(parg);               /* End variable argument process      */
  return sum/count;
}
```

If you compile and run this, you should get the following output:

```
Average = 5.250000
Average = 1.500000
Average = 9.100000
```

How It Works

This output is as a result of three calls to average with different numbers of arguments. Remember, you need to ensure that you cast the variable arguments to the type double, because this is the argument type assumed by the function average(). You can call the average() function with as many arguments as you like as long as the last one is 0.

You might be wondering how printf() manages to handle a mix of types. Well, remember the first argument is a control string with format specifiers. This supplies the information necessary to determine the types of the arguments that follow, as well as how many there are. The number of arguments following the first must match the number of format specifiers in the control string. The type of each argument after the first must match the type implied by the corresponding format specifier. You've seen how things don't work out right if you specify the wrong format for the type of variable you want to output.

Copying a va_list

It is possible that you may need to process a variable argument list more than once. The <stdarg.h> header file defines a routine for copying an existing va_list for this purpose. Suppose you have created and initialized a va_list object, parg, within a function by using va_start(). You can now make a copy of parg like this:

```
va_list parg_copy;
copy(parg_copy, parg);
```

The first statement creates a new va_list variable, parg_copy. The next statement copies the contents of parg to parg_copy. You can then process parg and parg_copy independently to extract argument values using va_arg() and va_end().

Note that the copy() routine copies the va_list object in whatever state it's in, so if you have executed va_arg() with parg to extract argument values from the list prior to using the copy() routine, parg_copy will be in an identical state to parg with some argument values already extracted. Note also that you must not use the va_list object parg_copy as the destination for another copy operation before you have executed pa_end() for parg_copy.

Basic Rules for Variable-Length Argument Lists

Here's a summary of the basic rules and requirements for writing functions to be called with a variable number of arguments:

! There needs to be at least one fixed argument in a function that accepts a variable number of arguments.

! You must call va_start() to initialize the value of the variable argument list pointer in your function. This pointer also needs to be declared as type va_list.

! There needs to be a mechanism to determine the type of each argument. Either there can be a default type assumed or there can be a parameter that allows the argument type to be determined. For example, in the function average(), you could have an extra fixed argument that would have the value 0 if the variable arguments were double, and 1 if they were long. If the argument type specified in the call to va_arg() isn't correct for the argument value specified when your function is called, your function won't work properly.

! You have to arrange for there to be some way to determine when the list of arguments is exhausted. For example, the last argument in the variable argument list could have a fixed value called a **sentinel** value that can be detected because it's different from all the others, or a fixed argument could contain a count of the number of arguments in total or in the variable part of the argument list.

! The second argument to va_arg() that specifies the type of the argument value to be retrieved must be such that the pointer to the type can be specified by appending * to the type name. Check the documentation for your compiler for other restrictions that may apply.

! You must call va_end() before you exit a function with a variable number of arguments. If you fail to do so, the function won't work properly.

You could try a few variations in Program 9.7 to understand this process better. Put some output in the function average() and see what happens if you change a few things. For example, you could display value and count in the loop in the function average(). You could then modify main() to use an argument that isn't double, or you could introduce a function call in which the last argument isn't 0.

The main() Function

You already know that the main() function is where execution starts. What I haven't discussed up to now is that main() can have a parameter list so that you can pass arguments to main() when you execute a program from the command line. You can write the main() function either with no parameters or with two parameters.

When you write main() with parameters, the first parameter is of type int and represents a count of the number of arguments that appear in the command that is used to execute main(), including the name of the program itself. Thus, if you add two arguments following the name of the program on the command line, the value of the first argument to main() will be 3. The second parameter to main() is an array of pointers to strings. The argument that will be passed when you write two arguments following the name of the program at the command line will be an array of three pointers. The first will point to the name of the program, and the second and third will point to the two arguments that you enter at the command line.

```
/* Program 9.8 A program to list the command line arguments */
#include <stdio.h>
int main(int argc, char *argv[])
{
  printf("Program name: %s\n", argv[0]);
  for(int i = 1 ; i<argc ; i++)
    printf("\nArgument %d: %s", i, argv[i]);
  return 0;
}
```

The value of argc must be at least 1 because you can't execute a program without entering the program name. You therefore output argv[0] as the program name. Subsequent elements in the argv array will be the arguments that were entered at the command line, so you output these in sequence within the for loop.

My source file for this program had the name Program9_08.c so I entered the following command to execute it :

```
Program9_08   first   second_arg   "Third is this"
```

Note the use of double quotes to enclose an argument that includes spaces. This is because spaces are normally treated as delimiters. You can always enclose an argument between double quotes to ensure it will be treated as a single argument.

The program then produces the following output as a result of the preceding command:

```
Program name: Program9_08

Argument 1: first
Argument 2: second_arg
Argument 3: Third is this
```

As you can see, putting double quotes around the last argument ensures that it is read as a single argument and not as three arguments.

All command-line arguments will be read as strings, so when numerical values are entered at the command line, you'll need to convert the string containing the value to the appropriate numerical type. You can use one of the functions shown in Table 9-1 that are declared in <stdlib.h> to do this.

Table 9-1. *Functions That Convert Strings to Numerical Values*

Function	Description
atof()	Converts the string passed as an argument to type double
atoi()	Converts the string passed as an argument to type int
atof()	Converts the string passed as an argument to type long

For example, if you're expecting a command-line argument to be an integer, you might process it like this:

```
int arg_value = 0;          /* Stores value of command line argument */
if(argc>1)                  /* Verify we have at least one argument  */
  arg_value = atoi(argv[1]);
else
{
  printf("Command line argument missing.");
  return 1;
}
```

Note the check on the number of arguments. It's particularly important to include this before processing command-line arguments, as it's very easy to forget to enter them.

Ending a Program

There are several ways of ending a program. Falling off the end of the body of main() is equivalent to executing a return statement in main(), which will end the program. There are two standard library functions that you can call to end a program, both of which are declared in the <stdlib.h> header. Calling the abort() function terminates the program immediately and represents an abnormal end to program operations, so you shouldn't use this for a normal end to a program. You would call abort() to end a program like this:

```
abort();                        /* Abnormal program termination */
```

This statement can appear anywhere in your program.

Calling the exit() function results in a normal end to a program. The function requires an integer argument that will be returned to the operating system. A value of 0 usually represents a completely normal program end. You may use other values to indicate the status of the program in some way. What happens to the value returned by exit() is determined by your operating system. You could call the exit() function like this:

```
exit(1);                        /* Normal program end - status is 1 */
```

You can call exit() to terminate execution from anywhere in your program.

As you have seen, you can also end a program by executing a return statement with an integer value in main(), for example:

```
return 1;
```

The return statement has a special meaning in main() (and *only* in main(), not in any other function), and it's the equivalent of calling exit() with the value specified in the return statement as the argument. Thus, the value in the return statement will be passed back to the operating system.

Libraries of Functions: Header Files

I've already mentioned that your compiler comes with a wide range of standard functions that are declared in **header files**, sometimes called **include files**. These represent a rich source of help for you when you're developing your own applications. You've already come across some of these because header files are such a fundamental component of programming in C. So far you have used functions declared in the header files listed in Table 9-2.

Table 9-2. *Standard Header Files You Have Used*

Header File	Functions
<stdio.h>	Input/output functions
<stdarg.h>	Macros supporting a variable number of arguments to a function
<math.h>	Mathematical floating-point functions
<stdlib.h>	Memory allocation functions
<string.h>	String-handling functions
<stdbool.h>	bool type and Boolean values true and false
<complex.h>	Complex number support
<ctype.h>	Character classification functions
<wctype.h>	Wide character conversion functions

All the header files in Table 9-2 contain declarations for a range of functions, as well as definitions for various constants. They're all ISO/IEC standard libraries, so all standard-conforming compilers will support them and provide at least the basic set of functions, but typically they'll supply much more. To comprehensively discuss the contents of even the ISO/IEC standard library header files and functions could double the size of this book, so I'll mention just the most important aspects of the standard header files and leave it to you to browse the documentation that comes with your compiler.

The header file <stdio.h> contains declarations for quite a large range of high-level input/output (I/O) functions, so I'll devote the whole of Chapter 10 to exploring some of these further, particularly for working with files.

As well as memory allocation functions, <stdlib.h> provides facilities for converting character strings to their numerical equivalents from the ASCII table. There are also functions for sorting and searching. In addition, functions that generate random numbers are available through <stdlib.h>.

You used the <string.h> file in Chapter 6. It provides functions for working with null-terminated strings.

A header file providing a very useful range of functions also related to string processing is <ctype.h>, which you also saw in Chapter 6. The <ctype.h> header includes functions to convert characters from uppercase to lowercase (and vice versa) and a number of functions for checking for alphabetic characters, numeric digits, and so on. These provide an extensive toolkit for you to do your own detailed analysis of the contents of a string, which is particularly useful for dealing with user input.

The <wctype.h> header provides wide character classification functions, and <wchar.h> provides extended multibyte-character utility functions.

I strongly recommend that you invest some time in becoming familiar with the contents of these header files and the libraries that are supplied with your compiler. This familiarity will greatly increase the ease with which you can develop applications in C.

Enhancing Performance

You have two facilities that are intended to provide cues to your compiler to generate code with better performance. One relates to how short function calls are compiled, and the other is concerned with the use of pointers. The effects are not guaranteed though and depend on your compiler implementation. I'll discuss short functions first.

Declaring Functions inline

The functional structure of the C language encourages the segmentation of a program into many functions, and the functions can sometimes be very short. With very short functions it is possible to improve execution performance by replacing each function call of a short function with inline code that implements the effects of the function. You can indicate that you would like this technique to be applied by the compiler by specifying a short function as inline. Here's an example:

```
inline double bmi(double kg_wt, double m_height)
{
  return kg_wt/(m_height*m_height);
}
```

This function calculates an adult's Body Mass Index from their weight in kilograms and their height in meters. This operation is sensibly defined as a **function** but it is also a good candidate for **inline implementation of calls** because the code is so simple. This is specified by the inline keyword in the function header. There's no guarantee in general that the compiler will take note of a function being declared as inline though.

Using the restrict Keyword

Sophisticated C compilers have the capability to optimize the performance of the object code, and this can involve changing the sequence in which calculations occur compared to the sequence in which you specify operations in the code. For such code optimization to be possible, the compiler must be sure that such resequencing of operations will not affect the result of the calculations, and pointers represent something of a problem in this respect. To allow optimization of code involving pointers, the compiler has to be certain that the pointers are not aliased! in other words the data item that each pointer references is not referenced by some other means in a given scope. The restrict keyword provides a way for you to tell the compiler when this is the case and thus allows code optimization to be applied.

Here's an example of a function that is declared in <string.h>:

```
char *strcpy(char * restrict s1, char * restrict s2)
{
  /* Implementation of the function to copy s2 to s1 */
}
```

This function copies s2 to s1. The restrict keyword is applied to both parameters thus indicating that the strings referenced by s1 and s2 are only referenced through those pointers in the body of the function, so the compiler can optimize the code generated for the function. The restrict keyword only imparts information to the compiler and does not guarantee that any optimization will be applied. Of course, if you use the restrict keyword where the condition does not apply, your code may produce incorrect results.

Most of the time you won't need to use the restrict keyword. Only if your code is very computationally intensive will it have any appreciable effect, and even then it depends on your compiler.

Designing a Program

At this point, you've finished with functions, and because you're more than halfway through the capabilities of C, an example of reasonable complexity wouldn't come amiss. In this program, you're going to put to practical use the various elements of C that you've covered so far in the book.

The Problem

The problem that you're going to solve is to write a game. There are several reasons for choosing to write a game. First, games tend to be just as complex, if not more so, as other types of programs, even when the game is simple. And second, games are more fun.

The game is in the same vein as Othello or, if you remember Microsoft Windows 3.0, Reversi. The game is played by two players who take turns placing a colored counter on a square board. One player has black counters and the other has white counters. The board has an even number of squares along each side. The starting position, followed by five successive moves, is shown in Figure 9-4.

You can only place a counter adjacent to an opponent's counter, such that one or more of your opponent's counters! in a line diagonally, horizontally, or vertically! are enclosed between two of your own counters. The opponent's counters are then changed to counters of your own color. The person with the most counters on the board at the end of the game wins. The game ends when all the squares are occupied by counters. The game can also end if neither player can place a counter legally, which can occur if you or your opponent manage to convert all the counters to the same color.

The game can be played with any size of board, but you'll implement it here on a 6 × 6 board. You'll also implement it as a game that you play against the computer.

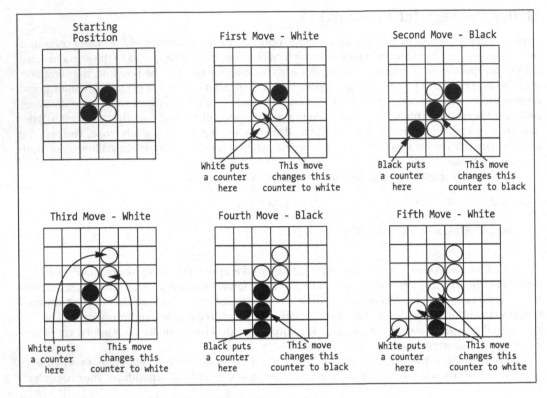

Figure 9-4. *Starting position and initial moves in Reversi*

The Analysis

This problem's analysis is a little different from those you've seen up to now. The whole point of this chapter is to introduce the concept of **structured programming**! in other words, breaking a problem into small pieces! which is why you've spent so long looking at functions.

A good way to start is with a diagram. You'll start with a single box, which represents the whole program, or the main() function, if you like. Developing from this, on the next level down, you'll show the functions that will need to be directly called by the main() function, and you'll indicate what these functions have to do. Below that, you'll show the functions that those functions in turn have to use. You don't have to show the actual functions; you can show just the tasks that need to be accomplished. However, these tasks *do* tend to be functions, so this is a great way to design your program. Figure 9-5 shows the tasks that your program will need to perform.

You can now go a step further than this and begin to think about the actual sequence of actions, or functions, that the program is going to perform. Figure 9-6 is a flowchart that describes the same set of functions but in a manner that shows the sequence in which they're executed and the logic involved in deciding that. You're moving closer now to a more precise specification of how the program will work.

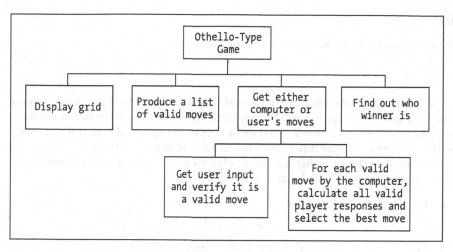

Figure 9-5. *Tasks in the Reversi program*

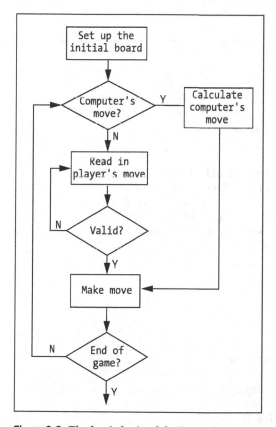

Figure 9-6. *The basic logic of the Reversi program*

This isn't absolutely fixed, of course. There's a lot of detail that you'll need to fill in. This sort of diagram can help you get the logic of the program clear in your mind, and from there you can progress to a more detailed definition of how the program will work.

The Solution

This section outlines the steps you'll take to solve the problem.

Step 1

The first thing to do is to set up and display the initial board. You'll use a smaller-than-normal board (6 × 6), as this makes the games shorter, but you'll implement the program with the board size as a symbol defined by a preprocessor directive. You'll then be able to change the size later if you want. You'll display the board using a separate function, as this is a self-contained activity.

Let's start with the code to declare, initialize, and display the grid. The computer will use '@' as its counter, and the player will have 'O' for his counter:

```c
/* Program 9.9 REVERSI An Othello type game */
#include <stdio.h>

const int SIZE = 6;                /* Board size - must be even */
const char comp_c = '@';           /* Computer's counter        */
const char player_c = 'O';         /* Player's counter          */

/* Function prototypes */
void display(char board[][SIZE]);

int main(void)
{
  char board [SIZE][SIZE] = { 0 };   /* The board           */
  int row = 0;                       /* Board row index     */
  int col = 0;                       /* Board column index  */

  printf("\nREVERSI\n\n");
  printf("You can go first on the first game, then we will take turns.\n");
  printf("   You will be white - (%c)\n   I will be black   - (%c).\n",
                                          player_c, comp_c);
  printf("Select a square for your move by typing a digit for the row\n "
                   "and a letter for the column with no spaces between.\n");
  printf("\nGood luck!  Press Enter to start.\n");
  scanf("%c", &again);

  /* Blank all the board squares */
  for(row = 0; row < SIZE; row++)
    for(col = 0; col < SIZE; col++)
      board[row][col] = ' ';

  /* Place the initial four counters in the center */
  int mid = SIZE/2;
  board[mid - 1][mid - 1] = board[mid][mid] = player_c;
  board[mid - 1][mid] = board[mid][mid - 1] = comp_c;
  display(board);                       /* Display the board  */
  return 0;
}
```

```c
/**********************************************
 * Function to display the board in its       *
 * current state with row numbers and column  *
 * letters to identify squares.               *
 * Parameter is the board array.              *
 **********************************************/
void display(char board[][SIZE])
{
  /* Display the column labels */
  char col_label = 'a';                 /* Column label   */
  printf("\n ");                        /* Start top line */
  for(int col = 0 ; col<SIZE ;col++)
    printf("   %c", col_label+col);     /* Display the top line */
  printf("\n");                         /* End the top line     */

  /* Display the rows… */
  for(int row = 0; row < SIZE; row++)
  {
    /* Display the top line for the current row */
    printf("  +");
    for(int col = 0; col<SIZE; col++)
      printf("---+");
    printf("\n%2d|",row + 1);

    /* Display the counters in current row */
    for(int col = 0; col<SIZE; col++)
      printf(" %c |", board[row][col]);  /* Display counters in row */
    printf("\n");
  }

  /* Finally display the bottom line of the board */
  printf("  +");                         /* Start the bottom line   */
  for(int col = 0 ; col<SIZE ; col++)
    printf("---+");                      /* Display the bottom line */
  printf("\n");                          /* End the bottom  line    */
}
```

The function display() outputs the board with row numbers to identify the rows and the letters from 'a' onward to identify each column. This will be the reference system by which the user will select a square to place his counter.

The code looks complicated, but it's quite straightforward. The first loop outputs the top line with the column label, from 'a' to 'f' with the board size. The next loop outputs the squares that can contain counters, a row at a time, with a row number at the start of each row. The last loop outputs the bottom of the last row. Notice how you've passed the board array as an argument to the display() function rather than making board a global variable. This is to prevent other functions from modifying the contents of board accidentally. The function will display a board of any size.

Step 2

You need a function to generate all the possible moves that can be made for the current player. This function will have two uses: first, it will allow you to check that the move that the player enters is valid, and second, it will help you to determine what moves the computer can make. But first you must decide how you're going to represent and store this list of moves.

So what information do you need to store, and what options do you have? Well, you've defined the grid in such a way that any cell can be referenced by a row number and a column letter. You could therefore store a move as a string consisting of a number and a letter. You would then need to accommodate a list of moves of varying length, to allow for the possibility that the dimensions of the board might change to 10 × 10 or greater.

There's an easier option. You can create a second array with elements of type bool with the same dimensions as the board, and store true for positions where there is a valid move, and false otherwise. The function will need three parameters: the board array, so that it can check for vacant squares; the moves array, in which the valid moves are to be recorded; and the identity of the current player, which will be the character used as a counter for the player.

The strategy will be this: for each blank square, search the squares around that square for an opponent's counter. If you find an opponent's counter, follow a line of opponent counters (horizontal, vertical, or diagonal) until you find a player counter. If you do in fact find a player counter along that line, then you know that the original blank square is a valid move for the current player.

You can add the function definition to the file following the definition of the display() function:

```
/* Program 9.9 REVERSI An Othello type game */
#include <stdio.h>
#include <stdbool.h>

const int SIZE = 6;                 /* Board size - must be even */
const char comp_c = '@';            /* Computer's counter        */
const char player_c = 'O';          /* Player's counter          */

/* Function prototypes */
void display(char board[][SIZE]);
int valid_moves(char board[][SIZE], bool moves[][SIZE], char player);

int main(void)
{
  char board [SIZE][SIZE] = { 0 };       /* The board          */
  bool moves[SIZE][SIZE] = { false };     /* Valid moves        */
  int row = 0;                            /* Board row index      */
  int col = 0;                            /* Board column index   */

  /* Other code for main as before... */
}

/* Code for definition of display() as before... */

/***********************************************
 * Calculates which squares are valid moves    *
 * for player. Valid moves are recorded in the  *
 * moves array - true indicates a valid move,   *
 * false indicates an invalid move.             *
 * First parameter is the board array           *
 * Second parameter is the moves array          *
 * Third parameter identifies the player        *
 * to make the move.                            *
 * Returns valid move count.                    *
 ***********************************************/
```

```
int valid_moves(char board[][SIZE], bool moves[][SIZE], char player)
{
  int rowdelta = 0;                    /* Row increment around a square   */
  int coldelta = 0;                    /* Column increment around a square */
  int x = 0;                           /* Row index when searching        */
  int y = 0;                           /* Column index when searching      */
  int no_of_moves = 0;                 /* Number of valid moves           */

  /* Set the opponent          */
  char opponent = (player == player_c) ? comp_c : player_c;

  /* Initialize moves array to false */
  for(int row = 0; row < SIZE; row++)
    for(int col = 0; col < SIZE; col++)
      moves[row][col] = false;

  /* Find squares for valid moves.                          */
  /* A valid move must be on a blank square and must enclose */
  /* at least one opponent square between two player squares */
  for(int row = 0; row < SIZE; row++)
    for(int col = 0; col < SIZE; col++)
    {
      if(board[row][col] != ' ')      /* Is it a blank square? */
        continue;                     /* No - so on to the next */

      /* Check all the squares around the blank square  */
      /* for the opponents counter                      */
      for(rowdelta = -1; rowdelta <= 1; rowdelta++)
        for(coldelta = -1; coldelta <= 1; coldelta++)
        {
          /* Don't check outside the array, or the current square */
          if(row + rowdelta < 0 || row + rowdelta >= SIZE ||
             col + coldelta < 0 || col + coldelta >= SIZE ||
                              (rowdelta==0 && coldelta==0))
            continue;

          /* Now check the square */
          if(board[row + rowdelta][col + coldelta] == opponent)
          {
            /* If we find the opponent, move in the delta direction  */
            /* over opponent counters searching for a player counter */
            x = row + rowdelta;       /* Move to          */
            y = col + coldelta;       /* opponent square  */

            /* Look for a player square in the delta direction */
            for(;;)
            {
              x += rowdelta;          /* Go to next square */
              y += coldelta;          /* in delta direction*/

              /* If we move outside the array, give up */
              if(x < 0 || x >= SIZE || y < 0 || y >= SIZE)
                break;
```

```
          /* If we find a blank square, give up */
          if(board[x][y] == ' ')
            break;

          /*  If the square has a player counter */
          /*  then we have a valid move         */
          if(board[x][y] == player)
          {
            moves[row][col] = true;   /* Mark as valid */
            no_of_moves++;            /* Increase valid moves count */
            break;                    /* Go check another square     */
          }
        }
      }
    }
  }
  return no_of_moves;
}
```

You have added a prototype for the valid_moves() function and a declaration for the array moves in main().

Because the counters are either player_c or comp_c, you can set the opponent counter in the valid_moves() function as the one that isn't the player counter that's passed as an argument. You do this with the conditional operator. You then set the moves array to false in the first nested loop, so you only have to set valid positions to true. The second nested loop iterates through all the squares on the board, looking for those that are blank. When you find a blank square, you search for an opponent counter in the inner loop:

```
/* Check all the squares around the blank square  */
/* for the opponents counter                      */
for(rowdelta = -1; rowdelta <= 1; rowdelta++)
  for(coldelta = -1; coldelta <= 1; coldelta++)
      ...
```

This will iterate over all the squares that surround the blank square and will include the blank square itself, so you skip the blank square or any squares that are off the board with this if statement:

```
/* Don't check outside the array, or the current square */
if(row + rowdelta < 0 || row + rowdelta >= SIZE ||
   col + coldelta < 0 || col + coldelta >= SIZE ||
                         (rowdelta==0 && coldelta==0))
    continue;
```

If you get past this point, you've found a nonblank square that's on the board. If it contains the opponent's counter, then you move in the same direction, looking for either more opponent counters or a player counter. If you find a player counter, the original blank square is a valid move, so you record it. If you find a blank or run off the board, it isn't a valid move, so you look for another blank square.

The function returns a count of the number of valid moves, so you can use this value to indicate whether the function returns any valid moves. Remember, any positive integer is true and 0 is false.

Step 3

Now that you can produce an array that contains all the valid moves, you can fill in the game loop in main(). You'll base this on the flowchart that you saw earlier. You can start by adding two nested do-while loops: the outer one will initialize each game, and the inner one will iterate over player and computer turns.

```c
/* Program 9.9 REVERSI An Othello type game */
#include <stdio.h>
#include <stdbool.h>

const int SIZE = 6;                    /* Board size - must be even */
const char comp_c = '@';               /* Computer's counter        */
const char player_c = 'O';             /* Player's counter          */

/* Function prototypes */
void display(char board[][SIZE]);
int valid_moves(char board[][SIZE], bool moves[][SIZE], char player);

int main(void)
{
  char board [SIZE][SIZE] = { 0 };     /* The board              */
  bool moves[SIZE][SIZE] = { false };  /* Valid moves            */
  int row = 0;                         /* Board row index        */
  int col = 0;                         /* Board column index     */
  int no_of_games = 0;                 /* Number of games        */
  int no_of_moves = 0;                 /* Count of moves         */
  int invalid_moves = 0;               /* Invalid move count     */
  int comp_score = 0;                  /* Computer score         */
  int user_score = 0;                  /* Player score           */
  char again = 0;                      /* Replay choice input    */

  /* Player indicator: true for player and false for computer */
  bool next_player = true;

  /* Prompt for how to play - as before */

  /* The main game loop */
  do
  {
    /* On even games the player starts; */
    /* on odd games the computer starts */
    next_player = !next_player;
    no_of_moves = 4;                   /* Starts with four counters */

    /* Blank all the board squares */
    for(row = 0; row < SIZE; row++)
      for(col = 0; col < SIZE; col++)
        board[row][col] = ' ';

    /* Place the initial four counters in the center */
    int mid = SIZE/2;
    board[mid - 1][mid - 1] = board[mid][mid] = player_c;
    board[mid - 1][mid] = board[mid][mid - 1] = comp_c;
    /* The game play loop */
    do
    {
      display(board);                  /* Display the board  */
```

```
      if(next_player = !next_player)
      { /*   It is the player's turn                    */
        /* Code to get the player's move and execute it */
      }
      else
      { /* It is the computer's turn                   */
        /* Code to make the computer's move            */
      }
    }while(no_of_moves < SIZE*SIZE && invalid_moves<2);

    /* Game is over */
    display(board);                    /* Show final board  */

    /* Get final scores and display them */
    comp_score = user_score = 0;
    for(row = 0; row < SIZE; row++)
      for(col = 0; col < SIZE; col++)
      {
        comp_score += board[row][col] == comp_c;
        user_score += board[row][col] == player_c;
      }
    printf("The final score is:\n");
    printf("Computer %d\n    User %d\n\n", comp_score, user_score);

    printf("Do you want to play again (y/n): ");
    scanf(" %c", &again);             /* Get y or n            */
  }while(tolower(again) == 'y');      /* Go again on y         */

  printf("\nGoodbye\n");
  return 0;
}


/* Code for definition of display() */

/* Code for definition of valid_moves() */
```

I recommend that you don't run this program yet because you haven't written the code to handle input from the user or moves from the computer. At the moment, it will just loop indefinitely, printing a board with no new moves being made. You'll sort out those parts of the program next.

The variable player determines whose turn it is. When player is false, it's the computer's turn, and when player is true, it's the player's turn. This is set initially to true, and setting player to !player in the do-while loop will alternate who goes first. To determine who takes the next turn, you invert the value of the variable player and test the result in the if statement, which will alternate between the computer and the player automatically.

The game ends when the number of counters in no-of_moves reaches SIZE*SIZE, the number of squares on the board. It will also end if invalid_moves reaches 2. You set invalid_moves to 0 when a valid move is made and increment it each time no valid move is possible. Thus, it will reach 2 if there's no valid option for two successive moves, which means that neither player can go. At the end of a game, you output the final board and the results and offer the option of another game.

You can now add the code to main() that will make the player and computer moves:

```
/* Program 9.9 REVERSI An Othello type game */
#include <stdio.h>
#include <stdbool.h>
#include <ctype.h>
#include <string.h>

const int SIZE = 6;                    /* Board size - must be even */
const char comp_c = '@';               /* Computer's counter        */
const char player_c = 'O';             /* Player's counter          */

/* Function prototypes */
void display(char board[][SIZE]);
int valid_moves(char board[][SIZE], bool moves[][SIZE], char player);
void make_move(char board[][SIZE], int row, int col, char player);
void computer_move(char board[][SIZE], bool moves[][SIZE], char player);

int main(void)
{
  char board [SIZE][SIZE] = { 0 };     /* The board             */
  bool moves[SIZE][SIZE] = { false }; /* Valid moves           */
  int row = 0;                         /* Board row index       */
  int col = 0;                         /* Board column index    */
  int no_of_games = 0;                 /* Number of games       */
  int no_of_moves = 0;                 /* Count of moves        */
  int invalid_moves = 0;               /* Invalid move count    */
  int comp_score = 0;                  /* Computer score        */
  int user_score = 0;                  /* Player score          */
  char y = 0;                          /* Column letter         */
  int x = 0;                           /* Row number            */
  char again = 0;                      /* Replay choice input */

  /* Player indicator: true for player and false for computer */
  bool next_player = true;

  /* Prompt for how to play - as before */

  /* The main game loop */
  do
  {
    /* The player starts the first game */
    /* then they alternate         */
    next_player = !next_player;
    no_of_moves = 4;                   /* Starts with four counters */

    /* Blank all the board squares */
    for(row = 0; row < SIZE; row++)
      for(col = 0; col < SIZE; col++)
        board[row][col] = ' ';

    /* Place the initial four counters in the center */
    board[SIZE/2 - 1][SIZE/2 - 1] = board[SIZE/2][SIZE/2] = 'O';
    board[SIZE/2 - 1][SIZE/2] = board[SIZE/2][SIZE/2 - 1] = '@';
```

```
      /* The game play loop */
      do
      {
        display(board);                /* Display the board  */
        if(next_player=!next_player)    /* Flip next player */
        { /*   It is the player's turn                    */
          if(valid_moves(board, moves, player_c))
          {
            /* Read player moves until a valid move is entered */
            for(;;)
            {
              printf("Please enter your move (row column): ");
              scanf(" %d%c", &x, &y);     /* Read input        */
              y = tolower(y) - 'a';       /* Convert to column index */
              x--;                         /* Convert to row index    */
              if( x>=0 && y>=0 && x<SIZE && y<SIZE && moves[x][y])
              {
                make_move(board, x, y, player_c);
                no_of_moves++;             /* Increment move count */
                break;
              }
              else
                printf("Not a valid move, try again.\n");
            }
          }
          else                      /* No valid moves */
            if(++invalid_moves<2)
            {
              printf("\nYou have to pass, press return");
              scanf("%c", &again);
            }
            else
              printf("\nNeither of us can go, so the game is over.\n");
        }
        else
        { /* It is the computer's turn                     */
          if(valid_moves(board, moves, '@')) /* Check for valid moves */
          {
            invalid_moves = 0;                /* Reset invalid count   */
            computer_move(board, moves, '@');
            no_of_moves++;                    /* Increment move count  */
          }
          else
          {
            if(++invalid_moves<2)
              printf("\nI have to pass, your go\n"); /* No valid move */
            else
              printf("\nNeither of us can go, so the game is over.\n");
          }
        }
      }while(no_of_moves < SIZE*SIZE && invalid_moves<2);

      /* Game is over */
      display(board);                /* Show final board */
```

```
      /* Get final scores and display them */
      comp_score = user_score = 0;
      for(row = 0; row < SIZE; row++)
        for(col = 0; col < SIZE; col++)
        {
          comp_score += board[row][col] == comp_c;
          user_score += board[row][col] == player_c;
        }
      printf("The final score is:\n");
      printf("Computer %d\n    User %d\n\n", comp_score, user_score);

      printf("Do you want to play again (y/n): ");
      scanf(" %c", &again);                    /* Get y or n              */
    }while(tolower(again) == 'y');             /* Go again on y           */

    printf("\nGoodbye\n");
    return 0;
}


/* Code for definition of display() */

/* Code for definition of valid_moves() */
```

The code to deal with game moves uses two new functions for which you add prototypes. The function make_move() will execute a move, and the computer_move() function will calculate the computer's move. For the player, you calculate the moves array for the valid moves in the if statement:

```
        if(valid_moves(board, moves, player_c))
        ...
```

If the return value is positive, there are valid moves, so you read the row number and column letter for the square selected:

```
            printf("Please enter your move: "); /* Prompt for entry       */
            scanf(" %d%c", &x, &y);             /* Read input             */
```

You convert the row number to an index by subtracting 1 and the letter to an index by subtracting 'a'. You call tolower() just to be sure the value in y is lowercase. Of course, you must include the ctype.h header for this function. For a valid move, the index values must be within the bounds of the array and moves[x][y] must be true:

```
            if( x>=0 && y>=0 && x<SIZE && y<SIZE && moves[x][y])
            ...
```

If you have a valid move, you execute it by calling the function make_move(), which you'll write in a moment (notice that the code won't compile yet, because you make a call to this function without having defined it in the program).

If there are no valid moves for the player, you increment invalid_moves. If this is still less than 2, you output a message that the player can't go, and continue with the next iteration for the computer's move. If invalid_moves isn't less than 2, however, you output a message that the game is over, and the do-while loop condition controlling game moves will be false.

For the computer's move, if there are valid moves, you call the computer_move() function to make the move and increment the move count. The circumstances in which there are no valid moves are handled in the same way as for the player.

Let's add the definition of the make_move() function next. To make a move, you must place the appropriate counter on the selected square and flip any adjacent rows of opponent counters that are bounded at the opposite end by a player counter. You can add the code for this function at the end of the source file! I won't repeat all the other code:

```c
/********************************************************************
 * Makes a move. This places the counter on a square and reverses   *
 * all the opponent's counters affected by the move.                *
 * First parameter is the board array.                              *
 * Second and third parameters are the row and column indices.      *
 * Fourth parameter identifies the player.                          *
 ********************************************************************/
void make_move(char board[][SIZE], int row, int col, char player)
{
  int rowdelta = 0;               /* Row increment               */
  int coldelta = 0;               /* Column increment            */
  int x = 0;                      /* Row index for searching     */
  int y = 0;                      /* Column index for searching  */

  /* Identify opponent */
  char opponent = (player == player_c) ? comp_c : player_c;

  board[row][col] = player;       /* Place the player counter    */

  /* Check all the squares around this square */
  /* for the opponents counter               */
  for(rowdelta = -1; rowdelta <= 1; rowdelta++)
    for(coldelta = -1; coldelta <= 1; coldelta++)
    {
      /* Don't check off the board, or the current square */
      if(row + rowdelta < 0 || row + rowdelta >= SIZE ||
         col + coldelta < 0 || col + coldelta >= SIZE ||
                       (rowdelta==0 && coldelta== 0))
        continue;

      /* Now check the square */
      if(board[row + rowdelta][col + coldelta] == opponent)
      {
        /* If we find the opponent, search in the same direction */
        /* for a player counter                                  */
        x = row + rowdelta;       /* Move to opponent */
        y = col + coldelta;       /* square           */

        for(;;)
        {
          x += rowdelta;          /* Move to the      */
          y += coldelta;          /* next square      */

          /* If we are off the board give up */
          if(x < 0 || x >= SIZE || y < 0 || y >= SIZE)
            break;

          /* If the square is blank give up */
          if(board[x][y] == ' ')
            break;
```

```
                    /* If we find the player counter, go backward from here  */
                    /* changing all the opponents counters to player          */
                     if(board[x][y] == player)
                     {
                       while(board[x-=rowdelta][y-=coldelta]==opponent) /* Opponent? */
                          board[x][y] = player;    /* Yes, change it */
                       break;                       /* We are done    */
                     }
                   }
                 }
               }
            }
     }
```

The logic here is similar to that in the valid_moves() function for checking that a square is a valid move. The first step is to search the squares around the square indexed by the parameters row and col for an opponent counter. This is done in the nested loops:

```
for(rowdelta = -1; rowdelta <= 1; rowdelta++)
  for(coldelta = -1; coldelta <= 1; coldelta++)
  {
    ...
  }
```

When you find an opponent counter, you head off in the same direction looking for a player counter in the indefinite for loop. If you fall off the edge of the board or find a blank square, you break out of the for loop and continue the outer loop to move to the next square around the selected square. If you do find a player counter, however, you back up, changing all the opponent counters to player counters.

```
                    /* If we find the player counter, go backward from here  */
                    /* changing all the opponents counters to player          */
                    if(board[x][y] == player)
                    {
                      while(board[x-=rowdelta][y-=coldelta]==opponent) /* Opponent? */
                         board[x][y] = player;    /* Yes, change it */
                      break;                       /* We are done    */
                    }
```

The break here breaks out of the indefinite for loop.

Now that you have this function, you can move on to the trickiest part of the program, which is implementing the function to make the computer's move. You'll adopt a relatively simple strategy for determining the computer's move. You'll evaluate each of the possible valid moves for the computer. For each valid computer move, you'll determine what the best move is that the player could make and determine a score for that. You'll then choose the computer move for which the player's best move produces the lowest score.

Before you get to write computer_move(), you'll implement a couple of helper functions. Helper functions are just functions that help in the implementation of an operation, in this case implementing the move for the computer. The first will be the function get_score() that will calculate the score for a given board position. You can add the following code to the end of the source file for this:

```
/******************************************************************
 * Calculates the score for the current board position for the    *
 * player. player counters score +1, opponent counters score -1   *
 * First parameter is the board array                             *
 * Second parameter identifies the player                         *
 * Return value is the score.                                     *
 ******************************************************************/
int get_score(char board[][SIZE], char player)
{
  int score = 0;                          /* Score for current position */

  /* Identify opponent */
  char opponent = (player == player_c) ? comp_c : player_c;

  /* Check all board squares */
  for(int row = 0; row < SIZE; row++)
    for(int col = 0; col < SIZE; col++)
    {
      score -= board[row][col] == opponent; /* Decrement for opponent */
      score += board[row][col] == player;   /* Increment for player   */
    }
  return score;
}
```

This is quite simple. The score is calculated by adding 1 for every player counter on the board, and subtracting 1 for each opponent counter on the board.

The next helper function is best_move(), which will calculate and return the score for the best move of the current set of valid moves for a player. The code for this is as follows:

```
/******************************************************************
 * Calculates the score for the best move out of the valid moves  *
 * for player in the current position.                            *
 * First parameter is the board array                             *
 * Second parameter is the moves array defining valid moves.      *
 * Third parameter identifies the player                          *
 * The score for the best move is returned                        *
 ******************************************************************/
int best_move(char board[][SIZE], bool moves[][SIZE], char player)
{
  /* Identify opponent */
  char opponent = (player == player_c) ? comp_c : player_c;

  char new_board[SIZE][SIZE] = { 0 }; /* Local copy of board    */
  int score = 0;                      /* Best score             */
  int new_score = 0;                  /* Score for current move */

  /* Check all valid moves to find the best */
  for(int row = 0 ; row<SIZE ; row++)
    for(int col = 0 ; col<SIZE ; col++)
    {
      if(!moves[row][col])             /* Not a valid move? */
        continue;                      /* Go to the next    */
```

```
    /* Copy the board */
    memcpy(new_board, board, sizeof(new_board));

    /* Make move on the board copy */
    make_move(new_board, row, col, player);

    /* Get score for move */
    new_score = get_score(new_board, player);

    if(score<new_score)              /* Is it better?              */
      score = new_score;             /* Yes, save it as best score */
  }
  return score;                      /* Return best score          */
}
```

Remember that you must add function prototypes for both of these helper functions to the other function prototypes before main():

```
/* Function prototypes */
void display(char board[][SIZE]);
int valid_moves(char board[][SIZE], bool moves[][SIZE], char player);
void make_move(char board[][SIZE], int row, int col, char player);
void computer_move(char board[][SIZE], bool moves[][SIZE], char player);
int best_move(char board[][SIZE], bool moves[][SIZE], char player);
int get_score(char board[][SIZE], char player);
```

Step 4

The last piece to complete the program is the implementation of the computer_move() function. The code for this is as follows:

```
/****************************************************************
 * Finds the best move for the computer. This is the move for   *
 * which the opponent's best possible move score is a minimum.  *
 * First parameter is the board array.                          *
 * Second parameter is the moves array containing valid moves.  *
 * Third parameter identifies the computer.                     *
 ****************************************************************/
void computer_move(char board[][SIZE], bool moves[][SIZE], char player)
{
  int best_row = 0;                  /* Best row index         */
  int best_col = 0;                  /* Best column index      */
  int new_score = 0;                 /* Score for current move */
  int score = 100;                   /* Minimum opponent score */
  char temp_board[SIZE][SIZE];       /* Local copy of board    */
  bool temp_moves[SIZE][SIZE];       /* Local valid moves array */

  /* Identify opponent */
  char opponent = (player == player_c) ? comp_c : player_c;
```

```
/* Go through all valid moves */
for(int row = 0; row < SIZE; row++)
  for(int col = 0; col < SIZE; col++)
  {
    if( !moves[row][col] )
      continue;

    /* First make copies of the board array */
    memcpy(temp_board, board, sizeof(temp_board));

    /* Now make this move on the temporary board */
    make_move(temp_board, row, col, player);

    /* find valid moves for the opponent after this move */
    valid_moves(temp_board, temp_moves, opponent);

    /* Now find the score for the opponent's best move */
    new_score = best_move(temp_board, temp_moves, opponent);

    if(new_score<score)             /* Is it worse?                       */
    {                               /* Yes, so save this move             */
      score = new_score;            /* Record new lowest opponent score   */
      best_row = row;               /* Record best move row               */
      best_col = col;               /* and column                         */
    }
  }
  /* Make the best move */
  make_move(board, best_row, best_col, player);
}
```

This isn't difficult with the two helper functions. Remember that you're going to choose the move for which the opponent's subsequent best move is a minimum.

In the main loop that is controlled by the counters row and col, you make each valid move, in turn, on the copy of the current board that's stored in the local array temp_board. After each move, you call the valid_moves() function to calculate the valid moves for the opponent in that position and store the results in the temp_moves array. You then call the best_move() function to get the score for the best opponent move from the valid set stored in the array temp_moves. If that score is less than any previous score, you save the score, the row, and the column index for that computer move, as a possible best move.

The variable score is initialized with a value that's higher than any possible score, and you go about trying to minimize this (because it's the strength of the opponent's next move) to find the best possible move for the computer. After all of the valid computer moves have been tried, best_row and best_col contain the row and column index for the move that minimizes the opponent's next move. You then call make_move() to make the best move for the computer.

You can now compile and execute the game. The game starts something like this:

```
     a   b   c   d   e   f
   +---+---+---+---+---+---+
 1 |   |   |   |   |   |   |
   +---+---+---+---+---+---+
 2 |   |   |   |   |   |   |
   +---+---+---+---+---+---+
 3 |   |   | O | @ |   |   |
   +---+---+---+---+---+---+
 4 |   |   | @ | O |   |   |
   +---+---+---+---+---+---+
 5 |   |   |   |   |   |   |
   +---+---+---+---+---+---+
 6 |   |   |   |   |   |   |
   +---+---+---+---+---+---+
Please enter your move: 3e
     a   b   c   d   e   f
   +---+---+---+---+---+---+
 1 |   |   |   |   |   |   |
   +---+---+---+---+---+---+
 2 |   |   |   |   |   |   |
   +---+---+---+---+---+---+
 3 |   |   | O | O | O |   |
   +---+---+---+---+---+---+
 4 |   |   | @ | O |   |   |
   +---+---+---+---+---+---+
 5 |   |   |   |   |   |   |
   +---+---+---+---+---+---+
 6 |   |   |   |   |   |   |
   +---+---+---+---+---+---+
```

The computer doesn't play too well because it looks only one move ahead, and it doesn't have any favoritism for edge and corner cells.

Also, the board is only 6 × 6. If you want to change the board size, just change the value of SIZE to another even number. The program will work just as well.

Summary

If you've arrived at this point without too much trouble, you're well on your way to becoming a competent C programmer. This chapter and the previous one have covered all you really need to write well-structured C programs. A functional structure is inherent to the C language, and you should keep your functions short with a well-defined purpose. This is the essence of good C code. You should now be able to approach your own programming problems with a functional structure in mind right from the outset.

Don't forget the flexible power that pointers give you as a C programmer. They can greatly simplify many programming problems, and you should frequently find yourself using them as function arguments and return values. After a while, it will be a natural inclination. The real teacher is experience, so going over the programs in this chapter again will be extremely useful if you don't feel completely confident. And once you feel confident with what's in this book, you should be raring to have a go at some problems of your own.

There's still one major new piece of language territory in C that you have yet to deal with, and it's all about data and how to structure it. You'll look at data in Chapter 11. But before you do that, you need to cover I/O in rather more detail than you have so far. Handling input and output is an important and fascinating aspect of programming, so that's where you're headed next.

Exercises

The following exercises enable you to try out what you've learned in this chapter. If you get stuck, look back over the chapter for help. If you're still stuck, you can download the solutions from the Source Code/Download area of the Apress web site (http://www.apress.com), but that really should be a last resort.

Exercise 9-1. A function with the prototype

```
double power(double x, int n);
```

should calculate and return the value of x^n. That is, the expression power(5.0, 4) will evaluate 5.0 * 5.0 * 5.0 * 5.0, which will result in the value 625.0.

Implement the power() function as a recursive function (so it should call itself) and demonstrate its operation with a suitable version of main().

Exercise 9-2. Implement functions with the prototypes

```
double add(double a, double b);       /* Returns a+b */
double subtract(double a, double b);  /* Returns a-b */
double multiply(double a, double b);  /* Returns a*b */
double array_op(double array[], int size, double (*pfun)(double,double));
```

The parameters for the array_op() function are the array to be operated on, the number of elements in the array, and a pointer to a function defining the operation to be applied between successive elements. The array_op() function should be implemented so that when the subtract() function is passed as the third argument, the function combines the elements with alternating signs. So for an array with four elements, x1, x2, x3, and x4, it computes the value of x1 - x2 + x3 - x4.

Demonstrate the operation of these functions with a suitable version of main().

Exercise 9-3. Define a function that will accept an array of pointers to strings as an argument and return a pointer to a string that contains all the strings joined into a single string, each terminated by a newline character. If an original string in the input array has newline as its last character, the function shouldn't add another to the string. Write a program to demonstrate this function in operation by reading a number of strings from the keyboard and outputting the resultant combined string.

Exercise 9-4. Implement a function that has the prototype

```
char *to_string(int count, double first, ...);
```

This function should return a string that contains string representations of the second and subsequent arguments, each to two decimal places and separated by commas. The first argument is a count of the number of arguments that follow. Write a suitable version of main() to demonstrate the operation of your function.

CHAPTER 10

∎∎∎

Essential Input and Output Operations

In this chapter you're going to look in more detail at input from the keyboard, output to the screen, and output to a printer. The good news is that everything in this chapter is fairly easy, although there may be moments when you feel it's all becoming a bit of a memory test. Treat this as a breather from the last two chapters. After all, you don't have to memorize everything you see here; you can always come back to it when you need it.

Like most modern programming languages, the C language has no input or output capability within the language. All operations of this kind are provided by functions from standard libraries. You've been using many of these functions to provide input from the keyboard and output to the screen in all the preceding chapters.

This chapter will put all the pieces together into some semblance of order and round it out with the aspects I haven't explained so far. I'll also add a bit about printing because it's usually a fairly essential facility for a program. You don't have a program demonstrating a problem solution with this chapter for the simple reason that I don't really cover anything that requires any practice on a substantial example (it's that easy).

In this chapter you'll learn the following:

!   How to read data from the keyboard

!   How to format data for output on the screen

!   How to deal with character output

!   How to output data to a printer

Input and Output Streams

Up to now you've primarily used scanf() for keyboard input and printf() for output to the screen. Actually, there has been nothing in particular about the way you've used these functions to specify where the input came from or where the output went. The information that scanf() received could have come from anywhere, as long as it was a suitable stream of characters. Similarly, the output from printf() could have been going anywhere that could accept a stream of characters. This is no accident: the standard input/output functions in C have been designed to be device-independent, so that the transfer of data to or from a specific device isn't a concern of the programmer. The C library functions and the operating system make sure that operations with a specific device are executed correctly.

Each input source and output destination in C is called a **stream**. An **input stream** is a source of data that can be read into your program, and an **output stream** is a destination for data that originates in your program. A stream is independent of the physical piece of equipment involved, such as the display or the keyboard. Each device that a program uses will usually have one or more streams associated with it, depending on whether it's simply an input device such as a keyboard, or an output device such as a printer, or a device that can have both input and output operations, such as a disk drive. This is illustrated in Figure 10-1.

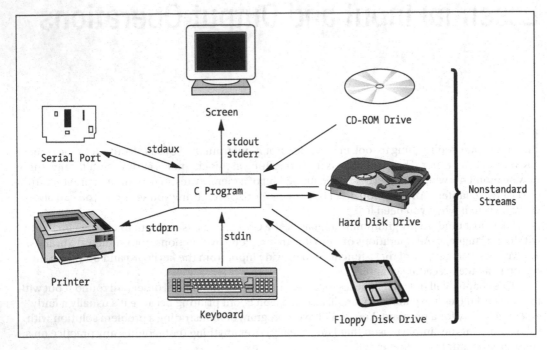

Figure 10-1. *Standard and nonstandard streams*

A disk drive can have multiple input and output streams because it can contain multiple files. The correspondence is between a stream and a file, not between a stream and the device. A stream can be associated with a specific file on the disk. The stream that you associate with a particular file could be an input stream, so you could only read from the file; it could be an output stream, in which case you could only write to the file; or the stream might allow input and output so reading and writing the file would both be possible. Obviously, if the stream that is associated with a file is an input stream, the file must have been written at some time so it contained some data. You could also associate a stream with a file on a CD-ROM drive. Because this device is typically read-only, the stream would, of necessity, be an input stream.

There are two further kinds of streams: **character streams**, which are also referred to as **text streams**, and **binary streams**. The main difference between these is that data transferred to or from character streams is treated as a sequence of characters and may be modified by the library routine concerned, according to a format specification. Data that's transferred to or from binary streams is just a sequence of bytes that isn't modified in any way. I discuss binary streams in Chapter 12 when I cover reading and writing disk files.

Standard Streams

C has three predefined **standard streams** that are automatically available in any program, provided, of course, that you've included the <stdio.h> header file, which contains their definitions, into your program. These standard streams are stdin, stdout, and stderr. Two other streams that are available with some systems are identified by the names stdprn and stdaux, but these are not part of the C language standard so your compiler may not support them.

No initialization or preparation is necessary to use these streams. You just have to apply the appropriate library function that sends data to them. They are each preassigned to a specific physical device, as shown in Table 10-1.

Table 10-1. *Standard Streams*

Stream	Device
stdin	Keyboard
stdout	Display screen
stderr	Display screen
stdprn	Printer
stdaux	Serial port

In this chapter I concentrate on how you can use the standard input stream, stdin, the standard output stream, stdout, and the printer stream, stdprn.

The stderr stream is simply the stream to which error messages from the C library are sent, and you can direct your own error messages to stderr if you wish. The main difference between stdout and stderr is that output to stdout is buffered in memory so the data that you write to it won't necessarily be transferred immediately to the device, whereas stderr is unbuffered so any data you write to it is always transferred immediately to the device. With a buffered stream your program transfers data to or from a buffer area in memory, and the actual data transfer to or from the physical device can occur asynchronously. This makes the input and output operations much more efficient. The advantage of using an unbuffered stream for error messages is that you can be sure that they will actually be displayed but the output operations will be inefficient; a buffered stream is efficient but may not get flushed when a program fails for some reason, so the output may never be seen. I won't discuss this further, other than to say stderr points to the display screen and can't be redirected to another device. Output to the stream stdaux is directed to the serial port and is outside the scope of this book for reasons of space rather than complexity.

Both stdin and stdout can be reassigned to files, instead of the default of keyboard and screen, by using operating system commands. This offers you a lot of flexibility. If you want to run your program several times with the same data, during testing for example, you could prepare the data as a text file and redirect stdin to the file. This enables you to rerun the program with the same data without having to re-enter it each time. By redirecting the output from your program to a file, you can easily retain it for future reference, and you could use a text editor to access it or search it.

Input from the Keyboard

There are two forms of input from the keyboard on stdin that you've already seen in previous chapters: **formatted input**, which is provided primarily by the scanf() function and **unformatted input**, in which you receive the raw character data from a function such as getchar(). There's rather more to both of these possibilities, so let's look at them in detail.

Formatted Keyboard Input

As you know, the function scanf() reads characters from the stream stdin and converts them to one or more values according to the format specifiers in a format control string. The prototype of the scanf() function is as follows:

```
int scanf(char *format, ... );
```

The format control string parameter is of type char *, a pointer to a character string as shown here. However, this usually appears as an explicit argument in the function call, such as

```
scanf("%lf", &variable);
```

But there's nothing to prevent you from writing this:

```
char str[] = "%lf";
scanf(str, &variable);
```

The scanf() function makes use of the facility of handling a variable number of arguments that you learned about in Chapter 9. The format control string is basically a coded description of how scanf() should convert the incoming character stream to the values required. Following the format control string, you can have one or more optional arguments, each of which is an address in which a corresponding converted input value is to be stored. As you've seen, this implies that each of these arguments must be a pointer or a variable name prefixed by & to define the address of the variable rather than its value.

The scanf() function reads from stdin until it comes to the end of the format control string, or until an error condition stops the input process. This sort of error is the result of input that doesn't correspond to what is expected with the current format specifier, as you'll see. Something that I haven't previously noted is that scanf() returns a value that is the count of the number of input values read. This provides a way for you to detect when an error occurs by comparing the value returned by scanf() with the number of input values you are expecting.

The wscanf() function provides exactly the same capabilities as scanf() except that the first argument to the function, which is the format control string, must be a wide character string of type wchar_t *.

Thus you could use wscanf() to read a floating-point value from the keyboard like this:

```
wscanf(L"%lf", &variable);
```

The first argument is a wide character string constant and in all other respects the function works like scanf(). If you omit the L for the wide character string literal, you will get an error message from the compiler because your argument does not match the type of the first parameter.

Of course, you could also write this:

```
wchar_t wstr[] = L"%lf";
wscanf(wstr, &variable);
```

Input Format Control Strings

The format control string that you use with scanf() or wscanf() isn't precisely the same as that used with printf(). For one thing, putting one or more whitespace characters! blank ' ', tab '\t', or newline '\n'! in the format control string causes scanf() to read and ignore whitespace characters up to the next nonwhitespace character in the input. A single whitespace character in the format control string causes any number of consecutive whitespace characters to be ignored. You can therefore include as many whitespace characters as you wish in the format string to make it more readable. Note that whitespace characters are ignored by scanf() by default except when you are reading data using %c, %[], or %n specifications (see Table 10-2).

Any nonwhitespace character other than % will cause scanf() to read but not store successive occurrences of the character. If you want scanf() to ignore commas separating values in the input for instance, just precede each format specifier by a comma. There are other differences too, as you'll see when I discuss formatted output in the section •Output to the Screen! a bit later in this chapter.

The most general form of a format specifier is shown in Figure 10-2.

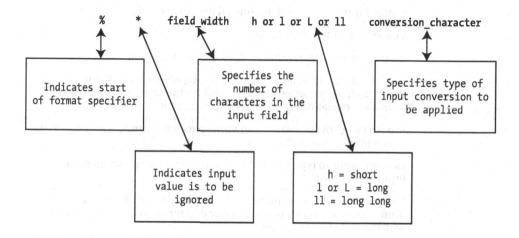

Figure 10-2. *The general form of an output specifier*

Let's take a look at what the various parts of this general form mean:

! The % simply indicates the start of the format specifier. It must always be present.

! The next * is optional. If you include it, it indicates that the next input value is to be ignored. This isn't normally used with input from the keyboard. It does become useful, however, when stdin has been reassigned to a file and you don't want to process all the values that appear within the file in your program.

! The field width is optional. It's an integer specifying the number of characters that scanf() should assume makes up the current value being input. This allows you to input a sequence of values without spaces between them. This is also often quite useful when reading files.

! The next character is also optional, and it can be h, L, l (the lowercase letter L), or ll (two lowercase Ls). If it's h, it can only be included with an integer conversion specifier (d, I, o, u, or x) and indicates that the input is to be converted as short. If it's l, it indicates long when preceding an int conversion specifier, and double when preceding a float conversion specifier. Prefixing the c specification with l specifies a wide character conversion so the input is read as wchar_t. The prefix L applied to e, E, f, g, or G specifies the value is of type long double. The ll prefix applies to integer conversions and specifies that the input is to be stored as type long long.

! The conversion character specifies the type of conversion to be carried out on the input stream and therefore must be included. The possible characters and their meanings are shown in Table 10-2.

Table 10-2. *Conversion Characters and Their Meanings*

Conversion Character	Meaning
d	Convert input to int.
i	Convert input to int. If preceded by 0, then assume octal digits input. If preceded by 0x or 0X, then assume hexadecimal digits input.
o	Convert input to int and assume all digits are octal.
u	Convert input to unsigned int.
x	Convert to int and assume all digits are hexadecimal.
c	Read the next character as char (including whitespace). If you want to ignore whitespace when reading a single character, just precede the format specification by a whitespace character.
s	Input a string of successive nonwhitespace characters, starting with the next nonwhitespace character.
e, f, or g	Convert input to type float. A decimal point and an exponent in the input are optional.
n	No input is read but the number characters that have been read from the input source up to this point are stored in the corresponding argument, which should be of type int*.

You can also read a string that consists of specific characters by placing all the possible characters between square brackets in the specification. For example, the specification %[0123456789.-] will read a numerical value as a string, so if the input is –1.25 it will be read as "-1.25". To read a string consisting of the lowercase letters *a* to *z*, you could use the specification %[abcdefghijklmnopqrstuvwxyz]. This will read any sequence of the characters that appear between the square brackets as a string, and the first character in the input that isn't in the set between the square brackets marks the end of the input. Although it isn't required by the standard, many C library implementations support the form %[a-z] to read a string consisting of any lowercase letters.

A specification using square brackets is also very useful for reading strings that are delimited by characters other than whitespace. In this case, you can specify the characters that are *not* in the string by using the ^ character as the first character in the set. Thus, the specification %[^,] will include everything in the string except a comma, so this form will enable you to read a series of strings separated by commas.

Table 10-3 shows a few examples of applying the various options.

Table 10-3. *Examples of Options in Conversion Specifications*

Specification	Description
%lf	Read the next value as type double
%*d	Read the next integer value but don't store it
%lc	Read the next character as type wchar_t
%\nc	Read the next character as type char ignoring whitespace characters
%10lld	Reads the next ten characters as an integer value of type long long

Table 10-3. *Examples of Options in Conversion Specifications*

Specification	Description
%5d	Read the next five characters as an integer
%Lf	Read the next value as a floating-point value of type long double
%hu	Read the next value as type unsigned short

Let's exercise some of these format control strings with practical examples.

TRY IT OUT: EXERCISING FORMATTED INPUT

To start, let's read a variety of data and then output the result:

```
/* Program 10.1        Exercising formatted input */
#include <stdio.h>

const size_t SIZE - 20;       /* Max characters in a word */

int main(void)
{
  int value_count = 0;        /* Count of input values read */
  float fp1 = 0.0;            /* Floating-point value read  */
  int i = 0;                  /* First integer read         */
  int j = 0;                  /* Second integer read        */
  char word1[SIZE] = " ";     /* First string read          */
  char word2[SIZE] = " ";     /* Second string read         */
  int byte_count = 0;         /* Count of input bytes read   */

  value_count = scanf("%f %d %d %[abcdefghijklmnopqrstuvwxyz] %*1d %s%n",
                       &fp1, &i , &j, word1, word2, &byte_count);
  printf("\nCount of bytes read = %d\n", byte_count);
  printf("\nCount of values read = %d\n", k);
  printf("\nfp1 = %f   i = %d   j = %d", fp1, i, j);
  printf("\nword1 = %s   word2 = %s\n", word1, word2);
  return 0;
}
```

Here's an example of the output from this program:

```
-2.35 15 25 ready2go

Count of bytes read = 20

Count of values read = 5

fp1 = -2.350000   i = 15   j = 25
word1 = ready   word2 = go
```

How It Works

The first three input values are read in a straightforward way. The fourth input value is read using the specifier "%[abcdefghijklmnopqrstuvwxyz]", which will read a sequence of lowercase letters as a string. This reads the string "ready" because the character that follows, '2', isn't in the set between the square brackets. The '2' in the input is read using the specifier "%*1d". The * in the specification causes the input to be read but not stored, and the field width is one character. The word "go" is read and stored in word2 using the "%s" specifier. The %n specifier does not extract data from the input stream; it just stores the number of bytes that the scanf() function has read from the input stream up to that point so that value is stored in byte_count.

The value of value_count holds the count of the number of values processed that is returned by the scanf() function. As you can see, the value reflects the number of values stored and doesn't include the value read by the "%*1d" specification.

It isn't essential that you enter all the data on a single line. If you key in the first two values and press Enter, the scanf() function will wait for you to enter the next value on the next line.

Now let's change the program a little bit by altering one statement. Replace the input statement with

```
value_count = scanf(
                "%4f %d %d %*d %[abcdefghijklmnopqrstuvwxyz] %*1d %[^o]%n",
                &fp1, &i , &j, word1, word2, &byte_count);
```

Now run the program with exactly the same input line as before. You should get the following output:

```
-2.35 15 25 ready2go

Count of bytes read = 19

Count of values read = 5

fp1 = -2.300000    i = 5    j = 15
word1 = ready    word2 = g
```

Because you specified a field width of 4 for the floating-point value, the first four characters are taken as defining the value of the first input variable. The following integer value to be input is read as 5, the last digit following the value read as –2.3. The integer that's stored in j is 15, and the value 25 is read and ignored by the "%*d" specification. The last string is read now as just "g" because the specification "%[^o]" accepts any character in the string except the letter 'o'. Because the letter 'o' is not read as part of the input the byte count is now 19.

Let's try another variation. Change the input statement to this:

```
value_count = scanf(
                "%4f %4d %d %*d %[abcdefghijklmnopqrstuvwxyz] %*1d %[^o]%n",
                &fp1, &i , &j, word1, word2, &byte_count);
```

With exactly the same input line as before, you should now get the following output:

```
-2.35 15 25 ready2go

Count of bytes read = 19

Count of values read = 5

fp1 = -2.300000    i = 5    j = 15
word1 = ready    word2 = g
```

So what can you conclude from this case? The first floating-point value has clearly been defined by the first four characters of input. The next two values result in the integers 5 and 15. This shows that in spite of the fact that you specified a field width of 4 for the second integer, it appears to have been overridden. This is a consequence of the blank following digit 5, which terminates the input scanning for the value being read. So whatever value you put as a field width, the scanning of the input line for a given value stops as soon as you meet the first blank. You could change the specifiers for the integer values to %12d and the result would still be the same for the given input.

You can demonstrate one further aspect of numerical input processing by running the last version of the previous example with a slightly different input line:

```
-2.3A 15 25 ready2go

Count of bytes read = 0

Count of values read = 1

fp1 = -2.300000    i = 0   j = 0
word1 =      word2 =
```

The count of the number of input values is 1, corresponding to a value for the variable fp1 being read. The count of the number of bytes read is zero, which is clearly incorrect, the reason being that we never got to store a value in byte_count. The A in the input stream is invalid in numerical input, and so the whole process stops dead. No values for variables i and j, word1 and word2, are processed, and no value is stored for the byte count. This demonstrates how unforgiving scanf() really is. A single invalid character in the input stream will stop your program in its tracks. If you want to be able to recover from the situation in which invalid input is entered, you can use the return value from scanf() as a measure of whether all the necessary input has been processed correctly and include some code to retrieve the situation when necessary.

The simplest approach would perhaps be to print an irritable message and then demand the whole input be repeated. But beware of errors in your code getting you into a permanent loop in this circumstance. You'll need to think through all of the possible ways that things might go wrong if you're going to produce a robust program.

You could also read the input using wscanf(). The only difference is that you must specify the format string to be a wide character string:

```
value_count = wscanf(L"%f %d %d %[abcdefghijklmnopqrstuvwxyz] %*1d %s%n",
                     &fp1, &i , &j, word1, word2, &byte_count);
```

For this statement to compile, you need an #include directive for the <wchar.h> header file. The L prefix specifies in the first argument the string constant to be a wide character string, so it will occupy twice as much memory as a regular string. You would probably only use wscanf() if you were using wide character strings in your program, and in this case you would also be storing the strings read as wide character strings. Here's a fragment that illustrates how you could read strings as wide character strings:

```
wchar_t wword1[SIZE] = L" ";
wchar_t wword2[SIZE] = L" ";
value_count = wscanf(L"%l[abcdefghijklmnopqrstuvwxyz] %*1d %ls%n",
                     wword1, wword2, &byte_count);
printf("\nwword1 = %ls   wword2 = %ls\n", wword1, wword2);
```

Here you have two arrays that store elements of type wchar_t to hold the strings. The type specifiers in the format string for the two strings have l (lowercase L) as the prefix so the input is read as wide character strings. If you enter **ready2go**, then ready and go will be stored in wword1 and wword2 as wide character strings and the 2 between them will be discarded, as in the example. To output the strings, the printf() function uses %ls as the format specification, because the function needs to know they are wide character strings. If you were to use %s, the output would be incorrect. You could try it to see what you get.

Characters in the Input Format String

You can include a sequence of one or more characters that isn't a format conversion specifier within the input format string. If you do this, you're indicating that you expect the same characters to appear in the input and that the scanf() function should read them but not store them. These have to be matched exactly, character for character, by the data in the input stream. Any variation will terminate the input scanning process in scanf().

TRY IT OUT: CHARACTERS IN THE INPUT FORMAT STRING

You can illustrate the effect of including characters in the input format string with the following example:

```
/* Program 10.2 Characters in the format control string */
#include <stdio.h>

int main(void)
{
  int i = 0;
  int j = 0;
  int value_count = 0;
  float fp1 = 0.0;

  printf("Input:\n");
  value_count = scanf("fp1 = %f i = %d %d", &fp1, &i , &j);

  printf("\nOutput:\n");
  printf("\nCount of values read = %d", value_count);
  printf("\nfp1 = %f\ti = %d\tj = %d\n", fp1, i, j);
  return 0;
}
```

Here's an example of the output:

```
Input:
fp1 = 3.14159 i = 7 8

Output:

Count of values read = 3
fp1 = 3.141590  i = 7   j = 8
```

How It Works

It doesn't matter whether the blanks before and after the = are included in the input—they're whitespace characters and are therefore ignored. The important thing is to include the same characters that appear in the format control string in the correct sequence and at the correct place in the input. Try an input line in which this isn't the case:

```
Input:
fp1 = 3.14159 i = 7 j = 8

Output:

Count of values read = 2
fp1 = 3.141590  i = 7   j = 0
```

Now only two values are read. This is because the character j in the input stops processing immediately, and no value is received by the variable j. The input processing of characters by scanf() is also case sensitive. If you input Fp1= instead of fp1=, no values will be processed at all, because the mismatch with the capital F will stop scanning before any values are entered.

Variations on Floating-Point Input

When you're reading floating-point values formatted using scanf(), you not only have a choice of specification that you use, but also you can enter the values in a variety of forms. You can see this with a simple example.

TRY IT OUT: FLOATING-POINT INPUT

With this example you can try various forms of specifier and various ways in which you can enter the input values.

```
/* Program 10.3 Floating-Point Input */
#include <stdio.h>

int main(void)
{
  float fp1 = 0.0f;
  float fp2 = 0.0f;
  float fp3 = 0.0f;
  int value_count = 0;

  printf("Input:\n");
  value_count = scanf("%f %f %f", &fp1, &fp2, &fp3);

  printf("\nOutput:\n");
  printf("Return value = %d", value_count);
  printf("\nfp1 = %f   fp2 = %f   fp3 = %f\n", fp1, fp2, fp3);
  return 0;
}
```

Here's an example of output from this program with the same input value written three different ways:

```
Input:
3.14.314E1.0314e+02

Output:
Return value = 3
fp1 = 3.140000  fp2 = 3.140000  fp3 = 3.140000
```

How It Works

This example demonstrates three different ways of entering the same value. The first way is a straightforward decimal value, the second has an exponent value defined by the E1 that indicates that the value is to be multiplied by 10, and the third has an exponent value of e+02 and therefore is to be multiplied by 100. As you can see, when you're reading a floating-point value with the "%f" specification, you have the option of whether to include an exponent. If you do include an exponent, you can define it beginning with either an e or an E. You also have the option to include a sign for the exponent value, + or -, and, of course, the value can be signed too. There are countless variations possible here.

You could try changing the scanf() statement to the following:

```
value_count = scanf("%e %g %f", &fp1, &fp2, &fp3);
```

Here's the output with this statement in the program:

```
Input:
3.14.314E1.0314e+02

Output:
Return value = 3
fp1 = 3.140000  fp2 = 3.140000  fp3 = 3.140000
```

Clearly all three format specifications work equally well with the various input forms. The variation between these is only when you use them for output with the printf() function.

I recommend that you experiment with the various possibilities here. In particular, try experimenting with floating-point numbers and the field-width specifiers for reading integers.

Reading Hexadecimal and Octal Values

As you saw earlier, you can read hexadecimal values from the input stream using the format specifier %x. For octal values you use %o. These are very straightforward, but let's see them working in an example.

TRY IT OUT: READING HEXADECIMAL AND OCTAL VALUES

Try the following example:

```
/* Program 10.4 Reading hexadecimal and octal values */
#include <stdio.h>

int main(void)
{
  int i = 0;
```

```
  int j = 0;
   int k = 0;
   int n = 0;

   printf("Input:\n");
   n = scanf(" %d %x %o", &i , &j, &k );

   printf("\nOutput:\n");
   printf("%d values read.", n);
   printf("\ni = %d   j = %d   k = %d\n", i, j, k );
   return 0;
}
```

Here's some sample output:

```
Input:
12 12 12

Output:
3 values read.
i = 12   j = 18   k = 10
```

How It Works

You read the three values entered as 12. The first is read with a decimal format specifier %d, the second with a hexadecimal format specifier %x, and the third with an octal format specifier %o. The output shows that 12 in hexadecimal is 18 in decimal notation, whereas 12 in octal is 10 in decimal notation.

Hexadecimal data entry can be useful when you want to enter bit patterns (sequences of 1s and 0s), as they're easier to specify in hexadecimal than in decimal. Each hexadecimal digit corresponds to 4 bits, so you can specify a 16-bit word as four hexadecimal digits. Octal is hardly ever used, and it appears here mainly for historical reasons.

Note the following example of output:

```
Input:
18 18 18

Output:
3 values read.
i = 18   j = 24   k = 1
```

Here, the first two values are read correctly as 18, as a hexadecimal value is indeed 24 in decimal notation. However, the third value is read as 1. This is because 8 isn't a legal octal digit. Octal digits are 0 to 7.

You can enter hexadecimal values using A to F, or a to f, or even a mixture if you're so inclined. Here's another example of output:

```
Input:
12 aA 17

Output:
3 values read.
i = 12   j = 170   k = 15
```

The value aA is 10 × 16 + 10, which is 170 as a decimal value. The octal value 17 is 1 × 8 + 7, which is 15 as a decimal value.

There's no difference between using "%x" and "%X" with scanf(), but they'll have a different effect when you use them with printf() for output. You can demonstrate this by changing the last printf() statement to the following:

```
printf("\ni = %x   j = %X   k = %d\n", i, j, k );
```

This now outputs the first two values in hexadecimal notation. You can get the following output with the input shown:

```
Input:
26 AE 77

Output:
3 values read.
i = 1a   j = AE   k = 63
```

So "%x" produces hexadecimal output using hexadecimal digits a to e, and "%X" produces output using hexadecimal digits A to E.

Reading Characters Using scanf()

You tried reading strings in the first example, but there are more possibilities. You know that there are three format specifiers for reading one or more single-byte characters. You can read a single character and store it as type char using the format specifier %c and as type wchar_t using %lc. For a string of characters, you use either the specifier %s or the specifier %[ ], or if you are storing the input as wide characters, %ls or %l[ ], where the prefix to the conversion specification is lowercase L. In this case, the string is stored as a null-terminated string with '\0' as the last character. With %[ ] or %l[ ] format specification, the string to be read must include only the characters that appear between the square brackets, or if the first character between the square brackets is ^, the string must contain only characters that are *not* among those following the ^ characters. Thus, %[aeiou] will read a string that consists only of vowels. The first character that isn't a vowel will signal the end of the string. The specification %[^aeiou] reads a string that contains any character that isn't a vowel. The first vowel will signal the end of the string.

Note that one interesting aspect of the %[ ] specification is it enables you to read a string containing spaces, something that the %s specification can't do. You just need to include a space as one of the characters between the square brackets.

TRY IT OUT: READING CHARACTERS AND STRINGS

You can see these character-reading capabilities in operation with the following example:

```
/* Program 10.5 Reading characters with scanf() */
#include <stdio.h>

int main(void)
{
  char initial = ' ';
  char name[80] = { 0 };
```

```
  char age[4] = { 0 };
  printf("Enter your first initial: ");
  scanf("%c", &initial );
  printf("Enter your first name: " );
  scanf("%s", name );

  if(initial  != name[0])
    printf("\n%s,you got your initial wrong.", name);
  else
    printf("\nHi, %s. Your initial is correct. Well done!", name );
  printf("\nEnter your full name and your age separated by a comma:\n" );
  scanf("%[^,] , %[0123456789]", name, age );
  printf("\nYour name is %s and you are %s years old\n", name, age );
  return 0;
}
```

Here's some output from this program:

```
Enter your first initial: I
Enter your first name: Ivor

Hi, Ivor. Your initial is correct. Well done!
Enter your full name and your age separated by a comma:
Ivor Horton     ,  99

Your name is
Ivor Horton       and you are 99 years old
```

How It Works

This program first expects you to enter your first initial and then your first name. It checks that the first letter of your name is the same as the initial you entered. This works in a straightforward way, as you can see from the output.

Next, you're asked to enter your full name followed by your age, separated by a comma. The read operation is carried out by the following statement:

```
scanf("%[^,] , %[0123456789]", name, age );
```

I deliberately spaced out the input data so you could see that the first input specification, %[^,], reads any character as part of the string that isn't a comma, including spaces. Hence the extra spaces following the name in the last line of output. You then have a comma in the control string that will cause scanf() to read the comma (or several commas in succession) in the input and not store it. The input for age is read as a string with the specifier %[0123456789]. This will read any sequence of consecutive digits as a string.

Note that the comma in the input string is essential for the input to be read properly. If you leave it out, scanf() will attempt to read the comma as part of the input for age. Because a comma is evidently not a digit, this will stop input for age so it will just consist of an empty string.

If you try entering a space and then your initial as the first input, the program will treat the blank as the value for initial and the single character you entered as your name. With the way the control string is defined, the first character that you enter when using the %c specifier is taken to be the character, whatever it is. If you don't want a space to be accepted as the initial, you can fix this by writing the input statement as follows:

```
scanf(" %c", &initial );
```

Now the first character in the control string is a space, so scanf() will read and ignore any number of spaces and read the first character that isn't a space into initial.

Pitfalls with scanf()

There are two very common mistakes people make when using scanf() that you should keep in mind:

! Don't forget that the arguments *must* be pointers. Perhaps the most common error is to forget the ampersand (&) when specifying single variables as arguments to scanf(), particularly because you don't need it with printf(). Of course, the & isn't necessary if the argument is an array name or a pointer variable.

! When reading a string, remember to ensure that there's enough space for the string to be read in, *plus* the terminating '\0'. If you don't do this, you'll overwrite something in memory, possibly even some of your program code.

String Input from the Keyboard

As you've seen, the gets() function in <stdio.h> will read a complete line of text as a string. The prototype of the function is as follows:

```
char *gets(char *str);
```

This function reads successive characters into the memory pointed to by str until you press the Enter key. It appends the terminating null, '\0', in place of the newline character that is read when you press the Enter key. The return value is identical to the argument, which is the address where the string has been stored. The following example provides a reminder of how it works.

TRY IT OUT: READING A STRING WITH GETS()

Here's a simple program using gets():

```
/* Program 10.6 Reading a string with gets() */
#include <stdio.h>

int main(void)
{
  char initial[2] = {0};
  char name[80] = {0};

  printf("Enter your first initial:  ");
  gets(initial);
  printf("Enter your name:  " );
  gets(name);
  if(initial[0] != name[0])
    printf("\n%s,you got your initial wrong.\n", name);
  else
    printf("\nHi, %s. Your initial is correct. Well done!\n", name);
  return 0;
}
```

Here's some output from this program:

```
Enter your first initial:  M
Enter your name:  Mephistopheles

Hi, Mephistopheles. Your initial is correct. Well done!
```

How It Works

You read the initial and the name as strings using gets(). The function is very easy to use because there's no format specification involved. Because gets() will read characters until you press Enter, you can now enter your full name if you wish.

Of course, the downside to using gets() is that you have no control over how many characters are stored. This implies that you must be sure to create an array to receive the data with sufficient space for the maximum length string that might be entered. Where you want to be sure that your array length will not be exceeded, you have the option of using the fgets() function. You could replace the statements that manage the input with the following:

```
printf("Enter your first initial: ");
fgets(initial, sizeof(initial), stdin);      /* Read 1 character max        */
fflush(stdin);                               /* Flush the newline           */

printf("Enter your name: " );
fgets(name, sizeof(name), stdin);            /* Read max name-1 characters */
size_t length = strlen(name);
name[length-1] = name[length];               /* Overwrite the newline       */
```

The fgets() function will read up to one less than the number of characters specified by the second argument and append the terminating '\0'. This ensures that the length of the array you pass as the first argument is not exceeded. You need to remember that the fgets() function stores a newline character in the input string corresponding to the Enter key being pressed, whereas the gets() function does not. With the first read operation, the newline will be left in the input buffer so the call to fflush() will flush stdin and remove it. Without this, the newline would be read as the input for name. The last character before the null in name will be the newline character, so copying the terminating null one position back will overwrite it.

For string input, using gets() or fgets() is usually the preferred approach unless you want to control the content of the string, in which case you can use %[]. The %[] specification is more convenient to use when the nonstandard %[a-z] form is supported, but remember, because this is nonstandard, your code is no longer as portable as it is if you use the standard form for reading a string of lowercase letters, %[abcdefghijklmnopqrstuvwxyz].

Unformatted Input from the Keyboard

The getchar()function reads one character at a time from stdin. The getchar() function is defined in <stdio.h>, and its general syntax is as follows:

```
int getchar(void);
```

The getchar() function requires no arguments, and it returns the character read from the input stream. Note that this character is returned as int, and the character is displayed on the screen as it is entered from the keyboard.

With many implementations of C, the nonstandard header file <conio.h> is often included. This provides additional functions for character input and output. One of the most useful of these is getch(), which reads a character from the keyboard without displaying it on the screen. This is particularly useful when you need to prevent others from being able to see what's being keyed in! for example, when a password is being entered.

The standard header <stdio.h> also declares the ungetc() function that enables you to put a character that you have just read back into an input stream. The function requires two arguments: the first is the character to be pushed back onto the stream, and the second is the identifier for the stream, which would be stdin for the standard input stream. The ungetc() returns a value of type int that corresponds to the character pushed back onto the stream, or a special character, EOF (end-of-file), if the operation fails.

In principle you can push a succession of characters back into an input stream but only one character is guaranteed. As I noted, a failure to push a character back onto a stream will be indicated by EOF being returned by the function, so you should check for this if you are attempting to return several characters to a stream.

The ungetc() function is useful when you are reading input character by character and don't know how many characters make up a data unit. You might be reading an integer value, for example, but don't know how many digits there are. In this situation the ungetc() function makes it possible for you to read a succession of characters using getchar(), and when you find you have read a character that is not a digit, you can return it to the stream. Here's a function that ignores spaces and tabs from the standard input stream using the getchar() and ungetc() functions:

```
void eatspaces(void)
{
  char ch = 0;
  while(isspace(ch = getchar()));   /* Read as long as there are spaces */
  ungetc(ch, stdin);               /* Put back the nonspace character */
}
```

The isspace() function that is declared in the <ctype.h> header file returns true when the argument is a space character. The while loop continues to read characters as long as they are spaces or tabs, storing each character in ch. The first nonspace character that is read will end the loop, and the character will be left in ch. The call to ungetc() returns the nonblank character back to the stream for future processing.

Let's try out the getchar() and ungetc() functions in a working example.

TRY IT OUT: READING AND UNREADING CHARACTERS

This example will assume the input from the keyboard consists of some arbitrary sequence of integers and names:

```
/* Program 10.7 Reading and unreading characters */
#include <stdio.h>
#include <ctype.h>
#include <stdbool.h>
#include <string.h>

const size_t LENGTH = 50;

/* Function prototypes */
void eatspaces(void);
bool getinteger(int *n);
char *getname(char *name, size_t length);
bool isnewline(void);

int main(void)
```

```
{
  int number;
  char name[LENGTH];
  printf("Enter a sequence of integers and alphabetic names:\n");
  while(!isnewline())
    if(getinteger(&number))
      printf("\nInteger value:%8d", number);
    else if(strlen(getname(name, LENGTH)) > 0)
      printf("\nName: %s", name);
    else
    {
      printf("\nInvalid input.");
      return 1;
    }
  return 0;
}

/* Function to check for newline */
bool isnewline(void)
{
  char ch = 0;
  if((ch = getchar()) == '\n')
    return true;

  ungetc(ch, stdin);
  return false;
}

/* Function to ignore spaces from standard input */
void eatspaces(void)
{
  char ch = 0;
  while(isspace(ch = getchar()));
  ungetc(ch, stdin);
}

/* Function to read an integer from standard input */
bool getinteger(int *n)
{
  eatspaces();
  int value = 0;
  int sign = 1;
  char ch = 0;

  /* Check first character */
  if((ch=getchar()) == '-')              /* should be minus */
    sign = -1;
  else if(isdigit(ch))                   /* ...or a digit   */
   value = 10*value + (ch - '0');
  else  if(ch != '+')                    /* ...or plus      */
  {
    ungetc(ch, stdin);
    return false;                        /* Not an integer  */
  }
```

```
  /* Find more digits */
  while(isdigit(ch = getchar()))
    value = 10*value + (ch - '0');

  /* Push back first nondigit character */
  ungetc(ch,stdin);
  *n = value*sign;
  return true;
}

/* Function to read an alphabetic name from input */
char *getname(char *name, size_t length)
{

  eatspaces();                          /* Remove leading spaces */
  size_t count = 0;
  char ch = 0;
  while(isalpha(ch=getchar()))          /* As long as there are letters */
  {
    name[count++] = ch;                 /* store them in name          */
    if(count == length-1)
      break;
  }

  name[count] = '\0';                   /* Append string terminator    */
  if(count < length-1)
    ungetc(ch, stdin);                  /* Return nonletter to stream  */
  return name;
}
```

Here's an example of output from the program:

```
Enter a sequence of integers and alphabetic names:
12              Jack Jim   234 Jo Janet 99   88

Integer value:     12
Name: Jack
Name: Jim
Integer value:     234
Name: Jo
Name: Janet
Integer value:     99
Integer value:     88
```

Here's another sample:

```
Enter a sequence of integers and alphabetic names:
Jim     Jo Will Bert

Name: Jim
Name: Jo
Name: Will
Name: Bert
```

How It Works

There are four functions using the getchar() and ungetc() functions to read from stdin. You saw the eatspaces() function in the previous section. The isnewline() function just reads a character from the keyboard and returns true if it is a newline character. This function is used to control when input ends in main().

The getinteger() function reads an integer of arbitrary length from the keyboard that is optionally preceded by a sign. The first step is to remove leading spaces by calling the eatspaces() function. After checking for a sign or the first digit, the function continues to read digits from the keyboard in a loop:

```
while(isdigit(ch = getchar()))
    value = 10*value + (ch - '0');
```

The digits are read from left to right, so the latest digit is the low-order digit in the number. The digit value is obtained by subtracting the code value for the 0 digit from the code value for the current digit. This works because the code values for digits are in ascending sequence. To insert the digit, you multiply the current accumulated value by 10 and add the new digit value. Of course, storing the result as type int is a constraint. You could implement the function to store the value as type long long to accommodate a wider range of values. You could also include code to check for how large the number is getting and to output an error message if it cannot be stored as type int.

The first character read that is not a digit ends the loop, and this character is returned to the stream so that it can be read again.

The getname() function reads an alphabetic name from the keyboard. The arguments are an array in which the name is to be stored, and the length of the array so the function can ensure the capacity is not exceeded. The function returns the address of the first byte of the string as a convenience to the calling program. The process is, in principle, the same as the getinteger() function. The function continues to read characters in a loop as long as they are alphabetic characters:

```
while(isalpha(ch=getchar()))          /* As long as there are letters */
{
    name[count++] = ch;               /* store them in name           */
    if(count == length-1)
      break;
}
```

The count variable tracks the number of characters stored in the name array, and when only one element is still free, the loop ends. After the loop, the code appends a '\0' to terminate the string. Of course, the last character read will have been alphabetic and therefore stored in the array if the value of count reaches length-1. You therefore only restore the last character back to the stream by calling ungetc() when this is not the case.

The main() function reads an arbitrary sequence of names and integers in a loop:

```
while(!isnewline())
  if(getinteger(&number))
    printf("\nInteger value:%8d", number);
  else if(strlen(getname(name, LENGTH)) > 0)
    printf("\nName: %s", name);
  else
  {
    printf("\nInvalid input.");
    return 1;
  }
}
```

The loop continues as long as the current character is not a newline signaling the end of the current line. The program expects to read either an integer or a name on each loop iteration. The loop first tries to read an integer by calling the getinteger() function. This function returns false if an integer is not found, in which case the getname() function is called to read a name. If no name is found, the input is neither a name nor an integer, so the program ends after outputting a message.

Output to the Screen

Writing data to the command line on the screen is much easier than reading input from the keyboard. You know what data you're writing, whereas with input you have all the vagaries of possible incorrect entry of the data. The primary function for formatted output to the stdout stream is printf().

Fortunately! or unfortunately, depending how you view the chore of getting familiar with this stuff! printf() provides myriad possible variations for the output you can obtain, much more than the scope of the format specifiers associated with scanf().

Formatted Output to the Screen Using printf()

The printf() function is defined in the header file <stdio.h>, and its general form is the following:

```
int printf(char *format, ...);
```

The first parameter is the format control string. The argument for this parameter is usually passed to the function as an explicit string constant, as you've seen in all the examples, but it can be a pointer to a string that you specify elsewhere. The optional arguments to the function are the values to be output in sequence, and they must correspond in number and type with the format conversion specifiers that appear in the string that is passed as the first argument. Of course, as you've also seen in earlier examples, if the output is simply the text that appears in the control string, there are no additional arguments after the first. But where there are argument values to be output, there must be *at least* as many arguments as there are format specifiers. If not, the results are unpredictable. If there are *more* arguments than specifiers, the excess is ignored. This is because the function uses the format string as the determinant of how many arguments follow and what type they have.

■Note The fact that the format string alone determines how the data is interpreted is the reason why you get the wrong result with a %d specifier combined with a long long argument.

The <stdio.h> header also declares the wprintf() function. Analogous to the situation you saw with scanf(), the wprintf() function works in exactly the same way as printf() except that it expects the first argument to be a wide character string. The format specifications are exactly the same for both functions.

The format conversion specifiers for printf() and wprintf() are a little more complicated than those you use for input with scanf() and wscanf(). The general form of an output format specifier is shown in Figure 10-3.

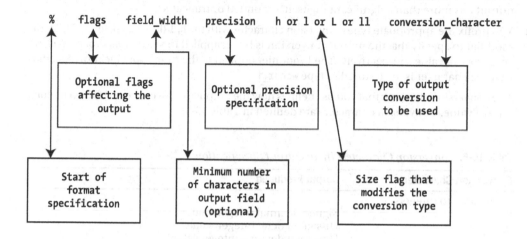

Figure 10-3. *Format specifications for the printf() and wprintf() functions*

You've seen most of the details before, but let's take a quick pass through the elements of this general format specifier:

! The % sign indicates the start of the specifier, as it does for output.

! The optional flag characters are +, -, #, and space. These affect the output, as shown in Table 10-4.

Table 10-4. *Effects of the Optional Flag Characters in an Output Specification*

Character	Use
+	Ensures that, for signed output values, there's always a sign preceding the output value! either a plus or a minus sign. By default, only negative values have a sign.
-	Specifies that the output value is left-justified in the output field and padded with blanks on the right. The default positioning of the output is right-justified.
0	Prefixes a field_width value to specify that the value should be padded with zeros to fill out the field width to the left.
#	Specifies that 0 is to precede an octal output value, 0x; or 0X is to precede a hexadecimal output value; or a floating-point output value will contain a decimal point. For the g or G floating-point conversion characters, trailing zeros will also be omitted.
space	Specifies that positive or zero output values are preceded by a space rather than a plus sign.

! The optional field_width specifies the minimum number of characters for the output value. If the value requires more characters, the field is simply expanded. If it requires less than the minimum specified, it is padded with blanks, unless the field width is specified with a leading zero, as in 09, for example, where it would be filled on the left with zeros.

! The precision specifier is also optional and is generally used with floating-point output values. A specifier of .n indicates that n decimal places are to be output. If the value to be output has more than n significant digits, it's rounded or truncated.

! You prefix the appropriate type conversion character with the h, l (lowercase letter *L*), ll, or L modifier to specify that the output conversion is being applied to short, long, long long, or long double values, respectively. The l modifier applied to the c type specification specifies that the character is to be stored as type wchar_t.

! The conversion character that you use defines how the output is to be converted for a particular type of value. Conversion characters are defined in Table 10-5.

Table 10-5. *Conversion Characters in an Output Specification*

Conversion Character	Output Produced
Applicable to integers	
d	Signed decimal integer value
o	Unsigned octal integer value
u	Unsigned decimal integer value
x	Unsigned hexadecimal integer value with lowercase hexadecimal digits a, b, c, d, e, f
X	As x but with uppercase hexadecimal digits A, B, C, D, E, F
Applicable to floating-point	
f	Signed decimal value
e	Signed decimal value with exponent
E	As e but with E for exponent instead of e
g	As e or f depending on size of value and precision
G	As g but with E for exponent values
Applicable to characters	
c	Single character
s	All characters until '\0' is reached or precision characters have been output

Believe it or not, this set of output options includes only the most important ones. If you consult the documentation accompanying your compiler, you'll find a few more.

Escape Sequences

You can include whitespace characters in the format control string for printf() and wprintf(). The characters that are referred to as whitespace are the newline, carriage return, and form-feed characters; blank (a space); and tab. Some of these are represented by escape sequences that begin with \. Table 10-6 shows the most common escape sequences.

You use the escape sequence \\ in format control strings when you want to output the backslash character \. If this weren't the case, it would be impossible to output a backslash, because it would always be assumed that a backslash was the start of an escape sequence. To write a % character to stdout, use %%. You can't use % by itself as this would be interpreted as the start of a format specification.

Table 10-6. *Common Escape Sequences*

Escape Sequence	Description
\a	Bell sound (a beep on your computer not used much these days)
\b	Backspace
\f	Form-feed or page eject
\n	Newline
\r	Carriage return (for printers) or move to the beginning of the current line for output to the screen
\t	Horizontal tab

■**Note** Of course, you can use escape sequences within any string, not just in the context of the format string for the printf() function.

Integer Output

Let's take a look at some of the variations that you haven't made much use of so far. Those with field width and precision specifiers are probably the most interesting.

TRY IT OUT: OUTPUTTING INTEGERS

Let's try a sample of integer output formats first:

```
/* Program 10.8 Integer output variations */
#include <stdio.h>

int main(void)
{
  int i = 15;
  int j = 345;
  int k = 4567;
  long li = 56789L;
  long lj = 678912L;
  long lk = 23456789L;

  printf("\ni = %d    j = %d    k = %d    i = %6.3d    j = %6.3d    k = %6.3d\n",
                                   i ,j, k, i, j, k);
  printf("\ni = %-d    j = %+d    k = %-d    i = %-6.3d    j = %-6.3d    k ="
                       " %-6.3d\n",i ,j, k, i, j, k);
  printf("\nli = %d    lj = %d    lk = %d\n", li, lj, lk);
  printf("\nli = %ld    lj = %ld    lk = %ld\n", li, lj, lk);
  return 0;
}
```

When you execute this example, you should see something like this:

```
i = 15    j = 345    k = 4567    i =     015    j =      345    k =     4567

i = 15    j = +345    k = 4567    i = 015        j = 345        k = 4567

li = -8747    lj = 23552    lk = -5099

li = 56789    lj = 678912    lk = 23456789
```

How It Works

This example illustrates a miscellany of options for integer output. You can see the effects of the - flag by comparing the first two lines produced by these statements:

```
printf("\ni = %d    j = %d    k = %d    i = %6.3d    j = %6.3d    k = %6.3d\n",
                                i ,j, k, i, j, k);
printf("\ni = %-d    j = %+d    k = %-d    i = %-6.3d    j = %-6.3d    k ="
                    " %-6.3d\n",i ,j, k, i, j, k);
```

The - flag causes the output to be left-justified. The effect of the field width specifier is also apparent from the spacing of the last three outputs in each group of six. Note that the default width provides just enough output positions to accommodate the number of digits to be output, so the - flag has no effect.

You get a leading plus in the output of j on the second line because of the flag modifier. You can use more than one flag modifier if you want. With the second output of the value of i, you have a leading 0 inserted due to the minimum precision being specified as 3. You could also have obtained leading zeroes by preceding the minimum width value with a 0 in the format specification.

The third output line is produced by the following statement:

```
printf("\nli = %d    lj = %d    lk = %d\n", li, lj, lk);
```

Here, you can see that failure to insert the l (lowercase letter L) modifier when outputting integers of type long results in apparent garbage, because the output value is assumed to be a 2-byte integer. Of course, if your system implements type int as a 4-byte integer, the values will be correct here. The problem arises only if long and int are differentiated. You should get a warning from your compiler if there is a mismatch. The same problem can arise when you use the wrong type conversion when outputting values of type long long.

You get the correct values from this statement:

```
printf("\nli = %ld    lj = %ld    lk = %ld\n", li, lj, lk);
```

It's unwise to specify inadequate values for the width and the precision of the values to be displayed. Weird and wonderful results may be produced if you do. Try experimenting with this example to see just how much variation you can get.

TRY IT OUT: VARIATIONS ON A SINGLE INTEGER

You'll try one more integer example to run the gamut of possibilities with a single integer value:

```
/* Program 10.9 Variations on a single integer */
#include <stdio.h>

int main(void)
{
  int k = 678;

  printf("%%d    %%o    %%x    %%X");  /* Display format as heading */
  printf("\n%d  %o  %x  %X", k, k, k, k );      /* Display values */

  /* Display format as heading then display the values */
  printf("\n\n%%8d       %%-8d       %%+8d       %%08d       %%-+8d");
  printf("\n%8d  %-8d  %-+8d  %08d  %-+8d\n", k, k, k, k, k );
  return 0;
}
```

How It Works

This program may look a little confusing at first because the first of each pair of `printf()` statements displays the format used to output the number appearing immediately below. The %% specifier simply outputs the % character.

When you execute this example, you should get something like this:

%d	%o	%x	%X		
678	1246	2a6	2A6		
%8d		%-8d	%+8d	%08d	%-+8d
678		678	+678	00000678	+678

The first row of output values is produced by this statement:

```
printf("\n%d  %o  %x  %X", k, k, k, k );      /* Display values */
```

The outputs are decimal, octal, and two varieties of hexadecimal for the value 678, with the default width specification. The corresponding format appears above each value in the output.

The next row of output values is produced by this:

```
printf("\n%8d  %-8d  %-+8d  %08d  %-+8d\n", k, k, k, k, k );
```

This statement includes a variety of flag settings with a width specification of 8. The first is the default right-justification in the field. The second is left-justified because of the - flag. The third has a sign because of the + flag. The fourth has leading zeroes because the width is specified as 08 instead of 8, and it also has a sign because of the + flag. The last output value uses a specifier with all the trimmings, %-+8d, so the output is left-justified in the field and also has a leading sign.

Tip When you're outputting multiple rows of values on the screen, using a width specification—possibly with tabs—will enable you to line them up in columns.

Outputting Floating-Point Values

If plowing through the integer options hasn't started you nodding off, then take a quick look at the floating-point output options through working examples.

TRY IT OUT: OUTPUTTING FLOATING-POINT VALUES

Look at the following example:

```
/* Program 10.10 Outputting floating-point values */
 #include <stdio.h>

int main(void)
{
  float fp1 = 345.678f;
  float fp2 = 1.234E6f;
  double fp3 = 234567898.0;
  double fp4 = 11.22334455e-6;

  printf("\n%f  %+f  %-10.4f  %6.4f\n", fp1, fp2, fp1, fp2);
  printf("\n%e  %+E\n", fp1, fp2);
  printf("\n%f  %g  %#+f  %8.4f  %10.4g\n", fp3,fp3, fp3, fp3, fp4);
  return 0;
}
```

How It Works

With my compiler, I get this output:

345.678009	+1234000.000000 345.6780		1234000.0000
3.456780e+002	+1.234000E+006		
234567898.000000	2.34568e+008	+234567898.000000	234567898.0000

1.122e-005

It's possible that you may not get exactly the same output, but it should be close. Most of the output is a straightforward demonstration of the effects of the format conversion specifiers that I've discussed, but a few points are noteworthy.

The value of the first output for fp1 differs slightly from the value that you assigned to the variable. This is typical of the kind of small difference that can creep in when floating-point numbers are converted from decimal to binary. With fractional decimal values, there isn't always an exact equivalent in binary floating-point.

In the output generated by the statement

```
printf("\n%f  %+f  %-10.4f  %6.4f\n", fp1, fp2, fp1, fp2);
```

the second output value for fp1 shows how the number of decimal places after the point can be constrained. The output in this case is left-justified in the field. The second output of fp2 has a field width specified that is too small for the number of decimal places required and is therefore overridden.

The second printf() statement is as follows:

```
printf("\n%e  %+E\n", fp1, fp2);
```

This outputs the same values in floating-point format with an exponent. Whether you get an uppercase E or a lowercase e for the exponent indicator depends on how you write the format specifier.

In the last line, you can see how the g-specified output of fp3 has been rounded up compared to the f specified output.

■Note There are a huge number of possible variations for the output obtainable with `printf()`. It would be very educational for you to play around with the options, trying various ways of outputting the same information.

Character Output

Now that you've looked at the various possibilities for outputting numbers, let's have a look at outputting characters. There are basically four flavors of output specifications you can use with printf() and wprintf() for character data: %c and %s for single characters and strings, and %lc and %ls for single wide characters and wide character strings, respectively. You have seen how to use %s and %ls, so let's just try out single character output in an example.

TRY IT OUT: OUTPUTTING CHARACTER DATA

This example outputs all the printable characters, then all the lower and uppercase letters:

```
/* Program 10.11 Outputting character data */
#include <stdio.h>
#include <limits.h>
#include <wchar.h>
#include <ctype.h>
#include <wctype.h>

int main(void)
{
  int count = 0;
  char ch = 0;
  printf("\nThe printable characters are the following:\n");

  /* Iterate over all values of type char */
  for(int code = 0 ; code <= CHAR_MAX ; code++)
  {
    ch = (char)code;
    if(isprint(ch))
    {
      if(count++ % 32 == 0)
        printf("\n");
      printf("%c", ch);
    }
  }
```

```
/* Use wprintf() to output wide characters */
count = 0;
wchar_t wch = 0;
wprintf(
    L"\n\nThe alphabetic characters and their codes are the following:\n");

/* Iterate over the lowercase wide character letters */
for(wchar_t wch = L'a' ; wch <= L'z' ; wch++)
{
  if(count++ % 3 == 0)
    wprintf(L"\n");

  wprintf(L" %lc    %#x    %lc    %#x", wch, (long)wch, towupper(wch),
                                              (long)towupper(wch));

}
  return 0;
}
```

The output from this program is the following:

The printable characters are the following:

```
 !"#$%&'()*+,-./0123456789:;<=>?
@ABCDEFGHIJKLMNOPQRSTUVWXYZ[\]^_
`abcdefghijklmnopqrstuvwxyz{|}~
```

The alphabetic characters and their codes are the following:

a	0x61	A	0x41	b	0x62	B	0x42 c	0x63	C	0x43
d	0x64	D	0x44	e	0x65	E	0x45 f	0x66	F	0x46
g	0x67	G	0x47	h	0x68	H	0x48 i	0x69	I	0x49
j	0x6a	J	0x4a	k	0x6b	K	0x4b l	0x6c	L	0x4c
m	0x6d	M	0x4d	n	0x6e	N	0x4e o	0x6f	O	0x4f
p	0x70	P	0x50	q	0x71	Q	0x51 r	0x72	R	0x52
s	0x73	S	0x53	t	0x74	T	0x54 u	0x75	U	0x55
v	0x76	V	0x56	w	0x77	W	0x57 x	0x78	X	0x58
y	0x79	Y	0x59	z	0x7a	Z	0x5a			

How It Works

The first block of output for the printable characters is generated in the for loop:

```
for(int code = 0 ; code <= CHAR_MAX ; code++)
{
  ch = (char)code;
  if(isprint(ch))
  {
    if(count++ % 32 == 0)
      printf("\n");
    printf("%c", ch);
  }
}
```

First, note the type of the loop control variable, code. You might be tempted to use type char here but this would be a serious mistake, as the loop would run indefinitely. The reason for this is that the condition for ending the loop is checked after the value of code has been incremented. On the last good iteration, code has the value CHAR_MAX, which is the maximum value that can be stored as type char. If code is type char, when 1 is added to CHAR_MAX the result would be 0, so the loop would continue instead of ending as it should.

Within the loop you cast the value of code to type char and store the result in ch. The explicit cast is not required for the code to compile, as the compiler will insert the conversion, but it does indicate that it is intentional. You then use the isprint() function that is declared in the <ctype.h> header to test for a printable character. When isprint() returns true, you output the character using the %c format specification. You also arrange to output a newline character each time 32 characters have been output so that you don't have output just spilling arbitrarily from one line to the next.

The second loop uses the wprintf() function to output alphabetic wide characters and their character code values:

```
for(wchar_t wch = L'a' ; wch <= L'z' ; wch++)
{
  if(count++ % 3 == 0)
    wprintf(L"\n");

  wprintf(L" %lc    %#x    %lc    %#x", wch, (long)wch, towupper(wch),
                                        (long)towupper(wch));
}
```

This time you can use a loop control variable wch of type wchar_t that iterates over the code values from L'a' to L'z'. You use essentially the same trick as you used in the previous loop to output three success groups of output on each line. The wprintf() outputs the character using the %lc specification and the code value as %ld. To output the code value you cast the value stored in wch to type long and use the %ld format specification to display it. You use the towupper() function that is declared in the <wctype.h> header to get the uppercase equivalent of wch.

Don't forget, the only difference between the wprintf() and printf() functions is that the former requires the first argument to be a wide character string. All of the last output operation could be done just as well with printf(); you would just need to remove the L prefix from the format string that is the first argument.

Other Output Functions

In addition to the string output capabilities of printf() and wprintf(), you have the puts() function that is also declared in <stdio.h>, and which complements the gets() function. The name of the function derives from its purpose: **put** string. The general form of puts() is as follows:

```
int puts(const char *string);
```

The puts() function accepts a pointer to a string as an argument and writes the string to the standard output stream, stdout. The string must be terminated by '\0'. The parameter to puts() is const so the function does not modify the string you pass to it. The function returns a negative integer value if any errors occur on output, and a nonnegative value otherwise. The puts() function is very useful for outputting single-line messages, for example:

```
puts("Is there no end to input and output?");
```

This will output the string that is passed as the argument and then move the cursor to the next line. The function printf() requires an explicit '\n' to be included at the end of the string to do the same thing.

■ Note The function puts() will process embedded '\n' characters in the string you pass as the argument to generate output on multiple lines.

Unformatted Output to the Screen

Also included in <stdio.h>, and complementing the function getchar(), is the function putchar(). This has the following general form:

```
int putchar(int c);
```

The putchar() function outputs a single character, c, to stdout and returns the character that was displayed. This allows you to output a message one character at a time, which can make your programs a bit bigger, but gives you control over whether or not you output particular characters. For example, you could simply write the following to output a string:

```
char string[] = "Beware the Jabberwock, \nmy son!";
puts(string);
```

Alternatively, you could write:

```
char string[] = " Beware the Jabberwock, \nmy son!";
int i = 0;
while( string[i] != '\0')
  if(string[i] != '\n')
    putchar(string[i++]);
```

The first fragment outputs the string over two lines, like this:

```
Beware the Jabberwock,
my son!
```

The second fragment skips newline characters in the string so the output will be the following:

```
Beware the Jabberwock, my son!
```

Your use of putchar() need not be as simple as this. With putchar() you could choose to output a selected sequence of characters from the middle of a string bounded by a given delimiter, or you could selectively transform the occurrences of certain characters within a string before output, converting tabs to spaces, for example.

Formatted Output to an Array

You can write formatted data to an array of elements of type char in memory using the sprintf() function that is declared in the <stdio.h> header file. This function has the prototype:

```
int sprintf(char *str, const char *format, . . .);
```

The function writes the data specified by the third and subsequent arguments formatted according to the format string second argument. This works identically to printf() except that the data is written to the string specified by the first argument to the function. The integer returned is a count of the number of characters written to str, excluding the terminating null character.

Here's a fragment illustrating how this works:

```
char result[20];                    /* Output from sprintf */
int count = 4;
int nchars = sprintf(result, "A dog has %d legs.", count);
```

The effect of this is to write the value of count to result using the format string that is the second argument. The effect is that result will contain the string "A dog has 4 legs.". The variable nchars will contain the value 17, which is the same as the return value you would get from strlen(result) after the sprintf() call has executed. The sprintf() function will return a negative integer if an encoding error occurs during the operation.

One use for the sprintf() function is to create format strings programmatically. You'll see a simple example of this in Program12.8 in Chapter 12.

Formatted Input from an Array

The sscanf() function complements the sprintf() function because it enables you to read data under the control of a format string from an array of elements of type char. The prototype looks like this:

```
int sscanf(const char *str, const char *format, . . .);
```

Data will be read from str into variables that are specified by the third and subsequent arguments according to the format string format. The function returns a count of the number of items actually read, or EOF if a failure occurs before any data values are read and stored. The end of the string is recognized as the end-of-file condition, so reaching the end of the str string before any values are converted will cause EOF to be returned.

Here's a simple illustration of how the sscanf() function works:

```
char *source = "Fred 94";
char name[10];
int age = 0;
int items = sscanf(source, " %s %d", name, age);
```

The result of executing this fragment is that name will contain the string "Fred" and age will contain the value 94. The variable items will contain the value 2 because two items are read from source.

One use for the sscanf() function is to try various ways of reading the same data. You can always read an input line into an array as a string. You can then use sscanf() to reread the same input line from the array with different format strings as many times as you like.

Sending Output to the Printer

Writing to a printer is not part of standard C, but some C libraries do support it, so it's worth mentioning. To write output to the default printer, you can use a more generalized form of the printf() function called fprintf(). This function is designed to send formatted output to *any* stream, and more often to files on disk, but I'll stick to printing for now. For the purpose of printing, the general form for using fprintf() is as follows:

```
fprintf(stdprn, format_string, argument1, argument2, ..., argumentn);
```

The function will return a value of type int that is a count of the number of values that were sent to stdprn. With the exception of the first argument and the extra f in the function name, fprintf() looks exactly like printf(). And so it is. If you don't have stdprn defined with your compiler and library, you'll need to consult your documentation to see how to handle printing, but many C libraries do define stdprn. You can use the same format string with the same set of specifiers to output data to your printer in exactly the same way that you display results with printf(). However, there are a couple of minor variations you need to be aware of. I'll illustrate these in the next example.

TRY IT OUT: PRINTING ON A PRINTER

This program shows how you can get programs to output to a printer:

```
/* Program 10.12 Printing on a printer - where else? */
#include <stdio.h>
int main(void)
{
  fprintf(stdprn, "The barber shaves all those who do not"
                                      " shave themselves.");
  fprintf(stdprn, "\n\rQuestion: Who shaves the barber?\n\r");
  fprintf(stdprn, "\n\rAnswer: She doesn't need to shave.\f");
  return 0;
}
```

How It Works

The only oddities here are the new escape sequences \r and \f. The sequence \n\r is equivalent to newline/carriage return on a printer, and the \f is form-feed character, which produces a page eject on printers where this is necessary.

Summary

Although I chose the various specifications for formatting that you've seen in this chapter with the idea of them being as meaningful as possible, there are a lot of them. The only way you're going to become comfortable with them is through practice, and ideally this practice needs to take place in a real-world context. Understanding the various codes is one thing, but they'll probably become really familiar to you only once you've used them a few times in real programs. In the meantime, when you need a quick reminder you can always look them up in the summary Appendix D.

Exercises

The following exercises enable you to try out what you've learned in this chapter. If you get stuck, look back over the chapter for help. If you're still stuck, you can download the solutions from the Source Code/Download area of the Apress web site (http://www.apress.com), but that really should be a last resort.

Exercise 10-1. Write a program that will read, store, and output the following five types of strings on separate lines, when one of each type of string is entered on a single line without spaces between the lines:

! *Type 1*: A sequence of lowercase letters followed by a digit (e.g., number1)

! *Type 2*: Two words that both begin with a capital letter and have a hyphen between them (e.g., Seven-Up)

! *Type 3*: A decimal value (e.g., 7.35)

! *Type 4*: A sequence of upper- and lowercase letters and spaces (e.g., Oliver Hardy)

! *Type 5*: A sequence of any characters except spaces and digits (e.g., floating-point)

The following is a sample of input that should be read as five separate strings:

babylon5John-Boy3.14159Stan Laurel'Winner!'

Exercise 10-2. Write a program that will read the numerical values in the following line of input, and output the total:

$3.50 , $4.75 , $9.95 , $2.50

Exercise 10-3. Define a function that will output an array of values of type double that is passed as an argument along with the number of elements in the array. The prototype of the function will be the following:

```
void show(double array[], int array_size, int field_width);
```

The values should be output 5 to a line, each with 2 decimal places after the decimal point and in a field width of 12. Use the function in a program that will output the values from 1.5 to 4.5 in steps of 0.3 (i.e., 1.5, 1.8, 2.1, and so on, up to 4.5).

Exercise 10-4. Define a function using the getchar() function that will read a string from stdin terminated by a character that is passed as the second argument to the function. Thus the prototype will be the following:

```
char *getString(char *buffer, char end_char);
```

The return value is the pointer that is passed as the first argument. Write a program to demonstrate the use of the function to read and output five strings that are from the keyboard, each terminated by a colon.

CHAPTER 11

■■■

Structuring Data

So far, you've learned how to declare and define variables that can hold various types of data, including integers, floating-point values, and characters. You also have the means to create arrays of any of these types and arrays of pointers to memory locations containing data of the types available to you. Although these have proved very useful, there are many applications in which you need even more flexibility.

For instance, suppose you want to write a program that processes data about breeding horses. You need information about each horse such as its name, its date of birth, its coloring, its height, its parentage, and so on. Some items are strings and some are numeric. Clearly, you could set up arrays for each data type and store them quite easily. However, this has limitations!   for example, it doesn't allow you to refer to Dobbin's date of birth or Trigger's height particularly easily. You would need to synchronize your arrays by relating data items through a common index. Amazingly, C provides you with a better way of doing this, and that's what I'll discuss in this chapter.

In this chapter you'll learn the following:

!   What structures are

!   How to declare and define data structures

!   How to use structures and pointers to structures

!   How you can use pointers as structure members

!   How to share memory between variables

!   How to define your own data types

!   How to write a program that produces bar charts from your data

Data Structures: Using struct

The keyword struct enables you to define a collection of variables of various types called a **structure** that you can treat as a single unit. This will be clearer if you see a simple example of a structure declaration:

```
struct horse
{
  int age;
  int height;
} Silver;
```

This example declares a **structure** type called horse. This isn't a variable name; it's a new type. This type name is usually referred to as a **structure tag**, or a **tag name**. The naming of the structure tag follows the same rules as for a variable name, which you should be familiar with by now.

■ **Note** It's legal to use the same name for a structure tag name and another variable. However, I don't recommend that you do this because it will make your code confusing and difficult to understand.

The variable names within the structure, age and height, are called **structure members**. In this case, they're both of type int. The members of the structure appear between the braces that follow the struct tag name horse.

In the example, an instance of the structure, called Silver, is declared at the same time that the structure is defined. Silver is a variable of type horse. Now, whenever you use the variable name Silver, it includes both members of the structure: the member age and the member height.

Let's look at the declaration of a slightly more complicated version of the structure type horse:

```
struct horse
{
  int age;
  int height;
  char name[20];
  char father[20];
  char mother[20];
} Dobbin = {
          24, 17, "Dobbin", "Trigger", "Flossie"
        };
```

Any type of variable can appear as a member of a structure, including arrays. As you can see, there are five members to this version of the structure type called horse: the integer members age and height, and the arrays name, father, and mother. Each member declaration is essentially the same as a normal variable declaration, with the type followed by the name and terminated by a semicolon. Note that initialization values can't be placed here because you aren't declaring variables; you're defining members of a type called horse. A structure type is a kind of specification or blueprint that can then be used to define variables of that type! in this example, type horse.

You define an instance of the structure horse after the closing brace of the structure definition. This is the variable Dobbin. Initial values are also assigned to the member variables of Dobbin in a manner similar to that used to initialize arrays, so initial values *can* be assigned when you define instances of the type horse.

In the declaration of the variable Dobbin, the values that appear between the final pair of braces apply, in sequence, to the member variable age (24), height (17), name ("Dobbin"), father ("Trigger"), and mother ("Flossie"). The statement is finally terminated with a semicolon. The variable Dobbin now refers to the complete collection of members included in the structure. The memory occupied by the structure Dobbin is shown in Figure 11-1, assuming variables of type int occupy 4 bytes. You can always find out the amount of memory that's occupied by a structure using the sizeof operator.

Structure Variable Dobbin

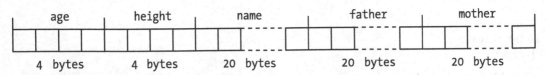

Figure 11-1. *Memory occupied by Dobbin*

Defining Structure Types and Structure Variables

You could have separated the declaration of the structure from the declaration of the structure variable. Instead of the statements you saw previously, you could have written the following:

```
struct horse
{
  int age;
  int height;
  char name[20];
  char father[20];
  char mother[20];
};

struct horse Dobbin = {
                24, 17,"Dobbin", "Trigger", "Flossie"
                };
```

You now have two separate statements. The first is the definition of the structure tag horse, and the second is a declaration of one variable of that type, Dobbin. Both the structure definition and the structure variable declaration statements end with a semicolon. The initial values for the members of the Dobbin structure tell you that the father of Dobbin is Trigger and his mother is Flossie.

You could also add a third statement to the previous two examples that would define another variable of type horse:

```
struct horse Trigger = {
                30, 15, "Trigger", "Smith", "Wesson"
                };
```

Now you have a variable Trigger that holds the details of the father of Dobbin, where it's clear that the ancestors of Trigger are "Smith" and "Wesson".

Of course, you can also declare multiple structure variables in a single statement. This is almost as easy as declaring variables of one of the standard C types, for example

```
struct horse Piebald, Bandy;
```

declares two variables of type horse. The only additional item in the declaration, compared with standard types, is the keyword struct. You haven't initialized the values! to keep the statement simple! but in general it's wise to do so.

Accessing Structure Members

Now that you know how to define a structure and declare structure variables, you need to be able to refer to the members of a structure. A structure variable name is *not* a pointer. You need a special syntax to access the members.

You refer to a member of a structure by writing the structure variable name followed by a period, followed by the member variable name. For example, if you found that Dobbin had lied about his age and was actually much younger than the initializing value would suggest, you could amend the value by writing this:

```
Dobbin.age = 12;
```

The period between the structure variable name and the member name is actually an operator that is called the **member selection operator**. This statement sets the age member of the structure

Dobbin to 12. Structure members are just the same as variables of the same type. You can set their values and use them in expressions in the same way as ordinary variables.

TRY IT OUT: USING STRUCTURES

You can try out what you've learned so far about structures in a simple example that's designed to appeal to horse enthusiasts:

```c
/* Program 11.1 Exercising the horse */
#include <stdio.h>

int main(void)
{
  /* Structure declaration */
  struct horse
  {
    int age;
    int height;
    char name[20];
    char father[20];
    char mother[20];
  };

  struct horse My_first_horse;          /* Structure variable declaration   */

  /* Initialize the structure variable from input data */
  printf("Enter the name of the horse: " );
  scanf("%s", My_first_horse.name );              /* Read the horse's name    */

  printf("How old is %s? ", My_first_horse.name );
  scanf("%d", &My_first_horse.age );              /* Read the horse's age     */

  printf("How high is %s ( in hands )? ", My_first_horse.name );
  scanf("%d", &My_first_horse.height );           /* Read the horse's height */

  printf("Who is %s's father? ", My_first_horse.name );
  scanf("%s", My_first_horse.father );            /* Get the father's name    */

  printf("Who is %s's mother? ", My_first_horse.name );
  scanf("%s", My_first_horse.mother );            /* Get the mother's name    */

  /* Now tell them what we know */
  printf("\n%s is %d years old, %d hands high,",
      My_first_horse.name, My_first_horse.age, My_first_horse.height);
  printf(" and has %s and %s as parents.\n", My_first_horse.father,
                                        My_first_horse.mother );
  return 0;
}
```

Depending on what data you key in, you should get output approximating to the following:

```
Enter the name of the horse: Neddy
How old is Neddy? 12
How high is Neddy ( in hands )? 14
Who is Neddy's father? Bertie
Who is Neddy's mother? Nellie

Neddy is 12 years old, 14 hands high, and has Bertie and Nellie as parents.
```

How It Works

The way you reference members of a structure makes it very easy to follow what is going on in this example. You define the structure horse with this statement:

```
struct horse
{
  int age;
  int height;
  char name[20];
  char father[20];
  char mother[20];
};
```

The structure has two integer members, age and height, and three char array members, name, father, and mother. Because there's just a semicolon following the closing brace, no variables of type horse are declared here.

After defining the structure horse, you have the following statement:

```
struct horse My_first_horse;        /* Structure variable declaration  */
```

This declares one variable of type horse, which is My_first_horse. This variable has no initial values assigned in the declaration.

You then read in the data for the name member of the structure My_first_horse with this statement:

```
scanf("%s", My_first_horse.name );          /* Read the horse's name   */
```

No address of operator (&) is necessary here, because the name member of the structure is an array, so you implicitly transfer the address of the first array element to the function scanf(). You reference the member by writing the structure name, My_first_horse, followed by a period, followed by the name of the member, which is name. Other than the notation used to access it, using a structure member is the same as using any other variable.

The next value you read in is for the age of the horse:

```
scanf("%d", &My_first_horse.age );          /* Read the horse's age    */
```

This member is a variable of type int, so here you must use the & to pass the address of the structure member.

■**Note** When you use the address of operator (&) for a member of a struct object, you place the & in front of the whole reference to the member, not in front of the member name.

The following statements read the data for each of the other members of the structure in exactly the same manner, prompting for the input in each case. Once input is complete, the values read are output to the display as a single line using the following statements:

```
printf("\n\n%s is %d years old, %d hands high,",
       My_first_horse.name, My_first_horse.age, My_first_horse.height);
  printf(" and has %s and %s as parents.", My_first_horse.father,
                                          My_first_horse.mother );
```

The long names that are necessary to refer to the members of the structure tend to make this statement appear complicated, but it's quite straightforward. You have the names of the member variables as the arguments to the function following the first argument, which is the standard sort of format control string that you've seen many times before.

Unnamed Structures

You don't have to give a structure a tag name. When you declare a structure and any instances of that structure in a single statement, you can omit the tag name. In the last example, instead of the structure declaration for type horse, followed by the instance declaration for My_first_horse, you could have written this statement:

```
struct
{                                        /* Structure declaration and... */
  int age;
  int height;
  char name[20];
  char father[20];
  char mother[20];
} My_first_horse;             /* ...structure variable declaration combined */
```

A serious disadvantage with this approach is that you can no longer define further instances of the structure in another statement. All the variables of this structure type that you want in your program must be defined in the one statement.

Arrays of Structures

The basic approach to keeping horse data is fine as far as it goes. But it will probably begin to be a bit cumbersome by the time you've accumulated 50 or 100 horses. You need a more stable method for handling a lot of horses. It's exactly the same problem that you had with variables, which you solved using an array. And you can do the same here: you can declare a horse array.

TRY IT OUT: USING ARRAYS OF STRUCTURES

Let's saddle up and extend the previous example to handle several horses:

```
/* Program 11.2   Exercising the horses */
#include <stdio.h>
#include <ctype.h>

int main(void)
{
  struct horse                     /* Structure declaration */
  {
    int age;
    int height;
```

```c
   char name[20];
      char father[20];
      char mother[20];
   };

   struct horse My_horses[50];       /* Structure array declaration   */
   int hcount = 0;                   /* Count of the number of horses */
   char test = '\0';                 /* Test value for ending         */

   for(hcount = 0; hcount<50 ; hcount++ )
   {
     printf("\nDo you want to enter details of a%s horse (Y or N)? ",
                                         hcount?"nother " : "" );
     scanf(" %c", &test );
     if(tolower(test) == 'n')
        break;

     printf("\nEnter the name of the horse: " );
     scanf("%s", My_horses[hcount].name );  /* Read the horse's name */

     printf("\nHow old is %s? ", My_horses[hcount].name );
     scanf("%d", &My_horses[hcount].age );  /* Read the horse's age  */

     printf("\nHow high is %s ( in hands )? ", My_horses[hcount].name );
     /* Read the horse's height*/
     scanf("%d", &My_horses[hcount].height );

     printf("\nWho is %s's father? ", My_horses[hcount].name );
     /* Get the father's name */
      scanf("%s", My_horses[hcount].father );

     printf("\nWho is %s's mother? ", My_horses[hcount].name );

     /* Get the mother's name  */
      scanf("%s", My_horses[hcount].mother );
   }

   /* Now tell them what we know. */
   for(int i = 0 ; i<hcount ; i++ )
   {
     printf("\n\n%s is %d years old, %d hands high,",
             My_horses[i].name, My_horses[i].age, My_horses[i].height);
     printf(" and has %s and %s as parents.", My_horses[i].father,
                                         My_horses[i].mother );
   }
   return 0;
}
```

The output from this program is a little different from the previous example you saw that dealt with a single horse. The main addition is the prompt for input data for each horse. Once all the data for a few horses has been entered, or if you have the stamina, the data on 50 horses has been entered, the program outputs a summary of all the data that has been read in, one line per horse. The whole mechanism is stable and works very well in the mane (almost an unbridled success, you might say).

How It Works

In this version of equine data processing, you first declare the horse structure, and this is followed by the declaration

```
struct horse My_horses[50]; /* Structure array declaration    */
```

This declares the variable My_horses, which is an array of 50 horse structures. Apart from the keyword struct, it's just like any other array declaration.

You then have a for loop controlled by the variable hcount:

```
for(hcount = 0; hcount<50 ; hcount++ )
{
   ...
}
```

This creates the potential for the program to read in data for up to 50 horses. The loop control variable hcount is used to accumulate the total number of horse structures entered. The first action in the loop is in these statements:

```
printf("\nDo you want to enter details of a%s horse (Y or N)? ",
                              hcount?"nother " : "" );
scanf(" %c", &test );
if(tolower(test) == 'n')
   break;
```

On each iteration the user is prompted to indicate if he or she wants to enter data for another horse by entering **Y** or **N**. The printf() statement for this uses the conditional operator to insert "nother" into the output on every iteration after the first. After reading the character that the user enters, using scanf(), the if statement executes a break, which immediately exits from the loop if the response is negative.

The succeeding sequence of printf() and scanf() statements are much the same as before, but there are two points to note in these. Look at this statement:

```
scanf("%s", My_horses[hcount].name );  /* Read the horse's name */
```

You can see that the method for referencing the member of one element of an array of structures is easier to write than to say! The structure array name has an index in square brackets, to which a period and the member name are appended. If you want to reference the third element of the name array for the fourth structure element, you would write My_horses[3].name[2].

■**Note** Of course, the index values start from 0, as with arrays of other types, so the fourth element of the structure array has the index value 3, and the third element of the member array is accessed by the index value 2.

Now look at this statement from the example:

```
scanf("%d", &My_horses[hcount].age );  /* Read the horse's age  */
```

Notice that the arguments to scanf() don't need the & for the string array variables, such as My_horses[hcount].name, but they *do* require them for the integer arguments My_horses[hcount].age and My_horses[hcount].height. It's very easy to forget the address of operator when reading values for variables like these.

Don't be misled at this point and think that these techniques are limited to equine applications. They can perfectly well be applied to porcine problems and also to asinine exercises.

Structures in Expressions

A structure member that is one of the built-in types can be used like any other variable in an expression. Using the structure from Program 11.2, you could write this rather meaningless computation:

```
My_horses[1].height = (My_horses[2].height + My_horses[3].height)/2;
```

I can think of no good reason why the height of one horse should be the average of two other horses' heights (unless there's some Frankenstein-like assembly going on) but it's a legal statement.

You can also use a complete structure element in an assignment statement:

```
My_horses[1] = My_horses[2];
```

This statement causes *all* the members of the structure My_horses[2] to be copied to the structure My_horses[1], which means that the two structures become identical. The only other operation that's possible with a whole structure is to take its address using the & operator. You can't add, compare, or perform any other operations with a complete structure. To do those kinds of things, you must write your own functions.

Pointers to Structures

The ability to obtain the address of a structure raises the question of whether you can have pointers to a structure. Because you can take the address of a structure, the possibility of declaring a pointer to a structure does, indeed, naturally follow. You use the notation that you've already seen with other types of variables:

```
struct horse *phorse;
```

This declares a pointer, phorse, that can store the address of a structure of type horse.

You can now set phorse to have the value of the address of a particular structure, using exactly the same kind of statement that you've been using for other pointer types, for example

```
phorse = &My_horses[1];
```

Now phorse points to the structure My_horses[1]. You can immediately reference elements of this structure through your pointer. So if you want to display the name member of this structure, you could write this:

```
printf("\nThe name is %s.", (*phorse).name);
```

The parentheses around the dereferenced pointer are essential, because the precedence of the member selection operator (the period) is higher than that of the pointer-dereferencing operator *.

However, there's another way of doing this, and it's much more readable and intuitive. You could write the previous statement as follows:

```
printf("\nThe name is %s.", phorse->name );
```

So you don't need parentheses or an asterisk. You construct the operator -> from a minus sign immediately followed by the greater-than symbol. The operator is sometimes called the **pointer to member** operator for obvious reasons. This notation is almost invariably used in preference to the usual pointer-dereferencing notation you used at first, because it makes your programs so much easier to read.

Dynamic Memory Allocation for Structures

You have virtually all the tools you need to rewrite Program 11.2 with a much more economical use of memory. In the original version, you allocated the memory for an array of 50 horse structures, even when in practice you probably didn't need anything like that amount.

To create dynamically allocated memory for structures, the only tool that's missing is an array of pointers to structures, which is declared very easily, as you can see in this statement:

```
struct horse *phorse[50];
```

This statement declares an array of 50 pointers to structures of type horse. Only memory for the pointers has been allocated by this statement. You must still allocate the memory necessary to store the actual members of each structure that you need.

TRY IT OUT: USING POINTERS WITH STRUCTURES

You can see the dynamic allocation of memory for structures at work in the following example:

```
/* Program 11.3 Pointing out the horses */
#include <stdio.h>
#include <ctype.h>
#include <stdlib.h>           /* For malloc() */

int main(void)
{
  struct horse              /* Structure declaration */
  {
    int age;
    int height;
    char name[20];
    char father[20];
    char mother[20];
  };

  struct horse *phorse[50]; /* pointer to structure array declaration */
  int hcount = 0;           /* Count of the number of horses          */
  char test = '\0';         /* Test value for ending input            */

  for(hcount = 0; hcount < 50 ; hcount++ )
  {
    printf("\nDo you want to enter details of a%s horse (Y or N)? ",
                                        hcount?"nother " : "" );
    scanf(" %c", &test );
    if(tolower(test) == 'n')
      break;

    /* allocate memory to hold a structure    */
    phorse[hcount] = (struct horse*) malloc(sizeof(struct horse));

    printf("\nEnter the name of the horse: " );
    scanf("%s", phorse[hcount]->name );  /* Read the horse's name */
```

```
    printf("\nHow old is %s? ", phorse[hcount]->name );
    scanf("%d", &phorse[hcount]->age );  /* Read the horse's age  */

    printf("\nHow high is %s ( in hands )? ", phorse[hcount]->name );
    scanf("%d", &phorse[hcount]->height ); /* Read the horse's height */

    printf("\nWho is %s's father? ", phorse[hcount]->name );
    scanf("%s", phorse[hcount]->father );  /* Get the father's name */

    printf("\nWho is %s's mother? ", phorse[hcount]->name );
    scanf("%s", phorse[hcount]->mother );  /* Get the mother's name */
  }

  /* Now tell them what we know. */
  for(int i = 0 ; i < hcount ; i++ )
  {
    printf("\n\n%s is %d years old, %d hands high,",
                  phorse[i]->name, phorse[i]->age, phorse[i]->height);
    printf(" and has %s and %s as parents.",
                           phorse[i]->father, phorse[i]->mother);
    free(phorse[i]);
  }
  return 0;
}
```

The output should be exactly the same as that from Program 11.2, given the same input.

How It Works

This looks very similar to the previous version, but it operates rather differently. Initially, you don't have any memory allocated for any structures. The declaration

```
struct horse *phorse[50]; /* pointer to structure array declaration */
```

defines only 50 pointers to structures of type horse. You still have to find somewhere to put the structures to which these pointers are going to point:

```
phorse[hcount] = (struct horse*) malloc(sizeof(struct horse));
```

In this statement, you allocate the space for each structure as it's required. Let's have a quick reminder of how the malloc() function works. The malloc() function allocates the number of bytes specified by its argument and returns the address of the block of memory allocated as a pointer to type void. In this case, you use the sizeof operator to provide the value required.

It's very important to use sizeof when you need the number of bytes occupied by a structure. It doesn't necessarily correspond to the sum of the bytes occupied by each of its individual members, so you're likely to get it wrong if you try to work it out yourself.

Variables other than type char are often stored beginning at an address that's a multiple of 2 for 2-byte variables, a multiple of 4 for 4-byte variables, and so on. This is called **boundary alignment** and it has nothing to do with C but is a hardware requirement where it applies. Arranging variables to be stored in memory like this makes the transfer of data between the processor and memory faster. This arrangement can result in unused bytes occurring between member variables of different types, though, depending on their sequence. These have to be accounted for in the number of bytes allocated for a structure. Figure 11-2 presents an illustration of how this can occur.

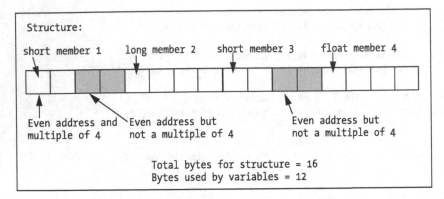

Figure 11-2. *The effect of boundary alignment on memory allocation*

As the value returned by `malloc()` is a pointer to `void`, you then cast this to the type you require with the expression (`struct horse*`). This enables the pointer to be incremented or decremented correctly, if required.

```
scanf("%s", phorse[hcount]->name );  /* Read the horse's name    */
```

In this statement, you use the new notation for selecting members of a structure through a pointer. It's much clearer than (`*phorse[hcount]`)`.name`. All subsequent references to members of a specific `horse` structure use this new notation.

Lastly in this program, you display a summary of all the data entered for each horse, freeing the memory as you go along.

More on Structure Members

So far, you've seen that any of the basic data types, including arrays, can be members of a structure. But there's more. You can also make a structure a member of a structure. Furthermore, not only can pointers be members of a structure, but also a pointer to a structure can be a member of a structure.

This opens up a whole new range of possibilities in programming with structures and, at the same time, increases the potential for confusion. Let's look at each of these possibilities in sequence and see what they have to offer. Maybe it won't be a can of worms after all.

Structures As Members of a Structure

At the start of this chapter, you examined the needs of horse breeders and, in particular, the necessity to manage a variety of details about each horse, including its name, height, date of birth, and so on. You then went on to look at Program 11.1, which carefully avoided date of birth and substituted age instead. This was partly because dates are messy things to deal with, as they're represented by three numbers and hold all the complications of leap years. However, you're now ready to tackle dates, using a structure that's a member of another structure.

You can define a structure type designed to hold dates. You can specify a suitable structure with the tag name Date with this statement:

```
struct Date
{
  int day;
  int month;
  int year;
};
```

Now you can define the structure horse, including a date-of-birth variable, like this:

```
struct horse
{
  struct Date dob;
  int height;
  char name[20];
  char father[20];
  char mother[20];
};
```

Now you have a single variable member within the structure that represents the date of birth of a horse, and this member is itself a structure. Next, you can define an instance of the structure horse with the usual statement:

```
struct horse Dobbin;
```

You can define the value of the member height with the same sort of statement that you've already seen:

```
Dobbin.height = 14;
```

If you want to set the date of birth in a series of assignment statements, you can use the logical extension of this notation:

```
Dobbin.dob.day = 5;
Dobbin.dob.month = 12;
Dobbin.dob.year = 1962;
```

You have a very old horse. The expression Dobbin.dob.day is referencing a variable of type int, so you can happily use it in arithmetic or comparative expressions. But if you use the expression Dobbin.dob, you would be referring to a struct variable of type date. Because this is clearly not a basic type but a structure, you can use it only in an assignment such as this:

```
Trigger.dob = Dobbin.dob;
```

This *could* mean that they're twins, but it doesn't guarantee it.

If you can find a good reason to do it, you can extend the notion of structures that are members of a structure to a structure that's a member of a structure that's a member of a structure. In fact, if you can make sense of it, you can continue with further levels of structure. Your C compiler is likely to provide for at least 15 levels of such convolution. But beware: if you reach this depth of structure nesting, you're likely to be in for a bout of repetitive strain injury just typing the references to members.

Declaring a Structure Within a Structure

You could declare the Date structure within the horse structure definition, as in the following code:

```
struct horse
{
  struct Date
  {
    int day;
    int month;
    int year;
  } dob;

  int height;
  char name[20];
  char father[20];
  char mother[20];
};
```

This has an interesting effect. Because the declaration is enclosed within the scope of the horse structure definition, it doesn't exist outside it, and so it becomes impossible to declare a Date variable external to the horse structure. Of course, each instance of a horse type variable would contain the Date type member, dob. But a statement such as this

```
struct date my_date;
```

would cause a compiler error. The message generated will say that the structure type date is undefined. If you need to use date outside the structure horse, its definition must be placed outside of the horse structure.

Pointers to Structures As Structure Members

Any pointer can be a member of a structure. This includes a pointer that points to a structure. A pointer structure member that points to the same type of structure is also permitted. For example, the horse type structure could contain a pointer to a horse type structure. Interesting, but is it of any use? Well, as it happens, yes.

TRY IT OUT: POINTERS TO STRUCTURES AS STRUCTURE MEMBERS

You can demonstrate a structure containing a pointer to a structure of the same type with a modification of the last example:

```
/* Program 11.4   Daisy chaining the horses */
#include <stdio.h>
#include <ctype.h>
#include <stdlib.h>

int main(void)
{
  struct horse                    /* Structure declaration      */
  {
    int age;
    int height;
    char name[20];
    char father[20];
    char mother[20];
```

```c
    struct horse *next;                /* Pointer to next structure   */
};

struct horse *first = NULL;           /* Pointer to first horse     */
struct horse *current = NULL;         /* Pointer to current horse   */
struct horse *previous = NULL;        /* Pointer to previous horse  */

char test = '\0';                     /* Test value for ending input */

for( ; ; )
{
  printf("\nDo you want to enter details of a%s horse (Y or N)? ",
                              first != NULL?"nother " : "" );
  scanf(" %c", &test );
  if(tolower(test) == 'n')
    break;

  /* Allocate memory for a structure */
  current = (struct horse*) malloc(sizeof(struct horse));

  if(first == NULL)
    first = current;                  /* Set pointer to first horse  */

  if(previous != NULL)

    previous -> next = current; /* Set next pointer for previous horse */

  printf("\nEnter the name of the horse: ");
  scanf("%s", current -> name);       /* Read the horse's name       */

  printf("\nHow old is %s? ", current -> name);
  scanf("%d", &current -> age);       /* Read the horse's age        */

  printf("\nHow high is %s ( in hands )? ", current -> name );
  scanf("%d", &current -> height);  /* Read the horse's height       */

  printf("\nWho is %s's father? ", current -> name);
  scanf("%s", current -> father);   /* Get the father's name         */

  printf("\nWho is %s's mother? ", current -> name);
  scanf("%s", current -> mother);   /* Get the mother's name         */

  current->next = NULL;               /* In case it's the last...    */
  previous = current;                 /* Save address of last horse  */
}

/* Now tell them what we know. */
current = first;                      /* Start at the beginning      */

while (current != NULL)       /* As long as we have a valid pointer */
{ /* Output the data*/
  printf("\n\n%s is %d years old, %d hands high,",
                  current->name, current->age, current->height);
```

```
  printf(" and has %s and %s as parents.", current->father,
                                        current->mother);
    previous = current;    /* Save the pointer so we can free memory */
    current = current->next;        /* Get the pointer to the next */
    free(previous);                 /* Free memory for the old one */
  }
  return 0;
}
```

This example should produce the same output as Program 11.3 (given the same input), but here you have yet another mode of operation.

How It Works

This time, not only do you have no space for structures allocated, but also you have only three pointers defined initially. These pointers are declared and initialized in these statements:

```
struct horse *first = NULL;      /* Pointer to first horse      */
struct horse *current = NULL;    /* Pointer to current horse    */
struct horse *previous = NULL;   /* Pointer to previous horse   */
```

Each of these pointers has been defined as a pointer to a horse structure. The pointer first is used solely to store the address of the first structure. The second and third pointers are working storage: current holds the address of the current horse structure that you're dealing with, and previous keeps track of the address of the previous structure that was processed.

You've added a member to the structure horse with the name next, which is a pointer to a horse type structure. This will be used to link together all the horses you have, where each horse structure will have a pointer containing the address of the next. The last structure will be an exception, of course: its next pointer will be NULL. The structure is otherwise exactly as you had previously. It's shown in Figure 11-3.

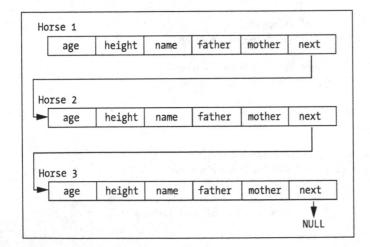

Figure 11-3. *A sequence of linked horses*

The input loop is the following:

```
for( ; ; )
{
    ...
}
```

The input loop is now an indefinite loop, because you don't have an array to worry about. You don't need to mess around with indexes. It's also unnecessary to keep count of how many sets of data are read in, so you don't need the variable hcount or the loop variable i. Because you allocate memory for each horse, you can just take them as they come.

The initial statements in the loop are the following:

```
printf("\nDo you want to enter details of a%s horse (Y or N)? ",
                             first != NULL?"nother " : "" );
scanf(" %c", &test );
if(tolower(test) == 'n')
    break;
```

After the prompt, you exit from the loop if the response 'N' or 'n' is detected. Otherwise, you expect another set of structure members to be entered. You use the pointer first to get a slightly different prompt on the second and subsequent iterations, because the only time it will be NULL is on the first loop iteration.

Assuming you get past the initial question in the loop, you execute these statements:

```
current = (struct horse*) malloc(sizeof(struct horse));

if(first == NULL)
    first = current;                    /* Set pointer to first horse  */

if(previous != NULL)
    previous -> next = current; /* Set next pointer for previous horse */
```

On each iteration, you allocate the memory necessary for the current structure. To keep things short, you don't check for a NULL return from malloc(), although you ought to do this in practice.

If the pointer first is NULL, you must be on the first loop iteration, and this must be the first structure about to be entered. Consequently, you set the pointer first to the pointer value that you've just obtained from malloc(), which is stored in the variable current. The address in first is the key to accessing the first horse in the chain. You can get to any of the others by starting with the address in first and then looking in the member pointer next to obtain the address of the next structure. You can step from there to the next structure and so on to any horse in the sequence.

The next pointer always needs to point to the next structure if there is one, but the address of the next structure can be determined only once you actually have the next structure. Therefore, on the second and subsequent iterations, you store the address of the current structure in the next member of the previous structure, whose address you'll have saved in previous. On the first iteration, the pointer previous will be NULL at this point, so of course you do nothing.

At the end of the loop, following all the input statements, you have these statements:

```
current->next = NULL;         /* In case it's the last...   */
previous = current;           /* Save address of last horse  */
```

The pointer next in the structure pointed to by current, which you're presently working with, is set to NULL in case this is the last structure and there's no next structure. If there is a next structure, this pointer next will be filled in on the next iteration. The pointer previous is set to current and is ready for the next iteration, when the current structure will indeed be the previous structure.

The strategy of the program is to generate a daisy chain of horse structures, in which the next member of each structure points to the next structure in the chain. The last is an exception because there's no next horse, so the next pointer contains NULL. This arrangement is called a **linked list**.

Once you have the horse data in a linked list, you process it by starting with the first structure and then getting the next structure through the pointer member next. When the pointer next is NULL, you know that you've reached the end of the list. This is how you generate the output list of all the input.

Linked lists are invaluable in applications in which you need to process an unknown number of structures, such as you have here. The main advantages of a linked list relate to memory usage and ease of handling. You occupy only the minimum memory necessary to store and process the list. Even though the memory used may be fragmented, you have no problem progressing from one structure to the next. As a consequence, in a practical situation in which you may need to deal with several different types of objects simultaneously, each can be handled using its own linked list, with the result that memory use is optimized. There is one small cloud associated with this—as there is with any silver lining—and it's that you pay a penalty in slower access to the data, particularly if you want to access it randomly.

The output process shows how a linked list is accessed as it steps through the linked list you've created with these statements:

```
current = first;                        /* Start at the beginning      */

while (current != NULL)      /* As long as we have a valid pointer */
{ /* Output the data*/
  printf("\n\n%s is %d years old, %d hands high,",
                   current->name, current->age, current->height);
  printf(" and has %s and %s as parents.", current->father,
                                      current->mother);
  previous = current;      /* Save the pointer so we can free memory */
  current = current->next;        /* Get the pointer to the next */
  free(previous);                 /* Free memory for the old one */
}
```

The current pointer controls the output loop, and it's set to first at the outset. Remember that the first pointer contains the address of the first structure in the list. The loop steps through the list, and as the members of each structure are displayed, the address stored in the member next, which points to the next structure, is assigned to current.

The memory for the structure displayed is then freed. It's obviously fairly essential that you only free the memory for a structure once you have no further need to reference it. It's easy to fall into the trap of putting the call of the function free() immediately after you've output all of the member values for the current structure. This would create some problems, because then you couldn't legally reference the current structure's next member to get the pointer to the next horse structure.

For the last structure in the linked list, the pointer next will contain NULL and the loop will terminate.

Doubly Linked Lists

A disadvantage of the linked list that you created in the previous example is that you can only go forward. However, a small modification of the idea gives you the **doubly linked list**, which will allow you to go through a list in either direction. The trick is to include an extra pointer in each structure to store the address of the previous structure in addition to the pointer to the next structure.

TRY IT OUT: DOUBLY LINKED LISTS

You can see a doubly linked list in action in a modified version of Program 11.4:

```c
/* Program 11.5 Daisy chaining the horses both ways */
#include <stdio.h>
#include <ctype.h>
#include <stdlib.h>

int main(void)
{
  struct horse                         /* Structure declaration      */
  {
    int age;
    int height;
    char name[20];
    char father[20];
    char mother[20];
    struct horse *next;          /* Pointer to next structure      */
    struct horse *previous;      /* Pointer to previous structure */
  };

  struct horse *first = NULL;      /* Pointer to first horse       */
  struct horse *current = NULL;    /* Pointer to current horse     */
  struct horse *last = NULL;       /* Pointer to previous horse    */

  char test = '\0';                /* Test value for ending input */

  for( ; ; )
  {
    printf("\nDo you want to enter details of a%s horse (Y or N)? ",
                              first == NULL?"nother " : "");
    scanf(" %c", &test );
    if(tolower(test) == 'n')
      break;

    /* Allocate memory for each new horse structure */
    current = (struct horse*)malloc(sizeof(struct horse));

    if( first == NULL )
    {
      first = current;                 /* Set pointer to first horse  */
     current->previous = NULL;
    }
    else
    {
      last->next = current;     /* Set next address for previous horse */
      current->previous = last; /* Previous address for current horse */
    }

    printf("\nEnter the name of the horse: ");
    scanf("%s", current -> name );     /* Read the horse's name    */
```

```
    printf("\nHow old is %s? ", current -> name);
    scanf("%d", &current -> age);      /* Read the horse's age     */

    printf("\nHow high is %s ( in hands )? ", current -> name);
    scanf("%d", &current -> height);  /* Read the horse's height */

    printf("\nWho is %s's father? ", current -> name);
    scanf("%s", current -> father);    /* Get the father's name    */

    printf("\nWho is %s's mother? ", current -> name);
    scanf("%s", current -> mother);    /* Get the mother's name    */

    current -> next = NULL;      /* In case it's the last horse..*/
    last = current;              /* Save address of last horse   */
  }

  /* Now tell them what we know. */
  while(current != NULL)         /* Output horse data in reverse order */
  {
    printf("\n\n%s is %d years old, %d hands high,",
              current->name, current->age, current->height);
    printf(" and has %s and %s as parents.", current->father,
                                    current->mother);
    last = current;        /* Save pointer to enable memory to be freed */
    current = current->previous; /* current points to previous in list */
    free(last);                  /* Free memory for the horse we output */
  }
  return 0;
}
```

For the same input, this program should produce the same output as before, except that the data on horses entered is displayed in reverse order to that of entry—just to show that you can do it.

How It Works

The initial pointer declarations are now as follows:

```
  struct horse *first = NULL;      /* Pointer to first horse     */
  struct horse *current = NULL;    /* Pointer to current horse   */
  struct horse *last = NULL;       /* Pointer to previous horse  */
```

You change the name of the pointer recording the horse structure entered on the previous iteration of the loop to last. This name change isn't strictly necessary, but it does help to avoid confusion with the structure member previous.

The structure horse is declared as follows:

```
  struct horse                     /* Structure declaration      */
  {
    int age;
    int height;
    char name[20];
    char father[20];
    char mother[20];
```

```
    struct horse *next;          /* Pointer to next structure    */
    struct horse *previous;      /* Pointer to previous structure */
};
```

The horse structure now contains two pointers: one to point forward in the list, called next, the other to point backward to the preceding structure, called previous. This allows the list to be traversed in either direction, as you demonstrate by the fact that you output the data at the end of the program in reverse order.

Aside from the output, the only changes to the program are to add the statements that take care of the entries for the pointer structure member previous. In the beginning of the input loop you have the following:

```
if( first == NULL )
{
  first = current;                /* Set pointer to first horse    */
  current->previous = NULL;
}
else
{
  last->next = current;     /* Set next address for previous horse */
  current->previous = last; /* Previous address for current horse */
}
```

Here, you take the option of writing an if with an else, rather than the two ifs you had in the previous version. The only material difference is setting the value of the structure member previous. For the first structure, previous is set to NULL, and for all subsequent structures it's set to the pointer last, whose value was saved on the preceding iteration.

The other change is at the end of the input loop:

```
last = current;                       /* Save address of last horse   */
```

This statement is added to allow the pointer previous in the next structure to be set to the appropriate value, which is the current structure that you're recording in the variable last.

The output process is virtually the same as in the previous example, except that you start from the last structure in the list and work back to the first.

Bit-Fields in a Structure

Bit-fields provide a mechanism that allows you to define variables that are each one or more binary bits within a single integer word, which you can nevertheless refer to explicitly with an individual member name for each one.

■Note Bit-fields are used most frequently when memory is at a premium and you're in a situation in which you must use it as sparingly as possible. This is rarely the case these days so you won't see them very often. Bit-fields will slow your program down appreciably compared to using standard variable types. You must therefore assess each situation upon its merits to decide whether the memory savings offered by bit-fields are worth this price in execution speed for your programs. In most instances, bit-fields won't be necessary or even desirable, but you need to know about them.

An example of declaring a bit-field is shown here:

```
struct
{
  unsigned int flag1 : 1;
  unsigned int flag2 : 1;
  unsigned int flag3 : 2;
  unsigned int flag4 : 3;
} indicators;
```

This defines a variable with the name `indicators` that's an instance of an anonymous structure containing four bit-fields with the names `flag1` through `flag4`. These will all be stored in a single word, as illustrated in Figure 11-4.

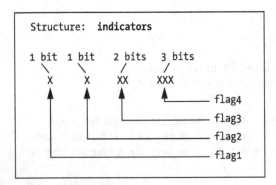

Figure 11-4. *Bit-fields in a structure*

The first two bit-fields, being a single bit specified by the 1 in their definition, can only assume the values 0 or 1. The third bit-field, `flag3`, has 2 bits and so it can have a value from 0 to 3. The last bit-field, `flag4`, can have values from 0 to 7, because it has 3 bits. These bit-fields are referenced in the same manner as other structure members, for example

```
indicators.flag4 = 5;
indicators.flag3 = indicators.flag1 = 1;
```

You'll rarely, if ever, have any need for this facility. I've included bit-fields here for the sake of completeness and for that strange off chance that one day bit-fields will be just what you need in a particularly tight memory situation.

Structures and Functions

Because structures represent such a powerful feature of the C language, their use with functions is very important. You'll now look at how you can pass structures as arguments to a function and how you can return a structure from a function.

Structures As Arguments to Functions

There's nothing unusual in the method for passing a structure as an argument to a function. It's exactly the same as passing any other variable. Analogous to the `horse` structure, you could create this structure:

```
struct family
{
  char name[20];
  int age;
  char father[20];
  char mother[20];
};
```

You could then construct a function to test whether two members of the type family are siblings:

```
bool siblings(struct family member1, struct family member2)
{
  if(strcmp(member1.mother, member2.mother) == 0)
    return true;
  else
    return false;
}
```

This function has two arguments, each of which is a structure. It simply compares the strings corresponding to the member mother for each structure. If they're the same, they are siblings and 1 is returned. Otherwise, they can't be siblings so 0 is returned. You're ignoring the effects of divorce, in vitro fertilization, cloning, and any other possibilities that may make this test inadequate.

Pointers to Structures As Function Arguments

Remember that a copy of the value of an argument is transferred to a function when it's called. If the argument is a large structure, it can take quite a bit of time, as well as occupying whatever additional memory the copy of the structure requires. Under these circumstances, you should use a pointer to a structure as an argument. This avoids the memory consumption and the copying time, because now only a copy of the pointer is made. The function will access the original structure directly through the pointer. More often than not, structures are passed to a function using a pointer, just for these reasons of efficiency. You could rewrite the siblings() function like this:

```
bool siblings(struct family *member1, struct family *member2)
{
  if(strcmp(member1->mother, member2->mother) == 0)
    return true;
  else
    return false;
}
```

Now, there is a downside to this. The pass-by-value mechanism provides good protection against accidental modification of values from within a called function. You lose this if you pass a pointer to a function. On the upside, if you don't need to modify the values pointed to by a pointer argument (you just want to access and use them, for instance), there's a technique for getting a degree of protection, even though you're passing pointers to a function.

Have another look at the last siblings() function. It doesn't need to modify the structures passed to it! in fact, it only needs to compare members. You could therefore rewrite it like this:

```
bool siblings(struct family const *pmember1, struct family const *pmember2)
{
  if(strcmp(pmember1->mother, pmember2->mother) == 0)
    return true;
  else
    return false;
}
```

You'll recall the const modifier from earlier in the book, where you used it to make a variable effectively a constant. This function declaration specifies the parameters as type •pointer to constant family structure.! This implies that the structures pointed to by the pointers transferred to the function will be treated as constants within the function. Any attempt to change those structures will cause an error message during compilation. Of course, this doesn't affect their status as variables in the calling program, because the const keyword applies only to the values while the function is executing.

Note the difference between the previous definition of the function and this one:

```
bool siblings(struct family *const pmember1, struct family *const pmember2)
{
  if(strcmp(pmember1->mother, pmember2->mother) == 0)
    return true;
  else
    return false;
}
```

The indirection operator in each parameter definition is now in front of the keyword const, rather than in front of the pointer name as it was before. Does this make a difference? You bet it does. The parameters here are •constant pointers to structures of type family,! not •pointers to constant structures.! Now you're free to alter the structures themselves in the function, but you must not modify the addresses stored in the pointers. It's the pointers that are protected here, not the structures to which they point.

A Structure As a Function Return Value

There's nothing unusual about returning a structure from a function either. The function prototype merely has to indicate this return value in the normal way, for example:

```
struct horse my_fun(void);
```

This is a prototype for a function taking no arguments that returns a structure of type horse.

Although you can return a structure from a function like this, it's often more convenient to return a pointer to a structure. Let's explore this in more detail through a working example.

TRY IT OUT: RETURNING A POINTER TO A STRUCTURE

To demonstrate how returning a pointer to a structure works, you can rewrite the previous horse example in terms of humans and perform the input in a separate function:

```
/* Program 11.6 Basics of a family tree */
#include <stdio.h>
#include <ctype.h>
#include <stdlib.h>

struct Family *get_person(void);        /* Prototype for input function */

struct Date
{
  int day;
   int month;
  int year;
};
```

```c
struct Family                         /* Family structure declaration */
{
  struct Date dob;
  char name[20];
  char father[20];
  char mother[20];
  struct Family *next;                /* Pointer to next structure   */
  struct Family *previous;            /* Pointer to previous structure */
};

int main(void)
{
  struct Family *first = NULL;        /* Pointer to first person     */
  struct Family *current = NULL;      /* Pointer to current person   */
  struct Family *last = NULL;         /* Pointer to previous person  */
  char more = '\0';                   /* Test value for ending input */

  for( ; ; )
  {
    printf("\nDo you want to enter details of a%s person (Y or N)? ",
                                    first != NULL?"nother" : "");
    scanf(" %c", &more);
    if(tolower(more) == 'n')
      break;

    current = get_person();

    if(first == NULL)
    {
      first = current;                /* Set pointer to first Family */
      last = current;                 /* Remember for next iteration */
    }
    else
    {
      last->next = current;   /* Set next address for previous Family */
      current->previous = last;   /* Set previous address for current */
      last = current;                 /* Remember for next iteration     */
    }
  }

  /* Now tell them what we know */

  /* Output Family data in reverse order */
  while (current  != NULL)
  {
    printf("\n%s was born %d/%d/%d, and has %s and %s as parents.",
            current->name, current->dob.day, current->dob.month,
            current->dob. year, current->father,  current->mother );

    last = current;        /* Save pointer to enable memory to be freed */
    current = current->previous;   /* current points to previous list */
    free(last);            /* Free memory for the Family we output     */
  }
```

```
  return 0;
}

/*   Function to input data on Family members    */
struct Family *get_person(void)
{
  struct Family *temp;            /* Define temporary structure pointer */

  /* Allocate memory for a structure */
  temp = (struct Family*) malloc(sizeof(struct Family));

  printf("\nEnter the name of the person: ");
  scanf("%s", temp -> name );         /* Read the Family's name       */

  printf("\nEnter %s's date of birth (day month year); ", temp->name);
  scanf("%d %d %d", &temp->dob.day, &temp->dob.month, &temp->dob.year);

  printf("\nWho is %s's father? ", temp->name );
  scanf("%s", temp->father );         /* Get the father's name        */

  printf("\nWho is %s's mother? ", temp->name );
  scanf("%s", temp -> mother );        /* Get the mother's name       */

  temp->next = temp->previous = NULL; /* Set pointers to NULL          */

  return temp;                     /* Return address of Family structure */
}
```

How It Works

Although this looks like a lot of code, you should find this example quite straightforward. It operates similarly to the previous example, but it's organized as two functions instead of one.

The first structure declaration is the following:

```
struct Date
{
  int day;
  int month;
  int year;
};
```

This defines a structure type Date with three members, day, month, and year, which are all declared as integers. No instances of the structure are declared at this point. The definition precedes all the functions in the source file so it is accessible from within any function that appears subsequently in the file.

The next structure declaration is the following:

```
struct Family                        /* Family structure declaration  */
{
  struct Date dob;
  char name[20];
  char father[20];
  char mother[20];
  struct Family *next;                    /* Pointer to next structure    */
  struct Family *previous;               /* Pointer to previous structure */
};
```

This defines a structure type Family, which has a Date type structure as its first member. It then has three conventional char arrays as members. The last two members are pointers to structures. They're intended to allow a doubly linked list to be constructed, being pointers to the next and previous structures in the list, respectively.

The fact that both structure declarations are external to all the functions and are therefore available globally is an important difference between this and the previous examples. This is necessary here because you want to define Family structure variables in both the functions main() and get_person().

■**Note** Only the specification of the structure type is accessible globally. All the variables of type Family declared within each function are local in scope to the function in which they're declared.

The function get_person() has this prototype:

```
struct Family *get_person(void);   /* Prototype for input function   */
```

This indicates that the function accepts no arguments but returns a pointer to a Family structure.

The process parallels the operation of Program 11.5, with the differences that you have global structure type declarations and you input a structure within a separate function.

After verifying that the user wants to enter data by checking his or her response in more, the function main() calls the function get_person(). Within the function get_person(), you declare this pointer:

```
struct Family *temp;        /* Define temporary structure pointer */
```

This is a "pointer to a Family type structure" and it has local scope. The fact that the declaration of the structure type is global has no bearing on the scope of actual instances of the structure. The scope of each instance that you declare will depend on where the declaration is placed in the program.

The first action within the function get_person() is the following:

```
temp = (struct Family*) malloc(sizeof(struct Family));
```

This call to malloc() obtains sufficient memory to store a structure of type Family and stores the address that's returned in the pointer variable, temp. Although temp is local and will go out of scope at the end of the function get_person(), the memory allocated by malloc() is more permanent. It remains until you free it yourself within the program somewhere, or until you exit from the program completely.

The function get_person() reads in all the basic data for a person and stores that data in the structure pointed to by temp. As it stands, the function will accept any values for the date, but in a real situation you would include code for data validity checking. You could verify that the month value is from 1 to 12 and the day value is valid for the month entered. Because a birth date is being entered, you might verify that it isn't in the future.

The last statement in the function get_person() is the following:

```
return temp;                /* Return address of Family structure */
```

This returns a copy of the pointer to the structure that it has created. Even though temp will no longer exist after the return, the address that it contains that points to the memory block obtained from malloc() is still valid.

Back in main(), the pointer that's returned is stored in the variable current and is also saved in the variable first if this is the first iteration. You do this because you don't want to lose track of the first structure in the list. You also save the pointer current in the variable last, so that on the next iteration you can fill in the backward pointer member, previous, for the current person whose data you've just obtained.

After all the input data has been read, the program outputs a summary to the screen in reverse order, in a similar fashion to the previous examples.

An Exercise in Program Modification

Perhaps we ought to produce an example combining both the use of pointers to structures as arguments and the use of pointers to structures as return values. You can declare some additional pointers, p_to_pa and p_to_ma, in the structure type Family in the previous example, Program 11.6, by changing that structure declaration as follows:

```
struct Family                        /* Family structure declaration  */
{
  struct Date dob;
  char name[20];
  char father[20];
  char mother[20];
  struct Family *next;               /* Pointer to next structure     */
  struct Family *previous;           /* Pointer to previous structure */
  struct Family *p_to_pa;            /* Pointer to father structure   */
  struct Family *p_to_ma;            /* Pointer to mother structure   */
};
```

Now you can record the addresses of related structures in the pointer members p_to_pa and p_to_ma. You'll need to set them to NULL in the get_person() function by adding the following statement just before the return statement:

```
  temp->p_to_pa = temp->p_to_ma = NULL;        /* Set pointers to NULL  */
```

You can now augment the program with some additional functions that will fill in your new pointers p_to_pa and p_to_ma once data for everybody has been entered. You could code this by adding two functions. The first function, set_ancestry(), will accept pointers to Family structures as arguments and check whether the structure pointed to by the second argument is the father or mother of the structure pointed to by the first argument. If it is, the appropriate pointer will be updated to reflect this, and true will be returned; otherwise false will be returned. Here's the code:

```
bool set_ancestry(struct Family *pmember1, struct Family *pmember2)
{
  if(strcmp(pmember1->father, pmember2->name) == 0)
  {
    pmember1->p_to_pa = pmember2;
    return true;
  }

  if( strcmp(pmember1->mother, pmember2->name) == 0)
  {
    pmember1->p_to_ma = pmember2;
    return true;
  }
  else
    return false;
}
```

The second function will test all possible relationships between two Family structures:

```
/* Fill in pointers for mother or father relationships */
bool related (struct Family *pmember1, struct Family *pmember2)
{
  return set_ancestry(pmember1, pmember2) ||
                     set_ancestry(pmember2, pmember1);
}
```

The `related()` function calls `set_ancestry()` twice in the return statement to test all possibilities of relationship. The return value will be `true` if either of the calls to `set_ancestry()` return the value `true`. A calling program can use the return value from `related()` to determine whether a pointer has been filled in.

Note Because you use the library function `strcmp()` here, you must add an `#include` directive for `<string.h>` at the beginning of the program. You'll also need an `#include` directive for the `<stdbool.h>` header because you use the `bool` type and the values `true` and `false`.

You now need to add some code to the `main()` function that you created in Program 11.6 to use the function `related()` to fill in all the pointers in all the structures where valid addresses can be found. You can insert the following code into `main()` directly after the loop that inputs all the initial data:

```
current = first;

while(current->next != NULL) /* Check for relation for each person in */
{                            /* the list up to second to last         */
  int parents = 0;        /* Declare parent count local to this block */
  last = current->next;   /* Get the pointer to the next              */

  while(last != NULL)     /* This loop tests current person           */
  {                       /* against all the remainder in the list    */
    if(related(current, last))          /* Found a parent ?           */
      if(++parents == 2)    /* Yes, update count and check it         */
        break;              /* Exit inner loop if both parents found  */

    last = last->next;      /* Get the address of the next            */
  }
  current = current->next;  /* Next in the list to check              */
}

/* Now tell them what we know etc. */
/* rest of output code etc.  ...   */
```

This is a relatively self-contained block of code to fill in the parent pointers where possible. Starting with the first structure, a check is made with each of the succeeding structures to see if a parent relationship exists. The checking stops for a given structure if two parents have been found (which would have filled in both pointers) or the end of the list is reached.

Of necessity, some structures will have pointers where the values can't be updated. Because you don't have an infinite list, and barring some very strange family history, there will always be someone whose parent records aren't included. The process will take each of the structures in the list in turn and check it against all the following structures to see if they're related, at least up to the point where the two parents have been discovered.

Of course, you also need to insert prototypes for the functions `related()` and `set_ancestry()` at the beginning of the program, immediately after the prototype for the function `get_person()`. These prototypes would look like this:

```
bool related(struct Family *pmember1, struct Family *pmember2);
bool set_ancestry(struct Family *pmember1, struct Family *pmember2);
```

To show that the pointers have been successfully inserted, you can extend the final output to display information about the parents of each person by adding some additional statements immediately after the last printf(). You can also amend the output loop to start from first so the output loop will thus be as follows:

```
/* Output Family data in correct order */
current = first;

while (current != NULL)                /* Output Family data in correct order */
{
  printf("\n%s was born %d/%d/%d, and has %s and %s as parents.",
              current->name, current->dob.day, current->dob.month,
            current->dob. year, current->father,  current->mother);
  if(current->p_to_pa != NULL )
    printf("\n\t%s's birth date is %d/%d/%d  ",
            current->father, current->p_to_pa->dob.day,
                            current->p_to_pa->dob.month,
                            current->p_to_pa->dob.year);
  if(current->p_to_ma != NULL)
    printf("and %s's birth date is %d/%d/%d.\n  ",
            current->mother, current->p_to_ma->dob.day,
                            current->p_to_ma->dob.month,
                            current->p_to_ma->dob.year);

  current = current->next;             /* current points to next in list     */
}
```

This should then produce the dates of birth of both parents for each person using the pointers to the parents' structures, but only if the pointers have been set to valid addresses. Note that you don't free the memory in the loop. If you do this, the additional statements to output the parents' dates of birth will produce junk output when the parent structure appears earlier in the list. So finally, you must add a separate loop at the end of main() to delete the memory when the output is complete:

```
/* Now free the memory */
current = first;
while(current != NULL)
{
  last = current;     /* Save pointer to enable memory to be freed */
  current = current->next; /* current points to next in list      */
  free(last);         /* Free memory for last                     */
}
```

If you've assembled all the pieces into a new example, you should have a sizeable new program to play with. Here's the sort of output that you should get:

```
Do you want to enter details of a person (Y or N)? y

Enter the name of the person: Jack

Enter Jack's date of birth (day month year); 1 1 65

Who is Jack's father? Bill

Who is Jack's mother? Nell

Do you want to enter details of another person (Y or N)? y

Enter the name of the person: Mary

Enter Mary's date of birth (day month year); 3 3 67

Who is Mary's father? Bert

Who is Mary's mother? Moll

Do you want to enter details of another person (Y or N)? y

Enter the name of the person: Ben

Enter Ben's date of birth (day month year); 2 2 89

Who is Ben's father? Jack

Who is Ben's mother? Mary

Do you want to enter details of another  person (Y or N)? n

Jack was born 1/1/65, and has Bill and Nell as parents.
Mary was born 3/3/67, and has Bert and Moll as parents.
Ben was born 2/2/89, and has Jack and Mary as parents.
        Jack's birth date is 1/1/65  and Mary's birth date is 3/3/67.
```

You could try to modify the program to output everybody in chronological order or possibly work out how many offspring each person has.

Binary Trees

A binary tree is a very useful way of organizing data because you can arrange that the data that you have stored in the tree can be extracted from the tree in an ordered fashion. A binary tree is also a very interesting mechanism because it is basically very simple. Implementing a binary tree can involve recursion as well as dynamic memory allocation. We'll also use pointers to pass structures around.

A binary tree consists of a set of interconnected elements called **nodes**. The starting node is the base of the tree and is called a **root node**, as shown in Figure 11-5.

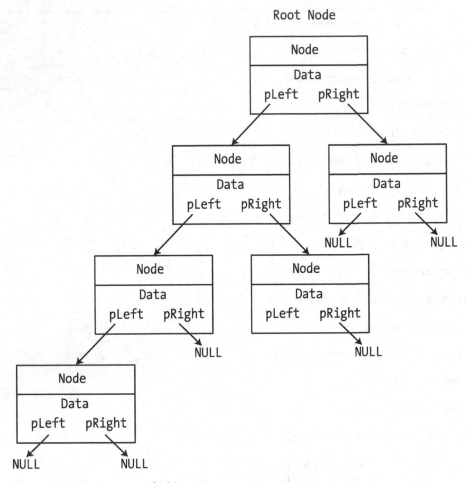

Figure 11-5. *The structure of a binary tree*

Each node typically contains an item of data, plus pointers to two subsidiary nodes, a **left node** and a **right node**. If either subsidiary node does not exist, the corresponding pointer is NULL. A node may also include a counter that records when there are duplicates of data items within the tree.

A struct makes it very easy to represent a binary tree node. Here's an example of a struct that defines nodes that store integers of type long:

```
struct Node
{
  long item;            /* The data item             */
  int count;            /* Number of copies of item  */
  struct Node *pLeft;   /* Pointer to left node      */
  struct Node *pRight;  /* Pointer to right node     */
};
```

When a data item is to be added to the binary tree and that item already exists somewhere, a new node is not created; the count member of the existing node is simply incremented by 1. I'll use the previous definition of a struct that represents a node holding an integer when we get to creating a binary tree in practice in Program 11.7, which is the next working example in this chapter.

Ordering Data in a Binary Tree

The way in which you construct the binary tree will determine the order of data items within the tree. Adding a data item to a tree involves comparing the item to be added with the existing items in the tree. Typically items are added so that for every node, the data item stored in the subsidiary left node when it exists is less than the data item in the current node, and the data item stored in the right node when it exists is greater than the item stored in the node. An example of a tree containing an arbitrary sequence of integers is shown in Figure 11-6.

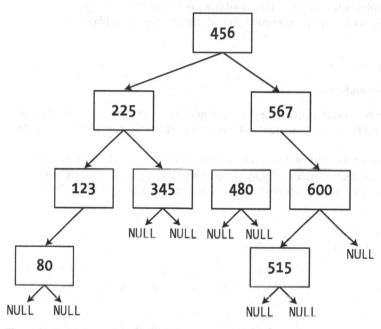

Figure 11-6. *A binary tree storing integers*

The structure of the tree will depend on the sequence in which the data items are added to the tree. Adding a new item involves comparing the data item with the values of the nodes in the tree starting with the root node. If it's less than a given node you then inspect the left subsidiary node, whereas if it's greater you look at the right subsidiary node. This process continues until either you find a node with an equal value, in which case you just update the count for that node, or you arrive at a left or right node pointer that is NULL, and that's where the new node is placed.

Constructing a Binary Tree

The starting point is the creation of the root node. All nodes will be created in the same way so the first step is to define a function that creates a node from a data item. I will assume we are creating a tree to store integers, so the struct definition you saw earlier will apply. Here's the definition of a function that will create a node:

```
struct Node *createnode(long value)
{
  /* Allocate memory for a new node */
  struct Node *pNode = (struct Node *)malloc(sizeof(struct Node));
```

```
  pNode->item = value;                   /* Set the value         */
  pNode->count = 1;                      /* Set the count         */
  pNode->pLeft = pNode->pRight = NULL;   /* No left or right nodes */
  return pNode;
}
```

The function allocates memory for the new Node structure and sets the item member to value. The count member is the number of duplicates of the value in the node so in the first instance this has to be 1. There are no subsidiary nodes at this point so the pLeft and pRight members are set to NULL. The function returns a pointer to the Node object that has been created.

To create the root node for a new binary tree you can just use this function, like this:

```
long newvalue;
printf("Enter the node value: ");
scanf(" %ld", newvalue);
struct Node *pRoot = createnode(newvalue);
```

After reading the value to be stored from the keyboard, you call the createnode() function to create a new node on the heap. Of course, you must not forget to release the memory for the nodes when you are done.

Working with binary trees is one of the areas where recursion really pays off. The process of inserting a node involves inspecting a succession of nodes in the same way, which is a strong indicator that recursion may be helpful. You can add a node to a tree that already exists with the following function:

```
/* Add a new node to the tree */
struct Node *addnode(long value, struct Node* pNode)
{
  if(pNode == NULL)                      /* If there's no node             */
    return createnode(value);           /* ...create one and return it    */

  if(value ==pNode->item)
  {                                      /* Value equals current node      */
    ++pNode->count;                      /* ...so increment count and      */
    return pNode;                        /* ...return the same node        */
  }

  if(value < pNode->item)                /* If less than current node value */
  {
    if(pNode->pLeft == NULL)             /* and there's no left node       */
    {
      pNode->pLeft = createnode(value);  /* create a new left node and     */
      return pNode->pLeft;               /* return it.                     */
    }
    else                                 /* If there is a left node...      */
      return addnode(value, pNode->pLeft); /* add value via the left node   */
  }
  else                                   /* value is greater than current  */
  {
    if(pNode->pRight == NULL)            /* so the same process with       */
    {                                    /* the right node.                */
      pNode-> pRight = createnode(value);
      return pNode-> pRight;
    }
```

```
        else
          return addnode(value, pNode-> pRight);
    }
}
```

The arguments to the addnode() function when you call it in the first instance are the value to be stored in the tree and the address of the root node. If you pass NULL as the second argument it will create and return a new node so you could also use this function to create the root node. When there is a root node passed as the second argument, there are three situations to deal with:

1. If value equals the value in the current node, no new node needs to be created, so you just increment the count in the current node and return it.

2. If value is less than the value in the current node, you need to inspect the left subsidiary node. If the left node pointer is NULL, you create a new node to hold value and make it the left subsidiary node. If the left node exists, you call addnode() recursively with the pointer to the left subsidiary node as the second argument.

3. If value is greater than the value in the current node, you proceed with the right node in the same way as with the left node.

Whatever happens within the recursive function calls, the function will return a pointer to the node where value is inserted. This may be a new node or one of the existing nodes if value is already in the tree somewhere.

You could construct a complete binary tree storing an arbitrary number of integers with the following code:

```
long newvalue = 0;
struct Node *pRoot = NULL;
char answer = 'n';
do
{
  printf("Enter the node value: ");
  scanf(" %ld", &newvalue);
  if(pRoot == NULL)
    pRoot = createnode(newvalue);
  else
    addnode(newvalue, pRoot);

  printf("\nDo you want to enter another (y or n)? ");
  scanf(" %c", &answer);
} while(tolower(answer) == 'y');
```

The do-while loop constructs the complete tree including the root node. On the first iteration pRoot will be NULL, so the root node will be created. All subsequent iterations will add nodes to the existing tree.

Traversing a Binary Tree

You can traverse a binary tree to extract the contents in ascending or descending sequence. I'll discuss how you extract the data in ascending sequence and you'll see how you can produce an descending sequence by analogy. At first sight it seems a complicated problem to extract the data from the tree because of its arbitrary structure but using recursion makes it very easy.

I'll start the explanation of the process by stating the obvious: the value of the left subnode is always less than the current node, and the value of the current node is always less than that of the right subnode. You can conclude from this that the basic process is to extract the values in the sequence: left subnode, followed by current node, followed by right subnode. Of course, where the subnodes have subnodes, the process has to be applied to those too, from left through current to right. It will be easy to see how this works if we look at some code.

Suppose we want to simply list the integer values contained in our binary tree in ascending sequence. The function to do that looks like this:

```c
/* List the node values in ascending sequence */
void listnodes(struct Node *pNode)
{
  if(pNode->pLeft != NULL)
    listnodes(pNode->pLeft);             /* List nodes in the left subtree */

  for(int i = 0; i<pNode->count ; i++)
    printf("\n%10ld", pNode->item);    /* Output the current node value  */

  if(pNode->pRight != NULL)
    listnodes(pNode->pRight);            /* List nodes in the right subtree */
}
```

It consists of three simple steps:

1. If the left subnode exists, you call listnodes() recursively for that node.

2. Write the value for the current node.

3. If the right subnode exists, call listnodes() recursively for that node.

The first step repeats the process for the left subnode of the root if it exists, so the whole subtree to the left will be written before the value of the current node. The value of the current node is repeated count times in the output to reflect the number of duplicate values for that node. The values for the entire right subtree to the root node will be written after the value for the current node. You should be able to see that this happens for every node in the tree, so the values will be written in ascending sequence. All you have to do to output the values in ascending sequence is to call listnodes() with the root node pointer as the argument, like this:

```c
listnodes(pRoot);           /* Output the contents of the tree */
```

In case you find it hard to believe that such a simple function will output all the values in any binary tree of integers you care to construct, let's see it working.

TRY IT OUT: SORTING USING A BINARY TREE

This example drags together the code fragments you have already seen:

```c
/* Program 11.7 Sorting integers using a binary tree */
#include <stdio.h>
#include <stdlib.h>
#include <ctype.h>

/* Function prototypes */
struct Node *createnode(long value);                    /* Create a tree node */
struct Node *addnode(long value, struct Node* pNode);  /* Insert a new node   */
void listnodes(struct Node *pNode);                     /* List all nodes      */
void freenodes(struct Node *pNode);                     /* Release memory      */
```

```c
/* Defines a node in a binary tree sotring integers */
struct Node
{
  long item;                  /* The data item            */
  int count;                  /* Number of copies of item */
  struct Node *pLeft;         /* Pointer to left node     */
  struct Node *pRight;        /* Pointer to right node    */
};

/* Function main - execution starts here */
int main(void)
{
  long newvalue = 0;
  struct Node *pRoot = NULL;
  char answer = 'n';
  do
  {
    printf("Enter the node value: ");
    scanf(" %ld", &newvalue);
    if(pRoot == NULL)
      pRoot = createnode(newvalue);
    else
      addnode(newvalue, pRoot);
    printf("\nDo you want to enter another (y or n)? ");
    scanf(" %c", &answer);
  } while(tolower(answer) == 'y');

  printf("The values in ascending sequence are: ");
  listnodes(pRoot);           /* Output the contents of the tree */
  freenodes(pRoot);           /* Release the heap memory         */

  return 0;
}

struct Node *createnode(long value)
{
  struct Node *pNode = (struct Node *)malloc(sizeof(struct Node));
  pNode->item = value;                  /* Set the value          */
  pNode->count = 1;                     /* Set the count          */
  pNode->pLeft = pNode->pRight = NULL;  /* No left or right nodes */
  return pNode;
}

/* Add a new node to the tree */
struct Node *addnode(long value, struct Node* pNode)
{
  if(pNode == NULL)                     /* If there's no node      */
    return createnode(value);           /* ...create one and return it */

  if(value ==pNode->item)
  {                                     /* Value equals current node   */
    ++pNode->count;                     /* ...so increment count and   */
    return pNode;                       /* ...return the same node     */
  }
```

```
  if(value < pNode->item)                /* If less than current node value */
  {
    if(pNode->pLeft == NULL)             /* and there's no left node        */
    {
      pNode->pLeft = createnode(value);  /* create a new left node and      */
      return pNode->pLeft;               /* return it.                      */
    }
    else                                 /* If there is a left node...      */
      return addnode(value, pNode->pLeft); /* add value via the left node   */
  }
  else                                   /* value is greater than current   */
  {
    if(pNode->pRight == NULL)            /* so the same process with        */
    {                                    /* the right node.                 */
      pNode-> pRight = createnode(value);
      return pNode-> pRight;
    }
    else
      return addnode(value, pNode-> pRight);
  }
}

/* List the node values in ascending sequence */
void listnodes(struct Node *pNode)
{
  if(pNode->pLeft != NULL)
    listnodes(pNode->pLeft);

  for(int i = 0; i<pNode->count ; i++)
    printf("\n%10ld", pNode->item);

  if(pNode->pRight != NULL)
    listnodes(pNode->pRight);
}

/* Release memory allocated to nodes */
void freenodes(struct Node * pNode)
{
  if(pNode == NULL)                 /* If there's no node...          */
    return;                         /* we are done.                   */

  if(pNode->pLeft != NULL)          /* If there's a left sub-tree     */
    freenodes(pNode->pLeft);        /* free memory for those nodes.   */

  if(pNode->pRight != NULL)         /* If there's a right sub-tree    */
    freenodes(pNode->pRight);       /* free memory for those nodes.   */

  free(pNode);                      /* Free current node memory       */
}
```

Here is some typical output from this example:

```
Enter the node value: 56

Do you want to enter another (y or n)? y
Enter the node value: 33

Do you want to enter another (y or n)? y
Enter the node value: 77

Do you want to enter another (y or n)? y
Enter the node value: -10

Do you want to enter another (y or n)? y
Enter the node value: 100

Do you want to enter another (y or n)? y
Enter the node value: -5

Do you want to enter another (y or n)? y
Enter the node value: 200

Do you want to enter another (y or n)? n
The values in ascending sequence are:
    -10
     -5
     33
     56
     77
    100
    200
```

How It Works

The do-while loop in main() constructs the binary tree from the values that are entered in the way I discussed earlier. The loop continues as long as you enter 'y' or 'Y' when prompted. Calling listnodes() with the address of the root node as the argument outputs all the values in the tree in ascending sequence. You then call the freenodes() function to release the memory that is allocated for the nodes for the tree.

The freenodes() function is the only new code in the example. This is another recursive function that works in a similar way to the listnodes() function. It is essential to delete the memory for the subsidiary nodes of each node before freeing the memory for the node itself, because once you have freed a memory block, it could be used immediately by some other program that is executing concurrently. This means that the addresses for the subsidiary nodes are effectively unavailable once the memory has been released. The function therefore always calls freenodes() for the subsidiary node pointers if they are not NULL before releasing the memory for the current node.

You can construct binary trees to store any kind of data including struct objects and strings. If you want to organize strings in a binary tree for example, you could use a pointer in each node to refer to the string rather than making copies of the strings within the tree.

Sharing Memory

You've already seen how you can save memory through the use of bit-fields, which are typically applied to logical variables. C has a further capability that allows you to place several variables in the same memory area. This can be applied somewhat more widely than bit-fields when memory is short, because circumstances frequently arise in practice in which you're working with several variables, but only one of them holds a valid value at any given moment.

Another situation in which you can share memory between a number of variables to some advantage is when your program processes a number of different kinds of data record, but only one kind at a time, and the kind to be processed is determined at execution time. A third possibility is that you want to access the same data at different times, and assume it's of a different type on different occasions. You might have a group of variables of numeric data types, for instance, that you want to treat as simply an array of type char so that you can move them about as a single chunk of data.

Unions

The facility in C that allows the same memory area to be shared by a number of different variables is called a **union**. The syntax for declaring a union is similar to that used for structures, and a union is usually given a tag name in the same way. You use the keyword union to define a union. For example, the following statement declares a union to be shared by three variables:

```
union u_example
{
  float decval;
  int *pnum;
  double my_value;
} U1;
```

This statement declares a union with the tag name u_example, which shares memory between a floating-point value decval, a pointer to an integer pnum, and a double precision floating-point variable my_value. The statement also defines one instance of the union with a variable name of U1. You can declare further instances of this union with a statement such as this:

```
union u_example U2, U3;
```

Members of a union are accessed in exactly the same way as members of a structure. For example, to assign values to members of U1 and U2, you can write this:

```
U1.decval = 2.5;
U2.decval = 3.5 * U1.decval;
```

TRY IT OUT: USING UNIONS

Here's a simple example that makes use of a union:

```
/* Program 11.8 The operation of a union */
#include <stdio.h>

int main(void)
{
  union u_example
  {
    float decval;
    int pnum;
    double my_value;
  } U1;
```

```
    U1.my_value = 125.5;
    U1.pnum = 10;
    U1.decval = 1000.5f;
    printf("\ndecval = %f    pnum = %d    my_value = %lf",
                    U1.decval, U1.pnum, U1.my_value );

    printf("\nU1 size = %d\ndecval size = %d    pnum size = %d    my_value"
                        " size = %d",sizeof U1, sizeof U1.decval,
                            sizeof U1.pnum, sizeof U1.my_value);
    return 0;
}
```

How It Works

This example demonstrates the structure and basic operation of a union. You declare the union U1 as follows:

```
union u_example
{
  float decval;
  int pnum;
  double my_value;
} U1;
```

The three members of the union are of different types and they each require a different amount of storage (assuming your compiler assigns 2 bytes to variables of type int).

With the assignment statements, you assign a value to each of the members of the union instance U1 in turn:

```
  U1.my_value = 125.5;
  U1.pnum = 10;
  U1.decval = 1000.5f;
```

Notice that you reference each member of the union in the same way as you do members of a structure.

The next two statements output each of the three member values, the size of the union U1, and the size of each of its members. You get this output (or something close if your machine assigns 4 bytes to variables of type int):

```
decval = 1000.500000    pnum = 8192    my_value = 125.50016
U1 size = 8
decval size = 4    pnum size = 2    my_value size = 8
```

The first thing to note is that the last variable that was assigned a value is correct, and the other two have been corrupted. This is to be expected, because they all share the same memory space. The second thing to notice is how little the member my_value has been corrupted. This is because only the least significant part of my_value is being modified. In a practical situation, such a small error could easily be overlooked, but the ultimate consequences could be dire. You need to take great care when using unions that you aren't using invalid data.

Note You can see from the output of the sizes of the union and its members that the size of the union is the same as the size of the largest member.

Pointers to Unions

You can also define a pointer to a union with a statement such as this:

```
union u_example *pU;
```

Once the pointer has been defined, you can modify members of the union, via the pointer, with these statements:

```
pU = &U2;
U1.decval = pU->decval;
```

The expression on the right of the second assignment is equivalent to U2.decval.

Initializing Unions

If you wish to initialize an instance of a union when you declare it, you can initialize it only with a constant of the same type as the first variable in the union. The union just declared, u_example, can be initialized only with a float constant, as in the following:

```
union u_example U4 = 3.14f;
```

You can always rearrange the sequence of members in a definition of a union so that the member that you want to initialize occurs first. The sequence of members has no other significance, because all members overlap in the same memory area.

Structures As Union Members

Structures and arrays can be members of a union. It's also possible for a union to be a member of a structure. To illustrate this, you could write the following:

```
struct my_structure
{
  int num1;
  float num2;
  union
  {
    int *pnum;
    float *pfnum;
  } my_U
} samples[5];
```

Here you declare a structure type, my_structure, which contains a union without a tag name, so instances of the union can exist only within instances of the structure. This is often described as an **anonymous union**. You also define an array of five instances of the structure, referenced by the variable name samples. The union within the structure shares memory between two pointers. To reference members of the union, you use the same notation that you used for nested structures. For example, to access the pointer to int in the third element of the structure array, you use the expression appearing on the left in the following statement:

```
samples[2].my_U.pnum = &my_num;
```

You're assuming here that the variable my_num has been declared as type int.

It's important to realize that when you're using a value stored in a union, you always retrieve the last value assigned. This may seem obvious, but in practice it's all too easy to use a value as float that has most recently been stored as an integer, and sometimes the error can be quite subtle, as shown by the curious output of my_value in Program 11.7. Naturally, you'll usually end up with garbage if you do this. One technique that is often adopted is to embed a union in a struct that also has a member that specifies what type of value is currently stored in the union. For example

```
/* Type code for data in union */
#define TYPE_LONG    1
#define TYPE_FLOAT   2
#define TYPE_CHAR    3

struct Item
{
  int u_type;
  union
  {
    long integer;
    float floating;
    char ch;
  } u;
} var;
```

This defines the Item structure type that contains two members: a value u_type of type int, and an instance u of an anonymous union. The union can store a value of type long, type float or type char, and the u_type member is used to record the type that is currently stored in u.

You could set a value for var like this:

```
var.u.floating = 2.5f;
var.u_type = TYPE_FLOAT;
```

When you are processing var, you need to check what kind of value is stored. Here's an example of how you might do that:

```
switch(var.u_type)
{
  case TYPE_FLOAT:
  printf("\nValue of var is %10f", var.u.floating);
  break;
  case TYPE_LONG:
  printf("\nValue of var is %10ld", var.u.integer);
  break;
  case TYPE_CHAR:
  printf("\nValue of var is %10c", var.u.ch);
  break;
  default:
  printf("\nInvalid union type code.");
  break;
}
```

When working with unions is this way it is usually convenient to put code such as this in a function.

Defining Your Own Data Types

With structures you've come pretty close to defining your own data types. It doesn't look quite right because you must use the keyword struct in your declarations of structure variables. Declaration of a variable for a built-in type is simpler. However, there's a feature of the C language that permits you to get over this and make the declaration of variables of structure types you've defined follow exactly the same syntax as for the built-in types. You can apply this feature to simplify types derived from the built-in types, but here, with structures, it really comes into its own.

Structures and the typedef Facility

Suppose you have a structure for geometric points with three coordinates, x, y, and z, that you define with the following statement:

```
struct pts
{
  int x;
  int y;
  int z;
};
```

You can now define an alternative name for declaring such structures using the keyword typedef. The following statement shows how you might do this:

```
typedef struct pts Point;
```

This statement specifies that the name Point is a synonym for struct pts.

When you want to declare some instances of the structure pts, you can use a statement such as this:

```
Point start_pt;
Point end_pt;
```

Here, you declare the two structure variables start_pt and end_pt. The struct keyword isn't necessary, and you have a very natural way of declaring structure variables. The appearance of the statement is exactly the same form as a declaration for a float or an int.

You could combine the typedef and the structure declaration as follows:

```
typedef struct pts
{
  int x;
  int y;
  int z;
} Point;
```

Don't confuse this with a basic struct declaration. Here, Point isn't a structure variable name! this is a type name you're defining. When you need to declare structure variables, as you've just seen, you can use a statement such as this:

```
Point my_pt;
```

There's nothing to prevent you from having several types defined that pertain to a single structure type, or any other type for that matter, although this can be confusing in some situations. One application of this that can help to make your program more understandable is where you're using a basic type for a specific kind of value and you would like to use a type name to reflect the kind of variable you're creating. For example, suppose your application involves weights of different kinds, such as weights of components and weights of assembly. You might find it useful to define a type name, weight, as a synonym for type double. You could do this with the following statement:

```
typedef double weight;
```

You can now declare variables of type weight:

```
weight piston = 6.5;
weight valve = 0.35;
```

Of course, these variables are all of type double because weight is just a synonym for double, and you can still declare variables of type double in the usual way.

Simplifying Code Using typedef

Another useful application of typedef is to simplify complicated types that can arise. Suppose you have occasion to frequently define pointers to the structure pts. You could define a type to do this for you with this statement:

```
typedef struct pts *pPoint;
```

Now, when you want to declare some pointers, you can just write this:

```
pPoint pfirst;
pPoint plast;
```

The two variables declared here are both pointers to structures of type pts. The declarations are less error-prone to write and they're also easier to understand.

In Chapter 9 I discussed pointers to functions, which are declared with an even more complicated notation. One of the examples has the pointer declaration:

```
int(*pfun)(int, int);               /* Function pointer declaration */
```

If you are expecting to use several pointers to functions of this kind in a program, you can use typedef to declare a generic type for such declarations with this statement:

```
typedef int (*function_pointer)(int, int);    /* Function pointer type */
```

This doesn't declare a variable of type •pointer to a function.! This declares function_pointer as a type name that you can use to declare a •pointer to function! , so you can replace the original declaration of pfun with this statement:

```
function_pointer pfun;
```

This is evidently much simpler than what you started with. The benefit in simplicity is even more marked if you have several such pointers to declare, because you can declare three pointers to functions with the following statements:

```
function_pointer pfun1;
function_pointer pfun2;
function_pointer pfun3;
```

Of course, you can also initialize them, so if you assume you have the functions sum(), product(), and difference(), you can declare and initialize your pointers with the following:

```
function_pointer pfun1 = sum;
function_pointer pfun2 = difference;
function_pointer pfun3 = product;
```

The type name that you've defined naturally only applies to •pointers to functions! with the arguments and return type that you specified in the typedef statement. If you want something different, you can simply define another type.

Designing a Program

You've reached the end of another long chapter, and it's time to see how you can put what you've learned into practice in the context of a more substantial example.

The Problem

Numerical data is almost always easier and faster to understand when it's presented graphically. The problem that you're going tackle is to write a program that produces a vertical bar chart from a set of data values. This is an interesting problem for a couple of reasons. It will enable you to make use of structures in a practical context. The problem also involves working out how to place and present the bar chart within the space available, which is the kind of messy manipulation that comes up quite often in real-world applications.

The Analysis

You won't be making any assumptions about the size of the •page! that you're going to output to, or the number of columns, or even the scale of the chart. Instead, you'll just write a function that accepts a dimension for the output page and then makes the set of bars fit the page, if possible. This will make the function useful in virtually any situation. You'll store the values in a sequence of structures in a linked list. In this way, you'll just need to pass the first structure to the function, and the function will be able to get at them all. You'll keep the structure very simple, but you can embellish it later with other information of your own design.

Assume that the order in which the bars are to appear in the chart is going to be the same as the order in which the data values are entered, so you won't need to sort them. There will be two functions in your program: a function that generates the bar chart, and a function main() that exercises the bar chart generation process.

These are the steps required:

1. Write the bar-chart function.

2. Write a main() function to test the bar-chart function once you've written it.

The Solution

This section outlines the steps you'll take to solve the problem.

Step 1

Obviously, you're going to use a structure in this program because that's what this chapter is about. The first stage is to design the structure that you'll use throughout the program. You'll use a typedef so that you don't have to keep reusing the keyword struct.

```
/* Program 11.9 Generating a bar chart */
#include <stdio.h>

typedef struct barTAG
{
  double value;
  struct barTAG *pnextbar;
}bar;
```

```
int main(void)
{
  /* Code for main */
}
```

```
/* Definition of the bar-chart function */
```

The barTAG structure will define a bar simply by its value. Notice how you define the pointer in the structure to the next structure. This will enable you to store the bars as a linked list, which has the merit that you can allocate memory as you go so none will be wasted. This suits this situation because you'll only ever want to step through the bars from the first to the last. You'll create them in sequence from the input values and append each new bar to the tail of the previous one. You'll then create the visual representation of the bar chart by stepping through the structures in the linked list. You may have thought that the typedef statement would mean that you could use the bar type name that you're defining here. However, you have to use struct barTAG here because at this point the compiler hasn't finished processing the typedef yet, so bar isn't defined. In other words, the barTAG structure is analyzed first by the compiler, after which the typedef can be expedited to define the meaning of bar.

Now you can specify the function prototype for the bar-chart function and put the skeleton of the definition for the function. It will need to have parameters for a pointer to the first bar in the linked list, the page height and width, and the title for the chart to be produced:

```
/* Program 11.9 Generating a bar chart */
#include <stdio.h>

#define PAGE_HEIGHT  20
#define PAGE_WIDTH   40
typedef struct barTAG
{
  double value;
  struct barTAG *pnextbar;
}bar;

typedef unsigned int uint;    /* Type definition*/

/* Function prototype */
int bar_chart(bar *pfirstbar, uint page_width, uint page_height, char *title);

int main(void)
{
  /* Code for main */
}

int bar_chart(bar *pfirstbar, uint page_width, uint page_height,
                                            char *title)
{
  /* Code for function... */
  return 0;
}
```

You've added a typedef to define uint as an alternative to unsigned int. This will shorten statements that declare variables of type unsigned int.

Next, you can add some declarations and code for the basic data that you need for the bar chart. You'll need the maximum and minimum values for the bars and the vertical height of the chart, which will be determined by the difference between the maximum and minimum values. You also need to calculate the width of a bar, given the page width and the number of bars, and you must adjust the height to accommodate a horizontal axis and the title:

```c
/* Program 11.9 Generating a bar chart */
#include <stdio.h>

#define PAGE_HEIGHT 20
#define PAGE_WIDTH  40

typedef struct barTAG
{
  double value;
  struct barTAG *pnextbar;
}bar;

typedef unsigned int uint;       /* Type definition */

/* Function prototype */
int bar_chart(bar *pfirstbar, uint page_width, uint page_height,
                                              char *title);

int main(void)
{
   /* Code for main */
}

int bar_chart(bar *pfirstbar, uint page_width, uint page_height,
                                              char *title)
{
  bar *plastbar = pfirstbar;   /* Pointer to previous bar        */
  double max = 0.0;            /* Maximum bar value              */
  double min = 0.0;            /* Minimum bar value              */
  double vert_scale = 0.0;     /* Unit step in vertical direction */
  uint bar_count = 1;          /* Number of bars - at least 1    */
  uint barwidth = 0;           /* Width of a bar                 */
  uint space = 2;              /* spaces between bars            */

   /* Find maximum and minimum of all bar values */

   /* Set max and min to first bar value */
   max = min = plastbar->value;

   while((plastbar = plastbar->pnextbar) != NULL)
   {
     bar_count++;                  /* Increment bar count */
     max = (max < plastbar->value)? plastbar->value : max;
     min = (min > plastbar->value)? plastbar->value : min;
   }
   vert_scale = (max - min)/page_height; /* Calculate step length */
```

```
/* Check bar width */
if((barwidth = page_width/bar_count - space) < 1)
{
  printf("\nPage width too narrow.\n");
  return -1;
}

/* Code for rest of the function... */
return 0;
}
```

The space variable stores the number of spaces separating one bar from the next, and you arbitrarily assign the value 2 for this.

You will, of necessity, be outputting the chart a row at a time. Therefore, you'll need a string that corresponds to a section across a bar that you can use to draw that bar row by row, and a string of the same length, containing spaces to use when there's no bar at a particular position across the page. Let's add the code to create these:

```
/* Program 11.9 Generating a bar chart */
#include <stdio.h>
#include <stdlib.h>

#define PAGE_HEIGHT   20
#define PAGE_WIDTH    40

typedef struct barTAG
{
  double value;
  struct barTAG *pnextbar;
}bar;

typedef unsigned int uint;    /* Type definition */

/* Function prototype */
int bar_chart(bar *pfirstbar, uint page_width, uint page_height,
                                               char *title);

int main(void)
{
  /* Code for main */
}

int bar_chart(bar *pfirstbar, uint page_width, uint page_height,
                                               char *title)
{
  bar *plastbar = pfirstbar;  /* Pointer to previous bar          */
  double max = 0.0;           /* Maximum bar value                */
  double min = 0.0;           /* Minimum bar value                */
  double vert_scale = 0.0;    /* Unit step in vertical direction  */
  uint bar_count = 1;         /* Number of bars - at least 1      */
  uint barwidth = 0;          /* Width of a bar                   */
  uint space = 2;             /* spaces between bars              */
  uint i = 0;                 /* Loop counter                     */
  char *column = NULL;        /* Pointer to bar column section    */
  char *blank = NULL;         /* Blank string for bar+space       */
```

```
/* Find maximum and minimum of all bar values */

/* Set max and min to first bar value */
max = min = plastbar->value;

while((plastbar = plastbar->pnextbar) != NULL)
{
  bar_count++;                   /* Increment bar count */
  max = (max < plastbar->value)? plastbar->value : max;
  min = (min > plastbar->value)? plastbar->value : min;
}
vert_scale = (max - min)/page_height; /* Calculate step length */

/* Check bar width */
if((barwidth = page_width/bar_count - space) < 1)
{
  printf("\nPage width too narrow.\n");
  return -1;
}

/* Set up a string that will be used to build the columns */

/* Get the memory */
if((column = malloc(barwidth + space + 1)) == NULL)
{
  printf("\nFailed to allocate memory in barchart()"
                     " - terminating program.\n");
  exit(1);
}
for(i = 0 ; i<space ; i++)
  *(column+i)=' ';            /* Blank the space between bars */
for( ; i<space+barwidth ; i++)
  *(column+i)='#';            /* Enter the bar characters    */
*(column+i) = '\0';           /* Add string terminator       */

/* Set up a string that will be used as a blank column */

/* Get the memory */
if((blank = malloc(barwidth + space + 1)) == NULL)
{
  printf("\nFailed to allocate memory in barchart()"
                     " - terminating program.\n");
  exit(1);
}

for(i = 0 ; i<space+barwidth ; i++)
  *(blank+i) = ' ';           /* Blank total width of bar+space */
*(blank+i) = '\0';            /* Add string terminator          */

/* Code for rest of the function... */
free(blank);                  /* Free memory for blank string  */
free(column);                 /* Free memory for column string */
return 0;
}
```

You'll draw a bar using '#' characters. When you draw a bar, you'll write a string containing space spaces and barwidth '#' characters. You allocate the memory for this dynamically using the library function malloc(), so you must add an #include directive for the header file stdlib.h. The string that you'll use to draw a bar is column, and blank is a string of the same length containing spaces. After the bar chart has been drawn and just before you exit, you free the memory occupied by column and blank.

Next, you can add the final piece of code that draws the chart:

```
/* Program 11.9 Generating a bar chart */
#include <stdio.h>
#include <stdlib.h>
#include <stdbool.h>

#define PAGE_HEIGHT  20
#define PAGE_WIDTH   40

typedef struct barTAG
{
  double value;
  struct barTAG *pnextbar;
}bar;

typedef unsigned int uint;     /* Type definition */

/* Function prototype */
int bar_chart(bar *pfirstbar, uint page_width, uint page_height,
                                              char *title);
int main(void)
{
  /* Code for main */
}

int bar_chart(bar *pfirstbar, uint page_width, uint page_height,
                                              char *title)
{
  bar *plastbar = pfirstbar;  /* Pointer to previous bar           */
  double max = 0.0;           /* Maximum bar value                 */
  double min = 0.0;           /* Minimum bar value                 */
  double vert_scale = 0.0;    /* Unit step in vertical direction   */
  double position = 0.0;      /* Current vertical position on chart */
  uint bar_count = 1;         /* Number of bars - at least 1       */
  uint barwidth = 0;          /* Width of a bar                    */
  uint space = 2;             /* spaces between bars               */
  uint i = 0;                 /* Loop counter                      */
  uint bars = 0;              /* Loop counter through bars         */
  char *column = NULL;        /* Pointer to bar column section     */
  char *blank = NULL;         /* Blank string for bar+space        */
  bool axis = false;          /* Indicates axis drawn              */

  /* Find maximum and minimum of all bar values */

  /* Set max and min to first bar value */
  max = min = plastbar->value;
```

```
while((plastbar = plastbar->pnextbar) != NULL)
{
  bar_count++;                   /* Increment bar count */
  max = (max < plastbar->value)? plastbar->value : max;
  min = (min > plastbar->value)? plastbar->value : min;
}
vert_scale = (max - min)/page_height; /* Calculate step length */

/* Check bar width */
if((barwidth = page_width/bar_count - space) < 1)
{
  printf("\nPage width too narrow.\n");
  return -1;
}

/* Set up a string that will be used to build the columns */

/* Get the memory */
if((column = malloc(barwidth + space + 1)) == NULL)
{
  printf("\nFailed to allocate memory in barchart()"
                      " - terminating program.\n");
  exit(1);
}
for(i = 0 ; i<space ; i++)
  *(column+i)=' ';             /* Blank the space between bars */
for( ; i < space+barwidth ; i++)
  *(column+i)='#';             /* Enter the bar characters      */
*(column+i) = '\0';            /* Add string terminator         */

/* Set up a string that will be used as a blank column */

/* Get the memory */
if((blank = malloc(barwidth + space + 1)) == NULL)
{
  printf("\nFailed to allocate memory in barchart()"
                      " - terminating program.\n");
  exit(1);
}

for(i = 0 ; i<space+barwidth ; i++)
  *(blank+i) = ' ';            /* Blank total width of bar+space */
*(blank+i) = '\0';            /* Add string terminator         */

printf("^ %s\n", title);    /* Output the chart title       */
```

```
/* Draw the bar chart */
position = max;
for(i = 0 ; i <= page_height ; i++)
{
  /* Check if we need to output the horizontal axis */
  if(position <= 0.0 && !axis)
  {
    printf("+");              /* Start of horizontal axis   */
    for(bars = 0; bars < bar_count*(barwidth+space); bars++)
      printf("-");            /* Output horizontal axis     */
    printf(">\n");
    axis = true;             /* Axis was drawn             */
    position -= vert_scale;/* Decrement position         */
    continue;
  }
  printf("|");               /* Output vertical axis       */
  plastbar = pfirstbar;      /* start with the first bar   */

  /* For each bar... */
  for(bars = 1; bars <= bar_count; bars++)
  {
    /* If position is between axis and value, output column */
    /* otherwise output blank                               */
    printf("%s", position <= plastbar->value &&
                 plastbar->value >= 0.0 && position > 0.0 ||
                 position >= plastbar->value &&
                 plastbar->value <= 0.0 &&
                 position <= 0.0 ? column: blank);
    plastbar = plastbar->pnextbar;
  }
  printf("\n");              /* End the line of output     */
  position -= vert_scale;  /* Decrement position         */
}
if(!axis)                  /* Have we output the horizontal axis? */
{                          /* No, so do it now           */
  printf("+");
  for(bars = 0; bars < bar_count*(barwidth+space); bars++)
    printf("-");
  printf(">\n");
}

free(blank);              /* Free memory for blank string  */
free(column);             /* Free memory for column string */
return 0;
}
```

The `for` loop outputs `page_height` lines of characters. Each line will represent a distance of `vert_scale` on the vertical axis. You get this value by dividing `page_height` by the difference between the maximum and minimum values. Therefore, the first line of output corresponds to `position` having the value `max`, and it's decremented by `vert_scale` on each iteration until it reaches `min`.

On each line, you must decide first if you need to output the horizontal axis. This will be necessary when position is less than or equal to 0 and you haven't already displayed the axis.

On lines other than the horizontal axis, you must decide what to display for each bar position. This is done in the inner for loop that repeats for each bar. The conditional operator in the printf() call outputs either column or blank. You output column if position is between the value of the bar and 0, and you output blank otherwise. Having output a complete row of bar segments, you output '\n' to end the line and decrement the value of position.

It's possible that all the bars could be positive, in which case you need to make sure that the horizontal axis is output after the loop is complete, because it won't be output from within the loop.

Step 2

Now you just need to implement main() to exercise the bar_chart() function:

```c
/* Program 11.9 Generating a bar chart */
#include <stdio.h>
#include <string.h>
#include <stdlib.h>
#include <stdbool.h>

#define PAGE_HEIGHT  20
#define PAGE_WIDTH   40

typedef struct barTAG        /* Bar structure       */
{
  double value;              /* Value of bar        */
  struct barTAG *pnextbar;   /* Pointer to next bar */
}bar;                        /* Type for a bar      */

typedef unsigned int uint;   /* Type definition     */

/* Function prototype */
int bar_chart(bar *pfirstbar, uint page_width, uint page_height, char *title);

int main()
{
  bar firstbar;              /* First bar structure */
  bar *plastbar = NULL;      /* Pointer to last bar */
  char value[80];            /* Input buffer        */
  char title[80];            /* Chart title         */

  printf("\nEnter the chart title: ");
  gets(title);               /* Read chart title    */

  for( ;; )                  /* Loop for bar input  */
  {
    printf("Enter the value of the bar, or use quit to end: ");
    gets(value);
```

```
    if(strcmp(value, "quit") == 0)    /* quit entered?      */
     break;                           /* then input finished */

    /* Store in next bar */
    if(!plastbar)                      /* First time?        */
    {
      firstbar.pnextbar = NULL;  /* Initialize next pointer */
      plastbar = &firstbar;        /* Use the first            */
    }
    else
    {
      /* Get memory */
      if(!(plastbar-> = malloc(sizeof(bar))))
      {
        printf("Oops! Couldn't allocate memory\n");
        return -1;
      }
      plastbar = plastbar->pnextbar;    /* Old next is new bar  */
      plastbar->pnextbar = NULL;        /* New bar next is NULL */
    }
    plastbar->value = atof(value);      /* Store the value      */
  }

  /* Create bar-chart */
  bar_chart(&firstbar, PAGE_WIDTH, PAGE_HEIGHT, title);

  /* We are done, so release all the memory we allocated */
  while(firstbar.pnextbar)
  {
    plastbar = firstbar.pnextbar;                /* Save pointer to next */
    firstbar.pnextbar = plastbar->pnextbar; /* Get one after next    */
    free(plastbar);                              /* Free next memory      */
  }
  return 0;
}


int bar_chart(bar *pfirstbar, uint page_width, uint page_height, char *title)
{
  /* Implementation of function as before... */
}
```

After reading the chart title using gets(), you read successive values in the for loop. For each value other than the first, you allocate the memory for a new bar structure before storing the value. Of course, you keep track of the first structure, firstbar, because this is the link to all the others, and you track the pointer to the last structure that you added so that you can update its pnextbar pointer when you add another. Once you have all the values, you call bar_chart() to produce the chart. Finally, you delete the memory for the bars. Note that you need to take care to not delete firstbar, as you didn't allocate the memory for this dynamically. You need an #include directive for string.h because you use the gets() function.

All you do then is add a line to main() that actually prints the chart from the values typed in. Typical output from the example is shown here:

```
Enter the chart title: Trial Bar Chart
Enter the value of the bar, or use quit to end: 6
Enter the value of the bar, or use quit to end: 3
Enter the value of the bar, or use quit to end: -5
Enter the value of the bar, or use quit to end: -7
Enter the value of the bar, or use quit to end: 9
Enter the value of the bar, or use quit to end: 4
Enter the value of the bar, or use quit to end: quit


^ Trial Bar Chart
|                             ####
|                             ####
|                             ####
|                             ####
|    ####                     ####
|    ####                     ####
|    ####                     ####
|    ####                     #### ####
|    #### ####                #### ####
|    #### ####                #### ####
|    #### ####                #### ####
|    #### ####                #### ####
+----------------------------------->
|             #### ####
|             #### ####
|             #### ####
|             #### ####
|             #### ####
|             ####
|             ####
|             ####
```

Summary

This has been something of a marathon chapter, but the topic is extremely important. Having a good grasp of structures rates alongside understanding pointers and functions in importance, if you want to use C effectively.

Most real-world applications deal with things such as people, cars, or materials, which require several different values to represent them. Structures in C provide a ready tool for dealing with these sorts of complex objects. Although some of the operations may seem a little complicated, remember that you're dealing with complicated entities, so the complexity isn't implicit in the programming capability; rather, it's built into the problem you're tackling.

In the next chapter, you'll look at how you can store data in external files. This will, of course, include the ability to store structures.

Exercises

The following exercises enable you to try out what you've learned in this chapter. If you get stuck, look back over the chapter for help. If you're still stuck, you can download the solutions from the Source Code/Download area of the Apress web site (http://www.apress.com), but that really should be a last resort.

Exercise 11-1. Define a struct type with the name Length that represents a length in yards, feet, and inches. Define an add() function that will add two Length arguments and return the sum as type Length. Define a second function, show(), that will display the value of its Length argument. Write a program that will use the Length type and the add() and show() functions to sum an arbitrary number of lengths in yards, feet, and inches that are entered from the keyboard and output the total length.

Exercise 11-2. Define a struct type that contains a person's name consisting of a first name and a second name, plus the person's phone number. Use this struct in a program that will allow one or more names and corresponding numbers to be entered and will store the entries in an array of structures. The program should allow a second name to be entered and output all the numbers corresponding to the name, and optionally output all the names with their corresponding numbers.

Exercise 11-3. Modify or reimplement the program from the previous exercise to store the structures in a linked list in ascending alphabetical order of the names.

Exercise 11-4. Write a program to use a struct to count the number of occurrences of each different word in a paragraph of text that's entered from the keyboard.

Exercise 11-5. Write a program that reads an arbitrary number of names consisting of a first name followed by a last name. The program should use a binary tree to output the names in ascending alphabetical sequence ordered by first name within second name (i.e., second name takes precedence in the ordering so Ann Choosy comes after Bill Champ and before Arthur Choosy).

CHAPTER 12

■ ■ ■

Working with Files

If your computer could only ever process data stored within the main memory of the machine, the scope and variety of applications that you could deal with would be severely limited. Virtually all serious business applications require more data than would fit into main memory and depend on the ability to process data that's stored on an external device, such as a fixed disk drive. In this chapter, you'll explore how you can process data stored in files on an external device.

C provides a range of functions in the header file <stdio.h> for writing to and reading from external devices. The external device you would use for storing and retrieving data is typically a fixed disk drive, but not exclusively. Because, consistent with the philosophy of the C language, the library facilities that you'll use for working with files are device-independent, so they apply to virtually any external storage device. However, I'll assume in the examples in this chapter that we are dealing with disk files.

In this chapter you'll learn the following:

! What a file is in C

! How files are processed

! How to write and read formatted files and binary files

! How to retrieve data from a file by direct random access to the information

! How to use temporary work files in a program

! How to update binary files

! How to write a file viewer program

The Concept of a File

With all the examples you've seen up to now, any data that the user enters when the program is executed is lost once the program finishes running. At the moment, if the user wants to run the program with the same data, he or she must enter it again each time. There are a lot of occasions when this is not only inconvenient, but also makes the programming task impossible.

If you want to maintain a directory of names, addresses, and telephone numbers, for instance, a program in which you have to enter all the names, addresses, and telephone numbers each time you run it is worse than useless! The answer is to store data on permanent storage that continues to be maintained after your computer is switched off. As I'm sure you know, this storage is called a **file**, and a file is usually stored on a hard disk.

You're probably familiar with the basic mechanics of how a disk works. If so, this can help you recognize when a particular approach to file usage is efficient and when it isn't. On the other hand, if you know nothing about disk file mechanics, don't worry at this point. There's nothing in the concept of file processing in C that depends on any knowledge of physical storage devices.

A file is essentially a serial sequence of bytes, as illustrated in Figure 12-1.

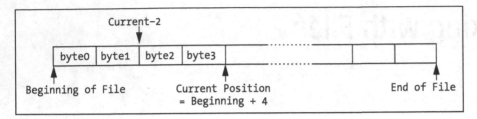

Figure 12-1. *Structure of a file*

Positions in a File

A file has a beginning and an end, and it has a **current position**, typically defined as so many bytes from the beginning, as Figure 12-1 illustrates. The current position is where any file action (a read from the file or a write to the file) will take place. You can move the current position to any other point in the file. A new current position can be specified as an offset from the beginning of the file or, in some circumstances, as a positive or negative offset from the previous current position.

File Streams

The C library provides functions for reading and writing to or from data streams. A **stream** is an abstract representation of any external source or destination for data, so the keyboard, the command line on your display, and files on disk are all examples of streams. You therefore use the same input/output functions for reading and writing any external device that is mapped to a stream.

There are two ways of writing data to a stream that is a disk file. Firstly, you can write a file as a **text file**, in which case data is written as a characters organized as lines, where each line is terminated by a newline character. Obviously, binary data such as values of type int or type double have to be converted to characters to allow them to be written to a text file, and you've already seen how this formatting is done with the printf() function. Secondly you can write a file as a **binary file**. Data that is written to a binary file is always written as a series of bytes, exactly as it appears in memory, so a value of type double for example would be written as the 8 bytes that appear in memory.

Of course, you can write any data you like to a file, but once a file has been written, it just consists of a series of bytes on disk. Regardless of whether you write a file as a binary file or as a text file, it ultimately ends up as just a series of bytes, whatever the data is. This means that when the file is read, the program must know what sort of data the file represents. You've seen many times now that exactly what a series of bytes represents is dependent upon how you interpret it. A sequence of 12 bytes in a binary file could be 12 characters, 12 8-bit signed integers, 12 8-bit unsigned integers, 6 16-bit signed integers, a 32-bit integer followed by an 8-byte floating-point value, and so on. All of these will be more or less valid interpretations of the data, so it's important that a program that is reading a file has the correct assumptions about how it was written.

Accessing Files

The files that are resident on your disk drive each have a name, and the rules for naming files will be determined by your operating system. When you write a program to process a file, it would not be particularly convenient if the program would only work with a specific file with a particular name. If it did, you would need to produce a different program for each file you might want to process. For this reason, when you process a file in C, your program references a file through a **file pointer**. A file pointer is an abstract pointer that is associated with a particular file when the program is run so that the program can work with different files on different occasions. A file pointer points to a struct that represents a stream. In the examples in this chapter, I'll use Microsoft Windows file names. If you're using a different operating system environment, such as UNIX, you'll need to adjust the names of the files appropriately.

If you want to use several files simultaneously in a program, you need a separate file pointer for each file, although as soon as you've finished using one file, you can associate the file pointer you were using with another file. So if you need to process several files, but you'll be working with them one at a time, you can do it with one file pointer.

Opening a File

You associate a specific external file name with an internal file pointer variable through a process referred to as **opening a file**. You open a file by calling the standard library function fopen(), which returns the file pointer for a specific external file. The function fopen() is defined in <stdio.h>, and it has this prototype:

```
FILE *fopen(char *name, char *mode);
```

The first argument to the function is a pointer to a string that is the name of the external file that you want to process. You can specify the name explicitly as an argument, or you can use an array, or a variable of type pointer to char that contains the address of the character string that defines the file name. You would typically obtain the file name through some external means, such as from the command line when the program is started, or you could arrange to read it in from the keyboard. Of course, you can also define a file name as a constant at the beginning of a program when the program always works with the same file.

The second argument to the fopen() function is a character string called the **file mode** that specifies what you want to do with the file. As you'll see, this spans a whole range of possibilities, but for the moment I'll introduce just three file modes (which nonetheless comprise the basic set of operations on a file). Table 12-1 lists these three file modes.

Table 12-1. *File Modes*

Mode	Description
"w"	Open a text file for write operations. If the file exists, its current contents are discarded.
"a"	Open a text file for append operations. All writes are to the end of the file.
"r"	Open a text file for read operations.

■**Note** Notice that a file mode specification is a character string between double quotes, not a single character between single quotes.

These three modes only apply to text files that are files that are written as characters. You can also work with binary files that are written as a sequence of bytes and I'll discuss that in the section •Binary File Input and Output! later in this chapter. Assuming the call to fopen() is successful, the function returns a pointer of type File * that you can use to reference the file in further input/output operations, using other functions in the library. If the file cannot be opened for some reason, fopen() returns a null pointer.

■Note The pointer returned by fopen() is referred to as a **file pointer**, or a **stream pointer**.

So a call to fopen() does two things for you: it creates a file pointer that identifies the specific file on disk that your program is going to operate on, and it determines what you can do with that file within your program.

The pointer that's returned by fopen() is of type FILE * or •pointer to FILE,! where FILE specifies a structure type that has been predefined in the header file <stdio.h> through a typedef. The structure that a file pointer points to will contain information about the file. This will be such things as the open mode you specified, the address of the buffer in memory to be used for data, and a pointer to the current position in the file for the next operation. You don't need to worry about the contents of this structure in practice. It's all taken care of by the input/output functions. However, if you really want to know about the FILE structure, you can browse through the library header file.

As I mentioned earlier, when you want to have several files open at once, they must each have their own file pointer variable declared, and you open each of them with a separate call to fopen () with the value that is returned stored in a separate file pointer. There's a limit to the number of files you can have open at one time that will be determined by the value of the constant FOPEN_MAX that's defined in <stdio.h>. FOPEN_MAX is an integer that specifies the maximum number of streams that can be open at one time. The C language standard requires that the value of FOPEN_MAX be at least 8, including stdin, stdout and stderr. Thus, as a minimum, you will be able to be working with up to 5 files simultaneously.

If you want to write to an existing text file with the name myfile.txt, you would use these statements:

```
FILE *pfile = fopen("myfile.txt", "w");   /* Open file myfile.txt to write it */
```

This statement opens the file and associates the physical file specified by the file name myfile.txt with your internal pointer pfile. Because you've specified the mode as "w", you can only write to the file; you can't read from it. The string that you supply as the first argument is limited to a maximum of FILENAME_MAX characters, where FILENAME_MAX is defined in the <stdio.h> header file. This value is usually sufficiently large enough that it isn't a real restriction.

If a file with the name myfile.txt does not already exist, the call to the function fopen() in the previous statement will create a new file with this name. Because you have just provided the file name without any path specification as the first argument to the fopen() function, the file is assumed to be in the current directory, and if the file is not found there, that's where it will be created. You can also specify a string that is the full path and name for the file, in which case the file will be assumed to be at that location and a new file will be created there if necessary. Note that if the directory that's supposed to contain the file doesn't exist when you specify the file path, neither the directory nor the file will be created and the fopen() call will fail. If the call to fopen() does fail for any reason, NULL will be returned. If you then attempt further operations with a NULL file pointer, it will cause your program to terminate.

■Note So here you have the facility to create a new text file. Simply call fopen() with mode "w" and the first argument specifying the name you want to assign to the new file.

On opening a file for writing, the file is positioned at the beginning of any existing data for the first operation. This means that any data that was previously written to the file will be overwritten when you initiate any write operations.

If you want to add to an existing text file rather than overwrite it, you specify mode "a", which is the append mode of operation. This positions the file at the end of any previously written data. If the file specified doesn't exist, as in the case of mode "w", a new file will be created. Using the file pointer that you declared previously, to open the file to add data to the end, use the following statement:

```
pfile = fopen("myfile.txt", "a");      /* Open file myfile.txt to add to it */
```

When you open a file in append mode, all write operations will be at the end of the data in the file on each write operation. In other words, all write operations append data to the file and you cannot update the existing contents in this mode.

If you want to read a file, once you've declared your file pointer, open it using this statement:

```
pfile = fopen("myfile.txt", "r");
```

Because you've specified the mode argument as "r", indicating that you want to read the file, you can't write to this file. The file position will be set to the beginning of the data in the file.

Clearly, if you're going to read the file, it must already exist. If you inadvertently try to open a file for reading that doesn't exist, fopen() will return NULL. It's therefore a good idea to check the value returned from fopen() in an if statement, to make sure that you really are accessing the file you want.

Renaming a File

There are many circumstances in which you'll want to rename a file. You might be updating the contents of a file by writing a new, updated file, for instance. You'll probably want to assign a temporary name to the new file while you're creating it, and then change the name to that of the old file once you've deleted it. Renaming a file is very easy. You just use the rename() function, which has the following prototype:

```
int rename(const char *oldname, const char *newname);
```

The integer that's returned will be 0 if the name change is successful, and nonzero otherwise. The file must be closed when you call rename(), otherwise the operation will fail.

Here's an example of using the rename() function:

```
if(rename( "C:\\temp\\myfile.txt", "C:\\temp\\myfile_copy.txt"))
  printf("Failed to rename file.");
else
  printf("File renamed successfully.");
```

The preceding code fragment will change the name of the myfile.txt file in the temp directory on drive C to myfile_copy.text. A message will be produced that indicates whether the name change succeeded. Obviously, if the file path is incorrect or the file doesn't exist, the renaming operation will fail.

■**Caution** Note the double backslash in the file path string. If you forget to use the escape sequence for a backslash when specifying a Microsoft Windows file path you won't get the file name that you want.

Closing a File

When you've finished with a file, you need to tell the operating system that this is the case and free up your file pointer. This is referred to as **closing** a file. You do this by calling the fclose()function which accepts a file pointer as an argument and returns a value of type int, which will be EOF if an error occurs and 0 otherwise. The typical usage of the fclose() function is as follows:

```
fclose(pfile);                          /* Close the file associated with pfile */
```

The result of executing this statement is that the connection between the pointer, pfile, and the physical file name is broken, so pfile can no longer be used to access the physical file it represented. If the file was being written, the current contents of the output buffer are written to the file to ensure that data isn't lost.

■**Note** EOF is a special character called the **end-of-file character**. In fact, the symbol EOF is defined in <stdio.h> and is usually equivalent to the value –1. However, this isn't necessarily always the case, so you should use EOF in your programs rather than an explicit value. EOF generally indicates that no more data is available from a stream.

It's good programming practice to close a file as soon as you've finished with it. This protects against output data loss, which could occur if an error in another part of your program caused the execution to be stopped in an abnormal fashion. This could result in the contents of the output buffer being lost, as the file wouldn't be closed properly. You must also close a file before attempting to rename it or remove it.

■**Note** Another reason for closing files as soon as you've finished with them is that the operating system will usually limit the number of files you may have open at one time. Closing files as soon as you've finished with them minimizes the chances of you falling afoul of the operating system in this respect.

There is a function in <stdio.h> that will force any unwritten data left in a buffer to be written to a file. This is the function fflush(), which you've already used in previous chapters to flush the input buffer. With your file pointer pfile, you could force any data left in the output buffer to be written to the file by using this statement:

```
fflush(pfile);
```

The fflush() function returns a value of type int, which is normally 0 but will be set to EOF if an error occurs.

Deleting a File

Because you have the ability to create a file in your code, at some point you'll want to be able to delete a file programmatically, too. The remove() function that's declared in <stdio.h> does this. You use it like this:

```
remove("pfile.txt");
```

This will delete the file from the current directory that has the name pfile.txt. Note that the file should not be open when you call remove() to delete it. If the file is open, the effect of calling remove is implementation-defined, so consult your library documentation.

You always need to double-check any operations on files, but you need to take particular care with operations that delete files.

Writing to a Text File

Once you've opened a file for writing, you can write to it any time from anywhere in your program, provided you have access to the pointer for the file that has been set by fopen(). So if you want to be able to access a file from anywhere in a program that contains multiple functions, you need to ensure the file pointer has global scope or arrange for it to be passed as an argument to any function that accesses the file.

■**Note** As you'll recall, to ensure that the file pointer has global scope you place the declaration for it outside of all of the functions, usually at the beginning of the source file.

The simplest write operation is provided by the function fputc(), which writes a single character to a text file. It has the following prototype:

```
int fputc(int c, FILE *pfile);
```

The fputc() function writes the character specified by the first argument to the file defined by the second argument, which is a file pointer. If the write is successful, it returns the character that was written. Otherwise it returns EOF.

In practice, characters aren't written to the physical file one by one. This would be extremely inefficient. Hidden from your program and managed by the output routine, output characters are written to an area of memory called a **buffer** until a reasonable number have been accumulated; they are then all written to the file in one go. This mechanism is illustrated in Figure 12-2.

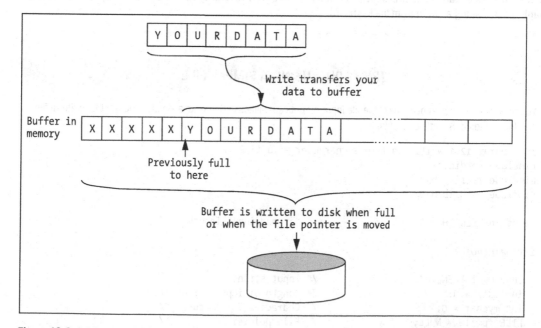

Figure 12-2. *Writing a file*

Note that the putc()function is equivalent to fputc(). It requires the same arguments and the return type is the same. The difference between them is that putc() may be implemented in the standard library as a macro, whereas fputc() is definitely a function.

Reading from a Text File

The fgetc() function is complementary to fputc() and reads a character from a text file that has been opened for reading. It takes a file pointer as its only argument and returns the character read as type int if the read is successful; otherwise, it returns EOF. The typical use of fgetc() is illustrated by the following statement:

```
mchar = fgetc(pfile);                     /* Reads a character into mchar */
```

You're assuming here that the variable mchar has been declared to be of type int.

Behind the scenes, the actual mechanism for reading a file is the inverse of writing to a file. A whole block of characters is read into a buffer in one go. The characters are then handed over to your program one at a time as you request them, until the buffer is empty, whereupon another block is read. This makes the process very fast, because most fgetc() operations won't involve reading the disk but simply moving a character from the buffer in main memory to the place where you want to store it.

Note that the function getc() that's equivalent to fgetc() is also available. It requires an argument of type FILE* and returns the character read as type int, so it's virtually identical to fgetc(). The only difference between them is that getc() may be implemented as a macro, whereas fgetc() is a function.

Caution Don't confuse the function getc() with the function gets(). They're quite different in operation: getc() reads a single character from the stream specified by its argument, whereas gets() reads a whole line of input from the standard input stream, which is the keyboard. You've already used the gets() function in previous chapters for reading a string from the keyboard.

TRY IT OUT: USING A SIMPLE FILE

You now have enough knowledge of the file input/output capabilities in C to write a simple program that writes a file and then reads it. So let's do just that:

```
/* Program 12.1 Writing a file a character at a time */
#include <stdio.h>
#include <string.h>
#include <stdlib.h>

const int LENGTH = 80;                    /* Maximum input length    */

int main(void)
{
  char mystr[LENGTH];                     /* Input string            */
  int lstr = 0;                           /* Length of input string  */
  int mychar = 0;                         /* Character for output     */
  FILE *pfile = NULL;                     /* File pointer            */
  char *filename = "C:\\myfile.txt";
```

```
  printf("\nEnter an interesting string of less than 80 characters:\n");
  fgets(mystr, LENGTH, stdin);           /* Read in a string       */

  /* Create a new file we can write */

  if(!(pfile = fopen(filename, "w")))
  {
    printf("Error opening %s for writing. Program terminated.", filename);
    exit(1);
  }

  lstr = strlen(mystr);
  for(int i = lstr-1 ; i >= 0 ; i--)
    fputc(mystr[i], pfile);              /* Write string to file backward  */

  fclose(pfile);                         /* Close the file                 */

  /* Open the file for reading */
  if(!(pfile = fopen(filename, "r")))
{
    printf("Error opening %s for reading. Program terminated.", filename);
    exit(1);
  }

  /* Read a character from the file and display it */
  while((mychar = fgetc(pfile)) != EOF)
    putchar(mychar);                     /* Output character from the file */
  putchar('\n');                         /* Write newline                  */

  fclose(pfile);                         /* Close the file                 */
  remove(filename);                      /* Delete the physical file       */
  return 0;
}
```

Here's an example of some output from this program:

```
Enter an interesting string.
Too many cooks spoil the broth.
.htorb eht liops skooc ynam ooT
```

How It Works

The name of the file that you're going to work with is defined by this statement:

```
char *filename = "C:\\myfile.txt";
```

This statement defines the file with the name myfile.txt on drive C with the Microsoft Windows notation for file names. As I noted earlier, you must use the escape sequence '\\' to get a backslash character. If you forget to do this and just use a single backslash, the compiler will think that you're writing an escape sequence '\m' in this case, which it won't recognize as valid.

Before running this program—or indeed any of the examples working with files—do make sure you don't have an existing file with the same name and path. If you have a file with the same name as that used in the example, you should change the initial value for filename in the example; otherwise, your existing file will be overwritten.

After displaying a prompt, the program reads a string from the keyboard. It then executes the following statements:

```
if(!(pfile = fopen(filename, "w")))
{
  printf("Error opening %s for writing. Program terminated.", filename);
  exit (1);
}
```

The condition in this if statement calls fopen() to create the new file myfile.txt on drive C, opens it for writing, and stores the pointer that is returned in pfile. The second argument to fopen() determines the mode as writing the file. The block of statements will be executed if fopen() returns NULL, so in this case you display a message and call the exit() function that is declared in <stdlib.h> for an abnormal end to the program.

After determining the length of the string using strlen() and storing the result in lstr, you have a loop defined by these statements:

```
for(int i = lstr-1 ; i >= 0 ; i--)
  fputc(mystr[i], pfile);          /* Write string to file backward  */
```

The loop index is varied from a value corresponding to the last character in the string lstr-1 back to 0. Therefore, the putc() function call within the loop writes to the new file character-by-character, in reverse order. The particular file you're writing is specified by the pointer pfile as the second argument to the function call.

After closing the file with a call to fclose(), it's reopened in reading mode by these statements:

```
if(!(pfile = fopen(filename, "r")))
{
  printf("Error opening %s for reading. Program terminated.", filename);
  exit(1);
}
```

The mode specification "r" indicates that you intend to read the file, so the file position will be set to the beginning of the file. You have the same check for a NULL return value as when you wrote the file.

Next, you use the getc() function to read characters from the file within the while loop condition:

```
while((mychar = fgetc(pfile)) != EOF)
  putchar(mychar);                 /* Output character from the file */
```

The file is read character-by-character. The read operation actually takes place within the loop continuation condition. As each character is read, it's displayed on the screen using the function putc() within the loop. The process stops when EOF is returned by getc() at the end of the file.

The last two statements before the return in the main() function are the following:

```
fclose(pfile);                 /* Close the file               */
remove(filename);              /* Delete the physical file     */
```

These statements provide the necessary final tidying up, now that you've finished with the file. After closing the file, the program calls the remove() function, which will delete the file identified by the argument. This avoids cluttering up the disk with stray files. If you want to check the contents of the file that was written using a text editor, just remove or comment out the call to remove().

Writing Strings to a Text File

Analogous to the puts() function for writing a string to stdout, you have the fputs() function for writing a string to a text file. Its prototype is as follows:

```
int fputs(char *pstr, FILE *pfile);
```

   The first argument is a pointer to the character string that's to be written to the file, and the second argument is a file pointer. The operation of the function is slightly odd, in that it continues to write characters from a string until it reaches a '\0' character, which it doesn't write to the file. This can complicate reading back variable-length strings from a file that have been written by fputs(). It works this way because it's a character write operation, not a binary write operation, so it's expecting to write a line of text that has a newline character at the end. A newline character isn't required by the operation of the function, but it's very helpful when you want to read the file back (using the complementary fgets() function, as you'll see).

   The fputs() function returns EOF if an error occurs, and 0 under normal circumstances. You use it in the same way as puts(), for example

```
fputs("The higher the fewer", pfile);
```

   This will output the string appearing as the first argument to the file pointed to by pfile.

Reading Strings from a Text File

Complementing fputs() is the function fgets() for reading a string from a text file. It has the following prototype:

```
char *fgets(char *pstr, int nchars, FILE *pfile);
```

   The fgets() function has three parameters. The function will read a string into the memory area pointed to by pstr, from the file specified by pfile. Characters are read from the file until either a '\n' is read or nchars-1 characters have been read from the file, whichever occurs first.

   If a newline character is read, it's retained in the string. A '\0' character will be appended to the end of the string in any event. If there is no error, fgets() will return the pointer, pstr; otherwise, NULL is returned. The second argument to this function enables you to ensure that you don't overrun the memory area that you've assigned for input in your program. To prevent the capacity of your data input area from being exceeded, just specify the length of the area or the array that will receive the input data as the second argument to the function.

TRY IT OUT: TRANSFERRING STRINGS TO AND FROM A TEXT FILE

You can exercise the functions to transfer strings to and from a text file in an example that also uses the append mode for writing a file:

```
/* Program 12.2  As the saying goes...it comes back! */
#include <stdio.h>
#include <stdlib.h>
#include <stdbool.h>

const int LENGTH = 80;                  /* Maximum input length */

int main(void)
{
  char *proverbs[] =
```

```c
                { "Many a mickle makes a muckle.\n",
                  "Too many cooks spoil the broth.\n",
                  "He who laughs last didn't get the joke in"
                                      " the first place.\n"
                };

char more[LENGTH];                  /* Stores a new proverb */
FILE *pfile = NULL;                 /* File pointer         */
char *filename = "C:\\myfile.txt";

/* Create a new file( if myfile.txt does not exist */
if(!(pfile = fopen(filename, "w")))    /* Open the file to write it */
{
  printf("Error opening %s for writing. Program terminated.", filename);
  exit(1);
}

/* Write our first three sayings to the file. */
int count = sizeof proverbs/sizeof proverbs[0];
for(int i = 0 ; i < count ; i++)
  fputs(proverbs[i], pfile);

fclose(pfile);                      /* Close the file */

/* Open the file to append more proverbs */
if(!(pfile = fopen(filename, "a")))
{
  printf("Error opening %s for writing. Program terminated.", filename);
  exit(1);
}

printf("Enter proverbs of less than 80 characters or press Enter to end:\n");
while(true)
{
  fgets(more, LENGTH, stdin);       /* Read a proverb       */
  if(more[0] == '\n')               /* If its empty line    */
    break;                          /* end input operation  */
  fputs(more, pfile);               /* Write the new proverb */
}

fclose(pfile);                      /* Close the file        */

if(!(pfile = fopen(filename, "r")))    /* Open the file to read it */
{
  printf("Error opening %s for writing. Program terminated.", filename);
  exit(1);
}

/* Read and output the file contents */
printf("The proverbs in the file are:\n\n");
while(fgets(more, LENGTH, pfile))    /* Read a proverb */
  printf("%s", more);                /* and display it */
```

```
   fclose(pfile);                         /* Close the file */
   remove(filename);                      /* and remove it  */
   return 0;
}
```

Here is some sample output from this program:

```
Enter proverbs of less than 80 characters or press Enter to end:
Least said, soonest mended.
A nod is as good as a wink to a blind horse.

The proverbs in the file are:

Many a mickle makes a muckle.
Too many cooks spoil the broth.
He who laughs last didn't get the joke in the first place.
Least said, soonest mended.
A nod is as good as a wink to a blind horse.
```

How It Works

You initialize the array of pointers, `proverbs[]`, in the following statement:

```
char *proverbs[] =
        {  "Many a mickle makes a muckle.\n",
           "Too many cooks spoil the broth.\n",
           "He who laughs last didn't get the joke in"
                              " the first place.\n"
        };
```

You specify the three sayings as initial values for the array elements, and this causes the compiler to allocate the space necessary to store each string.

You have a further declaration of an array that will store a proverb that will be read from the keyboard:

```
char more[LENGTH];                    /* Stores a new proverb */
```

This initializes a conventional `char` array with another proverb. You also include `'\n'` at the end for the same reason as before.

After creating and opening a file on drive C for writing, the program writes the initial three proverbs to the file in a loop:

```
int count = sizeof proverbs/sizeof proverbs[0];
for(int i = 0 ; i < count ; i++)
   fputs(proverbs[i], pfile);
```

The contents of each of the memory areas pointed to by elements of the `proverbs[]` array are written to the file in the `for` loop using the function `fputs()`. This function is extremely easy to use; it just requires a pointer to the string as the first argument and a pointer to the file as the second.

The number of proverbs in the array is calculated by the following expression:

```
sizeof proverbs/sizeof proverbs[0]
```

The expression `sizeof proverbs` will evaluate to the total number of bytes occupied by the complete array, and `sizeof proverbs[0]` will result in the number of bytes required to store a single pointer in one element of the array. Therefore, the whole expression will evaluate to the number of elements in the pointer array. You could have manually counted how many initializing strings you supplied, of course, but doing it this way means that the correct number of iterations is determined automatically, and this expression will still be correct even if the array dimension is changed by adding more initializing strings.

Once the first set of proverbs has been written, the file is closed and then reopened with this statement:

```
if(!(pfile = fopen(filename, "a")))
{
  printf("Error opening %s for writing. Program terminated.", filename);
  exit(1);
}
```

Because you have the mode specified as "a", the file is opened in append mode. Note that the current position for the file is automatically set to the end of the file in this mode, so that subsequent write operations will be appended to the end of the existing data in the file.

After prompting for input, you read more proverbs from the keyboard and write them to the file with the following statements:

```
while(true)
{
  fgets(more, LENGTH, stdin);      /* Read a proverb          */
  if(more[0] == '\n')              /* If its empty line       */
    break;                         /* end input operation     */
  fputs(more, pfile);              /* Write the new proverb   */
}
```

Each additional proverb that's stored in the more array is written to the file using fputs(). As you can see, the function fputs() is just as easy to use with an array as it is with a pointer. Because you're in append mode, each new proverb will be added at the end of the existing data in the file. The loop terminates when an empty line is entered. An empty line will result in a string containing just '\n' followed by the string terminator.

Having written the file, you close it and then reopen it for reading, using the mode specifier "r". You then have the following loop:

```
while(fgets(more, LENGTH, pfile))    /* Read a proverb */
  printf("%s", more);                /* and display it */
```

You read strings successively from the file into the more array within the loop continuation condition. After each string is read, you display it on the screen by the call to printf() within the loop. The reading of each proverb by fgets() is terminated by detecting the '\n' character at the end of each string. The loop terminates when the function fgets() returns NULL.

Finally, the file is closed and then deleted using the function remove() in the same fashion as the previous example.

Formatted File Input and Output

Writing characters and strings to a text file is all very well as far as it goes, but you normally have many other types of data in your programs. To write numerical data to a text file, you need something more than you've seen so far, and where the contents of a file are to be human readable, you need a character representation of the numerical data. The mechanism for doing just this is provided by the functions for formatted file input and output.

Formatted Output to a File

You already encountered the function for formatted output to a file when I discussed standard streams back in Chapter 10. It's virtually the same as the printf() statement, except that there's one extra parameter and a slight name change. Its typical usage is the following:

```
fprintf(pfile, "%12d%12d%14f", num1, num2, fnum1);
```

As you can see, the function name has an additional f (for *file*), compared with printf(), and the first argument is a file pointer that specifies the destination of the data to be written. The file pointer obviously needs to be set through a call to fopen() first. The remaining arguments are identical to that of printf(). This example writes the values of the three variables num1, num2, and num3 to the file specified by the file pointer pfile, under control of the format string specified as the second argument. Therefore, the first two variables are of type int and are to be written with a field width of 12, and the third variable is of type float and is to be written to the file with a field width of 14.

Formatted Input from a File

You get formatted input from a file by using the function fscanf(). To read three variable values from a file pfile you would write this:

```
fscanf(pfile, "%12d%12d%14f", &num1, &num2, &fnum1);
```

This function works in exactly the same way as scanf() does with stdin, except that here you're obtaining input from a file specified by the first argument. The same rules govern the specification of the format string and the operation of the function as apply to scanf(). The function returns EOF if an error occurs such that no input is read; otherwise, it returns the number of values read as a value of type int.

TRY IT OUT: USING FORMATTED INPUT AND OUTPUT FUNCTIONS

You can demonstrate the formatted input and output functions with an example that will also show what's happening to the data in these operations:

```
/* Program 12.3 Messing about with formatted file I/O */
#include <stdio.h>
#include <stdlib.h>

int main(void)
{
  long num1 = 234567L;                  /* Input values...            */
  long num2 = 345123L;
  long num3 = 789234L;

  long num4 = 0L;                       /* Values read from the file... */
  long num5 = 0L;
  long num6 = 0L;

  float fnum = 0.0f;                    /* Value read from the file   */
  int   ival[6] = { 0 };                /* Values read from the file  */
  FILE *pfile = NULL;                   /* File pointer               */
  char *filename = "C:\\myfile.txt";
```

```
pfile = fopen(filename, "w");                    /* Create file to be written */
if(pfile == NULL)
{
  printf("Error opening %s for writing. Program terminated.", filename);
  exit(1);
}
fprintf(pfile, "%6ld%6ld%6ld", num1, num2, num3);    /* Write file          */
fclose(pfile);                                        /* Close file          */
printf("\n %6ld %6ld %6ld", num1, num2, num3);    /* Display values written */

pfile = fopen(filename, "r");                        /* Open file to read    */
fscanf(pfile, "%6ld%6ld%6ld", &num4, &num5 ,&num6);  /* Read back            */
printf("\n %6ld %6ld %6ld", num4, num5, num6);       /* Display what we got */

rewind(pfile);                                /* Go to the beginning of the file */
fscanf(pfile, "%2d%3d%3d%3d%2d%2d%3f", &ival[0], &ival[1], /* Read it again */
                  &ival[2], &ival[3], &ival[4] , &ival[5], &fnum);
fclose(pfile);                                       /* Close the file and   */
remove(filename);                                    /* delete physical file. */

/* Output the results */
printf("\n");
for(int i = 0 ; i < 6 ; i++ )
  printf("%sival[i] = %d", i == 4 ? "\n\t" : "\t", i, ival[i]);
printf("\nfnum = %f\n", fnum);
return 0;
}
```

The output from this example is the following:

```
234567 345123 789234
234567 345123 789234
        ival[i] = 0    ival[i] = 1    ival[i] = 2    ival[i] =3
        ival[i] = 4    ival[i] = 5
fnum = 234.000000
```

How It Works

This example writes the values of num1, num2, and num3, which are defined and assigned values in their declaration, to the file myfile.txt on drive C. This is referenced through the pointer pfile. The file is closed and reopened for reading, and the values are read from the file in the same format as they are written. You then have the following statement:

```
rewind(pfile);
```

This statement calls the rewind() function, which simply moves the current position back to the beginning of the file so that you can read it again. You could have achieved the same thing by closing the file then reopening it again, but with rewind() you do it with one function call and the operation will be a lot faster.

Having repositioned the file, you read the file again with this statement:

```
fscanf(pfile, "%2d%3d%3d%3d%2d%2d%3f", &ival[0], &ival[1], /* Read it again */
                  &ival[2], &ival[3], &ival[4] , &ival[5], &fnum);
```

This statement reads the same data into the array ival[] and the variable fnum, but with different formats from those that you used for writing the file. You can see from the effects of this that the file consists of just a string of characters once it has been written, exactly the same as the output to the screen from printf().

■**Note** You can lose information if you choose a format specifier that outputs fewer digits precision than the stored value holds.

You can see that the values you get back from the file when you read it will depend on both the format string that you use and the variable list that you specify in the fscanf() function.

None of the intrinsic source information that existed when you wrote the file is necessarily maintained. Once the data is in the file, it's just a sequence of bytes in which the meaning is determined by how you interpret them. This is demonstrated quite clearly by this example, in which you've converted the original three values into eight new values.

Lastly, you leave everything neat and tidy in this program by closing the file and using the function remove() to delete it.

Dealing with Errors

The examples in this book have included minimal error checking and reporting because the code for comprehensive error checking and reporting tends to take up a lot of space in the book and make the programs look rather more complicated than they really are. In real-world programs, however, it's essential that you do as much error checking and reporting as you can.

Generally, you should write your error messages to stderr, which is automatically available to your program and always points to your display screen. Even though stdout may be redirected to a file by an operating system command, stderr continues to be assigned to the screen. It's important to check that a file you want to read does in fact exist and you have been doing this in the examples, but there's more that you can do. First of all, you can write error messages to stderr rather than stdin, for example

```
char *filename = "C:\\MYFILE.TXT";    /* File name    */
FILE *pfile = NULL;                    /* File pointer */

if(!(pfile = fopen(filename, "r")))
{
  fprintf(stderr, "\nCannot open %s to read it.", filename);
  exit(1);
}
```

The merit of writing to stderr is that the output will always be directed to the display and it will always be written immediately to the display device. This means that you will always see the output directed to stderr, regardless of what happens in the program. The stdin stream is buffered, so there is the risk that data could be left in the buffer and never displayed if your program crashes. Terminating a program by calling exit() ensures that output stream buffers will be flushed so output will be written to the ultimate destination. The stream stdin can be redirected to a file, but stderr can't be redirected simply to ensure that the output always occurs.

Knowing that some kind of error occurred is useful, but you can do more than this. The perror() function outputs a string that you pass as an argument plus an implementation-defined error message corresponding to the error that occurred. You could therefore rewrite the previous fragment as follows:

```
if(!(pfile = fopen(myfile, "r")))
{
  perror(strcat("Error opening ", filename));
  exit(1);
}
```

This will output your message consisting of the file name appended to the first argument to strcat(), plus a system-generated message relating to the error. The output will be written to stderr.

If an error occurs when you're reading a file, you can check whether the error is due to reaching the end of file. The feof() function will return a nonzero integer if the end of file has been reached, so you can check for this with statements such as these:

```
if(feof(pfile))
  printf("End of file reached.");
```

Note that I didn't write the message to stderr here because reaching the end of the file isn't necessarily an error.

The ferror() function returns a nonzero integer if an error occurrs with an operation on the stream that's identified by the file pointer that you pass as the argument. Calling this function enables you to establish positively that an error did occur. The <errno.h> header file defines a value with the name errno that may indicate what kind of file error has occurred. You need to read the documentation for your C implementation to find out the specifics of this. The value of errno may be set for errors other than just file operations.

You should always include some basic error checking and reporting code in all of your programs. Once you've written a few programs, you'll find that including some standard bits of code for each type of operation warranting error checks is no hardship. With a standard approach, you can copy most of what you need from one program to another.

Further Text File Operation Modes

Text mode is the default mode of operation with the open modes you have seen up to now, but in earlier versions of C you could specify explicitly that a file is to be opened in text mode. You could do this by adding t to the end of the existing specifiers. This gives you the mode specifiers "wt", "rt", and "at" in addition to the original three. I am only mentioning this because you may come across it in other C programs. Although most compilers will support this, it's not specifically part of the current C standard so it is best not to use this option in your code.

You can also open a text file for update! that is, for both reading and writing! using the specifier "r+". You can also specify the open mode as "w+" if you want to both read and write a new file, or when you want to discard the original contents of an existing file before you start. Opening a file with the mode "w+" truncates the length of an existing file to zero, so only use this mode when you want to discard the current file contents. In older programs you may come across these modes written as "rt+" or "r+t" and "wt+" or "w+t".

As I've said, in update mode you can both read and write a text file. However, you can't write to the file immediately after reading it or read from the file immediately after writing it, unless the EOF has been reached or the position in the file has been changed by some means. (This involves calling a function such as rewind() or some other function that modifies the file position.) The reason for this is that writing to a file doesn't necessarily write the data to the external device. It simply transfers it to a buffer in memory that's written to the file once it's full, or when some other event causes it to be written. Similarly, the first read from a file will fill a buffer area in memory, and subsequent reads will transfer data from the buffer until it's empty, whereupon another file read to fill the buffer will be initiated. This is illustrated in Figure 12-3.

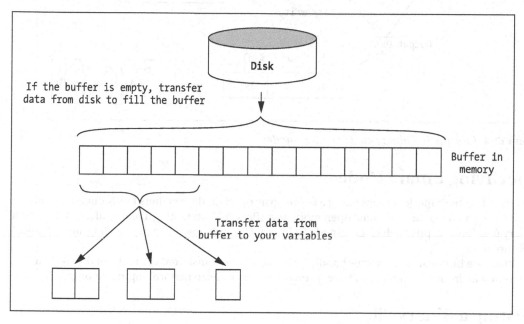

Figure 12-3. *Buffered input operations*

This means that if you were able to switch immediately from write mode to read mode, data would be lost because it would be left in the buffer. In the case of switching from read mode to write mode, the current position in the file may be different from what you imagine it to be, and you may inadvertently overwrite data on the file. A switch from read to write or vice versa, therefore, requires an intervening event that implicitly flushes the buffers. The fflush() function will cause the bytes remaining in an output buffer for the stream you pass as the argument to be written to an output file.

Binary File Input and Output

The alternative to text mode operations on a file is **binary mode**. In this mode, no transformation of the data takes place, and there's no need for a format string to control input or output, so it's much simpler than text mode. The binary data as it appears in memory is transferred directly to the file. Characters such as '\n' and '\0' that have specific significance in text mode are of no consequence in binary mode.

Binary mode has the advantage that no data is transformed or precision lost, as can happen with text mode due to the formatting process. It's also somewhat faster than text mode because no transformation operations are performed. The two modes are contrasted in Figure 12-4.

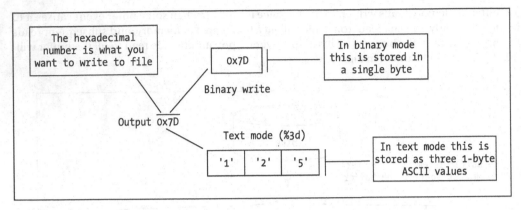

Figure 12-4. *Contrasting binary mode and text mode*

Specifying Binary Mode

You specify binary mode by appending b to the basic open mode specifiers I introduced initially. Therefore, you have the additional open mode specifiers "wb" for writing a binary file, "rb" to read a binary file, "ab" to append data to the end of a binary file, and "rb+" to enable reading and writing of a binary file.

Because binary mode involves handling the data to be transferred to and from the file in a different way from text mode, you have a new set of functions to perform input and output.

Writing a Binary File

You use the fwrite() function to write a binary file. This is best explained with an example of its use. Suppose that you open the file to be written with the following statements:

```
char *filename = "myfile.bin";
FILE *pfile = fopen(filename, "wb");
```

The filename variable points to the string that defines the name of the file, and pfile is a variable to store a pointer to an object of type FILE as before.

You could write to the file with these statements:

```
long pdata[] = {2L, 3L, 4L};
int num_items = sizeof(pdata)/sizeof(long);
FILE *pfile = fopen(filename, "wb");
size_t wcount = fwrite(pdata, sizeof(long), num_items, pfile);
```

The fwrite() function operates on the principle of writing a specified number of binary data items to a file, where each item is a given number of bytes long. The first argument, pdata, is a pointer containing the starting address in memory of where the data items to be written are stored. The second argument specifies the size in bytes of each item to be written. The third argument, num_items, defines a count of the number of items to be written to the file. The file to which the data is to be transferred is identified by the last argument, pfile. The function fwrite() returns the count of the number of items actually written as a value of type size_t. If the operation is unsuccessful for some reason, this value will be less than num_items.

Note that there is no check that you opened the file in binary mode when you call the fwrite() function. The write operation will write binary data to a file that you open in text mode. Equally, there is nothing to prevent you from writing text data to a binary file. Of course, if you do this a considerable amount of confusion is likely to result.

The return value and the second and third arguments to the function are all of the same type as that returned by the sizeof operator. This is defined as type size_t, which you probably remember is an unsigned integer type.

The code fragment above uses the sizeof operator to specify the size in bytes of the objects to be transferred and also determines the number of items to be written using the expression sizeof(pdata)/sizeof(long). This is a good way of specifying these values when this is possible, because it reduces the likelihood of error. Of course, in a real context, you should also check the return value in wcount to be sure the write is successful.

The fwrite() function is geared to writing a number of binary objects of a given length to a file. You can write in units of your own structures as easily as you can write values of type int, values of type double, or sequences of individual bytes.

This doesn't mean that the values you write in any given output operation all have to be of the same type. You might allocate some memory using malloc(), for instance, into which you assemble a sequence of data items of different types and lengths. You could then write the whole block of memory in one go as a sequence of bytes. Of course, when you come to read them back, you need to know the precise sequence and types for the values in the file if you are to make sense of them.

Reading a Binary File

You use the fread() function to read a binary file once it has been opened in read mode. Using the same variables as in the example of writing a binary file, you could read the file using a statement such as this:

```
size_t wcount = fread( pdata, sizeof(long), num_items, pfile);
```

This operates exactly as the inverse of the write operation. Starting at the address specified by data, the function reads num_items objects, each occupying the number of bytes specified by the second argument. The function returns the count of the number of items that were read. If the read isn't completely successful, the count will be less than the number of objects requested.

TRY IT OUT: READING A BINARY FILE

You can apply the binary file operations to a version of the Program 7.11 you saw in Chapter 7 for calculating primes. This time, you'll use a disk file as a buffer to calculate a larger number of primes. You can make the program automatically spill primes on to a disk file if the array assigned to store the primes is insufficient for the number of primes requested. In this version of the program to find primes, you'll improve the checking process a little.

In addition to the main() function that will contain the prime finding loop, you'll write a function to test whether a value is prime called test_prime(), a helper function that will check a given value against a block of primes called check(), and a function called put_primes(), which will retrieve the primes from the file and display them.

As this program consists of several functions and will work with variables at global scope, let's take a look at it piece by piece. We'll start with the function prototypes and global data before we look at detail of the functions:

```
/* Program 12.4  A prime example using binary files */
#include <stdio.h>
#include <stdlib.h>
#include <math.h >                          /* For square root function sqrt() */

/* Function prototypes */
int test_prime(unsigned long long N);
void put_primes(void);
int check(unsigned long long buffer[], size_t count, unsigned long long N);
```

```
/* Global data */
const unsigned int MEM_PRIMES = 100;   /* Count of number of primes in memory */

struct
{
  char *filename;                              /* File name for primes     */
  FILE *pfile;                                 /* File stream pointer       */
  int nrec;                                    /* Number of file records */

  unsigned long long primes[MEM_PRIMES];       /* Array to store primes    */
  size_t index;                    /* Index of free location in array primes */

} global = { "C:\\myfile.bin",                 /* Physical file name       */
             NULL,                             /* File pointer value        */
             0,                                /* File record count         */
             {2ULL, 3ULL, 5ULL},               /* primes array values       */
             3                                 /* Number of primes          */
          };

int main(void)
{
  /* Code for main()... */
}

/*******************************************************************
 * Function to test if a number, N, is prime using primes in      *
 * memory and on file                                             *
 * First parameter N - value to be tested                         *
 * Return value - a positive value for a prime, zero otherwise     *
 *******************************************************************/
int test_prime(unsigned long long N)
{
  /* Code for test_prime()... */
}

/*******************************************************************
 * Function to check whether an integer, N, is divisible by any   *
 * of the elements in the array pbuffer up to the square root of N.*
 * First parameter buffer - an array of primes                    *
 * second parameter count - number of elements in pbuffer         *
 * Third parameter N - the value to be checked                    *
 * Return value - 1 if N is prime, zero if N is not a prime,       *
 *              -1 for more checks                                 *
 *******************************************************************/
int check(unsigned long long buffer[], size_t count, unsigned long long N)
{
  /* Code for check()... */
}
```

```
/*******************************************
 * Function to output primes from the file *
 *******************************************/
void put_primes(void)
{
  /* Code for put_primes()... */
}
```

After the usual #include statements, you have the prototypes for three functions used in the program:

```
int test_prime(unsigned long long N);
void put_primes(void);
int check(unsigned long long buffer[], size_t count, unsigned long long N);
```

You write just the parameter types within the prototypes without using a parameter name. Function prototypes can be written either with or without parameter names, but the parameter types must be specified. Generally, it's better to include names, because they give a clue to the purpose of the parameter. The names in the prototype can be different from the names used in the definition of the function, but you should only do this if it helps to make the code more readable. To allow the maximum range of possible prime values you'll store them as values of type unsigned long long.

It is often convenient to define variables at global scope when they need to be accessed by several functions. This avoids the need for long parameter lists for the functions where you would pass the data as arguments in each function call. However, the more names you declare at global scope, the greater the risk of collisions with local names in your program or names used in the standard libraries, so it is always a good idea to keep the number of names at global scope to a minimum. One way to reduce the number of names at global scope is to put your global variables inside a struct. Here we have defined a struct without a type name, and the struct variable has the name global. All the variables defined as members of the struct therefore do not appear at global scope because they must be qualified by the name global.

The first three members of the struct are filename that points to the name of the file that will store primes, the file stream pointer, pfile, and the nrec variable to store the number of records in the file. You then have the primes array that will hold up to MEM_PRIMES values in memory before they need to be written to the file followed by the index variable that records the current free element in the primes array.

You can see how we initialize the members of the struct using an initializer list. Note how the initial values for three elements in the primes array appear between braces; because there are only three initializers for the array, the remaining elements will be set to 0.

Here's the definition for main():

```
int main(void)
{
  unsigned long long trial = 5ULL;                  /* Prime candidate */
  unsigned long num_primes = 3UL;                   /* Prime count     */
  unsigned long total = 0UL;                        /* Total required  */

  printf("How many primes would you like?  ");
  scanf("%lu", &total);                /* Total is how many we need to find */
  total = total<4UL ? 4UL:total;       /* Make sure it is at least 4        */
```

```
/* Prime finding and storing loop */
while(num_primes < total)              /* Loop until we get total required  */
{
  trial += 2ULL;                       /* Next value for checking          */
  if(test_prime(trial))                /* Check if trial is prime          */
  {                                    /* Positive value means prime       */
     global.primes[global.index++] = trial;  /* so store it               */
     num_primes++;                     /* Increment total number of primes */

     if(global.index == MEM_PRIMES)    /* Check if array is full            */
     {
       /* File opened OK?   */
       if(!(global.pfile = fopen(global.filename, "ab")))
       { /* No, so explain and end the program */
         printf("\nUnable to open %s to append\n", global.filename);
         exit(1);
       }
       /* Write the array   */
       fwrite(global.primes, sizeof(unsigned long long),
                                      MEM_PRIMES, global.pfile);

       fclose(global.pfile);           /* Close the file                   */
       global.index = 0U;              /* Reset count of primes in memory  */
       global.nrec++;                  /* Increment file record count      */
     }
  }
}

if(total>MEM_PRIMES)                    /* If we wrote some to file          */
  put_primes();                         /* Display the contents of the file  */
if(global.index)                        /* Display any left in memory        */
  for(size_t i = 0; i<global.index ; i++)
  {
    if(i%5 == 0)
      printf("\n");
    printf("%12llu", global.primes[i]); /* Newline after five               */
  }                                     /* Output a prime                   */

if(total>MEM_PRIMES)                              /* Did we need a file?      */
  if(remove(global.filename))                     /* then delete it.          */
    printf("\nFailed to delete %s\n", global.filename); /* Delete failed     */
  else
    printf("\nFile %s deleted.\n", global.filename);    /* Delete OK         */
return 0;
}
```

How It Works

The definition of the function main() follows the global declarations. When the program executes, you enter the number of primes you want to find, and this value controls the loop for testing prime candidates. Checking for a prime is performed by the function test_prime(), which is called in the if statement condition within the loop. The function returns 1 if the value tested is prime, and 0 otherwise. If a prime is found, then you execute these statements:

```
    global.primes[global.index++] = trial;   /* so store it              */
    num_primes++;                             /* Increment total number of primes */
```

The first statement stores the prime that you've found in the global.primes[] array. You keep track of how many primes you have in total with the variable num_primes, and the struct member variable global.index records how many you have in memory at any given time.

Every time you find a prime and add it to the primes[] array, you perform the following check:

```
    if(global.index == MEM_PRIMES)        /* Check if array is full          */
    {
      /* File opened OK?   */
      if(!(global.pfile = fopen(global.filename, "ab")))
      { /* No, so explain and end the program */
        printf("\nUnable to open %s to append\n", global.filename);
        exit(1);
      }
      /* Write the array    */
      fwrite(global.primes, sizeof(unsigned long long),
                                    MEM_PRIMES, global.pfile);

      fclose(global.pfile);            /* Close the file               */
      global.index = 0U;               /* Reset count of primes in memory */
      global.nrec++;                   /* Increment file record count    */
    }
```

If you've filled the global.primes array, the if condition will be true and you'll execute the associated statement block. In this case, the file is opened in binary mode to append data. The first time this occurs, a new file will be created. On subsequent calls of the fopen() function file, the existing file will be opened with the current position set at the end of any existing data in the file, ready for the next block to be written. After writing a block, the file is closed, as it will be necessary to reopen it for reading in the function that performs the checking of prime candidates.

Finally in this group of statements, the count of the number of primes in memory is reset to 0 because they've all been safely stowed away, and the count of the number of blocks of primes written to the file is incremented.

When sufficient primes have been found to fulfill the number requested, you display the primes with the following statements:

```
  if(total>MEM_PRIMES)                  /* If we wrote some to file        */
    put_primes();                       /* Display the contents of the file */
  if(global.index)                      /* Display any left in memory       */
    for(size_t i = 0; i<global.index ; i++)
    {
      if(i%5 == 0)
        printf("\n");                              /* Newline after five    */
      printf("%12llu", global.primes[i]);          /* Output a prime        */
    }
```

It's quite possible that the number of primes requested can be accommodated in memory, in which case you won't write to a file at all. You must therefore check whether total exceeds MEM_PRIMES before calling the function put_primes() that outputs the primes in the file. If the value of global.index is positive, there are primes in the global.primes array that haven't been written to the file. In this case, you display these in the for loop, five to a line.

Finally in main(), you remove the file from the disk with the following statements:

```
   if(total>MEM_PRIMES)                            /* Did we need a file?  */
     if(remove(global.filename))                   /* then delete it.      */
       printf("\nFailed to delete %s\n", global.filename); /* Delete failed  */
     else
       printf("\nFile %s deleted.\n", global.filename);    /* Delete OK       */
```

The first if ensures that you don't attempt to delete the file if you didn't create one.

The implementation of the function to check whether a value is prime is as follows:

```
int test_prime(unsigned long long N)
{
  unsigned long long buffer[MEM_PRIMES]; /* local buffer for primes from file */

  int k = 0;

  if(global.nrec > 0)                             /* Have we written records? */
  {
    if(!(global.pfile = fopen(global.filename, "rb"))) /* Then open the file */
    {
      printf("\nUnable to open %s to read\n", global.filename);
      exit(1);
    }

    for(size_t i = 0; i < global.nrec ; i++)
    { /* Check against primes in the file first */
      /* Read primes */
      fread(buffer, sizeof( long long), MEM_PRIMES, global.pfile);
      if((k = check(buffer, MEM_PRIMES, N)) >= 0)  /* Prime or not?      */
      {
        fclose(global.pfile);                      /* Yes, so close the file */
        return k;                                  /* 1 for prime, 0 for not */
      }
    }
    fclose(global.pfile);                          /* Close the file          */
  }

  /* Check against primes in memory */
  return check(global.primes, global.index, N);
}
```

The test_prime() function accepts a candidate value as an argument and returns 1 if it's prime and 0 if it isn't.

If you've written anything to the file, this will be indicated by a positive value of global.nrec. In this case, the primes in the file need to be used as divisors first, because they are lower than those currently in memory as you compute them in sequence.

■ **Note** As you may remember, a prime is a number with no factors other than 1 and itself. It's sufficient to check whether a number is divisible by any of the primes less than the square root of the number to verify that it's prime. This follows from the simple logic that any exact divisor greater than the square root must have an associated factor (the result of the division) that's less than the square root.

To read the file, the function executes this statement:

```
fread(buffer, sizeof( long long), MEM_PRIMES, global.pfile);
```

This reads one block of primes from the file into the array buffer. The second argument defines the size of each object to be read, and MEM_PRIMES defines the number of objects of the specified size to be read.

Having read a block, the following check is executed:

```
if((k = check(buffer, MEM_PRIMES, N)) >= 0)    /* Prime or not?            */
{
  fclose(global.pfile);                        /* Yes, so close the file */
  return k;                                    /* 1 for prime, 0 for not */
}
```

Within the if condition, the check() function is called to determine if any of the array elements divide into the prime candidate with no remainder. This function returns 0 if an exact division is found, indicating the candidate isn't prime. If no exact division is found with primes up to the square root of the candidate value, 1 is returned, indicating that the candidate must be prime. Whatever value is returned from check(), in both cases you've finished checking so the file is closed and the same value is returned to main().

The value –1 is returned from check() if no exact division has been found, but the square root of the test value hasn't been exceeded. You don't need to check for the –1 return explicitly, because it's the only possibility left if the value returned from check() isn't 0 or 1. In this case, the next block, if there is one, is read from the file in the next iteration of the for loop.

If the contents of the file have been exhausted without determining whether N is prime, the for loop will end, and you'll close the file and execute the following statement:

```
return check(global.primes, global.index, N);
```

Here, the test value is tried against any primes in the primes array in memory by the function check(). If a prime is found, the check() function will return 1; otherwise, the function will return 0. The value that's returned by the check() function will be returned to main().

The code for the check() function is as follows:

```
int check(unsigned long long buffer[], size_t count, unsigned long long N)
{
  /* Upper limit */
  unsigned long long root_N = (unsigned long long)(1.0 + sqrt(N));

  for(size_t i = 0 ; i<count ; i++)
  {
    if(N % buffer[i] == 0ULL )              /* Exact division?             */
      return 0;                             /* Then not a prime            */

    if(buffer[i] > root_N)                  /* Divisor exceeds square root? */
      return 1;                             /* Then must be a prime         */
  }
  return -1;                                /* More checks necessary...    */
}
```

The role of this function is to check if any of the primes contained in the buffer array that's passed as the first argument divide exactly into the test value supplied as the second argument. The local variable in the function is declared in this statement:

```
/* Upper limit */
unsigned long long root_N = (unsigned long long)(1.0 + sqrt(N));
```

The integer variable, root_N, will hold the upper limit for divisors to be checked against the trial value. Only divisors less than the square root of the test value N are tried.

The checking is done in the for loop:

```
for(size_t i = 0 ; i<count ; i++)
{
  if(N % buffer[i] == 0UL )          /* Exact division?              */
    return 0;                        /* Then not a prime             */

  if(buffer[i] > root_N)             /* Divisor exceeds square root? */
    return 1;                        /* Then must be a prime         */
}
```

This loop steps through each of the divisors in the buffer array. If an exact divisor for N is found, the function will end and return 0 to indicate that the value isn't prime. If you arrive at a divisor that's greater than root_N, you've tried all those lower than this value, so N must be prime and the function returns 1. If the loop ends without executing a return statement then you haven't found an exact divisor but you haven't tried all values up to root_N. In this case the function returns −1 to indicate there's more checking to be done.

The last function that you need to define will output all the primes to the file:

```
void put_primes(void)
{
  unsigned long long buffer[MEM_PRIMES];      /* Buffer for a block of primes */

  if(!(global.pfile = fopen( global.filename, "rb"))) /* Open the file         */
  {
    printf("\nUnable to open %s to read primes for output\n", global.filename);
    exit(1);
  }

  for (size_t i = 0U ; i< global.nrec ; i++)
  {
    /* Read a block of primes    */
    fread(buffer, sizeof( unsigned long long), MEM_PRIMES, global.pfile);

    for(size_t j = 0 ; j<MEM_PRIMES ; j++)           /* Display the primes */
    {
      if(j%5 == 0U)                                  /* Five to a line     */
        printf("\n");
      printf("%12llu", buffer[j]);                   /* Output a prime     */
    }
  }
  fclose(global.pfile);                              /* Close the file     */
}
```

The operation of the put_primes() function is very simple. Once the file is opened, blocks of primes are read into the buffer array and as each is read, the for loop outputs the values to the screen, five to a line with a field width of 12. After all records have been read, the file is closed.

To run the program, you need to assemble all the functions that you've described into a single file and compile it. You'll be able to get as many primes as your computer and your patience permit.

A disadvantage of this program is that when you have a large number of primes, the output whizzes by on the screen before you can inspect it. You can do several things to fix this. You can write the output to the printer for a permanent record, instead of writing it to the screen. Or perhaps you can arrange for the program to display a prompt and wait for the user to press a key, between the output of one block and the next.

Moving Around in a File

For many applications, you need to be able to access data in a file other than in the sequential order you've used up to now. You can always find some information that's stored in the middle of a file by reading from the beginning and continuing in sequence until you get to what you want. But if you've written a few million items to the file, this may take some time.

Of course, to access data in random sequence requires that you have some means of knowing where the data that you would like to retrieve is stored in the file. Arranging for this is a complicated topic in general. There are many different ways of constructing pointers or indexes to make direct access to the data in a file faster and easier. The basic idea is similar to that of an index to a book. You have a table of keys that identify the contents of each record in the file you might want, and each key has an associated position in the file defined that records where the data is stored.

Let's look at the basic tools in the library that you need to enable you to deal with this kind of file input/output.

Note You cannot update a file in append mode. Regardless of any operations you may invoke to move the file position, all writes will be to the end of the existing data.

File Positioning Operations

There are two aspects to file positioning: finding out where you are at a given point in a file, and moving to a given point in a file. The former is basic to the latter: if you never know where you are, you can never decide how to get to where you want to go.

A random position in a file can be accessed regardless of whether the file concerned was opened in binary mode or in text mode. However, working with text mode files can get rather complicated in some environments, particularly Microsoft Windows. This is because the number of characters recorded in the file can be greater than the number of characters you actually write to the file. This is because a newline ('\n' character) in memory can translate into two characters when written to a file in text mode (carriage return, CR, followed by linefeed, LF). Of course, your C library function for reading the information sorts everything out when you read the data back. A problem only arises when you think that a point in the file is 100 bytes from the beginning. Whether writing 100 characters to a file in text mode results in 100 bytes actually appearing in the file depends on whether the data includes newline characters. If you subsequently want to write some different data that is the same length in memory as the original data written to the file, it will only be the same length on the file if it contains the same number of '\n' characters.

Thus writing to text files randomly is best avoided. For this reason, I'll sidestep the complications of moving about in text files and concentrate the examples on the much more useful!   and easier! context of randomly accessing the data in binary files.

Finding Out Where You Are

You have two functions to tell you where you are in a file, both of which are very similar but not identical. They each complement a different positioning function. The first is the function ftell(), which has the prototype

```
long ftell(FILE *pfile);
```

This function accepts a file pointer as an argument and returns a long integer value that specifies the current position in the file. This could be used with the file that's referenced by the pointer pfile that you've used previously, as in the following statement:

```
fpos = ftell(pfile);
```

The fops variable of type long now holds the current position in the file and, as you'll see, you can use this in a function call to return to this position at any subsequent time. The value is actually the offset in bytes from the beginning of the file.

The second function providing information on the current file position is a little more complicated. The prototype of the function is the following:

```
int fgetpos(FILE *pfile, fpos_t *position);
```

The first parameter is your old friend the file pointer. The second parameter is a pointer to a type that's defined in <stdio.h> called fpos_t. fpos_t will be a type other than an array type that is able to record every position within a file. It is typically an integer type and with my library it is type long. If you're curious about what type fpos_t is on your system, then have a look at it in <stdio.h>.

The fgetpos() function is designed to be used with the positioning function fsetpos(), which I'll come to very shortly. The function fgetpos() stores the current position and file state information for the file in position and returns 0 if the operation is successful; otherwise, it returns a nonzero integer value. You could declare a variable here to be of type fpos_t with a statement such as this:

```
fpos_t here = 0;
```

You could now record the current position in the file with the statement

```
fgetpos(pfile, &here);
```

This records the current file position in the variable here that you have defined.

Caution Note that you must declare a variable of type fpos_t. It's no good just declaring a pointer of type fpos_t*, as there won't be any memory allocated to store the position data.

Setting a Position in a File

As a complement to ftell(), you have the function fseek(), which has the following prototype:

```
int fseek(FILE *pfile, long offset, int origin);
```

The first parameter is a pointer to the file that you're repositioning. The second and third parameters define where you want to go in the file. The second parameter is an offset from a reference point specified by the third parameter. The reference point can be one of three values that are specified by the predefined names SEEK_SET, which defines the beginning of the file; SEEK_CUR, which defines the current position in the file; and SEEK_END, which, as you might guess, defines the end of the file. Of course, all three values are defined in the header file <stdio.h>. For a text mode file, the second argument must be a value returned by ftell() if you're to avoid getting lost. The third argument for text mode files must be SEEK_SET. So for text mode files, all operations with fseek() are performed with reference to the beginning of the file.

For binary files, the offset argument is simply a relative byte count. You can therefore supply positive or negative values for the offset when the reference point is specified as SEEK_CUR.

You have the fsetpos() function to go with fgetpos(). This has the rather straightforward prototype

```
int fsetpos(FILE *pfile, fpos_t *position);
```

The first parameter is a pointer to the file opened with fopen(), and the second is a pointer of the type you can see, where the value was obtained by calling fgetpos().

You can't go far wrong with this one really. You could use it with a statement such as this:

```
fsetpos(pfile, &here);
```

The variable here was previously set by a call to fgetpos(). As with fgetpos(), a nonzero value is returned on error. Because this function is designed to work with a value that is returned by fgetpos(), you can only use it to get to a place in a file that you've been before, whereas fseek() allows you to go to any specific position.

Note that the verb **seek** is used to refer to operations of moving the read/write heads of a disk drive directly to a specific position in the file. This is why the function fseek() is so named.

With a file that you've opened for update by specifying the mode as "rb+" or "wb+", for example, either a read or a write may be safely carried out on the file after executing either of the file positioning functions, fsetpos() or fseek(). This is regardless of what the previous operation on the file was.

TRY IT OUT: RANDOM ACCESS TO A FILE

To exercise your newfound skills with files, you can create a revised version of Program 11.6 from the previous chapter to allow you to keep a dossier on family members. In this case, you'll create a file containing data on all family members, and then you'll process the file to output data on each member and that member's parents. The structures used only extend to a minimum range of members in each case. You can, of course, embellish these to hold any kind of scuttlebutt you like on your relatives.

Let's look at the function main() first:

```
/* Program 12.5 Investigating the family.*/
#include <stdio.h>
#include <ctype.h>
#include <stdlib.h>
#include <string.h>

/* Global Data */
const int NAME_MAX = 20;

struct
{
  char *filename;                    /* Physical file name   */
  FILE *pfile;                       /* File pointer         */
} global = {"C:\\myfile.bin", NULL };
```

```
/* Structure types */
struct Date                              /* Structure for a date       */
{
  int day;
  int month;
  int year;
};

typedef struct family                    /* Structure for family member */
{
  struct Date dob;
  char name[NAME_MAX];
  char pa_name[NAME_MAX];
  char ma_name[NAME_MAX];
}Family;

/* Function prototypes */
bool get_person(Family *pfamily);        /* Input function          */
void getname(char *name);                /* Read a name             */
void show_person_data(void);             /* Output function         */
void get_parent_dob(Family *pfamily);    /* Function to find pa & ma */

int main(void)
{
  Family member;                         /* Stores a family structure */

  if(!(global.pfile = fopen(global.filename, "wb")))
  {
    printf("\nUnable to open %s for writing.\n", global.filename);
    exit(1);
  }

  while(get_person(&member))             /* As long as we have input */
    fwrite(&member, sizeof member, 1, pfile);   /*    write it away      */

  fclose(global.pfile);                  /* Close the file now its written */

  show_person_data();                    /* Show what we can find out     */

  if(remove(global.filename))
    printf("\nUnable to delete %s.\n", global.filename);
  else
    printf("\nDeleted %s OK.\n", global.filename);
  return 0;
}
```

How It Works

After the #include statements, you have the global variables and structure definitions. You've seen all of these in previous examples. Family isn't a variable, but it has been declared as a type name for the structure family. This will allow you to declare Family type objects without having to use the keyword struct. Following the structure declarations, you have the prototypes for the three functions that you're using in addition to main().

Because you want to try out the file-positioning functions in addition to the basic file read and write operations, the example has been designed to exercise these as well. You get the input on one person at a time in the get_person() function, where the data is stored in the member structure object. You write each structure to the file as soon as it is received, and the input process ceases when the function get_person() returns 0.

When the while loop ends, the input file is closed and the function show_person_data() is called. You use the file position getting and setting functions within this function. Lastly, the file is deleted from the disk by the function remove().

The code for the input function, get_person(), is as follows:

```
/* Function to input data on Family members */
bool get_person(Family *temp)
{
  static char more = '\0';                    /* Test value for ending input */

  printf("\nDo you want to enter details of a%s person (Y or N)? ",
                           more != '\0'?"nother " : "" );
  scanf(" %c", &more);

  if(tolower(more) == 'n')
    return false;

  printf("\nEnter the name of the person: ");
  getname(temp->name);                        /* Get the person's name */
  printf("\nEnter %s's date of birth (day month year); ", temp->name);
  scanf("%d %d %d", &temp->dob.day, &temp->dob.month, &temp->dob.year);

  printf("\nWho is %s's father? ", temp->name);
  getname(temp->pa_name);                     /* Get the father's name  */
  printf("\nWho is %s's mother? ", temp->name);
  getname(temp->ma_name);                     /* Get the mother's name  */
return true;
}
```

This function is fairly self-explanatory. None of the mechanisms involved in this function is new to you. An indicator, more, controls whether reading data continues, and it's set by the input following the first prompt. It's defined as static so the variable and its value persists in the program from one call of get_person() to the next. This allows the prompt to work correctly in selecting a slightly different message for the second and subsequent iterations.

If no data input takes place, which is triggered when **N** or **n** is entered in response to the initial prompt in the function, false is returned. If more data entry occurs, it's entered into the appropriate structure members and true is returned.

The names are read by the getname() function that can be implemented like this:

```
/* Read a name from the keyboard */
void getname(char *name)
{
  fflush(stdin);                       /* Skip whitespace            */
  fgets(name, NAME_MAX, stdin);
  int len = strlen(name);
  if(name[len-1] == '\n')              /* If last char is newline */
    name[len-1] = '\0';               /* overwrite it            */
}
```

This reads a name using fgets() to allow whitespace in the input and also to ensure the capacity of the storage for a name is not exceeded. If the input exceeds NAME_MAX characters, including the terminating null, the name will be truncated. The fgets() function stores the newline that arises when the Enter key is pressed, so when this is present as the last string character, you overwrite it with a terminating null.

The next function generates the output for each person, including the date of birth of both parents, if they've been recorded. The code for this function is as follows:

```
/* Function to output data on people on file    */
void show_person_data(void)
{
  Family member;                          /* Structure to hold data from file  */
  fpos_t current = 0;                     /* File position                     */

  /* Open file for binary read */
  if(!(global.pfile = fopen(global.filename, "rb")))
  {
    printf("\nUnable to open %s for reading.\n", global.filename);
    exit(1);
  }

  /* Read data on person */
  while(fread(&member, sizeof member, 1, global.pfile))
  {
    fgetpos(global.pfile, &current);    /* Save current position        */
    printf("\n\n%s's father is %s, and mother is %s.",
            member.name, member.pa_name, member.ma_name);
    get_parent_dob(&member);             /* Get parent data             */
    fsetpos(global.pfile, &current);    /* Position file to read next  */
  }
   fclose(global.pfile);                 /* Close the file              */
}
```

This function processes each structure in sequence from the file.

After declaring a variable of type Family, you declare a variable, current, with the following statement:

```
  fpos_t current = 0;                         /* File position                    */
```

This statement declares current as type fpos_t. This variable will be used to remember the current position in the file. The get_parent_dob() function is called later in this function, which also accesses the file. It's therefore necessary to remember the file position of the next structure to be read on each iteration before calling get_parent_dob().

After opening the file for binary read operations, all of the processing takes place in a loop controlled by the following:

```
  while(fread(&member, sizeof member, 1, global.pfile))
```

This uses the technique of reading the file within the loop condition and using the value returned by the function fread() as the determinant of whether the loop continues. If the function returns 1, the loop continues, and when 0 is returned, the loop is terminated.

Within the loop you have these statements:

```
  fgetpos(global.pfile, &current);    /* Save current position          */
  printf("\n\n%s's father is %s, and mother is %s.",
         member.name, member.pa_name, member.ma_name);
  get_parent_dob(&member);            /* Get parent data                */
  fsetpos(global.pfile, &current);    /* Position file to read next     */
```

First, the current position in the file is saved, and the parents of the current person stored in member are displayed. You then call the function get_parent_dob(), which will search the file for parent entries. On returning after the call to this function, the file position is unknown, so a call to fsetpos() is made to restore it to the position required for the next structure to be read. After all the structures have been processed, the while loop terminates and the file is closed.

The function to find the dates of birth for the parents of an individual is as follows:

```
/* Function to find parents' dates of birth. */
void get_parent_dob(Family *pmember)
{
  Family relative;                         /* Stores a relative           */
  int num_found = 0;                        /* Count of relatives found   */

  rewind(global.pfile);                     /* Set file to the beginning */

  /* Get the stuff on a relative */
  while(fread(&relative, sizeof(Family), 1, global.pfile))
  {
    if(strcmp(pmember->pa_name, relative.name) == 0)    /*Is it pa?        */
    { /* We have found dear old dad */
      printf("\n Pa was born on %d/%d/%d.",
          relative.dob.day, relative.dob.month, relative.dob.year);

      if(++num_found == 2)                   /* Increment parent count    */
        return;                              /* We got both so go home     */
    }
    else
      if(strcmp(pmember->ma_name, relative.name) == 0) /*Is it ma?        */
      { /* We have found dear old ma */
        printf("\n Ma was born on %d/%d/%d.",
              relative.dob.day, relative.dob.month, relative.dob.year);

        if(++num_found == 2)                  /* Increment parent count    */
          return;                             /* We got both so go home     */
      }
  }
}
```

As the file has already been opened by the calling program, it's only necessary to set it back to the beginning with the rewind() function before beginning processing. The file is then read sequentially, searching each structure that's read for a match with either parent name. The search mechanism for the father is contained in the following statements:

```
    if(strcmp(pmember->pa_name, relative.name) == 0)    /*Is it pa?        */
    { /* We have found dear old dad */
      printf("\n Pa was born on %d/%d/%d.",
          relative.dob.day, relative.dob.month, relative.dob.year);
```

```
    if(++num_found == 2)              /* Increment parent count   */
      return;                         /* We got both so go home    */
  }
```

The name entry for the father of the person indicated by pmember is compared with the name member in the structure object relative. If the father check fails, the function continues with an identical mother check.

If a parent is found, the date of birth information is displayed. A count is kept in num_found of the number of parents discovered in the file, and the function is exited if both have been found. The function ends in any event after all structures have been read from the file.

To run this program, you need to assemble the code for main() and the other functions into a single file. You can then compile and execute it. Of course, the example could be written equally well using ftell() and fseek() as positioning functions.

As in the previous examples in this chapter, the program uses a specific file name, on the assumption that the file doesn't already exist when the program is run. There's a way in C to create temporary files that get around this so let's look into that next.

Using Temporary Work Files

Very often you need a work file just for the duration of a program. You use it only to store intermediate results and you can throw it away when the program is finished. The program that calculates primes in this chapter is a good example; you really only need the file during the calculation.

You have a choice of two functions to help with temporary file usage, and each has advantages and disadvantages.

Creating a Temporary Work File

The first function will create a temporary file automatically. Its prototype is the following:

```
FILE *tmpfile(void);
```

The function takes no arguments and returns a pointer to the temporary file. If the file can't be created for any reason! for example, if the disk is full! the function returns NULL. The file is created and opened for update, so it can be written and read, but obviously it needs to be in that order. You can only ever get out what you have put in. The file is automatically deleted on exit from your program, so there's no need to worry about any mess left behind. You'll never know what the file is called, and because it doesn't last this doesn't matter.

The disadvantage of this function is that the file will be deleted as soon as you close it. This means you can't close the file, having written it in one part of the program, and then reopen it in another part of the program to read the data. You must keep the file open for as long as you need access to the data. A simple illustration of creating a temporary file is provided by these statements:

```
FILE pfile;                  /* File pointer                */
pfile = tmpfile();           /* Get pointer to temporary file */
```

Creating a Unique File Name

The second possibility is to use a function that provides you with a unique file name. Whether this ends up as the name of a temporary file is up to you. The prototype for this function is the following:

```
char *tmpnam(char *filename);
```

If the argument to the function is NULL, the file name is generated in an internal static object, and a pointer to that object is returned. If you want the name stored in a char array that you declare yourself, it must be at least L_tmpnam characters long, where L_tmpnam is an integer constant that is defined in <stdio.h>. In this case, the file name is stored in the array that you specify as an argument, and a pointer to your array is also returned. If the function is unable to create a unique name, it will return NULL.

So to take the first possibility, you can create a unique file with the following statements:

```
FILE *pFile = NULL;
char *filename = tmpnam(NULL);
if(filename != NULL)
  pfile = fopen(filename, "wb+");
```

Here you declare your file pointer pfile and then your pointer filename that is initialized with the address of the temporary file name that the tmpnam() function returns. Because the argument to tmpnam() is NULL, the file name will be generated as an internal static object whose address will be placed in the pointer filename. As long as filename is not NULL you call fopen() to create the file with the mode "wb+". Of course, you can also create temporary text files, too.

Don't be tempted to write this:

```
pfile = fopen(tmpnam(NULL), "wb+");    /* Wrong!! */
```

Apart from the fact there is a possibility that tmpnam() may return NULL, you also no longer have access to the file name, so you can't use remove() to delete the file.

If you want to create the array to hold the file name yourself, you could write this:

```
FILE *pfile = NULL;
char filename[L_tmpnam];
if(tmpnam(filename) != NULL)
  pfile = fopen(filename, "wb+");
```

Remember, the assistance that you've obtained from the standard library is just to provide a unique name. It's your responsibility to delete any files created.

Note You should note that you'll be limited to a maximum number of unique names from this function in your program. You can access the maximum number through TMP_MAX that is defined in <stdio.h>.

Updating Binary Files

You have three open modes that provide for updating binary files:

- ! The mode "r+b" (or you can write it as "rb+") opens an existing binary file for both reading and writing. With this open mode you can read or write anywhere in the file.

- ! The mode "w+b" (or you can write "wb+") truncates the length of an existing binary file to zero so the contents will be lost; you can then carry out both read and write operations but, obviously because the file length is zero, you must write something before you can read the file. If the file does not exist, a new file will be created when you call fopen() with mode "w+b".

- ! The third mode "a+b" (or "ab+") opens an existing file for update. This mode only allows write operations at the end of the file.

While you can write each of the open modes for updating binary files in either of two ways, I prefer to always put the + at the end because for me it is more obvious that the + is significant and means update. We can first put together an example that uses mode "wb+" to create a new file that we can then update using the other modes.

TRY IT OUT: WRITING A BINARY FILE WITH AN UPDATE MODE

The file will contain names of people and their ages, the data being read from the keyboard. A name will be stored as a single string containing a first name and a second name. I have specified a full file path to the temp directory on drive C: in the code so you should check that this will be satisfactory on your system or change it to suit your environment. Note that if the directory in the path does not exist, the program will fail. Here's the code for the example:

```
/* Program 12.6 Writing a binary file with an update mode */
#include <stdio.h>
#include <ctype.h>
#include <string.h>
#include <stdlib.h>

const int MAXLEN = 30;                      /* Size of name buffer    */

void listfile(char *filename);              /* List the file contents */

int main(void)
{
  const char *filename = "C:\\temp\\mydata.bin";
  char name[MAXLEN];                        /* Stores a name      */
  size_t length = 0;                        /* Length of a name */
  int age = 0;                              /* Person's age       */
  char answer = 'y';

  FILE *pFile = fopen(filename, "wb+");

  do
  {
    fflush(stdin);                          /* Remove whitespace */

    printf("\nEnter a name less than %d characters:", MAXLEN);
    gets(name);                             /* Read the name      */

    printf("Enter the age of %s: ", name);
    scanf(" %d", &age);                     /* Read the age       */

    /* Write the name & age to file */
    length = strlen(name);                  /* Get name length    */
    fwrite(&length, sizeof(length), 1, pFile);  /* Write name length */
    fwrite(name, sizeof(char), length, pFile);  /* then the name     */
    fwrite(&age, sizeof(age), 1, pFile);        /* then the age      */

    printf("Do you want to enter another(y or n)?  " );
    scanf("\n%c", &answer);
  } while(tolower(answer) == 'y');
```

```
    fclose(pFile);                                /* Close the file    */

    listfile(filename);                           /* List the contents */
    return 0;
}

/* List the contents of the binary file */
void listfile(char *filename)
{
    size_t length = 0;                            /* Name length       */
    char name[MAXLEN];                            /* Stores a name     */
    int age = 0;
    char format[20];                              /* Format string     */

    /* Create the format string for names up to MAXLEN long */
    sprintf(format, "\n%%-%ds Age:%%4d", MAXLEN);

    FILE *pFile = fopen(filename, "rb");          /* Open to read      */
    printf("\nThe contents of %s are:", filename);

    /* Read records as long as we read a length value */
    while(fread(&length, sizeof(length), 1, pFile) == 1)
    {
      if(length+1>MAXLEN)
      {
        printf("\nName too long.");
        exit(1);
      }
      fread(name, sizeof(char), length, pFile);   /* Read the name     */
      name[length] = '\0';                        /* Append terminator */
      fread(&age, sizeof(age), 1, pFile);         /* Read the age      */
      printf(format, name, age);                  /* Output the record */
    }
    fclose(pFile);
}
```

Here's some sample output from this program:

```
Enter a name less than 30 characters:Bill Bloggs
Enter the age of Bill Bloggs: 21
Do you want to enter another(y or n)?  y

Enter a name less than 30 characters:Yolande Dogsbreath
Enter the age of Yolande Dogsbreath: 27
Do you want to enter another(y or n)?  y

Enter a name less than 30 characters:Ned Nudd
Enter the age of Ned Nudd: 33
Do you want to enter another(y or n)?  y

Enter a name less than 30 characters:Binkie Huckerback
Enter the age of Binkie Huckerback: 18
Do you want to enter another(y or n)?  y
```

```
Enter a name less than 30 characters:Mary Dunklebiscuit
Enter the age of Mary Dunklebiscuit: 29
Do you want to enter another(y or n)?  n

The contents of C:\temp\mydata.bin are:
Bill Bloggs                 Age:  21
Yolande Dogsbreath          Age:  27
Ned Nudd                    Age:  33
Binkie Huckerback           Age:  18
Mary Dunklebiscuit          Age:  29
```

How It Works

The file is opened for binary update operations with the mode specified as "rb+". In this mode the file contents will be overwritten because the file length is truncated to zero. If the file does not exist, a file will be created. The data is read from the keyboard and the file is written in the do-while loop. The first statement in the loop flushes stdin:

```
fflush(stdin);                              /* Remove whitespace */
```

This is necessary because the read operation for a single character that appears in the loop condition will leave a newline character in stdin on all loop iterations after the first. If you don't get rid of this character, the read operation for the name will not work correctly because the newline will be read as an empty name string.

After reading a name and an age from the keyboard, the information is written to the file as binary data with these statements:

```
length = strlen(name);                      /* Get name length    */
fwrite(&length, sizeof(length), 1, pFile);  /* Write name length */
fwrite(name, sizeof(char), length, pFile);  /* then the name      */
fwrite(&age, sizeof(age), 1, pFile);        /* then the age       */
```

The names are going to vary in length and you have basically two ways to deal with this. You can write the entire name array to the file each time and not worry about the length of a name string. This is simpler to code but means that there would be a lot of spurious data in the file. The alternative is to adopt the approach used in the example. The length of each name string is written preceding the name itself, so to read the file you will first read the length, then read that number of characters from the file as the name. Note that the '\0' string terminator is not written to the file, so you have to remember to add this at the end of each name string when you read the file back.

The loop allows as many records as you want to be added to the file because it continues as long as you enter 'y' or 'Y' when prompted. When the loop ends you close the file and call the listfile() function that lists the contents of the file on stdout.

The listfile() function opens the file for binary read operations with the mode "rb". In this mode the file pointer will be positioned at the beginning of the file and you can only read it.

The maximum length of a name is specified by the MAXLEN symbol so it would be helpful to use the format %-MAXLENs for outputting names. This would output a name left-justified in a field that has a width that is the maximum name length, so the names would line up nicely and they would always fit in the field. Of course, you can't really write this as part of the format string because the letters in the MAXLEN symbol name would be interpreted as just that, a sequence of letters, and not the value of the symbol. To achieve the required result, the listfile() function uses the sprintf() function to write to the format array to create a format string:

```
sprintf(format, "\n%%-%ds Age:%%4d", MAXLEN);
```

The sprintf() function works just like printf() except that the output is written to an array of char elements that you specify as the first argument. This operation therefore writes the value of MAXLEN to the format array, using the format string:

```
"\n%%-%ds Age:%%4d"
```

After the \n for a newline there is %% which specifies a single % symbol in the output. The - will appear next in the output followed by the value of MAXLEN formatted using the %d specification. This will be followed by s, then a space followed by Age:. Finally the output will contain a % character followed by 4d. Because the MAXLEN symbol is defined as 30, after executing the sprintf() function the format array will contain the following string:

```
"\n%-30s Age:%d"
```

The file is read and the contents listed on stdout in the while loop that is controlled by the value of an expression that reads the name length from the file:

```
while(fread(&length, sizeof(length), 1, pFile) == 1)
{
...
}
```

The call to fread() reads one item of sizeof(length) bytes into the location specified by &length. When the operation is successful the fread() function returns the number of items read but when the end-of-file is reached the function will return less than the number requested because there is not more data to be read. Thus when we reach the end of file, the loop will end.

An alternative way of recognizing when the end-of-file is reached is to code the loop like this:

```
while(true)
{
  fread(&length, sizeof(length), 1, pFile);
  /* Now check for end of file */
  if(feof(pFile))
    break;
...
}
```

The feof() function tests the end-of-file indicator for the stream specified by the argument and returns nonzero if the indicator is set. Thus when end-of-file is reached, the break will be executed and the loop will end.

After reading the length value from the file, you check that you have space to accommodate the name that follows with the following statements:

```
if(length+1>MAXLEN)
{
  printf("\nName too long.");
  exit(1);
}
```

Remember that the name in the file does not have a terminating '\0' character so you have to allow for that in the name array. Hence you compare length+1 with MAXLEN.

You read the name and age from the file with these statements:

```
fread(name, sizeof(char), length, pFile);    /* Read the name      */
name[length] = '\0';                          /* Append terminator */
fread(&age, sizeof(age), 1, pFile);           /* Read the age       */
```

Finally in the loop, you write the name and age to stdout using the format string that you created using the sprintf() function.

```
printf(format, name, age);                             /* Output the record */
```

Changing the File Contents

We could revise and extend the previous example so that it uses the other two binary update modes. Let's add capability to update the existing records in the file as well as add records or delete the file. This program will be rather more complicated so it will be helpful to break the operations down into more functions. We will still write the file so the names are recorded as they are, so the records consisting of a name and an age will vary in length. This will provide an opportunity to see some of the complications this introduces when we want to change the contents of the file.

To give you an idea of where we are headed, let's look at the program in outline. The program will consist of the following nine functions:

listfile(): Controls overall operation of the program and allows the user to select from a range of operations on the file.

listfile(): Outputs the contents of the file to stdin.

writefile(): Operates in two modes, either writes a new file with records read from stdin, or appends a record to the existing file.

getrecord(): Reads a record from stdin.

getname(): Reads a name from stdin.

writerecord(): Writes a record to the file.

readrecord(): Reads a record from the file.

findrecord(): Find the record in the file with a name that matches input.

duplicatefile(): Reproduces the file replacing a single updated record. This function is used to update a record when the new record will be a different length from the record being replaced.

Figure 12-5 shows the call hierarchy for the functions in the application.

The three functions called by main() implement the basic functionality of the program. The functions to the right of these three provide functionality that helps to simplify the three primary functions.

It will simplify the code if we define a structure that we can use to pass a name and age between functions:

```
struct Record
{
  char name[MAXLEN];
  int age;
};
```

We could easily write objects of type Record to the file, but this would mean the whole name array of MAXLEN elements would be written each time, so the file would contain a lot of spurious bytes for names shorter than MAXLEN characters. However, the structure will provide a very convenient way of passing a name and the associated age value to a function. There will be several functions in the new example, so let's first look at the code for each function before we put the example together. You can assemble the code for the functions into a single source file as you read through the following sections.

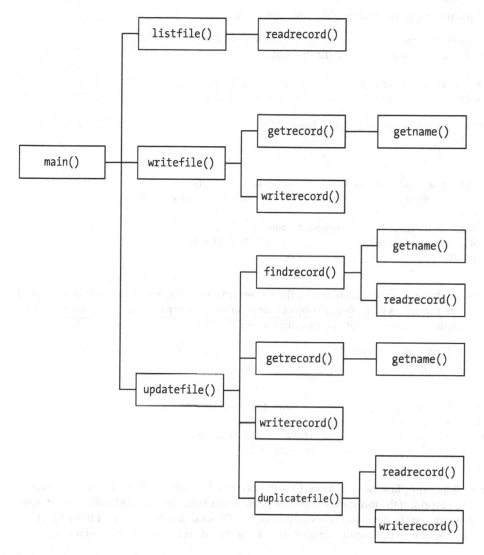

Figure 12-5. *The hierarchy of function calls in Program 12.8*

Reading a Record from the Keyboard

We can write a function that will read a name string and age value from stdin and store them in a Record object. The prototype of the function will be the following:

```
struct Record *getrecord(struct Record *precord);
```

The function requires an argument that is a pointer to an existing Record structure object and it returns the address of the same object. By returning the address of the Record object you make it possible to use a call to this function as an argument to another function that expects an argument of type Record *.

Here's how the implementation of the function looks:

```
/* Read the name and age for a record from the keyboard */
struct Record *getrecord(struct Record *precord)
{
  /* Verify the argument is good */
  if(!precord)
  {
    printf("No Record object to store input.");
    return NULL;
  }

  printf("\nEnter a name less than %d characters:", MAXLEN);
  getname(precord->name);                          /* readf the name    */

  printf("Enter the age of %s: ", precord->name);
  scanf(" %d", &precord->age);                      /* Read the age      */
  return precord;
}
```

This is a straightforward operation where the name and age that are read from stdin are stored in the appropriate members of the Record object that is pointed to by precord. The name is read by the auxiliary function getname() that you can implement like this:

```
/* Read a name from the keyboard */
void getname(char *pname)
{
  fflush(stdin);
  fgets(pname, MAXLEN, stdin);           /* Read the name      */
  int len = strlen(pname);
  if(pname[len-1] == '\n')               /* if there's a newline */
    pname[len-1] = '\0';                 /* overwrite it        */
}
```

The only slight complication in getname() is the need to deal with the '\n' that may be stored by the fgets() function. If the input exceeds MAXLEN characters then the '\n' will still be in the input buffer and not stored in the array pointed to by pname. You'll need to read a name at more that one location in the program so packaging the operation in the getname() function is convenient.

Writing a Record to a File

You can now define a function that will write the members of a record object to a file identified by a pointer of type FILE *. The prototype would look like this:

```
void writerecord(struct Record *precord, FILE *pFile);
```

The first parameter is a pointer to a Record structure that has the name and age that are to be written to the file as members. The second argument is the file pointer.

The implementation looks like this:

```
/* Write a new record to the file at the current position */
void writerecord(struct Record *precord, FILE *pFile)
{
```

```
  /* Verify the arguments are good */
  if(!precord)
  {
    printf("No Record object to write to the file.");
    return;
  }
  if(!pFile)
  {
    printf("No stream pointer for the output file.");
    return;
  }

  /* Write the name & age to file */
  size_t length = strlen(precord->name);              /* Get name length   */
  fwrite(&length, sizeof(length), 1, pFile);          /* Write name length */
  fwrite(precord->name, sizeof(char), length, pFile);   /* then the name     */
  fwrite(&precord->age, sizeof(precord->age), 1, pFile); /* then the age      */
}
```

The function checks that the file pointer exists and the file will be written at the current position. It is therefore the responsibility of the calling function to ensure that the file has been opened in the correct mode and the file position has been set appropriately. The function first writes the length of the string to the file, followed by the string itself, excluding the terminating '\0'. This is to enable the code that will read the file to determine first how many characters are in the name string. Finally the age value is written to the file.

Reading a Record from a File

Here's the prototype of a function to read a single record from a file:

```
struct Record *readrecord(struct Record *precord, FILE *pFile);
```

The file to be read is identified by the second parameter, a file pointer. Purely as a convenience, the return value is the address that is passed as the first argument.

The implementation of the readrecord() function looks like this:

```
/* Reads a record from the file at the current position */
struct Record * readrecord(struct Record *precord, FILE *pFile)
{
  /* Verify the arguments are good */
  if(!precord)
  {
    printf("No Record object to store data from the file.");
    return NULL;
  }
  if(!pFile)
  {
    printf("No stream pointer for the input file.");
    return NULL;
  }

  size_t length = 0;                          /* Name length       */
  fread(&length, sizeof(length), 1, pFile);   /* Read the length   */
  if(feof(pFile))                             /* If it's end file  */
    return NULL;                              /* return NULL       */
```

```
  /* Verify the name can be accommodated */
  if(length+1>MAXLEN)
  {
    fprintf(stderr, "\nName too long. Ending program.");
    exit(1);
  }

  fread(precord->name, sizeof(char), length, pFile);     /* Read the name       */
  precord->name[length] = '\0';                          /* Append terminator  */
  fread(&precord->age, sizeof(precord->age), 1, pFile); /* Read the age        */

  return precord;
}
```

Like the `writerecord()` function, the `readrecord()` function assumes the file has been opened with the correct mode specified and by default attempts to read a record from the current position. Each record starts with a length value that is read first. Of course, the file position could be at the end of the file, so you check for EOF by calling `feof()` with the file pointer as the argument after the read operation. If it is the end-of-file, the `feof()` function returns a nonzero integer value, so in this case you return NULL to signal the calling program that EOF has been reached.

The function then checks for the possibility that the length of the name exceeds the length of the name array. If it does, the program ends after outputting a message to the standard error stream.

If all is well, the name and age are read from the file and stored in the members of the record object. A `'\0'` has to be appended to the name string to avoid disastrous consequences when working with the string subsequently.

Writing a File

Here's the prototype of a function that will write an arbitrary number of records to a file, where the records are entered from the keyboard:

```
void writefile(char *filename, char *mode);
```

The first parameter is the name of the file to be written, so this implies that the function will take care of opening the file. The second parameter is the file open mode to be used. By passing "wb+" as the mode, the `writefile()` function will write to a file discarding any existing contents or create a new file with the specified name if it does not already exist. If the mode is specified as "ab+", records will be appended to an existing file, and a new file will be created if there isn't one already.

Here's the implementation of the function:

```
/* Write to a file */
void writefile(char *filename, char *mode)
{
  char answer = 'y';

  FILE *pFile = fopen(filename, mode);    /* Open the file              */
  if(pFile == NULL)                       /* Verify file is open        */
  {
    fprintf(stderr, "\n File open failed.");
    exit(1);
  }
```

```
  do
  {
    struct Record record;                    /* Stores a record name & age    */

    writerecord(getrecord(&record), pFile); /* Get record & write the file */

    printf("Do you want to enter another(y or n)?  " );
    scanf("\n%c", &answer);
    fflush(stdin);                           /* Remove whitespace             */
  } while(tolower(answer) == 'y');

  fclose(pFile);                             /* Close the file                */
}
```

After opening the file with the mode passed as the second argument, the function writes the file in the do-while loop. The read from stdin and the write to the file are done in the single statement that calls writerecord() with a call to getdata() as the first argument. The pointer to a Record object that getdata() returns is passed directly to the writerecord() function. The operation ends when the user enters 'n' or 'N' to indicate that no more data is to be entered. The file is closed before returning from the function.

Listing the File Contents

The prototype of a function that will list the records in a file on the standard output stream looks like this:

```
void listfile(char *filename);
```

The parameter is the name of the file, so the function will take care of opening the file initially and then closing it when the operation is complete.

Here's the implementation:

```
/* List the contents of the binary file */
void listfile(char *filename)
{
  /* Create the format string for names up to MAXLEN long */
  /* format array length allows up to 5 digits for MAXLEN */
  char format[15];                              /* Format string             */
  sprintf(format, "\n%%-%ds Age:%%4d", MAXLEN);

  FILE *pFile = fopen(filename, "rb");       /* Open file to read         */
  if(pFile == NULL)                          /* Check file is open        */
  {
    printf("Unable to open %s. Verify it exists.\n", filename);
    return;
  }

  struct Record record;                        /* Stores a record           */
  printf("\nThe contents of %s are:", filename);

  while(readrecord(&record, pFile) != NULL)  /* As long as we have records */
    printf(format, record.name, record.age); /* Output the record          */
```

```
  printf("\n");                            /* Move to next line       */

  fclose(pFile);                           /* Close the file          */
}
```

The function generates a format string that will adjust the name field width to be MAXLEN characters. The sprintf() function writes the format string to the format array.

The file is opened in binary read mode so the initial position will be at the beginning of the file. If the file is opened successfully, records are read from the file in the while loop by calling the readrecord() function that we defined earlier. The call to readrecord() is done in the loop condition so when NULL is returned signaling end-of-file has been detected, the loop ends. Within the loop you write the members of the Record object that was read by readrecord() to stdout using the string in the format array that was created initially. When all the records have been read, the file is closed by calling fclose() with the file pointer as the argument.

Updating the Existing File Contents

Updating existing records in the file adds a complication because of the variable length of the names in the file. You can't just arbitrarily overwrite an existing record because the chances are it won't fit in the space occupied by the record to be replaced. If the length of the new record is the same as the original, you can overwrite it. If they are different, the only solution is to write a new file. Here's the prototype of the function to update the file:

```
void updatefile(char *filename);
```

The only parameter is the file name, so the function will handle finding out which record is to be changed, as well as opening and closing the file. Here's the code:

```
/* Modify existing records in the file */
void updatefile(char *filename)
{  char answer = 'y';

  FILE *pFile = fopen(filename, "rb+");    /* Open the file for update   */
  if(pFile == NULL)                        /* Check file is open         */
  {
    fprintf(stderr, "\n File open for updating records failed.");
    return;
  }
  struct Record record;                    /* Stores a record            */
  int index = findrecord(&record, pFile);  /* Find the record for a name */
  if(index<0)                              /* If the record isn't there  */
  {
    printf("\nRecord not found.");         /* ouput a message            */
    return;                                /* and we are done.           */
  }

  printf("\n%s is aged %d,", record.name, record.age);
  struct Record newrecord;                            /* Stores replacement record */
  printf("\nYou can now enter the new name and age for %s.", record.name);
  getrecord(&newrecord);                   /* Get the new record         */
```

```
/* Check if we can update in place */
if((strlen(record.name) == strlen(newrecord.name)))
{ /* Name lengths are the same so we can */
  /* Move to start of old record         */
  fseek(pFile,
        -(long)(sizeof(size_t)+strlen(record.name)+sizeof(record.age)),
        SEEK_CUR);
  writerecord(&newrecord, pFile);          /* Write the new record    */
  fflush(pFile);                           /* Force the write         */
}
else
  duplicatefile(&newrecord, index, filename, pFile);

printf("File update complete.\n");
}
```

There's quite a lot of code in this function but it consists of a sequence of fairly simple steps:

1. Open the file for update.

2. Find the index (first record at index 0) for the record to be updated.

3. Get the data for the record to replace the old record.

4. Check if the record can be updated in place. This is possible when the lengths of the names are the same. If so move the current position back by the length of the old record and write the new record to the old file.

5. If the names are different lengths duplicate the file with the new record replacing the old in the duplicate file.

After opening the file for update, the function reads the name corresponding to the record that is to be changed. The findrecord() function, which I'll get to in a moment, reads the name for the record to be updated, then returns the index value for that record, if it exists, with the first record at index 0. The findrecord() function will return –1 if the record is not found.

If the old and new names are the same length, move the file position back by the length of the old record by calling fseek(). Then write the new record to the file and flush the output buffer. Calling fflush() for the file forces the new record to be transferred from the file.

If the old and new records are different lengths, call duplicatefile() to copy the file with the new record replacing the old in the copy. You can implement the function like this:

```
/* Duplicate the existing file replacing the record to be update */
/* The record to be replaced is index records from the start     */
void duplicatefile(struct Record *pnewrecord, int index,
                                        char *filename, FILE *pFile)
{
  /* Create and open a new file */
  char tempname[L_tmpnam];
  if(tmpnam(tempname) == NULL)
  {
    printf("\nTemporary file name creation failed.");
    return;
  }
  char tempfile[strlen(dirpath)+strlen(tempname)+1];
  strcpy(tempfile, dirpath);                /* Copy original file path */
  strcat(tempfile, tempname);              /* Append temporary name   */
  FILE *ptempfile = fopen(tempfile, "wb+");
```

```
/* Copy first index records from old file to new file */
rewind(pFile);                              /* Old file back to start    */
struct Record record;                       /* Store for a record        */
for(int i = 0 ; i<index ; i++)
  writerecord(readrecord(&record, pFile), ptempfile);


writerecord(pnewrecord, ptempfile);         /* Write the new record      */
readrecord(&record,pFile);                  /* Skip the old record       */

/* Copy the rest of the old file to the new file */
while(readrecord(&record,pFile))
  writerecord(&record, ptempfile);

/* close the files */
if(fclose(pFile)==EOF)
  printf("\n Failed to close %s", filename);
if(fclose(ptempfile)==EOF)
  printf("\n Failed to close %s", tempfile);

if(!remove(filename))                        /* Delete the old file       */
{
  printf("\nRemoving the old file  failed. Check file in %s", dirpath);
  return;
}

/* Rename the new file same as original */
if(!rename(tempfile, filename))
  printf("\nRenaming the file copy failed. Check file in %s", dirpath);
}
```

This function carries the update through the following steps:

1. Create a new file with a unique name in the same directory as the old file. The dirpath variable will be a global that contains the path to the original file.

2. Copy all records preceding the record to be changed from the old file to the new file.

3. Write the new record to the new file and skip over the record to be updated in the old file.

4. Write all the remaining records from the old file to the new file.

5. Close both files.

6. Delete the old file and rename the new file with the name of the old file.

Once the new file is created using the name generated by tmpnam( ), records are copied from the original file to the new file, with the exception that the record to be updated is replaced with the new record in the new file. The copying of the first index records is done in the for loop where the pointer that is returned by readrecord() reading the old file is passed as the argument to writerecord() for the new file. The copying of the records that follow the updated record is done in the while loop. Here you have to continue copying records until the end-of-file is reached in the old file. Finally, after closing both files, delete the old file to free up its name and then rename the new file to the old. If you want to do this more safely, you can rename the old file in some way rather than deleting it, perhaps by appending "_old" to the existing file name. You can then rename the new file as you do here. This would leave a backup file in the directory that would be useful if the update goes awry.

The implementation of the findrecord() function that is called by updatefile() to find the index for the record that matches the name that is entered looks like this:

```
/* Find a record                           */
/* Returns the index number of the record */
/* or -1 if the record is not found.       */
int findrecord(struct Record *precord, FILE *pFile)
{
  char name[MAXLEN];
  printf("\nEnter the name for the record you wish to find: ");
  getname(name);

  rewind(pFile);                      /* Make sure we are at the start */
  int index = 0;                      /* Index of current record       */

  while(true)
  {
    readrecord(precord, pFile);
    if(feof(pFile))                   /* If end-of-file was reached     */
      return -1;                      /* record not found               */
    if(!strcmp(name, precord->name))
      break;
    ++index;
  }
  return index;                       /* Return record index            */
}
```

This function reads a name for the record that is to be changed, then reads records looking for a name that matches the name that was entered. If end-of-file is reached without finding the name, −1 is returned to signal to the calling program that the record is not in the file. If a name match is found, the function returns the index value of the matching record.

You can now assemble the complete working example.

TRY IT OUT: READING, WRITING, AND UPDATING A BINARY FILE

I won't repeat all the functions I have just described. You can add the following to the beginning of the source file containing the code for the functions other than main():

```
/* Program 12.7 Writing, reading and updating a binary file */
#include <stdio.h>
#include <ctype.h>
#include <string.h>
#include <stdlib.h>
#include <stdbool.h>

const int MAXLEN = 30;                        /* Size of name buffer      */
const char *dirpath = "C:\\temp\\";           /* Directory path for file */
const char *file = "mydata.bin";              /* File name                */

/* Structure encapsulating a name and age */
struct Record
{
```

```
    char name[MAXLEN];
    int age;
};

void listfile(char *filename);                    /* List the file contents   */
void updatefile(char *filename);                  /* Update the file contents */
struct Record *getrecord(struct Record *precord); /* Read a record from stdin */
void getname(char *pname);                         /* Read a name from stdin   */
void writefile(char *filename, char *mode);       /* Write records to a file  */
void writerecord(struct Record *precord, FILE *pFile);
struct Record * readrecord(struct Record *precord, FILE *pFile);
int findrecord(struct Record *precord, FILE *pFile);
void duplicatefile(struct Record *pnewrecord,
                              int index, char *filename, FILE *pFile);

int main(void)
{
    char filename[strlen(dirpath)+strlen(file)+1];  /* Stores file path      */
    strcpy(filename, dirpath);                       /* Copy directory path    */
    strcat(filename, file);                          /*  and append file name  */

    /* Choose activity option */
    char answer = 'q';
    while(true)
    {
        printf("\nChoose from the following options:"
                "\nTo list the file contents enter  L"
                "\nTo create a new file enter       C"
                "\nTo add new records enter         A"
                "\nTo update existing records enter U"
                "\nTo delete the file enter         D"
                "\nTo end the program enter         Q\n : ");
        scanf("\n%c", &answer);

        switch(tolower(answer))
        {
            case 'l':                               /* List file contents      */
                listfile(filename);
                break;
            case 'c':                               /* Create new file         */
                writefile(filename,"wb+");
                printf("\nFile creation complete.");
                break;
            case 'a':                               /* Append records          */
                writefile(filename, "ab+");
                printf("\nFile append complete.");
                break;
            case 'u':                               /* Update existing records */
                updatefile(filename);
                break;
            case 'd':
                printf("Are you sure you want to delete %s (y or n)? ", filename);
                scanf("\n%c", &answer);
                if(tolower(answer) == 'y')
                    remove(filename);
```

```
          break;
        case 'q':                                /* Quit the program        */
          printf("\nEnding the program.", filename);
          return 0;
        default:
          printf("Invalid selection. Try again.");
          break;
      }
    }
    return 0;
}
```

Here's some sample output from a session using the main options offered by the program:

```
Choose from the following options:
To list the file contents enter  L
To create a new file enter       C
To add new records enter         A
To update existing records enter U
To delete the file enter         D
To end the program enter         Q
 : c

Enter a name less than 30 characters:Bill Bloggs
Enter the age of Bill Bloggs: 22
Do you want to enter another(y or n)?  y

Enter a name less than 30 characters:Kitty Malone
Enter the age of Kitty Malone: 23
Do you want to enter another(y or n)?  n

File creation complete.
Choose from the following options:
To list the file contents enter  L
To create a new file enter       C
To add new records enter         A
To update existing records enter U
To delete the file enter         D
To end the program enter         Q
 : l

The contents of C:\temp\mydata.bin are:
Bill Bloggs                  Age:  22
Kitty Malone                 Age:  23

Choose from the following options:
To list the file contents enter  L
To create a new file enter       C
To add new records enter         A
To update existing records enter U
To delete the file enter         D
To end the program enter         Q
 : a

Enter a name less than 30 characters:Jack Flash
Enter the age of Jack Flash: 30
Do you want to enter another(y or n)?  n
```

```
File append complete.
Choose from the following options:
To list the file contents enter  L
To create a new file enter       C
To add new records enter         A
To update existing records enter U
To delete the file enter         D
To end the program enter         Q
 : l

The contents of C:\temp\mydata.bin are:
Bill Bloggs                Age:  22
Kitty Malone               Age:  23
Jack Flash                 Age:  30

Choose from the following options:
To list the file contents enter  L
To create a new file enter       C
To add new records enter         A
To update existing records enter U
To delete the file enter         D
To end the program enter         Q
 : u

Enter the name for the record you wish to find: Kitty Malone

Kitty Malone is aged 23,
You can now enter the new name and age for Kitty Malone.
Enter a name less than 30 characters:Kitty Moline
Enter the age of Kitty Moline: 24
File update complete.

Choose from the following options:
To list the file contents enter  L
To create a new file enter       C
To add new records enter         A
To update existing records enter U
To delete the file enter         D
To end the program enter         Q
 : l

The contents of C:\temp\mydata.bin are:
Bill Bloggs                Age:  22
Kitty Moline               Age:  24
Jack Flash                 Age:  30

Choose from the following options:
To list the file contents enter  L
To create a new file enter       C
To add new records enter         A
To update existing records enter U
To delete the file enter         D
To end the program enter         Q
 : q
```

How It Works

There's a lot of code in main but it's very simple. The global strings dirpath and file identify the directory and file name respectively for the file that contains the data. These are concatenated in main() with the result stored in filename.

The indefinite while loop offers a series of choices of action and the choice entered is determined in the switch statement. Depending on the character entered, one of the functions you developed for the program is called. Execution continues until the option 'Q' or 'q' is entered to end the program.

File Open Modes Summary

You probably will need a little practice before the file open mode strings come immediately to mind, so Table 12-2 contains a summary that you can refer back to when necessary.

Table 12-2. *File Modes*

Mode	Description
"w"	Open or create a text file for write operations.
"a"	Open a text file for append operations, adding to the end of the file.
"r"	Open a text file for read operations.
"wb"	Open or create a binary file for write operations.
"ab"	Open a binary file for append operations.
"rb"	Open a binary file for read operations.
"w+"	Open or create a text file for update operations. An existing file will be truncated to zero length.
"a+"	Open or create a text file for update operations, adding to the end of the file.
"r+"	Open a text file for update operations (read and write anywhere).
"w+b" or "wb+"	Open or create a binary file for update operations. An existing file will be truncated to zero length.
"a+b" or "ab+"	Open a binary file for update operations, adding to the end of the file.
"r+b" or "rb+"	Open a binary file for update operations (read and write anywhere).

Designing a Program

Now that you've come to the end of this chapter, you can put what you've learned into practice with a final program. This program will be shorter than the previous example, but nonetheless it's an interesting program that you may find useful.

The Problem

The problem you're going to solve is to write a file-viewer program. This will display any file in hexadecimal representation and as characters.

The Analysis

The program will open the file as binary read-only and then display the information in two columns, the first being the hexadecimal representation of the bytes in the file, and the second being the bytes represented as characters. The file name will be supplied as a command line argument or, if that isn't supplied, the program will ask for the file name.

The stages are as follows:

1. If the file name isn't supplied, get it from the user.

2. Open the file.

3. Read and display the contents of the file.

The Solution

This section outlines the steps you'll take to solve the problem.

Step 1

You can easily check to see if the file name appears at the command line by specifying that the function main() has parameters. Up until now, we have ignored the possibility of parameters being passed to main(), but here you can use it as the means of identifying the file that's to be displayed. You'll recall that when main() is called, two parameters are passed to it. The first parameter is an integer indicating the number of words in the command line, and the second is an array of pointers to strings. The first string contains the name that you use to start the program at the command line, and the remaining strings represent the arguments that follow at the command line. Of course, this mechanism allows an arbitrary number of values to be entered at the command line and passed to main().

If the value of the first argument to main() is 1, there's only the program name on the command line, so in this case you'll have to prompt for the file name to be entered:

```
/* Program 12.8 Viewing the contents of a file */
#include <stdio.h>

const int MAXLEN = 256;                        /* Maximum file path length    */

int main(int argc, char *argv[])
{
  char filename[MAXLEN];                       /* Stores the file path        */

  if(argc == 1)                                /* No file name on command line? */
  {
    printf("Please enter a filename: ");       /* Prompt for input            */
    fgets(filename, MAXLEN, stdin);            /* Get the file name entered   */
```

```
    /* Remove the newline if it's there */
    int len = strlen(filename);
    if(filename[len-1] == '\n')
      filename[len-1] = '\0';
  }
  return 0;
}
```

This allows for a maximum file path length of 256 characters.

Step 2

If the first argument to main() isn't 1, then you have at least one more argument, which you assume is the file name. You therefore copy the string pointed to by argv[1] to the variable openfile. Assuming that you have a valid file name, you can open the file and start reading it:

```
/* Program 12.8 Viewing the contents of a file */
#include <stdio.h>

const int MAXLEN = 256;                   /* Maximum file path length     */

int main(int argc, char *argv[])
{
  char filename[MAXLEN];                  /* Stores the file path         */
  FILE *pfile;                            /* File pointer                 */

  if(argc == 1)                           /* No file name on command line? */
  {
    printf("Please enter a filename: ");  /* Prompt for input             */
    fgets(filename, MAXLEN, stdin);       /* Get the file name entered    */

    /* Remove the newline if it's there */
    int len = strlen(filename);
    if(filename[len-1] == '\n')
      filename[len-1] = '\0';
  }
  else
    strcpy(filename, argv[1]);            /* Get 2nd command line string   */

  /* File can be opened OK? */
  if(!(pfile = fopen(filename, "rb")))
  {
    printf("Sorry, can't open %s", filename);
    return -1;
  }
  fclose(pfile);                          /* Close the file               */
  return 0;
}
```

You put the call to the fclose() function to close the file at the end of the program so that you don't forget about it later. Also, you use a return value of –1 for the program to indicate when an error has occurred.

Step 3

You can now output the file contents. You do this by reading the file one byte at a time and saving this data in a buffer. Once the buffer is full or the end of file has been reached, you output the buffer in the format you want. When you output the data as characters, you must first check that the character is printable, otherwise strange things may start happening on the screen. You use the function isprint(), declared in ctype.h, for this. If the character isn't printable, you'll print a period instead.

Here's the complete code for the program:

```
/* Program 12.8 Viewing the contents of a file */
#include <stdio.h>
#include <ctype.h>
#include <string.h>

const int MAXLEN = 256;                     /* Maximum file path length    */
const int DISPLAY = 80;                     /* Length of display line      */
const int PAGE_LENGTH = 20;                 /* Lines per page              */

int main(int argc, char *argv[])
{
  char filename[MAXLEN];                    /* Stores the file path        */
  FILE *pfile;                              /* File pointer                */
  unsigned char buffer[DISPLAY/4 - 1];      /* File input buffer           */
  int count = 0;                            /* Count of characters in buffer */
  int lines = 0;                            /* Number of lines displayed   */

  if(argc == 1)                             /* No file name on command line? */
  {
    printf("Please enter a filename: ");    /* Prompt for input            */
    fgets(filename, MAXLEN, stdin);         /* Get the file name entered   */

    /* Remove the newline if it's there */
    int len = strlen(filename);
    if(filename[len-1] == '\n')
      filename[len-1] = '\0';
  }
  else
    strcpy(filename, argv[1]);              /* Get 2nd command line string */

    /* File can be opened OK?        */
    if(!(pfile = fopen(filename, "rb")))
    {
      printf("Sorry, can't open %s", filename);
      return -1;
    }
  while(!feof(pfile))                       /* Continue until end of file  */
  {
    if(count < sizeof buffer)               /* If the buffer is not full   */
      buffer[count++] = (unsigned char)fgetc(pfile);    /* Read a character */
    else
    { /* Output the buffer contents, first as hexadecimal */
      for(count = 0; count < sizeof buffer; count++)
        printf("%02X ", buffer[count]);
      printf("| ");                         /* Output separator            */
```

```
        /* Now display buffer contents as characters */
        for(count = 0; count < sizeof buffer; count++)
          printf("%c", isprint(buffer[count]) ? buffer[count]:'.');
        printf("\n");                          /* End the line         */
        count = 0;                             /* Reset count          */

        if(!(++lines%PAGE_LENGTH))             /* End of page?         */
          if(getchar()=='E')                   /* Wait for Enter       */
            return 0;                          /* E pressed            */
    }
  }

  /* Display the last line, first as hexadecimal */
  for(int i = 0; i < sizeof buffer; i++)
    if(i < count)
      printf("%02X ", buffer[i]);             /* Output hexadecimal   */
    else
      printf("   ");                           /* Output spaces        */
  printf("| ");                                /* Output separator     */

  /* Display last line as characters */
  for(int i = 0; i < count; i++)
    /* Output character    */
    printf("%c",isprint(buffer[i]) ? buffer[i]:'.');

  /* End the line */
  printf("\n");
  fclose(pfile);                               /* Close the file       */
  return 0;
}
```

The symbol DISPLAY specifies the width of a line on the screen for output, and the symbol PAGE_LENGTH specifies the number of lines per page. You arrange to display a page, and then wait for Enter to be pressed before displaying the next page, thus avoiding the whole file whizzing by before you can read it.

You declare the buffer to hold input from the file as

```
unsigned char buffer[DISPLAY/4 - 1];    /* File input buffer          */
```

The expression for the array dimension arises from the fact that you'll need four characters on the screen to display each character from the file, plus one separator. Each character will be displayed as two hexadecimal digits plus a space, and as a single character, making four characters in all.

You continue reading as long as the while loop condition is true:

```
while(!feof(pfile))                      /* Continue until end of file  */
```

The library function, feof(), returns true if EOF is read from the file specified by the argument; otherwise, it returns false.

You fill the buffer array with characters from the file in the if statement:

```
if(count < sizeof buffer)                /* If the buffer is not full   */
  buffer[count++] = (unsigned char)fgetc(pfile);   /* Read a character  */
```

When count exceeds the capacity of buffer, the else clause will be executed to output the contents of the buffer:

```
  else
  { /* Output the buffer contents, first as hexadecimal */
    for(count = 0; count < sizeof buffer; count++)
      printf("%02X ", buffer[count]);
    printf("| ");                              /* Output separator        */

    /* Now display buffer contents as characters */
    for(count = 0; count < sizeof buffer; count++)
      printf("%c", isprint(buffer[count]) ? buffer[count]:'.');
    printf("\n");                              /* End the line            */
    count = 0;                                 /* Reset count             */

    if(!(++lines%PAGE_LENGTH))                 /* End of page?            */
      if(getchar()=='E')                       /* Wait for Enter          */
        return 0;                              /* E pressed               */
  }
```

The first for loop outputs the contents of buffer as hexadecimal characters. You then output a separator character and execute the next for loop to output the same data as characters. The conditional operator in the second argument to printf() ensures that nonprinting characters are output as a period.

The if statement increments the line count, lines, and for every PAGE_LENGTH number of lines, wait for a character to be entered. If you press Enter, the next pageful will be displayed, but if you press E and then Enter, the program will end. This provides you with an opportunity to escape from continuing to output the contents of a file that's larger than you thought.

The final couple of for loops are similar to those you've just seen. The only difference is that spaces are output for array elements that don't contain file characters. An example of the output is as follows. It shows part of the source file for the self-same program and you can deduce from the output that the file path was entered as a command line argument.

```
2F 2A 20 50 72 6F 67 72 61 6D 20 31 32 2E 38 20 56 69 65 | /* Program 12.8 Vie
77 69 6E 67 20 74 68 65 20 63 6F 6E 74 65 6E 74 73 20 6F | wing the contents o
66 20 61 20 66 69 6C 65 20 2A 2F 0D 0A 23 69 6E 63 6C 75 | f a file */..#inclu
64 65 20 3C 73 74 64 69 6F 2E 68 3E 0D 0A 23 69 6E 63 6C | de <stdio.h>..#incl
75 64 65 20 3C 63 74 79 70 65 2E 68 3E 0D 0A 23 69 6E 63 | ude <ctype.h>..#inc
6C 75 64 65 20 3C 73 74 72 69 6E 67 2E 68 3E 0D 0A 0D 0A | lude <string.h>....
63 6F 6E 73 74 20 69 6E 74 20 4D 41 58 4C 45 4E 20 3D 20 | const int MAXLEN =
32 35 36 3B 20 20 20 20 20 20 20 20 20 20 20 20 20 20 20 | 256;
20 20 20 20 20 2F 2A 20 4D 61 78 69 6D 75 6D 20 66 69 6C |      /* Maximum fil
65 20 70 61 74 68 20 6C 65 6E 67 74 68 20 20 20 20 20 20 | e path length
2A 2F 0D 0A 63 6F 6E 73 74 20 69 6E 74 20 44 49 53 50 4C | */..const int DISPL
41 59 20 3D 20 38 30 3B 20 20 20 20 20 20 20 20 20 20 20 | AY = 80;
20 20 20 20 20 20 20 20 20 2F 2A 20 4C 65 6E 67 74 68 20 |          /* Length
6F 66 20 64 69 73 70 6C 61 79 20 6C 69 6E 65 20 20 20 20 | of display line
20 20 20 20 2A 2F 0D 0A 63 6F 6E 73 74 20 69 6E 74 20 50 |     */..const int P
41 47 45 5F 4C 45 4E 47 54 48 20 3D 20 32 30 3B 20 20 20 | AGE_LENGTH = 20;
20 20 20 20 20 20 20 20 20 20 20 20 20 2F 2A 20 4C 69 6E |              /* Lin
65 73 20 70 65 72 20 70 61 67 65 20 20 20 20 20 20 20 20 | es per page
20 20 20 20 20 20 20 20 2A 2F 0D 0A 0D 0A 69 6E 74 20 6D |         */....int m
61 69 6E 28 69 6E 74 20 61 72 67 63 2C 20 63 68 61 72 20 | ain(int argc, char
```

A lot more output follows, ending with this:

```
66 65 72 5B 69 5D 3A 27 2E 27 29 3B 0D 0A 20 20 2F 2A 20 | fer[i]:'.');..  /*
45 6E 64 20 74 68 65 20 6C 69 6E 65 20 20 20 20 20 20 20 | End the line
20 20 20 2A 2F 0D 0A 20 20 70 72 69 6E 74 66 28 22 5C 6E |    */..  printf("\n
22 29 3B 0D 0A 20 20 66 63 6C 6F 73 65 28 70 66 69 6C 65 | ");..  fclose(pfile
29 3B 20 20 20 20 20 20 20 20 20 20 20 20 20 20 20 20 20 | );
20 20 20 20 20 20 20 20 20 20 2F 2A 20 43 6C 6F 73 65 20 |          /* Close
74 68 65 20 66 69 6C 65 20 20 20 20 20 20 20 20 20 20 20 | the file
20 20 20 20 20 2A 2F 0D 0A 20 20 72 65 74 75 72 6E 20 30 |    */..  return 0
3B 0D 0A 7D 0D 0A 0D 0A FF                               | ;..}.....
```

Summary

Within this chapter I've covered all of the basic tools necessary to provide you with the ability to program the complete spectrum of file functions. The degree to which these have been demonstrated in examples has been, of necessity, relatively limited. There are many ways of applying these tools to provide more sophisticated ways of managing and retrieving information in a file. For example, it's possible to write index information into the file, either as a specific index at a known place in the file, often the beginning, or as position pointers within the blocks of data, rather like the pointers in a linked list. You should experiment with file operations until you feel confident that you understand the mechanisms involved.

Although the functions I discussed in this chapter cover most of the abilities you're likely to need, you'll find that the input/output library provided with your compiler offers quite a few additional functions that give you even more options for handling your file operations.

Exercises

The following exercises enable you to try out what you've learned in this chapter. If you get stuck, look back over the chapter for help. If you're still stuck, you can download the solutions from the Source Code/Download area of the Apress web site (http://www.apress.com), but that really should be a last resort.

Exercise 12-1. Write a program that will write an arbitrary number of strings to a file. The strings should be entered from the keyboard and the program shouldn't delete the file, as it will be used in the next exercise.

Exercise 12-2. Write a program that will read the file that was created by the previous exercise, and retrieve the strings one at a time in reverse sequence and write them to a new file in the sequence in which they were retrieved. For example, the program will retrieve the last string and write that to the new file, then retrieve the second to last and retrieve that from the file, and so on, for each string in the original file.

Exercise 12-3. Write a program that will read names and telephone numbers from the keyboard and write them to a new file if a file doesn't already exist and add them if the file does exist. The program should optionally list all the entries.

Exercise 12-4. Extend the program from the previous exercise to implement retrieval of all the numbers corresponding to a given second name. The program should allow further enquiries, adding new name/number entries and deleting existing entries.

CHAPTER 13

■■■

Supporting Facilities

At this point you've covered the complete C language, as well as the important library functions. You should be reasonably confident in programming all aspects of the language. If you aren't, that's simply because you need more practice. Once you've learned the elements of the language, competence comes down to practice, practice, practice.

In this final chapter, I'll tie up a few loose ends. You'll delve deeper into the capabilities you have available through the preprocessor, and you'll look at a few more library functions that you're sure to find useful.

In this chapter you'll learn the following:

!   More about the preprocessor and its operation

!   How to write preprocessor macros

!   What logical preprocessor directives are and how you can use them

!   What conditional compilation is and how you can apply it

!   More about the debugging methods that are available to you

!   How you use some of the additional library functions available

Preprocessing

As you are certainly aware by now, preprocessing of your source code occurs before it's compiled to machine instructions. The preprocessing phase can execute a range of service operations specified by preprocessing directives, which are identified by the # symbol as the first character of each preprocessor directive. The preprocessing phase provides an opportunity for manipulating and modifying your C source code prior to compilation. Once the preprocessing phase is complete and all directives have been analyzed and executed, all such preprocessing directives will no longer appear in the source code that results. The compiler begins the compile phase proper, which generates the machine code equivalent of your program.

You've already used preprocessor directives in all the examples, and you're familiar with both the #include and #define directives. There are a number of other directives that add considerable flexibility to the way in which you specify your programs. Keep in mind as you proceed that all these are preprocessing operations that occur before your program is compiled. They modify the set of statements that constitute your program. They aren't involved in the execution of your program at all.

Including Header Files in Your Programs

A header file is any external file whose contents are included into your program by use of the #include preprocessor directive. You're completely familiar with statements such as this:

```
#include <stdio.h>
```

This fetches the standard library header file supporting input/output operations into your program. This is a particular case of the general statement for including standard libraries into your program:

```
#include <standard_library_file_name>
```

Any library header file name can appear between the angled brackets. If you include a header file that you don't use, the only effect, apart from slightly confusing anyone reading the program, is to extend the compilation time.

You can include your own source files into your program with a slightly different #include statement. A typical example might be this:

```
#include "myfile.h"
```

This statement will introduce the contents of the file named between double quotes into the program in place of the #include directive. The contents of any file can be included into your program by this means. You simply specify the name of the file between quotes as shown in the example.

You can also give the file whatever name you like within the constraints of the operating system. In theory you don't have to use the extension .h, although it's a convention commonly adhered to by most programmers in C, so I strongly recommend that you use it too. The difference between using this form and using angled brackets lies in the source that will be assumed for the required file. The precise operation is compiler-dependent and will be described in the compiler documentation, but usually the first form will search the default header file directory for the required file, whereas the second form will search the current source directory before the default header file directory is searched.

Header files cannot include implementation, by which I mean executable code. You use header files to contain declarations, not function definitions or initialized global data. All your function definitions and initialized globals are placed in source files with the extension .c. You can use the header file mechanism to divide your program source code into several files and, of course, to manage the declarations for any library functions of your own. A very common use of this facility is to create a header file containing all the function prototypes and type declarations for a program. These can then be managed as a separate unit and included at the beginning of any source file for the program. You need to avoid duplicating information if you include more than one header file into a source file. Duplicate code will often cause compilation errors. You'll see later in this chapter in the •Conditional Compilation! section how you can ensure that any given block of code will appear only once in your program, even if you inadvertently include it several times.

■**Note** A file introduced into your program by an #include directive may also contain another #include directive. If so, preprocessing will deal with the second #include in the same way as the first and continue replacing such directives with the contents of the corresponding file until there are no more #include directives in the program.

External Variables and Functions

With a program that's made up of several source files, you'll frequently find that you want to use a global variable that's defined in another file. You can do this by declaring the variable as external to the current file using the extern keyword. For example, if you have variables defined in another file as **global** (which means outside of any of the functions) using the statements

```
int number = 0;
double in_to_mm = 2.54;
```

then in a function in which you want to access these, you can specify that these variable names are external by using these statements:

```
extern int number;
extern double in_to_mm;
```

These statements don't create these variables! they just identify to the compiler that these names are defined elsewhere, and this assumption about these names should apply to the rest of this source file. The variables you specify as extern must be declared and defined somewhere else in the program, usually in another source file. If you want to make these external variables accessible to all functions within the current file, you should declare them as external at the very beginning of the file, prior to any of the function definitions. With programs consisting of several files, you could place all initialized global variables at the beginning of one file and all the extern statements in a header file. The extern statements can then be incorporated into any program file that needs access to these variables by using an include statement for the header file.

■**Note** Only one declaration of each global variable is allowed in a file. Of course, the global variables may be declared as external in as many files as necessary.

Substitutions in Your Program Source Code

There are preprocessor directives for replacing symbols in your source code before it is compiled. The simplest kind of symbol substitution you can make is one you've already seen. For example, the preprocessor directive to substitute the specified numeric value, wherever the character string PI occurs, is as follows:

```
#define PI 3.14159265
```

Although the identifier PI *looks* like a variable, it is not a variable and has nothing to do with variables. Here PI is a token, rather like a voucher, that is exchanged for the sequence of digits specified in the #define directive during the preprocessing phase. When your program is ready to be compiled after preprocessing has been completed, the string PI will no longer appear, having been replaced by its definition wherever it occurs in the source file. The general form of this sort of preprocessor directive is the following:

```
#define identifier sequence_of_characters
```

Here, identifier conforms to the usual definition of an identifier in C: any sequence of letters and digits, the first of which is a letter, and underline characters count as letters. Note that sequence_of_characters, which is the replacement for identifier, is any sequence of characters and need not be just digits.

A very common use of the #define directive is to define array dimensions by way of a substitution, to allow a number of array dimensions to be determined by a single token. Only one directive in the program then needs to be modified to alter the dimensions of a number of arrays in the program. This helps considerably in minimizing errors when such changes are necessary, as shown in the following example:

```
#define MAXLEN 256
char *buffer[MAXLEN];
char *str[MAXLEN];
```

Here, the dimensions of both arrays can be changed by modifying the single #define directive, and of course the array declarations that are affected can be anywhere in the program file. The advantages of this approach in a large program involving dozens or even hundreds of functions should be obvious. Not only is it easy to make a change, but also using this approach ensures that the same value is being used through a program. This is especially important with large projects involving several programmers working together to produce the final product.

Of course, you can also define a value such as MAXLEN as a const variable:

```
const size_t MAXLEN = 256;
```

The difference between this approach and using the #define directive is that MAXLEN here is no longer a token but is a variable of a specific type with the name MAXLEN. The MAXLEN in the #define directive does not exist once the source file has been preprocessed because all occurrences of MAXLEN in the code will be replaced by 256.

I use numerical substitution in the last two examples, but as I said, you're in no way limited to this. You could, for example, write the following:

```
#define Black White
```

This will cause any occurrence of Black in your program to be replaced with White. The sequence of characters that is to replace the token identifier can be anything at all.

Macro Substitutions

A **macro** is based on the ideas implicit in the #define directive examples you've seen so far, but it provides a greater range of possible results by allowing what might be called **multiple parameterized substitutions**. This not only involves substitution of a fixed sequence of characters for a token identifier, but also allows parameters to be specified, which may themselves be replaced by argument values, wherever the parameter appears in the substitution sequence.

Let's look at an example:

```
#define Print(My_var) printf("%d", Myvar)
```

This directive provides for two levels of substitution. There is the substitution for Print(My_var) by the string immediately following it in the #define statement, and there is the possible substitution of alternatives for My_var. You could, for example, write the following:

```
Print(ival);
```

This will be converted during preprocessing to this statement:

```
printf("%d", ival);
```

You could use this directive to specify a printf() statement for an integer variable at various points in your program. A common use for this kind of macro is to allow a simple representation of a complicated function call in order to enhance the readability of a program.

Macros That Look Like Functions

The general form of the kind of substitution directive just discussed is the following:

```
#define macro_name( list_of_identifiers ) substitution_string
```

This shows that in the general case, multiple parameters are permitted, so you're able to define more complex substitutions.

To illustrate how you use this, you can define a macro for producing a maximum of two values with the following directive:

```
#define max(x, y) x>y ? x : y
```

You can then put the statement in the program:

```
result = max(myval, 99);
```

This will be expanded during preprocessing to produce the following code:

```
result = myval>99 ? myval : 99;
```

It's important to be conscious of the substitution that is taking place and not to assume that this is a function. You can get some strange results otherwise, particularly if your substitution identifiers include an explicit or implicit assignment. For example, the following modest extension of the last example can produce an erroneous result:

```
result = max(myval++, 99);
```

The substitution process will generate this statement:

```
result = myval++>99 ? myval++ : 99;
```

The consequence of this is that if the value of myval is larger than 99, myval will be incremented twice. Note that it does *not* help to use parentheses in this situation. If you write the statement as

```
result = max((myval++), 99);
```

preprocessing will convert this to

```
result = (myval++>99) ? (myval++) : 99;
```

You need to be very cautious if you're writing macros that generate expressions of any kind. In addition to the multiple substitution trap you've just seen, precedence rules can also catch you out. A simple example will illustrate this. Suppose you write a macro for the product of two parameters:

```
#define product(m, n)  m*n
```

You then try to use this macro with the following statement:

```
result = product(x, y + 1);
```

Of course, everything works fine so far as the macro substitution is concerned, but you don't get the result you want, as the macro expands to this:

```
result = x*y + 1;
```

It could take a long time to discover that you aren't getting the product of the two parameters at all in this case, as there's no external indication of what's going on. There's just a more or less erroneous value propagating through the program. The solution is very simple. If you use macros to generate expressions, put parentheses around everything. So you should rewrite the example as follows:

```
#define product(m, n)  ((m)*(n))
```

Now everything will work as it should. The inclusion of the outer parentheses may seem excessive, but because you don't know the context in which the macro expansion will be placed, it's better to include them. If you write a macro to sum its parameters, you will easily see that without the outer parentheses, there are many contexts in which you will get a result that's different from what you expect. Even with parentheses, expanded expressions that repeat a parameter, such as the one you saw earlier that uses the conditional operator, will still not work properly when the argument involves the increment or decrement operators.

Preprocessor Directives on Multiple Lines

A preprocessor directive must be a single logical line, but this doesn't prevent you from using the statement continuation character, \.

You could write the following:

```
#define min(x, y) \
                ((x)<(y) ? (x) : (y))
```

Here, the directive definition continues on the second line with the first nonblank character found, so you can position the text on the second line wherever you feel looks like the nicest arrangement. Note that the \ must be the last character on the line, immediately before you press Enter.

Strings As Macro Arguments

String constants are a potential source of confusion when used with macros. The simplest string substitution is a single-level definition such as the following:

```
#define MYSTR "This string"
```

Suppose you now write the statement

```
printf("%s", MYSTR);
```

This will be converted during preprocessing into the statement

```
printf("%s", "This string");
```

This should be what you are expecting. You couldn't use the #define directive without the quotes in the substitution sequence and expect to be able to put the quotes in your program text instead. For example, suppose you write the following:

```
#define  MYSTR  This string
...
printf("%s", "MYSTR" );
```

There will be no substitution for MYSTR in the printf() function in this case. Anything in quotes in your program is assumed to be a literal string, so it won't be analyzed during preprocessing.

There's a special way of specifying that the substitution for a macro argument is to be implemented as a string. For example, you could specify a macro to display a string using the function printf() as follows:

```
#define PrintStr(arg) printf("%s", #arg)
```

The # character preceding the appearance of the arg parameter in the macro expansion indicates that the argument is to be surrounded by double quotes when the substitution is generated. Therefore, if you write the following statement in your program

```
PrintStr(Output);
```

it will be converted during preprocessing to

```
printf("%s", "Output");
```

You may be wondering why this apparent complication has been introduced into preprocessing. Well, without this facility you wouldn't be able to include a variable string in a macro definition at all. If you were to put the double quotes around the macro parameter, it wouldn't be interpreted as a variable; it would be merely a string with quotes around it. On the other hand, if you put the quotes in the macro expansion, the string between the quotes wouldn't be interpreted as an identifier for a parameter; it would be just a string constant. So what might appear to be an unnecessary complication at first sight is actually an essential tool for creating macros that allow strings between quotes to be created.

A common use of this mechanism is for converting a variable name to a string, such as in this directive:

```
#define show(var) printf("\n%s = %d", #var, var);
```

If you now write

```
show(number);
```

this will generate the statement

```
printf("\n%s = %d", "number", number);
```

You can also generate a substitution that would allow you to display a string with double quotes included. Assuming you've defined the macro PrintStr as shown previously and you write the statement

```
PrintStr("Output");
```

it will be preprocessed into the statement

```
printf("%s", "\"Output\"");
```

This is possible because the preprocessing phase is clever enough to recognize the need to put \" at each end to get a string that includes double quotes to be displayed correctly.

Joining Two Results of a Macro Expansion

There are times when you may wish to generate two results in a macro and join them together with no spaces between them. Suppose you try to define a macro to do this as follows:

```
#define join(a, b) ab
```

This can't work in the way you need it to. The definition of the expansion will be interpreted as ab, not as the parameter a followed by the parameter b. If you separate them with a blank, the result will be separated with a blank, which isn't what you want either. The preprocessing phase provides you with another operator to solve this problem. The solution is to specify the macro as follows:

```
#define join(a, b) a##b
```

The presence of the operator consisting of the two characters ## serves to separate the parameters and to indicate that the result of the two substitutions are to be joined. For example, writing the statement

```
strlen(join(var, 123));
```

will result in the statement

```
strlen(var123);
```

This might be applied to synthesizing a variable name for some reason, or generating a format control string from two or more macro parameters.

Logical Preprocessor Directives

The last example you looked at appears to be of limited value, because it's hard to envision when you would want to simply join var to 123. After all, you could always use one parameter and write var123 as the argument. One aspect of preprocessing that adds considerably more potential to the previous example is the possibility for multiple macro substitutions where the arguments for one macro are derived from substitutions defined in another. In the last example, both arguments to the join() macro could be generated by other #define substitutions or macros. Preprocessing also supports directives that provide a logical if capability, which vastly expands the scope of what you can do during the preprocessing phase.

Conditional Compilation

The first logical directive I'll discuss allows you to test whether an identifier exists as a result of having been created in a previous #define directive. It takes the following form:

```
#if defined identifier
```

If the specified identifier is defined, statements that follow the #if are included in the program code until the directive #endif is reached. If the identifier isn't defined, the statements between the #if and the #endif will be skipped. This is the same logical process you use in C programming, except that here you're applying it to the inclusion or exclusion of program statements in the source file.

You can also test for the absence of an identifier. In fact, this tends to be used more frequently than the form you've just seen. The general form of this directive is:

```
#if !defined identifier
```

Here, the statements following the #if down to the #endif will be included if the identifier hasn't previously been defined. This provides you with a method of avoiding duplicating functions, or other blocks of code and directives, in a program consisting of several files, or to ensure bits of code that may occur repeatedly in different libraries aren't repeated when the #include statements in your program are processed.

The mechanism is simply to top and tail the block of code you want to avoid duplicating as follows:

```
#if !defined block1
  #define block1
  /* Block of code you do not */
  /* want to be repeated.     */
#endif
```

If the identifier block1 hasn't been defined, the block following the #if will be included and processed, and block1 will be defined. The following block of code down to the #endif will also be included in your program. Any subsequent occurrence of the same group of statements won't be included because the identifier block1 now exists.

The #define directive doesn't need to specify a substitution value in this case. For the conditional directives to operate, it's sufficient for block1 to appear in a #define directive. You can now include this block of code anywhere you think you might need it, with the assurance that it will never be duplicated within a program. The preprocessing directives ensure this can't happen.

Note It's a good idea to get into the habit of always protecting code in your own libraries in this fashion. You'll be surprised how easy it is to end up duplicating blocks of code accidentally, once you've collected a few libraries of your own functions.

You aren't limited to testing just one value with the #if preprocessor directive. You can use logical operators to test if multiple identifiers have been defined. For example, the statement

```
#if defined block1 && defined block2
```

will evaluate to true if both block1 and block2 have previously been defined, and so the code that follows such a directive won't be included unless this is the case.

A further extension of the flexibility in applying the conditional preprocessor directives is the ability to undefine an identifier you've previously defined. This is achieved using a directive such as #undef block1.

Now, if block1 was previously defined, it is no longer defined after this directive. The ways in which these directives can all be combined to useful effect is only limited by your own ingenuity.

There are alternative ways of writing these directives that are slightly more concise. You can use whichever of the following forms you prefer. The directive #ifdef block is the same as #if defined block. And the directive #ifndef block is the same as #if !defined block.

Directives Testing for Specific Values

You can also use a form of the #if directive to test the value of a constant expression. If the value of the constant expression is nonzero, the following statements down to the next #endif are included in the program code. If the constant expression evaluates to zero, the following statements down to the next #endif are skipped. The general form of the #if directive is the following:

```
#if constant_expression
```

This is most frequently applied to test for a specific value being assigned to an identifier by a previous preprocessing directive. You might have the following sequence of statements, for example:

```
#if CPU == Pentium4
  printf("\nPerformance should be good." );
#endif
```

The printf() statement will be included in the program here only if the identifier CPU has been defined as Pentium4 in a previous #define directive.

Multiple-Choice Selections

To complement the #if directives, you have the #else directive. This works in exactly the same way as the else statement does, in that it identifies a group of directives to be executed or statements to be included if the #if condition fails, for example:

```
#if CPU == Pentium4
  printf("\nPerformance should be good." );
#else
  printf("\nPerformance may not be so good." );
#endif
```

In this case, one or the other of the printf() statements will be included, depending on whether CPU has been defined as Pentium4.

The preprocessing phase also supports a special form of the #if for multiple-choice selections, in which only one of several choices of statements for inclusion in the program is required. This is the #elif directive, which has the general form

```
#elif constant_expression
```

An example of using this would be as follows:

```
#define US 0
#define UK 1
#define Australia 2
#define Country US
#if Country == US
  #define Greeting "Howdy, stranger."
#elif Country == UK
  #define Greeting "Wotcher, mate."
#elif Country == Australia
  #define Greeting "G'day, sport."
#endif
printf("\n%s", Greeting );
```

With this sequence of directives the output of the printf() statement will depend on the value assigned to the identifier Country, in this case US.

Standard Preprocessing Macros

There are usually a considerable number of standard preprocessing macros defined, which you'll find described in your compiler documentation. I'll just mention two that are of general interest and that are available to you.

The __DATE__ macro provides a string representation of the date in the form Mmm dd yyyy when it's invoked in your program. Here Mmm is the month in characters, such as Jan, Feb, and so on. The pair of characters dd is the day in the form of a pair of digits 1 to 31, where single-digit days are preceded by a blank. Finally, yyyy is the year as four digits! 2006, for example.

A similar macro, __TIME__, provides a string containing the value of the time when it's invoked, in the form hh:mm:ss, which is evidently a string containing pairs of digits for hours, minutes, and seconds, separated by colons. Note that the time is when the compiler is executed, not when the program is run.

You could use this macro to record when your program was last compiled with a statement such as this:

```
printf("\nProgram last compiled at %s on %s", __TIME__, __DATE__ );
```

Note that both __DATE__ and __TIME__ have two underscore characters at the beginning and the end. Once the program containing this statement is compiled, the values that will be output by the printf() statement are fixed until you compile it again. On subsequent executions of the program, the then current time and date will be output. Don't confuse these macros with the time function I discuss later in this chapter in the section •The Date and Time Function Library.!

Debugging Methods

Most of your programs will contain errors, or **bugs**, when you first complete them. Removing such bugs from a program can represent a substantial proportion of the time required to write the program. The larger and more complex the program, the more bugs it's likely to contain, and the more time it will take to get the program to run properly. Very large programs, such as those typified by operating systems, or complex applications, such as word processing systems or even C program development systems, can be so involved that all the bugs can never be eliminated. You may already have experience of this in practice with some of the systems on your own computer. Usually these kinds of residual bugs are relatively minor, with ways in the system to work around them.

Your approach to writing a program can significantly affect how difficult it will be to test. A well-structured program consisting of compact functions, each with a well-defined purpose, is much easier to test than one without these attributes. Finding bugs will also be easier in a program that has extensive comments documenting the operation and purpose of its component functions and has well-chosen variable and function names. Good use of indentation and statement layout can also make testing and fault finding simpler.

It's beyond the scope of this book to deal with debugging comprehensively, but in this section I introduce the basic ideas that you need to be aware of.

Integrated Debuggers

Many compilers are supplied with extensive debugging tools built into the program development environment. These can be very powerful facilities that can dramatically reduce the time required to get a program working. They typically provide a varied range of aids to testing a program that include the following:

Tracing program flow: This capability allows you to execute your program one source statement at a time. It operates by pausing execution after each statement and continuing with the next statement after you press a designated key. Other provisions of the debug environment will usually allow you to display information easily, pausing to show you what's happening to the data in your program.

Setting breakpoints: Executing a large or complex program one statement at a time can be very tedious. It may even be impossible in a reasonable period of time. All you need is a loop that executes 10,000 times to make it an unrealistic proposition. Breakpoints provide an excellent alternative. With breakpoints, you define specific selected statements in your program at which a pause should occur to allow you to check what's happening. Execution continues to the next breakpoint when you press a specified key.

Setting watches: This sort of facility allows you to identify variables that you want to track the value of as execution progresses. The values of the variables that you select are displayed at each pause point in your program. If you step through your program statement by statement, you can see the exact point at which values are changed, or perhaps not changed when you expect them to be.

Inspecting program elements: It may also be possible to examine a wide variety of program components. For example, at breakpoints the inspection can show details of a function such as its return type and its arguments. You can also see details of a pointer in terms of its address, the address it contains, and the data stored at the address contained in the pointer. Seeing the values of expressions and modifying variables may also be provided for. Modifying variables can help to bypass problem areas to allow other areas to be executed with correct data, even though an earlier part of the program may not be working properly.

The Preprocessor in Debugging

By using conditional preprocessor directives, you can arrange for blocks of code to be included in your program to assist in testing. In spite of the power of the debug facilities included with many C development systems, the addition of tracing code of your own can still be useful. You have complete control of the formatting of data to be displayed for debugging purposes, and you can even arrange for the kind of output to vary according to conditions or relationships within the program.

TRY IT OUT: USING PREPROCESSOR DIRECTIVES

I can illustrate how you can use preprocessor directives to control execution and switch debugging output on and off through a program that calls functions at random through an array of function pointers:

```
/* Program 13.1 Debugging using preprocessing directives */
#include <stdio.h>
#include <stdlib.h>
#include <time.h>

/* Macro to generate pseudo-random number from 0 to NumValues */
#define random(NumValues) ((int)(((double)(rand())*(NumValues))/(RAND_MAX+1.0)))

#define iterations 6
#define test                        /* Select testing output     */
#define testf                       /* Select function call trace */
#define repeatable                  /* Select repeatable execution */

/* Function prototypes */
int sum(int, int);
int product(int, int);
int difference(int, int);

int main(void)
{
  int funsel = 0;                   /* Index for function selection */
  int a = 10, b = 5;                /* Starting values              */
  int result = 0;                   /* Storage for results          */

  /* Function pointer array declaration */
  int (*pfun[])(int, int) = {sum, product, difference};

  /* Conditional code for repeatable execution */
  #ifdef repeatable
  srand(1);
  #else
  srand((unsigned int)time(NULL));  /* Seed random number generation  */
  #endif

  /* Execute random function selections */
  int element_count = sizeof(pfun)/sizeof(pfun[0]);
  for(int i = 0 ; i < iterations ; i++)
  {
    /* Generate random index to pfun array */
```

```
    funsel = random(element_count);
    if( funsel>element_count-1 )
    {
      printf("\nInvalid array index = %d", funsel);
      exit(1);
    }

    #ifdef test
     printf("\nRandom index = %d", funsel);
    #endif

    result = pfun[funsel](a , b);       /* Call random function         */
    printf("\nresult = %d", result );
    }
   return 0;
}

/* Definition of the function sum */
int sum(int x, int y)
{
#ifdef testf
  printf("\nFunction sum called args %d and %d.", x, y);
#endif

  return x + y;
}

/* Definition of the function product */
int product( int x, int y )
{
  #ifdef testf
  printf("\nFunction product called args %d and %d.", x, y);
  #endif

  return x * y;
}

/* Definition of the function difference */
int difference(int x, int y)
{
  #ifdef testf
  printf("\nFunction difference called args %d and %d.", x, y);
  #endif

  return x - y;
}
```

How It Works

You have a macro defined at the beginning of the program:

```
#define random(NumValues) ((int)(((double)(rand())*(NumValues))/(RAND_MAX+1.0)))
```

This defines the macro random() in terms of the function rand() that's declared in stdlib.h. The function rand() generates random numbers in the range 0 to RAND_MAX, which is a constant defined in <stdlib.h>. The macro maps values from this range to produce values from 0 to NumValues-1. You cast the value from rand() to double to ensure that computation will be carried out as type double, and you cast the result overall back to int because that's what you want in the program. It's quite possible that your version of <stdlib.h> may already contain a macro for random() that does essentially the same thing. If so, you'll get an error message as the compiler won't allow two different definitions of the same macro. In this case, just delete the definition from the program.

I defined random() as a macro to show how you do it, but it would be better defined as a function because this would eliminate any potential problems that might arise with argument values to the macro.

You then have four directives that define symbols:

```
#define iterations 6
#define test                /* Select testing output     */
#define testf               /* Select function call trace */
#define repeatable          /* Select repeatable execution */
```

The first of these defines a symbol that specifies the number of iterations in the loop that executes one of three functions at random. The last three are all symbols that control the selection of code to be included in the program. Defining the test symbol causes code to be included that will output the value of the index that selects a function. Defining testf causes code that traces function calls to be included in the function definitions. When the repeatable symbol is defined, the srand() function is called with a fixed seed value, so the rand() function will always generate the same pseudo-random sequence and the same output will be produced on successive runs of the program. Having repeatable output during test runs of the program obviously makes the testing process somewhat easier. If you remove the directive that defines the repeatable symbol, srand() will be called with the current time value as the argument, so the seed will be different each time the program executes, and you will get different output on each execution of the program.

After setting up the initial variables used in main() you have the following statement declaring and initializing the pfun array:

```
int (*pfun[])(int, int) = {sum, product, difference};
```

This declares an array of pointers to functions with two parameters of type int and a return value of type int. The array is initialized using the names of the three functions so the array will contain three elements.

Next you have a directive that includes one of two alternative statements depending on whether the repeatable symbol is defined:

```
#ifdef repeatable
  srand(1);
#else
  srand((unsigned int)time(NULL));     /* Seed random number generation     */
#endif
```

If repeatable is defined, the statement that calls srand() with the argument value 1 will be included in the source for compilation. This will result in the same output each time you execute the program. Otherwise the statement with the result of the time() function as the argument will be included and you will get different output each time you run the program.

Look at the loop in main() that follows. The number of iterations is determined by the value of the iterations symbol; in this case it corresponds to 6. The first action in the loop is the following:

```
  funsel = random(element_count);
  if( funsel>element_count-1 )
  {
    printf("\nInvalid array index = %d", funsel);
    exit(1);
  }
```

This uses the `random()` macro with `element_count` as the argument. This is the number of elements in the `pfun` array and is calculated immediately prior to the loop. The preprocessor will substitute `element_count` in the macro expansion before the code is compiled. For safety, there is a check that we do indeed get a valid index value for the `pfun` array.

The next three lines are the following:

```
#ifdef test
  printf("\nRandom index = %d", funsel);
#endif
```

These include the `printf()` statement in the code when the `text` symbol is defined. If you remove the directive that defines `text`, the `printf()` will not be included in the program that is compiled.

The last two statements in the loop call a function through one of the pointers in the `pfun` array and output the result of the call:

```
  result = pfun[funsel](a , b);        /* Call random function            */
  printf("\nresult = %d", result );
```

Let's look at one of the functions that may be called, `product()` for example:

```
int product( int x, int y )
{
  #ifdef testf
  printf("\nFunction product called args %d and %d.", x, y);
  #endif

  return x * y;
}
```

The function definition includes an output statement if the `testf` symbol is defined. You can therefore control whether the statements in the `#ifdef` block are included here independently from the output block in `main()` that is controlled by `test`. With the program as written with both `test` and `testf` defined, you'll get trace output for the random index values generated and a message from each function as it's called, so you can follow the sequence of calls in the program exactly.

You can have as many different symbolic constants defined as you wish. As you've seen previously in this chapter, you can combine them into logical expressions using the `#if defined` form of the conditional directive.

Using the assert() Macro

The `assert()` macro is defined in the standard library header file `<assert.h>`. This macro enables you to insert tests of arbitrary expressions in your program that will cause the program to be terminated with a diagnostic message if a specified expression is false (that is, evaluates to 0). The argument to the `assert()` macro is an expression that results in an integer value, for example:

```
assert(a == b);
```

The expression will be true (nonzero) if a is equal to b. If a and b are unequal, the argument to the macro will be false and the program will be terminated with a message relating to the assertion. Termination is achieved by calling abort(), so it's an abnormal end to the program. When abort() is called, the program terminates immediately. Whether stream output buffers are flushed, open streams are closed, or temporary files are removed, it is implementation-dependent, so consult your compiler documentation on this.

In program 13.1 I could have used an assertion to verify that funsel is valid:

```
assert(funsel<element_count);
```

If funsel is not less than element_count, the expression will be false, so the program will assert. Typical output from the assertion looks like this:

```
Assertion failed:  funsel<element_count d:\examples\program13_01.c 44
```

The assertion facility allowing assertions to occur can be switched off by defining the symbol NDEBUG before the #include directive for assert.h, like this:

```
#define NDEBUG                        /* Switch off assertions */
#include <assert.h>
```

This will cause all assertions to be ignored.

With some systems, assertions are disabled by default, in which case you can enable them by undefining NDEBUG:

```
#undef NDEBUG                         /* Switch on assertions */
#include <assert.h>
```

By including the directive to undefine NDEBUG, you ensure that assertions are enabled for your source file. The #undef directive must appear before the #include directive for assert.h to be effective.

I can demonstrate this in operation with a simple example.

TRY IT OUT: DEMONSTRATING THE ASSERT() MACRO

Here's the code for a program that uses the assert() macro:

```
/* Program 13.2 Demonstrating assertions */
#undef NDEBUG                         /* Switch on assertions */
#include <stdio.h>
#include <assert.h>

int main(void)
{
  int y = 5;
  for(int x = 0 ; x < 20 ; x++)
  {
    printf("\nx = %d   y = %d", x, y);
    assert(x<y);
  }
  return 0;
}
```

Compiling and executing this with my compiler produces the following output:

```
x = 0    y = 5
x = 1    y = 5
x = 2    y = 5
x = 3    y = 5
x = 4    y = 5
x = 5    y = 5
Assertion failed: x<y , file Prog13_02.C, line 12
```

How It Works

At this point, apart from the assert() statement, the program shouldn't need much explanation, as it simply displays the values of x and y in the for loop.

The program is terminated by the assert() macro as soon as the condition x < y becomes false. As you can see from the output, this is when x reaches the value 5. The macro displays the output on stderr, which is always the display screen. Not only do you get the condition that failed displayed, but you also get the file name and line number in the file where the failure occurred. This is particularly useful with multifile programs in which the source of the error is pinpointed exactly.

Assertions are often used for critical conditions in a program in which, if certain conditions aren't met, disaster will surely ensue. You would want to be sure that the program wouldn't continue if such errors arise.

You could switch off the assertion mechanism in the example by replacing the #undef directive with #define NDEBUG. This must be placed before the #include statement for <assert.h> to be effective, although assertions may be disabled by default. With this #define at the beginning of Program 13.2, you'll see that you get output for all the values of x from 0 to 19, and no diagnostic message.

Additional Library Functions

The library functions are basic to the power of the C language. Although I've covered quite a range of standard library functions so far, it's beyond the scope of this book to discuss all the standard libraries. However, I can introduce a few more of the most commonly used functions you haven't dealt with in detail up to now.

The Date and Time Function Library

Because time is an important parameter to measure, C includes a standard library of functions called <time.h> that deal with time and dates. They provide output in various forms from the hardware timer in your PC.

The simplest function has the following prototype:

```
clock_t clock(void);
```

This function returns the processor time (not the elapsed time) used by the program since execution began, as a value of type clock_t. Your computer will typically be executing multiple processes at any given moment. The processor time is the total time the processor has been executing on behalf of the process that called the clock() function. The type clock_t is defined in <time.h> and is equivalent to type size_t. The value that is returned by the clock() function is measured in **clock ticks**, and to convert this value to seconds, you divide it by the value that is produced by the macro CLOCKS_PER_SEC, which is also defined in the library <time.h>. The value that results from executing CLOCKS_PER_SEC is the number of clock ticks in one second and is of type clock_t. The clock() function returns -1 if an error occurs.

To determine the processor time used in executing a process, you need to record the time when the process starts executing and subtract this from the time returned when the process finishes. For example

```
clock_t start, end;
double cpu_time;
start = clock();

/* Execute the process for which you want the processor time */

end = clock();
cpu_time = ((double)(end-start)/CLOCKS_PER_SEC;
```

This fragment stores the total processor time used in cpu_time. The cast to type double is necessary in the last statement to get the correct result.

As you've seen, the time() function returns the calendar time as a value of type time_t. The calendar time is the current time in seconds since a fixed time and date. The fixed time and date is often 00:00:00GMT on January 1, 1970, for example, and this is typical of how time values are defined.

The prototype of the time() function is the following:

```
time_t time(time_t *timer);
```

If the argument isn't NULL, the current calendar time is also stored in the location pointed to by the argument. The type time_t is defined in the header file and is equivalent to long.

To calculate the elapsed time in seconds between two successive time_t values returned by time(), you can use the function difftime(), which has this prototype:

```
double difftime(time_t T2, time_t T1);
```

The function will return the value of T2 - T1 expressed in seconds as a value of type double. This value is the time elapsed between the two time() function calls that produce the time_t values, T1 and T2.

TRY IT OUT: USING TIME FUNCTIONS

You could define a function to log the elapsed time and processor time used between successive calls by using functions from <time.h> as follows:

```
/* Program 13.3 Test our timer function */
#include <stdio.h>
#include <time.h>
#include <math.h>
#include <ctype.h>

int main(void)
{
  time_t calendar_start = time(NULL);    /* Initial calendar time    */
  clock_t cpu_start = clock();           /* Initial processor time   */
  int count = 0;                         /* Count of number of loops */
  const int iterations = 1000000;        /* Loop iterations          */
  char answer = 'y';
```

```
    printf("Initial clock time = %lu Initial calendar time = %lu\n",
                                cpu_start, calendar_start);

    while(tolower(answer) == 'y')
    {
      for(int i = 0 ; i<iterations ; i++)
      {
        double x = sqrt(3.14159265);
      }
      printf("\n%ld square roots completed.", iterations*(++count));
      printf("\nDo you want to run some more(y or n)? ");

      scanf("\n%c", &answer);
    }

    clock_t cpu_end = clock();              /* Final cpu time        */
    time_t calendar_end = time(NULL);       /* Final calendar time   */

    printf("\nFinal clock time = %lu Final calendar time = %lu\n",
                                        cpu_end, calendar_end);
    printf("\nCPU time for %ld iterations is %.2lf seconds\n",
            count*iterations, ((double)(cpu_end-cpu_start))/CLOCKS_PER_SEC );

    printf("\nElapsed calendar time to execute the program is %8.2lf\n",
                                difftime(calendar_end, calendar_start));
    return 0;
}
```

On my machine I get the following output:

```
Initial clock time = 0 Initial calendar time = 1155841882

1000000 square roots completed.
Do you want to run some more(y or n)? y

2000000 square roots completed.
Do you want to run some more(y or n)? n

Final clock time = 7671 Final calendar time = 1155841890

CPU time for 2000000 iterations is 7.67 seconds

Elapsed calendar time to execute the program is     8.00
```

How It Works

This program illustrates the use of the functions clock(), time(), and difftime(). The time() function returns the current time in seconds, so you won't get values less than 1 second. Depending on the speed of your machine, you may want to adjust the number of iterations in the loop to reduce or increase the time required to execute this program. Note that the clock() function may not be a very accurate way of determining the processor time used in the program. You also need to keep in mind that measuring elapsed time using the time() function can be a second out.

You record and display the initial values for the processor time and the calendar time and set up the controls for the loop that follows with these statements:

```
time_t calendar_start = time(NULL);      /* Initial calendar time   */
clock_t cpu_start = clock();             /* Initial processor time  */
int count = 0;                           /* Count of number of loops */
const int iterations = 1000000;          /* Loop iterations         */
char answer = 'y';
printf("Initial clock time = %lu Initial calendar time = %lu\n",
                          cpu_start, calendar_start);
```

With my C library, the types `clock_t` and `time_t` are defined as type `unsigned long` in the `time.h` header file. You should check how the types are defined in your library and adjust the format specifications for these values if necessary.

You then have a loop controlled by the character stored in `answer`, so the loop will execute as long as you want it to continue:

```
while(tolower(answer) == 'y')
{
  for(int i = 0 ; i<iterations ; i++)
  {
    double x = sqrt(3.14159265);
  }

  printf("\n%ld square roots completed.", iterations*(++count));
  printf("\nDo you want to run some more(y or n)? ");

  scanf("\n%c", &answer);
}
```

The inner loop calls the `sqrt()` function that is declared in the `<math.h>` header `iterations` times, so this is just to occupy some processor time. If you are leisurely in your entry of a response to the prompt for input, this should extend the elapsed time. Note the newline escape sequence in the beginning of the first argument to `scanf()`. If you leave this out, your program will loop indefinitely, because `scanf()` will not ignore whitespace characters in the input stream buffer.

Finally, you output the final values returned by `clock()` and `time()`, and calculate the processor and calendar time intervals:

```
clock_t cpu_end = clock();               /* Final cpu time        */
time_t calendar_end = time(NULL);        /* Final calendar time   */

printf("\nFinal clock time = %lu Final calendar time = %lu\n",
                                      cpu_end, calendar_end);
printf("\nCPU time for %ld iterations is %.2lf seconds\n",
          count*iterations, ((double)(cpu_end-cpu_start))/CLOCKS_PER_SEC );

printf("\nElapsed calendar time to execute the program is %8.2lf\n",
                          difftime(calendar_end, calendar_start));
```

The library that comes with your C compiler may well have additional nonstandard functions for obtaining processor time that are more reliable than the `clock()` function.

■**Caution** Note that the processor clock can wrap around, and the resolution with which processor time is measured can vary between different hardware platforms. For example, if the processor clock is a 32-bit value that has a microsecond resolution, the clock will wrap back to zero roughly every 72 minutes.

Getting the Date

Having the time in seconds since a date over a quarter of a century ago is interesting, but it's often more convenient to get today's date as a string. You can do this with the function ctime(), which has this prototype:

```
char *ctime(const time_t *timer);
```

The function accepts a pointer to a time_t variable as an argument that contains a calendar time value returned by the time() function. It returns a pointer to a 26-character string containing the day, the date, the time, and the year, which is terminated by a newline and a '\0'.

A typical string returned might be the following:

```
"Mon Aug 25  10:45:56 2003\n\0"
```

You might use the ctime() function like this:

```
time_t calendar = 0;
calendar = time(NULL);              /* Store calendar time              */
  printf("\n%s", ctime(&calendar)); /* Output calendar time as date string */
```

You can also get at the various components of the time and date from a calendar time value by using the library function localtime(). This function has the following prototype:

```
struct tm *localtime(const time_t *timer);
```

This function accepts a pointer to a time_t value and returns a pointer to a structure type tm, which is defined in the <time.h> header file. The structure contains the members listed in Table 13-1.

Table 13-1. *Members of the tm Structure*

Member	Description
tm_sec	Seconds after the minute on 24-hour clock
tm_min	Minutes after the hour on 24-hour clock (0 to 59)
tm_hour	The hour on 24-hour clock (0 to 23)
tm_mday	Day of the month (1 to 31)
tm_mon	Month (0 to 11)
tm_year	Year (current year minus 1900)
tm_wday	Weekday (Sunday is 0; Saturday is 6)
tm_yday	Day of year (0 to 365)
tm_isdst	Daylight saving flag. Positive for daylight saving time 0 for not daylight saving time −1 for not known

All these structure members are of type int. The localtime() function returns a pointer to the same structure each time you call it and the structure members are overwritten on each call. If you want to keep any of the member values, you need to copy them elsewhere before the next call to localtime(), or you could create your own tm structure and save the whole lot if you really need to.

The time that the localtime() function produces is local to where you are. If you want to get the time in a tm structure that reflects UTC (Coordinated Universal Time) you can use the gmtime() function. This also expects an argument of type time_t and returns a pointer to a tm structure.

Here's a code fragment that will output the day and the date from the members of the tm structure:

```
time_t calendar = 0;                   /* Holds calendar time        */
struct tm *time_data;                  /* Holds address of tm struct */
const char *days[] = {"Sunday",    "Monday", "Tuesday", "Wednesday",
                      "Thursday", "Friday", "Saturday"            };
constchar *months[] = {"January", "February", "March",
                      "April",    "May",       "June",
                      "July",     "August",    "September",
                      "October", "November", "December"  };

calendar = time(NULL);                 /* Get current calendar time */
printf("\n%s", ctime(&calendar));
time_data = localtime(&calendar);
printf("Today is %s %s %d %d\n",
                  days[time_data->tm_wday], months[time_data->tm_mon],
                  time_data->tm_mday,       time_data->tm_year+1900);
```

You've defined arrays of strings to hold the days of the week and the months. You use the appropriate member of the structure that has been set up by the call to the localtime() function. You use the day in the month and the year values from the structure directly. You can easily extend this to output the time.

TRY IT OUT: GETTING THE DATE

It's very easy to pick out the members you want from the structure of type tm returned from the function localtime(). You can demonstrate this with the following example:

```
/* Program 13.4        Getting date data with ease */
#include <stdio.h>
#include <time.h>
int main(void)
{
  const char *Day[7] = {
                  "Sunday"   , "Monday", "Tuesday", "Wednesday",
                  "Thursday", "Friday", "Saturday"
                       };
  const char *Month[12] = {
                  "January",   "February", "March",     "April",
                  "May",       "June",     "July",      "August",
                  "September", "October",  "November", "December"
                       };
  const char *Suffix[4] = { "st", "nd", "rd", "th" };
  enum sufindex { st, nd, rd, th } sufsel = th;      /* Suffix selector */
```

```
struct tm *OurT = NULL;              /* Pointer for the time structure */
time_t Tval = 0;                     /* Calendar time                  */

Tval = time(NULL);                   /* Get calendar time              */
OurT = localtime(&Tval);             /* Generate time structure        */

switch(OurT->tm_mday)
{
  case 1: case 21: case 31:
    sufsel= st;
    break;
  case 2: case 22:
    sufsel= nd;
    break;
  case 3: case 23:
    sufsel= rd;
    break;
  default:
    sufsel= th;
    break;
}

printf("Today is %s the %d%s %s %d", Day[OurT->tm_wday],
  OurT->tm_mday, Suffix[sufsel], Month[OurT->tm_mon], 1900 + OurT->tm_year);
printf("\nThe time is %d : %d : %d",
  OurT->tm_hour, OurT->tm_min, OurT->tm_sec );
return 0;
}
```

Here's an example of output from this program:

```
Today is Friday the 18th August 2006
The time is 11 : 49 : 53
```

How It Works

In this example, the first declarations in main() are as follows:

```
const char *Day[7] = {
                "Sunday"   , "Monday", "Tuesday", "Wednesday",
                "Thursday", "Friday", "Saturday"
                };
const char *Month[12] = {
                "January",   "February", "March",     "April",
                "May",       "June",     "July",      "August",
                "September", "October",  "November",  "December"
                };
const char *Suffix[] = { "st", "nd", "rd", "th" };
```

Each defines an array of pointers to char. The first holds the days of the week, the second contains the months in the year, and the third holds the suffixes to numerical values for the day in the month when representing dates. You could leave out the array dimensions in the first two declarations and the compiler would compute them for you, but in this case you're reasonably confident about both these numbers, so this is an instance in which putting them in helps to avoid an error. The const qualifier specifies that the strings pointed to are constants and should not be altered in the code.

The enumeration provides a mechanism for selecting an element from the Suffix array:

```
enum sufindex { st, nd, rd, th } sufsel = th;        /* Suffix selector */
```

The enumeration constants, st, nd, rd, and th will be assigned values 0 to 3 by default, so we can use the sufsel variable as an index to access elements in the Suffix array.

You also declare a structure variable in the following declaration:

```
struct tm *OurT = NULL;                  /* Pointer for the time structure */
```

This provides space to store the pointer to the structure returned by the function local_time().

You first obtain the current time in Tval using the function time(). You then use this value to generate the values of the members of the structure returned by the function localtime(). If you want to keep the data in the structure, you need to copy it before calling the localtime() function again, as it would be overwritten. Once you have the structure from localtime(), you execute the switch:

```
switch( OurT->tm_mday )
{
    case 1: case 21: case 31:
        sufsel= st;
        break;
    case 2: case 22:
        sufsel= nd;
        break;
    case 3: case 23:
        sufsel= rd;
        break;
    default:
        sufsel= th;
        break;
}
```

The sole purpose of this is to select what to append to the date value. Based on the member tm_mday, the switch selects an index to the array Suffix[ ] for use when outputting the date by setting the sufsel variable to the appropriate enumeration constant value.

The day, the date, and the time are displayed, with the day and month strings obtained by indexing the appropriate array with the corresponding structure member value. The addition of 1900 to the value of the member tm_year is because this value is measured relative to the year 1900.

You can also use the mktime() function to determine the day of the week for a given date. The function has the following prototype:

```
time_t mktime(struct tm *ptime);
```

You can pass a pointer to a tm structure to a function with the tm_mon, tm_day, and tm_year values set to a date you are interested in. The values of the tm_wkday and tm_yday members of the structure will be ignored, and if the operation is successful, the values will be replaced with the values that are correct for the date you have supplied. The function returns the calendar time as a value of type time_t if the operation is successful, or –1 if the date cannot be represented as a time_t value, causing the operation to fail. Let's see it working in an example.

TRY IT OUT: GETTING THE DAY FOR A DATE

It's very easy to pick out the members you want from the structure of type tm returned from the function localtime(). You can demonstrate this with the following example:

```
/* Program 13.5          Getting the day for a given date */
#include <stdio.h>
#include <time.h>
int main(void)
{
  const char *Day[7] = {
                 "Sunday"   , "Monday", "Tuesday", "Wednesday",
                 "Thursday", "Friday", "Saturday"
                   };
  const char *Month[12] = {
                   "January",   "February", "March",     "April",
                   "May",       "June",     "July",      "August",
                   "September", "October",  "November", "December"
                     };
  const char *Suffix[4] = { "st", "nd", "rd", "th" };
  enum sufindex { st, nd, rd, th } sufsel = th;  /* Suffix selector */

  int day = 0;                       /* Stores a day...          */
  int month = 0;                     /* month...                 */
  int year = 0;                      /* and year for a date      */

  struct tm birthday;                /* A birthday time structure */

  /* Set the structure members we don't care about */
  birthday.tm_hour = birthday.tm_min = 0;
  birthday.tm_sec = 1;
  birthday.tm_isdst = -1;

  printf("Enter your birthday as integers, day month year."
          "\ne.g. Enter 1st February 1985 as 1 2 1985. : ");
  scanf(" %d %d %d", &day, &month, &year);

  birthday.tm_mon = month-1;
  birthday.tm_mday = day;
  birthday.tm_year = year-1900;

  if(mktime(&birthday) == (time_t)-1)
  {
    printf("\nOperation failed.");
    return 0;
  }

  switch(birthday.tm_mday)
  {
      sufsel= st;
      break;
    case 2: case 22:
      sufsel= nd;
      break;
```

```
case 3: case 23:
    sufsel= rd;
    break;
  default:
    sufsel= th;
    break;
}

printf("\nYour birthday, the %d%s %s %d, was a %s",
              birthday.tm_mday, Suffix[sufsel], Month[birthday.tm_mon],
                         1900 + birthday.tm_year, Day[birthday.tm_wday]);

  return 0;
}
```

Here's a sample of output from this example:

```
Enter your birthday as integers, day month year.
e.g. Enter 1st February 1985 as 1 2 1985. : 15 6 1985

Your birthday, the 15th June 1985, was a Saturday
```

How It Works

You create arrays of constant strings for the day month and date suffixes as you did in Program 13.4. You then create a tm structure and initialize some of its members:

```
struct tm birthday;                     /* A birthday time structure */

/* Set the structure members we don't care about */
birthday.tm_hour = birthday.tm_min = 0;
birthday.tm_sec = 1;
birthday.tm_isdst = -1;
```

You set the value of the tm_isdst member to −1 because you don't know whether it applies for the date that will be entered.

After outputting a prompt, you read values for the day, month, and year of a birthday date from the keyboard and set the values entered in the birthday structure:

```
printf("\nEnter your birthday as integers, day month year."
          "\ne.g. Enter 1st February 1985 as 1 2 1985. : ");
scanf(" %d %d %d", &day, &month, &year);

birthday.tm_mon = month-1;
birthday.tm_mday = day;
birthday.tm_year = year-1900;
```

With the date set, you can get the tm_wday and tm_yday members set according by calling the mktime() function:

```
if(mktime(&birthday) == (time_t)-1)
{
  printf("\nOperation failed.");
  return 0;
}
```

The if statement checks whether the function returns –1, indicating that the operation has failed. In this case you simply output a message and terminate the program.

Finally, the day corresponding to the birth date entered is displayed in the same way as in the previous example.

Summary

In this chapter I discussed the preprocessor directives that you use to manipulate and transform the code in a source file before it is compiled. Your standard library header files are an excellent source of examples of coding preprocessing directives. You can view these examples with any text editor. Virtually all of the capabilities of the preprocessor are used in the libraries, and you'll find a lot of C source code there too. It's also useful to familiarize yourself with the contents of the libraries, as you can find many things not necessarily described in the library documentation. If you aren't sure what the type clock_t is, for example, just look in the library header file <time.h>, where you'll find the definition.

The debugging capability that the preprocessor provides is useful, but you will find that the tools that are provided for debugging with many C programming systems are much more powerful. For serious program development the debugging tools are as important as the efficiency of the compiler.

If you've reached this point and are confident that you understand and can apply what you've read, you should now be comfortable with programming in C. All you need now is more practice to improve your expertise. To get better at programming, there's no alternative to practice, and the more varied the types of programs you write, the better. You can always improve your skills, but, fortunately! or unfortunately, depending on your point of view! it's unlikely that you'll ever reach perfection in programming, as it's almost impossible to sit down and write a bug-free program of any size from the outset. However, every time you get a new piece of code to work as it should, it will always generate a thrill and a feeling of satisfaction. Enjoy your programming!

Exercises

The following exercises enable you to try out what you learned in this chapter. If you get stuck, look back over the chapter for help. If you're still stuck, you can download the solutions from the Source Code/Download area of the Apress web site (http://www.apress.com), but that really should be a last resort.

Exercise 13-1. Define a macro, COMPARE(x, y), that will result in the value –1 if x < y, 0 if x == y, and 1 if x > y. Write an example to demonstrate that your macro works as it should. Can you see any advantage that your macro has over a function that does the same thing?

Exercise 13-2. Define a function that will return a string containing the current time in 12-hour format (a.m./p.m.) if the argument is 0, and in 24-hour format if the argument is 1. Demonstrate that your function works with a suitable program.

Exercise 13-3. Define a macro, print_value(expr), that will output on a new line exp = result where result is the value that results from evaluating expr. Demonstrate the operation of your macro with a suitable program.

APPENDIX A

■ ■ ■

Computer Arithmetic

In the chapters of this book, I've deliberately kept discussion of arithmetic to a minimum. However, it's important, so I'm going to quickly go over the subject in this appendix. If you feel confident in your math skills, this review will be old hat to you. If you find the math parts tough, this section should show you how easy it really is.

Binary Numbers

First, let's consider exactly what you intend when you write a common, everyday decimal number such as 324 or 911. Obviously what you mean is *three hundred and twenty-four* or *nine hundred and eleven*. Put more precisely, you mean the following:

324 is $3 \times 10^2 + 2 \times 10^1 + 4 \times 10^0$, which is $3 \times 10 \times 10 + 2 \times 10 + 4$

911 is $9 \times 10^2 + 1 \times 10^1 + 1 \times 10^0$, which is $9 \times 10 \times 10 + 1 \times 10 + 1$

We call this **decimal notation** because it's built around powers of 10. (This is derived from the Latin **decimalis**, meaning •of tithes,! which was a tax of 10 percent. Ah, those were the days . . .)

Representing numbers in this way is very handy for people with 10 fingers and/or 10 toes, or indeed 10 of any kind of appendage. However, your PC is rather less handy, being built mainly of switches that are either on or off. It's OK for counting up to 2, but not spectacular at counting to 10. I'm sure you're aware that this is the primary reason why your computer represents numbers using base 2 rather than base 10. Representing numbers using base 2 is called the **binary** system of counting. With numbers expressed using base 10, digits can be from 0 to 9 inclusive, whereas with binary numbers digits can only be 0 or 1, which is ideal when you only have on/off switches to represent them. In an exact analogy to the system of counting in base 10, the binary number 1101, for example, breaks down like this:

$1 \times 2^3 + 1 \times 2^2 + 0 \times 2^1 + 1 \times 2^0$

which is

$1 \times 2 \times 2 \times 2 + 1 \times 2 \times 2 + 0 \times 2 + 1$

This amounts to 13 in the decimal system. In Table A-1 you can see the decimal equivalents of all the possible numbers you can represent using eight binary digits (a binary digit is more commonly known as a **bit**).

Notice that using the first seven bits you can represent numbers from 0 to 127, which is a total of 2^7 numbers, and that using all eight bits you get 256 or 2^8 numbers. In general, if you have n bits, you can represent 2^n integers, with values from 0 to $2^n - 1$.

Table A-1. *Decimal Equivalents of 8-Bit Binary Values*

Binary	Decimal	Binary	Decimal
0000 0000	0	1000 0000	128
0000 0001	1	1000 0001	129
0000 0010	2	1000 0010	130
...	...	...	...
0001 0000	16	1001 0000	144
0001 0001	17	1001 0001	145
...	...	...	...
0111 1100	124	1111 1100	252
0111 1101	125	1111 1101	253
0111 1110	126	1111 1110	254
0111 1111	127	1111 1111	255

Adding binary numbers inside your computer is a piece of cake, because the •carry! from adding corresponding digits can only be 0 or 1, and very simple circuitry can handle the process. Figure A-1 shows how the addition of two 8-bit binary values would work.

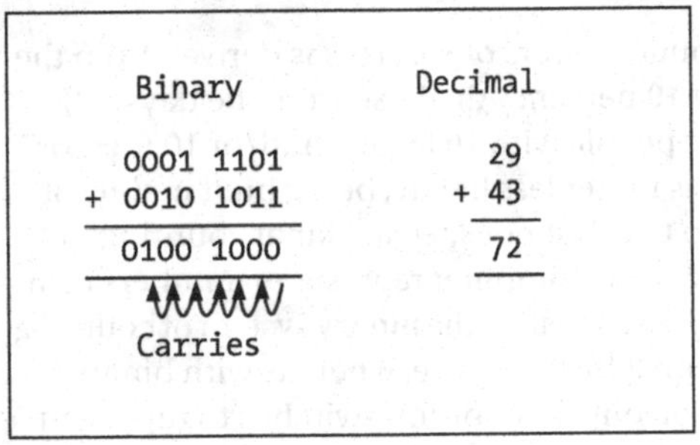

```
        Binary           Decimal

      0001  1101            29
    + 0010  1011          + 43
      0100  1000            72
      wwwww
      Carries
```

Figure A-1. *Adding binary values*

Hexadecimal Numbers

When you start dealing with larger binary numbers, a small problem arises. Look at this one:

1111 0101 1011 1001 1110 0001

Binary notation here starts to be more than a little cumbersome for practical use, particularly when you consider that if you work out what this is in decimal, it's only 16,103,905! a miserable eight decimal digits. You can sit more angels on the head of a pin than that. Clearly we need a more economical way of writing this, but decimal isn't always appropriate. Sometimes (as you saw in Chapter 3) you might need to be able to specify that the 10th and 24th bits from the right are set to 1, but without the overhead of writing out all the bits in binary notation. To figure out the decimal integer required to do this sort of thing is hard work, and there's a good chance you'll get it wrong anyway. A much easier solution is to use hexadecimal notation in which the numbers are represented using base 16.

Arithmetic to base 16 is a much more convenient option, and it fits rather well with binary. Each hexadecimal digit can have values from 0 to 15 (the digits from 10 to 15 being represented by letters A to F, as shown in Table A-2), and values from 0 to 15 correspond nicely with the range of values that four binary digits can represent.

Table A-2. *Hexadecimal Digits and Their Values in Decimal and Binary*

Hexadecimal	Decimal	Binary
0	0	0000
1	1	0001
2	2	0010
3	3	0011
4	4	0100
5	5	0101
6	6	0110
7	7	0111
8	8	1000
9	9	1001
A	10	1010
B	11	1011
C	12	1100
D	13	1101
E	14	1110
F	15	1111

Because a hexadecimal digit corresponds to four binary digits, you can represent a large binary number as a hexadecimal number simply by taking groups of four binary digits starting from the right and writing the equivalent hexadecimal digit for each group. Look at the following binary number:

1111 0101 1011 1001 1110 0001

Taking each group of four bits in turn and replacing it with the corresponding hexadecimal digit from the table, this number expressed in hexadecimal notation will come out as follows:

F   5   B   9   E   1

You have six hexadecimal digits corresponding to the six groups of four binary digits. Just to prove that it all works out with no cheating, you can convert this number directly from hexadecimal to decimal by again using the analogy with the meaning of a decimal number. The value of this hexadecimal number therefore works out as follows:

F5B9E1 as a decimal value is given by

$15 \times 16^5 + 5 \times 16^4 + 11 \times 16^3 + 9 \times 16^2 + 14 \times 16^1 + 1 \times 16^0$

This turns out to be

$15{,}728{,}640 + 327{,}680 + 45{,}056 + 2{,}304 + 224 + 1$

Thankfully, this adds up to the same number you get when converting the equivalent binary number to a decimal value: 16,103,905.

Negative Binary Numbers

There's another aspect to binary arithmetic that you need to understand: negative numbers. So far, you've assumed that everything is positive! the optimist's view, if you will! and so the glass is still half full. But you can't avoid the negative side of life! the pessimist's perspective! that the glass is already half empty. How can a negative number be represented inside a computer? Well, you have only binary digits at your disposal, so the solution has to be to use one of those to indicate whether the number is negative or positive.

For numbers that you want to allow to have negative values (referred to as **signed numbers**), you must first decide on a fixed length (in other words, the number of binary digits) and then designate the leftmost binary digit as a **sign bit**. You have to fix the length to avoid any confusion about which bit is the sign bit.

Because your computer's memory consists of 8-bit bytes, the binary numbers are going to be stored in some multiple (usually a power of 2) of 8 bits. Thus, you can have some numbers with 8 bits, some with 16 bits, and some with 32 bits (or whatever), and as long as you know what the length is in each case, you can find the sign bit! it's just the leftmost bit. If the sign bit is 0, the number is positive, and if it's 1, the number is negative.

This seems to solve the problem, and in some computers it does. Each number consists of a sign bit that is 0 for positive values and 1 for negative values, plus a given number of bits that specify the absolute value of the number! unsigned, in other words. Changing +6 to –6 just involves flipping the sign bit from 0 to 1. Unfortunately this representation carries a lot of overhead with it in terms of the complexity of the circuits that are needed to perform arithmetic with this number representation. For this reason, most computers take a different approach.

Ideally when two integers are added, you don't want the computer to be messing about, checking whether either or both of the numbers are negative. You just want to use simple **add** circuitry, regardless of the signs of the operands. The add operation will combine corresponding binary digits to produce the appropriate bit as a result, with a carry to the next digit where necessary. If you add –8 in binary to +12, you would really like to get the answer +4, using the same circuitry that would apply if you were adding +3 and +8.

If you try this with your simplistic solution, which is just to set the sign bit of the positive value to 1 to make it negative, and then perform the arithmetic with conventional carries, it doesn't quite work:

12 in binary is 0000 1100.

–8 in binary (you suppose) is 1000 1000.

If you now add these together, you get 1001 0100.

This seems to be –20, which isn't what you wanted at all. It's definitely not +4, which you know is 0000 0100. •Ah,! I hear you say, •you can't treat a sign just like another digit.! But that is just what you *do* want to do.

Let's see how the computer would like you to represent –8 by trying to subtract +12 from +4, as that should give you the right answer:

+4 in binary is 0000 0100.

+12 in binary is 0000 1100.

Subtract the latter from the former and you get 1111 1000.

For each digit from the fourth from the right onward, you had to •borrow! 1 to do the subtraction, just as you would when performing ordinary decimal arithmetic. This result is supposed to be –8, and even though it doesn't look like it, that's exactly what it is. Just try adding it to +12 or +15 in binary, and you'll see that it works.

Of course, if you want to produce –8 you can always do so by subtracting +8 from 0.

What *exactly* did you get when you subtracted 12 from 4 or +8 from 0, for that matter? It turns out that what you have here is called the **2's complement** representation of a negative binary number, and you can produce this from any positive binary number by a simple procedure that you can perform in your head. At this point, I need to ask a little faith on your part and avoid getting into explanations of *why* it works. I'll just show you how the 2's complement form of a negative number can be constructed from a positive value, and you can prove to yourself that it does work. Let's return to the previous example, in which you need the 2's complement representation of –8.

You start with +8 in binary:

0000 1000

You now •flip! each binary digit, changing 0s to 1s and vice versa:

1111 0111

This is called the **1's complement** form, and if you now add 1 to this, you'll get the 2's complement form:

1111 1000

This is exactly the same as the representation of –8 you get by subtracting +12 from +4. Just to make absolutely sure, let's try the original sum of adding –8 to +12:

+12 in binary is 0000 1100.

Your version of –8 is 1111 1000.

If you add *these* together, you get 0000 0100.

The answer is 4! magic. It works! The •carry! propagates through all the leftmost 1s, setting them back to 0. One fell off the end, but you shouldn't worry about that! it's probably compensating for the one you borrowed from the end in the subtraction operation that produced the –8 in the first place. In fact, what's happening is that you're making an assumption that the sign bit, 1 or 0, repeats forever to the left. Try a few examples of your own; you'll find it always works automatically. The really great thing about using 2's complement representation of negative numbers is that it makes arithmetic very easy (and fast) for your computer.

Big-Endian and Little-Endian Systems

As I've discussed, integers generally are stored in memory as binary values in a contiguous sequence of bytes, commonly groups of 2, 4, or 8 bytes. The question of the sequence in which the bytes appear can be very important! it's one of those things that doesn't matter until it matters, and then it *really* matters.

Let's consider the decimal value 262,657 stored as a 4-byte binary value. I chose this value because in binary it happens to be

0000 0000 0000 0100 0000 0010 0000 0001

Each byte has a pattern of bits that is easily distinguished from the others.
If you're using an Intel PC, the number will be stored as follows:

Byte address:	00	01	02	03
Data bits:	0000 0001	0000 0010	0000 0100	0000 0000

As you can see, the most significant eight bits of the value! the one that's all 0s! are stored in the byte with the highest address (last, in other words), and the least significant eight bits are stored in the byte with the lowest address, which is the leftmost byte. This arrangement is described as **little-endian**.

If you're using a mainframe computer, a RISC workstation, or a Mac machine based on a Motorola processor, the same data is likely to be arranged in memory as follows:

Byte address:	00	01	02	03
Data bits:	0000 0000	0000 0100	0000 0010	0000 0001

Now the bytes are in reverse sequence with the most significant eight bits stored in the leftmost byte, which is the one with the lowest address. This arrangement is described as **big-endian**.

■**Note** Within each byte, the bits are arranged with the most significant bit on the left and the least significant bit on the right, regardless of whether the byte order is big-endian or little-endian.

This is all very interesting, you may say, but why should it matter? Most of the time it doesn't. More often than not you can happily write your C program without knowing whether the computer on which the code will execute is big-endian or little-endian. It *does* matter, however, when you're processing binary data that comes from another machine. Binary data will be written to a file or transmitted over a network as a sequence of bytes. It's up to you how you interpret it. If the source of the data is a machine with a different endian-ness from the machine on which your code is running, you must reverse the order of the bytes in each binary value. If you don't, you have garbage.

■**Note** For those who collect curious background information, the terms **big-endian** and **little-endian** are drawn from the book *Gulliver's Travels* by Jonathan Swift. In the story, the emperor of Lilliput commands all his subjects to always crack their eggs at the smaller end. This is a consequence of the emperor's son having cut his finger following the traditional approach of cracking his egg at the big end. Ordinary law-abiding Lilliputian subjects who cracked their eggs at the smaller end were described as Little Endians. The Big Endians were a rebellious group of traditionalists in the Lilliputian kingdom who insisted on continuing to crack their eggs at the big end. Many were put to death as a result.

Floating-Point Numbers

We often have to deal with very large numbers! the number of protons in the universe, for example! which need around 79 decimal digits. Clearly there are a lot of situations in which you'll need more than the 10 decimal digits you get from a 4-byte binary number. Equally, there are a lot of very small numbers! for example, the amount of time in minutes it takes the typical car salesperson to accept your generous offer on a 1982 Ford LTD (and it's covered only 380,000 miles . . .). A mechanism for handling both these kinds of numbers is, as you may have guessed, **floating-point** numbers.

A floating-point representation of a number in decimal notation is a decimal value 0 with a fixed number of digits multiplied by a power of 10 to produce the number you want. It's easier to demonstrate than to explain, so let's look at some examples. The number 365 in normal decimal notation could be written in floating-point form as follows:

0.3650000E03

The *E* stands for **exponent** and precedes the power of 10 that the 0.3650000 (the mantissa) part is multiplied by to get the required value. That is

0.3650000 × 10 × 10 × 10

which is clearly 365.

The mantissa in the number here has seven decimal digits. The number of digits of precision in a floating-point number will depend on how much memory it is allocated. A single precision floating-point value occupying 4 bytes will provide approximately seven decimal digits accuracy. I say *approximately* because inside your computer these numbers are in binary floating-point form, and a binary fraction with 23 bits doesn't exactly correspond to a decimal fraction with seven decimal digits.

Now let's look at a small number:

0.3650000E-04

This is evaluated as $.365 \times 10^{-4}$, which is .0000365! exactly the time in minutes required by the car salesperson to accept your cash.

Suppose you have a large number such as 2,134,311,179. How does this look as a floating-point number? Well, it looks like this:

0.2134311E10

It's not quite the same. You've lost three low-order digits and you've approximated your original value as 2,134,311,000. This is a small price to pay for being able to handle such a vast range of numbers, typically from 10^{-38} to 10^{+38} either positive or negative, as well as having an extended representation that goes from a minute 10^{-308} to a mighty 10^{+308}. They're called floating-point numbers for the fairly obvious reason that the decimal point •floats! and its position depends on the exponent value.

Aside from the fixed precision limitation in terms of accuracy, there's another aspect you may need to be conscious of. You need to take great care when adding or subtracting numbers of significantly different magnitudes. A simple example will demonstrate this kind of problem. You can first consider adding .365E–3 to .365E+7. You can write this as a decimal sum:

0.000365 + 3,650,000.0

This produces the following result:

3,650,000.000365

When converted back to floating-point with seven digits of precision, this becomes the following:

0.3650000E+7

So you might as well not have bothered. The problem lies directly with the fact that you carry only seven digits precision. The seven digits of the larger number aren't affected by any of the digits of the smaller number because they're all further to the right. Funnily enough, you must also take care when the numbers are nearly equal. If you compute the difference between such numbers, you may end up with a result that has only one or two digits precision. It's quite easy in such circumstances to end up computing with numbers that are totally garbage.

APPENDIX B

■ ■ ■

ASCII Character Code Definitions

The first 32 American Standard Code for Information Interchange (ASCII) characters provide control functions. Many of these haven't been referenced in this book but are included here for completeness. In Table B-1, only the first 128 characters are included. The remaining 128 characters include further special symbols and letters for national character sets.

Table B-1. *ASCII Character Code Values*

Decimal	Hexadecimal	Character	Control
000	00	Null	NUL
001	01	☺	SOH
002	02	●	STX
003	03	♥	ETX
004	04	♦	EOT
005	05	♣	ENQ
006	06	♠	ACK
007	07	•	BEL (audible bell)
008	08	--	Backspace
009	09	--	HT
010	0A	--	LF (linefeed)
011	0B	--	VT (vertical tab)
012	0C	--	FF (form feed)
013	0D	--	CR (carriage return)
014	0E	--	SO
015	0F	--	SI
016	10	--	DLE
017	11	--	DC1
018	12	--	DC2
019	13	--	DC3

Table B-1. *ASCII Character Code Values (Continued)*

Decimal	Hexadecimal	Character	Control
020	14	--	DC4
021	15	--	NAK
022	16	--	SYN
023	17	--	ETB
024	18	--	CAN
025	19	--	EM
026	1A	→	SUB
027	1B	←	ESC (escape)
028	1C	L	FS
029	1D	--	GS
030	1E	--	RS
031	1F	--	US
032	20	--	Space
033	21	!	--
034	22	"	--
035	23	#	--
036	24	$	--
037	25	%	--
038	26	&	--
039	27	'	--
040	28	(	--
041	29	)	--
042	2A	*	--
043	2B	+	--
044	2C	'	--
045	2D	-	--
046	2E	.	--
047	2F	/	--
048	30	0	--
049	31	1	--
050	32	2	--
051	33	3	--

Table B-1. *ASCII Character Code Values (Continued)*

Decimal	Hexadecimal	Character	Control
052	34	4	--
053	35	5	--
054	36	6	--
055	37	7	--
056	38	8	--
057	39	9	--
058	3A	:	--
059	3B	;	--
060	3C	<	--
061	3D	=	--
062	3E	>	--
063	3F	?	--
064	40	@	--
065	41	A	--
066	42	B	--
067	43	C	--
068	44	D	--
069	45	E	--
070	46	F	--
071	47	G	--
072	48	H	--
073	49	I	--
074	4A	J	--
075	4B	K	--
076	4C	L	--
077	4D	M	--
078	4E	N	--
079	4F	O	--
080	50	P	--
081	51	Q	--
082	52	R	--
083	53	S	--

Table B-1. *ASCII Character Code Values (Continued)*

Decimal	Hexadecimal	Character	Control
084	54	T	--
085	55	U	--
086	56	V	--
087	57	W	--
088	58	X	--
089	59	Y	--
090	5A	Z	--
091	5B	[	--
092	5C	\	--
093	5D	]	--
094	5E	^	--
095	5F	_	--
096	60	'	--
097	61	a	--
098	62	b	--
099	63	c	--
100	64	d	--
101	65	e	--
102	66	f	--
103	67	g	--
104	68	h	--
105	69	i	--
106	6A	j	--
107	6B	k	--
108	6C	l	--
109	6D	m	--
110	6E	n	--
111	6F	o	--
112	70	p	--
113	71	q	--
114	72	r	--
115	73	s	--

Table B-1. *ASCII Character Code Values (Continued)*

Decimal	Hexadecimal	Character	Control
116	74	t	--
117	75	u	--
118	76	v	--
119	77	w	--
120	78	x	--
121	79	y	--
122	7A	z	--
123	7B	{	--
124	7C	|	--
125	7D	}	--
126	7E	~	--
127	7F	Delete	--

Note that the null character in the table is not necessarily the same as NULL, which is defined in the C library and whose value is implementation-dependent.

■ ■ ■

Reserved Words in C

The words in the following list are keywords in C, so you must not use them for other purposes, such as variable names or function names.

auto	for	struct
break	goto	switch
case	if	typedef
char	inline	union
const	int	unsigned
continue	long	void
default	register	volatile
do	restrict	while
double	return	_Bool
else	short	_Complex
enum	signed	_Imaginary
extern	sizeof	
float	static	

APPENDIX D

▪ ▪ ▪

Input and Output Format Specifications

This appendix summarizes all the format specifications you have available for stream input and output. You use these with the standard streams stdin, stdout, and stderr, as well as text file streams.

Output Format Specifications

There are three standard library functions for formatted output: the printf() that writes to the standard output stream stdout (which by default is the command line), the sprintf() function that writes to a string, and the fprintf() function that writes to a file. These functions have the following form:

```
int printf(const char* format_string, . . .);
int sprintf(char* source_string, const char* format_string, . . .);
int fprintf(FILE* file_stream, const char* format_string, . . .);
```

The ellipsis at the end of the parameter list indicates that there can be zero or more arguments supplied. These functions return the number of bytes written, or a negative value if an error occurs. The format string can contain ordinary characters (including escape sequences) that are written to the output, together with format specifications for outputting the values of succeeding arguments.

An output format specification always begins with a % character and has the following general form:

```
%[flags][width][.precision][size_flag]type
```

The items between square brackets are all optional, so the only mandatory bits are the % character at the beginning and the type specifier for the type of conversion to be used.

The significance of each of the optional parts is as follows:

[flags] are zero or more conversion flags that control how the output is presented. The flags you can use are shown in Table D-1.

Table D-1. *Conversion Flags*

Flag	Description
+	Include the sign in the output, + or-. For example, %+d will output a decimal integer with the sign always included.
space	Use space or – for the sign, that is, a positive value is preceded by a space. This is useful for aligning output when there may be positive and negative values in a column of output. For example, % d will output a decimal integer with a space for the sign with positive values.

Table D-1. *Conversion Flags (Continued)*

Flag	Description
–	Left-justify the output in the field width with spaces padding to the right if necessary. For example, %-10d will output an integer as a decimal value left-justified in a field width of ten characters. The %-+10d specification will output a decimal integer with the sign always appearing, and left-justified in a field width of ten characters.
#	Prefix hexadecimal output values with 0x or 0X (corresponding to x and X conversion type specification respectively), and octal values with 0.
0	Use 0 as the pad character to the left in a right-justified output. For example, %012d will output a decimal integer right-justified in a field width of 12 characters, padded to the left with zeros as necessary.

[width] specifies the minimum field width for the output value. The width you specify will be exceeded if the value does not fit within the specified minimum width. For example, %15u outputs an unsigned integer value right-justified in a field width of 15 characters padded to the left with spaces as necessary.

[.precision] specifies the number of places following the decimal point in the output for a floating-point value. For example, %15.6f outputs a floating-point value in a minimum field width of 15 characters with four places after the decimal point.

[size_flag] is a size specification for the value that modifies the meaning of the type specification. Possible size specifications are l (lowercase *L*), L, ll (two lowercase *L*'s), or h. The size specification you can use in any given situation depends on the type specification you are using, as shown in Table D-2.

type is a character specifying the type of conversion to be applied to the value to be output, as shown in Table D-2.

Table D-2. *Conversion Type and Size Specifications*

Conversion Type	Description
d, i	The value is assumed to be of type int and the output is as a decimal integer. With the h size modifier (hd or hi) the argument is assumed to be type short. With the l size modifier (ld or li) the argument is assumed to be type long. With the ll modifier (lld or lli) the argument is assumed to be type long long.
u	The value is assumed to be of type unsigned int and the output is as an unsigned decimal integer. With the h size modifier (hu) the argument is assumed to be type unsigned short. With the l size modifier (lu) the argument is assumed to be type unsigned long. With the ll modifier (llu) the argument is assumed to be type unsigned long long.
o	The value is assumed to be of type unsigned int and the output is as an unsigned octal value. With the h size modifier (ho) the argument is assumed to be type unsigned short. With the l size modifier (lo) the argument is assumed to be type unsigned long. With the ll modifier (llo) the argument is assumed to be type unsigned long long.

Table D-2. *Conversion Type and Size Specifications*

Conversion Type	Description
x or X	The value is assumed to be of type unsigned int and the output is as an unsigned hexadecimal value. The hexadecimal digits a to f are used if the lowercase type conversion specification is used, and A to F otherwise.
	With the h size modifier (ho) the argument is assumed to be type unsigned short.
	With the l size modifier (lo) the argument is assumed to be type unsigned long.
	With the ll modifier (llo) the argument is assumed to be type unsigned long long.
c	The value is assumed to be of type char and the output is as a character.
	With the l size modifier (lc) the argument is assumed to be the wide character type wchar_t.
e or E	The value is assumed to be of type double and the output is as a floating-point value in scientific notation (with an exponent). The exponent value in the output will be preceded by e when you use the lowercase type conversion, e, and E otherwise.
	With the L modifier (Le or LE) the argument is assumed to be type long double.
f or F	The value is assumed to be of type double and the output is as a floating-point value in ordinary notation (without an exponent).
	With the L modifier (Lf or LF) the argument is assumed to be type long double.
g or G	The value is assumed to be of type double and the output is as a floating-point value in ordinary notation (without an exponent) unless the exponent value is greater than the precision (default value 6) or is less than –4, in which case the output will be in scientific notation.
	With the L modifier (Lg or LG) the argument is assumed to be type long double.
s	The argument is assumed to be a null-terminated string of characters of type char and characters are output until the null character is found or until the precision specification is reached if it is present. The optional precision specification represents the maximum number of characters that may be output.
S	When used with printf() the argument is assumed to be a null-terminated string of characters of type wchar_t and characters are output until the null character is found or until the precision specification is reached if it is present. The optional precision specification represents the maximum number of characters that may be output.
p	The argument is assumed to be a pointer, and because the output is an address it will be a hexadecimal value.
n	The argument is assumed to be a pointer of type int* (pointer to int) and the number of characters in the output so far is stored at the address pointed to by the argument.
	If you use the h modifier (hn) the argument is assumed to be type short* (pointer to short).
	If you use the l modifier (ln) the argument is assumed to be type long* (pointer to long).
	If you use the ll modifier (lln) the argument is assumed to be type long long* (pointer to long long).
%	No argument is expected and the output is the % character.

Input Format Specifications

For the scanf() function that reads data from the standard input stream, stdin (which by default is the keyboard), the sscanf() function that reads data from a string in memory, and the fscanf() function that reads data from a file, data is read from the source controlled by a format string that is passed as an argument to the function. These input functions have the following form:

```
int scanf(const char* format_string, pArg1, ...);
int sscanf(const char* destination_string, const char* format_string, ...);
int fscanf(FILE* file_stream, const char* format_string, ...);
```

Each of these functions returns a count of the number of data items read by the operation. The ellipsis at the end of the parameter list indicates that there can be zero or more arguments here. Don't forget, the arguments that follow the format string must always be pointers. It is a common error to use a variable that is not a pointer as an argument to one of these input functions.

The format string controlling how the input is processed can contain spaces, other characters, and format specifications, beginning with a % character, for data items.

A single whitespace character in the format string causes the function to ignore successive whitespace characters in the input. The first nonwhitespace character found will be interpreted as the first character of the next data item. When a newline character in the input follows a value that has been read, for example, when you are reading a single character from the keyboard using the %c format specification, any newline, tab, or space character that is entered will be read as the input character. This will be particularly apparent when you are reading a single character repeatedly, where the newline from the Enter key will be left in the buffer. If you want the function to ignore the whitespace in such situations, you can force the function to skip whitespace by including at least one whitespace character preceding the %c in the format string.

You can also include nonwhitespace characters in the input format string that are not part of a format specification. Any nonwhitespace character in the format string that is not part of a format specification must be matched by the same character in the input, otherwise the input operation ends.

The format specification for an item of data is of the following form:

```
%[*][width][size_flag]type
```

The items enclosed between square brackets are optional. The mandatory parts of the format specification are the % character marking the start of the format specification and the type conversion type specification at the end. The meanings of the optional parts are as follows:

[*] indicates that that the input data item corresponding to this format specification should be scanned but not stored. For example, %*d will scan an integer value and discard it.

[width] specifies the maximum number of characters to be scanned for this input value. If a whitespace character is found before width characters have been scanned, it is the end of the input for the current data item. For example, %2d reads up to two characters as an integer value. The width specification is useful for reading multiple inputs that are not separated by whitespace characters. You could read 12131415 and interpret it as the values 12, 13, 14, and 15 by using "%2d%2d%2d%2d" as the format string.

[size_flag] modifies the input type specified by the type part of the specification. Possible size_flag specifications include h, l, (lowercase L), ll (lowercase L's), and L. Which of these you can use depends on the type specifier you are using, as described in Table D-3.

Table D-3. *Input Conversion Type Specifications and Modifiers*

Conversion Type	Description
c	Reads a single character as type char.
	When you use the l modifier (%lc) a single character is read as type wchar_t.
	You can also precede the c or lc specification with a decimal integer, m, to read m successive characters as a string not terminated by null. For example, %20c will read 20 successive characters. The corresponding argument should be a pointer to a character array with sufficient elements to accommodate the number of characters to be read.
d	Reads successive decimal digits as a value of type int.
	With the h modifier (%hd), successive digits are read and interpreted as type short.
	With the l modifier (%ld), successive digits are read and interpreted as type long.
	With the ll modifier (%lld), successive digits are read and interpreted as type long long.
u	Reads successive decimal digits as a value of type unsigned int.
	With the h modifier (%hu), successive digits are read and interpreted as type unsigned short.
	With the l modifier (%lu), successive digits are read and interpreted as type unsigned long.
	With the ll modifier (%llu), successive digits are read and interpreted as type unsigned long long.
o	Reads successive octal digits as a value of type unsigned int.
	With the h modifier (%ho), successive octal digits are read and interpreted as type unsigned short.
	With the l modifier (%lo), successive octal digits are read and interpreted as type unsigned long.
	With the ll modifier (%llo), successive octal digits are read and interpreted as type unsigned long long.
x or X	Reads successive hexadecimal digits as a value of type unsigned int.
	With the h modifier (%hx or %hX), successive hexadecimal digits are read and interpreted as type unsigned short.
	With the l modifier (%lx or %lX), successive hexadecimal digits are read and interpreted as type unsigned long.
	With the ll modifier (%llx or %llX), successive digits are read and interpreted as type unsigned long long.
s	Reads successive characters until a whitespace is reached and stores the address of the null-terminated string that results in the corresponding argument.
	If you use the l modifier (%ls) the characters are read and stored as a null-terminated wide character string.
n	Reads no input, but the number of characters that have been read from the input source up to this point is stored as an integer at the address specified by the corresponding argument, which should be of type int*.

Note that if you want to read a string that includes whitespace characters, you have the %[set_of_characters] form of specification available. With this specification, successive characters are read from the input source as long as they appear in the set you supply between the square brackets. Thus, the specification %[abcdefghijklmnopqrstuvwxyz] will read any sequence of lower-case letters and spaces as a single string. A more useful variation on this is to precede the set of characters with a caret, ^, as in %[^set_of_characters], in which case the set of characters represents the characters that will be interpreted as ending the string input. For example, the specification %[^,!] will read a sequence of characters until either a comma or an exclamation point is found, which will end the string input.

Index

■T